WHISPERS OF THE
LONG DEPARTED

Other books by the author

IN THIS SMALL PLACE:
*Amazing Tales of the First 300 Years of Havelock
and Craven County, North Carolina*

NEW BERN HISTORY 101
*The Essential Facts for the Native, Newcomer or
Visitor to the Colonial Capital of North Carolina*

HISTORIC IMAGES OF HAVELOCK AND
CHERRY POINT
A Photographic Tour of the Community's Past

WHISPERS OF THE LONG DEPARTED

Untold History of Southern Craven County, N.C.

Edward Barnes Ellis, Jr.

McBryde Publishing
NEW BERN, NORTH CAROLINA USA

McBryde Publishing
NEW BERN-NORTH CAROLINA USA

Whispers of the Long Departed:
Untold History of Southern Craven County, N.C.

Set in Times New Roman and Palatino Linotype
Printed in the United States

ISBN: 978-1-7339824-3-6

Book graphic design by the author
Maps, and artwork by the author, unless otherwise noted.
Photographs from the collection of the author, unless otherwise noted.

Cover design: Bill Benners
Cover photograph: A farmer in his field, thought to be Abner P. Whitehead of Bachelor, N.C., with an unidentified African American farm hand. Photo courtesy of John B. Green III and the New Bern-Craven County Public Library from the Mrs. Margaret Wall Collection

First Edition

For Harriet Veronica Jones Ellis
My wife and boon companion, Ronnie

Table of Contents

Before Computers

The original Havelock cemetery and burial record, begun by Eddie Ellis in 1976, is this low-tech set of 3" x 5" index cards in a gray metal file box. Most of the information was transcribed over time from old tombstones and grave markers at burial grounds and individual sites in the fields, woodlands, and rural roadsides in the southern half of Craven County.

Graves were searched for and recorded from time to time by the author but he made a major push for discoveries in 1983-1984. The project expanded further in 1985 when a group of archaeologists came to survey MCAS Cherry Point, consulting during the process with Ellis, by then the local newspaperman and historian.

The hunt for graves and cemeteries continued through the years.

In 2018, Ellis sat down, at last, to sort and compile the information in the box. The intention was to type a simple list to be posted on the Havelock history website and be provided for use in local libraries.

The result was this book.

On the Matter of Language & Spelling

Regarding language and the quotations of speech, the author grew up in the South and developed a great affinity for the way Southern people talk. In some of the quotes herein, the tense of verbs, for example, may be off from "standard English." We quote these imperfections and anomalies both for accuracy and to preserve the traditional words and dialect which country people, both black and white, have spoken to one another. Either overemphasizing or diminishing these peculiarities of speech would be false.

Herein also the reader will find Barbados sometimes spelled with an "e" and Godette spelled without. You'll find New Bern spelled in a variety of ways: the old-style being Newbern, the victors-of-the-Civil-War-style being New Berne, and the compromise version being the present one.

Names like Hancock and Slocum show up with quite a bit of variety: Handcock and Slocumbe being examples. There's Wynne, Wynn, Wyn, Winn, and Win. Kennedy, Cannady, and Canada; all the same family. Ballenger, Belangia, Belanga, even Blanger; ditto. Row, Rowe, and Roe; same-same. And many more.

Clubfoot Creek can be Cutfoot or even Clumsford. Cherry Point is occasionally spelled as one word. Cherrypoint. Go figure. Adams Creek is found as Adam's, Adams', and Adams's. Neuse is spelled Nuse sometimes. Or Neus. We even found it – in an old Civil War-era New York City newspaper – spelled *Noose*, but wrote our way around that usage.

The key takeaway is that words were spelled phonetically; the way they sounded. And they sounded differently to different people, and, therefore, were spelled every possible way. We wind up with a family called *Dickinson* living next door to the family *Dickerson*, who believe, after a generation or two, that they are not related to one another.

Moving from one old document to another, we have chosen to spell them as we find them with confidence that you'll figure it out. But in many old documents, things are just plain misspelled or spelled two or even three different ways within the same document. And words are often Capitalized for No reason Whatsoever. We have let it be.

We must proceed with the understanding that language is fluid, and that astonishing mutations of original spellings are to be expected.

Abbreviations:

AAF = African American female
AAM = African American male
a.k.a. = also known as
AMA/ARC = American Missionary Association records at the Amistad
    Research Center, Tulane University
ARC = Archaeological Resource Consultants report 1985
c. or circa = about, approximately
COD = cause of death
CP = Cherry Point
CP with number = Old Cherry Point cemetery. See map on previous page
EBE/ECU = Edward B. Ellis, Jr. Papers, Joyner Library, ECU
ENCGS = Eastern North Carolina Genealogical Society
Esq. = Esquire, often means the person is an attorney
FUMC = First United Methodist Church Cemetery, Havelock
HIHCP = *Historic Images of Havelock & Cherry Point* - Ellis
ITSP = *In This Small Place* - Ellis
i.e. = in other words
inst. or instant = when referring to date means *this month*
KR = Kellenberger Room, New Bern-Craven County Public Library
MCAS = Marine Corps Air Station
MUM = mulatto male
MUF = mulatto female
OR = Official Records of the War of the Rebellion
ORN = Official Records, Navy, War of the Rebellion
q.v. = which see
SHC = Southern Historical Collection, UNC-Chapel Hill
SOHP = Southern Oral History Program, Collection 4007, SHC, UNC-CH
ult. or ultimo = when referring to date means *the previous month*
USFS = United States Forest Service
WF = white female
WM = white male

"When the old people pass, there go the history."

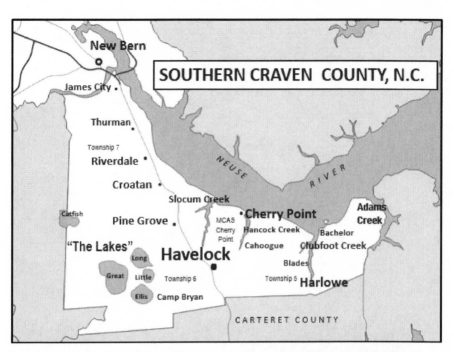

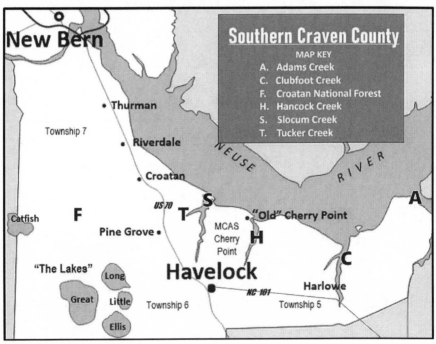

Cemeteries and Farms at Cherry Point, 1941

Below is a map showing the positions of the old cemeteries, homes, farms, and other land tracts existing on MCAS Cherry Point in 1941 along with some other sites referred to in the text.

Cemeteries are represented by numbers 1-15 assigned to each in the military survey of that year and a re-survey in 1985. Locations of places – some from the 1800s and 1900s; some from today – are marked with letters and identified in the key box at the lower right of the page.

A list of Cherry Point burials corresponding to the map, plus some headstone photographs, can be found in Part IV of this book.

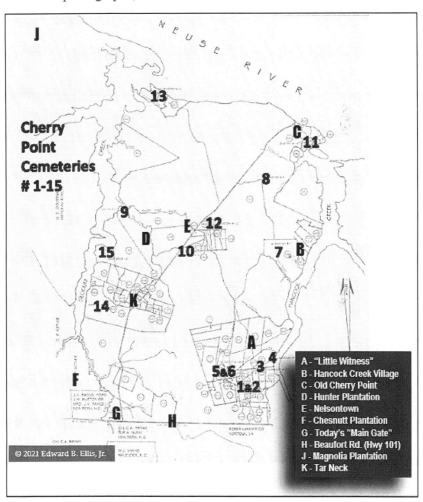

Cherry Point Cemeteries # 1-15

A - "Little Witness"
B - Hancock Creek Village
C - Old Cherry Point
D - Hunter Plantation
E - Nelsontown
F - Chesnutt Plantation
G - Today's "Main Gate"
H - Beaufort Rd. (Hwy 101)
J - Magnolia Plantation
K - Tar Neck

© 2021 Edward B. Ellis, Jr.

PART I

UNTOLD STORIES

A Man Named Sparks

In 1941, men used dynamite to make ditches at Cherry Point.

Construction of the brand-new Marine Corps air station was largely a drainage operation. There was a vast swampy open savannah where the runways are today. That deadly place – a mile long, 400 feet wide, and three feet deep – will be revealed later as important to our understanding of local history, but in 1941 it just needed to be dried out, and quickly. War was creating unholy hell in Europe. Sabers were rattling. America was on the brink. It was a few months yet before Pearl Harbor would be mercilessly attacked by the Japanese. But there was a sense of urgency; that collective feeling of the hair saluting on the back of your neck. They had to get the job done.

So, in 1941, at Cunningham Field – the temporary name for the place – men were using dynamite to make ditches.

I saw a treatise on it once. It instructed how long to cut the sticks, how far apart to bury them and how deep. Here, I'll let them tell it:

> "The mucky soil along the proposed line of ditch was almost completely underwater. Stumps of green sweetgum, black gum, and pine, up to 2 ½ feet in diameter, stood above, about 6 to 8 feet apart.

"Owing to the presence of large roots the entire 1,500 feet of ditch was not blown at one time, but in ten sections, with the resulting economy in the size of charge. One stick of 50 percent nitroglycerin dynamite was used in each hole. The holes were 24 inches deep, and in a straight line, with spacing of 10 to 16 inches, averaging 12.

"A No. 3 blasting machine was used as detonator, and No. 6 electric blasting caps as primers. The immersion of some of the dynamite in water for as long as four hours between loading and firing was not apparently detrimental to the dynamite.

"Within 30 minutes after the last shot there was a freely running stream in the bed. The resulting ditch averaged 7 ½ feet at the top, 2 ½ at the bottom, and 3 ½ deep. Approximately 970 cubic yards of material was removed, or 0.65 cubic yards per linear foot.

"No hand trimming of the sides was found necessary, as is often the case." [a]

Forget about shovels.

Forget the wheelbarrows.

Forget about trenching machines.

Just push a plunger and *BOOM!*; two million pounds of dirt loft skyward and a perfect channel, half the length of a football field, appears with water flowing through it.

But they weren't ditching by the foot at Cherry Point. Hoo-boy! They were ditching by the mile. And then they began blowing up the tree stumps. Thousands of them. It sounded like a war out there.

Though the base property was littered with small farms, much of the initial 8,046.8 acres was woodlands thick enough to get lost in. All of it needed clearing.

The place was huge. It's three miles across Cherry Point from Hancock Creek to Slocum Creek. All twelve-and-a-half square miles of it had to be clear-cut, drained and brought to a set of standard elevations. Timber crews took out enough of the trees to make what was estimated to be five million board feet of lumber. That was still only one-tenth the amount of wood necessary to complete the thousands of buildings going up over the next few months. Every one of the extracted trees left its stump, some of them huge, and pulling them out by hand would've taken forever. So, they started using dynamite on those, too. Aerial photos taken during the base clearing process show white craters pockmarking the earth as far as the eye could see.

---

[a] Rector, N.H., *Anti-Malarial Ditching with Dynamite*, Journal of the National Malaria Society, Vol. 2., No.2., 1943; Public Health Reports, Vol. 36, March 18, 1921, pg. 1.

Aerial photograph shows white craters where trees were dynamited during the land clearing operation for the new Marine air base at Cherry Point, N.C., late 1941. *Edward Ellis Collection, Joyner Library, ECU.*

Almost a thousand workers were hired in one single early month. Before it was done, many thousands more were laboring five days a week and that pace quickened to seven after Pearl Harbor, December 7, 1941.

Contemporary accounts of the construction of Cherry Point often use the words like *colossal* and *controlled chaos* to describe what was going on there. Pick your analogy. A bee-hive. An ant mound. Whatever. A military city for 20,000-plus was being built from scratch in the middle of North Carolina coastal pinelands.

Among the top objectives was the creation of runways so spectacular that even in the twenty-first century they'd have handled the largest vehicle NASA ever built. But the entire length of one runway, and the center where all of them were to intersect, was pure wetlands. Some bean counter once estimated ten million cubic yards of earth were moved. [*The writer's inner bean counter wants you to know that that's ten million* tons (!) *of dirt, and in pounds, it's a number that will put an* E *on your calculator.*] The mind-scrambling amount of concrete – mixed and hauled and poured – has spawned local legends about how many hundreds of miles of theoretical highway could have been built with it.

Battalions of trucks and countless pieces of heavy equipment – brigades of bulldozers, tractor-scrapers, and graders – thundered about alternately making curtains of dust or getting stuck in the bottomless quagmire. A railroad spur was routed across a quickly-trestled creek's prong and into the midst of the ordered disorder. Three asphalt and concrete plants were under construction. These would require mountains of sand and stone that only locomotives could efficiently deliver.

A coal-fired electrical power station was going up on the east bank of Slocum Creek. Lengthy thoroughfares and dense grids of roads – by the tens of miles – were being cut, filled, tamped, rolled, and paved.

Sprawling "temporary buildings" were already under roof and built to such a standard that some of them were in use more than thirty years later. Some 4,300 buildings were in various stages of construction or on drawing boards, including a hospital – called the *dispensary* – a colossal movie theater, chow halls, warehouses, echelons of barracks, and a headquarters building worthy of a potentate. Several structures were the largest ever built in Craven County; the largest ever built in eastern North Carolina for that matter. To belabor the point, there were few edifices in all of North Carolina that wouldn't have fit inside a single Cherry Point aircraft hangar.

With the ground this stirred up and the terrain this rugged, one base inspector decided that the most efficient form of transportation was horseback. The United States was not yet at war but with the noisy uproar, the smoke, the dust, and the exploding nitroglycerine, it would not have been hard for an onlooker of the period to think otherwise.

Amid this construction whirlwind, a small team of U. S. Forestry Service surveyors had their heads down, working diligently to record the old property boundaries of the evicted landowners. Scratched, sweaty and bug-bitten, the surveyors were also finding and making note of a hodge-podge of cemeteries, some dating back to colonial times. Several of the cemeteries were neat and well-arranged with burials marked by gracefully carved stones, some waist-high. In others, there were smaller headstones and white marble cubes the size of a loaf of bread with names and dates etched on them. There were wooden markers, some still barely legible, others ravaged beyond decipherment by rain, sun, and insects. These surveyors were also seeing unmarked "sinks," depressions that indicated individuals were buried there. In some cases, dozens of sinks aligned in rows. In one old cemetery, they estimated forty or fifty burials but found only a single headstone. Some graves were marked with

Temporary grave marker at Cherry Point, 1941.

small metal stakes where rectangular crowns held paper inserts intended to be temporary. In many cases, mildew had long since rendered illegible the names and dates that had been typed or handwritten in ink. Then there were ancient graveyards full of forgotten people; completely overgrown with scrub pines and a dense understory of wax myrtle and thorny smilax.

Disenfranchised African American residents were still about in June of 1941. All of them were upset about losing the farms where their families had lived for generations; the only homes they'd ever known. They were fearful, bewildered, and confused, as later avowals made evident. But in the survival mechanism of the day, nearly all kept their anger to themselves. Though some were already gone, others were in the process. A number hadn't moved or made any attempt to do so. But, with a deadline to be off their land by September, people salvaged for use elsewhere the metal roofs from otherwise-functional tobacco barns, and windows and doors from still-serviceable houses.

As circumstance allowed, the surveyors gathered information from the long-time landowners still there. They asked questions. Working one day within a black settlement near Hancock Creek in the southeastern quadrant of the emerging airbase, one of them had a brief interview with a woman named Emma Hill Stevens. Under her maiden name, Emma Hill owned a 21.3-acre farm that the government designated Tract 475. She'd lived all her life in the village of Little Witness or Melvin or Toon Neck, whichever name one preferred. Her house was next door to the Little Witness Baptist Church and within sight of two of the village graveyards.

Notes from a yellowed government report:

> CEMETERY 4: This cemetery also lacks markers, but the survey-ors in 1941 estimated that three or four graves were present. Ac-cording to their informant, Emma Hill Stevens, one of the graves is the burial place of a man named Sparks.

A man named Sparks.

In 1941, nothing remained of the man in an unmarked grave except one stubborn connection that had hung on inside Emma Hill's brain. She re-called two facts. That a man was buried there. And his name was Sparks. He was otherwise forgotten, unknown. What could we know of him? That he was almost certainly a black man buried in a cemetery at the nexus of an isolated African American outpost in the wet pine forest of southern Craven County. Possibly a former slave, though many here had not been slaves.

But nothing else was recorded.

Nothing else was known.

A man named Sparks.

No first name, no race, no life story. Gone. Nearly forgotten. He was so invisible, so ephemeral – just six letters typed on a piece of paper – that he might well have never even been at all.

We'll return to the curiosity of Mr. Sparks and Cherry Point in a moment but first, let it be said that this work of investigating and recording the past sometimes becomes more than mere history. It begins to feel personal. These can be deep, existential matters if you let them. After all, it's life and death were talking about.

What does it mean that so many people have walked upon the earth and are now gone? And despite the trite line "Gone, But Not Forgotten" carved on headstones, many *are* forgotten ... until someone digs up and considers the facts about them. Otherwise, lives evaporate; graves are lost. The stories of individuals, families, groups of people, and whole communities slip from memory, vanished as if they never were.

Does it matter? I don't know. But there's a pull deep within me that says there is merit and value and, maybe, even some sort of uprightness in preserving the past and in remembering the things – blissful and horrid – that make up this story of mankind upon the planet. And so, I find this pocket of the world – half of an ancient American county – in which little effort has been made to record or memorialize or even acknowledge the fact that thousands of people are buried beneath our feet. In southern Craven County, I've found the overlooked burials of our forebears in thick, deep woods, under convenience store parking lots, beneath residential streets, and airfield runways.

And I've found them cared for in neat cemeteries with their names and dates faded beyond legibility. But even when burials are well-preserved, there's scant information to know and understand – to remember – the lives, beliefs, expectations, and ambitions of those who have gone before.

For instance, consider the implications of four old graves from the 1860s; all by themselves, out in an open field off Adams Creek Road, in Havelock's eastern orbit. Take a moment. Ponder the names. See the dates. The whole story is there.

George T. Willis	Sylvester Willis
Born March 5, 1833	Born February 27, 1867
Died November 21, 1867	Died November 12, 1867
Mary E. Willis	James V. Willis
Born March 25, 1837	Born November 28, 1861
Died April 6, 1867	Died November 30, 1865

George Thomas Willis married Mary E. Ellis on September 19, 1860.[b] Willis was a turpentine farmer with 150 acres of fertile land near Adams Creek. At just 27, he was well off compared to his peers. And according to his census filings, he was *very* well off compared to his neighbors overall. Perhaps he'd inherited the family farm. But his prospects must have appeared bright when he transported his beautiful new 23-year-old bride to their stately country home that fall.

Eleven months later, the Willises – with the deep joy common to any new parents – welcomed their first baby, a boy they named James.

But in less than three months – with the threat of Northern invasion growing by the day – Willis felt compelled to join Company H of the 3rd North Carolina Artillery on January 20, 1862. In mere weeks, a Union armada sailed by on the Neuse River and bombarded the shoreline with all the artillery a sixty-ship fleet could muster. The blue-clad Federal horde landed a few miles from the Willis farm on March 13. More than ten thousand of them attacked New Bern the following day leaving death and smoke and ruin in their wake. They'd stay four years.

Pvt. Willis joined for the duration of the war. He was part of Capt. Alexander C. Latham's six-gun light field artillery outfit. On the morning of March 14, 1862, Latham's men and artillery were on the Fort Thompson front line south of New Bern. They were set up on both sides of the Beaufort Road. There's evidence that Latham's Parrott gun fired the first shot at the advancing Union enemy. To say that Pvt. Willis and the other Latham men were actively engaged in the battle is an understatement. They were in the thick of the melee and fought to the bitter end. Willis was there as ten of his fellows were shot to pieces around him and eleven more were grievously wounded. In the end, all of their guns were lost and their position was overrun. Willis was taken prisoner on the field. [c]

We don't know what Mary and the baby endured alone while the young husband and father was gone to war. We don't know what other horrors George lived through. Or how much of his young son's life he missed. Or what shape the father was in when he finally returned home.

But we know from the evidence of the gravestones that within months of war's end – and a cruel two days passed his fourth birthday – little James V. Willis was dead. They buried him at home; in a field at the edge of the farm; a common practice in that era.

---

b This book is full of people named Ellis and Barnes, and the writer is directly related to none of them.

c *North Carolina Troops 1861-1865, A Roster*, Louis Manarin. 1966, Vol. 1, Artillery, pp. 464, 465, 478; Richard Sauers, *The Burnside Expedition in North Carolina,* pp. 259, 262, 284, & 298; Fold3.

Heart-rending as that must have been, life goes on.

Within six months George and Mary were expecting … maybe even hopeful, again.

Baby Sylvester was born in February 1867. But thirty-eight days later, Mary Ellis Willis, aged only 30 years, was shuffled off to the promise beyond. There might have been an accident. There might have been a fever, but death in childbirth, and from complications of childbirth – some unhealed wound; some infection – was in those times as common as the rain.

Though divorce was almost unknown, childbirth claimed enough women that many husbands were married twice. Some a third time. That makes it no less painful.

So, Mary's grave was added in April 1867 to the little field next to her firstborn.

More was to come. Within eight months, all of them had passed to that great unknown.

Infant Sylvester died in November. God knows why. He was buried in the field, the third fresh grave there.

And what took George just nine days later? Epidemics were recurrent, but they usually came in warmer weather. Still, a disease could have caused the father and son to die one after another. Was it starvation? Or was it that a once-strong man – who'd had his whole life ahead of him – came home only to see his wife and two sons die before his war-weary eyes? Did yellow fever take both George and Sylvester, one after the other, or did George Thomas Willis – unable the bear another day of life on the glorious planet Earth – stumble out into that sad field of graves on November 21, 1867, with a Navy Colt revolver he'd carried during the war?

In the end, we cannot know more than the tragic facts carved on the gravestones.

And the stories of people of African descent. They were close to half the population. Consider them.

In 1880, at Havelock, there's John R. Holland, a farmer. Of course. Farmer was the default occupation. You had to be some sort of maverick – a preacher or a blacksmith – to be otherwise.

So, there's John, 34, on any census website you choose. A hundred and forty years ago. Married to his beloved Emily Jane, 29. How do we know that? Well, he liked her enough to have Joshua, 13; Matilda, 11; Mulvina, 9; David, seven; Millie, five; and Joseph John, three. And John R. Holland is living in the village of Melvin, N.C., also known as "Little Witness," on what is now MCAS Cherry Point, He's among others of his race named Hammond and Fisher and Lovick and Dove and Batts and Nelson; among a huge community of African people, some of whom had never been slaves … and were proud of it.

He served as deacon of the Craven Corner Missionary Baptist Church and when he died in 1911, his friends and neighbors didn't just see to an obituary; they published a long "Resolution of Respect" in the newspaper.

His big brother, Joseph, aged 36, is next door with his wife Jane and their Biblically-named children: Jesse, Isaac, Noah, Abraham, and Sarah.

Look in the census and there they are. Alive. Breathing. Farming. Walking upon the land. Having children. Making their lives.

The written records confirm them. It's undeniable.

But today, all of these people are dead and gone. All but forgotten. Some of their very graves – their final resting places – either carelessly unmarked or inexcusably desecrated.

Where is even so much as the memory of them?

George Willis and John Holland, and Mary and Emily Jane – and this unknown Sparks – existed and walked upon the earth. They were men. They were women. They had dreams and aspirations. They loved and were loved. And now they're gone. Virtually no remnant of them remains.

Unless we make it so.

But what of Sparks? The solitary surname buried in an old report. What could be known?

As it turns out, answering that question gives a glimpse of the method, the magic, and the sometimes-mad obsession inherent in historical research.

The only Sparks, male or female. listed in the United States Census for Craven County between 1870 and 1930 is a blacksmith named A. J. Sparks. He's in Township 6 in 1889. This Sparks was a white man, age 58. So that wouldn't be him buried in the cemetery of a black village.

Would it?

In that year, Sparks is living with his wife, Martha, 42, and Lovey Davis – shown as a black female, age 49 – is in the household as a *domestic*. Based on the census takers numbering of households, Sparks appears to be living close to the southwest prong of Slocum Creek near the central part of old Havelock.

Then – later and far away – in 1900, we find a woman named Martha Sparks, 65, in the twelve-member household of her nephew, James Harrell, 43, a farmer in Upper Conetoe, Edgecombe County, about seven miles from Tarboro. She's listed as *aunt* [spelled *ant* by the census taker] and *housekeeper*. Her marital status is shown as "single" and her birthdate is given as January 1835. Among the dozen people living there is Sallie A. Harrell, aged 70, listed as James's mother.

It's about 85 miles from Havelock to Upper Conetoe, which is pronounced con-KNEE-toe. Martha Sparks is still living among the Harrells in 1910 and now correctly listed as a widow.

Using Edgecombe County as a clue, Martha Mayo Sparks is found buried among family members in the Harrell Cemetery, Tarboro, N.C. Her death certificate from the same county documents her birth there in 1837 and records her date of death as February 15, 1916, age 79.

And then comes the drumroll ...

Under Martha's name, the headstone reads *"Wife of A. J. Sparks."*

Further checking finds a marriage bond in Edgecombe County dated November 21, 1860, documenting the nuptials of Martha Ann Mayo and Andrew J. Sparks. They had a son, William A., and two daughters, Martha Luzetta, and Elizabeth Henrietta.

Based upon all the information, we can surmise that A. J. Sparks of Havelock died after June 1880 – when the census was taken – and before June 1900 having moved to or near Little Witness. (See the Cherry Point Cemetery Map for location, p. xv). Though white, in 1880 all of Spark's neighbors, according to the census, were African American so he may have successfully provided blacksmithing services for that community.

Matters cascade quickly after that. A search of old newspapers finds the notice of the executor for the estate of Andrew J. Sparks. His date of demise is given in the ad as September 3, 1884.

His will comes next. It's dated June 19, 1883, and states he was "of sound mind"

NOTICE.

STATE OF NORTH CAROLINA,
          Craven County.

The subscriber having qualified as Executor of the estate of Andrew J. Sparks, deceased, on the 3d day of September, A.D. 1884, before the Probate Court of Craven county, hereby notifies all persons having claims against said Estate, to present them for payment on or before the 3d day of September, 1885, or this notice will be pleaded in bar of their recovery.

All persons indebted to said Estate will make immediate payment.

Done this 3d day of September, 1884.

sep4 d0w   R. C. GARNER, Executor.

The Daily Journal (New Bern)
September 11, 1884

and in his "proper senses." He named R. C. Garner, then 41, of Carteret County to be his executor and that name appears in the notices that run in the newspaper the weeks following Sparks's death. Richard C. Garner was a "Dealer in Groceries" who lived on Sixth Street in Newport. Whatever else their relationship was, Garner's trade suggests Sparks knew he could trust the man's skills in the handling of business affairs. The train ran through downtown Newport giving Garner ease in traveling to Havelock and New Bern for probate matters.

And Sparks's hand-written will holds the key piece of information. In it he says:

"... that my wife Martha A. Sparks is to have the use and control of my land where I now live on Hancocks Creek containing seventy-five acres more or less during her natural life ..."[d]

The boundaries described in the will have the Sparks land bordered by Hancock Creek and Shop Branch. Shop Branch runs through Little Witness. Thus, the Sparks farm was directly adjacent to the old black settlement. Standing on his land, Andrew Sparks could have seen the Little Witness Baptist Church and the graveyard where we now know he was buried.

The people of Little Witness knew him. They'd lived with him, had seen and smelled the smoke from Sparks's blacksmith shop. They'd have heard his hammer ringing on the anvil as he pounded horseshoes into shape.

Sparks left his blacksmith tools – the bellows, tongs, hammers and draw dogs – to black neighbor Amos Bryant. Bryant was a 63-year-old farmer in 1880; married to Affie, 39; with three daughters, Caroline, 16, Emily Jane, 13, and Emeline, 11; and son, James Edward, eight.

From his land at Little Witness, Andrew J. Sparks could have seen the home of the woman – Emma Hill Stevens – who has now brought him back to life, by recalling his name, by a single spark of her memory.

Here's the most curious part of the story.

Emma Hill did not know A. J. Sparks. When she was born on May 29, 1891, he'd been dead six years and eight months.

Somehow a man named Sparks – or more accurately, the life of a man named Sparks – had meant enough, had made enough of an impression on people in a small pocket of southeastern Craven County, that the unmarked place of his burial was known to people born after he was gone.

Despite that bit of serendipity, we don't know today where Sparks is buried. Through the jumble of the creation of a military base, all that's left of him is a single line written in a forest service surveyor's report ... and now what has been written here.

For this writer, Andrew Jacob Sparks, George, Mary, Sylvester, and James Willis, and John Holland and his beloved brood – and Emma Hill Stevens, too – are emblematic of the many thousands of southern Craven County people who have lived, died, and been forgotten; whose final resting places have gone unmarked, been overgrown, trammeled by time, or unceremoniously and intentionally dishonored. They're emblematic also of an entire history of half a county that has been overlooked, unrecorded, and even had its very place in history denied.

---

[d] Craven County records, Will of A.J. Sparks, pg. 364.

The misstatements and denials that anything happened – at least anything meaningful – on the south shore of the Neuse River before 1941, or that anything was, or had ever been there at all, were at times frustrating, at other times exasperating, but ultimately inspiring. Perhaps this book will, finally, put an end to such misconceptions, misunderstandings, and myths.

May it be so.

In any event, beyond the bare facts to be presented in this book – beyond the enumerated details to be reckoned with – life is filled with mystery. It's left for us, the living, to parse out what meaning there may be as we quiet ourselves and listen for the whispers of the long departed.

SOUTH SHORE NEUSE RIVER 1733. Excerpted from *A New and Correct Map of the Province of North Carolina* by Edward Moseley. Used by permission of Special Collections, J. Y. Joyner Library, East Carolina University.

Moonrise on the Neuse

In all of God's vast creation, there are few wonders more spectacular, stunning, or gorgeous than the rise of the full moon above the banks of the Neuse River's south shore. The effect is perfect only a few times a year; when it's still, quiet, and flat calm. But when a golden harvest or blood-red, or, particularly, the impossibly white bright moon comes up suddenly into an otherwise black and empty sky, and when its bottom edge moves just this much above the Earth's horizon, and the improbably-large lunar disc is reflected on the dusky plane of the miles-wide Neuse, there comes an exquisite perfume of timelessness, a refrain of eternity, a hush of infinity, in which the Moon is no longer the Earth's distant cold satellite, but instead a near and vital sibling.

There's a sense in this solitary moment that every person – every living creature – on the river's shore, stands transmuted to exquisite unity, communing, and anointed in speechless awe.

Know this: From the earliest days of America, Europeans and Africans were here in southern Craven County and that they were surely touched and left dumbstruck by that moon.

From the Trent River to Adams Creek – in the place we now call Havelock, on what is today Cherry Point, at Harlowe, on the banks of creeks called Clubfoot and Hancock and Slocum – up and down the entire south shore of the Neuse River – immigrants were settled, even before New Bern's founding in 1710.

How early? 1707 surely. 1702 probably. 1701. Maybe before.

But that's nothing.

There were human beings on the banks of this river *thousands* of years before it was even called the Neuse. They were here so long ago they weren't even Indians. Archaeologists call them Paleo-Indians.

Anthropologists tell us you could take a man and a woman from the Stone Age, comb their hair, dress them in contemporary fashions, and they wouldn't draw a second glance walking down Middle Street. They looked like us. They were smart. They felt hunger and thirst. They felt the love of family and fear of things that make noise in the dark. Just as we do.

It's something to ponder. The United States of America is not yet 300 years old and things have been found along the Neuse River made by human beings that date to 7,000 years in the past.

That long ago, in 5,000 B.C., the Sahara in Africa was green. Humans in China were just beginning to cultivate rice. Aboriginals in Australia were carving patterns on rocks. Linguists believe a precursor of the oldest-known language was being spoken in Europe but it left no written form and no known structure. The Egyptians and Assyrians were millennia in the future.

In that long-ago epoch, along what we now call the Neuse, human beings lived in villages. They raised children. They hunted. They gathered. They fished. They wove cloth and they made pottery.

And, ever so often, they must have stood in amazement, momentarily silenced by the magnificent moonrise over the river.

The Ancient Ones

The evidence we have – good evidence – tells us the entire Neuse basin was active and alive with humans for longer than many of us are equipped to imagine. We happen to know the most about the area around Slocum Creek and Hancock Creek because federal regulations have required, and federal dollars have afforded, one archaeological study after another on the Marine Corps airbase. The land there has been surveyed and mapped and dug and sifted. The things found have been drawn and photographed and analyzed and carbon-dated more than any other local place we know.

What has been discovered at MCAS Cherry Point can be extrapolated to be true for all the county's riverine habitats but it's from those plus-or-minus 11,000 acres that we have hard data.

Archaeological shovel tests in 2003 yielded from a single site near Slocum Creek 2,329 prehistoric artifacts. When assembled, there were 2,142 pieces of pottery – what the scientists call "ceramic sherds" – 131 stone tools or items left from stone tool making – what they call "lithic artifacts – and

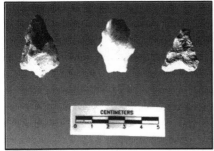

Prehistoric fabric-impressed ceramics, at right, and lithic biface projectile points, above, recovered during an MCAS Cherry Point archeological survey in 2003. Multiple sites were investigated. A single location near Slocum Creek yielded more than 2,000 stone and pottery artifacts during the dig by a research team.
Goodwin & Associates; R-10-Davis-2003.

"65 fragments of organic material." The artifact inventory from the single site ran to hundreds of pages.[a]

The pottery sherds are ingeniously made ceramic items. The south shore of the Neuse is an abundant source of clay for making pots. Several different kinds can be identified today during a casual walk on a riverside beach. When made hard with fire, the handmade clay vessels have the same utility as bowls and pots found in a modern kitchen. But the ancient ones figured out methods for "tempering" the clay; adding materials to make it stronger. A local favorite was quartz. Many of the sherds found at Cherry Point were quartz-tempered. Others were tempered with fiber, red hematite, shells, or sand.

Pottery was decorated by different groups and even by different potters. By pressing fabric or cords over the surface of the clay before firing, unique patterns were created. Experts use the patterns of the pottery pieces to classify age ranges. One of the time ranges, the Woodland Period – divided by archaeologists into subgroups of Early, Middle, and Late – runs from 1,600 A.D. to 1,000 B.C.[b]

---

[a] Thomas W. Davis, PhD., R. Christopher Goodwin & Associates, Inc., *Archeological Investigations at MCAS Cherry Point*, April 2003, pg. 63. R-10-Davis-2003.

[b] Ibid, pg. 38.

Of the pottery that could be identified from this single Cherry Point site, all of it fell into one of the three Woodland categories. [c]

Matters were even more interesting in the stone material.

Archaeologists don't call them arrowheads. They call them "bifaces." A biface is any kind of tool that has been worked and chipped on both sides to make it sharp. Bifaces can be arrow points, spear points, scrapers, and awls. A palm-sized biface made round on one side and sharp on the other could be used to butcher meat. It could scrape hides for curing and for later use in clothing or for shelter.

One of the bifaces found at the Slocum Creek site was classified as a Morrow Mountain II projectile point. That doesn't mean it was made in the mountains. Morrow Mountain is a style of arrow point-making and it goes back to the Stone Age. Of course, scientists don't call it that. They call it the Middle Archaic. The Middle Archaic will get you back to 5,000 B.C. Add 2,000 years for the current era and we are deep into prehistory.[d]

Exploration of the Slocum Creek site convinced the study team that they'd identified a village location of about one thousand feet square. And it had been occupied for at least 700 years … much more than twice as long as the United States has existed.

This is all from a single location on the south shore of the Neuse River.

Those charged with studying and preserving cultural resources are guarded about revealing precise locations to the public. We know from a variety of sources that as many as two dozen prehistoric sites have been identified on MCAS Cherry Point alone. Also, prehistoric material has been found on Hancock Creek, Cahoogue Creek, Clubfoot Creek, Adams Creek, Otter Creek, and the Catfish Lake area. Similar locations have been identified throughout the Croatan National Forest.

As one archaeologist once told us, "Indians were everywhere."

That goes for Paleo-Indians, too.

A Few Thousand Years Later

Fast-forward several millennia and the still-Stone Age culture of the coastal Carolina natives is suddenly thrown into close contact with "civilized" Europeans who begin coming up the river looking for a place to settle. The Native Americans have taken their name from the big river where they live, or vice versa. In any event, the tribal Neusiok look on, at first with curiosity, later with amusement, and finally with something bordering on

---

[c] Ibid, pg. 83.
[d] Ibid, pg. 106.

horror as the number of arriving white people increases from a trickle to a flood.

A clash is inevitable.

When it comes, it will be as brutal as it is decisive.

Take a look at the 1733 map that heads this chapter. Starting from the left on the south shore of "Neus River" are C. Glover, A. Hatch, and W. Hancock. Capt. William Handcock – as you can see – was on land between Handcock's Creek and Slocumb's Creek. That's the exact site of today's Cherry Point airbase. Charlesworth Glover and Anthony Hatch were land-holders on each side of a watercourse then known as Glover's Creek but now called Otter Creek.

Otter Creek – in line with today's Catfish Lake Road off US 70 near Croatan – would be the position of the southernmost fortifications in defense of New Bern from Northern invasion in 1862. But that's a long time in the future of this story, and we'll get back to it later.

The illustration above is part of *A New and Correct Map of the Province of North Carolina* created by Edward Moseley in 1733. The original Moseley Map is one of the treasures of the manuscript collection at East Carolina University in Greenville. It verifies that by the year of its creation people named Glover, Hatch, Slocumb, and Hancock were on the south shore at the river's tributaries already called Slocumbs, Handcocks, Club-foot, Adams, and South River. But these familial names are merely land-marks because by 1733 there were scores of farmers and planters, grant-holders, and speculators who had already cleared land, built homes, and were raising children in the abundant woodlands of southern Craven County.

In fact, by the 1730s, this was a hot real estate market. Large tracts of raw land and ready-for-move-in plantations were changing hands like kids' trading cards. To see this for oneself – as recently as the 1990s – it was necessary to go to the Craven County Register of Deeds office in New Bern and thumb through very old, very thick, and very heavy ledgers turning the leaves of the yellowed, handwritten documents one by one. Now, the old index books are all searchable online at the office's website.

In Book 1 at page 100, for instance, is a 1738 deed wherein William Handcock is transferring 300 acres of land – a plantation called Wormitt Fields – to his beloved son, appropriately named William Handcock, Jr. It's at the mouth of Slocumb's Creek, on the creek's east side and bounded to the south by Duck Creek. In it, William, Sr. described the land as "being part of a large tract, granted to John Slocumb by a patent bearing the date the 13th of December 1716."

Few at the helm of their gleaming golf carts, sipping a favorite adult beverage, while cruising down the macadam paths of the Sound of Freedom course aboard Marine Corps Air Station Cherry Point in, say, 2019, imagined they were traversing an ancient plantation called Wormitt Fields.[e]

And few before now have fathomed that all of the lands on the river's south shore have been traversed, occupied, inhabited, and worked by immigrant settlers since the early 1700s. There's a persistent impression that the entire area was pristine wilderness into the modern era. The truth is – as we shall see – that there have been several waves of settlement and outmigration in southern Craven County. The third wave of outmigration, propelled by the Great Depression, was at its peak in 1940. This wave was initially *accelerated* by the coming of the Marine Corps airbase. No one arriving at Cherry Point after 1941 had any reason to suspect that four named villages had been leveled to make way for the base. Or that it had once been among the most densely settled slave plantation areas in the South. Or that it had been a red-hot real estate market when Louis XV was King of France.

Dating South Shore Settlement by Europeans

Slocumb, Slocombe, Slokum, Slocum. We've seen the name of this key family of early settlement on the south shore of the Neuse River spelled eight or ten different ways. The most common forms have been Slocumb and Slocum with the latter winning out in modern times. But it's not just the spelling of the name that's convoluted. Both the history of the family and its genealogy are difficult to untangle as well. Though we know that John Slocum was among the earliest settlers of the Neuse River basin, documentation is scant. Matters aren't helped any by the most authoritative book on the Slocums – a tome massive enough to be used as a doorstop – which claims that Slocum Creek in Craven County, North Carolina was named for a soldier of the Revolutionary War.[f]

Ezekiel Slocumb was a hero indeed. He was born on Slocum Creek. He and his wife, Mary, were both notables of the Battle of Moore's Creek Bridge near Wilmington. But by the time Sgt. (later Col.) Slocum helped defeat the British – and his wife made her celebrated ride to care for wounded soldiers – people had been referring to the creek by his family's name for six or seven decades. As the 1733 map detail above makes clear, the waterway that transects modern Havelock and has played such a

---

[e] Wormitt, or Wormit, is a small town on the banks of the Firth of Tay in northeast Fife, Scotland. The Tay actually looks a bit like the Neuse.

[f] *A Short History of the Slocums, Slocumbs and Slocombes in America*; Charles Elihu Slocum, 1882.

prominent role in the area's history was named Slocumb's Creek well before Ezekiel's 1760 birth.

The best decipherment of surviving documents suggests the creek's namesake is John Slocum – a forebear of Ezekiel to be sure – who moved to "Neus River" from more northern Carolina circa 1700. How *circa* we don't know, but he was among a group of stalwarts living here even before the Swiss and German Palatines, who in 1710 founded the famous colony of New Bern a little more than a dozen miles upstream.

John Slocum was William Hancock's cousin and both were well connected to the source of all land grants in the Carolinas because they were relatives of Old Anthony Slocum. Old Anthony was the Lords Proprietors Deputy, the Lords Proprietors of England being the "owners" of North and South Carolina.[g]

Why "old" Anthony? Well, he lived to be 97 or 98 (1590-1688), a rare feat in those times. He's come down to us as Anthony *Slocombe*. But his own will spells his name *Slokum*. For simplicity, we're going to stick with the modern version here – Slocum.

A few of the key pieces of evidence are the will of Old Anthony of Edenton, N. C. in which he names his offspring, and some early land grant abstracts preserved in the North Carolina Historical and Genealogical Register (NCHGR) of January 1900. In his will proved November 26, 1688, he bequeathed land to his son John and his grandsons, John and Samuel.[h]

The Slocums were evidently in the Pamlico Sound area of the state by

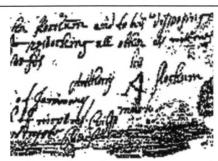

Anthony Slocumb, an ancestor and benefactor of one of southern Craven County's founding settlers, John Slocumb, signed his will with a big letter "A" at Edenton in the late 1600s.

1684 because three land patents were issued to them in that year at Chowan: 600 acres to Anthony Slocum; 200 acres to Joseph Slocum; and 400 acres to John Slocum. We can be sure that John Slocum was on the South Shore of the Neuse River by or before 1706 because a land grant on Dam Creek to William Glover, Esq. in May of that year describes the land as "adjoining" John Slocum and Charlesworth Glover. Dam Creek divides present-day residential subdivisions of

---

[g] J. Bryan Grimes, Secretary of State, *Abstract of North Carolina Wills*, 1910, pg. 149; NCHGR, page 224.

[h] Grimes, Abstract, 1910, pg. 343.

Carolina Pines and Stately Pines and, among other things, the 1733 Moseley Map labels the location of both Slocum Creek and Charlesworth Glover.

In further evidence of John Slocum's early arrival, he was among a group of his neighbors who petitioned the colonial government for "a court at Neuse River" in 1706.

After the establishment of the court for which they petitioned, it met at people's residences. During the period 1713-1715, the court often assembled at Jacob Miller's Green Springs house on the river south of New Bern. Sometimes, the court was held at William Hancock's house. Invariable, John Slocum was a justice of the court along with others like William Brice, John Nelson, George Bell, or Richard Graves. [i]

Minutes of one such meeting read, "Court held at the house of Capt. Jacob Miller, Esqr., the third Tuesday in August 1713. Present: John Nelson, Judge; Col. William Brice, John Slocum, George Bell, Jacob Miller."

In 1715, "the Vestrymen of Craven Parish" were named upon the passage of the North Carolina colonial assembly's act establishing the church of the "Anglican or Episcopal faith." The vestry was the organizing men of the church; in this case, Christ Church in New Bern. These men included John Slocumb, William Hancock, Col. William Brice, John Nelson, Capt. Richard Graves, Daniel McFarlan, John Smith, John Mackey, Thomas Smith, Joseph Bell, Martin Frank, and Jacob Sheets. [j]

In the Craven County tax list of 1720, Slocum claimed the second largest family with eight members, next in line after William Brice's nine "taxables." One modern researcher counted Slocum among the county's "wealthy landowners." [k]

In "Craven Precinct" in September 1722 Anthony Slocum's son, John, left "my dwelling plantation" on Slocum Creek to his son John. He left land there to other sons and a daughter: "land known as Josias Slocum's" to Joseph, "land on Mill Branch" to Jeseway, Josias, and Elizabeth. The will was proven before "Capt. William Handcock" and signed by Clerk of Court Caleb Metcalf.

When Anthony Slocum's grandson John died at Slocum Creek about December 1759, he mentioned his cousins, Joseph and John Charles Slocumb, and his mother, Mary, and his wife, also named Mary. The will was witnessed by Grigg Yarborough. [l]

---

[i] *Carolina and the Southern Cross*, Vol. 1, No. 12, March 1914, pg. 16.

[j] Gertrude Carraway, *Crown of Life: History of Christ Church*, 1940, pg. 25.

[k] Watson, Alan, *A History of New Bern and Craven County*, Tryon Palace Commission, 1987, pg. 616, item 2.

[l] Grimes, Abstracts, 1910, pg. 343.

While the exact date of the first John Slocum's arrival is unclear, he was certainly among the earliest on the south shore since everyone else's deeds and grants reference the creek already named for him.

Early Land Grants on the South Shore of the Neuse River

In 1706, Charlesworth Glover received a land grant described as follows, "West side of Dam Creek. 640 acres ye South side of Neuse River, joining mouth of Otter Creek, ye wood, ye mouth of Dam Creek and ye said river." All existing land grants can be found by searching. They're recorded and cited like this one: Patent Book 1, 420, page 154, May 11. ᵐ

The same year, "Ye Honorable W[illiam] Glover, Esq." received an interesting grant on the "East side of Dam Creek. 860 acres on ye South side of Neuse River, joining Dam Creek, ye mouth of the river, John Slocumbe, a branch of said creek and Charlesworth Glover." Patent Book 1, 419, page 153, May 11, 1706.

William Glover (1653–1713), an attorney, was Governor of North Carolina from 1706 to 1708. His administration was overthrown by Thomas Cary in "Cary's Rebellion" of 1708-1711. Glover was driven out of the state and confusion within the fledgling North Carolina government hampered the state's response to the Tuscarora Indian uprising in 1711.

Charlesworth Glover was his son. William Glover also had a son named William but the titles "ye honorable" and "esquire" indicates that the governor was the one granted the Neuse River land during his first year in office.

Other early land grants:

- In 1707, Robert Coleman – "250 acres, in Slocumbe Creek in New Beginning at Coleman's Creek, joining Glover's and Coleman's Creek." Patent Book 1, grant number 404, page 148, September 10. Also, Book 1, 458, page 165.
  Coleman's Creek would later be called Tucker Creek.
- Alexander Goodgroom – "220 acres, up Hancock's Creek in Neuse, joining the creek." Book 1, 429, pg. 157.
- William Handcock – 1,320 acres, "in Neuse on Hancock Creek."
- William Handcock, Jr. – "640 acres adjoining his father in Neuse, King's Creek and the river." Book 1, 430, pg. 158.
- Edward Beicheino – "15 ½ acres on Slocumb's Creek above Mr. Coleman joining a little creek, small gut or run and the main creek." Book1, 431, pg. 158.

ᵐ **For locations of watercourses mentioned, see the alphabetical list in the Part IV.**

- Christopher Dawson – "200 acres in Adams Creek in Neuse joining John Kiton." Book 1, grant 424, pg. 156.
- Dutton Lane – "220 acres in the fork of Hancocks Creek in Neuse, joining a little creek." 1, 438, 160.
- Amy Thurle – "300 acres at Hancocks creek, joining the river, Slocumb, the head of a little creek and ye said creek." 1, 452, 164.[n]
- Edward Haynes – "640 acres above Mr. Hancock on Hancocks Creek in Neuse." 1, 453, 164.
- John Kiton – "640 acres, Adams Creek, Neuse, joining Thomas Lewis." 1, 455, 164.
- James Walker – "640 acres in Neuse, joining Kings Creek to ye creek's mouth." 1, 457, 165.

Other early records lodged at New Bern were lost in the Tuscarora Indian attacks beginning September 22, 1711.

Historian Emma Powell wrote, "In 1710 came a colony of Welsh Quakers and settled below New Bern, on Clubfoot and Hancock creek, on the south side of the Neuse. Among these were Thomas and John Lovick, the latter of whom was one of the North Carolina Boundary Commission in 1728 to settle the line between Virginia and North Carolina." [o]

Also in this group were brothers Evan and Roger Jones, who settled on the Neuse River near the mouth of Slocum Creek.

Selected land grants continue:

- In 1713, Anthony Hatch – "640 acres, south side of Neuse, joining ye mouth of Otter Creek, ye head, ye woods, and a branch of the River." Book 1, 711, page 245.
- In 1716, John Slocumb – "820 acres at Neuse River and ye East Side of Slocumbs Creek, joining ye mouth of Mill Creek, the main creek, ye main gutt, his other land, and a branch." 1, 1362, 343.
- John Slocum – "350 acres on the South side of Neuse River, joining his land on ye East Side of Slocumb Creek, ye fork of a branch and the main course." 1, 1363, 343.
- John Slocum – "640 acres next to Wm. Glover." 1, 1367, 344.
- William Booth – 380 acres at Clubfoot Creek.
- In 1717, Simon Keeler – "60 acres joining Dennis O'Dier on Coleman's Creek and the fork of said creek." 1, 1349, 339.
- 1720: Christian Isler – 390 acres at the head of Coleman's Creek [*formerly survey of Dennis O'Dier "but elapsed."*] 1, 1273, 313.

---

[n] Amy, in this case, is the name of a man. The last name variously appears in other places as *Thirel* and *Thurel*.

[o] *New Bern, N. C. Founded by De Graffenried in 1710*, Emma H. Powell, 1905.

- John Tannyhill – "Mouth of Adams Creek." 1, 1276, 314.

During these same years, partial records and references indicate others received land grants and these mention patents for individuals not recorded elsewhere. Among them were grants on Hancock Creek to Martin Frank, two parcels totaling 230 acres on the west side of the creek and another joining the land of Dalton [Dutton] Lane; Jacob Sweet, 230 acres on the west side "above Bryan Lee"; and 200 acres to Edward Hays. Robert Jones received a grant for 100 acres on the west side of Slocum Creek in 1730 "joining Dennis O'Dier" with a reference to land at Adams Creek that Jones had acquired from a grant in 1716. [p]

The famous explorer and co-founder of New Bern, John Lawson, received a 640-acre grant on Clubfoot Creek in 1706, the documentation of which gives us its old Indian name – *Hutosquock*. While the original name is interesting so is the fact that the creek had taken on the name "Clubfoot" by 1706.

William Hancock's October 10, 1707 grants for 1,320 acres on his self-named creek included a home that he'd already built there. It was on the creek's east side near the Neuse. The mention of a dwelling house in a land grant is exceedingly rare. While Hancock was granted and sold numerous and sizable parcels of land in the area, he lived at Hancock's Creek.

Some people never settled their land but sold it to other settlers. William Glover, for example, may not have lived on or cultivated his Neuse River tract granted in 1706 to the west of Slocum Creek's mouth. He later sold it as he did thousands of other acres from dozens of land grants he received across the colony. [q]

Colonial surveyor John Lovick acquired in 1719 the first 190-acre parcel of plantation land that would one day stretch from Dam Creek to Slocum Creek. One historian described Lovick as being among "other leaders who afterward became prominent." [r]

Lovick family holdings on the Neuse grew into a successful and long-lived 1,250-acre farm called Magnolia Plantation and became the central part of the successful agricultural region west of Slocum Creek that came to be known as *The Croatan*.

As mentioned above, Lovick, a surveyor by trade was chosen in 1728 by the colony's governor to be one of the four commissioners charged with settling the disputed border between Virginia and North Carolina.

---

[p] O'Dier, whose name is found elsewhere as *O'Dyer* and *O'Dia*, appears to have been a speculator in land with property on both sides of the river. He later sold 300 acres of his land on Hancock Creek to settler John Clark. O'Dier was the step-son of Robert Coleman.

[q] ARC, pg. 22.

[r] Descendent Mary McGrath interview, and county records of Elizabeth Moore.

In 1707, French Huguenots arrived in the Neuse basin followed in 1710 by the aforementioned Quaker settlers from Wales, the same year that Swiss and German Palatines led by Christopher DeGraffenried settled New Bern at the intersection of the Neuse and Trent rivers.

The Massacres of 1711

The wave of settlement that resulted in the founding of New Bern was the most important, most successful, and longest-lasting in the Neuse basin. New Bern became the capital of the colony of North Carolina and one of the important towns and vital ports of early America. It's been continuously occupied since 1710 and has, through good time and bad, developed a rich and interesting history.

Still, in considering early pioneers, even New Bern must be seen as one of the waves of settlement among many.

People were streaming out of Europe by the boatload, undertaking the dangerous voyage to escape the nightmares of war, disease, and hunger. Surviving letters from a few Neuse River colonists illuminate the reason so many undertook the "difficult journey over the fearful and wild sea." Repeatedly, they talk about food.

Christen Engel wrote in 1711, "I would also wish that the poor neighbors were with us and then they would not need to suffer hunger if they would only be willing to work a little."

The same year, Jacob Gabley wrote to relatives in Europe, "I will say that for the workman or poor man it is then better here. He can get as much land as he needs. He can keep as much stock as he is able. Swine cost nothing to keep. Cattle go the whole year on pasture, become fat and good to butcher by themselves."

Another urged, "Therefore, whoever has the desire for it, let him just venture boldly under the protection of the Most High."

And Christen Jantz wrote, "We lie on a stream called Neuss. That is where 6 years ago they started cultivating, the English until 2 years ago, and then the Swiss people; most of them were as poor as we. They are, it seems to me, all of them rich enough with livestock, all kinds of crops, and the best tree fruit, and work about two months during the whole year." [s]

Others came seeking religious freedom and safety. For decades Catholics and Protestants in Europe had been relentlessly carrying out slaughters, reprisals, and repression against one another. French Huguenots, Quakers, Calvinists, Puritans, and other dissenters like Presbyterians,

---

[s] *Swiss American Historical Society Review*, Volume 45, No. 3, November 2009.

Baptists, Methodists, and Lutherans came seeking relief from religious persecution on the old continent. [t]

Tensions created by the influx of land-hungry Europeans soon coalesced into a pitiless uprising by the indigenous Tuscarora Indians and their satellite tribes. The horrific attacks began at sunrise on September 22, 1711. They were well-coordinated with the Native American warriors striking simultaneously across a multi-county area. Settlers and livestock were killed. Mutilation was common. Plantation homes and outbuildings were burned. The nascent settlement of New Bern was particularly hard hit with many killed and much of it put to the torch by the marauders.

Hundreds of settlers – men, women, children, and infants – met their deaths in the countryside within the first few hours, but the attacks continued in the following weeks and months. On their riverfront farm just to the east of Slocum Creek trouble came for Evan and Roger Jones. Jones's family history says, "While these brothers were burning a tar-kiln they were surprised by Indians ... They caught Roger and cut off his head." [u]

Following the devastating 1711 attacks, survivors sent an obsequious plea to Virginia Lieutenant Governor Alexander Spotswood seeking military aid. While the word "ye" appears repeatedly in the original and the spelling is amusing (*Vergeney* for Virginia; *masecre* for massacre; and *voyse* for voice, *releafe* for relief, for example), the spelling, punctuation and capitalizations have been edited here to something more familiar to the modern reader. It's all worth reading but boldface is added to the most dramatic parts.

*To the Right Honorable Alexander Spotswood, Lt. Gov of Virginia, The humble petition of **the poor distressed inhabitants of Neuse River** ... most humbly shows your Excellency— That whereas there has, by the permission of Almighty God for our sins and disobedience, been **a most horrid massacre committed by the Tuscarora Indians** upon Her Majesty's poor subjects in the said province of North Carolina, and we, **Her Majesty's** [Queen Anne of Great Britain] **poor subjects, who by God's providence have survived, are in continual dread and do suffer daily destruction in our stocks and horses and fencing being burned—which if not speedily prevented, we must all likewise perish with our brethren**, for we have not force, nor indeed any speedy care taken to prevent it in our country, but, for as much as we are Her Majesty's subjects, and ready at all times to be observant to Her Majesty's royal commands, we do therefore with one voice, knowing your Excellency's care and paternal tenderness towards all Her Majesty's subjects, **most humbly beseech***

---

[t] Carraway, *Crown of Life*, 1940, pg. 19.

[u] *The Jones Family of Craven County, N.C.*, Catherine Boyd Brown - Mary C. Roberts.

*and implore your Honor as you tender the welfare of Her Majesty's poor subjects, forthwith **to send to our relief some considerable force of men, arms and ammunition to detect the barbarous insolvency of those rebellious rogues**, and as for provision, we are ready to the uttermost of our ability to assist the army if your Excellency pleases to send them— which we shall daily pray for: So hoping your Excellency will take into your sage consideration our destressed condition, we your poor petition- ers as in duty bound shall ever pray—* [v]

Among the numerous signers on the south shore were William Han- cock, John Slocum, Adam Ferguson, and Adam Ferguson, Jr. The Fergu- sons hailed from, and are considered the namesakes of, Adams Creek. Wil- liam Hancock, Jr. may also have signed the letter though the signatures have been partially obscured by time.

Spotswood never sent help. Relief came in the form of South Carolina soldiers and their Native American allies. It was mid-1713 before major hostilities wound down.

Deciphering the Old Records

With insects, rodents, mildew, hurricanes, human error, fire, and war, it's fortunate that anything has been preserved so long.

J. Bryan Grimes served as North Carolina's secretary of state from 1901-1923. During his tenure in office, he oversaw a project to secure the valuable information contained in the state's oldest wills. Writing in his office's book on the subject, Grimes cited the General Assembly of 1754 as having found – even at that early date – that "many of the original wills, patents and deeds have been lost for want of convenient offices to keep the same." Grimes suggested "the various migrations" of the North Carolina capital from New Bern to Hillsborough to Raleigh had "undoubtedly added to the losses." He said that many of the documents on hand in 1910 were "in bad order, decayed, foxed and faded, and some of them are illegible." [w]

The problems of lost records also devolve from the shift in political divisions in the colony. Beginning in 1696, the south shore of the Neuse River was part of Bath County. Later Bath County was divided into three parts – Pamplicough, Wyckham, and Archdale – with the south shore being in the latter. Thus, land records might say the property was in Bath County or Archdale Precinct. Then, in 1712. the names were changed again to the

---

[v] *Petition from the inhabitants of the Neuse River area concerning attacks by Native Americans*, Benjamin Simson, et al., 1711, Vol. 1, pgs. 819-820; *The Calendar of Vir- ginia State Papers*, Vol. 1. Pg. 154.
[w] Grimes, Abstracts, 1910, Introduction, pg. v.

precincts of Beaufort, Hyde, and Craven. As these shifts occurred, some records probably stayed in place while others made perilous journeys over muddy roads and various waterways. Finally, in 1739, Bath County became extinct.

Remarkably, Craven County deeds are intact from 1739.

That's still a gap of nearly four decades from the earliest known and suspected settlement activity along the south shore of the Neuse River. Some of the records destroyed in the Indian war or otherwise lost were re-recorded or stipulated by affidavit, in Craven County Deed Book Two.

One example of this process is the following document inserted in Craven County records:

"WHEREAS in the year 1711 there was acknowledged in Open Court in Craven Precinct a conveyance of six hundred and forty acres of land from John Keaton by Capt. John Nelson, lawful attorney to the said Keaton, to Adam Ferguson, the said land being in Adams Creek upon Neuse River and by Misfortune of the War in this Government with the Indians the office of the aforementioned Precinct of Craven being burnt, wherein was the above-mentioned conveyance of the above tract of land Recorded according to the law: Therefore, to prevent all trouble and incumbrances of ill-minded people, John Slocum, Esq. being then one of the members of the said Court when the above acknowledgment was made as above mentioned as well as at the time in Open Court made Oath on the Holy Evangelist that he saw the above-mentioned conveyance proved in Open Court by the oath of John Smith and Thomas Lewis and acknowledged to Adam Ferguson, and by Capt. John Nelson, attorney to the said Keaton, as above said and John Smith made oath on the Holy Evangelist in Open Court that said John Keaton sign, seal, and deliver the above-mentioned conveyance unto Adam Ferguson as his act and deed."

Some Craven Precinct deeds are recorded in other places, such as Beaufort County. A few loose records are held in various archives around the state. But, it's more than fair to say the record is incomplete.

Nevertheless, some 170 land grants are known to have been made along the Neuse River between 1705 and 1711. Fourteen of these were acquired by William Hancock alone.

The future Craven County was organized at New Bern in 1712, virtually from the ashes of the Tuscarora war. In a pattern that became the norm during western expansion, once the Native American competition was eliminated, settlers poured in. The number of Craven County's taxable residents grew ten-fold from 1720 to 1755. The influx created a land boom of major proportion along the river's south shore. [x]

A Southern Craven County Land Rush

The existing land records fill an entire library-like hall at the Craven County Register of Deeds Office. Likewise, the list of North Carolina land grants from the colonial period up to the beginning of the United States of America is voluminous enough to have its own website. Thus, only a tiny fraction can be offered here as examples of the dramatic influx of people that followed the conclusion of the Tuscarora War.

Because their names are interesting, we begin with Florence Swellwant who sold one hundred acres on the west side of Hancock Creek to Job Taner in December 1733.

In 1755, Robert Roe of Virginia sold 2,050 acres to John Physioc for "fifty pounds proclamation money." The land was on the west side of Slocumb's Creek. Other property owners mentioned in the deed include James Keith and his patent of 1714, William Hancock, George Keith, Edward Beichenoe, and Thomas Lee.

In 1760, Butler Smith of Virginia sold 860 acres at the mouth of Dam Creek next to John Slocumb "on Nuce River" to George Phenney Lovick for 400 pounds.

On October 2, 1765, "Jacob Taylor, carpenter, purchased from Samuel Collins & Joseph Collins – 250 acres on Slocumb Ck." The land is described as having been "patented by Robert Coleman, dated 10 Sept. 1707."

In 1766, Henry Always acquired 175 acres next to William Rutledge on the east side of "Mockcock branch," a tributary of Hancock Creek.

Lydia Guard acquired her 300 acres "on the Westernmost branch of Slocums Creek" in 1771.

Susannah Goodett (Godette) received fifty acres near the head of Mitchell Creek on the south side of the Neuse River in 1799.

At Coleman's Creek, later known as Tucker Creek, we find Robert Coleman, 1720, 620 acres; Peter Smith, 1756, 410 acres; and later Stephen Gooding, 1808, 100 acres. In 1758, George Barber and James Davis took up land there. Roger Bratcher received a grant for 300 acres in 1772 and Absalom Taylor received 65 acres in 1774.

Hancock Creek was desirable because of the many fine landing places along its banks. Here are names, dates, and acreages on the creek during the

---

[x] *A Phase 1 Archeological Survey of Three U.S. Marine Corps Housing Locations, Craven County, North Carolina*, John Milner Associates. R-21-Reeves et al, 1994, pg. 5.

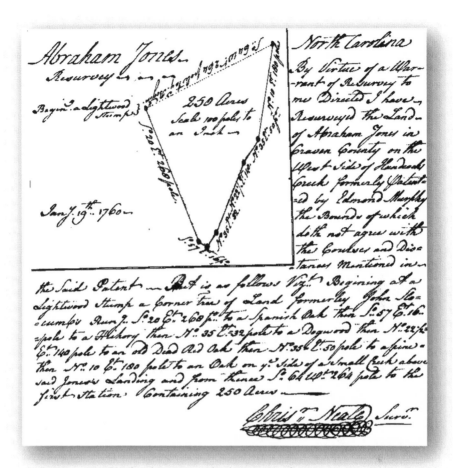

A January 19, 1760, land grant to Abraham Jones for 250 acres on the west side of Hancock Creek, a tract that today lies within MCAS Cherry Point. The property is described as having a common corner with land formerly owned by John Slocum. The grant uses a lightwood stump, a Spanish oak, a hickory tree, a dogwood, and a dead red oak as landmarks. It's stylishly signed by Christopher Neale, county clerk, soldier, and politician; one of the important men of early colonial affairs. *Craven County Register of Deeds Office.*

busy land rush period: John Blake, 1766, 100 acres; James Black, 1759, 90 acres; Joseph Masters, 1745, 150 acres; Leonard Loftin, 1745, 400 acres; Obadiah Yarbrough, 1761, 340 acres; Roger James, 1792, 250 acres; Thomas Lovick, 1750, 690 acres, and 1758, 200 acres; William Bardon (Borden) 1791, 600 acres; William Routledge, 1761, 80 acres; William Stewart, 1757, 200 acres; and Charles Physioc, 1770, 230 acres. And the list goes on and on.

Other names on Hancock Creek during this time are Edmond Murphey, Frederick Acreman, Grigg Yarbrough, Isaac Perkins, James Davis, James Hancock, John Benners, John Lane, Joseph Loftin, Abner Neal, Jr., Adam Tooley, and Bazil Smith.

Robert Coleman's grandson, David Dupuis, had a tract on the west side of Hancock Creek immediately south of Jack's Branch that had a landing named for him. Dupuis Landing shows up on later property maps as does Hyman's Landing just north of it.

We've found Cahoogue Creek spelled three different ways in the same document. In other places, it's appeared as Cahookey, Cohuka, Cohoque, Cahowqua, Cowhukey, and so on. The tributary of Hancock Creek drew many settlers despite the difficulties of spelling. Abner Whitehead, the heirs of Roger Jones, Bartholomew Howard, James Black, Joseph Bishop, William Physioc, Sr., William Herritage, and William Stewart each patented land thereon of between 90 and 560 acres.

At Adams Creek, there's Abner Neal, 1759 and 1788, 840 acres; Abner Neal, Jr., 1759-60, 300 acres; Alley Collins, 1790, 125 acres; Bartholemew Coin (Cain?), 1761, 1280 acres; Benjamin Mason, 1791 and 1798, 840 acres; Charles McLin, 1791, 200 acres; Edmund Cullen, 1764, 100 acres; James Godfrey, 1766, 100 acres; John Kerney, 1761-1762, 430 acres; John Stanton, 1762, 100 acres; Thomas Cook, 1760, 200 acres; Thomas Masters, 1775, 200 acres; Thomas Nelson 1741 and 1798, 400 acres; Thomas Whitledge, 1758, 90 acres; William Cottle, 1793, 100 acres; and many more.

Abner Neal also patented 200 acres on the east side of Coats (Coates) Creek in 1787, while George Burgess acquired 580 acres there,

Taking up land at Clubfoot Creek in the mid-1700s were Bartholomew Howard, Benners Vail, George Godett, Sr., Humphry Smith, James Reed, John Benners, John Bishop, John Howard, John Lovett, John Rice, John Tannyhill, Joseph Smith, Lovick Jones, Matthew Moore, Nathan Moore, Parmenas Horton, Patrick Conner, Robert Welch, Roger Jones, Sr., Simon Bright, Thomas Baker, and William Stewart.

John Bishop acquired 25 acres on the west side of Mitchell Creek in 1770 and Natham Moore took ownership of a 250 acres parcel at the head of Mitchell Creek in 1766.

In the lake country of the southwest quadrant of the county, large tracts, most of 640 acres, were acquired from 1775-1794. Some people got several of the parcels. Owners there included David Barron, James and John Biggleston, Richard Ellis, Joseph Leech, Josiah Henry Martin, Richard Dobbs Spaight, Robert Howe, William Dry, and Wright Stanly.

Rivaling all the others in desirability, however, was Slocum Creek. Between 1756 and 1793, fifty-four land grants were issued. Some people wanted them for settlement and the establishment of a farm or plantation.

Others were pure speculators taking advantage of the availability of ready buyers. Some of the grants sold shortly after being issued. Some were sold over and over again. Typical sizes were two or three hundred acres. One to Christopher Neale was just 23 acres. The largest was 850 acres to Richard Dobbs Spaight. The influential Spaight gobbled up eleven grants for a total of 5,440 acres along Slocum Creek.

Others acquiring Slocum Creek land during the four decades were Absalom Taylor, Elinor McDowell, Basil (Bazell) Smith, Charles Thompson, David Jones, Frederick Acreman, Edward Kennedy, Henry Sikes, Jacob Sikes, John Donelson, John Norwood, Joshua Taylor, Lydia Guard, Obadiah Yarbrough, Samuel Potter, Thomas Bratcher, Thomas Hampton, Thomas Roe, Thomas Ryall, William Brice, William Routledge, William Smith, William Wynn (Wynne), and William Whitehurst.

Earliest Records on the Neuse

As mentioned, some early land records for Craven County didn't survive. We are left to take our clues where we can.

While bold explorer John Lawson stayed for a time at the future site of New Bern in 1701, most researchers have placed settlement and land transactions at a later date. A noted historian wrote, "The date of the earliest land transaction in the region was November 26, 1702, when William Powell purchased a tract from Thomas Lepper." [y]

While researching an unrelated matter, we recently found a tantalizing clue within an 1887 deed for the sale of land from John J. and Mary Killibrew of Edgecomb County to William H. and Fanny Mallison of Craven. The tract was 860 acres from the mouth of Dam Creek, along Anderson Creek, to the Mouth of Slocum Creek.

After describing the twists and turns of the property boundaries using degrees of the compass and numbers of surveyor's poles, the deed further describes the acreage as "being the same patented by William Glover A.D., 1701." [z]

A portion of an 1887 deed makes reference to a south shore land grant of 1701.

---

[y] Watson, *A History of New Bern and Craven County*, pg.4.
[z] Craven County Deed Book 97, page 82.

Up the Creek

Money doesn't just talk. It gets you waterfront property.

Affluent or politically influential planters managed to settle on prime river tracts, especially on those with good landing places for boats. Travel by water was necessary because of the normally wretched condition of roads. Watercourses provided the only reliable means of transportation. Most early roads, if they could be called that at all, were the ancient Indian trading paths that developed over eons as human beings found the shortest, safest, and simplest routes that avoided obstacles like deep water. What became the Beaufort-to-New Bern road – after colonists were mandated to work on and improved it – very likely followed the course of a trail pounded down by the feet of native people through centuries uncounted. Such winding tracks through the forest were unmarked, ungraded, and often impassable by horse and wagon.

The embryonic county government required landowners along the main road to contribute labor and-or funds for construction and maintenance. As an example, in 1816 overseers of the roads and its wooden bridges were named: Jesse Collins "from Slocumb's Creek Bridge to Hancock's Creek Bridge"; William Physioc, from Hancock's Creek to Jumping Run," a tributary of Clubfoot Creek; and James Smith "from Benner's Vail Mills to Adams Creek Ferry."

Old letters referring to the New Bern-to-Beaufort Road illustrate the challenges.

- "It snowed all night then the snow melted, making the roads muddy."
- "It rained almost without intermission and meanwhile snowed so heavily that the roads were already bad and became impassable."
- "For three days the post has not come because of the bad roads." [a]

Bad roads meant prime locations on the water were the most desirable for trade and for travel, especially those with a good place to load and unload watercraft. The creeks along the south shore of the Neuse abounded with such places.

While land grants were initially limited to 50- and 100-acre parcels, instances are easily found where a single individual received a series of grants or ones that were colossal in size. Or they simply bought granted land from others. The Glovers, John Lovick, Slocum, and Hancock are examples. Soon the prime river and creek frontage was taken up by the affluent. The

---

[a] Elizabeth Moore, *Records of Craven County, North Carolina, Vol. 1.*

middle class typically occupied land more in the central parts of the stream. The lower-class "subsistence" farmers, well, they were "up the creek." [b]

Evan and Sally Jones epitomized the more fortunate. The Joneses lived near the junction of Slocum Creek and the Neuse. Evan's estate papers, created shortly after his death in 1817, list herds of livestock including pigs, cattle, horses, and sheep. Like many planters, he had beehives. There were two canoes, furniture of mahogany, a tarpot, barrels of corn, a cotton machine, and an impressive library. Books and mirrors were luxury items in those days. Jones had a law book, two Bibles, two Quaker books, a book on travel, and a thirteen-volume set called *The World Displayed*, which appears to be something like an early encyclopedia focusing on history and geography. The papers also list the plantation's slaves: Silbey, Bill, Harriet, Shadrack, Hannah, Primas, Betty, Old Betty, John, Henney, Godfrey, Phillis, Rose, London, Tom, Molly, Manville, Eliza, Isaac, and Cerene. [c]

Evan Jones was named for his father. Evan Jones the elder, and his brother Roger took up land at Slocum Creek in 1710. As we read in the previous chapter, Roger Jones was killed by Indians near the brother's turpentine still and tar kiln overlooking the Neuse River during the Tuscarora uprising of 1711. Evan named one of his children Roger to keep the name alive. A prosperous planter, the older Evan Jones passed his successes in the form of land and possessions to his children.

Lot Holton lived near both the river and Hancock Creek. Holton's estate papers list an impressive array of luxuries including mirrors, silver pitchers, and silver tableware. Guns, swords, and pistols are inventoried, as well as two canoes, two copper stills, a cotton gin, and a fishing seine net. Plantation appointments included 21 beehives and farming, carpentry, and cooper's tools. On hand were potatoes, peas, corn, and cotton. There were 29 barrels of turpentine, 80 cows, more than 100 sheep. There were 26 slaves and a strongbox bolted to the floor with $7,000 in cash inside, about $213,000 today.

Holton, "an eccentric old gentleman," had a remarkable windmill that served for a time as a landmark to boats passing Hancock Creek on the river. The revolving arms of the windmill were highly-burnished iron rods decorated by bits of shiny tin that flashed the reflected sun and could be seen for miles. [d]

---

[b] *The History of a Southern State*, H.T. Lefler and A.R. Newsome, UNC Press, 1954 pp. 82 and 96; T. Davis, *Archeological Investigation at MCAS Cherry Point*, 2003, pg. 25.

[c] Craven County estate record, Evan Jones, 1817.

[d] Craven estate papers of Lot Holton, 1849; *Daily Journal*, August 20, 1884. Note: Another man of the same name on the Neuse's northside can cause confusion for researchers.

At the other end of the financial spectrum, and in the upper reaches of Hancock and Cahoogue Creek, were Obadiah Always (Allways) and his neighbor, William Rutledge. Rutledge, probably a cooper, left behind a few tools, a few barrels, and timber dressed to assemble 30 more. His 1811 will listed a deerskin, a raccoon skin, and a canoe. Nearly everyone had a canoe, including Always, who also had some livestock and five beehives. But even a man of modest means like Obadiah Always left land and slaves, dividing his estate among his children, John, Meshack, Boneda, and Aquilla, and grandchildren John and Betsy Ivy. [e]

Obadiah's brother, Henry, owned an inn on the Old Beaufort Road near today's Ferry Road. It was a stage stop between New Bern and Beaufort that was operating in the years around 1783 when a Spanish traveler wrote about it. Obadiah and Henry, who married Sarah Loftin, were the children of early south shore settlers Francis and Mary Always. [f]

The Always family intermarried with other early immigrant families including Jones, Wynn, Whitehead, Collins, Parson, and Bailey.

Free People of Color

There were several ways for enslaved people to become free. *Manumission* means being released from slavery. A slaveholder might manumit a slave or a slave family for long or distinguished service. This could occur at any time but often was accomplished in the owner's will.

A good number of African Americans were set free in return for enlisting to fight the British during the American Revolution.

Freedom could be purchased. Sometimes skilled slaves were allowed to keep a portion of the wages they earned when hired out for others or might be allowed to work or trade on their own account, eventually earning enough to pay the owner an agreed-upon value. Some slaves ran away, changed their identities, and started a new life in a place that accommodated free blacks. The southeastern part of Craven County was such a place. One other route to freedom was for a slave's child to be born to a white or Indian mother. The status of the child followed that of its mother. Such circumstances were not as rare as they may sound. [g]

However they got there, the south shore of the Neuse became a haven and a place of opportunity for free people of color. One example is William Dove. The Doves arrived via Virginia in the 1700s and became a large, well-

---

[e] Craven County estate papers of O. Always 1812, W. Rutledge, undated.

[f] *Travels of Francisco de Miranda in the United States, 1783-1784.*

[g] Lefler and Newsome, pg. 117.

known family in southern Craven County. Many Doves were still living there in the 21st century.

In February 1775, William Dove bought ninety acres on Cahoogue Creek from Martin Black, another free African American. Through this deed, William is one of the earliest Doves for whom we have a record. The 1790 census shows him as the head of a family of nine "Free Persons."

He added another fifty acres to his farm in 1794. This one touched Little John Creek, just to the north of his first holding. Dove paid ten pounds to the white seller, John Gatlin. His deed was witnessed by two prominent white neighbors, John Physioc and John Bishop.

His deed for another transaction the next year is interesting for several reasons. It's a small tract along Deep Creek of just eight acres, and it's referred to in the deed as a "Messuage of Land." The term "messuage" is Norman French for "household" and often refers to a dwelling house. A legal dictionary said it means a "plot of land as the site for a house; later, a residential building taken together with its outbuildings and assigned land." The fact that Dove paid ten pounds for fifty acres one year before and paid six pounds for the nine-acre "messuage" – more than three times as much per acre – argues in favor of the property having been improved by a home and other buildings.

In a nice touch, the 1795 deed said the messuage adjoined "the Dove Plantation," which had now grown to 148 acres. The final eight acres were purchased from William Thomson, Sr., a white resident of Carteret County. The transaction was witnessed by Roger Jones, Jr., another neighbor and a descendent of one of the earliest local settler families. [h]

When Southern Craven County Was Like Saudi Arabia

"Naval stores" is an odd term to our ears, but it's a simple idea. *Naval* refers to ships and boats of all sizes, and *stores* mean "supplies" or "products." So, naval stores are products – such as tar, pitch, turpentine, and rosin – used in the building and maintaining ships and boats. The stuff preserved wood and ropes, prevented leaks, made caulking work, and repelled ship-eating sealife.

And, in a time when the products were as vital and valuable as oil is now, Craven County was the Saudi Arabia of its day.

Nearly all the local farmers, from the 1700s to the War Between the States in the mid-1800s, were busy with it: creating tar, pitch, turpentine, rosin, and other derivatives of the long-leaf pine tree's sap; products that were essential in building and maintaining all the fleets that sailed the seven

---

[h] Craven County deed books and pages 22/73-74; 32/732; 32/794.

A turpentine distillery of southern Craven County is shown at top left in a vintage *Harper's Weekly* newspaper illustration. A tar kiln, above right, was a simpler affair. Logs covered with dirt were burned slowly forcing the tar to ooze out. Ditches directed the tar to a collection pit where it was dipped into barrels. Many old tar kiln sites have been found by archeologists in local woodlands.

seas. Wills and estate records prove that many farmers here did nothing but "turpentine farming" or "tar burning." And many grew rich from it.

Historian Alan Watson calculated the naval stores flowing out of the Port of Beaufort in 1764. He listed 30,043 barrels of tar, 3,303 barrels of turpentine, 3,721 barrels of pitch, 1,279 barrels of spirits of turpentine, and 619 barrels of rosin, "most of which probably came from Craven County."

The numbers – and profits – jumped significantly as time went by. In 1840, 139,000 barrels of naval stores of all kinds were shipped from Craven County, amounting to one-quarter of the production for the entire country. At 31½ gallons to the barrel, that's 4,378,000 gallons. At 320 pounds to the barrel, 44,480,000 pounds of naval stores were produced and shipped out of the Neuse River in a single antebellum year.

Based on these numbers, the 1764 shipments also required 38,965 locally-produced barrels. By 1840, that number more than tripled. Cooperage, the production of barrels, was a busy subsidiary industry of the turpentine trade. A significant portion of the local labor force, perhaps twenty-five percent, spent all their days engaged only in making barrels to ship naval store. A good hand was expected to make six barrels a day.

In 1845, a widow on Hancock's Creek, Mary C. Hyman, tried to make some money by offering at a "very low" price "a large quantity of Hoop Poles now growing on the plantation of the late Samuel Hyman." Hoop poles were straight, thin lengths of green saplings, often hickory or white oak, used as stock to make barrel hoops. [i]

A Union soldier named William Draper wrote in his Civil War memoirs what he'd learned on the subject from a man name Pelatier near Havelock.

Draper said, *"Turpentine farming was the principal business of eastern North Carolina. The pine forest of that section are, or have been, great sources of wealth to its people. A kind of cup was cut in one side of the tree, into which the sap ran and from which it was daily dipped. Each year a fresh strip of bark, half an inch wide, was cut off above this cut to allow the sap to run. When one side of the tree was cut as high as a man could reach, a new cup was cut on the other side, and the same process repeated there, and this was continued until the tree was girdled. It was then cut down and into lengths, and burned in a peculiar kind of pit when the remaining sap became tar and the residuum charcoal. The crude turpentine was dipped from the cups and distilled and refined, the residuum being rosin, the business, Mr. Pelatier said, was very profitable before the war." [j]*

In addition to refining the long-leaf pine tree sap into turpentine, tar was extracted by covering stacks of split pine logs with earth, setting the wood on fire, and "sweating" the tar out. The extracted tar was sold as is or cooked further to create pitch. The depleted wood became charcoal. Tar kilns were a less sophisticated process requiring no distillation equipment, thus tar was the simplest naval store to produce. Both operations were labor-intensive, however, but both were lucrative. The tar kilns and turpentine distilleries – *stills* as they were known – were common on every farm and in the woodlands all over southern Craven County.

So much money could be made that there was a strong financial incentive for farmers to multiply their naval stores' labor through the use of slaves. Many did so.

In the 1700s and 1800s, the products were absolutely vital to shipping. Naval stores were so ubiquitous on ships that the sailors – who were in constant contact with black, sticky materials – picked up the nickname *tars*. The children of North Carolina got the goo on their bare feet and grown men got it on their boots. The natives soon picked up the sobriquet *Tar Heels*.

---

[i] *The Newbernian and North Carolina Advocate,* June 17, 1845.
[j] *Recollections of a Varied Career*, William F. Draper, 1908, pp. 71-72.

In 1843, Hardy Loftin Jones (1793-1854) of Slocum Creek made a patent application for an improved method of pine sap extraction. Jones, the son of Roger Jones, Sr. (1731-1801) and Comfort Always Jones (d. 1826), explained that the elimination of "boxing" and reduction in "chipping" would make the tree live longer.

Grist for the Mill

If the reader knows anything about Richard Dobbs Spaight at all, it's probably that he's one of the main characters of New Bern history. Perhaps you know he was a governor of North Carolina. Perhaps you know that he was fabulously wealthy. Or that, with so much accomplished and so much potential, he died at just 44 in an infamous pistol duel with a political rival.

Spaight was one of the key representatives of the people in the formation of the United States of America. At 29 years of age, he stood in the same ornate Philadelphia chamber with George Washington, Benjamin Franklin, James Madison, and Alexander Hamilton as a signer of the Constitution of the United States. In Howard Chandler Christy's famous painting of the signing, with Washington presiding over a room full of patriot luminaries at Independence Hall in 1787, it is Richard Spaight who is captured in the act of inscribing his signature on the foundation document of the land.

Richard Dobbs Spaight

The year before, Spaight petitioned the Craven County court for permission to dam the southwest prong of Slocum Creek. The location chosen, he said in his 1786 petition, was "very convenient for a mill which might benefit the neighborhood of said creek."

Waterpower was used to operate grist mills where people ground corn, wheat, and other grains. Since everyone traveled on foot – either their own or that of a horse – having a mill close by was a great convenience. Mill power was also used to saw lumber. A good mill became a focal point of local business and often a centerpiece and gathering place for villages of the era. The courts agreed and Spaight built his dam and mill.

A major portion of the dam can still be seen today. It's just across the parking lot from the Havelock Tourist and Events Center. It's walkable and at this writing is open to the public free of charge.

Let's illustrate just how colossal this structure is. What remains today is 636 feet long; longer than two football fields. It's 24 feet wide at the top; wide enough that oxcarts were driven upon it. It's 12 to 16 feet taller than the surrounding bottomland and it carried a 25 foot deep head of water at the mill end in its heyday.

An estimated one-quarter to one-third of the dam has been washed away over time, but what remains today equals 407,040 cubic feet of dirt. It

Spaight's Mill Dam at Havelock dates from 1786. It's one of two mill dams still existing on the southwest prong of Slocum Creek. Photograph by the author.

would require 1,508 dump truck loads to equal the amount of soil from which it was built. The dam is estimated to weigh 20,350 tons, which is 40.7 million pounds, or the weight of 3,100 African elephants. The cost of the dirt in 2018 at $130 a load, would be $196,040. In the same year, the earthwork for construction would have cost from $375,000-$450,000. [k]

There are several matters to ponder in the story of why a New Bern politician built a mill and dam so far down into the county. The first thing to know is that while Spaight's palatial Clermont Plantation home was on the south bank of the Trent River – placing him within our definition of southern Craven County – Richard Dobbs Spaight owned a lion's share of southern Craven County itself. His property sprawled from Clermont past present-day Havelock to and beyond the Carteret County line. He owned much the of lake district we will talk so much about in this book. He owned much of what is now Havelock and the present-day Croatan National Forest. Nailing down exactly how much land he owned is difficult because he had so many parcels, some with partners, and he bought and sold large acreage tracts frequently. It's no stretch to say, however, that he owned more than 100,000 acres of land.

Spaight inherited much wealth and multiplied it. He was the grandson of Madam Mary Moore (1705-1761) who previously owned Clermont and thousands of acres on the Trent River's south bank. She was wealthy enough

---

[k] Spaight's Dam calculations by John Thomas, Thomas Engineering, PA, New Bern.

to have the honorific title "Madam" before her name. One of her husbands was so rich that he was known as "King" Roger Moore. Through Mary Vail Jones Willson Moore, Spaight was descended from the state's highest-ranking families, including the Blounts, Dobbs, and Nashes, and was further related to the Donnells, the Bryans, and others.

Slocum Creek was Spaight's mill land. Lake Ellis was one of his plantations. The number of slaves he owned approached one hundred. Canals were dug from the lakes southwest of present-day Havelock and drained into Slocum Creek. This not only emptied the lakes for agricultural planting but also provided even more water power for the mill's operation. The ditching and drainage projects were large enough that one old name for Lake Road was the "Canal Road." One canal from the lakes, the Blackledge Canal, ran many miles and emptied into Dam Creek and the Neuse River.

The first map of North Carolina made from an actual survey was published by Jonathan Price and John Strother in 1808. It featured Spaight's Mill as a landmark. By that year, Richard Spaight had lost his life to his dueling opponent's bullet. Richard Dobbs Spaight, Jr. inherited the mill, which by the time of the Civil War was owned by Dr. Samuel Masters.

Spaight's Mill wasn't the only one on Slocum Creek, however. It wasn't even the first. Bazell Smith applied for a mill there in 1767. There's no evidence it was completed. On December 18, 1772, John Bishop and Peter Physioc petitioned the "Worshipfull Justices of the Inferior Court of

The remnant of an old colonial-era mill dam is visible on Tucker Creek, then called Coleman's Creek. Modern Farina Drive homes are at lower left. Such dams were sometimes broken during hurricanes when the storm's winds built up water against the front of the dam until it was over-washed. After the storm, pent up waters rushed out around one end of the dam eroding the bank. In 1822, this mill dam was owned by William Holland who said it was 130 yards long and put its date of construction as 1787. *Newbern Sentinel*, November 9, 1822, page 4.

Craven County" for permission to dam the creek and build "a public grist mill" beside the main county road. That road ran from New Bern to Beaufort, or as they put it "from New Bern to Core Sound." At Havelock, the modern equivalent of Greenfield Heights Blvd. and Miller Blvd. was the course of the main county road because that route skirted the deepest parts of Slocum Creek.

In colonial times, a wooden bridge crossed Slocum Creek on what is today Greenfield Height's Blvd. in Havelock. A modern concrete box bridge crosses the creek today near Gray Road. The 250-year-old remains of the Bishop-Physioc dam still rest quietly on the west side of the road in low woods now controlled by the United States Forest Service.

Not all dams and grist mills are recorded in old county records.

The extent of early mill building activity might make a geologist wonder if Ordnance Point near Slocum Road on base is a natural or man-made structure. An aerial of Slocum Creek shows the Ordnance Point peninsula, above. It was "Long Point" when the U.S. Coast & Geodetic Survey chart below was printed in 1878.

Go West Fever

It was adventurous, ambitious, and sometimes desperate people of Europe who set out on the dangerous voyage across the Atlantic Ocean into the New World. By the late 1700s, the offspring of these brave souls began to look for broader horizons as coastal places became well-settled.

When the best tracts of land along the river and creeks had been taken up and the competition from the larger plantations pinched upon the productivity and profits of the smaller farm, word began to circulate of new territory opening in the west. Talk of vast open spaces and cheap homesteads in places like western North Carolina, Tennessee, Kentucky, and Alabama drew the attention of the second and third generation of the original pioneer families. Many were on the move by 1789.

Familiar names from the county's first records began to vanish during this period of outmigration; most of the Slocums, for example.

Even some who stayed wanted to go. Adam Tooley lived near Cahoogue Creek. On March 16, 1799, Tooley placed a curious announcement in the *Newbern Gazette* that read, "I intend to leave this state shortly." He didn't. Though he eventually moved to Greene County near Snow Hill, he was still advertising his 350-acre plantation for sale in 1811.

In the same year, magistrate and justice of the peace Joseph Physioc offered to sell his plantation "containing 606 acres, with a good dwelling house, and all necessary Out Houses." It never sold and he never went west. He was buried on his land east of Hancock Creek thirty years later.

We haven't done justice to the major influence of the Quakers, who for a time were numerous, well-organized, and prosperous settlers along the river's south shore, especially around Clubfoot Creek, Harlowe, Core Creek, and in western Carteret County. Nevertheless, the proliferation of slavery, which they generally opposed, made the newly-opened and slave-free Northwest Territory attractive to those of the Quaker faith. This vast frontier around the Great Lakes became the states of Ohio, Illinois, Indiana, Michigan, Wisconsin, and Minnesota. Many of the Quakers left in a series of migrations in 1799, 1802, and after.

While some of the migrants moved by water, the major visual for this is the horse- or ox-drawn wagon trains that became iconic as the United States enacted its "manifest destiny" during the 19th century.

The western exodus of the population drove county land values downward – from $3.81 per acre in 1815 to just ninety-eight cents by 1836.

Some of the pioneer families didn't go so far. The Slocums began their trek west by moving to Wayne County, a distance of about a hundred miles, or a week's journey. One of the main thoroughfares of old Goldsboro is Slocumb Street. Some of their descendants are today in Alabama.

One Pioneer Family

To be practical in writing this book, choices had to be made. A chain of title couldn't be run for every tract of land in southern Craven County, although it would be possible to do so. In theory. The deeds are there. But it would take half a lifetime and fill hundreds of books. Likewise, there's neither time nor space to create the genealogy of every family that has lived on the south shore of the river. For now, we'll focus on one.

In 1750, James Wynn bought 150 acres of land on the east side of Slocum Creek, south of the river. The land was purchased from Joseph Pearson. The deed was witnessed by James Handcock and Joseph Slocumb, descendants of two of the earliest settlers. Simon Wynn also witnessed the deed.[l]

The county recording clerk styled the date as "the twenty-second year of his Majesties reign, May 3rd 1750." The colony of North Carolina was still ruled by George II of Great Britain at the time of Wynn's purchase. [m]

Wynn was on the south shore of the Neuse before he bought the land from Pearson. We aren't certain when he arrived but by the deed we know he was here on that date, 26 years before the Declaration of Independence.

Six years later, James Wynn added substantially to his Slocum Creek plantation with the purchase from Joseph Slocum of 500 acres for 35 pounds in "proclamation money." The deed, witnessed by John Slocum and Grigg Yarbrough, said the land was "situated on the south side of the Neuse River and the east side of Slocumb Creek." The boundaries were described as "at the mouth of Mill Branch; running up Slocumb Creek its several courses to the second branch above the Mill Branch; thence up that branch to a white oak at the head of the branch, then south 50 degrees east 100 poles to a pine, then 49 degrees east to a red oak on the Mill Branch; thence down the Mill Branch to the beginning." [n]

He added another hundred acres with a 1759 land grant. The description is less than vague: "On the So. side of the Neuse River beginning at a Pine." Recorded the same day was the grant of another hundred acres beginning "in Jno. Slocumbs line." [o]

Wynn used his 850 acres to engage in the turpentine trade. He had nine barrels of turpentine on hand when he died, according to his estate papers. We know he was also a barrel-maker. He left instruction in his will that certain of his possessions were to be sold upon his death to pay off his land debts. These items included his horse, hogs, sheep, gun, and cooper's tools.

[l] The family name is spelled Winn, Wynn, and Wynne in official records.

[m] Craven County Deed Book 1, pg. 486.

[n] Craven County Deed Bool 10, pg. 307.

[o] Land Grant 2266, Book 16, pg. 286; 2776, Book 18, page 411.

Barrels were much in demand for storage and shipping. Cooperage – the making of barrels – required a shed-full of specialized and valuable tools. For example, draw knives, saws, particular axes and hammers, planes, gauges and measuring tools, files and rasps, borers, rivets and punches, and hoop drivers were typical.

We don't have the name of Wynn's wife, but she's mentioned as his widow in one of his estate papers in 1761 and as having remarried to a man named John Reed. Wynn and his wife had three children: a son, William; and daughters, Lazell and Catherine.

Upon his death in 1758, the estate was divided among the children. William received the largest portion. In the will, his father left him "my land and plantation that I now live on" as well as other property. The will also left specific instructions about the disposition of his body. He instructed his executors to bury him "touching said Estate as it hath been pleased God to bless me in this world." In other words, he wanted to be buried on his land. [p]

Though his grave is unmarked, Dr. Thomas W. Davis, an archaeologist who studied the matter wrote in 2002, "This explicit instruction suggests strongly that James Winn, the family progenitor, was interred in the cemetery overlooking Mill Branch at Cherry Point MCAS."

James's son, William Wynn, expanded the plantation in the late 1700s and early 1800s. In 1793, he received a patent for 200 acres "on the east side of Slocumb's Creek, part being surplus of John Slocumb's patent." Between 1774 and 1801, he acquired more than 1,300 additional acres, making the Wynn Plantation near 2,500 acres in total. [q]

William Wynn was overseer of the county road from the "Hancock Creek Bridge up to East branch" in 1782. He appears to have married Elizabeth "Betsie" Foscue in 1793. When he died in 1801, they had three minor children: a son, Stephen; and two daughters, Sallie and Cressy Ann. The wife, Elizabeth, received one-quarter of the estate and the manor house, plus one-fourth of all the slaves and livestock. Another farmer, Meshack Allways, was appointed guardian of the children's portion of the estate, which was common practice at the time. Ultimately, as was the right of the sole son, Stephen Wynn inherited all the land when he turned 21. Cressy Ann married affluent planter Joseph Brittain in 1814. [r]

Stephen married Elizabeth Jones in 1817. In 1820, a prosperous Stephen Winn had 15 slaves working on his east Slocum Creek plantation. Stephen and Elizabeth had four children: Sarah, William, James, and

---

[p] Craven County Deed Book 8, pg. 219.

[q] Craven County Grants Book 3, pg. 36; Book 58, pg. 347.

[r] County estates and wills; Elizabeth Moore, *Records of Craven County Vol. 1*; Frances T. Ingmire, *Craven County Marriage Records, 1780-1867*.

Tryphenia. Stephen Wynn's early death at age 45 in 1833 began an unwinding of the family's hold on the land. Ownership of the plantation passed to sons James and William. William appears to have incurred personal financial setbacks that forced the division of the land and sale of his half to pay debts. Neighbor John Ferguson purchased a considerable portion of the former Wynn land in 1850. Other death, marriages, and acts by surviving heirs reduced the estate. By the 1870s, all of the land, except the picturesque family cemetery, had passed to other owners. [s]

Nevertheless, Wynne descendants of more modest circumstances lived and farmed on other parcels between and around Slocum Creek and Hancock Creek into the modern era.

The Wynne Family Cemetery near Slocum Creek as it appeared in 1992. Nine burials were still marked with elaborate headstones in the modern era, but other interments were suspected to exist. The cemetery was also used for burials of the Dutch immigrant Buys and Brandt family, and others in the late 1800s and early 1900s. The location of the cemetery can be seen on a map at the front of the book. It was called Cherry Point Cemetery 9, Tract 199 in 1985, and later designated by archaeologists as Site 31CV343. The one-acre graveyard was surrounded with metal fencing. More information on the Wynne, Buys, and Brandt burials can be found in *Part II: The Whisperers* and in *Burials at MCAS Cherry Point* in Part IV. Photograph by the author.

---

[s] Craven County deeds, wills and estate records; Thomas W. Davis, Ph.D., *Archeological Investigations at MCAS Cherry Point and MCHOLF Oak Grove in Craven and Jones County, North Carolina*, April 2003.

Sailing vessels like this were once an everyday sight on the Neuse River.

Marine Intelligence

For more than a hundred and fifty years it was customary for newspapers in port towns and cities to run a daily or weekly column called by names like *Shipping News* or *Marine Intelligence*. Before the advent of modern communication, such as radio and telegraph, these lists of ships entering and exiting ports not only informed residents but also confirmed the whereabouts of vessels for shipowners, government officials, and worried families. News and newspapers traveled port-to-port and thus the progress of a ship – or in some cases, its last sighting – was documented by the columns of shipping news.

The formula for the announcements was the type of ship, its name, the last name of the "master" or captain of the ship, its port, and its cargo, like this one from 1867: Schooner *Emma Elizabeth*, Black, master, from Slocum's Creek, with wood to master.

Hundreds, if not thousands, of examples are available from newspapers published in New Bern and elsewhere during the eighteenth to the twentieth century. The few provided below are to illustrate the flow of sailing – and later steam and gasoline – vessels and their goods from the lower Neuse to New Bern. A full listing of the shipping news on any given day records crafts, large and small, arriving in and leaving the port of New Bern for

Boston, Rhode Island, New York City, Philadelphia, Baltimore, Alexandria or Charleston, and for more distant places like St. Lucia, Jamaica, Bermuda, St. Kitts, and Guadeloupe.

The bulk of the maritime trade entering the Neuse River "came from the northern colonies and the West Indies," according to historian Joe Mobley. "Little commerce originated in the British Isles, for the deep-draft vessels from England could not navigate the shallow swash at Ocracoke. Small craft – sloops and schooners of 20 to 50 tons – predominated the New Bern maritime trade. These vessels frequently stopped at

MARINE LIST.
PORT of NEW BERN.
ENTERED
Brig Fanny, Wade, Boston .
Ship Tillman, Cook, Jamaica.
CLEARED.
Sch'r. Newbern, Hall, St. Croix.

Newbern Gazette August 25, 1764

plantation wharves along the Neuse and Trent rivers to collect cargo." [a]

Some of the goods delivered from the creeks of Slocum, Hancock, Clubfoot, and Adams, and South River, were consumed in New Bern. But, as we've said in the previous chapter, large quantities of products – such as naval stores – were loaded onto larger vessels and shipped all over the world. These valuable products were derived from the sap of the long-leaf and other varieties of pine trees found in abundance in the surrounding countryside. The endless forests of North Carolina supplied the raw materials that the enterprising entrepreneurs of southern Craven County used to become world-class producers of naval stores.

William Benjamin Thorpe and his wife, Elizabeth, appear elsewhere in this book. In their time, they were mainstays of the community. The Thorpes raised a large brood, shepherded their plantation upon the west bank of Hancock Creek, and were in the thick of the naval stores business. After Benjamin's 1856 death, Elizabeth described their land in an estate filing as "not adapted to agricultural purposes except a small portion … it is adapted almost exclusively to tar and turpentine." And many of their neighbors on the Neuse River's south shore were busy with the same work. We already discussed the amazing quantities of these goods that were transported out of Craven County.

Below are the outgoing vessels for the past few days from the shipping news exactly as they appeared in the *Eastern Carolina Republican* for Wednesday, October 13, 1847. It's written in a kind of short-hand, but again the formula is date, ship, captain, port of destination, product, and merchant:

Oct. 7th, Schr. *E. Piggott,* Hall, Baltimore, n[aval] sto[res] by A. Wade.

---

[a] *Pamlico County: A Brief History*, Joe A, Mobley, pg. 12.

7th, *S. Carolinian*, Powers, N. Y., nav. sto., by J. Harvey & Sons.

8th, *Cora*, Guthrie, N. Y., nav. sto., by J. C. & M. Stevenson.

8th, *Amanda*, Davis, N. Y., nav. sto., by Wm. P. Moore.

9th, *Mary*, Sirman, Philad., nav. sto., by M. W. Jarvis.

12th, *Ione*, Hartick, N. Y., nav. sto., by Wm. Dunn.

That's a lot of "nav. sto."

The same paper reported that 3,000 barrels of the naval stores had come into Wilmington during the previous week. And the price was rising.

"On Friday and Saturday, it commanded $2.50; on Monday, $3; Tuesday, $3.05; Wednesday, $3.10; and today (Thursday), $3.10 and $3.15, closing at the latter price," the *Republican* announced.

Naval stores, though lucrative and important, were not the only products going out of southern Craven County. Corn and other varieties of produce, cotton, "crabgrass" used as cattle feed, and timber were also common shipments. Timber became more and more important in the second half of the 1800s when national lumbermen – like Roper and Blades – discovered the vast and untouched old-growth forests around southern Craven County.

As the naval stores industry waned with the coming of metal-hulled ships, the lumber business – or "working in the log-woods," as the locals called it – became big business. As double-mast, square-sail brigs – some approaching two hundred feet in length – disappeared from the river and were replaced by vessels propelled with steam, products being transshipped evolved along with them. With the coming of prohibition in the early twentieth century, a clear liquid – produced in a distillation process identical to turpentine's – would begin to be secreted in the holds of ships plying the river. Southern Craven County corn liquor – quite powerful, quite desirable, and quite illegal – is reputed to have been distributed widely enough to gain the trusted, but underground trademark "C.C.C."

Regardless of the products, the ships moved it daily in and out of one of the nation's widest rivers, the mighty Neuse. People standing on the river's south shore saw the sails of cooners, skiffs, sloops, and schooners every day. It was a picturesque scene. The river was the highway and a much more reliable

Thompson Little Stagecoach ad, 1850

one than dirt roads that quickly turned to mire with heavy rains and became nearly impassable at times, especially in winter.

This isn't to say the roads weren't open. Thundering four-horse stage-coaches – the driver sitting up high with both hands full of reins; the shotgun rider and strongbox beside him – ferried mail, and passengers in suits and bonnets, on regular routes to Beaufort and other places. Farmers' buggies and wagons of every description were drawn by horses, mules, and oxen. Still, much of the travel was by boat, even for matters like attending church, visiting relatives, and doing business.

For commerce, travel, and fishing, it's fair to say that nearly everyone had a boat. Nearly every old will in Craven County mentions a canoe. Many of the farms of southern Craven County had piers or even wharves. And boats were measured not so much by feet as by their carrying capacity.

In December 1818, John I. Pasteur, publisher of the New Bern weekly newspaper *Carolina Centinel,* posted this advertisement:

> FOR SALE: A small Sloop Boat
> burthen about one hundred and seventy
> barrels. She is eighteen months old, well
> found and in good order. –
> Enquire of the PRINTER

That Pasteur referred to his vessel, capable of carrying 170 barrels of naval stores, molasses, or whatever else might need transporting, as "a *small sloop boat*" is illustrative of the volume of freight being moved about on the river.

Benjamin Franklin Borden owned one thousand acres on the Neuse River across Hancock Creek from the Thorpes. Noting the size of the hold, he offered a capacious and well-known craft in August 1848 via *The New-bernian and North Carolina Advocate*:

> FOR SALE.
> The vessel commonly known as the BUZZARD.
> She is 40 feet keel, 14 feet 4 inches beam, and
> 3 ft. 8 in. depth of hold, built of the best materials,
> live oak and Cedar. She is about 12 months old,
> and in good sailing order. Apply to B. F. BORDEN

Mary C. Hyman, executrix for the estate of her deceased husband, Samuel Hyman of Hancock Creek, advertised for the sale in December 1843 "one first rate Two Mast Boat, built of Live oak and Cedar – in good repair – will carry 140 barrels, or 10 cords of wood."

And the schooner *J. D. Flanner* touted in *The New Berne Times* October 30, 1865 – just after the close of the War Between the States – had a 225-barrel capacity, was "in good running order" and could be seen at the Old County Wharf each day after its trip down the river.

But if you didn't own a boat, or *want* to own one, space was available on watercraft owned by others. John Vail posted this notice in the *Carolina Federal Republic* of October 19, 1816: "The Subscriber's boat runs regular once a week from Clubfoot's Creek to Newbern. Any person wishing to send grain to the Mills will please call upon the Captain of the boat (D. Rice) who will receive the grain on board. – Attention shall be paid in fanning and grinding the grain, as the Subscriber assures those that may send, he will see to it." The freight was ten cents per bushel.

"W. S. Wynn is one of our successful merchants," *The Daily Journal* reported in August 1890. "He has a sharpie running all the time to New Berne, carrying turpentine and produce." Sharpies were shallow-draft, adjustable centerboard vessels, often open, and flexible in design. They had one or two masts. Lengths from 24 to 35 feet were typical.

As mentioned above, ships of all sizes were plying the Neuse River from major U.S. cities and foreign countries on a daily and weekly basis. They were also arriving at the port of New Bern from Hyde County, Hatteras, Currituck, Washington (N.C.), Pollocksville, Beaufort, Goose Creek, and Bay River; all sorts of North Carolina places.

Here's a little shipping news to help paint the picture of those bygone days:

Schooner *Wildcat*, [master not given], from Slocum Creek, with naval stores and corn meal. *The New Era and Commercial Advertiser* (New Bern) September 21, 1858

Schooner *Eagle*, Carter, from Hancock's Creek, with naval stores, to B. B. Lane. *ibid.*

Schooner *Susan*, Dove, from Hancock's Creek, with naval stores, to B. B. Lane. *ibid.*

Schooner *Monument*, from Slocum's Creek. *The New Berne Times* July 23, 1864.

Schooner *Dolphin*, Mackin, from Slocum's Creek. *ibid.* August 9, 1864

Schooner *Jenny Lind*, Jackson, from Slocum's Creek, turpentine and melons. *ibid.*

Sloop *Mary Francis*, Coleman, from Slocum's Creek, fish. *ibid.*

Schooner *Patty Martin*, Lawson, from Slocum's Creek, turpentine. *ibid.*

Schooner *Caper*, Hall, from Adam's Creek, turpentine. *ibid.*

Schooner *Fred Jones*, Barnes, from Clubfoot's Creek, turpentine. *ibid.*

Schooner *Leland*, Carter, from Hancock's Creek, produce. *ibid.*

Schooner *Ellen*, Johnson, from Slocum's Creek, naval stores. *ibid.*

Schooner *Champion*, Simpson, from Clubfoot's Creek, wood and naval stores. *ibid.*

Schooner *Fred Jones*, Barnes, from Clubfoot's Creek, naval stores. *ibid.* August 16, 1864.

Schooner *Ellen*, Johnson, from Slocum's Creek, naval stores. *ibid.*

Schooner *Leland*, Carter, from Hancock's Creek, naval stores, and melons. *ibid.*

Schooner *Mary Jane*, Coleman, Slocum's Creek. *ibid.* September 2, 1864.

Schooner *Fred Jones*, Barnes, from Slocum's Creek, with cotton. *ibid.* Oct. 11, 1866.

Schooner *Marietta*, Carter, from Hancock's Creek, cotton, turpentine, and wood. *ibid.*

Schooner *Margaret Jane*, Dove, from Hancock's Creek, wood and turpentine. *ibid.*

Schooner *Sam Hyman*, Fountain, from Slocum's Creek, with wood to master. *ibid.*

Schooner *Emma Elizabeth*, Black, master, from Slocum's Creek, with wood to master. *Newbern Journal of Commerce* May 4, 1867.

Schooner *Marietta*, Godett master, from Handcock's Creek with wood to master. *ibid.* May 10, 1867.

Schooner *Dolphin*, Hill master, from Slocum's Creek with wood to master. *ibid.*

Schooner *Henry Clay*, _____ master, from Clubfoots' Creek, with wood and turpentine, to master. *The New Berne Times* August 20, 1869.

Schooner *Fred I. Jones*, Willoughby master, from Hancock's Creek, with wood and turpentine, to order. *ibid.*

Schooner *Mary E. Queen*, Cully master, from Slocum's Creek with wood and turpentine to master. *ibid.* August 24, 1869.

Schooner *Travis*, Johnson master, from Hancock's Creek, with wood to steamer Cotton Plant. *ibid.* August 29, 1869.

Schooner *Jenny Lind*, Rice master, from Hancock's Creek, with wood to master. *ibid.*

Schooner *Little Lad*, Johnson master, from Slocum's Creek, with wood to order. *ibid.* August 31, 1869.

Schooner *Commence*, Rose master, from Adam's Creek, in ballast. *ibid.*

Schooner *Henry Clay*, Martin master, from Clubfoot's Creek, with turpentine to order. *ibid*, September 4, 1869.

Schooner *Star*, Lindsay master, from Hancock's Creek, with turpentine to order. *ibid*.

Schooner *Fred I. Jones*, Willoughby master, from Hancock's Creek, with turpentine, to order. *ibid*.

Schooner *Mary E. Queen*, Cully master, from Slocum's Creek with wood to master. *ibid*.

Schooner *Little Lad*, Bryan master, from Fisher's Landing, with wood to order. *ibid*. September 12, 1869.

Schooner *Travis*, Johnson master, wood from Hancock's Creek. *ibid*.

Schooner *Little Lad*, Dudley master, from Adams' Creek, with cotton for Mr. Holland. ibid. October 21, 1869.

Schooner *Marietta*, Godett master, from Clubfoot's Creek, turpentine to J. A. Bell. *ibid*.

Schooner *Josie Havens*, Cully master, from Slocum's Creek, wood to master, *ibid*. October 24, 1869.

Schooner *Commerce*, Lasta master, from South River, with staves to order. *ibid*.

Schooner *Cracker Box*, Ritch master, from South River with Sweet Potatoes to order. *ibid*.

Schooner *Josie Havens*, Cully master, from Hancock's Creek, with turpentine to J. H. Bell. *ibid*.

Schooner *Mary E. Queen*, Cully master, from Slocum's Creek with wood to master. *ibid*.

Schooner *Dime*, Martin master, from Clubfoot Creek, with wood to order. *ibid*. October 26, 1869.

Schooner *Isaac Havens*, Cully master, from Hancock's Creek, with wood to order. *ibid*. November 6, 1869.

Schooner *Harry Lee*, Barrett master, to Hancock's Creek, for a load of railroad ties, thence to Philadelphia. *ibid*. November 27, 1869.

Schooner *Dread*, Carraway master, with cotton and potatoes from Adams Creek. *ibid*. January 8, 1873.

Schooner *Little Lad*, Peed master, cotton, turpentine, and wood, from Adams Creek. *ibid*.

Schooner *Johnnie*, Moore master, wood from Handcock's Creek. *ibid*.

Sloop *Mattie*, Eborn master, wood and poultry from Adams Creek. *ibid*.

Schooner *Lady Gray*, Carraway master, from Adams Creek, watermelons, cotton, peaches. *ibid.* August 10, 1873. *"Lady Gray* has been decked over and much improved lately."

Steamer *Ellen S.* left port last night with the barge *Neptune* in tow for Slocumb's Creek. *The New Bern Sun* April 27, 1911.

The gas freight boats *Adele* from Clubfoot Creek and *Grace Leonard* from Slocum Creek arrived in port yesterday morning with cargoes of country produce. The *Daily Journal* (New Bern) July 26, 1914.

The gas freight boat *Captain Todd* arrived in port yesterday morning from Slocumbs Creeks with a cargo of pork. *The Daily Journal* December 24, 1914.

The River Turns Deadly

The railroad after 1858, and the new option of motor freight in the early twentieth century, eventually diminished the river shipping trade.

And even before that, it wasn't always smooth sailing.

Capt. Isaac Taylor of Clubfoot Creek caught a break in the weather on Tuesday, January 30, 1883, when he delivered what *The Daily Journal* claimed was "some of the finest and best sweet potatoes … that have been on the market this winter." Other sailors weren't so lucky. The paper explained that wood was in demand, high priced, and scarce because the daily fog was rendering the river almost impassable. "Several of [the wood boats] have recently been three days coming to the city from Hancock's Creek, a distance of only ten miles. The captains say the fog has been thick enough to cut it into blocks."

Fog, sudden wind and rainstorms, lightning, and even ice sometimes made manifest the malevolent potential of the normally bucolic river.

One of the themes of *The Waterman's Song* subtitled "Slavery and Freedom in Maritime North Carolina," and written by a nationally-respected historian – and Havelock native – David Cecelski, is the vital participation in the sea-faring life by slaves and freedmen of the South. Several of the names above, like Cully, Moore, Dove, Carter, and Martin – are recognizable as those of local African American families. The skills of black mariners of the Neuse River's south shore were critical to the freight-handling trade, but these individuals also faced the river's many dangers as well.

Anyone who has sailed on the Neuse River will confirm that the waters from Pamlico Sound into Craven County – though scenic and often tranquil

– can be transformed into a dangerous, even deadly, maelstrom in a span of times that may be measured in minutes. [b]

IN 1765, NEWSPAPER SUBSCRIBERS were advised of "a sad Accident happening near Town; a boat belonging to Joseph Bryan Esq.; with four of his most valuable Slaves, and one Paine, who had borrowed the Boat and Hands, coming to town with Pork, they were all unfortunately drowned, together with another white man, one who went to their Relief. It seems the Boat ran on a Log, and the Tide falling, could not be got off; a Canoe with two white Men going by, carried off Paine, and left the Negroes in the Boat; but the Weather being extreme cold, they went back to the Negroes, and in returning, the Canoe overset and Six of them were drowned." *The New Bern Gazette* Jan. 4, 1765.

"A SAD ACCIDENT. On Tuesday morning last, a boat load of colored people started in a little schooner-rigged boat, from New

☞ We learn that the bodies of Messrs. Phipps and Horton, drowned some time since, have been recovered. They were found in a shad net at the mouth of Hancock's creek.

Eastern Carolina Republican, March 13, 1850

Bern, for the purpose of carrying the body of a colored woman to Hancock's Creek, for burial. On reaching Hammond's Shoal [Hampton Shoal, where the depth was six feet or less], a short distance down the river, a squall struck the boat, which was under full sail, capsized the frail craft, and, sad to relate, seven of the party, consisting of women and children, were drowned. Two only escape. The bodies were recovered and brought to this city on Tuesday afternoon. We have been unable to ascertain their names." *The New Bern Times* June 11, 1864.

WRECK OF A SMALL SCHOONER. "Yesterday the schooner *Fred Jones*, Samuel Dove master, was coming up the Neuse River from Hancock's Creek for this port, loaded with turpentine, etc. etc. and as she was coming through the "blockade," her sails, main boom and all rigging were carried away by the heavy wind that was prevailing. She was subsequently driven ashore at Fort Point, where she now rests. Capt. Black, with the schooner *Elizabeth*, went down and took the cargo out of the wrecked schooner and brought it to this port. Although her sails, booms, rigging, etc., are carried away she is not totally wrecked." *The New Bern Times* September 21, 1873. [Note: The "blockade" was the remnant of a line of ships sunk in the river in 1862 in a failed attempt to prevent the invading Union Navy from reaching New Bern.]

---

[b] In a 1999 interview by Angela Hornsby, Dorcas E. Carter recalled that her grandfather, Henry Carter, was captain of a sailboat that ran regularly from North Harlowe by way of the Neuse River to New Bern. SOHP, 6.25.99-DC.

❧ ❧ ❧ ❧ ❧ ❧

The harrowing account of Capt. Haywood Dove of Clubfoot Creek and his two-masted working boat, the Isabella, *on the Neuse River one frigid evening before Thanksgiving 1892, was reported by the* Newbern Journal *but was picked up and reprinted by newspapers across the state. We first found the story in the December 1, 1892 issue of* The Standard *of Concord, N.C. It's presented here as it appeared locally more than 125 years ago, including its original headlines. The name of the reporter was not given.*

A TERRIBLE NIGHT

One Man Drowned – Three Frozen to Death

Wednesday night about 8 o'clock a small two-masted wood boat, the Isabella, was caught by a whirlwind and turned over on her side near Jessie Brooks landing about a mile below the city while on the way here with a load of wood. Six colored men were aboard at the time, two running the boat and four passengers. Only two out of this number lived to tell the story.

The men all succeeded in securing a hold on the boat. Some could swim, some could not, but owing to the cold no one felt able to reach the shore. One made the start but concluded immediately that he could never reach the land and came right back on the boat.

The youngest of the number, George Richards, who was but a boy, died from the exposure about 11 o'clock. Near midnight his stepfather, William Willoughby, who was the mate of the boat, went overboard without notification – it is thought, rendered desperate by his sufferings with the intention of trying to reach the shore anyhow. He appeared to those left on the boat to have gone down almost at once, evidently being so benumbed that he was powerless to make the needful exertion. His body has not yet been found.

These lived near Clubfoot Creek.

Two hours later another boy expired, and about day Henry Gaylor, of James City, making the fourth death. The bodies of the three dead ones on the boat were lain across it, their heads hanging on one side, their feet on the other so that they would not fall over and be carried away.

Remarkable as it appears, the men were not discovered and rescued until 10 o'clock the next day. Then Capt. Haywood Dove, from about Clubfoot Creek, and Ervin Green of this city, were the only ones left living, and they were covered with ice and suffering terribly.

❧ ❧ ❧ ❧ ❧ ❧

DEADLY LIGHTNING. "Capt. Terry Midgett, colored, from Slocum's Creek, was in route to New Bern on Friday evening in a boat belonging to W. B. Flanner, during the thunderstorm, when lightning struck the boat killing his son, Joe, a boy about 10 or 12 years old, and slightly damaging the boat. He went ashore at Johnson's Point and took the body of his son home, leaving the boat." *The New Bern Journal* September 27, 1885.

SECOND IN A WEEK. "This is the second case of drowning down Neuse River last week. The others, it will be remembered by readers, was a colored man named Henry Hardesty, who was knocked overboard by a boom, and drowned near Hancock's Creek Tuesday." *The Daily Journal* March 7, 1893.

"THREE MEN DROWNED. The schooner Molly B., Capt. James Bell, col., was turned over by the gale of Wednesday morning two miles from Cherry Point, Neuse River, while bringing a load of wood to Newbern and broken to pieces. Five men were aboard. The captain and another colored man escaped – one by clinging to the bottom of the small skiff, the other by clinging to a piece of the boat. Two colored men, Lewis Willowby and Cull Willowby were drowned. The body of the former was recovered; that of the latter has not been found. They lived at Clubfoot Creek. Mr. A. N. Weaver, a northern gentleman and proprietor of a sawmill at Cherry Point was also aboard and was drowned. He moved here we believe from Connecticut [*actually Pennsylvania*] about three years ago. He was about 35 years of age and was not a man of family. His body at last accounts had not been found." *The Herald* (Beaufort) November 16, 1893.

AND THREE MORE. "One of Fernie E. Gaskill & Co.'s fishing boats left their fishing ground in Slocumb's Creek Friday with a load for the city and three colored men aboard. The boat failed to reach the city and Mr.

Gaskill, learning that it had started, instituted a search and found it capsized in Neuse River off the mouth of the creek. As the men had never reported, of course, they were drowned. The drowned men are Alonzo Gaskins, Kitt Hewitt, and Jake Moore. Two of them leave families." *The Wilmington Messenger* January 4, 1895.

Small trading sailboat, Neuse River, 1908; New Bern-Craven County Public Library

A TERRIFIC GALE. "The storm of yesterday,

aside from blowing one of the most terrific gales that has been known here for very many years, cause damage to shipping even when anchored and placed as far from danger as possible. But many a good ship was the toy of the gale. In some cases, the wind blew the water out [of the Neuse] and left anchored boats on the ground and a few of the boats went over on their sides." *News and Observer* (Raleigh). January 10, 1908.

BOAT ADRIFT. "The boat Louise, used for transporting wood, and owned by Mr. Ben Richards, from Handcock's Creek, was found off Otter Creek in bad shape; her rigging had been torn loose and the boat had been turned into a little bay to weather the storm. It was anchored, but the waves were so obstreperous that the cable broke and the anchor was lost, the boat was drifting helplessly when picked up by the cutter." *News and Observer* (Raleigh) January 10, 1908.

AND SOMETIMES GOOD NEWS. "The schooner Arcadia, Capt. B. T. Bennett, which was reported missing has shown up with all hands safe. The Arcadia sailed from here for some point in Pamlico County, and baffling with contrary and strong wind was blown off her course taking harbor in Slocumb's Creek. A boat from Swansboro which arrived here yesterday reported speaking to Arcadia and that all was well." *New Bern Weekly Journal* May 11, 1905.

Other types of weather affected boatmen and the flow of goods. *The Federal Republican* advised on Saturday, February 8, 1817, that "on the night of the fourth instant, an unusual quantity of snow fell in this place. It is said by the oldest inhabitants of the town, that is the deepest that has fallen within the last 20 years. On the mornings of the sixth and seventh, the rivers Neuse and Trent were frozen across, so hard as to admit skating." The river was icebound again on New Year's Eve 1872 when the *New Bern Times* commented upon "the novel spectacle of a large schooner, under full sail, jammed in the ice, in the Neuse River, was witnessed by many citizens on Saturday." As fog once disturbed the supply of wood, "there seems to be a great scarcity of coal in our market; the cause of which, we learn is from the supposed fact that vessels already laden and en-route for this port, are delayed on accounts of navigation being so obstructed by ice."

Shipping News

Among the commodities traveling via boat and ship – such as naval stores, pork, wood and coal – was the news itself. Ship's captains earned ready cash by delivering newspapers from other cities, and across the sea from England, to printers always hungry for fresh copy. This teaser from *The Newbern Gazette* of July 13, 1764, illustrates how this worked.

"Yesterday arrived here, Capt. Bolton, from Philadelphia, with European Goods, and a Quantity of Rum. By him we have the late Act of Parliament for regulating the American Trade, and levying additional Duties on it; which will be inserted in our next [edition]."

And two weeks later: "Since our last, arrived Captain Hammond, in a Schooner from New-York, by whom we have the Papers of the 16th Instant: The Parliament broke up in good Humour ..."

And on the last day of the next month, this rumor: "By a Vessel in 7 days from Charles-town, we hear, just before she sailed, a Packet arrived there from England, which brought the disagreeable news, that the French, Dutch and Spaniards, have formed a Confederacy, and are on the point of declaring war against us."

Another type of "commodity" moving past the south shore of the Neuse was people. Passenger service was available to those who could afford it. And, of course, nearly all early immigrants came on ships. "Since our last [issue]," the *Gazette* stated December 14, 1764, "several Vessels arrived here from Northward, particularly a Sloop from Maryland with 57 Passengers, chiefly Families, who are to settle in the Province."

On August 24, the local paper carried this offer: "For Antigua, directly, the Sloop *Tryal*, John Scott, commander. Now lying at New Bern; very well accommodated for passengers. For freight or passage, inquire of the matter, at Richard Ellis's, Merchant."

As we are well aware, some of those making passage were not doing so voluntarily. For example, this item was run September 14, 1764, by Thomas Haslen, then mayor of the colonial borough of New Bern: "Advertisements. Just imported in the Sloop *New Bern Packet*, from Barbados, to be sold cheap for ready Money, or short Credit, at the Subscriber's store in New Bern; a Parcel of choice young SLAVES. Also, to be sold at said Store, wholesale or retail, old Barbadoes spirits, rum, sugar, and dry goods."

By land, Slocum Creek was equidistant from both Beaufort and New Bern. For some parts of the Neuse's south shore, Beaufort was even closer. Thus, in considering early trade from southern Craven County, it's useful and instructive to look at the Carteret County port as well. While the 1874 U. S. Coast Survey chart of the Neuse marked depths of 12 to 15 feet, with mid-stream shoals as shallow as six feet, Beaufort's harbor accommodated the largest ocean-going vessels of the day.

In the nearby chart, two "ships" are listed as having visited Port-Beaufort 1763-1764. To visualize a *ship* in this context, think of something with many masts and billowing sails that might have been commanded by captains with names like Hornblower or Ahab or if you must, Jack Sparrow. Snows were the largest of the old two-masted vessels, and though the lines between types of ships are sometimes a little fuzzy, snows were typically larger than brigs, which were the largest vessels that normally ventured into the shallower waters of the Neuse River

The chart also makes clear the kinds of things and their quantities being imported and exported. The colonists required salt, sugar, molasses, and flour, in addition to coffee, tea, rum, and beer; while exporting impressive amounts of wood products, such as staves, shingles, and boards. Several men in southern Craven County are listed in the census as shingle makers. Here we see over two hundred thousand wooden shingles being exported, along with significant quantities of hides, furs, skins, and beeswax. As we already know and reconfirm here, tar, turpentine, spirits of turpentine, and pitch measured in the tens of thousands of barrels were flowing outward. And the naval stores' trade thrived for another century.

Entered in Port-*Beaufort*, from the 1st of *October* 1763, to the 1st of *October* 1764, the following Vessels, viz.

2 Ships,	72 Sloops,
1 Snow,	43 Schooners,
9 Brigs.	
	In all 127

Imported in the said District, between the 1st of *October* 1763, and 1st of *October* 1764.

320 Hhds. Rum,	352 Barrels Floor,
318 Do Molasses,	1972 Do of Bread,
342 Bar. brown Sugar,	28000 lbs. of Iron,
18160 lbs. Loaf Do	179 Staves,
40 Casks of Wine,	2479 lbs. of Cheese,
913 Barrels Cyder,	96 Barrels of Beer,
10865 Bushels Salt,	1600 lbs. of Flax,
Exclusive of *European* Goods, Coffee, Tea, &c.	

Exported from the said District, between the 1st of *October* 1763, and 1st of *October* 1764.

30403 Barrels of Tar,	619 Barrels Rozin,
5363 Do Turpentine,	1279 Do Spirits Turp.
3721 Do Pitch,	47000 Feet Scantling,
4731 Do Pork,	87560 Do Boards,
495 Do Beef,	11305 lbs. Deer Skins,
32805 Bushels Corn,	1800 Furs Skins,
3556 Do Pease,	20 Barrels M Wax,
153161 Staves,	19 Do Bees Wax,
222150 Do Shingles,	190 Do Rice,
19900 lbs. of Tallow,	199731 Pieces Heading,
404 Hides,	160 Barrels Flour,
18732 lbs. tann'd Lea.	107 Do Hogs Fat,
Exclusive of Live Stock, &c.	

Around the time of the War Between the States, by the way, passengers traveled from the Neuse to New York City in just four days. Freight and mail moved just as quickly.

On December 14, 1865, Craven Moseley, identified in the notice he ran in *The New Berne Times* as "colored," announced the discovery he made in a waterway along the south shore of the Neuse.

"On Saturday morning last, December 9th, I found a Pilot Boat painted black, with white gunnels, containing eleven (11) barrels of scrape turpentine, sunk in Hancock's Creek near the mouth, in the neighborhood of Mr.

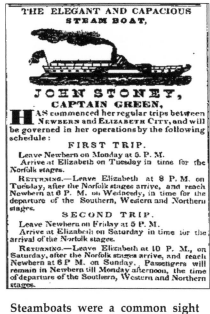

THE ELEGANT AND CAPACIOUS
STEAM BOAT,

JOHN STONEY,
CAPTAIN GREEN,

HAS commenced her regular trips between Newbern and Elizabeth City, and will be governed in her operations by the following schedule:

FIRST TRIP.

Leave Newbern on Monday at 5. P. M.
Arrive at Elizabeth on Tuesday in time for the Norfolk stages.

RETURNING.—Leave Elizabeth at 8 P. M. on Tuesday, after the Norfolk stages arrive, and reach Newbern at 6 P. M. on Wednesday, in time for the departure of the Southern, Western and Northern stages.

SECOND TRIP.

Leave Newbern on Friday at 5 P. M.
Arrive at Elizabeth on Saturday in time for the arrival of the Norfolk stages.

RETURNING.—Leave Elizabeth at 10 P. M., on Saturday, after the Norfolk stages arrive, and reach Newbern at 6 P. M. on Sunday. Passengers will remain in Newbern till Monday afternoon, the time of departure of the Southern, Western and Northern stages.

Steamboats were a common sight by the 1820s. The Neuse River Steamboat Company, chartered in 1817, ran daily to Elizabeth City.

Franklin Borden's Plantation. The owner will come forward, prove property, and pay the finder for his trouble, otherwise, it would be dealt with according to the law."

But the changes brought by time are inevitable. The torque and vibration of steam engines required vessels made of metal, not wood. The technological transition doomed the naval stores business and brought with it an aesthetic change lamented in 1868 by a newspaper correspondent who only identified himself as "Videns." In a letter to the editor of the *Charlotte (NC) Democrat*, the writer commented upon vicissitudes since his last visit before the War Between the States: "Steamers of large capacity have taken the place of the sail vessels which formerly dotted the waters of the Neuse and Trent, and added so much to the beauty of the picturesque river scenery."

Nevertheless, in one way or another, the people continued to live by, work on, and rely upon the river until the present day. But the dangers and challenges of doing so are ceaseless. In evidence, a news item of the *New Berne Weekly Journal*, January 14, 1908: "R. S. Hyman, a boatman, from Handcock's Creek, had the misfortune to drop his pocket-book overboard in the Trent River yesterday. He had just counted his money, the amount was $5.30, and was standing on the gunwale of his boat, when in returning his book to his pocket, he missed the pocket and dropped the book in the water. It sank and all efforts to recover it was to no avail."

Life (and Death) Before the Civil War

For thus sayeth the Lord concerning the sons and daughters who are born in this place, and concerning the mothers who bear them and the father who beget them in this land: They shall die of deadly disease.
                                        – Jeremiah 16:2-4 (NRSV)

On November 1, 1849, ten men sent a letter to the leaders of the Craven County school board asking permission to move the school house near Slocum Creek. These fathers of school-age children lived on both sides of the creek and all over plantation land that is now the Cherry Point military airbase.

In the letter, they made the case that a big swamp – *a low and wet savannah*, they called it – was causing problems for their childrens' navigation on foot to school and back, and that the distances involved were outside the parameters set by the school board itself. If the house for the school could not be moved, the signers suggested divvying up the district's money so they could build their own schoolhouse, or splitting out parts of districts 33 and 34 to form a new school district.

The handwritten letter in its difficult-to-read script is preserved on a seldom-reviewed microfilm reel at the public library in New Bern. The issue itself is mildly interesting but the big payoff is that the writers included a map showing where they and many of their neighbors lived. It's an incredible snapshot of life in southern Craven County 170 years ago; an immensely valuable document for the historical understanding of the community in a much earlier form. [a]

The map is no great work of art. It's a faded, smeared pencil sketch, not to scale, and out of proportion; the kind of drawing one might make quickly on a blank sheet of paper to explain the layout of a neighborhood to a visitor. Understanding it in its raw form requires someone who just happened to know Slocum Creek and Hancock Creek. And even then, the map is drawn upside down with the Neuse River at the bottom and the creeks pointing up the page as if they flowed from the north.

It's easy to imagine the rare researchers who even bothered to review the old school records over, say, a hundred years, glancing at the thing and simply moving to the next frame. What makes the letter stand out is that it

---

[a] Craven County Records (Misc.), Reel 1254, Kellenberger Room, New Bern-Craven County Public Library.

includes the only map found among hundreds and hundred of pages of minutes, notes, and lists chronicling the primitive system for public education in Craven County from the early 1800s.

"The petition has for its object," the letter began, "a change in District No. 34, as regards the School-House in a more central location among the citizens; a division of the moneys belonging to said district, or the formation of a new one, so that the area of ours may be diminished – either, or the best of which plans will be acceptable to the subscribers."

Subscribers meant the people who used and paid for the school and its house. They called their hand-drawn map a *draught*.

"By reference to the draught appended," the letter continued, "it will be readily perceived that the School-House is nearly in the center of the district and is not nearer than four to five miles from the subscribers' dwellings, which part is the most thickly settled, and that a large Savanna intervening (always wet) renders it nearly impassable for most of the pupils to avail themselves of the advantage of the school."

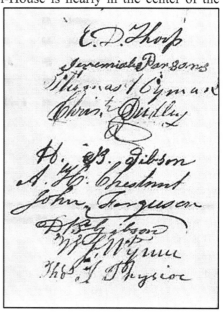

The writers pointed out that the chairman of the school board had ruled on the general matter two years before: "He distinctly says, 'The house for the school should be as near the center of the district as possible. Justice, the successful operation of the school, and the law requires this.' "

The signators, in the order in which they signed, were: Edwin D.

School house petitioners, 1849

Thorp(e), age 30; Jeremiah Parson, 44; Thomas Hyman, 24; Christopher Dudley, 28; H.B. Gibson, not found in the census; Alexander H. Chesnutt, 21; John Ferguson, 42; David B. Gibson, 54; W. J. Wynne, 25; and Thomas Physioc, 45. All were farmers except Physioc who was a blacksmith.

The signers represented only a small portion of the overall population. Their map identified more than two dozen farm families with children in school, but the number of plantations and farms was significantly larger. Census, agricultural and other records for 1850 list many more. Names found near the south shore of the Neuse River at the time include Holland, Ives, Hill, Stephens, Davis, Rowe, Oglesby, Marshall, Chesnutt, Peartree,

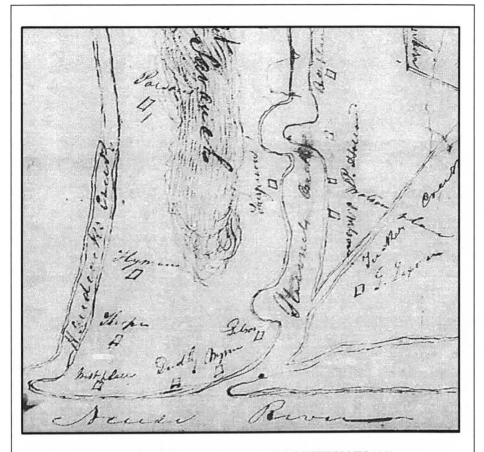

MAP SENT WITH SCHOOL HOUSE PETITION IN 1849

A portion of the school house petition map of 1849, above, gives an indication of what the orginal looks like. The entire map covers the area between Harlowe and Croatan. It's upside down with north at the bottom and south at the top. And it's not in proportion or to scale. The Neuse River is shown at the bottom with Slocum Creek at center and Hancock Creek at left going up the map. Tucker Creek is at right. Individual homes, mostly of the petitioners, are indicated by small squares with the names written out nearby. A hand-written note on the map reads: "The above is laid down only from a knowledge of the situation of the two districts, but I think very near right." In the top center of the map, the big swamp that the petitioners called a "low and wet savannah," is labelled in writing that runs down the page. The land between the creeks – Slocum and Hancock – is the present-day location of MCAS Cherry Point. Draining the big savannah was one of the challenges of base construction in 1940-41. That swamp is where Cherry Point's runways were built. The map is on microfilm reel 1254 in the Kellenberger Room of the New Bern-Craven County Public Library.

Franklin, Gooding, Parsons, Gibson, Brooks, McCabe, Mace, Cavenoe, Taylor, Conner, Whitehead, Caraway, Temple, Gibble, White, Merrit, Rigdon, Hampton, Loftin, Bratcher, Biger, Physioc, Read, Winn (Wynne), Williams, Utley, Hunter, West, Bell, Dudley, Latham, Piver, Lewis, Carman, Thorpe, Ferguson, Holton, and others.

The letter writers wished that they "might furnish our children with horses, and then they might reach the school but it must be recollected that many have not the means to do this."

Despite the poor-mouthing, this was a prosperous region of plantations, most engaged in the lucrative production of naval stores, some with slave labor. In 1850, the first signer, Edwin Thorpe, had 31 slaves; another, Christopher Dudley owned a dozen on his 700-acre plantation. While others who signed the petition appear in the slave census to be small yeomen farmers with no enslaved people, will and estate record tell a different story and indicate several of these families owned, hired out, or rented slaves. [b]

Pre-Civil War Schools of Southern Craven County

The law creating the Common School system in North Carolina passed the state legislature in 1839 and schools began operation in Craven County in 1840 and 1841.

By 1849, there were more than 40 school districts in the county. Each had a one-room schoolhouse and usually a single teacher. Most teachers were male and were paid about $22 per month. The school board – called the Board of Superintendents – elected the head superintendent, set policy, and picked the school books. The local three-member school committee in each district supervised the teacher, approved bills and the teacher's pay.

Districts 32 through 36 straddled the area from Croatan to Harlowe. District 32 was Deep Gully to Dam Creek; 33, Dam Creek to Slocum Creek;

34, Slocum Creek to Hancock Creek; and 35, Hancock Creek to Clubfoot Creek. The District 34 school was located on what is now Cherry Point. District 33, today's Havelock, was to the east and District 35 to the west.

In February 1848, school board member C. B. Wood reported to the Board of Superintendents that District No. 31 (Riverdale) had

A typical one-room school house.

b Craven County Slave Schedule, U.S. Census, 1850 and 1860.

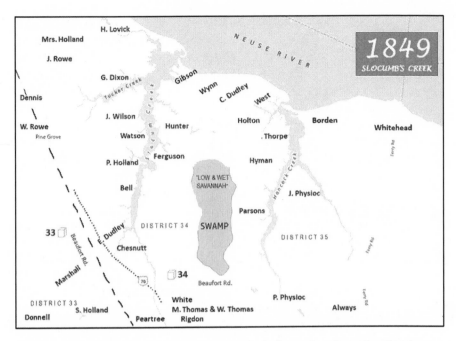

This is a map created by the author using the information from the sketch-map included with the 1849 school house petition. It represents the modern area from Carolina Pines to Ferry Road with USMC Cherry Point in the center between Slocum Creek and Hancock Creek. The names are those on just some of the farms and plantations in existence in 1849. The dashed line is the approximate route of the Atlantic & North Carolina Railroad which would open in 1858. The dotted line represents modern-day US 70, but approximates the main county road – the old Beaufort Road – that existed from colonial times. Three school districts are noted on the map: 33, 34 & 35, with the school house for 33 and 34 represented by boxes beside those numbers. The tributary of Slocum Creek that ran beside the District 34 school is still shown as "Schoolhouse Branch" on current government quadrangle maps.

built a schoolhouse and that Districts No. 32 and 33 (Croatan and the western side of Slocum Creek) were teaching orthography (spelling), reading, writing, arithmetic, English grammar, and geography. District 32 had "a flourishing school in operation, attended by 30 children." Wood reported that although District No. 34 (between Slocum Creek and Hancock Creek) had a schoolhouse they had no site for it and no school had been taught there since early 1847. Because of "natural inconveniences," District No. 35 had been divided in half. Each had a schoolhouse but no land for it, Wood reported, but in one part a school was in operation.

In the 1840s only men got to vote for school committee members, and for most anything else for that matter. The citizens – all men – met June 24, 1848, at the District No. 32 common schoolhouse at Croatan to elect the local school committee. Outgoing members were Vine A. Tolson, Stephen F. Hardison, and Charles C. Wilson. In attendance were L. Rowe, Vine Tolson, A. Taylor, B. Latham, C.B. Wood, John Baker, William Kincy, G.W. Rowe, William Bayley, Stephen F. Hardison, and Michael N. Fisher, Elijah Hardison, and Benjamin F. Williams, all residents of the district. Fisher, Tolson, Baker, Stephen Hardison, Williams, and Elijah Hardison were nominated for the committee. Vine Tolson (eleven votes), Stephen Hardison (nine votes), and Micheal Fisher (seven votes) were elected. This process was repeated in every district at least every two years.

The school committee lists are a fairly straightforward way to identify the prominent men of the communities. Voting, as noted, was an all-male enterprise. Getting elected normally meant being financially successful, owning property, and also having acquired a reasonably good reputation and the respect of one's peers. The lists, therefore, serve as a kind of "who's who" in southern Craven County.

Lists of students were also kept every year. For example, from 1841 Craven County school records, "a true list of the free white children in the 33rd school district between the age of five and 21 years of age."

William Holland Jr.	Philemon Holland
Nancy Holland	Stephen Holland
John Ives	Richard D.S Holland
Didama Hills	Kizia Holland
Betsy Davis	Jonathan Chesnutt
David D. Rowe	Redmon Chesnutt
Franklin V. Oglesby	John Chesnutt
Ann Oglesby	Thomas Peartree
George H. Rowe	Casandra Stephens
James W, Marshall	Abby Stephens
Matilda M. Marshall	Andrew J. Chesnutt
Sarah R. Marshall	

School Committee members for District 33 in 1841 were: William H. Marshall, Joseph R. Franklin, and John H. Gooding. James M. Rowe and James Marshall declined to serve that year.

The 1842 student list for District 34 included:

Susan Gibble	Needham M. White
Elizabeth D. Rowe	John Taylor
Peter Rowe	James Merrit
Haywood A. White	George Rigdon
Susan J. White	Betse Rigdon

Equillia Rigdon

Abaline Rigdon

Harriett Hampton

William Bratcher

Polly Bratcher

John H. Parsons

Nancy Parsons

Henry B. Gibson

David Gibson

William Gibson

John H. Physioc

Nancy Biger

Elisa Biger

Mary Read

William Read

Thomas Hyman

Trephina Parsons

William Winn

James Winn

John Hyman

[Note: The spelling of the prominent family name "Wynne" changed around 1850. In the 1840s the children appeared as *Winn*. In 1855, William S. *Wynne* declined his election to the school committee.]

Local school committee members in 1842 for District 34 were: N. B. White, Jeremiah Parsons, and Thomas J. Physioc.

District 35 school children for 1842 were:

Henry Brooks

Liddy Brooks

Sarah Brooks

Alexander Brooks

Samuel Brooks

Charlotte Brooks

Thomas C. Mace

Catherine McCabe

Sidney McCabe

William McCabe

Sidney Oglesby

Jesse W. Hibbs

Francis Mace

Abraham Cavener

Sarah Cavener

Sarah Ann Taylor

Elizabeth C. Taylor

Bryan Conner

John Whitehead

John Physioc

Caroline Gooding

Julia C. Caraway

1842 school committee members for District 34 were: John Whitehead, B. W. Thorpe, and William Temple. In 1841, Joseph Physioc had refused to accept his election. In 1845, Stephen Cavena(r), Joseph Taylor, and John S. Whitehead made up the committee.

On March 25, 1841, Clubfoot Creek's District 36 sent this message to the county school board: "Dear Sirs, I certify that Elijah Taylor, Joseph W. Brittain, and Joshua Neal each get five votes which was the highest number given. – Joseph W. Brittain." In 1844, the District 36 committee was Elijah Taylor, Oscar P. Dudley, and John Hasket who signed his name with an X. In 1845, Isaac Taylor, Alfred Casey, and Elijah Taylor served on the school committee.

In 1841, District 34 had just eight students: Jane Smith, daughter of Ezekiel Smith; Joshua and Hannah Taylor, children of Elijah Taylor; Nancy,

Catherine and Parker Smith, children of Nancy Smith; and Mary Jane Neal and John Casey, an orphan, in the household of Abner Neal. [a]

Gleaning Meaning from the School Records

Let's look at a few more batches of information before we re-cap why we're even considering this material.

First, "The Croatan." Before the Civil War, there was a huge farm community west of present-day Havelock and running up to Riverdale. Called *The Croatan*, this rich agricultural enclave of plantations and farms like Magnolia Plantation, which included the land where Carolina Pines is today, reached up to Riverdale with its massive Fisher Plantation. Other farms, large and small, coalesced into a thriving agrarian enterprise zone.

Naturally, the visuals for this are plows, horses, mules, oxen, and wagons. While that's a valid take on the idea, this was also a big area for slashing longleaf pine trees, gathering the sap, and distilling it into turpentine, or cooking it into tar and pitch. The reader, by now, knows well of the naval stores sold for export each year and that much of the income was produced in this manner. The busy residents were, by and large, prosperous.

Forty-five students were enrolled in the Croatan District No. 32's bustling school in 1845. Committeemen Stephen F. Hardison, Vine Allen Tolson, and John Baker certified the list for that year. The students were:

Christopher Kincy	Henry McTutch
Julia Kincy	William Bailey
Elizabeth Powell	Elizabeth Bailey
Nancy Powell	George Bailey
Mary A. McTutch	George W. Rowe
Eliza M. Baker	Susan Smith
John Baker	Benjamin Taylor
William Baker	Elijah Hardison
Bryant Baker	Bryant Williams
Nancy Tolson	George Wilson
Jacob Gibble	Mary A. Wilson
Alexander H. Chesnutt	James F. Williams
William H. Wood	Elizabeth W. Tolson
Charlotte W. Wood	Eveline Ebron
James Mozingo	George W. Hardison
Susan Mozingo	Gabriel Hardison

---

[a] Old Craven County school records, from which much of the material in this section is drawn, are preserved on microfilm reels 1252, 1253 & 1254 at the Kellenberger Room of the New Bern-Craven County Public Library.

Richard Whitford	David C. Williams
John P. Ives	Margaret Smith
Frances Ives	Richard B. Smith
Thomas Parsons	Beneter Smith
Kiziah Williams	Hardy Kincey
Robert Williams	Cliff Kincey

It's possible to draw some conclusions about this fragmented and seemingly random data. The first take-away is that there is enough information in old Craven County school records to easily fill a book of this size and there are many more names that could be highlighted. We have chosen to list *some* of the names from a *few* districts for a *limited number* of the years of the 1840s to illustrate in a small way the number of people who have populated southern Craven County. The area of the south shore of the Neuse River was an extension of the New Bern district. And it was far from being an isolated, uninhabited place. It had been settled in the early 1700s, as we have shown, experienced a land boom by the mid-1700s and then an out-migration in the early 1800s when descendants of the first settlers caught the fever to *Go West*.

Nevertheless, by the end of the antebellum era, the population had stabilized and much of the land of southern Craven County had been taken up. Productive farms and plantations had been established that were populated by hundreds of families amounting to thousands of people. Some of the prominent families of the area – but by no means all – have been mentioned herein.

The modern map created from the 1849 sketch map is tangible proof of the area's thorough settlement, especially when consideration is given to the fact that the family names listed are only a fraction of those who lived there.

Slavery in Southern Craven County

A few counties in eastern North Carolina had a higher concentration of slave labor than Craven County, but only a few. In 1756, Royal Governor Arthur Dobbs reported to the London Board of Trade that "there were 7,561 'Blacks' in the province of which 1,420 were in New Hanover, 1,091 in Edgecombe, and 934 in Craven." By 1790, it's estimated that 33-50 percent of the county's population was enslaved. [a]

As we have noted, the Neuse's lower shore was made up of numerous plantations dependent on slave labor. By the time of the Civil War, nearly

---

[a] *The History of a Southern State*, H.T. Lefler and A.R. Newsome, University of North Carolina Press, 1954, pp. 118-119.

WORK ON A CANAL - A striking antique print from *Harper's Weekly* shows former slaves digging a canal in March 1863. The sketch illustrates the heavy labor often done by slaves before the Civil War. In addition to the more common farm field work, dam building, land clearing, timbering, and "gathering turpentine" were all tasks performed by those in bondage.

a thousand slaves toiled daily in southern Craven County. [b]

While owning no slaves outright, schoolhouse petitioner Alexander Chesnutt still resided in 1849 on the plantation of his father, Owen Chesnutt, who owned fourteen slaves in 1860. The Chestnutt plantation was several hundred acres with a big stand of pecan trees at the fork of Slocum Creek.

Havelock's Graham Barden Elementary School and Slocum Village housing today occupy land that was once owned by Chesnutt. In 1860, Chesnutt had seven female slaves aged 50, 25, 16, 15, four, three, and four months and as many male slaves aged 24, 19, 18, 12, 10, eight, and six.

Henry J. Lovick, who owned Magnolia Plantation west of Havelock, had thirty-nine slaves including one female who was 100 years old. Only the age and sex of the slave – not names – were listed in the slave schedule, which was made with the census every ten years. In the case of this centenarian slave, however, the census taker made the handwritten note "Name Jane" next to her entry.

Lovick's slave plantation, as we shall see, was the landing point for the Union force that invaded Craven County in 1862.

The Flanner farmstead at Croatan had a whopping 72 slaves in 1860, and 23 were listed at the Riverdale plantation of Michael N. Fisher. B.F. Borden, whose farm was on the east side of Hancock Creek at the river, is shown with 41 in census records. Philemon Holland had 11 slaves on his Slocum Creek plantation.

While a few people owned large numbers of slaves, the majority of slave-holders in southern Craven had only a few. Dozens in the census – both male and female – owned a single slave; some owned two or three. Typically, these were personal or household servants. In other cases – like small farmer James H. Hunter of Slocum Creek who listed three men aged 24, 25, and 35 – the owner often worked shoulder-to-shoulder with the slaves to make the land productive. Rev. Jacob Utley had three slaves – males 45 and 18, and female, 16 – on his Havelock farm; W.H. Marshall at the head of Slocum Creek near the railroad also listed three; females, 17 and 20, and a single male aged 29.

In addition to working in farm fields and managing livestock, slaves performed a broad variety of occupations. Cooking, cleaning, sewing, caring for children and the sick, tending gardens or feeding chickens were routine chores. Larger slaveholders had crews clearing land for improved fields, harvesting timber, building dams for grist and sawmills, and operating the mills themselves. Before 1865, slaves also built railroads.

A phenomenal and much-ballyhooed internal improvements project, the Harlowe and Clubfoot Canal, was first opened to boat and barge traffic

---

[b] Craven County Slave Schedule, U.S. Census, 1860.

in 1790 and was widened and deepened in the 1820s. The canal linked Beaufort with New Bern by connecting the Neuse and Newport rivers. The canal not only made the trip between the two vital ports faster but also eliminated the need for vessels to cross dangerous ocean shoals in doing so.

It took years to dig the three-and-a-half-mile canal. Its dimensions, in one iteration, were 14 feet wide at its base, 26 feet wide at the water's surface, and while holding four feet of water, it was as much as fifteen feet deep from its highest natural elevation to the bottom.

It was built by – and probably would not have been built without – the labor of enslaved Africans and hired African Americans. [c]

Free Blacks Before the Civil War

It comes as a surprise to some that a large population of free people of African heritage inhabited the creek lands of the Neuse River's south shore long before the Civil War. They made up a significant percentage of the population from at least the time of the American Revolution. By the 1860s, many of these families had been out of bondage for generations.

As we have mentioned, some were descendants of volunteer soldiers who earned their freedom by fighting the British alongside the colonial patriots to create the United States of America. Others came from people who had been "manumitted"; that is, released from slavery by former masters for long service or good conduct.

In James Hyman's will of 1803, he wrote: "I give to my two negros Fender and Will their freedom." Hyman, whose expansive plantation was on Hancock Creek, also willed Fender and Will a hundred acres of land. [d]

Some purchased their freedom. And some surely escaped.

There was such a flow of runaways into North Carolina in the early 1700s that both the government of the Colony of Virginia and the British Board of Trade launched inquiries into why it was happening and how to stop it. Henderson Walker, colonial governor of North Carolina, vehemently denied it, writing: "Neither are there runaways harbored here, that one can discover by diligent inquiry, nor shall such thing be suffered so far as it is in our power to prevent it." [e]

In whatever way they came to be here, unfettered African Americans found opportunity and a hospitable social environment in southeastern

[c] *The Quaker Map: Harlowe to Mill Creek*, David Cecelski, davidcecelski.com, 2019; *Clubfoot & Harlowe Creek Canal (Part 1)*; John D. Whitford, *The Daily Journal*, New Bern, N.C., August 6, 1882.

[d] Craven County Wills, James Hyman, 1803, CR.801.22.

[e] Lefler and Newsome, *The History of a Southern State*, pp. 49-50.

Craven County. There they could live peaceful and largely un-harassed lives. The territory had originally held a large Quaker population that, for the most part, rejected slavery and thus made good neighbors for the freed people. Well before the 1860s, places like North Harlowe and Craven Corner had long-standing free black communities. They lived as neighbors with local white families. They got along together communally, did business with one another, trading in services, produce, livestock and land, despite living in a place where slave-holding was common. And there is a strong tradition that intermarriage was common with Native Americans who remained in the area after the Tuscarora War of 1711.

Many of these families today have the greatest longevity of residence in southern Craven County of any of the people who ever lived here. They are descendants of pioneers who came to the area in the 1700s.

As mentioned before, one of the earliest of these groups to emigrate from Virginia were people named Dove who arrived in the late 1700s. In 1850, census taker William H. Marshall found 62 members of this family living here.

The 1860 census lists free black and mulatto families and individuals in "Goodings District," roughly equivalent to today's Townships Five and Six. Most had a house full of children. Some of the heads of families were:

Andrew & Mary Godett	William & Charlotte Martin
Joseph & Mary Fenner	Jacob & Sarah Dove
Elijah & Sarah George	Abram & Sallie Costen
Jacob & Hettie Fenner	William & Sarah Dove
Mary George	Charity & Jacob Dove
Thomas & Penelope Fenner	Samuel & Margaret Dove
William Fenner	Edmund & Elizabeth George
Vestal & Rebeccah Gaskins	Louis & Hancy Willowby
James & Hannah Richards	Culbreth & Decy Willowby
Martin & Tabitha George	Alfred & Jane Willowby
Silas & Celia Richard	Silas & Crawford Moore
John & Lucinda Finner	Samuel & Judith Martin
William & Caroline Richard	Fanney Dove
Amos & Lila Costens	Abel Carter
James & Elizabeth Moore	Theophilus George
Isaac & Elizabeth Brown	Adam Culley
Stephen & Mary Godett	Solomon & Mary Chance

These and many more are listed in the September 1860 census as "Free Inhabitants of ... the County of Craven." The order in which the census is enumerated shows them living among and between the white families of Pittman, Holland, Wynne, Mayo, and Whitehead, to name only a few.

Their occupations, like most in that era, are farm-related. Farmers, farm laborers, day laborers, and coopers are common, but we also find boatmen (Levi Brown and Silas Moore), carpenters (Stephen Godett, George Frazier, and R. Davis), and a shoemaker (Anias Sampson) among the abbreviated list shown above.

Regardless of their successes and the niche they had carved out for themselves, for these families, education was a hit-and-miss matter. The North Carolina common school legislation of 1839 was for the benefit of free white children and did not make provision for people of color.

As we shall see in later chapters, the aftermath of the Civil War brought profound changes for both those in slavery and those already enjoying some of the fruits of freedom.

Death in a "Low & Wet Savannah"

A big, swampy plain was central to the argument of the petitioners of 1849 that, for convenience's sake, their school needed to be moved. In their letter to the board of superintendents, they included a note about the distances the children had to travel to school.

One solution the letter-writers suggested was the creation of a new district. They laid the corners for a proposed district on their map. It abutted the even-larger "pocosin," a particular and peculiar type of swamp that ran for miles to the south of their district.

"The superintendents should look to one fact not mentioned in the petition," the note read, "viz. that it is impossible for there ever to be any children south of Thomas and Rigdon in District 34 toward the pocosin as it is a place no person can live."

Distances were given from homes on the sketch map to the school.

- From Gibson to school house No. 34   4 miles or 5
- From Dudley, Physioc, and Thorpes, about the same
- From Hyman to do [*ditto*]   2 ½ miles
- From Parsons to do   1 ½ miles
- From White do   1 ¼ do
- From Thomas and Rigdon   2 ¼ do

It took the Board of Superintendents some time but eventually they acquiesced to the request of the schoolhouse petitioners by creating a new district – No. 46 – out of portions of District 33 and 34. In 1858, Owen Chesnutt, George Rigdon, and Stephen Peartree were the District 46 school committee.

The low and wet savannah complained about by the school house petitioners of 1849 had other implications more serious than blocking the way to school. It was a mosquito-breeding paradise. In that environment, undiagnosed illnesses – often referred to simply as "the fever" – were a common, seasonal cause of death.

In an era without air conditioning, mosquito abatement methods, or even window screens, flying, biting insects were a constant menace. No one in those days associated mosquitoes with the diseases that sometimes took out entire families. Many sicknesses were believed to be caused by bad air, the result of gases emanating from swampland. In fact, malaria means "bad air." Malaria *was* bad. But there were other more virulent illnesses.

In September 1841, Sally Rowe Holland lost, in the course of twenty-two days, her husband, two sons, and three servants who were part of her household on Slocum Creek. Thirteen-year-old Richard Dobbs Spaight Holland died September 6; Barney Holland, 25, died September 12; and her prosperous planter husband, Philemon Holland, 73, died on September 28. The "servants" – a euphemism for slaves – died about the same time. [a]

The deaths came during a period when the area around Slocum Creek was called Cravenville after a post office – the first ever established in southern Craven County – was opened for service by the Holland family on September 13, 1836.[b]

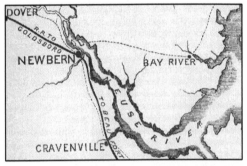

In a church newsletter, neighbor Cornelius Canaday reported the tragic events. He asked for comfort for Mrs. Holland, "her family having been visited by the monster death." Canady said "being left so desolate" the widow "earnestly solicits prayer of all the brethren and sisters of the Old

Detail from *Harper's Weekly* "Map of the Carolina Coast," February 1862, still shows Cravenville, the name of a defunct post office, at the head of Slocum Creek where Havelock already existed by that date. While known as Slocum Creek for much of its existence, many other names have been used for the area over time. See *Lists of Names in Southern Craven County* Part IV.

School Baptist faith, that she may be able to bear up under her affliction." [c]

[a] *The Primitive Baptist*, Saturday, April 23, 1842, pp. 126-127; KR.
[b] United States Post Office records, National Archives, Washington, D.C.
[c] "Old School Baptists" were a conservative sect also known as "hard shell" and "foot-washing" Baptists.

Canaday said Philemon Holland was born July 31, 1768 "and always sustained a reputable character until the year 1820, when he was baptized by Elder Jabez Weeks, and became a member of the Baptist church at Slocumb's Creek, Craven County, N.C." He listed the birth date of Barney Holland – "a very fine young man, much beliked by virtuous people" – as July 10, 1816, and the birth of Richard D.S. Holland as June 24, 1828.[d]

The sudden deaths of the Holland men doomed the Cravenville post office founded by Philemon's father, William Holland. U.S. post office records show that it was officially listed as closed as of January 28, 1842. Nevertheless, the name Cravenville – sometimes spelled Cravensville – lingered and continued to appear on maps and in print for years afterward as the *Harper's Weekly* Civil War map from 1862 illustrates on the previous page.

Victor T. Jones, Jr., research librarian of the Kellenberger Room of the New Bern-Craven County Public Library, suggested that the culprit in the Holland cases may have been yellow fever. The illness was seasonal, mosquito-borne, and responsible for recurrent fatal waves through two hundred years of local settlement. But malarial diseases were just as deadly.

Many of the old graves on Cherry Point are marked with dates of family members who died within days of one another and usually within periods of warm weather.

Bryan and Sarah Wynn Jones, who lived on the edge of the swamp, lost three baby girls in seven years; 1843, 1848, and 1850.

Though it's impossible to know with certainty the precise causes of deaths from the 1800s or even the early 1900s, a partial list of those close to the low, wet savannah who died young includes: Earnest Lee Berry, 16 months; Walter M. Toon, 7; Reta Bryant, 4; Jimmy Lee Richards, 20 months; Maudie E. Moore, 6; Nannie K. Moore, 6; Caroline E. Thorpe, 6 months, 22 days; Elizabeth Jones, 17 months; Martha E. Jones, 6; Gilley Jones, 18 months; Annie Virginia Weatherington, 21 months; Odious Moore, 5 months; Willie J. Barnes, 16 months; Benjamin Rowe, 8; Allen Jones, 7 months; and Winnifred Benners, 18 months. Teens and young adults: Etta Nunn Wynne, 12, suspected yellow fever; Guy Morton, 14; Thomas McCafity, 16; Addie George, 18; Blanche Borden Morton, 19, suspected yellow fever; Richard Hancock, 19; Jacob Holland 21; Charles Holland, 27; and Rosalee Pritchard, 27.

Consider 1849 school house petitioner Christopher Dudley, Sr. and his wife, Susan, who lived at the head of the swamp. They lost two children,

---

[d] The Hollands of Slocum Creek had several generations in a row of fathers and sons named *Philemon*.

Susan C., age 5, in 1853; and Christopher, age 3, in 1857. Then, Christopher Dudley, Sr. died on November 18, 1858, at the age of 37.

When teacher Margaret "Maggie" Fisher, 21, succumbed at Cherry Point in 1908, it was said that she "died of the dreaded fever." Two-month-old Wilber Russell died in September 1912. The doctor listed the cause of death as "convulsive fever, probably malarial in origin."

In a letter home during the Civil War, one Union soldier stationed at Havelock called the place an "ague hole," ague being a sometimes-fatal fever marked by an onset of chills, fits of shivering, sweating, aching, and malaise recurring at regular intervals.

To the Brink of War Between the States

In the years leading up to the conflagration of the War Between the States, the local schools not only functioned but matured. All of the community and school leaders – the prominent, propertied, family men of southern Craven County – listed here were mightily affected by the conflict. Some were drawn into the fighting itself. James Hunter of Slocum Creek is a notable example. Some of the students were as well.

Nevertheless, though it was a struggle, the schools continued to operate for the duration of the conflict.

Consider a few more names of the school board members and students from the last years before the war:
1857 School Committees
District 32: Benjamin R. Taylor, Vine A. Tolson, Benjamin Williams
District 33: Timothy Taylor, Rev. Jacob Utley, William H. Marshall
District 34: Christopher Dudley, John Ferguson, Edward M. Piver
District 35: Joshua Taylor, J. H. Wynne, William Temple
[*In District 33, Timothy Taylor, William H. Marshall, and Christopher Dudley were appointed, but Taylor and Dudley didn't live in the district. Marshall agreed to serve "provided that William Rowe and Jacob Utley are appointed. – School records.*]
1858 School Committees
District 31: (Riverdale) Gabriel Hardison, George Perry, Samuel Hill
District 32: B.A. Taylor, Vine Tolson, Benjamin Williams
District 33: Timothy G. Taylor, Jacob Utley, William Rowe
District 34: William H. Read, John Ferguson, Edward M. Piver
District 35: Joshua Taylor, J.W. Wynne, William Temple
District 36: Elijah Taylor, P.J. Smith, D.V. Dickinson

[*District 36 was east of Clubfoot Creek and defined as "Beginning at the Clubfoot's Creek Bridge, to the main road to include dwelling of Ezekiel Smith, which stands a few rods from the road to Elijah M. Dudley's Mill and with the Mill Creek to the River, to the mouth of Clubfoot Creek.*]

1859 School Committees

District 32: Vine A. Tolson, John Baker, John W. Williams

District 33: Rev. Jacob Utley, Henry Lovick, William R. Eborn

District 34: J.W. Wynne, Benjamin Borden, William Reade

District 35: Joshua Taylor, William Temple, Amos Bell

1861 School Committees

District 32: Vine A. Tolson, E. Mallett, James R. Moore

District 33: Jesse W. Leigh, Benjamin Bynum, William Belanga

District 34: Benjamin Borden, James H. Hunter, Edward M. Piver

District 35: Joshua Taylor, William Temple, Amos Bell

These are the children attending the District 33 (Havelock) school in June of 1860.

The District 33 schoolhouse was located on a parcel of about one acre on the west side of the Beaufort Road, which is today Greenfield Heights Blvd, at the head of Wolf Pit Branch, a tributary of Slocum Creek; thus between today's Greenfield Heights and US 70.

Males	
Spencer Harper	William H. Pitman
R.B. Jordan	William Belanga
Henry H. Rowe	William Meekins
John E. Lovick	
Hugh I. Lovick	*Females:*
Daniel M. Leigh	Linza Harper
Benjamin W. Leigh	Sarah Jordan
Charles N. Pitman	Catherine Rowe
John D. Pitman	Anna E. Leigh
Joshua W. Pitman	Emily Pitman
Murphy E. Pitman	Carolina Belanga
	Martha Meekins

Craven County's slave-based economy was part and parcel of the national forces driving a wedge between the North and the South. In the late 1860s, as anti-slavery sentiment and anti-slavery forces grew in strength, the issue became the key factor upsetting the political balance of the nation.

Nat Turner's infamous slave rebellion in Virginia, William Lloyd Garrison's publication of the "*Liberator*," Harriett Beecher Stowe's inflammatory *Uncle Tom's Cabin,* and the desperation of abolitionist John Brown's raid on a Federal arsenal in what is now West Virginia, sparked unrest, dread, and fury in the South.

Within North Carolina, the predominant party – the Democrats – while supporting slavery, were split over tax policies that favored the biggest slaveholders over small farmers. The 1860 N.C. gubernatorial contest between small-farmer-supported John Pool of Pasquotank County and big plantation candidate John W. Ellis of Rowan County became as divisive within the state as the presidential triumph of the anti-slavery Republican's candidate, Abraham Lincoln, was for the country as a whole.

Nationally, the Democrats were divided into factions of North and South. Even churches separated, like the Northern and Southern Baptists who fell out with one another over sectional issues.

While many citizens of North Carolina opposed secession from the federal union, Craven County voted to send pro-secession delegates to the state convention on the issue. On January 25, 1861, the New Bern *Daily Progress* predicted the outcome, declaring, "The Union is gone." [a]

Two and half months later – on April 12 – Confederate artillery was unleashed against the federal stronghold of Fort Sumter in the harbor of Charleston, S.C. Even North Carolinians who were opposed to secession were appalled when a few days later President Lincoln asked the state to support his raising of 75,000 soldiers to put down the rebellion.

"You can get no troops from North Carolina," Governor Ellis famously replied. Ellis immediately ordered the seizure of Fort Macon and dispatched a state militia unit, the Goldsboro Rifles, to do the job.

One of the odd coincidences of history is that when the train bearing the Goldboro Rifles crossed the Slocum Creek trestle at Havelock on April 16, 1861, one of the officers on board – Lt. Thomas Wright Slocumb – was descended from the early settler family for whom the creek had been named.

When the Goldsboro troops arrived at Fort Macon, they found that an armed group from Beaufort had already taken the initiative to seize the obsolete bastion from its lone federal caretaker.

The Tar Heel State followed South Carolina into the Confederate States of America on May 20, 1861.

An Old Testament quote from the Book of Jeremiah appears at the head of this chapter. In it, God warns against the settlement of a certain place because of the dangers of deadly disease. The warning might have been trumpeted for those who came to settle around the big savannah swamp between Slocum Creek and Hancock Creek. For more than 200 years, mosquito- and water-borne diseases were an invisible but constant peril, filling cemeteries with the corpses of infants, children, women, and men.

---

[a] Mobley, Joe A., *Pamlico County: A Brief History*, pp 33-34, North Carolina Dept. of Archives and History.

But as deathly as yellow fever, typhoid, cholera, pneumonia, smallpox and the other relentless ailments were, by the mid-1800s another mortal threat was bearing down upon not only the people of southern Craven County but also the United States as a whole: War.

During the four years of bloodshed from 1861-1865, southern Craven County was fundamentally transformed. Many residents stayed and tried to continue farming but ravenous armies confiscated food, livestock, and other necessities from country homes and farms. Warring troops, through both meanness and necessity, came to burden and prey upon the citizenry. Shortages of essentials like salt, sugar, flour, meat, leather, and cloth were commonplace.

So were arson, pillaging, and vandalism.

"The large plantations within Federal lines were devastated," Havelock resident Henry A. Marshall recalled in 1913. He said that the farmers "in reach of the Yankee foraging parties" were robbed of their cattle, horses, and other stock and "compelled to leave home." [b]

False assumptions have been made – and even incorrectly written in history books – that the colossal sixty-ship Union invasion flotilla of March 1862 bombarded barren woodlands below New Bern before Federal army forces came ashore in a desolate and uninhabited place on the Neuse River's south shore.

But, as we have just learned, General Ambrose Burnside and his Federal warriors landed at the center of the prosperous and well-populated plantation district of southern Craven County.

A detail of a much larger print entitled "Landing of Troops at Slocum's Creek" shows a Union gunboat firing near plantation homes on the Neuse River in the vicinity of Havelock. The perilous scene was witnessed and illustrated by a *Harper's Weekly* artist traveling with the invasion force on March 13, 1862.

[b] *Carolina and the Southern Cross*, Vol. 2, No. 1, pg. 17, April 1913.

The Invasion

The Battle of New Bern began on March 13, 1862.

Huge and ominous, the Union armada arrived and anchored in the flat-calm Neuse River off Slocum Creek the evening of March 12. By the wee hours of Thursday the 13th, offensive operations had begun. During that night and early morning, gunboats of the invasion force diligently and systematically shelled the riverfront between Havelock and Riverdale – wounding two troops of Southern cavalry and three soldiers, one later dying of his injuries – and attacking at least four defensive positions. Secret agents had been released by boat into the dark to create havoc up both the river and the creek, and a unit of troops worked before dawn tearing up the railroad line between Havelock and New Bern. In the daylight of the 13th, Union soldiers marching through muddy plantation country not only put the southern Craven County population to flight but also commandeered and wrecked their homes and farms. At the same time, Union sailors afloat on the river raked homes and woods with cannon fire. The guns are said to have thundered and echoed all day; so loudly that people in Beaufort heard them.[a]

By 8:00 p.m. on March 13, General Burnside and his federal forces had conducted an amphibious assault under cover of artillery at Slocum Creek – bringing ashore about 11,000 armed men.[b] They'd run off the defenders of the massive earthworks of the Croatan line and taken charge of it, repeatedly bombarded five miles of the river shore, engaged in a cannon duel with one of the occupied riverfront forts, and marched all of the regiments close enough to New Bern's main fortifications to have drawn picket fire on at least one group of mounted Yankee officers.

The next day would conclude the battle but the fighting was already underway.

The run-up to the invasion had been like waiting for water to boil.

Stories of the assembly of Burnside's fleet of ships had been national news for most of a year but no one in the South was sure where it was headed. Even after the brilliant victory in the attack and capture of Roanoke Island in early February 1862, the Union fleet could have been directed

---

[a] *The Southern Mind Under Northern Rule: The Diary of James Rumley, Beaufort, N.C., 1862-1865,* Judkin Browning, pg. 29.

[b] No one knows how many troops actually landed at Slocum Creek. Numbers cited range from 9,000-15,000. "The eleven thousand is an approximate figure. The official records are not clear as to the number of men Burnside used in the New Bern operation." John Barrett, *The Civil War in North Carolina,* pg. 97.

anywhere from Beaufort to Savannah. Still, people along the Neuse River – civilian and military alike – were alert and apprehensive.

Even with the foresight and sustained efforts of the leaders of the North Carolina troops, in the end, the state in general and Craven County, in particular, were woefully unprepared for the blue steamroller that was grinding inexorably forward.

By the second week of March, the fleet was finally sailing southwest from Roanoke Island. It was a mismatched collection of about five dozen watercraft that had been scrounged from every possible source. Richard A. Sauers in his influential study of the matter – *The Burnside Expedition in North Carolina* – lists the names of 58 vessels: nine Army gunboats (augmented by Navy gunboats bringing the total to 13 or 14); 12 Army transport steamships; 23 schooners; four barks; four ships; one brig; and five floating batteries. Other sources suggest there were even more. [c]

March 12, 1862, was a beautiful day to sail across Pamlico Sound toward the Neuse River. The ships' decks were crowded with thousands of blue-clad soldiers on what amounted, momentarily, to a sightseeing cruise.

Almost twenty military organizations made up Burnside's army forces; most of them regiments. And almost every one of them later produced a regimental history. In most of those, the beauty of the day is noted. The river is described as being like a mirror or a pond. The colors are commented upon. And the grandeur of the great fleet itself, flowing to its destiny in two long rows, and spread out, as one of them said, as far as the eye might see.

Onboard one of the steamers plowing forcefully through the water toward its anchorage at Slocum Creek was an unnamed reporter for *The New York Herald* who took in these things as well. He noted that the river was two to four miles wide and the banks were "covered in dense pine woods."

But the Herald's reporter also looked out upon the river with the keen sense that the fleet was being "most jealously watched and our movements telegraphed to the forces or to somebody in the rear." Every few miles, the reporter later wrote, large signal fires were set along the river shore "which threw up a most dense smoke and as we passed they were permitted to die away."

"There is one particular and most interesting feature connected with it," he wrote in his major news story published on March 19, 1862, "which is the number of farm houses scattered along its very edge and almost hidden in the foliage. I have made several attempts to get a peep at some of the inhabitants, as we would sometimes run in pretty close to the shore, so close in fact that had anybody been disposed they might have picked off some of

---

[c] For example, *The New York Herald* named the steamer *Jersey Blue*, the *Curlew* and the *Eagle,* as being on the sail from Roanoke Island to Slocum Creek. March 19, 1862.

us with a rifle. We attributed the total absence of human beings, where so many houses were, to the fact that all of the men were in the army or fortifications on the coast, and that the women were somewhat afraid to show themselves."

By nine o'clock that evening the fleet was anchored off Slocum Creek.

The first Union casualty of the Battle of New Bern was an Irishman named Reilly. The middle-aged private, a veteran of the recent fight at Roanoke Island, was found onboard the steamer *Jersey Blue* "with his throat cut from ear-to-ear and perfectly dead."

The fleet had anchored close to the south bank of the Neuse at Slocum Creek's mouth in the darkness of the evening. While General Burnside and his battle staff powwowed all night on his flagship – the steamer *Alice Price* – the men of the Union fleet distracted themselves by singing martial songs accompanied by the band. They sang *Hail, Columbia*; *The Star-Spangled Banner*; *My Country 'Tis of Thee*; and concluded with *Yankee Doodle*. Over the stillness of the tranquil, glassy waters, the sound of thousands of voices singing in unison traveled for miles. It was heard by many of the North Carolina defenders braced onshore for the primitive clash of politics that would soon manifest itself on an open plain between Havelock and New Bern.[d]

"A gentle roll gave motion to our craft," one soldier remembered, "sufficient to rock us to the deepest sleep ... while the noble, vigilant 'tars' in boats and launches, formed a cordon of videttes around the fleet to protect us from hostile intrusion." [e]

In the morning, while Yankee gunboats pounded the shoreline with cannon fire and the mass of Union troops prepared to disembark from their vessels, witnesses reported that Private Reilly ignored the preparation, kept to himself, and shuffled off below to lie down in his bunk.

"There was no question as to the method of his death – the unfortunate man having ended his own existence," one witness later wrote. "For some days past he had been observed to be very low-spirited, and kept aloof from the rest of his comrades ... it is supposed that in a fit of melancholy madness the man put an end to himself, his razor being found in his hand and a most frightful wound inflicted on his neck. He could have lived but a few moments after committing the act, as he made not the least noise and everyone supposing him to be sleeping." [f]

---

[d] *Philadelphia Inquirer*, March 20, 1862, pg. 4.
[e] "Tar" was a nickname for a Union sailor. Quote *from Bearing Arms in the 27th Mass. Regiment of Volunteer Infantry* by W.P Derby, 1883.
[f] *New York Herald*, March 19, 1862, pg. 4, col. 3

Pvt. Reilly's body was sewn into a canvas bag and, following a prayer by the vessel's captain, it was surrendered by crew members to the river's dark water.

"Had the rash man waited for a day," the witness said, "he might have died nobly on the field [*of battle*], without thus endangering his eternal happiness."

Overnight, while most of the Union troops slept, boatloads of special operatives were out on clandestine assignments. Some were spying to determine enemy locations and strength. One mission up Slocum Creek navigated many miles to deliver muscle bent on destroying a portion of the railroad between Havelock and New Bern to prevent reinforcements from Fort Macon. No such reinforcements had been planned but there was no way for the Union command to know that.

Better safe than sorry.

The foray up Slocum Creek seems to be responsible for an incorrect report published in the *Raleigh Standard* and reprinted in Confederate-leaning newspapers all over the state.

"On Wednesday evening [March 12] or Thursday morning [March 13] it is reported that the Yankees ascended Slocumb Creek, burnt Dr. Master's fine mill, and destroyed the railroad at Croatan and military preparations that had been made," the newspaper reported on page one.

Samuel Masters's mill was located near the railroad at Slocum Creek immediately adjacent to today's Havelock's Tourist and Events Center. Most of its old and massive dam dating from before the late 1700s and originally built by N.C. Governor Richard Dobbs Spaight is still there. However, after the fall of New Bern, when Company C of the Fifth Rhode Island Heavy Artillery occupied the railroad junction at Slocum Creek, it reported about the "abandoned grist mill, the machinery of which the rebels had attempted to destroy when they left that neighborhood."

The mill had not been burned, but someone had tried to wreck it. The Fifth assumed the Southerners had done the damage and had no way of knowing about a secret operation by their own forces the night before the landing.

In any event, the Fifth's mechanics soon had the Masters grist mill back in operation.[g]

The second clandestine mission of the night was a daring and dangerous attempt to burn the Trent River railroad bridge in the heart of New Bern.

---

[g] *Fayetteville (NC) Observer*, March 20, 1862; *History of the 5th R.I.*; *In This Small Place,* Edward Ellis, pg. 81.

"Corp[oral] L.L. Robbins, with the mate of the schooner *H.E. Pierce*, and a man named Baulsom, a tough specimen of the Hatteras stripe, embarked in a small skiff and at dark were towed by a tug as far as the first line of sunken vessels and piles," the report begins.

A line of ships had been scuttled in the Neuse by the Southern defenders to force invading Union ships to navigate close to their gun forts.

"From here we paddled up the river until near enough to throw up under the bridge one or two fire-balls of tow [*a fibrous material of flax or hemp*] dipped in tar." They failed in their mission of arson when sentries at the bridge discovered the trio but they made their escape and returned to the Union tug unscathed by 3:00 a.m.

The report of this mission has been disputed by a few modern writers, but its reporter, Herbert Valentine of the 23rd Massachusetts Volunteers, has been one of the most reliable chroniclers of the Burnside Expedition. Valentine served as General Burnside's quartermaster at New Bern, wrote much of the history of the Massachusetts regiment, and created some of the most iconic drawings and paintings of the expedition including the line of sunken ships mentioned above, and the only drawing of the blockhouse fort at Havelock.

MOUTH OF SLOCUM CREEK – A modern aerial photograph is used here to show where Gen. Ambrose Burnside's troops came ashore in 1862. *Graphic by the author.*

THE LANDING – Above and on the following page, three panels from one panoramic drawing show the off-loading of about 11,000 Burnside Expedition troops at Slocum Creek on the morning of March 13, 1862. The Union soldiers would overwhelm a much smaller Southern force in a pitched battle the next day on an open plain between Havelock and New Bern. Drawn by Francis Schell, a newspaper artist traveling with the fleet.

After the fog lifted on the chilly morning of March 13, and after the nearby wood had been thoroughly shelled by the gunboats, the disembarkation of the regiments began. This was the second amphibious landing of the war, Roanoke Island being the first. [h]

In the good-natured competition to be first ashore, General Burnside had the captain of his flagship run the *Alice Price* virtually onto the beach. While some boats were rowed toward the long fringe of pristine sand, others were strung in lines and hauled to the beach by shallow-draft steamers. The tugboat *Alert* steamed ahead hauling a line of twenty "surfboat" troop carriers. Once released, the boats glided to the shore. The Neuse being quite shallow for a long distance from the beach, many soldiers simply stepped

---

[h] It was, in fact, the second in American history and that it was occuring on land that one day would be occupied by the United States Marine Corps – the premier amphibious landing outfit in the world – is quite remarkable.

Southern Historical Collection, Wilson Library, UNC-Chapel Hill; *Frank Leslie's Illustrated Newspaper*, **Volume VIII, Number 334, pp 349-349, April 5, 1862.**

off their troop transports and made a bee-line for the beach.

"It was a singularly beautiful sight," Samuel H. Putman of the Massachusetts Regiment's Company A recalled years later. "The boats were crowded with men 'wearing the blue,' and their bayonets glistened as if tipped by sparks of sunshine." [i]

Putnam wondered at the fact that there was no resistance to the landing of the Union troops. "It was a mistake on the Rebels' part in allowing us to land on Roanoke Island; here was another one," he said. "We all landed, and not an opposing shot was fired."

Like the other units rallying around their distinctive flags, Company A quickly formed up in the woods that he described "as live oak trees from whose branches were long festoons of gray moss which waved in the slight breeze while vines crept tree to tree completely covering their tops."

Some of the Federal troops came ashore that March day on white sand while others had to slog through thick marsh grass or blue gumbo clay. Lucky troopers barely got their feet wet while hundreds were soaked from their necks down in water one soldier, Alfred S. Roe, remembered wryly as "quite cooling."

During the landing, the gunboats kept up an infernal racket "awakening lively echoes along the shore," according to Herbert Valentine, a soldier of and historian for the 23rd Massachusetts Volunteers previously mentioned. Valentine heard each shot echoing across the river and back, over and over, for as long as two minutes "before the reverberations aroused by the report of a single gun ceased."

Much has been written over the intervening years about this firing by the Federal navy on March 13 with most suggesting it was pro-forma; that the gunboats were simply going through the motions; being thorough in keeping potential Southern attackers at bay.

That is not the case, especially later in the day, when the gunboats were actively engaging three defensive positions of the North Carolina troops, as we shall soon see.

Official Records: "The men immediately formed on their respective colors, and as the several regiments landed they took up their line of march, following for some distance up the right bank of the Neuse River to a point where a company of the enemy's cavalry had been posted on advance-guard duty. Here the road leaves the river, and after passing one or two farmhouses in the pine woods, it strikes the road leading from Beaufort to New Berne." [j]

While the Union troops were going ashore – an operation that consumed about two hours – and unknown to those soldiers until they later came upon

---

[i] *The Story of Company A, 25th Regiment Massachusetts Volunteers*, 1886.
[j] OR, *Battle of New Berne, N.C.*, Chapter XX, pg. 233.

the aftermath, the gunboats had spotted and attacked an active camp of Southern cavalry on a knoll overlooking the landing.

The cavalry camp of Captain Peter G. Evans's mounted troops – Camp Gaston [k] – was situated on a river bluff about one mile west of the mouth of Slocum Creek. The cavalry troops were stationed on a farm called Magnolia Plantation. Its thirty-foot-high river bluffs gave a commanding view of the entire river. The horse soldiers had been housed for some time in a set of wooden barracks and stables as sentries for the advance of the Burnside expeditionary force. They had seen the bonfire signals of the previous day and relayed information on horseback to the headquarters of the local commander, General Lawrence O'Bryan Branch.

Peter Evans, later a renowned colonel of Confederate troops, owned the sprawling Evans Mill Plantation a few miles south of New Bern. He began the cavalry recruitment for his "Macon Mounted Guards" in 1861 and had positioned several camps around Havelock before Burnside's arrival.

Evans and his men were preparing breakfast at Camp Gaston – likely named in honor of famed Craven County jurist William Gaston – when the Union screw-steamer gunboat *Star and Stripes,* commanded by Lt. Reed Werden, along with the heavily-armed ferryboats *Perry* and *Southfield,* fired several large shells into their midst, wounding at least two of the mounted troops and scattering the rest in confusion. The *Southfield* alone carried a 100-pound Parrott rifle and three nine-inch smoothbore naval cannons.[1]

The Southern cavalry's Camp Gaston was on the direct line of march followed by most of the Northern troops after their landing as they made their way to the county road leading to New Bern. Many references are made to the abandoned camp and the aftermath of the firing in the Union's regimental histories. Some even claimed to have eaten portions of the Southern horse soldiers' breakfast.

Here are four excerpts:

■ "A deserted cavalry camp, with ample stores and breakfast still smoking on the table, was soon passed..." [m]

■ "We came on the camp of Rebel cavalry which the gunboats had routed precipitously. Everything lay around in magnificent disorder; fires still burning, breakfast cooking, and some served up and partly partaken of, showing the complete surprise by the landing of several unannounced 64-pound shells in the very heart of

---

[k] Identified on sketch map, *L. O'B. Branch Papers*, Univ. of Virginia-Roanoke. Marked by name and with a "U" horseshoe shape.

[1] ORN, Series 1, Vol. 7, pg. 115; *Wilmington (NC) Journal*, Mar. 20, 1862; *Fayetteville (NC) Observer,* Mar. 20, 1862; *Philadelphia Inquirer*, Mar. 20, 1862, pg. 4.

[m] *History of the 23rd Massachusetts Infantry*, James A. Emmerton.

the barracks. *We ransacked* the baggage of the Rebel officer and the "knappies" of the men." [n]

- "We passed large, rough buildings that had been used as barracks by the Rebels ... it had been a cavalry station, and their scouts had seen us land, and had given the alarm, when the whole crowd left for New Berne, and in such a hurry that their saddles, bridles and other equipment lay scattered around in great confusion. They left their tables standing with breakfast scarcely touched. We stopped but a few minutes, but long enough for some of us to pretty nearly finish that breakfast." [o]

- "Company G ... formed an advanced guard, and discovered a short distance into the woods ... a large number of wooden barracks which had been vacated about two hours before by Rebel cavalry whose equanimity had been disturbed by shells from the gunboat." [p]

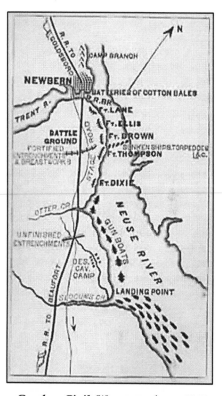

Greeley Civil War map from 1866 shows the deserted cavalry camp and other details of the operation.

The New York Herald reporter said the first soldiers who spotted the camp "peeping over the brow of a hill burst into loud cheers and dashed up the hill to enter the camp." The camp was deserted, of course, but "exhibited evidence of a most precipitous flight. The fires were still ablaze; breakfast was untouched; warm griddle cakes were ready for eating; beds, blankets, clothing, boots and shoes, were strewn."

[n] *History of the 51st Pennsylvania Volunteer Regiment*, Thomas H. Parker.
[o] *The Story of Company A, 25th Regiment of Mass. Vol*,. Samuel H. Putnam.
[p] *History of the 21st Regiment of Massachusetts Volunteers*, Charles F. Walcott.

He said the soldiers "soon ransacked the camp in search of trophies and relics, and took what suited them." This sort of ransacking would continue among the troops all day.

"From the documents I found in one of the tents," the reporter wrote, "I ascertained that the place had been occupied by a company of about eighty cavalry, under the command of Captain Evans."

The abandoned cavalry camp near Slocum Creek made an impression on many of the Union soldiers on the march to New Bern. So much so that it later appears on a map of "New Bern & the Neuse River" printed in the massive history of the Civil War by famous New York newspaperman Horace Greeley. Greeley's huge and hugely popular *The American Conflict* was published in 1866 and runs to more than 1,400 pages. Though neither to scale nor completely accurate, the map with the "Des. Cav. Camp" is on page 77 of his Volume II and is reproduced on the previous page of this one.

Another map showing Evans's cavalry camp was created after the war by an architect, Tristam Griffin, who served in Burnside's force. It was published in *A Record of the 23rd Regiment of Massachusetts Volunteer Infantry* just after its page 64. Griffin labeled it "Deserted Dragoon Camp," dragoon being another word referring to the cavalry. The map contains a scale for distance. Provided it's accurate, the location of Peter Evans's cavalry barracks and stables was near the end of present-day Boros Road in Carolina Pines, in the vicinity of the former country club's fifteenth green. Carolina Pines is within the boundaries of the old Magnolia Plantation established in the 1700s.

At the camp, the order finally came down to re-form the columns and move out. The troopers fell in line and once more resumed the march toward the main county road, or "stage route," toward New Bern, essentially the route of today's US 70. The distance to the road was two to four miles depending on the route. Others followed the railroad tracks that paralleled and sometimes crossed the main road.

What had been drizzle earlier in the day soon turned to hard rain. The rain morphed the roads to mush, especially with thousands of boots tromping over them. It was extremely hard going for wagons and artillery carriages and those charged with moving them through the deep mud.

Near the ruined Camp Gaston, Union soldier Albert Roe met a woman he described as "an ancient colored mammy." "She expressed her pleasure at seeing the Yankees, and praying the blessing of God upon them," Roe said. When asked how many rebels had been there, he was amused by her country dialect. He wrote that she replied there "was a right smart heap" of them and when the gunboats fired those "rotten shells" into the woods, the local troops had "right smart git" and were "a chance of a way off now."

Roe said the men nearby almost opened fire when a peacock strutting by surprised them with its loud screeching, "they not knowing what could be responsible for such unearthly yelling." He also noted encounters with other "colored people" from whom they tried to get information.

About a half-mile down the beach, one group encountered a large white family: a man, woman, and six children. The soldiers' hopes of getting some breakfast came to naught. "Eggs, fowl, and milk were luxuries we had not seen for many a day," one soldier said.

"Whether from a disinclination to satisfy us, or their not having the articles desired, we failed in our mission as far as the edibles are concerned. ... They appeared anything but pleased to see us and kept their eyes on us the whole time we remained, as if fearful that we came to rob them of the little they possessed. And even the house dog, as if in sympathy for his master, kept a most jealous and dangerous eye upon us. From these people we learned that the fleet was no unexpected visitor, the inhabitant being taught to look for its arrival at any moment but they did not expect an attack on this point, thinking the vessels would go much further up before stopping with any hostile intent. The master of the house disclaimed anything like secession sentiments, and the mistress, whose life was almost frightened out of her by the passage and explosion of shells over her house, was very anxious to know why they should be troubled, who had done nothing, and seemed to care a great deal more for the preservation of her pigs and chickens than for the safety of the Union ... if the soldiers could only be kept away from annoying them. The man was ignorant of everything pertaining to fortifications, and declared that he had not been up the river for a long time. He was very guarded and his only positive information was that a company of North Carolina cavalry had been on the point where our troops landed the day before, but he could not tell when they left or where they went." [a]

The second Union casualty of the Battle of New Bern was a sergeant named Charles Perrigo. As the 11,000-man parade made its way through the fertile countryside "quite a number of the men from different regiments indulged in considerable foraging." [b] It was a small city on the march; wet, muddy, and hungry. And it was passing through plantations with chicken yards, hog parlors, smokehouses, barns, and kitchens ripe for plunder.

While there are no records to prove it, Lovick family descendants would claim into the modern era that the stately main house of Magnolia

---

[a] *The New York Herald*, March 19, 1862

[b] *History of the Fifth Rhode Island Heavy Artillery*, Charles K. Burlingame.

Plantation was looted and burned by the invading Yankees.[c] We know others were pillaged by marauding troops because soldiers' memoirs say so.

Many of the homes were emptied of residents as their owners escaped to New Bern in response to the sound of cannon fire and just ahead of Federal troops swarming like blue locusts. Those who hadn't previously taken refuge in town were now on the run in near-panic because of the persistent shelling and the addled reports of the Southern defenders who had been moving rapidly up and down the county road all day.

At a halt near Croatan, two Union soldiers came upon a home from which the occupants had recently fled. The hungry soldiers "paid the house a visit." Troops who had gotten there first, they said, "had turned everything upside down." The lovely furniture had been wrecked; some of it was being rained on out in the muddy yard. Someone was playing a piano so hard that the instrument was already damaged. Few articles of food were left but the pair managed to salvage some pickles. "They were good," one said.[d]

As for Sgt. Perrigo of Company A, 5th Rhode Island, he was the victim of an overzealous hunter. The hunter – one of his very own troops busy pillaging a well-stocked farmyard – was trying to shoot a pig, though some say it was a turkey. The rifle shot missed the animal but struck and mortally wounded the company sergeant.

In the unit's official records, Charles Perrigo is listed as having died "from wounds received in the Battle of New Bern." [e]

Houses were commandeered wholesale for many reasons during the march and soon thereafter. In almost all cases, the homes were stripped of goods by the visitors. The roads were so heavy with mud that men claimed they weren't walking on the ground; they were walking on mire. The exertion took a toll on troops experiencing their first march of the war.

"There had been some falling out … a few being unable to stand up to the strain. One poor fellow going into spasms was carried to an old house and the surgeon summoned for his relief."

One lucky Yankee acquired a very small pony. And much to the delight of his compatriots, "proceeded to relieve the tedium of the march by riding it, though the combination was most ridiculous." [f]

A pair of valuable oxen were stolen from one farm to assist in pulling artillery pieces through the thick mud of the stage road.

William Marvel, in his biography of the expedition's commander titled *Burnside*, notes during the march the "many privates who scattered to

[c] Edward Ellis interview with Mary Hughes McGrath, 1988.
[d] *Diary of Capt. Levi Kent*, 4th Rhode Island Infantry Regiment.
[e] *History of the Fifth Rhode Island Heavy Artillery*, Burlingame.
[f] *History of the 24th Massachusetts Regiment.*

inspect some farmer's smokehouse" and the "Rhode Islanders who raided a barnyard full of squealing pigs."

Meanwhile, the gunboats were still firing for all they were worth. One of the points at which they were firing was the end of the Croatan earthworks at Otter Creek. This fortified line, anchored by an earthen fort on the railroad, extended from today's Catfish Lake Road at Croatan to the river. By about 10:00 a.m., just after shelling Capt. Evans's Macon Mounted Guards out of their barracks, the gunboats moved a few miles north and unleased at Otter Creek and Fisher's Landing.

The Southerners had pickets spread out for three miles on each side of Fisher's Landing in the mistaken expectation that Burnside's force would land there. When the gunboat opened up with heavy shelling on their positions, the defenders, armed only with rifles, began to fall back deeper into the woods. Before they got away, the gunboats' shells wounded three of the North Carolina soldiers; one of them mortally.[g]

Fisher's Landing was part of the massive Fisher Plantation at Riverdale. A stately white mansion was the plantation's centerpiece and lorded over the high river bluff.

"It seems strange that the gunboats of the Union forces under General Burnside would open fire on a dwelling house," family historian P. W. Fisher later wrote, "but such was the case, with the result that the main dwelling house of Michael N. Fisher was shelled and rendered useless as a home. The kitchen, a separate structure behind the main building and farther from the river, was not harmed."

Michael Fisher and his wife, Elizabeth, had fled their home and sought refuge in New Bern before the battle. Nevertheless, two of Fisher's sons and a number of their servants were on the plantation when the shelling occurred. They were uninjured.

Elizabeth Ann Pelletier Fisher, 42, died in New Bern during the yellow fever epidemic of 1863. After the war, Micheal Fisher – one of the state's richest men – and his remaining family was impoverished along with many others in Craven County, North Carolina, and the entire South. He lived the short remainder of his life in the kitchen house with his sons. In 1868, the boys buried the remains of their heartbroken father, age 59, in a homemade coffin of scrap wood.[h]

The shelling of the Fisher mansion appears nowhere within the official records of the war, nor do any of the other acts of wanton destruction of private property that were later memorialized in private correspondence, personal memoirs, and family lore. This isn't to say that the Burnside force

---

[g] OR, vol. 9, pg. 262.

[h] *One Dozen Eastern North Carolina Families*, P. W. Fisher, 1957.

was particularly ruthless. War is war. Plundering, looting, vandalism, and ruin are part and parcel of it and have been since the dawn of time.

Ultimately, the remarkably constructed Croatan works were abandoned by Southern forces due to confusion, poor communication, and a lack of manpower just ahead of the arrival of the first elements of the Union army. The face of the mile-long entrenchment was five feet high with a slope dipping into a trench as much as eight feet deep. Burnside's soldiers gawked at it like an archeological relic and thanked their lucky stars they didn't have to fight their way through it.

One Rhode Islander suggested that the Union could have held the Croatan line at Otter Creek with "5,000 men against all the soldiers in North Carolina." He said the works looked "absolutely impregnable" and marveled that the Rebels had given it up without a shot fired.[i]

Shots were being fired elsewhere though.

In the late afternoon of March 13, there was an artillery duel between Fort Dixie – one of the strongholds guarding New Bern – and two Union gunboats. Fort Dixie at Johnson Point was just under a mile south of Fort Thompson, New Bern's primary line of defense. The fort bristled with four 24-pounder smoothbore guns wielded by a heavy artillery company under Capt. Benjamin Leecraft.

The Union's naval commander, Commodore Stephen C. Rowan, on the gunboat *Delaware*, and accompanied by another, *Commodore Perry*, was steaming up the river to observe the city's defenses. As the enemy vessels approached Fort Dixie, Leecraft ordered his men to fire. *Delaware* and *Perry* returned the favor and were supported by the steamers *Lockwood, Underwriter,* and *Brinker*. Rowan called the duel "spirited and effective" though no losses were suffered by either side. The firing began about 4:15 p.m. and continued until "the battery was deserted" by the defenders. The gunboats then returned to guarding the fleet anchored at Slocum Creek.[j]

By late afternoon, a group of mounted officers sent out to scout by General Burnside had ridden up on two separate groups of North Carolina troops, one marching and one on horseback. The Union troopers had gotten close enough during one of the encounters to have drawn gunshots from enemy pickets.[k]

To recap, the firing began that morning at the cavalry camp at Slocum Creek, extended to Otter Creek and its Croatan earthworks. It continued at

---

[i] *History of the 5th Rhode Island Heavy Artillery*, Burlingame.

[j] OR, Navy, vol. 7, pp. 111, 116-117; *Battle of New Bern: Our Battery Was the Boast of the Day*, Steve Shaffer and Andrew Duppstadt, Civil War Navy, The Magazine, Winter 2020, Vol. 7, Issue 3; *Philadelphia Inquirer*, March 20, 1862, pg.4.

[k] OR, vol 9. Pag. 326; *Burnside*, William Marvel, pg. 70.

Fisher's Landing, escalated at Fort Dixie, and ended with the shots aimed at Burnside's scouts. There's no definitive list of damages from the all-day firing by the gunboats, but at least five Southerners were wounded. One died of his wounds, as did a Union sergeant shot by accident.

Late in the day, when the scouts reported back to Burnside that the Rebel fortifications were immediately at hand, the long march was halted.

The evening before the March 14 fight south of New Bern, most of the Union forces bedded down on the wet ground in the heavy rain and passed the chilly night the best they could. By 8:00 p.m. that night the regiments had made about 12 miles. The formation of their encampment roughly paralleled the Fort Thompson line. Both stretched from the river to the Atlantic and North Carolina Railroad.

"Many weary ones sank immediately to sleep on the wet ground; others cooked a little pork and coffee, and dried [in front of the fire] first one side and then the other," wrote the chroniclers of one Federal unit. "Still others wrapped in blankets, leaned against trees, and dozed away the dismal night. The bivouac was within the range of the rebel's works; but all night the rebel pickets watched the illuminated woods, and were silent." [1]

The more fortunate were sequestered in commandeered, fireplace-warmed farmhouses just below what would be tomorrow's battlefield. Many slept on porches out of the rain and upon interiors floorboards, with the most fortunate in feather beds. General Burnside was one of these and, in another requisitioned home, so was the reporter from the *New York Herald*. He wrote that he shared a bed with Francis "Frank" Schell, an artist from *Frank Leslie's Illustrated Newspaper*, who was there to create illustrations of the expedition's activities, including the dramatic panorama of the landing shown in three panels earlier in this chapter.

Slaves in the area directed the Northern forces to homes that had been deserted by owners and their families. In some cases, slaves cooked meals for the men making use of chickens supplied by foraging parties supplemented by groceries and dishes from the kitchen cupboards.

"In the morning another foraging party furnished more poultry for breakfast," the New York reporter wrote, "while those who desired went out into the garden and helped themselves to delightful honey from the beehives."

A few hours later, and less than a mile away, more than six hundred men lay dead or wounded.

---

[1] *Military and Civil History of Connecticut During the War of 1861-1865,* W. A. Croffut and John M. Morris.

Newbern, North Carolina, Taken by General Burnside.

THE NEW YORK HERALD

March 19, 1862 – The steamer Commodore arrived at Baltimore yesterday, direct from the Burnside expedition, and reports the capture of Newbern, N.C., the defeat of the enemy there and the capture of a large amount of artillery, after a hard-fought victory.

Newbern, N.C. was captured on the 14th inst. by the forces of General Burnside, with a loss of 300 killed and 450 wounded.[m]

The troops landed under the cover of gunboats on the morning of the 13th, at Slocum's Creek, marched some twelve miles and bivouacked on the railroad …[n]

The troops started again on the morning of the 14th. About five miles from Newbern, they encountered the enemy behind breastworks and batteries over two miles long, protecting the railroad. The battle lasted two and a half hours.

The enemy's flank was turned by a gallant charge of the Massachusetts Twenty-first and the New York 51st, supported by other regiments of the Second and Third brigades.

The rebels retreated to Newbern, crossing the railroad bridge over the Trent River … Our troops crossed in small boats to the town and took possession in the afternoon.

The greater part of the inhabitants fled. No opposition was made to its occupation.

The rebels retreated by trains toward Goldsboro, leaving about 300 prisoners in our hands. Their loss was nearly as great as the Union side.

The fight was one of the most desperate of the war.

Our troops behaved with steadfastness and courage, and after nearly four hours of hard fighting drove the rebels from their positions, capturing three light batteries of field artillery, forty-six heavy siege guns, large stores of fixed ammunition, three thousand stand of small arms, and two hundred prisoners, including one colonel, three captains and four lieutenants.[o]

---

[m] Modern sources put the losses at 154 killed and 481 wounded on both sides.

[n] Actually, on a long front between the railroad and the river.

[o] Though some details in *The New York Herald* are inaccurate, or even self-contradictory, the article gives a sense of the national interest in and importance of the invasion by the Burnside Expedition.

Rebel Spies of Southern Craven County

Ambrose Everett Burnside (1824-1881), the commanding general during the Union invasion of southern Craven County, was a graduate of West Point. All three of his subordinate commanders – also generals – were graduates of that top U. S. military academy as well. His battle-hardened forces were steeped in West Point doctrine and the battle was a case study of its use.

The Southern defenders – who, including their commanding general, had never been in combat – were largely farmers with some bankers, merchants, and lawyers thrown in for good measure. One of the flags captured by Union troops during the fighting belonged to an outfit called the Beaufort Plowboys. That might go some distance in explaining why the contest was so lopsided.

In addition to the mismatch in training, equipment, and skills, there was another factor that gave the North a major advantage in its campaign in Craven County: secret agents.

General Burnside had a vigorous clandestine force of scouts, spies, and couriers before the invasion of March 1862. He sent them in weeks and even months in advance to discover the lay of the land and the disposition of forces and fortifications. It was secret information about the latter that hatched the decision to land at Slocum Creek, just outside the limits of New Bern's defenses.

U.S. General A. E. Burnside

His intelligence network became even more energetic after he took New Bern and Beaufort. He had his soldiers and scouts, of course, but he was aided mightily by the recently-freed slaves and by the free people of color as well. Some of the local white citizens also remained loyal to the Union.

But it's the Southern secret agents of Craven County that we want to speak about here.[a]

---

[a] This chapter is adapted from presentations by the author to the New Bern Historical Society and at the Cullman Performance Hall - Tryon Palace, August 2018.

If you're at all familiar with this era, you know about Emeline Pigott. When it comes to the Confederate spies of this time and this place, it's the name Emeline Pigott we hear repeated over and over.

Pigott, a young woman from Harlowe – between Havelock and Beaufort – was captured, charged with smuggling, and held prisoner in New Bern at one of the homes now preserved in the Tryon Palace historic complex. Even in the most recent books, when the reader reaches the part about local clandestine operations, you'll see a picture of Emeline and read a repetition of the same small group of stories.[b]

Emeline Pigott

This is to take nothing away from Emeline Pigott. Quite the contrary. What she did was singularly remarkable. And dangerous. And useful. Her activities during the war were truly amazing. But while her exploits are the most well-known by far, there are others whose deeds were equally as daring.

Within a few months of the conclusion of the March 13-14, 1862 battle, New Bern was becoming one of the most fortified cities in the country. Several thousand freedmen worked for years building earthwork upon earthwork, defensive line inside defensive line.

New Bern becomes a fortress. Getting in and out was like going on and off a military base. There were well-guarded gates and checkpoints. There were sentries, lookouts, and roving patrols. All well-armed and all meaning business.

At the other end of the Department of North Carolina – as the Union called its new domain – was Fort Macon, a classic masonry fort growling with artillery. Two formidable strong points. But in between was another matter. The major connection for New Bern and Fort Macon/Beaufort was a vulnerable rail line; just two iron strips lying on split logs, over which had to pass virtually everything the U.S. Army required to maintain its eastern North Carolina stronghold.

To protect the rails, the Federals created or expanded a total of five outlying posts, marked by stars on the map. Five small forts of 50 to 200 men each, isolated in the middle of swamp and forest ... and threatened by four

---

[b] Lucy Worth London, *North Carolina Women of the Confederacy* (1928); Mildred Wallace, *The Sacrifice or Daring of a Southern Woman During the War Between the States*, Benjamin Royal Papers, Southern Historical Collection, UNC-CH.

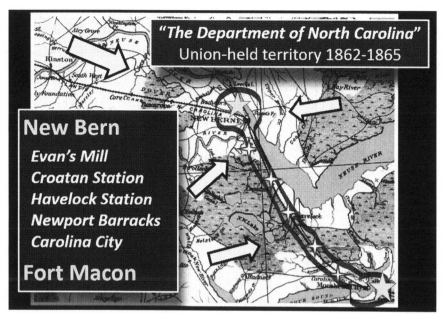

"*The Department of North Carolina*"
Union-held territory 1862-1865

New Bern

Evan's Mill
Croatan Station
Havelock Station
Newport Barracks
Carolina City

Fort Macon

Map by Edward Ellis

roving armies of Confederate soldiers – all angry that part of North Carolina had been occupied through invasion. Southern forces are shown as arrows.

Eastern North Carolina Confederates had headquarters in Kinston. The land in between there and the outskirts of New Bern was a no-man's-land to be scrapped over till war's end. By May 1862, the dog-bone-shaped piece of ground shown on the map was – for the Federals – the entire Department of North Carolina.

So, what about the spies?

Let's start by taking a look at Emeline and the factors that made her so well-known to us today.

To begin with, she stood out because she was female. In this calamity being acted out between 1861 and 1865, ninety-nine percent of the actors were men.

Second, she was pretty. Like it or not, our culture puts a premium on beauty.

And third, she was caught smuggling stuff in her undergarments!

You may have heard that Civil War women sometimes had secret pockets sewn in their petticoats for smuggling letters and such. Compared to Emeline Pigott, these folks were down-right underachievers. When arrested, she was taken to the marshal's office where she was searched by some ladies. What they found under her voluminous skirt has been reported many times before but we repeat it here because, well, it's just plain fun to do so.

The search revealed:

- One pair of fine boots.
- Two pairs of pants.
- One shirt.
- One naval cap.
- One dozen linen collars.
- One dozen linen pocket-handkerchiefs.
- Fifty skeins of sewing silk.
- A lot of spool cotton.
- Needles.
- Toothbrushes.
- Hair combs.
- Three pocket knives.
- Dressing pins.
- Several pairs of gloves.
- One razor.
- And four or five pounds of assorted candy.

Plus *"several letters addressed to rebels outside your lines, denouncing the federals, calling them Yankees and Buffalos, giving information about the movement of troops, etc."* [c]

The frivolity ends there. The last part was definitely a capital offense. After her arrest, she was imprisoned in an upstairs bedroom of the Frederick Jones house in New Bern but was later released. It's a miracle – and somewhat of a mystery – that she wasn't executed.

There are two additional factors responsible for Emeline being so familiar today. Those in the clandestine services were, by their very nature, unknown. Spies are nameless. Their identities are and must remain secret. And many of them continued to be a secret after the war.

But Emeline Pigott was caught. Her identity was made public. And loudly so. The news created quite a stir in Craven and Carteret counties. And far beyond.

Then, in addition to her cover being blown, Emeline lived until 1919; more than half a century after the war. During that time, she was busy in the United Daughters of the Confederacy. She supported them and donated money. They raised money off her fame and re-told her story, often in print, over and over and over again. Virtually all the details of what we know about Emeline Pigott today are those recited by the UDC in the late nineteenth and early twentieth centuries.

---

[c] "Beaufort Waiflets," *The Old North State*, February 18, 1865.

Because of those efforts, we know about this young woman who was in love with a Confederate soldier killed at Gettysburg. After which, she became even more dedicated to the cause of Southern Independence. She worked as a nurse. She organized fishermen to gather and deliver information. She was a lookout for special operations. She was a courier of food, supplies, letters, and secrets.

No matter how we view the War Between the States in light of the present day, by any standard, Emeline Pigott was, at the very least, brave and resourceful.

To illustrate what she and others like her were risking, consider what happened at the Union-occupied plantation of Evans Mill. Evans Mill Plantation was the former home of Peter Evans, the Southern cavalry commander introduced in the last chapter. Following the Battle of New Bern, Union troops built a blockhouse fort there and used the Evans home as a regimental headquarters.

During the summer of 1864, the 17th Massachusetts Volunteer Regiment of the Union army had outpost duty at Evans Mill. Years later, a Federal soldier maned William Eaton wrote a piece for the regiment's history.

As Eaton told it, that day a mounted patrol alerted the fort's guards that a suspicious person had been lurking about. They chased him but he'd hidden in the woods. Word was quickly sent to headquarters in the old Evans house and the company scrambled to find the intruder.

The soldiers surrounded the small pond where he was last seen, and all of them were surprised when the man simply stood up out of the water. They grabbed him, took his carbine, and marched him off to be interrogated and searched.

"In his pocket," Eaton said, "was found a waterproof tin can, in which, on oiled silk (waterproof cloth) were complete drawings of the camp and fortifications of Evans Mill, finely executed."

William Eaton's narrative concludes with the ominous line: "The prisoner, who did not reveal his name, was carried to New Bern, tried by court-martial, convicted as a spy … and shot."

This was serious business.

For both sides, information was like oxygen. They had to have it or die. The Southerners wanted to know what was going on inside the old Colonial Capital … and the Federals needed to know, just as badly, what the Confederates might do next. It was a ready-made environment for espionage.

So, what about these spies of southern Craven County? We are no doubt expected to name names. So here are some of them:

- William Henry Marshall

- Henry A. Marshall
- David Owen Dickinson
- James H. Hunter

Carolina and the Southern Cross

The names – and clues to others – appeared in 1913 when a brief article was published in a short-lived Kinston, N.C. magazine called *Carolina and the Southern Cross*. Produced by the United Daughters of the Confederacy, the magazine featured a seven-paragraph piece entitled *A Boy's Recollection of the Battle of New Bern*. In it, the writer named himself and others as having worked covertly for the South inside Union-occupied territory.[d]

The writer, Henry A. Marshall of Havelock, said the small group of amateur spies and couriers delivered messages to the Confederate headquarters in Kinston and that they smuggled coffee, cotton, letters, and firearms through Federal lines on foot, on horseback, and by boat.

"It was a dangerous business for which we were little qualified," Marshall wrote, "and would undoubtedly have been caught and executed as spies had our people within the Yankee lines been less loyal to the South."

Using Marshall's article as a starting point, additional research will now allow us to reveal the name of the leader of the spy ring inside occupied New Bern ... and prove that he gained access to highly secret information from a mole inside the Union headquarters itself.

We begin with William H. Marshall.

William Marshall is the article writer's father. Mentioned in the chapter about the schoolhouse of 1849, Marshall was a planter, a surveyor, and a map-maker. His maps are a major part of this story. He was born in 1817 on his family's large plantation near the southwest prong of Slocum Creek. How large? The Marshall plantation contained all of the current Greenfield Heights subdivision in Havelock, and farm fields still planted there to this day were part of it. In 1847, W. H. Marshall married Sarah J. Perkins of Cherry Point. They would raise two sons.

Before the war, he was an unsuccessful candidate for Craven County sheriff. He served as the census taker for the area east of New Bern in 1850. Called Gooding's District, Marshall's census territory ran from Riverdale and Croatan to Harlowe.

His 565-acre plantation was adjacent to the Atlantic and North Carolina Railroad track. The rail stop of Havelock Station was at his back door making travel to and from New Bern both simple and fast. Just before the Civil

---

[d] *Carolina and the Southern Cross*, Vol. 2, No. 1, pp. 17-18, April 1913.

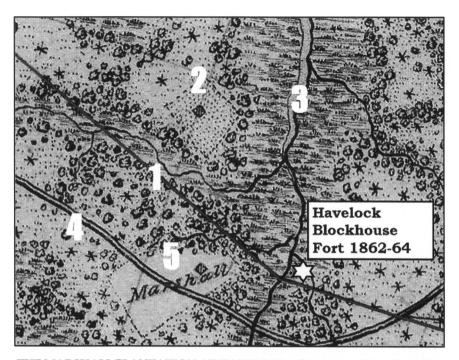

THE MARSHALL PLANTATION AT HAVELOCK. This is a small portion of the 1853 survey for the construction of the Atlantic and North Carolina Railroad, marked here for reference. W. H. Marshall was part of the survey crew and had his home identified on the map.

MAP KEY: 1) The A&NC Railroad line; New Bern would be to the left and Morehead City to the right. 2) A section of the Rev. Jacob Utley Plantation and the approximate location of the modern Havelock Tourist and Events Center. 3) The southwest prong of Slocum Creek. 4) The Old Beaufort Road; today's Greenfield Heights Blvd. 5) The W. H. Marshall Plantation; today's Greenfield Heights. The star indicates the location of the Union blockhouse at Slocum Creek.

[*Illustration by the author. The entire A&NC survey map of 1853 is preserved at the N.C. Department of Archives and History.*]

War, he established a George Street residence in New Bern and won a seat as a city alderman in 1861. He'd remain there for most of the war.

The plantation straddling the New Bern to Beaufort road is where Marshall grew up. It was a slave plantation with a large slave cemetery that was used by local African Americans into the modern era. Marshall seemed to want to get out of the planting business. He ran for sheriff. He was a surveyor and census taker. At the beginning of the war, he retreated to New Bern. But the area on the map above was his old stomping ground. He was intimately familiar with every inch of ground on the 1853 map. When the

Union invaded, they built a fort only a few hundred yards from Marshall's house. It will become clear shortly why this was important.

Some estimates are that seventy-five percent of New Bern's residents abandoned the city at the time of the Union attack. William Marshall, 44, was among the few who decided otherwise. He intentionally moved there and did not leave.

William H. Marshall was the leader of the Confederate spy ring inside Union-occupied New Bern.

While Union officers settled themselves into the fine homes of New Bern, Marshall was discovering that the fortified lines of the city, though formidable, were not exactly watertight. From the earliest days of the occupation, he worked to develop an underground network of couriers. Sometimes he made the dangerous trip through Union lines on his own. His secret correspondence provided much-needed details of the enemy's location, objectives, strengths, and weaknesses to Southern officers in Kinston.

The salutation of a letter smuggled out of the city a mere fifteen days after the battle is "Dear John." It mentions who was occupying which homes, what stores were closed or open, and who was now running them. It told about all the construction and earthwork that was going on, especially at the Fort Totten line, the morale of the Southerners left behind, and the latest gossip and rumors. The multipage correspondence is signed, not with a name, but with a symbol; an upside-down triangle. The recipient may have been Confederate Col. John N. Whitford. Marshall is known to have had a direct connection to Whitford in Kinston through one of Whitford's officers, Capt. James Henry Tolson.[e]

At the same time, Marshall was gun-running.

A young English metalsmith named Edward Want had a gun factory on Pollock Street. In late 1861, Want received an order from the Confederate government in Richmond for five thousand pistols. His dreams of being both useful and more prosperous were stymied by General Burnside's untimely arrival. So, Want was more than happy to offload some of his inventory to Confederate sympathizers.

On one occasion Marshall and his agents purchased a pair of Navy-style revolvers and a sword from the gunsmith and smuggled them out of town by boat. One of the pistols went to Lt. J.H. Marshall, probably William's younger brother. The swords and the other revolver were delivered to Capt. Tolson, the officer in Whitford's regiment. The sword was smuggled aboard the boat in the trouser leg of one of Marshall's co-conspirators.

---

[e] *Lawrence O'Bryan Branch Papers*, University of Virginia, Roanoke; *Carolina and the Southern Cross*, April 1913, page 18.

Marshall was heating things up. Soon enough, they'd boil.

The 12-year-old Spy

As we've noted, Henry A. Marshall was the son of William H. Marshall, the surveyor and budding spymaster we are speaking of. Henry is the author of *A Boys Recollection of the Battle of New Bern*, the short article published long after the war, when he was sixty years old. Henry's story is the skeleton we're hanging meat on here.

A model of the Civil War blockhouse complex is in a local history exhibit at Havelock Tourist and Events Center.

And, remarkably, he became a spy at the age of 12.

It happened this way.

Shortly after the fall of New Bern in 1862, William Marshall decided he was going to create maps of each of the new Union encampments. To do so, he sent his young son to gather intelligence.

The first location father and son targeted was the newly-built fort of the Ninth New Jersey Volunteer Infantry ... on Slocum Creek at Havelock ... just across the tracks from the Marshall family's plantation home. The boy used the sale of cigars and lemonade as a cover for his visit. His father told Henry the exact information to gather.

At Havelock Station, Henry
- counted the number of tents
- noted if they were round or walled tents
- determined the number of men assigned to each type

With this information, the total number of soldiers at Havelock Station was determined. Then Henry
- counted the number of guns of light artillery
- counted the cannons of the fort
- and counted and recorded his steps around the camp

No one paid any attention to a 12-year-old high-stepping across the grounds as if at play. But by measuring Henry's stride and multiplying by the number of steps, William Marshall derived the dimensions of the blockhouse fort, officers' quarters, outbuildings, and the camp overall; vital information for the creation of his map.

It turned out that Henry Marshall was a natural-born spy. This mission to Havelock was a big success. So much so that the father and son repeated the process, up and down the railroad, and all around New Bern.

In addition to the Ninth New Jersey, Henry ran ops on the camps of the 27th Massachusetts, the 10th Connecticut, the 2nd Maryland, the 3rd New Jersey Cavalry, the New York Artillery, and several regiments of Iowa, Wisconsin, Ohio, and Michigan.

William Marshall used his son's fresh information plus old maps of the city, along with notes from his survey files, to create detailed maps of all of the fortifications around New Bern. Then he sent them to Confederate headquarters in Kinston through the clandestine courier network he was perfecting.

The Lawrence O'Bryan Branch Map

Lawrence O'Bryan Branch was a general and commander of the Southern forces of North Carolina in the battle of New Bern. In the collection of his papers at the University of Virginia at Roanoke, there are 650 items. Six hundred and forty-eight are documents. Only two are maps.

General Branch, C.S.A.

The one reproduced on the next page was created to document the layout of the most eastern of New Bern's defenses before the Union invasion. It was made in late 1861; probably December 1861, about three months before the fall of New Bern; and about six months before young Henry's spy escapades.

The Branch Map of 1861 is focused on the Slocum Creek and Havelock area. On the left, it shows the location of the headquarters and camp of the 2nd North Carolina Cavalry just below the Spaightsville Post Office along the A&NC Railroad tracks.

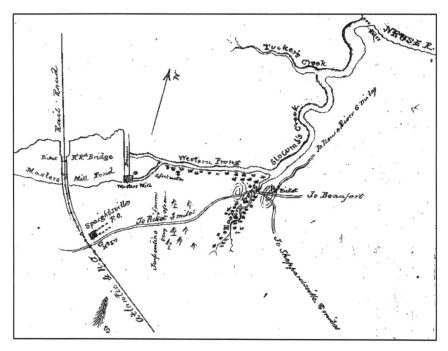

1861 map of Havelock defenses, L. O'B. Branch Papers, University of Virginia.

In 1861, local landowners were still growing accustomed to the name *Havelock* that had been foisted on them by the railroad when it opened for service from Goldsboro to Morehead City in 1858.

Upon establishing a post office in 1860, farmer A. J. Chesnutt called it *Spaightsville* in honor of colonial landowner and North Carolina governor, Richard Dobbs Spaight, who had built the nearby grist and sawmill on Slocum Creek. Chesnutt's post office did not survive the Civil War, but its location served as the community's mail stop into the 1940s.[f]

The 1861 map shows the mill, then owned by Dr. Samuel Masters, along with its mill pond going under the railroad trestle. According to the map, the vulnerable wooden trestle had its own picket post. Another Confederate picket post is shown as an oval at the intersection of Beaufort Road with Sheppardsville Road; Sheppardsville being another name for Newport.

The picket post at the roads' intersection is the precise location of today's MCAS Cherry Point main gate on Fontana Blvd. (Highway 101). The map shows the various courses of Tucker Creek and Slocum Creek to the Neuse River. At the mouth of Slocum Creek, defensive pilings are shown;

---

[f] U.S. Postal Service records, Library of Congress.

installed in the water by Southern forces before the Union invasion. Those pilings were later encountered and removed by Burnside's fleet.

The big mill pond was near the site where the Havelock blockhouse was built a few months later. The Marshall Plantation was also nearby.

The primary reason the Branch Map is being shown here is because of the likelihood that the artist was William Marshall. The style of the direction arrow and lettering suggests the artist was comfortable with both drafting and surveying. It's also easy to detect similarities in the handwriting on the Marshall plantation map of 1853 and the Branch map of 1861.

While none of the maps Marshall created of the Union fortifications are known to have survived, this one gives a tangible example of the type of map that the surveyor-spy turned, for a time, into a clandestine cottage industry.

David Dickinson: The Master Scout

David Owen Dickinson is all but a ghost of history. The paucity of information about him probably derives from the fact that this rough young family man was a Confederate scout; in other words, a spy on horseback; a secret agent working at the top levels of the South's clandestine services; a mere private reporting directly to commanding generals.

Dickinson was a farmer from Core Creek, which is just across the Carteret County line from Harlowe on the Beaufort Road (Hwy 101).

He's not named as an agent of William Marshall's spy operation by Henry Marshall's article. But his ties to the group will become evident as we move forward.

During the Civil War, Dickinson served with the 1st N.C. Artillery, Company H, 10th N.C. Troops. He joined early: July 15, 1861, just 90 days after the war's first shots. He served with distinction until the close of the war.

He was a strong young farmer, raised in the field, 21 years old and six feet tall. He was raised very close to Emeline Pigott's family home. During the Battle of Fort Macon, Dickinson was one of its defenders against Burnside's forces. He was captured and became a federal prisoner upon its surrender. But he was soon paroled and back on duty.

Cream rises, so they say, and he was chosen for detached duties as a "scout." For the remainder of the war, he ranged all over the counties of Craven, Carteret, Lenoir, and Wayne, and elsewhere, sometimes traveling on horseback a hundred miles in a day. [g]

As a Confederate scout, his duties were to:

---

[g] OR, various entries; Fold3 records.

- observe Federals in camp and in motion
- gather and report information
- observe lines of march and numbers of troops
- cross Federal lines
- deliver dispatches
- interview and interrogate individuals
- fight when necessary

Dickinson worked from and corresponded directly with Confederate regimental headquarters in Kinston, Goldsboro, and Wilmington. Even so, his details are very hard to find. Other than his name, historians at Fort Macon have no documentation on David Dickinson. For a time during the siege of Fort Fisher near Wilmington, Dickinson was one of its few outside contacts. But historians at Fort Fisher lacked details when asked about him. The 1st N.C. Artillery re-enactors knew nothing of him either.[h]

Dickinson has been unknown and his accomplishments unsung. For all these years, his exploits have remained as much a secret as they were during the Civil War.

The "official records" of the Union and Confederate armies and navies are chronicled in a 128-volume series entitled "The War of the Rebellion." It's nicknamed the *OR*. Some of the books run to more than 1,000 pages. They include dispatches, reports, orders, and letters of the main players during the 1861-1865 national tragedy. After a lot of digging, a researcher may occasionally find a gold nugget like the only document in the OR from Dickinson himself, signed without rank, as if by a civilian.

His middle initial is a typo. The transcriber had difficulty reading the handwritten "O" of his signature, but that's corrected in a footnote about 14

SWANSBOROUGH, N. C., *December 25, 1864—10 p. m.*
Capt. JOHN S. FAIRLY,
 Aide-de-Camp, Wilmington :

CAPTAIN: I have late intelligence from New Berne and Beaufort. The enemy has re-enforced at New Berne and is going to make a raid, 20,000 strong. I never heard where they were going. There is also an expedition for this place. It was within eight miles of here to-night at 8 o'clock. I will let you know more about it soon.

 I am, captain, very respectfully, your obedient servant,
        D. I. DICKINSON.

P. S.—The expedition for this place contains one gun-boat, one flat, and a lot of small boats. These coming up the sound.
        D. I. DICKINSON.

---

[h] Personal communications by the author, 2019.

volumes later. Here the scout reports to an intelligence officer in Wilmington that the Federals have re-enforced at New Bern and are planning to make a raid with an enormous force. At the bottom, his dispatch makes note of a Union flotilla he observed "coming up the sound."

Hard-to-find records show that Pvt. David Dickinson kept the news flowing throughout the entire war. Here are a few examples:

To Lieutenant General T.H. Holmes from regimental intelligence officer Col. Archer Anderson in Wilmington, December 25, 1864: "*General [Braxton] Bragg desires you to take care of the expedition on Swansboro, reported by Scout Dickinson, with your home guard.*"

To Col. Archer Anderson from Major A. Van Der Horst, Assistant Adjutant General, December 26, 1864: "*Scout Dickinson reports that the enemy have re-enforced at New Berne and are going to make a raid 20,000 strong; has not heard where they are going. Dickinson also states that at 8 o'clock last night the enemy were within eight miles of Swansboro. The expedition consists of one gunboat, one flat, and a lot of small boats. They were coming up the sound at the time he was writing, 10 o'clock last night. The letter containing this information will be sent to you at once by courier.*"

Lt. General Holmes to Colonel Anderson, December 28, 1864: "*Scout Dickinson reports that the rail cars have been running all the time from Morehead City to New Bern for the last four days.*"

From Colonel Anderson to Brigadier General L. S. Baker at Goldsboro, January 15, 1865: "*Scout Dickinson reports 1,000 troops at Morehead City, and 6,000 at New Bern. Raid in contemplation now.*"

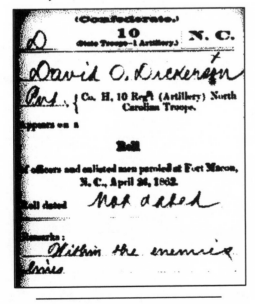

To General Baker from Colonel Anderson, January 27, 1865: "*Scout Dickinson reports 9,000 men at New Bern and Morehead City. Have been transporting troops from latter to former last three days. No cavalry re-enforcements.*"[i]

A few pay records remain. During the summer of 1863, he received payment of $375 for the previous five months of service as "expenses for self and horse while acting as a scout near New Bern NC."

---

[i] OR; Fold3 records; Dickinson's name often appears in records as *Dickerson.*

His base pay was $11 a month.

According to a voucher of December 1863, Dickinson's pay category was "for secret services rendered by him."

Normally pay records state where the soldier was serving, at a fort, camp, or city, for example. One quite interesting though undated entry from Dickinson's file simply states that he was "within the enemies lines." [sic].

Within the enemy's lines.

How much more of a secret agent can one be?

We'll return to Pvt. Dickinson shortly but first consider another scout.

James H. Hunter of Slocum Creek

James Howard Hunter was born in 1834 and raised on his family's 500-acre plantation on the east side of Slocum Creek. The Hunters and the Marshalls were long-time neighbors. Hunter may have taken over the plantation from his sea-captain father, John Hunter. Before the war, Jim Hunter was prosperous, bordering on wealth. He made his living from the production of tar, turpentine, timber, and farming.

He would suffer the loss of two wives with whom he had eight children before marrying again late in life.

Hunter initially joined the N.C. 3rd Cavalry in 1861 at age 28. He was assigned to Camp Gaston, just west of Slocum Creek, under the leadership of Peter G. Evans. Hunter's existing muster roll documents straddle the Battle of New Bern showing him in February 1862 as a corporal with "Capt. Peter G. Evans' Independent Company of Cavalry" and in March and April with Company E (Macon Mounted Guard) 41 Reg't North Carolina Cavalry." [j]

Based upon that information, it's reasonable to presume that Hunter was at the Camp Gaston cavalry barracks when it was shelled by Union gunboats on March 13, 1862.

Later, Hunter began service as a detached Confederate scout. Although we have evidence of his clandestine services during the war and know he was later called "Capt. Hunter," he mysteriously disappears from Confederate pay and enlistment records after the documents mentioned above.

Two years later, in 1864, James Hunter participated in the Confederate attempt to retake New Bern. It was a massive effort ordered by the South's top commander, General Robert E. Lee. Forces were scrounged from every possible reserve and converged on New Bern from three points of the compass. Many of the Southern attackers didn't know the local terrain, roads, or

---

[j] Fold3 records, James H. Hunter; *New Bern Weekly Journal*, August 28, 1905.

landmarks. They weren't from here and needed the knowledge of local scouts and guides to direct them where to go.

During the 1864 assault, a Confederate lieutenant colonel of the 5th South Carolina cavalry by the name of Robert J. Jeffords led his mounted troops up the Atlantic and North Carolina Railroad from Newport toward New Bern. By midnight February 3, 1864, Jeffords had reached the Havelock blockhouse fort complex at Slocum Creek and dispatched a message to his commanding officer.

In the dispatch, Jeffords gave a situation report. He said his unit was burning the blockhouse and quarters and that its Union company had fled toward New Bern. Then he writes: *"I have met Hunter this morning {Confederate scout so Dickinson says} ... he also says that a guide was sent Gen. Barton yesterday and he now was between Croatan and New Bern."*

Dickinson knows and is vouching for Hunter. Remarkably, we have scouts James Hunter and David Dickinson, and spy-master William Marshall together in a single dispatch.

We know that the guide who was sent to General Seth Barton is Marshall because Barton later reports that the man was one of the "scouts and spies deemed reliable" describing him as "one, in particular, a surveyor of the county and maker of the sketches and maps of the vicinity upon which we relied...." Not only does Barton describe Marshall as his guide, but also indicates that the entire movement of troops for the 1864 Confederate attack on New Bern relied upon Marshall's "sketches and maps." General Barton

---

(No. 12)

Havelock 12 o'clock M
February 3, 1864

General—I have reached this point. The fort has been deserted. One brass six pounder rifle gun spiked. The fort is now being burnt with quarters, the enemy (one company artillery) left this morning in the direction of Croatan, where from last information I can get, the enemy have a redoubt fort with one or two guns. I shall move forward immediately and see whether Croatan is occupied or not. It is six miles from this point. I met Hunter this morning (Confederate scout so Dickinson says) and he informed me that a terrible fight was going on from dawn until about 9 o'clock, he also says that a guide was sent Gen. Barton yesterday and he is now in between Croatan and Newbern. I shall forward you accurate information if it is possible to be obtained. A gentleman just brought in by my scout reports Croatan deserted. Troops going toward New Bern, he says he saw a dispatch from Newbern last night to Commanding Officer at Croatan stating that unless they get reinforcements by this Railroad last night they would be obliged to surrender the town this morning. I am fully impressed that the town is in our possession.

Very respectfully,
R.J. Jeffords, Lt. Col. Cavalry

1864 South Carolina cavalry LtCol. R. J. Jeffords' dispatch from Havelock mentions local scouts and spies. Underlining added for emphasis. Source: OR

> HEADQUARTERS BRIGADE,
> *February 21, 1864*
>
> MAJOR: I have the honor to make the following report of the part borne by the forces under my command in the recent advance against New Berne ...
>
> **Scouts and spies deemed reliable** had been examined and reported there were no works there. **One in particular, a surveyor of the county and maker of the sketches and maps of the vicinity, upon which we relied, was sent to ascertain the facts. He returned three days before the movement and reported that his maps were correct** ...
>
> Very respectfully, your obedient servant,
> S. M. BARTON,
> *Brigadier-General.*

Confederate General Seth Barton reports meeting with guide who is a surveyor for the county and maker of sketches and maps. Source: OR

sent Marshall out on another surveillance mission to review and update details of the existing maps. Marshall reported back to Barton three days before the attacks and re-confirmed the accuracy of his information.

One more interesting note about Jim Hunter. An article in the Person County (NC) Heritage Book shows James Hunter, born at Havelock, with the proper dates of birth and death along with a remarkable photograph. When the author interviewed Hunter's great-granddaughter and great-great-granddaughter – both historically and genealogically-aware individuals, they were adamant about the provenance of both the photo and the story of

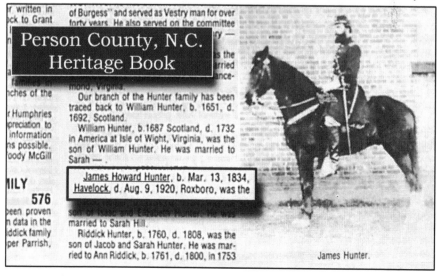

James Hunter.

their ancestor, Jim Hunter. And that the portrait had been passed down through the family from the time of the Civil War.

When they were told during the interview that the man in the picture was wearing a Union officer's uniform, the refined Southern ladies were suddenly horrified that ol' granddad might have been a Yankee! But then they were informed that he was a scout and spy for the Confederacy and that particularly daring spies sometimes wore the enemy uniform to cross their lines and do mischief, the ladies were both relieved and delighted.

Nevertheless, it's simply amazing that James Hunter had the nerve to sit for a portrait wearing the enemy's uniform – a hanging offense.

The Marshall Network

Business continued even during the Civil War and possibly it was under the guise of surveying jobs that William Marshall was able to move around, even in and out of Union-occupied lines. He traveled for business, to his Havelock plantation, and to visit friends in Confederate-held Kinston and Swift Creek.

We know that Marshall and Jim Hunter had known each other all their lives and lived within a few miles of one another. Henry Marshall colors the pair as working very closely together. In between the two lived Philemon Holland whose farm and large household were on the west bank of Slocum Creek. Holland's home was set close to both the Neuse River and the main county road, the road down which Emeline Pigott traveled to and from New Bern.

And here's a nice revelation: Philemon Holland's wife, Margaret Ann Pigott Holland, was Emeline's sister. It's more than a circumstantial case that Marshall, Hunter, Pigott, and Dickinson knew one another and were working hand-in-glove for the same cause.

In fact, on February 7, 1865, she wrote about a rendezvous with Rebel scouts. "I met Confederate scouts near the Neuse River with a Lady friend [and delivered] all the news I knew with letters & paper."[k]

Others were associated as well. Two sea captains were in the circle of influence. During part of the year, some roads were impassable making boats on the rivers and creeks the best way to travel. Boat captains, whose job it might be to fish or deliver goods and products, had quite a bit of freedom to move about. And just maybe to traffic in contraband, messages, and people.

One of the facts most known about Emeline Pigott is that she recruited and worked with ship's captains. In his article from *Carolina and the*

[k] Benjamin Franklin Royal Papers, Southern Historical Collection. UNC-CH.

Southern Cross, Henry Marshall names one sea captain and possibly names another. The first is Captain Solomon Broughton who lived on the north side of the Neuse River. During the Civil War, this area was a part of Craven County as Pamlico County wasn't formed until 1872. The second captain may have been James Hunter's elderly father. You will remember that one of gunsmith Edward Want's swords went on board a boat down someone's pants leg. The writer had just mentioned James Hunter so it's natural to assume it was with him that the sword went aboard the vessel "in the leg of Capt. Hunter's trousers." Another possibility is that the skipper of the boat, Captain John Hunter, concealed the sword.

There were others in the network of agents, spies, scouts, and couriers. Rufus Wilkinson Bell, also of Harlowe and Emeline's brother-in-law, was arrested with her for engaging in secret services. There was the mysterious agent, known to Marshall and the Confederate high command by the alias "Mrs. Meeker" and the "Lady of Swift Creek," who penetrated New Bern many times under the guise of a woman selling cotton. Mrs. Elizabeth Howland and her children were couriers as were Mary Francis Chadwick and Mrs. Alexander Taylor. Mrs. Julia Lewis was a spy. Lt. Franklin Foy was a scout around New Bern and three other 1st Artillery scouts, like David Dickinson, are known from official records: Joseph A. Bell and B. H. Bell of Company H and John Miller of Company B. The last three are said to have "frequently penetrated the enemy's lines and brought therefrom valuable information."

Then there was Jim Hunter, the detached scout dressed as a Federal officer; Scout Dickinson who was everywhere; young Henry, the boy spy; and fair Emeline of the big hoop skirts.

In the small world of 1860s Craven County, it's more than likely that all of these individuals knew, or knew of, one another. And all of them would have recognized William H. Marshall's unique role.

Union Commander Moves Against Spies

General John G. Foster was one of Burnside's three subordinate commanders at the Battle of New Bern. When Burnside was called to duty in Virginia in mid-1862, it was Foster he selected to take charge as the Union army commander for the Department of North Carolina. Foster was a West Point graduate and successful combat leader.

In 1863, Foster was nearly killed in an expedition near Washington, N.C. During the foray from New Bern into Confederate-held territory, Foster had been frustrated at every turn. His experience on that raid was like a football quarterback when the other team has stolen his game plan.

He felt that his every move had been anticipated. He found himself surrounded and barely able to escape on a steamer down the Pamlico River. Even his steamer was ambushed and hit with twenty-two rounds. The pilot of the vessel was struck and killed at General Foster's side. Foster was said to have been uncharacteristically emotional at the peak of the action. There's only so much anyone can take.

Major General John G. Foster

Upon his return to New Bern, he was convinced that clandestine operatives had compromised that operation and others. He hastily formulated a bold move to rid himself of the problem.

The author, Henry Marshall, described it well: "Mortified and furious (General Foster) arrived at New Bern and with savage brutality ordered forty families of women and children from their homes, and with one week's rations weighed from their own provisions, had them put out of the Federal lines on the side of the railroad about a mile below Cove Creek, where they remained for several hours, some of the time in the rain, until a Southern wagon train could come and take them to Kinston."

General Foster threw out suspected spies and their families. This included William Marshall, his wife, and three children, one of whom was his son, Henry. Foster also threw out people who were irritants, who wouldn't take the oath of loyalty to the union, and, in more than a few instances,

---

68 men, women & children expelled from Newbern, May, 1863

Mrs. Wallace & 2 children	Israel Disosway, wife & 6 children
Sam Cook, wife & two children	J. Gooding, Jr., wife & 2 children
Mrs. Connan, 72 years old	S. R. Street, wife & 7 children
Mrs. Russell & 2 children	L. Philips, wife & 2 children
W. H. Marshall, wife & 3 children	B. M. Cook, wife & 2 children
3 Misses Custis (sisters)	Mrs. Pittman & 2 children
Miss Justice	Major Phillips
Elijah W. Ellis & daughter	Mrs. Simpson, 70 years old
Mrs. Melvin, 80 years old	James Hancock, wife & 2 children
Mrs. Oliver	2 Misses Pittman (sisters)
Clifford Ball	James Armstrong, 68 years old
J. B. Oxley	Robert Lewis, 70 years old
Asa Bynum & wife	Needham Case, wife & 2 children
Jesse Bynum	Mrs. Stanley & infant
2 Miss Osgoods	

-- Weekly State Journal, Raleigh
May 27, 1863

people who had nice homes, thus creating additional housing for officers and Union families. The exiles lost all their property, furnishings, clothing, and personal possessions. Many were left with only the clothes on their backs and a little food.

More people were removed over the next few weeks and months. Southern papers called the exiles "Victims of Yankee brutality."

The event culminated in some remarkable and very high-level correspondence: a letter from Major General Daniel Harvey Hill to James Seddon, Confederate Secretary of War in Richmond, giving evidence that Marshall was the spymaster of Craven County … and revealing an even darker secret.

An extract of General Hill's letter, sent from his headquarters in Goldsboro, May 10, 1863, said: "… The other letter is from Mr. Marshall, until recently our only reliable source in New Berne. Foster has expelled him, however, and now my information is very vague."

It was a theory that William Marshall of Slocum Creek was the number one spy of occupied New Bern, but here is Maj. Gen. D. H. Hill confirming it. Others gathered information but Marshall was *the only reliable source*, the man with the organization, system, and contacts to get it out.

Continuing the letter, Gen. Hill drops this bombshell:

"We have an employee in Foster's military family who is as true to the South as President [Jefferson] Davis … but unfortunately, all communications from this person came through Mr. Marshall, and [now] I have no agent working in town."[1]

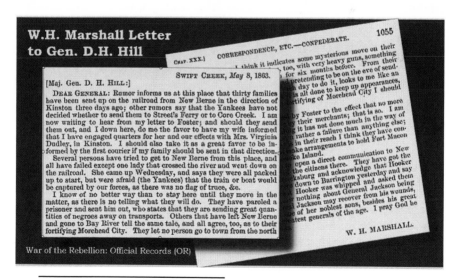

W.H. Marshall Letter to Gen. D.H. Hill

[CHAP. XXX.]   CORRESPONDENCE, ETC.—CONFEDERATE.   1055

SWIFT CREEK, *May* 8, 1863.

[Maj. Gen. D. H. HILL:]

DEAR GENERAL: Rumor informs us at this place that thirty families have been sent up on the railroad from New Berne in the direction of Kinston three days ago; other rumors say that the Yankees have not decided whether to send them to Street's Ferry or to Core Creek. I am now waiting to hear from my letter to Foster; and should they send them out, and I down here, do me the favor to have my wife informed that I have engaged quarters for her and our effects with Mrs. Virginia Dudley, in Kinston. I should also take it as a great favor to be informed by the first courier if my family should be sent in that direction.

Several persons have tried to get to New Berne from this place, and all have failed except one lady that crossed the river and went down on the railroad. She came up Wednesday, and says they were all packed up to start, but were afraid (the Yankees) that the train or boat would be captured by our forces, as there was no flag of truce, &c.

I know of no better way than to stay here until they move in the matter, as there is no telling what they will do. They have paroled a prisoner and sent him out, who states that they are sending great quantities of negroes away on transports. Others that have left New Berne and gone to Bay River tell the same tale, and all agree, too, as to their fortifying Morehead City. They let no person go to town from the north

I think it indicates some mysterious move on their ... too, with very heavy guns, something ..., for six months before. From their ... pretending to be on the eve of send- ... day to do it, looks to me like an ... is all done to keep up appearances, ... tifying of Morehead City I should

... by Foster to the effect that no more ... their merchants; that is so. I am ... it has not done much in the way of ... rather a failure than anything else; ... in their reach I think they have con- ... arrangements to hold Fort Macon

...ke Island.

...open a direct communication to New ... the citizens there. They have got the ...kaburg and acknowledge that Hooker ... down to Barrington yesterday and say ... Hooker was whipped and asked them ... nothing about General Jackson being ... Jackson may recover from his wounds, ... of her noblest sons, besides his great ...atest generals of the age. I pray God he

W. H. MARSHALL.

War of the Rebellion: Official Records (OR)

---

[1] Official Records, War of the Rebellion.

It was William Marshall who recruited and handled the mole in the Burnside/Foster headquarters. Furthermore, now that Marshall was no longer there, the Confederate command had "no agent," Hill stated.

"The other letter from Mr. Marshall" referred to by General Hill was considered important enough that it was preserved in the Official Records of the War of the Rebellion (OR).

Nearly all of the thousands of letters in the OR are from people with military ranks behind their names. It is rare for a civilian's letter to be found there. But Marshall's May 8, 1863 letter to Gen. D. H. Hill, from just after the exile of the New Bern townspeople, is today found on page 1054 of Chapter XXX – Correspondence, Etc. – Confederate.

The spymaster was in Rebel-held Kinston at the time of the expulsion, proving that Marshall was making clandestine movements of his own. Written from Swift Creek, the letter is a confidential report about recent activities in New Bern and promised, "I shall be able soon to open direct communications to New Berne, should they leave any of the citizens there." The letter is an excellent example of the type of messages he had been sending to the Confederate high command all along. Marshall indicated he and his compatriots would stay in the fight to the bitter end.

The Fates of the Secret Agents

WILLIAM HENRY MARSHALL: The reader may not be surprised to learn that after the war William H. Marshall was made the county surveyor. He spent most of the remainder of his life creating maps and surveys of New Bern and the boundaries of Craven County. One of his maps is in the Tryon Palace collection.

He became a passionate observer of the weather, keeping daily temperature records and appearing in the newspapers from time to time with words about hot and cold spells.

Then, an article from the *Newbernian* newspaper dated September 1877. The headline is Serious Accident. *"While a hand-car in charge of Capt. J.J. Roberson, who was accompanied by W.H. Marshall, Esq., was crossing the railroad bridge over the Trent, it was discovered that a negro woman was on the track, and every effort was made to stop the car. The woman instead of stepping off on one of the side-crossings became frightened and attempted to run to the shore, and upon her arrival on the Newbern side of the river, fell on the track, and the hand-car passed over her, throwing it off and precipitating its occupants down the railroad embankment. Capt. Roberson was severely bruised; but we regret to say that Mr. Marshall was seriously injured. The wind was blowing a gale at the time which added greatly to the speed of the car."*

The woman's fate wasn't revealed but we know Marshall survived. Three years later, in 1880, William Marshall, 63, is living at #5 George Street in New Bern with his wife, Sarah, and two sons, Henry and Francis. The home was on the street's west side near the old Tryon Palace stables.[m]

By the year 1900, when he was 83, Marshall had moved back to the family's land in Havelock, becoming Jim Hunter's neighbor once again. A widower now, his son Henry was listed as "head of household." The elder Marshall does not appear in the county voter rolls for 1902 or the 1910 census. No obituary for or portrait of William Marshall has been found. He was likely buried in the Marshall family cemetery just off the Old Beaufort Road in Havelock.

HENRY MARSHALL: In 1882, H. A. Marshall was still living in New Bern, earning his keep as a store clerk and in construction as a bricklayer. He married Elizabeth A. Harget, who was born in 1862. She died at the time of the 1884 birth of their daughter, Eleanor Eborn Marshall, the famed New Bern school teacher, and principal.

At age 50, he was living in Havelock where he'd spend the rest of his life. He joined his father's surveying business and became a civil engineer. He stayed active in Democratic politics and worked to register voters.

In 1899, Henry drew the important "Map of James A. Bryan's Land" preserving vital information about a huge swath of southwestern Craven County, as listed in Part IV of this book.

In April 1913, his valuable article "*A Boy's Recollection of the Battle of New Bern*" was published. He'd live until 1935. His grave, along with Elizabeth and Eleanor, is in New Bern's Cedar Grove Cemetery.

DAVID DICKINSON: After the fighting was over, the stalwart Confederate Scout, returned to his humble beginnings and hired himself out as a farm laborer at Core Creek, just outside Beaufort. We've been unable to discover the cause of his death at age 35, just ten years after the close of the conflict between the states. David is buried in the cemetery of the Core Creek United Methodist Church.

His wife, Lenoir County native Margaret Ann Tillman Dickinson, remarried soon after his

Bernd Doss photo

---

[m] U.S. Census of 1880; Records of Craven County, Vol. 1, Elizabeth Moore.

death, and his oldest son, who was 11 years old at the time of David's passing, was drawn into serious conflict with the new stepfather. At a young age, the boy left home and took to the sea working for two years on a square-rigged sailing ship. Coming ashore in New Jersey, he gained experience with several manufacturing companies over the next few years.

In 1897, with a partner, David Dickinson's son, Farleigh Dickinson, founded a company that grew to be the largest surgical instrument manufacturing business in the United States. The firm became the famed Fortune 500 medical technology company Becton Dickinson, today employing more than 50,000 people in 50 countries around the world.

The billionaire son of a Confederate scout became the benefactor of Fairleigh Dickinson University. And in 1938, he returned to the community of his birth and built the Core Creek church where David Dickinson now rests.

Fairleigh S. Dickinson

This portrait of the son may give an inkling of the looks of his soldier-spy father.

JAMES H. HUNTER: Well-known and respected for his wartime exploits, Jim Hunter became one of the county's wealthiest men and served as a magistrate, school board leader, and justice of the peace. He continued to make his home on Slocum Creek at Havelock for the next half-century.

Hunter was often mentioned in the newspaper, sometimes just for visiting New Bern by train. He worked as a real estate and timber agent and was later general manager of the nearby Lake Ellis Plantation, a massive farm southwest of Havelock owned by James Augustus Bryan.

After 1910, the old Rebel scout sold his acreage at Slocum Creek and moved to Roxboro, Person County, N.C. to live with his son, Collins. He died there in 1920 at age 86.

EMELINE PIGOTT: After the war, Emeline was the toast of the town from New Bern to Beaufort and everywhere in between. She was honored and talked about, talked about, and honored. Her stories were endlessly repeated, polished, and honed.

One was that she feigned protests upon her arrest against being searched by a black matron until a white woman could be found. But, the story goes, the protest was simply a stall for time during which she tore up and ate the most incriminating of the letters she was carrying that day.

And that she summoned some of the leaders of wartime New Bern to her jail cell and threatened to expose them as traitors if she was not released. Then an attempt was made on her life by pumping chloroform into the room, but after that failed, she was set free. Or so the stories go.

Around the turn of the last century, commemorative Emeline Pigott calendars were sold each year, and generations of school children in Craven and Carteret counties were taught her story. In her adult years, she lived in Morehead City and thus has been thoroughly embraced by Carteret County. The Emeline Pigott Chapter of the United Daughters of the Confederacy was founded in Morehead and she was made its honorary president.

Her one true love, Private Stokes MacRea, was killed in the war. She never married. His body was never identified. It's said that she perpetually tended the grave of an unknown Confederate soldier as an act of devotion to what might have been, but wasn't meant to be.

Emeline Jamison Pigott died on May 26, 1919, and was buried in a family cemetery in Morehead City. She was 82.

And now we know that she wasn't the only one. Now we know that William H. Marshall was the reliable conduit of intelligence from inside this Union-occupied territory. It was Marshall who recruited and handled an informant in the heart of Federal headquarters. It was his network of clandestine agents, scouts, and couriers who moved invisibly through enemy lines and whispered secrets to top Confederate generals. Marshall and his associates delivered the goods.

New Bern city map by William Marshall, 1875

Perhaps Henry Marshall memorialized his father best when he said, "He had much confidence, and no risk was too great for him to undertake to obtain information that he considered advantageous to the Southern cause."

As has been stated earlier, clandestine agents are, by their very nature, nameless. Today, an anonymous few who struggled here alongside folks like Emeline, in that dangerous, long-ago war of spies and secrets, are nameless no more.

Aftermath

In 1860, George Wolf Perry was sitting on top of the world.

Perry, 39, owned more than a thousand acres of land. He had a big, healthy family, forty-one "hands" on his farm, and the net worth of a millionaire. *Hands* was another euphemism for slaves.

His primary land holding was the turpentine plantation of the late Durant Hatch, a Revolutionary War general whose home had been south of the Trent River on the west side of Brice's Creek; land previously owned by Richard Dobbs Spaight, and Madam Mary Moore before him.

Perry was close enough to Havelock, though, to be counted in the 1860 census among those of Gooding's District using the Spaightsville post office. His wife, the former Sarah B. Koonce, went by the name Sally. Sally and George had four children in 1860: Hardy Hill, nine; Oliver Hazard, six, named in synchrony with U.S. Navy war hero, Commodore Oliver Hazard Perry; and daughters, Caroline, two; and Virginia, two months.

A Treatise On Turpentine Farming - Being A Review Of Natural And Artificial Obstructions, With Their Results, In Which Many Erroneous Ideas Are Exploded

G. W. Perry

George Perry was a naval stores man – a self-proclaimed expert on the subject – to the extent of having written a book about it. In an era when many people were scantily educated to the point of being illiterate, Perry penned the lucid and erudite *Treatise on Turpentine Farming* in 1859. The 163-page book of instruction was subtitled, *Being a Review of Natural and Artificial Obstructions, with their Results, in which Many Erroneous Ideas are Exploded: With Remarks on the Best Methods of Making Turpentine*. Its vocabulary and organization surpass many instructional volumes of the current era.

New Bern newspaper editor and publisher J. H. Muse advertised, "Having been appointed Agent for the above Work, we will furnish it for 50 cents per Copy; to purchase at a distance we will mail it on the receipt of 50

Cents, for the Book, and 8 Cents to pay the postage. It is the first Work of its kind ever published, and will prove an invaluable benefit to persons engaged in the business of Turpentine Making." [a]

Perry's treatise was wide-ranging in its advice and intended to help the novice as well as those actively engaged in naval stores production.

On preparing the land, "The land needs no cultivation, but every kind of turf should be turned over, such as huckleberry, gallberry, percosan bush, brier beds, reed beds, wire grass, savanna grass, and broom-sage grass."

On cutting boxes, "Boxes should be cut from about the first of November to the last of January, as there is less turpentine in the pines at that season than any other."

On types of trees, "Long [leaf] pines being best for turpentine."

Even tips on iron-handed labor management: "I let him repeat it until I felt satisfied that he knew I noticed it: I then had him whipped, without telling him the cause, and whether he understood or not, he never tried a repetition of the maneuver."

Of turpentine farming in general, Perry wrote, "It is a pleasant business to a man of industrious habits."

Census data indicates that his real estate assets, personal estate, and disposable income were exceeded by only a few of his peers in the county. His gross assets of $85,000 in 1860, adjusted for inflation, would exceed $2.5 million in today's dollars.

He wrote, "In short, good turpentine land is a fortune, and for those who have the cash, now is the time."

But the war began the next year; a war that rendered his labor practices obsolete. After four years of pillaging and abuse by occupying Federal troops, Perry had lost ninety-five percent of his assets. His farm was worth a fraction of what it had been before the war. And without his "hands," his income from turpentine production plummeted to a low ebb.[b]

Much of his property – his home, outbuildings, fences, and livestock – had been either damaged, confiscated, appropriated, or downright stolen. His post-war applications for compensation from the government went ignored and unpaid until after he died in 1877. In 1903, his son, Oliver, acting as administrator for the father's estate, was able to collect $8,600 from the U.S. Treasury. This was only possible because powerful U.S. Senator Furnifiold Simmons, who lived in New Bern, pushed a special relief bill through Congress to pay the family for "stores and supplies furnished to and used by the United States Army during the late war between the States." Four years later – and 41 years after the end of the Civil War – another war

[a] *Newbern Enquirer*, June 12, 1860, pg. 4.
[b] U.S. Census for Craven County of 1860 and 1870.

claims payment of $4,350 was received by the George W. Perry estate for "property destroyed by Union troops during the war or taken for the government during the conclusion of hostilities." [c]

While there can be little sympathy for those who had benefited through the enslavement of others, Perry's story illustrates the profound monetary and interpersonal landslide that rumbled over the county – and all of the South – as a result of the war.

Of southern Craven County, archeologist and historian Thomas Davis said, "The [Civil War] erased the last vestiges of the small antebellum landed aristocracy that existed in the area. As in much of the South, the Civil War left a legacy of social and economic dislocation, misery, and suffering in Craven County." [d]

Davis's words echo the angry pronouncement quoted previously from Henry Marshall of Havelock. Marshall decried the devastation of the large farms, the destruction and theft of property and livestock, and the forced scattering of plantation families.

One example of the war-wrought hardships is the attempts by formerly prosperous individuals to liquidate their turpentine-rich plantation lands at war's end, several here within days of one another.

- "Look Here: A GOOD TURPENTINE FARM FOR SALE. For Sale, on reasonable terms, 300 acres of the best and most desirable TURPENTINE LAND in the State. It is situated about 16 miles from New Berne, N.C., and one mile from Slocumbs Creek, which empties into the Neuse, near New Berne, and two miles from Havelock Station on the A. & N.C. R.R., adjoining the Turpentine Farm of Messrs. Lewis & Co. and lies nearby along the railroad and the old county road. For further particulars, apply to WM. H. OLIVER & CO., New Berne, N.C." [*The Lewises were the pre-war owners of the Lake Ellis Plantation.*] *The New Berne Times*, October 17, 1865.

- "FOR SALE PRIVATELY. OUR FARM, containing 1,000 Acres, lying immediately on the Railroad, 13 miles below New Berne, and also on Tucker's Creek, adapted to raising Cotton, Corn and Potatoes. Also, heavily timbered, consisting chiefly of Pine and Lightwood sufficient to burn from 500 to 100 Barrels of Tar, one Crop of Box Pine. Terms Cash. Immediate possession in order to enable the purchaser to work the Timber or

[c] *New Berne Weekly Journal*, February 17, 1903, pg. 4; *The Daily Journal*, New Bern, May 2, 1906, pg. 1.

[d] *Archeological Investigation at MCAS Cherry Point*, R-10-Davis-2003.

Lightwood. BENJAMIN BYNUM. T.H. MALLISON." *The New Berne Times* October 18, 1865.

- "FOR SALE – At $3,500. One Third on Time. 442 Acres of Land on Slocumb's Creek, 15 miles from New Berne, with Dwelling and Outhouses. Eight Acres are cleared, and produce good Cotton; the rest is well Timbered with Pine and Oak; four thousand [*turpentine*] Boxes now cut – Eight thousand can be cut. There is an abundance of marl on the place. One thousand cords of Oak, Ash, and Pine can be cut. This is a good chance for anyone who wants to embark in the Wood Business. W.D. WALLACE." *The New Berne Times* October 18, 1865.

- "FOR SALE OR LEASE. The following valuable Tracts of Land, in the County of Craven, State of North Carolina, belonging to the Estate of the late Thomas McLin are offered for sale or lease, viz: ... One other tract, located on Adams' Creek and its tributaries, embracing 1,060 acres, well timbered with pitch pine, live oak, and red cedar. There are on this tract 12,000 Turpentine Boxes, and enough lightwood to manufacture 1,000 barrels of Tar ... Henry McLin, Executor." *The New Berne Times* January 2, 1866.

The reader may recall that colonial surveyor John Lovick acquired land on the Neuse in 1719 whose wooded bluffs would one day stretch two-and-a-half miles from Anderson Creek to Dam Creek. [e]

The wealthy and successful Lovicks of Magnolia Plantation built a gristmill on Anderson Creek. Through the generations of the family, a blacksmith shop was created along with a complex of stables near the river built to accommodate sixty horses and mules.

According to descendant Mary Hughes McGrath in a 1990s interview with the author, by the time of the War Between the States, Magnolia Plantation was presided over by a "grand mansion" where the Lovick descendants lived. We've heard Mrs. McGrath say the burning of the graceful and capacious two-story home and the destruction of the war itself spelled the end of prosperity for the family that had been on the land for nearly a century and a half.

She added that though the liberated slaves moved away, many to the Hickman Hill area, they returned daily during certain times of the year to help the remaining Lovicks work the farm. Nevertheless, the efforts did not pay off in the long run. Tracts of the once-prosperous farm would be sold off piecemeal over the years to make ends meet.

We've heard also of the tragic losses of Michael N. Fisher of Riverdale.

---

[e] Dam Creek today divides Carolina Pines and Stately Pines.

Even the magnificent brick edifice of Clermont, the ancestral home of Governor Richard Dobbs Spaight and his mother-in-law Madam Mary Moore – the lands of which stretched from the Trent River well into the lake country beyond Havelock – was put to the torch by spiteful Northern troops.

Well-known, successful community mainstay Owen Chesnutt was the son of pioneers. His 500-acre plantation was in the heart of present-day Havelock. His prospects crushed by the war, the once well-to-do Chesnutt died insolvent in 1869. A Craven County court declared, "The personal estate of Owen Chesnutt is insufficient to pay his debts." It ordered the liquidation of the farm and its assets. It was duly sold at a courthouse auction in New Bern. The one bright spot in the story is that there was little appetite for plantation land so Chesnutt's son, Andrew Jackson Chesnutt, bought it back at the auction. James H. Hunter, a neighbor, and justice of the peace, later defended the sale testifying that A.J. had paid a fair price. [f]

The institution of slavery had to go, and by necessity so did the social, cultural, and financial constructs that derived from it and underpinned it. The morality of the cause, however, had no dampering effect upon the general dislocation necessary for its accomplishment.

The rending of the status quo drove off many of the familial names that had been woven into the fabric of southern Craven County since the dawn of the colonial era. The multi-generational Holland family was edged out of the plantation culture of Slocum Creek as were the Bells, the Hymans, and the Parsons. It was an ignominious end for people named Holton, Thorpe, Gibson, Wilson, Watson, Lovick, and Physioc. Of those who weren't gone at war's end, many soon would be.[g]

Scores of planters from Adams Creek, Clubfoot Creek, Kings Creek, and Hancock were either dead, impoverished … or headed to cities … or headed west. Families and individuals who decided to stay, or who had to stay, were economically downsized. Many of these faced the future for the first time as subsistence farmers.

Fending for Themselves

Left in the vacuum of deserted plantations were the suddenly-freed slaves. Hundreds of them. Former masters had been the source of their shelter, food, and clothing down to their shoes. And while aid flowed into

---

[f] Craven County wills, images 19, 21 & 30.

[g] Craven County census records, 1860-1880.

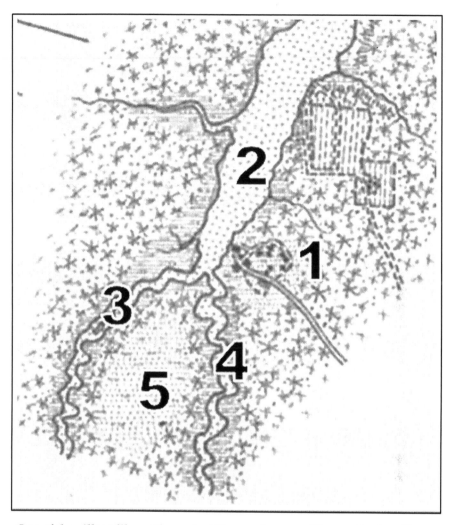

One of the village-like settlements of former slaves on Slocum Creek at Cherry Point is identified at the number 1 in a detail of a U.S. Coast & Geodetic Survey chart from 1878. It would become known as "Tar Neck." 2) The lower reaches of Slocum Creek. 3) The southwest prong of the creek. 4) The east prong of Slocum Creek, often called East Creek. 5) Location of Owen Chesnutt's plantation and today's Graham A. Barden Elementary School and Slocum military housing.

the South in the form of the Freedmen's Bureau, the American Missionary Association, and others, there were pockets of African Americans who suddenly had no alternative other than to make their own way. Most of the social largess was concentrated in populated places like New Bern. Those with access received basic necessities including food, clothes, medicine, and spiritual sustenance.

The embryonic settlement area south of the Trent River's junction with the Neuse, begun by missionary Vincent Collier, coalesced into an active and long-term community under the stewardship of its namesake Union chaplain Horace James. Shown as "Hayti" on some maps, James City grew into a picturesque settlement with a church and a school. One witness described James City as having the look of a Caribbean village.

Black folks in the hinterlands had to come up with different alternatives.

We know from the writings of Union soldiers that some of the slaves stayed close to their former plantations; some even continuing to live in what had been their quarters in slavery days. Some must have tended existing gardens and husbanded existing livestock of whatever kind might have been available. Those resources along with fishing and hunting would have at least kept starvation at bay.

Clusters of African American residences identifiable to the present day along US 70 and Highway 101 are the remnants of where freed people gathered in the immediate aftermath of the Civil War. The area around the forest service headquarters at Riverdale is one example.

Ultimately, three settlements were founded on former plantation lands between Hancock's Creek and Slocum's Creek. We'll speak in greater detail about these later in the book.

The Civil War Odyssey of Rev. Jacob Utley

Another man who lost a great deal to the war was Rev. Jacob Utley.

Rev. Utley owned much of what is modern west Havelock – from Slocum Creek to Slocum Road. Six hundred and fifteen acres in all; seventy-five acres cleared and the remainder in long-leaf "turpentine" pines.

On March 21, 1862, exactly one week after the fall of New Bern, a large force of blue-clad Northern soldiers was encamped on Reverend Utley's Havelock farm. A talented member of the Eighth Connecticut Volunteer Infantry

UTLEY

8⁰ Reg. C.V. Bivouac near Sloocombs Creek N.C. March 21ˢᵗ 1862.

Regiment, Cpl. Joseph Shadek, created this illustration of their camp at "Sloocombs Creek," as he spelled it. [h]

In this view, we are looking west with Slocum Creek at our backs. The A&NC railroad and the "main county road" are to the left. Today's course of US 70 would be off to the right. The Union forces lounging about with rifles stacked, and even playing in the background, were bivouacked on the Baptist minister's plantation on their way to Carteret County. The railroad tracks were torn up and the railroad bridge had burned at New Bern. General Burnside was using the Neuse River and Slocum Creek as his detour around the damage in moving men and materiel for the impending capture of Fort Macon.

The exact location of this field can be seen at Number 2 on the 1853 Marshall Plantation map in the previous chapter, "Rebel Spies." The big arrow above shows the 1862 home of Rev. Utley, age 57, his wife Aplis, 51, and the three slaves previously mentioned. Through a succession of owners

---

[h] Bridgeport History Center, Bridgeport (Connecticut) Public Library.

into modern times, the Utley property would remain an open farm field until the Wolf Creek subdivision, hotels, the Tourist and Events Center, and a U.S. Post Office were built immediately west of Slocum Creek well over one hundred years later.

Before the war, Rev. Utley had probably hired additional hands from other owners to work the turpentine plantation as needs dictated. In the county's 1860 agricultural census, he listed two horses, three milk cows, one ox, six other cattle, and eight hogs. The farm had produced twenty pounds of butter, five pounds of beeswax, and a hundred pounds of honey.

Beehives were known to have thrived on the property since the colonial era in a time it was the homeplace of the Rowe (Roe) family. The Rowes were multi-generational owners of the plantation, which they operated with enslaved labor on a scale much larger than Utley's.

Rev. Utley's corn harvest brought in one hundred and twenty-five bushels in 1860. They'd gathered twenty-five bushels of peas and beans, and four hundred bushels of sweet potatoes.

In addition to preaching, Rev. Utley had been active on the local school committee. He was a member of the St. John's Masonic Lodge in New Bern, having entered fellowship there in 1846.

At the approach of the Burnside Expedition, Rev. Utley and his wife abandoned their farm and sought refuge in Carteret County. He'd live out the war in Beaufort and Morehead City preaching on occasion and teaching school.

As stated previously, Union forces built a blockhouse fort, officers' quarters, and a substantial campground beside the railroad on the east side of Slocum Creek in 1862 keeping from fifty to 200 men there for the next two years. The fort at Havelock was one of a chain to protect the train tracks and trestles and, in its case, to secure the vital water link of Slocum Creek itself. The Northern troops occupied the site, as we have learned, until their fort was destroyed by Confederate raiders in 1864.

Another of the many outfits that moved up Slocum Creek, camping at Havelock on the way to the battle for Fort Macon, was the Fourth Rhode Island Infantry. One of its young officers – Capt. Levi Kent – described the movement in his journal and provides other telling details for this story.

March 23, 1862, Capt. Kent wrote, *"Our good Steamer left her anchorage* [at New Bern] *during the forenoon of the 20th steaming down the river as far as Slocoms Creek where we landed to commence our march ...*

"The Right Wing of the Regt. goes on board the Union; *the little stern-wheeler that has attended us so constantly, and preceded by the little Gun boat* Pickett *& followed by the Side wheel Steamer* Alice Price, *all small vessels, we commence, we steam away up [Slocum]Creek. After*

picking our tortuous winding for about two miles up the creek we made a landing. At the spot where we landed, the Creek was not of sufficient width to turn the Union *round in.*

"*After a successful landing and throwing out pickets, preparations were made for a comfortable bivouac. Capt. Brown was sent with his company to occupy the R.R. Depot about ¾ of a mile from us.*

"*We built bough huts to keep the rain off & tried to be comfortable.*

"*Before dark the* Union *worked herself out of the grass and returned to the River ... for the rest of the Regt.*

"*Was officer of the Day & made Grand Rounds at midnight and again at 3 A.M. Our Bush huts shed the rain finely. Fence rails were taken by the men and then covering their frames with Boughs the men got good comfortable quarters.*"

Split fence rails, as noted by Kent, were irresistible to soldiers. They made great posts, construction material, and easy firewood. And, in this case – at Slocum Creek – it was Rev. Utley's fence being consumed.

But it wasn't only fence rails that were missing at war's end.

Union soldiers stripping a rail fence for firewood. A pencil sketch by Alfred R. Waud, battlefield artist for *Harper's Weekly*, 1861-1865.

When Rev. and Mrs. Utley made it back to their Havelock plantation in 1865, their home and all of its outbuildings were gone. It wasn't that the structures had been damaged, or burned, or deteriorated for lack of maintenance.

No, they were indeed ... gone.

Absent.

Carted off.

Consumed.

Cannibalized ... for the construction of the big wooden fort, its officers' quarters, shelter for the men, and handy firewood for years of cooking and warmth. The once clear, fertile, productive fields were a jungle of head-high weeds, underbrush, and pine saplings. Strapped for cash after years of dislocation, there was no starting over.

Utley filed for relief from the Southern Claims Commission listing all the property and items the war had destroyed. In his claim number 13,333, Utley asked for compensation of $2,965. That's about $60,000 in current money. He was still trying to collect in 1874. There's no evidence that he was successful. His file in the Southern Claims Commission archives is empty.

So, he'd get no help from the government.

For Jacob Utley, salvation came in the form of a Connecticut minister named Bull.

The Curious Tale of Woodbridge

In the aftermath of the Civil War, a firebrand Northern pastor with the bearded countenance of an Old Testament prophet was sent to eastern North Carolina as a missionary to help the freedmen; to nurture the spiritual and educational well-being of former slaves.

For many years following his 1869 arrival, this minister and a series of dedicated missionary teachers labored to create a new town on the banks of Slocum Creek – on a former slave plantation – for the benefit of the "downtrodden" men, women, and children who had gained their freedom during the war.

As much as anything else, however, the records show that he sought to gain an advantage for himself.

In doing so, he became a man of business, of property, and a political power to be reckoned with.

He laid out a village on the main county road. There he built homes, a church, a school, a post office, a store, and a railroad stop.

This is the untold true story of a preacher from Connecticut who, for a time, made Havelock, N.C. disappear.

His name was Edward Bull.

He named his town Woodbridge.

The Yankee Preacher

"Please send check as I need more money…" —Edward Bull

Rev. Bull arrived on the Beaufort docks via steamship Tuesday, October 5, 1869, with his worldly goods packed neatly in wooden barrels. Barrels were sturdy, easily filled, and water-tight; ideal for loading and transporting aboard ships. All manner of things were packed in barrels: clothes, crackers, books, pickles, toys, tar, turpentine, or whiskey.

There would be no whiskey in Edward Bull's barrels. He was a temperance man, a confirmed man of the cloth, a missionary, a hearty Congregationalist minister, sent by Congregationalist ministers in New York City to do God's work among the recently-freed African slaves who made up more than one-third of the population of North Carolina. He was a white man, slight, but well-dressed, with a reedy voice and a bearded, Gothic face.

He came on a mission from the former abolitionists but harbored a grand vision of his own. He was seeking a main chance, opportunity, an increase. In the chaotic, rough, and tumble, impoverished postbellum South, he expected to find what he was looking for. The War Between the States had ended only four short years before and the minion of the vanquished Confederacy needed a man of vision, like him, he was sure.

Reverend Edward Bull.

While settling into the AMA's "neat and comfortable" home in Beaufort with the help of the black housekeeper, "Aunt Rachel, as they all call her," Bull took a look at the town. He met people. He talked softly. He listened. He traveled to little Morehead City the next day to pick up some of his barrels that had been delivered there. And he began to come to conclusions.

The political atmosphere was charged and turbulent. The competing interests he recognized, the very "busy-ness" of the place, did not fit with his vision. There were already powerful African American preachers with opposing churches and adamant coalitions of both races vying for control of the schools. A political structure had coalesced. Bull recognized the potential for further conflict and controversy. He would go forth, he decided, and as soon as possible, into a situation with fewer constraints, less contention, and more potential; to a place where a man could more freely mold his destiny. But, for now, he had duties to attend.

He set to work immediately doing an inventory of the textbooks at the American Missionary Association's—his association's—Beaufort school. He found them wanting. There were too many varieties of books and not enough of any one of them to do any good for the scholars. He wrote a detailed letter to "The Rooms," as the New York City offices of the American Missionary Association (AMA) were known among its preachers and teachers in the field.

Mail moved as fast in 1869 as it does today, sometimes faster, taking only three or four days for a letter to go from Beaufort to New York; a week or less for the round trip. The missionaries, scattered across the South like seeds sewn upon a fertile field, wrote often and about all manner of things and received immediate guidance from the great men doing the sowing.

The great men, Rev. E.M. Cravath, Rev. George Whipple, Rev. G.D. Pike, Rev. E.P. Smith, and those towering giants, Rev. Simeon S. Jocelyn, and Lewis Tappan, had grown their organization from a tiny band of idealists who fought to save the black men charged with mutiny after a revolt on a slave ship called the *Amistad* into a mighty union of saints. They claimed credit for opening the first freedmen's school in the South. Now they had scores of stations in dozens of states and the momentum to go worldwide spreading the Christian gospel.

The AMA's first freedmen's school opened in New Bern in July 1863. Before the year was done, it had scholars under instruction on Roanoke Island, in Morehead City, and Beaufort. From the start, Beaufort's Whipple School—named for Rev. Whipple, the AMA's corresponding secretary—was the eye of a squall swirling around the missionary-teachers and citizens of the town, both black and white.

In this tempest, Bull had taken his post.

"I do not find [the books] as suitable as I had hoped," Bull confidently informed The Rooms. "There are a great number that are only one of a kind. I find 23 Music Books all different, 16 Hymn Books, ditto. 38 Sabbath School question books, only four of a kind, 3 of another, et cetera. 35 different Readers generally only one of a kind."

He listed "19 Geographies, 38 Arithmetics, 20 Grammars, and 15 Spellers, nearly all different."

On and on he went for nearly three handwritten pages talking about the books at hand, his "preferences" personally and in the classroom, books suitable for "ordinary pupils" and the ones most useful to the teachers he had been sent to oversee as the new Beaufort minister and "head of station."

"...I am sure the prosperity of the school depends in a great degree upon a uniformity of the text books; by this means the scholars may be classified as to receive the fullest benefit of the teachers' labors."

Then, at the end of the dissertation, he added a line, the theme of which would become familiar over the coming months and years:

"Please send check as I shall need more money before the month closes."

Reverend Bull was a Yankee. Born in Saybrook, Connecticut on June 21, 1830, he was 39 upon his arrival in coastal Carolina. His first known letter to the AMA was written a year before from his home in Westbrook, Connecticut where he was already ministering to the members of a Congregationalist church. In it, he asked for a subscription to an AMA publication.

"We should like the paper if *free*, but do not care to pay for it," he wrote.

While many of the missionaries were single, Bull brought with him his second wife, Jane Susan Pratt Bull, 33, their two sons, Edward, Jr., age nine, and Fred W., age six. His oldest child, Hattie, 12, the daughter from his first marriage, would join them later. Hattie, whose full name was Harriet Beecher Bull, was named for Harriet Beecher Stowe, the ardent abolitionist, and author of the famous attack on the cruelty of slavery, *Uncle Tom's Cabin*.

The Reverend Edward Bull

N.C. Division of Archives & History

Edward Bull married Jane in 1859, four days following the death of his first wife, Mary. Hattie was two.

Research has yielded significant information about Reverend Bull. Of all the material, his letters, preserved at the Amistad Research Center, Tulane University in New Orleans, speak the loudest, especially when compared with the letters of hundreds of the other AMA missionaries. The entire fight against slavery had been altruistic, idealistic, and emotional. The Northern missionaries who volunteered to strike out into the Old South were true believers in the righteous championing of the poor and the "downtrodden," as they repeatedly called them. They were devoted to the divine and were not shy about it. Nearly every AMA missionary letter will lapse at some point into a discussion of faith. The letters to the AMA were supposed to be station reports. They listed numbers of students, the progress of the schools, numbers in church. But invariably the writer would comment about God, the Holy Spirit, or blessings being harvested out on the mission field.

"I hope God will bless our efforts…"

"May the good Lord help you in all your work…"

"Pray for us brother…"

"God has blessed us in all we have undertaken and we will give Him all the praise and glory."

"So, we trust God and take courage."

"The Lord's spirit has been in our midst ever since the Week of Prayer."

"Pray for us that the good work may go on."

"Let us live the Christian Life in all its abundance."

"We may have all things by God's blessings." [a]

---

[a] AMA mission reports, Amistad Research Center, Tulane University.

Sometimes the letters become outpourings of Christian faith tantamount to sermons. Some of the writers go on for pages caught up in the ecstasy of their spiritual experience. Sometimes they convey little factual information about the goings-on at the station but spend ink and paper on joyous flights in the realm of religion.

Bull never bothered with any of that. In fact, in his first eight dozen correspondences to the AMA, he penned the word "God" exactly one time and never made another religious reference of any kind. Repeatedly, monthly, sometimes weekly—one time twice on the same day—he wrote about something else.

"I am nearly out of funds."

"I am exceedingly hard-pressed for money."

"My finances are exceedingly low."

"As my family is *large* and my salary is *small*, I do not feel able to bear any part of the expense."

"I am without funds. Please send $100."

"Will you please send me $150?"

"I am *suffering* from want of *funds*."

"I am very much in need of funds."

"We are pretty short."

Reverend Edward Bull wrote about money.

They Must Have Land

Though money and his want of it was a constant theme in his letters, Bull also wrote about land. Bull had been sent as a missionary and one of the opportunities for missionaries was the establishment of settlements for the freedmen. On such settlements, on reasonable terms, the AMA wished to help the poor former slaves become owners of small homesteads with farming tracts on which they could learn to subsist on their own.

The AMA's idea was encapsulated in one of their publications, *The American Missionary*, by a writer in December 1868.

"The larger portion of the people are comfortable, but the poor among the Freedmen are poor indeed.

"Every year strengthens the conviction that the poorer portion of the people must be helped to land, or they will long be dependent. Hundreds of families are large, too large to be supported by one pair of hands. On land, every child above four years old is able to contribute, in various ways, to the support of the family.

"Four-fifths of North Carolina is howling wilderness. Lands, good lands, can be purchased at government prices, or a little above it. Even

Rev. Gustavus D. Pike

the poorest land, devoted to the raising of peanuts and sweet potatoes, becomes profitable."

Rev. Bull soon began to correspond with The Rooms about creating a freedmen's settlement in the country away from the perceived hustle and bustle of Beaufort. He looked at land in Newport and other places. The more he thought about the idea, the greater the possibilities grew in his mind.

He wouldn't simply create a farm community for the ex-slaves. He'd build a city. Two months after arriving in Beaufort, he wrote to Rev. Gustavus Pike, the New York minister acting as the AMA's land agent.

Beaufort, N.C. Dec. 11, 1869

Dear Bro. Pike

I am at length able to report something definite on the land acquisition... I have been offered a tract of land by Rev. Jacob Utley—a Baptist preacher here. It is situated about halfway between Morehead City and Newbern—19 m from Morehead—16 m from Newbern. It lies on both sides of the Rail Road, more than half being on the east side. The County Road from Newbern to Morehead also passes through it, on the west side of the R.R. The aspect of the land is very pleasant and beautiful. The soil is variable, in some parts equal to the best and good every where. The subsoil is clay, and in some places suitable for making brick. There is a good growth of timber—pine, gum, oak, hickory, poplar, cypress &c. The pine is mostly long-leaved suitable for R.R. ties, post &c. There is a considerable amount of cypress which is specially valuable.

The title I believe is perfect. An old estate was divided between two heirs. One of them sold his part—this tract—to the other person; that person sold to Mr. Utley the present proprietor.

The tract contains 681 acres. Before the war, Mr. Utley cleared and improved about 75 acres. He left it in 1861 to live at Morehead City. At that time he was offered $4,500 for it. During the war, his house was torn down, and all his fences burned up. Since then the fields he cultivated have grown over with pine now 15 to 20 feet high. He has become involved in debt and forced to lay a mortgage on it for $600.

He offered to sell the property for $2,500. He wants $1000 down, and the balance in one, two, and three years. I think the price is very reasonable, and the terms are certainly easy.

I believe this is an important place for us to occupy. It's situated on both sides of the R.R. and County Road, and nearly equidistant from Newbern and Morehead, is especially favorable for its prosperity and growth, if you should establish a Station here. And the necessity for occupying it is apparent from the fact—if I am correctly informed—that there is no school nearer than Newbern, and no preaching nearer, except as some colored preacher "holds forth" occasionally at one or more of the houses. The families around there desire very much to have someone to instruct them and care for them. I believe if the Association should purchase the property that enough good, faithful men could be found to settle it at once, and if wisely managed a thriving town could be built up there in a few years to the great advantage of the colored people.

So fully am I impressed with this idea that I would be willing to go there and commence the work, and grow up with it. More than this: if the Association wishes, I will buy $500 worth of the land, so as to make up the first payment –as you have told me that you have just $500 to invest in land. This would be 136 acres that I would take at the south part, on the east side of the R.R. which is a pleasant location and good though not the best land. *I could take my deed from Mr. Utley.*

I would recommend very strongly the purchase of this land. I have not seen so favorable an opportunity since I came south.

If we buy, there are many things which I wish to say in due time about it. Enough for now.

Let me hear from you as soon as you can.
Yours very truly,
Edw. Bull

On January 6, 1870, Bull wrote again to Rev. Pike in New York saying that he had "conversed with several leading men here both white and colored in reference to the whole plan and they heartily approve it."

Bull said the title for the Utley property had been examined by the post collectors of both Beaufort and New Bern – A.C. Davis and Orlando Hubbs respectively – and an attorney Robert F. Lehman, a native Pennsylvanian practicing law in New Bern.

Bull said, "The property can be traced for a long period of years since Thomas Rowe gave it by will to his sons. I have the utmost confidence in the validity of the title. Mr. Davis says *"it is the clearest title in North Carolina."* The papers will all be transferred to me when the business is complete, and forwarded to you in due time."

The survey Bull had completed showed 615 acres and he sent a plan with his letter on how the community might be designed.

He wrote," I wish you would give me permission to lay out the tract as indicated on the plan: that is, as squares of 10 acres each four together..., The roads by this plan will embrace 15¾ acres. I think there is wood and timber enough on them—which can be cut off by the people, furnishing them with employment so that they can secure money, and sold on the behalf of the Association, to more than pay for the cost of the land."

In post-war southern Craven County, land was selling for as little as one dollar per acre. Bull's deal with Rev. Utley was for a top-of-the-market price of three dollars per acre, or $1,845. Bull proposed to raise it even further; selling land to the potential settlers for six dollars per acre. Even at the high price, he assured Rev. Pike that he would "settle 25 or more families, comprising 100 to 150 persons, in two or three weeks."

He wrote, "I have made no effort to get men because it did not seem best to do so until we owned the land, but I have had as many as twenty applications which are under consideration. *They* think if they can begin now, they can get up a place to live and clear and fence and plant several acres this spring."

Rev. Bull said he would "locate" there and "devote myself to their interests, secular and intellectual and spiritual."

He wrote, "I have told them they must expect to work hard and live close for a year or two, but [*at*] the end of five years, when we expect the land will be all paid for, one can have a sober, progressive, and somewhat intelligent community."

Though Bull intended to charge his "somewhat intelligent community" more than double the going rate for their land, at least the terms seemed reasonable. It was a "no money down" deal for the settlers. Each would be required to pay one-fifth within three years, two-fifths within four years, and the remaining balance by the end of the fifth years of their contract.

Bull was taking about a quarter of the land – 167 acres – for himself. It was the acreage he had called "specially valuable" in his December 11 letter due to the amount of cypress that could be cut and sold from it. The tract he identified for himself also had the navigable creek frontage, was closest to the railroad stop, and adjacent to what Bull was proposing as the future center of town.

He said of his acreage, "It embraces all lying southerly of a line crossing the Rail Road at right angles 100 rods from the Wolf Pit culvert, except 10 acres marked *A.M.A.* which I hope you will reserve for a public square to contain school house, chapel, *Town Hall* &c. It is one of the highest and most eligible situations in the whole tract, and is really beautiful."

In addition to what Bull's plan reserved for himself and the AMA's town square, there were 51 ten-acre tracts for settlement by the freed people.

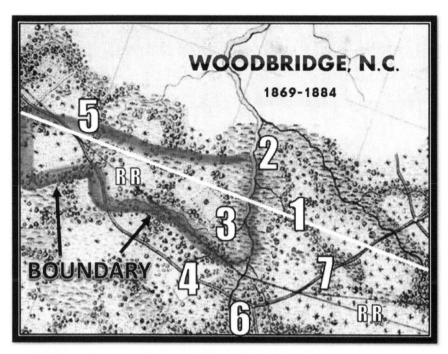

WOODBRIDGE – In 1869, the American Missionary Association purchased the 615-acre former slave plantation of Rev. Jacob Utley as a place of settlement for recently-freed slaves of southern Craven County. The plantation covered most of modern west Havelock from Slocum Creek to Slocum Road. Above, the dark gray outlined boundary of Woodbridge is indicated with black arrows. Today's route of US 70 is the white line marked with the numeral 1. The southwest prong of Slocum Creek is beside the number 2. Number 3 is the current location of the Havelock Tourist and Events Center. Numbers 4 and 7 indicate the old route of the road from New Bern to Beaufort but today 4 is Greenfield Heights Blvd. and 7 is Miller Blvd. Lake Road is just to the right of the number 6. Number 5 is the approximate location of today's Catawba Road, which in 2021 ran between the Westbrook Shopping Center and Walmart. The course of the A.&N.C. Railroad is the same today as it was in 1869 and is indicated with the letters RR. Today, among other things, all of the Wolf Creek and Don-Lee Heights subdivisions are within the old Woodbridge boundary.   Map by the author.

Bull assured Rev. Pike that getting the land sold to settlers would be no problem. The kindest thing to say about most of his claims is that he was overly optimistic.

Oh. And he wanted to name the place after his wife.

He closed with Rev. Pike saying, "One thing more. As everything must have a name and one must have a R.R. Station and P.O. to be called *something*—let me suggest that it be called *Janesville*. Is your wife named Jane? Perhaps not—mine is. Please advise." [a]

Slow Progress at "Janesville"

The American Missionary Association was founded in 1846 as an interdenominational missionary society devoted to abolitionist principles. In 1865, at the end of the Civil War, however, it became the official agency of the Congregationalist churches with the primary mission of providing educational resources to the Southern freedmen. A close second focus was the establishment of Congregationalist churches and gaining Congregationalist church members.

Different in tradition and practice from many churches of the South, Congregationalists traced their roots to the Puritans of New England. It was a Protestant, primarily Northern-based church. Scholars say Congregationalism resides in a theological position between Presbyterianism on one end of the scale and the Baptists and Quakers on the other end.

In the best of circumstances, the dry, formal Congregational church services were going to be a hard sell for Southern blacks used to emotional outpourings of the spirit including shouting, clapping, dancing, and energetic singing.

But ahead of the church and ahead of the school was the land.

Rev. Bull's goal of 25 or more families on the land in two to three weeks came to naught. His letter of mid-February was excuse-laden. Rainfall had held up his laying out of the land. He promised a new and better map would be supplied to the New York "Rooms" soon. He wrote, "Everything in regards to our colony looks favorable but as the matter was so long pending, and it has become so late in the season, that I shall not be able to settle as many persons on the tract this Spring as I had hoped."

Later in the month, he'd made scant progress but named the first three settlers to have begun their paperwork for the land: Moses Brooks, Collison Bryan, and Nelson Lovick. Lovick took Tract No. 3, 10 acres, for $60.

Seven months later on September 20, 1870, Rev. Bull wrote to New York, "Dear Sirs, I send below the names of persons who have recently taken up land at 'Janesville.' Please make out the papers and forward when convenient."

He listed the new handful of settlers, their lot numbers, and acreages:

Joseph Williams, No. 28, 10 acres.

---

[a] Amistad Research Center, Tulane University, American Missionary Association Archives # 102737.

Samuel Hogan, No. 24, 10 acres.
Robert Hogan, No. 25, 10 acres.
Amos Bryan, No. 9, 10 acres.
Kenyon Phillips, No. 16, 10 acres.
William Anderson, No. 21, 10 acres.
Once again, he promised to send a map of the settlement.[b]

Trouble at Woodbridge

It turned out there was already a place called Janesville. There was no other discussion of the name change, but a letter dated January 8, 1872, arrived in New York from Edward Bull addressed to AMA Field Secretary Rev. E.M. Cravath. It was return-addressed from "A.&N.C. R.R., Woodbridge, N.C." [c]

In it, Bull announced his closure of the "Free Public School" at the AMA station he had been running for black children in concert with Craven County. Bull wrote in the September 1872 *American Missionary* newsletter that he had "commenced with eight students, all barefooted and ragged, with only three books between them, and those out-of-date and worn out." He reported the school had grown to seventy-six pupils" and that, thanks to donations from the North, "the people have been generally well-clad."

As of the date of the letter, however, he had switched to a tuition school for which he would charge "10 cents a week per head ... though some will not be able to pay it." He said the night school, primarily for adult freedmen, had been stopped "to allow the people to gather their corn, which is five miles off, up at the "Lake." James A. Bryan's Ellis Lake Plantation was where many farmers, both black and white, rented land. But why anyone would be gathering corn at night in January, he did not say. He also asked for permission to move an organ from Beaufort to Woodbridge so that his daughter, "Hattie," could play it during Sabbath church services.

It's a small miracle that there are so many surviving letters from Woodbridge. Still, the record is not complete. There are gaps, like most of 1871, and we have only one side of the conversation. The letters from The Rooms are not known to exist in any archive. Only the letters from the ministers and teachers were saved by the AMA, not copies of the letters going out to them.

Thus, we do not know except by inference what sort of criticism the leaders of the AMA communicated to Rev. Bull about his conduct and

---

[b] AMA # 102773 February 16, 1870; 102744, February 23, 1870; 102858; September 20, 1870.

[c] AMA 102945, January 8, 1872.

performance at Woodbridge. For months, he had over-promised and under-delivered. His work as "head of station" at Beaufort had been lackluster. His station and school reports weren't coming monthly as required. It was clear by now to the leadership in New York that the Woodbridge experiment was not panning out as Bull, their on-scene agent, had promoted it.

A hot series of letters exchanged during 1872 marked the beginning of a downward spiral in the relationship between Rev. Bull and the AMA. From Bull's defensive responses, the letters from the New York leadership appear to allege numerous complaints and shortcomings, some bordering on charges of misconduct by the minister.

- That he was neglecting his duties at the Woodbridge station – resulting in poor attendance at the church and school – because he was busily engaging in personal enterprises.
- That he was failing to get settlers to take up land as he had promised.
- That he used freedman labor to cut timber and manufacture hundreds of railroad crossties and then sold them to the railroad.
- That he used freedman labor to cut hundreds of cords of wood to create a "wood station, the only one between New Bern and Beaufort" at the Woodbridge's twice-daily rail stop where he sold it as fuel for the A&NC Railroad's steam trains.
- That he had opened a store on AMA property, run largely by his sons, to sell groceries, provisions, and medicine to the Woodbridge settlers.
- That he had become deeply indebted to a grocery dealer named Bell and had failed to pay his bills so long that Mr. Bell had complained to and sought payment from the AMA in New York.
- That he had removed from the Beaufort Congregational Church a communion set that had been donated to it.
- That he had complained in writing to an important AMA donor – a particularly supportive patron of Rev. Bull named Mary Thomas - that he was being badly abused financially by the AMA resulting in her challenging the leadership in New York over the matter of money Bull claimed was due him.

The Rooms may have been displeased as well by the switcheroo Bull appears to have engineered concerning the 167-acre tract of Woodbridge land he reserved for himself. It was hard to fathom how a man so seemingly strapped for cash could offer to contribute $500 to the Woodbridge project. He had done just that to persuade the New York men to move forward. But eighteen months later, he convinced the AMA, somehow. to advance to him

Erastus M. Cravath, D.D.

Secretary George Whipple, D.D.

LEADERS OF THE AMA – Some of the principal men behind the American Missionary Association and its New York City-based operations were Rev. E.M. Cravath, Rev. George Whipple, and Rev. M.E. Strieby. Doctors of Divinity and abolitionists all, they pushed for war, if necessary, to end slavery, and after the war sent preachers and teachers into the former Confederacy to minister to the newly-freed slaves. The AMA established stations like Woodbridge throughout the South with varying degrees of success. Many letters penned by Rev. Edward Bull were addressed to these stern, white, Christian leaders who oversaw and, at times, were exasperated by the conduct of his mission in southern Craven County.

Secretary M.E. Strieby, D.D.

the entire purchase price of the land against a note he gave them. While maintaining possession of the whole tract, and being allowed to live and to farm upon it, Bull was required to pay only interest of his note. [d]

Except for one letter and a few school reports, all of Bull's 1871 correspondence is missing from the AMA records, so we have no way to discern the circumstances under which the new deal was struck. Although Bull would make periodic interest payments, existing records indicate the AMA never got its money back.

Nevertheless, of all the charges and complaints against Rev. Bull, one that seemed to have rankled the leadership, in particular, was that his Woodbridge store was selling snuff and tobacco. The AMA had a built-in temperance organization called the Band of Hope that included adults but was aimed primarily at youth. One of the Band of Hope's prime activities was a ceremonial pledge by the members to abstain from alcohol, tobacco, and profanity. A Band of Hope had been organized at Woodbridge – and here was one of the AMA's ministers selling tobacco to the people at one of its stations.

Bull's response about the tobacco issue was characteristic of the way he responded to all of the concerns raised by the men at The Rooms. He made excuses. He alternately blustered and made light of the issues. He lectured. He made himself out to be the offended party. And he criticized the settlers themselves.

Of his store, he said it was "for the accommodation of the people and to give a little more character and importance to the place." He claimed to the AMA that there was no place closer than New Bern to get supplies when Havelock was less than one mile away. This points up the curious fact that Bull never wrote the word *Havelock* a single time in his years of letters and once claimed that there was no town nearby.

Of tobacco, he said, "a store here at the South without tobacco would be like the play of Hamlet with the part of Hamlet left out."

Bull lectured the leaders, *"The prevailing and damning sins of the South are fornication and adultery, lying and stealing, Sabbath-breaking and profanity. These I wish to combat always and everywhere but the using of tobacco is not in itself a sin to be classed with these, and it is not well to advance it to such a place. It is well-known that I do not approve of the use of tobacco. I tell them frequently that I had rather forgo any profit that I may derive from it than to sell it. And I often tried to persuade them to buy meal or meat instead. And the children especially I [try] to dissuade from the using of a filthy, useless, and expensive habit. To do more than this, to refuse to sell it, among other articles of traffic, would be thought 'straining*

---

[d] Craven County deed book 72, pg. 243, June 10, 1871.

at a gnat' and 'exalting myself above measure,' and so neutralize my influence, and tend to defeat the object in view. This is my position upon the tobacco question. You may not accept my logic, but you will at least understand me."

Of the Beaufort Congregational Church's communion services, he wrote, "not trusting it to the servants – When we came here, I took it with us for safekeeping."

His explanation and excuses regarding his overdue grocery bill went on for several pages. Bull said that he had a great deal of expense for the construction of his new home at Woodbridge and that he thought he "might as well owe my grocer as my carpenter." He seemed to imply that his grocery bill had been run up by the Beaufort housekeeper, saying he "thought the bill was much larger than I supposed having been left with *Aunt Rachel* too much during my absence." He underlined the housekeeper's name.

He said that he had expected to be able to pay all his bills with the proceeds from the railroad crossties that were being cut. But speaking of the settler who had been working for him in the woods, he said, "I have *been outrageously cheated.*" He underlined that as well.

He said he had advanced the worker's rations enough for him to have produced 625 crossties but only found 276 to be on hand. This, along with the failure of Craven County to pay him his teaching salary, had left him with no ability to pay the grocer.

He wrote, "You know that I have $42 very unwillingly invested in the School Building – I have been a good deal straitened and troubled, but I hope the worst of it is over. I have a good degree of energy, and am working regularly eighteen hours a day, from 5 to 11, to get right, studying and writing morning and night – Keeping school from 9 to 1, and overseeing my work, and attending to the interests of the Station the balance of the time."

Rev. Bull deflected the leadership's questions about the settlement of Woodbridge. He wrote, "As to the land, I shall have to defer this to another time as this letter is already too long. I will only say that everything seems to be moving prosperously, but slowly. The 26th is the anniversary of the purchase and I intend soon after that time to 'take the census' and make up a full report. The papers need a thorough revision. Some have died, some have abandoned the land, and there are many new settlers this winter, whose papers are to be written."

And once again he promised, "I will send you a *map*, if I can find time to make a sufficiently nice one." [e]

Bull wrote to Rev. Cravath on February 1. He reported that the number of pupils in the school had been "very much reduced." He blamed the light

[e] AMA # 102953-102955, January 15, 1872.

attendance both on his new tuition charge and on the "circumstance that we have no stove." He said the recent cold had been "very severe for both teacher and pupils." He had, therefore, closed the night school altogether.

He wrote, "I would have bought a stove if I had had funds, but could not do it."

He complained that he hadn't received a response to his recent "long letter." Two days later, New York fired another shot.

It took Bull until March 1 to respond. "In your letter of February 3, *you do me great injustice* by intimating that the falling off in the school and the lack of interest in the preaching services is largely due to the fact that my 'best thoughts and strengths are given to private business.' I give my constant earnest personal attention to the educational and religious work of the station. My farm is mostly let out and on the few acres which I cultivate, I have nearly all the work done, simply directing it."

He continued, "The *store* is a small affair the very much needed for no article however simple or much-needed can be obtained near the New Bern, 15 miles off. It occupies little of my time or attention being *waited upon chiefly by my boys*. It is a great convenience to the people and important to the prosperity of the Station and I thought you would be glad to have me afford them such a privilege, but if otherwise, and you desire, I will close it altogether."

The disconnection between Rev. Bull's thinking and that of the leadership is distilled to its essence in a remarkable passage in which he told them that, instead of being censured, they should commend him on how hard he was working.

He closed, "Please send check for salary for February – *$50*." And then he suggested that the AMA "advance the amount of $150" from his next month's salary to pay his grocer's bill.[f]

Executive Action

It took them another year to get around to it, but the AMA fired Edward Bull.

His irregular 1872-1873 reports showed no growth in the First Congregational Church of Woodbridge where he was the preacher or at the Woodbridge School where he was the teacher, and but little change within the community. But there had been dozens of letters from Bull to the New York headquarters. These range in tone from optimistic and appeasing to defensive and belligerent.

---

[f] AMA # 102990, March 1, 1872.

He complained, made excuses, and asked for money but he also began to criticize the people he has been sent to support.

Of the school children, he said they "all are so ignorant."

Of the church members, he said they had been at first enthusiastic but that "after the season of special interest passed away, and the people fell back into their usual mode, I cannot say I saw in them many qualities that would make them eligible for church membership. They certainly are not exemplary Christians, and I do not believe the cause of religion, or of 'Congregationalism at the South,' would be subserved by receiving any more of the same sort."[g]

About continuing to spend money and labor on the Woodbridge settlers, he wrote, "I don't know that they are worth it. They are certainly the poorest people I ever saw, and I reckon about as ungrateful as other colored people, and how they are to keep from starving and freezing this winter, I hardly know. But I do not feel responsible for the *situation* ... they do not appreciate my labors nor the [association's] and are so gross and indifferent that it is exceedingly trying, and discouraging to labor for them."

The AMA concluded, however, "that the fault is more in the missionary than in the people." [h]

In August 1873, Rev. Cravath asked W.A.L. Campbell of the AMA station at Dudley – on the railroad line near Goldsboro – to visit Woodbridge and make a report. He wrote Cravath that after talking to, praying with, and preaching to the people, "I see no reason why a church cannot be gathered here."

He reported, "At present, there is a good Church building and that is about all. The members can be counted on the ends of my fingers who are regular attendants. Religious interest seems to be at a low ebb."

Campbell said the people "attribute this to the coldness of the Reverend Bull's preaching, two of them told me he had no strength of voice, i.e., no volume. They think a great deal of him as a citizen but not as a preacher. This I attribute to the very different way he preaches, to that which they have been accustomed, under the illiterate preachers of Methodist and Baptist denominations."

Of the settlers, he said, "They are very poor. They struggle for subsistence among the pines ... gathering the liquid goo of these trees, called turpentine, which they sell to the spirits distillers."[i]

---

[g] AMA # 103055, June 10, 1872; 103113, November 6, 1872.

[h] AMA # 103131-103133, December 1, 1872.

[i] AMA # 103326, August 30, 1873.

There's an ironic management joke that goes, "Firings will continue until morale improves." Bull's firing quickly adjusted his attitude.

Remember the map of the Woodbridge settlement he'd been promising for years? Well, he sent it in. His letters became more detailed and much more conciliatory. He suddenly got very busy updating land contract paperwork and even offered to become the AMA's land agent.

He delivered a list of the new settlers he had long promised:

Nelson Lovick, 10 acres

Perine Brooks, 10 acres

Eli Barrows, 20 acres

Aaron Hammond, 8.5 acres

Collison Bryan, 18 acres

James Chase, 10 acres

Larkins Manning, 14.5 acres

William Anderson, 10 acres

Joseph Williams, 20 acres

and Hogans Canada, eight acres.

He noted the Perine (Perrine) Brooks' land had originally been under contract to her husband, Moses Brooks. He "commenced building a house but before it was quite completed, he died." The neighbors finished the house for the widow Perine, who had been living there with "two or three children and an old Auntie." Perine had now married Hogans Canada and Canada wished to purchase the Brooks tract "if he can have a little more time to pay for it." [j]

Bull reported that twelve houses had been started or completed. He continued, of course, to live at Woodbridge and sent report after report about all manner of things. He offered suggestions. He offered to circulate among the churches. preaching wherever they needed him, though he said he couldn't take a reduction from his normal pay if he was to do so.

In one 1873 letter, he was able to proudly announce "I have just secured the establishment of a Post Office." As of April 21, he was the postmaster of Woodbridge, N.C. Bull soon delegated mail duties to one of the settlers, Joseph Williams. [k]

But in another letter in late 1873, he all but begged the New York leadership for work.

The leaders in New York ignored his solicitations. They informed Bull that a new schoolteacher named Alicia Blood was being sent to

---

[j] AMA # 103157, Jan. 1, 1873.

[k] AMA # 103258, May 13, 1873; AMA # 103355, September 30, 1873.

Woodbridge. Never one to miss an opportunity, he responded by offering to rent her a room.

Some Town of Woodbridge Settlers

The names of most of the freedman families who settled at Woodbridge are known through AMA records and Craven County deeds. Some named above also appear below with additional information. Others not previously listed above come from deeds and other records.

▶ Collison (Coleson) Bryant is in the 1870 Township 6 census as a 37-year-old farm laborer. Two children, John. H., 9, and Laura, 7, are in his home. In the 1880 agricultural census, he was on 17 acres, with five tilled and 12 in turpentine pines. He listed his farm's value at $150. He listed five dollars' worth of implements and machinery. Livestock worth $50 included an ox, two milk cows, six hogs, and ten chickens. He grew four acres of potatoes (50 bushels), four acres of cotton (two bales), and two acres of sweet potatoes (150 bushels).

▶ Perine – also found as Perrine and Pareny – Canada, the widow of Moses Brooks mentioned above, was listed with him in the census of 1870. Moses was 50 and Perrine was 35. Also in the home were Harriett, 16, Venturi, 16, Alis, 8, Elijah, 3, and Phebie, age one. After the death of Moses, she married a Woodbridge neighbor, Hogans Canada.

The Canada name is styled in various ways including Canady and Kannady. All her children took the Canada name. By the time of the 1880 U.S. census, Hogans Canada is dead. Perrine's additional children were Rachel, born 1862; Moses, born 1872; and Mary Jane, born 1875.

In the agricultural census of 1880, Perrine's Woodbridge farm totals 20 acres. She valued her land and buildings at $150. She has two milk cows, six hogs, six chickens and killed one cow that year for meat. She produced 15 bushels of corn on two acres and one bale of cotton on three acres.

▶ Aaron Hammond, like all the other Woodbridge settlers, was a former slave but from Grantsboro in Pamlico County. He was 30 in 1870. "Keeping house" was Betty, 40. In the home were Holland, 20; Frederick, 14; Albert, 11; Elizabeth 9; and Walter, 7.

▶ Nelson Lovick, 30, and Chuna Salone, 21, had a month-old baby, Thomas, in 1870. On ten acres in the Town of Woodbridge in 1880, they had a cow, two hogs, and five chickens. Rev. Bull married Nelson and Chuna in 1876.

▶ Joseph W. Williams was 35 in 1880. He had married Sena Williams who was 33 and keeping house. Their children were Henry, 15; Jenny, 13; Elizabeth, 8; Cherry (?) 3; Joseph, 4; and William, 2.

T H E
AMERICAN MISSIONARY ASSOCIATION

Has also under its care in the South,

3d. CHURCHES AT

VIRGINIA — Hampton.
NORTH CAROLINA — Beaufort,
    Woodbridge,
    Allemance,
    Dudley,
    Wilmington.
SOUTH CAROLINA — Charleston.
GEORGIA — Savannah,
    Ogeechee,
    Macon,
    Atlanta,
    Andersonville.
KENTUCKY — Berea,
    Bethesda,
    Walnut Chapel,
    Ariel.
TENNESSEE — Nashville,
    McMinneville,
    Chattanooga,
    Memphis.
ALABAMA — Talladega,
    Selma,
    Marion,
    Athens,
    Montgomery.

LOUISIANA — New Orleans,
    Greenville,
    Central,
    Zion,
    Howard,
    Jefferson City,
    Morris Brown,
    Lockport,
    Fance Point,
    Isle Piquant,
    New Iberia,
    Le Pigneur,
    Terrebonne,
    Gretna,
    Algiers.
MISSISSIPPI — Hamilton,
    Tougaloo.
MISSOURI — Westport,
    Lebanon.
KANSAS — Leavenworth,
    Lawrence,
    Topeka.
TEXAS —
    Corpus Christi,
    Brownsville.

SUMMARY.

Churches, ... 48
Chartered Institutions, ... 7
Graded and Normal Schools, ... 19
Common Schools, ... 63
Number of Pupils enrolled, 1871–72, ... 15,156
Students in Theology, ... 34
   " " College Course, ... 46
   " " College Preparatory, ... 154
   " " Normal Course, ... 219

E. M. CRAVATH, *Field Secretary,*
59 READE STREET, NEW YORK.

List of AMA stations in 1873 from the book *The Jubilee Singers* by Rev. G.D. Pike.

Active in Reconstruction politics, Williams became the first African American clerk of Township Six in 1871.

In 1880, they had seven acres tilled and 13 in turpentine woods. Joseph had a horse, 4 milk cows, 10 hogs, and 15 chickens. He produced a hundred bushels of corn on six acres but lost all the cotton planted on another eight.

He produced ten cords of wood. Wood was selling at a dollar a cord. After the establishment of the Woodbridge post office by Rev. Edward Bull, Williams assisted him and later served as its second and final postmaster beginning July 23, 1878. Born into slavery in 1845, Williams, nonetheless, had learned to read and write.

▶ In 1878, Tener (Fenner) Hammond contracted with the AMA for 8.5 acres of land in the Town of Woodbridge for $34.

▶ In January 1881, James Anderson agreed to pay $20 for five acres in the Town of Woodbridge.

▶ At the same time, Alsander Wallace took 12 acres for $48.

▶ In 1881, Mahala Dixon contracted with the AMA for ten acres in the Town of Woodbridge land at four dollars per acre.

▶ In 1881, Isaac Baatts (Batts) signed papers for 10 acres for $40.

▶ The Cully (Culley) family included Adam, 50, a farmer and mechanic; Eliza, 40, his wife, "keeping house"; and Octavious, 10. The family would grow.

Adam Cully became involved in Reconstruction Republican politics and, six years out of slavery, he was elected party chairman of Township Six in 1871. In the same year, he was made a justice of the peace.

In 1887, Eliza Ann Cully bought and paid for 17 AMA acres east of the railroad tracks and at the end of present-day Manila Street in Havelock. She paid $68 for the land. The family through several generations would own it into the modern era.

Craven County GIS maps still list the source as "Missionary Lands." The Cullys were one of the few families to pay for and hang onto their small AMA-Woodbridge farms.

Miss Blood's Bell

"Bells were part of the American tradition. Cast in iron, bronze, copper, and sometimes silver, they rang with hundreds of messages: summoning Americans to Sunday services, marking the harvest and holidays, signaling the prosperity of planting, tolling the sadness of death, chiming the happiness of marriage, clanging warnings of fire and flood, or booming out the celebration of victory."

—Jay Winik, American historian and author

Alicia Blood wanted a bell. She did not wish to mark the harvest or a holiday or signal the planting or toll death. She wanted a bell—a big one—because the Woodbridge settlers were so poor there were no timepieces among them.

"A bell should be of great service, for the people have no clocks," she informed her superior, Rev. E.M. Cravath of New York City. Acquiring the bell would become her great campaign. She would solicit funds. She would learn how they were sold: by weight. And she would conclude how loud she wanted the Woodbridge bell to be. But there were many other things to be accomplished, and getting a bell would not be easy.

In the early 1900s, a North Carolina historian explained, "Gunmetal being scarce, many of the bells in the South had been consumed early in the [Civil] war. At Edenton, for example, the army secured all the bells and sent them by wagon to the Tredegar Iron Works in Richmond to be cast into cannon. The town bell, the courthouse bell, the Academy bell, and the shipyard bells were all melted down. Only the bell at the Baptist church was spared by the vigorous objections of several of the members." [a]

Miss Blood, the new teacher, arrived at Woodbridge on Saturday, October 4, 1873, at about seven o'clock in the evening. Rev. Bull was at the rail stop when the train pulled to a halt. He told her he had not been expecting her so soon but was glad she had come.

Roused by the novelty of the new teacher about forty people attended the Sabbath School the next morning. She would report twice that number attended the "preaching service" Sunday evening.

Her first Monday was a busy day at Woodbridge. She wasted no time. The school term was convened with 15 of 18 scholars in attendance and before the morning was over, Jane Bull arrived at Woodbridge with Eddie and Freddie in tow to greet her.

---

[a] Dillard, Richard, *The Civil War in Chowan County, North Carolina*, pg. 5, 1916.

Miss Blood noted that "there were no books, hardly, and there are none to be had nearer than New Bern." What had become of the many books delivered since Rev. Bull's arrival is not known, but Miss Blood began the process of petitioning "The Rooms" for more.

"Could you make arrangements to send me some books for the school?" she wrote. "First, Second and Third Readers, Arithmetics, Geographies, Slates, Writing Books, Pen-holders and ink. If you have Primers, shall want them."

Not knowing how many books were needed she suggested two dozen of each "would do for the present." But she wanted even more slates.

Slates, the little hand-held blackboards, were the writing tablets of the day. The students marked them with chalk, then wiped the slates clean and wrote on them again.

"I want every scholar to have a slate," she said, noting that Rev. Bull, ever the optimist, had told her he thought she should plan for 60 students.

She also asked for a dozen illuminated mottoes. Popular at the time, mottoes were decorated with brightly colored letters of sayings and quotes.

"In God We Trust"

"Do unto others as you would have them do unto you"

"All things in moderation"

"Home Sweet Home"

"Live free or die"

"God bless America"

"United we stand, divided we fall"

Bull wasted no time either in getting down to business. Within five days of her arrival, he told Miss Blood he would need her to pay him $10.50 if she wanted the lamps in the schoolroom and the teacher's chair. He informed her he would be taking the school's blackboard to his house for the use of his children. He told her to order a new one for the school from a man he knew in New Bern, predicting the cost of a ten-foot by four-foot blackboard to be three or four dollars. He also offered to sell her the school's little stove for eight dollars more.

"I tried to have a fire yesterday as it was cold and rainy, but was almost smoked out," she wrote. "I concluded I could stand the cold better than the smoke so I extinguished the fire...I do not consider it suitable for a school room."

Bull tried to soothe her objection saying it had worked fine the previous winter and did not smoke "any more than any stove with the pipe running out of the window."

She would decide later whether or not to buy the goods Bull offered. For now, she bought a new broom and water bucket for the school and set to work.

"I came very near losing my patience."

Alicia Sarah Blood was part of a Northern missionary family. Her father, Abel Blood of Lyme, N.H., was a well-known, long-serving Congregational church deacon. Her sister, Carrie, was a teacher for the AMA, and several other members of the Blood family, both men and women, served at missions around the country.

Before the posting at Woodbridge, Alicia had been in Iowa. She had a brother and sister there. In 1871, she had been teaching at an AMA station in Monticello, Florida. From Florida she sent a lengthy report to the *American Missionary* commenting on the cold, the success of the school's temperance society she had founded, and the happy arrival of a barrel of clothing from supporters in Worcester, Massachusetts.

"Those kind friends can never see the comfort that barrel brought, but they will be richly rewarded in Heaven," she wrote.

It is striking to think of school teachers, young and elderly, in this early time in the country's history, leaving homes in New England and traveling by rail, steamboat, and buggy, moving from state to state, east to west, far and wide, to serve the poor and their beloved master, Jesus. In this era, travel was difficult, fraught with danger, and expensive. Many people never traveled. Some lived their entire lives without leaving the county in which they were born. The Civil War had ended only a few years before. Indians were still fighting the westward expansion. Communication was hit or miss. And these hearty souls left hearth and kin to venture out alone into the great unknown.

They surely did not do it for the money. Their accommodations were often only a little better than camping. They became ill. Some died of "fever" or in accidents. They were sometimes ostracized and sometimes attacked, verbally or physically. Separated from all they knew and loved; loneliness had to have been a constant companion. But a reader would seldom know this from the letters they wrote; for the great mass of them are filled with optimism, hope, and thanks for the chance to minister to what Miss Blood called "these downtrodden people."

From the record, one would think Miss Blood was a spinster up in years. One letter refers to her as an "old teacher." Nevertheless, when she arrived at Woodbridge, she was just 31. In another letter, though, D.D. Dodge, the AMA's "head of station" in Wilmington, wrote the New York leadership that she was "a hearty Congregationalist" and that "her rank of scholarship is such that she could fill a principal's place." [b]

---

[b] Find A Grave memorial 126792009;

Ill when she arrived in Woodbridge, she would suffer from chills, fever, weakness, and a cough for the next two years. At times, she could not work. On other occasions, she said she would sit up only when she was teaching.

Within 30 days of her arrival, she received a barrel of books. None of them were the ones she had ordered. She soon learned that she had received a shipment intended for Mr. Dodge. The books she ordered wound up in Wilmington. But in communicating with him about the mix-up, he offered a used organ for the Woodbridge station chapel. The shipment he sent languished in Goldsboro for two weeks "because the Freight Agent did not know where Woodbridge was."

"I came very near losing my patience," Miss Blood confessed.

In late November, she reported that the school, though small, was proceeding well with "a prospect of more scholars after Christmas." The parents seemed anxious for their children to go to school and nearly all have initially paid the small tuition charge. One gentleman sent three children to school, planned to send a fourth, and he attended Miss Blood's night classes himself. The teacher had one eleven-year-old girl who had earned her own tuition.

"Nearly all of the children within a mile each way attend the school," she reported, "and some that live three and four miles away."

Convinced the people needed more religious instruction she started a Wednesday evening prayer meeting. It was poorly attended with five or six people at any time. She lamented that few at Woodbridge professed any religion at all and even those who did, failed to "realize the necessity of *living* a Christian life."

She illustrated by telling this story: An old man, a Methodist minister, no less, shot and killed a deer that wandered up close to the AMA house on a Sunday. She confronted him and told him he should not have shot the deer there, especially not on the Sabbath. He said he agreed and did not believe in doing such things either, but that it appeared to him that God had sent that deer and he had to kill it.

"This is truly a field for missionary labor," she concluded.

The first time she mentioned the bell was about forty-five days after her arrival.

"There is one thing needed here very much. That is a bell for the school building. Sabbath days the people have very little idea of the time of day. When we appoint the Sabbath School for nine o'clock, they will not get there until ten, and if ten, then half-past ten."

She asked the AMA for permission to "lay the case before my friends" and see if they would contribute toward the purchase. A network of wealthy donors supported the AMA. Occasionally, on special projects, the AMA allowed money to be solicited and sent directly to a particular station.

"If there was a church bell within hearing distance, it would not be needed so much."

In 1873, however, there were no church bells to be heard anywhere in the vicinity of Slocum Creek.

Christmas 1873 at Woodbridge, N.C.

By early December 1873, just two months after her arrival, Miss Blood had decided she was going to show the people of Woodbridge a Christmas they would remember for a long, long time. She wrote the New York office and told the ministers there she hoped "to have a Christmas Tree for the children Christmas night." She had already informed friends in Worcester of her plans and requested their help. She asked New York to be on the lookout for a barrel she expected, requesting that they "hasten it on that I may get it in season."

There was no money at Woodbridge. The African American settlers lived in abject poverty barely able to scrape a subsistence living from the soil. They were repeatedly missing their land payments. They could seldom spare the monthly 25 cent tuition to keep their children in school. They lived in barely heated shacks where cold air moved at will between the rough-cut boards. Christmas had never been celebrated except in the crudest ways. Gifts were rare. Toys were nearly unknown.

Alicia Blood intended to change that.

Her letter describing the event now bears AMA Archive Number 103417. The few who have read it might have concluded that she succeeded admirably. Here we will allow Miss Blood to tell the story in her own words.

Woodbridge, Craven Co., N.C.
Jan. 3rd 1874

Christmas and New Years have come and gone, but will not soon be forgotten by these people.

Woodbridge being a new place is consequently thinly settled, and the people are all colored, except one family of northern people [the Bulls], and a few poor whites scattered here and there. Those days, so full of pleasure to the people of the northern states, had passed almost unnoticed here except in their usual way of celebrating them—firing guns and drinking whiskey.

I determined to have a Christmas Tree and wrote to friends asking assistance. They responded cheerfully informing me of the shipment of a barrel of clothing which was not all wearing apparel. A lady of Union Springs, N.Y. upon hearing of the intended Tree also sent money with which to purchase gifts.

Notice was given the previous Sabbath of the entertainment, but no mention was made of the Tree as we wished that to be a surprise.

Christmas night was very rainy; still a goodly number met in the Chapel; some coming three and four miles. The Tree was "Holly" with its beautiful red berries, with here and there a branch of Mistletoe with white berries, and moss hanging from the limbs. Although the barrel expected had been delayed, the gifts already obtained when hung upon the tree made it look really beautiful.

All passed a pleasant evening and went home to tell their friends how much they had missed by staying away.

Saturday night the delayed barrel arrived [on the train] *and we wondered while unpacking it how so much could be sent in so small a compass. What did it contain? Everything that loving hearts could suggest and busy hands make; it seemed half full of toys of every description, handsome ones, too. I saw plainly that the Tree must be refilled for New Years night, for it would please them more than receiving the gifts privately.*

Before that day arrived another barrel of clothing came from unknown friends, also a case of Illuminated Mottoes for the walls of the Chapel, which when up and framed with moss, made the room look cheerful and pleasant.

New Years night was all we could desire. The house was filled with the parents and friends of the scholars, the Tree was laden with gifts, and could our friends have seen the pleasure those two evenings gave to these people who have nothing at home from which to derive pleasure or instruction, they would have felt as I did: fully repaid for all the trouble and expense.

Before we separated all joined in singing "Praise God from whom all blessings flow" feeling that He was the Giver of all good.

Alicia S. Blood

Rev. Bull quickly submitted a glowing account of the event to the New Bern newspaper entitled *Christmas at Woodbridge*. He included much of the information above but did not mention Miss Blood. [c]

Bull continued to absent himself from responsibility and with Miss Blood in place he poured all his duties upon her. He was working steadily in enterprises of his own and becoming more and more involved in county politics. He told her that he had seen a bill for taxes of $9.46 against the AMA in New Bern. Not knowing what to do about it, she wrote New York for guidance. She worked on the stove and planned the construction of a chimney for the schoolhouse. She estimated materials and labor at $40. More pipe, she thought, would provide a temporary solution. Bull stayed after her until she paid him for the lamps and the chair. Although she had nothing to do with the arrangement, he hounded her for the $15 per month he was supposed to receive from the AMA for her board.

[c] *The New Berne Times*, December 28, 1873.

He also told her that she would now be the land agent in charge of real estate contracts, accounting, and collections of payments from the settlers. Stunned by this news, she immediately wrote again to New York and attempted to disqualify herself from the job. She urged them to arrange with Rev. Bull to continue as the land agent. Unknown to her, Bull was also writing "The Rooms" trying to make a better deal for himself.

Still feeling weak from her fevers and chills, Miss Blood soldiered on, teaching the children and adults, holding prayer meetings, and attending to the needs of her flock as best she could. She opened a night school charging twenty-five cents per month per pupil. She hoped to use the money for more pipe for a stove and for bookcases. Her Sabbath School books were piled on the floor.

The minister was less than encouraging. If you charge tuition, Bull told her, they will just take their children out of school. She felt she had the support of the settlers, however.

"The people seem *pleased* with the stove and they have reason to be. I hope to rouse their ideas about helping themselves somewhat."

She tried repeatedly in New Bern and Beaufort to get a blackboard built to replace the one Bull had taken from the school. All she got was excuses. The wood was too wet or they were too busy, she was told. Finally, she found a New Bern man who said he would make her one, but he proved to be slow. Once when she sent word to him, he responded by saying he was "almost" done and inquired if she wanted the board painted. His price, he now said, did not include painting.

Miss Blood boiled: "It seems to me he might have known I wanted him to paint it or I should not have written for a *black*-board."

As the warm weather of spring approached, she planned on closing the Woodbridge school for the summer. Her health had declined and so had enrollment.

"The scholars begin to leave the school because they are needed in the fields," she said. "My health is so poor. Have been fearful I would not be able to teach this month out. Some days I feel quite well and then I am so prostrated with weakness that it is all I can do to take care of eight scholars. Have been sick the whole year, therefore have not accomplished as much as I had hoped, but trust my labors have not been wholly in vain."

In the fall of 1874, Miss Blood began to press Reverend Bull about the state of the church. Bull made no bones about it. He said there was no church and never really had been. It had been "premature" to form one and that he had been pressed by The Rooms to do so. There were five or six members when Woodbridge was organized. They had drifted away and there had been no additions, no conversions, no souls saved. There were no tithes, no offerings, no contributions. The "Sacrament of the Lord's Supper" had never

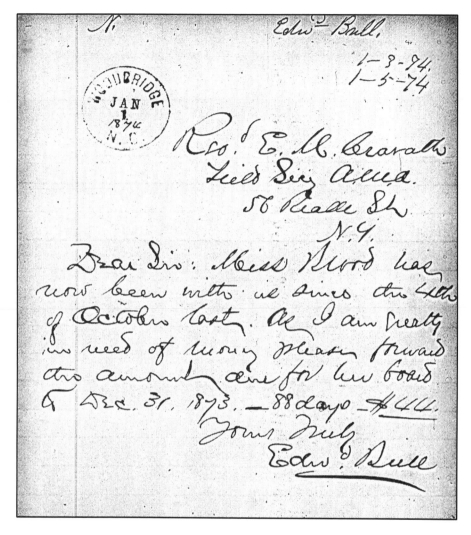

Above, one of about 90 letters to the American Missionary Association by Rev. Edward Bull from 1868-1875. Most are from Woodbridge. Only a few letters carry the rare postmark of the Woodbridge Post Office established by Rev. Bull, and which served the Havelock area from 1873-1881. In this short note, Bull writes to Rev. E.M. Cravath at AMA headquarters in New York on January 1, 1874 requesting the rent money he is charging for one of the missionary teachers. It reads, *"Dear Sirs: Miss Blood has been with us since the 4th of October last. As I am greatly in need of money, please forward the amount due for Miss Blood & Dec. 31, 1873. – 88 days – $44. Yours Truly, Edw'd Bull."* Adjusted for inflation, that was nearly a thousand dollars. Amistad Research Center, Tulane University. AMA #13411.

been observed. No one had asked him to preach, he said, so he only did that occasionally on Sunday evenings and no longer considered himself to be their pastor.

All in all, it's remarkable testimony from a man who had been paid to be a minister there for nearly four years.

One possible clue to the failure of the church is in a report Bull sent the AMA in September 1873. He was preaching only intermittently then and there had been no service for two weeks. When he opened the First Congregational Church again to the people, he told the leadership, "My Subject last night was Adultery and Fornication – crying evils in this region. I preached more *hell* to them

While this image is not from Woodbridge, but from a Freedmen's Bureau School in another part of the South, it is illustrative of the African American children who sought an education in the years following the Civil War. No images of the Woodbridge School or its "scholars" are known to exist but it is known that more than 60 students were enrolled at the AMA's school on the banks of Slocum Creek in 1878.

than in any other sermon I have ever delivered ... I trust it will do them good." [d]

Rev. Bull was not alone among the white, Northern ministers in failing to appreciate that the foundation of the former slaves' religion was hope, gladness, and thanksgiving, not shame, guilt, and self-denial. The tug of cultures and dissimilarity of worldviews left the black congregations longing for their own pastors and their own churches.

Miss Blood was living with the consequences. "I would like very much to see the church here prosperous and if I can do anything more than what I am doing, I shall be willing to try," she told the New York leadership.

And again, she asked about a bell. "The people are often late; they sometimes forget weekly prayer meeting."

She had gathered $30 in donations from friends and wrote to ask how much it would cost to get a bell loud enough to be heard two miles. The children were still in the cotton field, so school was sporadic. And then her chills and fever returned. She began to have thoughts of giving up.

---

[d] AMA # 103333, Amistad Research Center, Tulane University.

Alicia Blood was alone. The entire Woodbridge mission rested upon her tired shoulders. The minister had become all but a tormenter. She doubted her strength would return. It was November. Winter was coming and the darkness was lasting longer each day. She struggled to the conclusion that someone stronger should be sent to take her place. She believed God had decided to take the work from her hands and that "someone wiser and better" would be sent. She would do her best to keep the school and the Sabbath services going until a replacement was chosen, but resign she must.

Possibly it was the catharsis of surrender. Maybe it was a miracle. But a few days after posting her letter of resignation, her fever broke and did not return. There was an outpouring of grief from the settlers when she gave them the news that she was leaving. They visited her and asked her not to go. She began to get better each day. She wrote the AMA and told them she would stay on if it suited them. It did.

Something else was transpiring in her life as well. There is no mention of it in her letters; no reference at all. But her letter to the AMA on January 7, 1875, was signed by Alicia Brown. On December 19, 1874, the sick, lonely schoolmarm married Robert J. Brown, 39, in New Bern.

Bell and Farewell

Letter, April 1, 1875, Woodbridge, N.C.: "I have at last got enough money subscribed for a bell…Get a real bell, a metal bell that turns with a crank instead of a pulley, and get as good a one as can be bought for $60."

Letter, April 15, 1875, Woodbridge, N.C.: "I cannot give you the weight of the bell I desire; but want one that will be heard certain by 1½ miles and further if you can get it for $60. I am surprised that they cost so much per pound…Perhaps a bell weighing 100 lbs. will answer, but would like a heavier one if it can be had for the money. Please get as heavy a one as can be bought for $60."

Post Card, April 20, 1875, Woodbridge, N.C.: "I sent you a telegram the 19th not to order the bell. Since writing you the 15th, have heard of a good second-hand bell which we can get very cheap, or at least think we can get it. Will write you again when I know certainly."

Letter, April 26, 1875, Woodbridge N.C.: "I write to inform you that I can get a *good* second-hand bell here which weighs about 150 lbs. for less than $40 and I have concluded it is best for me to take it. Am very happy as I can have a heavier bell by the means."

On June 3, 1875, almost two years after she first stepped from the train at Woodbridge, Alicia Brown sent her second resignation letter to the Rooms. She knew she had done her best. But it was time to go home; to rest for a while; to see husband and family. She also sent her final financial report. It showed considerable tuition due. She would try to collect all she could before she left but did not expect much success.

"It is very hard to get hold of any money," she said. "They are doing the best they can, I truly believe."

Rev. George Lynch, the AMA pastor from Beaufort, would look after the place until they could send a new teacher – if they were going to send a new teacher – and she hoped they would. The people "desire it and are very interested in the school."

Lynch also reported to The Rooms, "The Church at Woodbridge has only one member. Those that are called members never left their churches to join any other church. Some are Baptist and some are Methodist. I have looked into the matter careful. I have no records of the church organization and no church book. And the last minister [Bull] tells me he has none. Do you have any records of the organization?

So little had been accomplished. But of the things that had, the teacher got her bell.

"The bell weighs 210 lbs. and can be heard over three miles on a clear day," she reported. "The people are very proud of it."

On that summer morning of 1875, Alicia Blood Brown boarded the steam train and waved farewell to the settlers. There had been hugs and handshakes and tears, but there was also poignant consolation from the Woodbridge schoolhouse. As the big bell pealed goodbye to her, its faithful ringing was heard, pure and strong, over most of the ground that is now modern-day Havelock.

Teacher Carrie and the Settlers

In October 1875, AMA headquarters sent word that a new teacher was on the way to Woodbridge to replace the departed Mrs. Brown. Carrie E. Waugh, 40, was from Scriba, New York, in the snow country on Lake Ontario 150 miles east of Buffalo.

Miss Waugh's first letters sent to Rev. Strieby were organizational; about books and supplies. Within three months, however, the reality of the situation at Woodbridge had made itself clear. On January 8, 1876, she penned a long, lonely letter to Rev. George Whipple, pouring her heart out about her concerns and those of the association.

She told Rev. Whipple that she was writing to him confidentially because, unlike the others in AMA leadership, she felt "a little acquainted" with him, having met "at Savannah two years ago." She asked for his prayers and his advice.

She wrote, "I have never been in a field where I was so utterly alone as to *human* help and sympathy as here in W."

Rev. Bull, in no official capacity, was still lurking about Woodbridge, preaching on occasion but spending much of his time engaged in Republican political affairs. When he did preach, hardly anyone came to hear him. Sent to teach at the school, Miss Waugh felt the call to hold religious services on her own. At first, all of the people were stand-offish but she began making inroads with the young. Over time, more adults began to come to Sabbath school. Enough had been coming that she invited Rev. Bull to preach one Sunday around Christmas. She said there was a good crowd.

She wrote, "I had had a grand day. In the Sabbath school and temperance meeting, God's Spirit had been with us in a greater measure than ever before and I felt that answers to prayers were coming ... Just as it was time to ring the last bell, he sent word that he could not come."

That Sunday evening, Miss Waugh held church services on her own. From the New Testament, she read the Parable of the Ten Talents to the group and was well-pleased with its reception. Inspired, she announced "a watch meeting" for New Year's Eve. The late-night service, while not unknown in the Congregational Church, was particularly significant in the African American community and black churches. It was a solemn time of deep reflection and prayer. Miss Waugh's moving watch night resulted in a profession of faith from five men and one woman at the Woodbridge Congregational Church. She was overjoyed and used ecstatic language to describe the event in her letter to Rev. Whipple.

But Bull crushed her.

She wrote the word "Private" over the next part of her letter.

"Mr. Bull has lost the confidence of the people here and they will not come out to hear him preach. He did not approve of me having watch meeting and told me he had no confidence in the conversion of the people or their Christianity and so I have no help or sympathy from him," she said.

In her desperation. she laid two questions before the Congregationalist ministers in New York that must have thundered through the all-white Rooms; "Would you think it best to ask any colored minister to speak? And if they asked the privilege, would you advise me to refuse?" [e]

We can only imagine Rev. Whipple's reaction.

As for Bull, he stopped preaching altogether. On the few occasions he attended her services, he would not speak even when asked to do so. His last letters in the AMA archive correspond to this period.

The Woodbridge teacher was known to be as capable in church as she was in the classroom. The words of one witness circulated and were discussed in Raleigh and New York. Teacher David Peebles visiting from Dudley said he had "attended the most joyful prayer meeting, conducted by Miss

[e] AMA # 103836, January 8, 1876, Amistad Research Center, Tulane University.

Waugh, that [I] ever saw. No one had to be called on. Everyone was ready. Old men bowed under it." Peebles was directly quoted as saying "I would give anything if I could have the association of such a person here. She is a woman that lives near to her God. She is a warrior." [f]

Miss Waugh battled on at Woodbridge for more than three years. She generated the second largest number of Woodbridge letters in the AMA archive – second only to Rev. Bull – so a great deal is known about her work at the settlement. She would serve there until the end of 1878.

The final entry in the Carrie E. Waugh letters on the final AMA film reel at Tulane University came as a surprise. It wasn't a letter. It was a list of her students, 64 girls and boys, at the Woodbridge School.

There was no apparent reason for a teacher to send a list of her students' names to The Rooms. But she did. No other list of the African American settlers' children of Woodbridge exists within the archive. We reproduce this treasure here without further comment:

Martha Anderson	Harlanda? Kornegay
Mary Anderson	Elisabeth Murry
Sarah Anderson	Ivey Manning
Margett Bryant	Jennie Williams
Betsy Bryant	Sally Williams
Mary Bryant	Rachel Williams
Emily Bryant	Lucinda Williams
Emiline Bryant	Carrie Williams
Sarah Batts	John Bryant
Pheba Brooks	Elijah Brooks
Clarasy Chase	Amos Batts
Frances Chance	Lennard Bennet
Delilah Chance	John Berry
Melvenia Cully	Henry Beltnar
Rebecca Canada	George Benjamin
Elisabeth Canada	Richard Chase
Caroline Canada	James Chase
Alvania Canada	James Canada
Sally Dixon	Isaac Canada
Harret Dixon	Charley Canada
Mary Frances Green	Squires Canada
Mary Halloway	John Canada
Caroline Jones	Louis Canada
Lettice Jones	Robert Dixon

[f] Rev. E.P. Hayes to Rev. E.P. Strieby, AMA # 104051, June 19, 1878.

Samuel Dixon	Alfred Murry
Louis George	Simon Stallion
Eli Hicks	Joseph Thomas
Tony (Tany) Hill	John Wallace
Henry Hammond	Alexander Wallace
Gilbert Jones	John Williams
Brice Kornegay	Henry Williams[a]
Willie Manning	Edward Laughinghouse

During her tenure in the little village along the A&NC Railroad and on the banks of Slocum Creek, Carrie Waugh began to receive help from other ministers who came to support her efforts to be all things to the people of Woodbridge.

But one of the major factors that helped Miss Waugh make it through three years at Woodbridge was that Rev. Bull was spending most of his time in New Bern.

North Carolina State Senator Edward Bull

The Republicans elected Abraham Lincoln President of the United States in 1860. A segment within the party, the "Radical Republicans," pushed for Civil War. The Radical Republicans – and abolitionists like those who organized the American Missionary Association – lobbied for the Emancipation Proclamation. And after Lincoln's assassination, the Radical Republicans pushed for a punitive "Reconstruction" of the South.

The states of the former Confederacy, including North Carolina, operated after the Civil War under federal military control. Unionists poured into the South, in some cases, to seek power and fortune. Many of them came carrying unique sets of fashionable luggage upholstered from sections of rugs. Most featured floral patterns and were called carpet bags. Thus, Northerners arriving by train and in ocean ports picked up the not-so-polite nickname "carpetbaggers."

Political control throughout the South quickly accrued to the carpetbaggers. In New Bern, the sheriff was a Republican. The editor of the newspaper was a Republican. Black voters naturally threw their support to the Republicans who had sent armies south to liberate them from slavery. With the voting power of the newly enfranchised African Americans, the Republicans, black and white, saw themselves elected to control of every board, commission, committee, including the delegations to the House of Representatives and the Senate, state and federal.

---

[a] AMA Archives # 104223.

While Edward Bull could win no popularity contest in the small town of Woodbridge, he quickly gained political power in New Bern, Craven County, and, ultimately, in the state of North Carolina.

Bull established a residence at 13 George St. in New Bern. That location today is on the grounds of the Tryon Palace Historic Site and Gardens.

In December 1876, Bull was named as one of the five new members of the Craven County Board of Education. He was later appointed as a magistrate, a justice of the peace, and a tax examiner, before being elected as a Craven County Commissioner. He was a census taker, which allowed him to visit every home and meet nearly every voting resident in southern Craven County.

So firm was the control of the ballot box by the Republican Party, Edward Bull won in a landslide with nearly three-quarters of the vote as a candidate for the N.C. Senate in the election of 1878. He would serve for years as a North Carolina senator beginning in the session of 1879. In Raleigh, he worked on the Committee of Military Affairs and the Committee on Engrossed Bills. By 1891, he was on the Committee on Finance, and the Committee on Agriculture, Mechanics, and Mining.

His portrait at the beginning of the chapter is cropped from a sort of class photo with the other North Carolina senators taken during one of his terms in the General Assembly and preserved ever since by the Division of Archives and History in Raleigh. His name is listed in the 1891 Senate session records as *E. W. Bull*, the only reference to a middle initial ever seen among hundreds of the documents about him.

The Wooden Bridge

Edward Bull won the election for the N.C. Senate the year following a controversy that might have disqualified him from further public service.

The night of Thursday, September 27, 1877, one of the two bridges over forks of Slocum Creek at Havelock was washed away by floodwaters from a remarkable, raging rainstorm. The storm, possibly a near-miss by a late-season hurricane, made headlines with the *Newbernian* newspaper saying two days later that nothing like the downpour was remembered "in the memory of our oldest citizens." Other bridges in the county were washed away as well, according to the newspaper.

Though newspaper stories don't say, the washed-out bridge at Havelock must have been the one over the southwest prong of the creek as the County Commissioners paid local merchant and postmaster Collins H.

Hunter $100 in May 1887 "for building bridge across east prong of Slo-cumb's Creek." [a]

The newspaper source does say that the bridge that washed away had been so "dilapidated" that the county commissioners had ordered its repair and that new lumber was delivered to the site in June. The lumber sat untouched on the creek bank for most of four months before it and the bridge were washed away in the deluge.

The contractor?

Edward Bull.

The Newbernian editor stormed on October 20, "the lumber was duly delivered and allowed to remain upon the premises for several months, and finally, in the freshet, to wash away, through the *neglect* of the Commissioner above mentioned. The result is that the people of that section are put at great inconvenience."

Bull responded on October 27 in typical style.

In a long article, he said the bridge had not washed away and was still "passable."

It wasn't dilapidated. It just needed some freshening up.

It wasn't his project. He had just been delegated "to use his discretion in the matter, both as to time and method."

And the lumber had not been washed away.

"Little of it was moved more than a few yards," he wrote.

A witness from Havelock who signed himself "Patrick" took serious issue with Bull's, well, bull.

"The bridge *was* washed down during the late storm, and, as I can prove by the traveling public, was both impassable and very dangerous," Patrick wrote in the same newspaper on November 3. He noted that some of the new lumber was found three miles down the creek.

Millwright L.M. Ward of the Bryan Mill at Havelock "being compelled to cross his team, bridged the old wreck with slabs, which being inadequate to hold the weight, gave way, and precipitated two of his oxen into the stream, and came near losing them," according to Patrick.

The reason Bull was holding up repairs was the most outrageous part, Patrick contended.

"Mr. Ward had waited on Mr. Bull, the County Commissioner at Woodbridge, who had contracted to repair the bridge and requested him to advance the work as rapidly as possible, as his business was suffering from its condition. Mr. Bull's reply was very unsatisfactory, and was to purport that as soon as he could induce Mr. George Biglow, a citizen of that township, to work out a private debt of five dollars, he would commence repairs."

---

[a] Craven County Commission records, May 2, 1887.

Patrick added, "The people of Newport, Harlowe Creek, and Havelock must wait uncomplainingly, the road to New Bern blocked up, while Mr. Bull uses his debt so outrageously."

The sawmill man, L.M. Ward, was awarded the new contract to replace the Slocum Creek crossing. He completed the 33-foot-wide bridge in about two months, and for half the price for which Bull had contracted.

When it was completed, the unflappable Rev. Bull wrote a glowing tribute to the structure.

In the *Newbernian* of January 12, 1878, he consumed most of two columns extolling its magnificent construction, its builder, its workmen, its history, and its importance to the community. He skillfully downplayed any negative aspects of the previous stories and, with a show of pride, dubbed it "the banner bridge of the county."

Havelock Replaced

By the late 1870s, Rev. Bull had made Havelock disappear.

In an annual mercantile guide, the *Charles Emerson and Company City Directory for 1880-1881*, New Bern is featured.

Riverdale is listed with its prominent citizens. So are Croatan and Dover and other familiar places. But not Havelock. Instead, *Woodbridge* is highlighted with a heading all its own.

Under the Woodbridge banner are the names of many leading men, black and white, of the entire Havelock area as well as characters from the AMA's Town of Woodbridge

"Woodbridge" farmers, the largest category, included Philip J. Armes (who lived at Hancock Creek), Eli Barrow, Isaac Batts, John Berry, George Berry, Daniel Best, Joseph Brinkley, Amos Bryan, George W. Bryan, Allen Canada, Morris Canada, Squires Canada, A.J. Chesnutt, John Cooper, Willis G. Copper, William Ebron, Michael N. Fisher, Squires George, Joseph Godwin, Joseph W. Holland, John W. Holland, John Hoover, John Lockey, Atlas Pate, Thomas H. Pate, Stephen Peartree, John D. Pittman, Edward Russell, A.J. Sparks, Benajah Taylor, Jabez Taylor, John M. Thorpe, James West, and William S. Wynne.

Others under the Woodbridge headline were Allen Atkinson and Adam Cully, listed as mechanics; James A. Bryan, as a steam lumber and grist mill operator; Edward Bull, of course, as a minister; William H. Ellis and C.R. Scott as ministers and teachers; Green Cox and Alex Mercer as blacksmiths; E.W. Howe, an insurance agent; James H. Hunter, a magistrate and overseer of the Lake Ellis Plantation; Frank Johnson, engineer; G.G. Lindsey, a pension agent; C.W. McLean of the N.C. colonization agency; Luke Neal, a steam sawyer; George Rigdon, a cooper; Jacob Smith, house carpenter, and wheelwright; Tolson & Heath, merchants; Joseph Williams, a cooper, and wheelwright; and citizen Jeremiah Simpson.

In that year, all that survived of Havelock was the name of the Atlantic and North Carolina rail stop nearby.

Other Missionaries and Teachers

1873 was the last year, however, that Bull was listed as the Woodbridge pastor in the AMA's annual publications. Teacher Alicia Blood was followed by Carrie Waugh.

Young fresh-faced William H. Ellis of Southfield, Massachusetts arrived in 1879 to replace Mrs. Waugh as the teacher while working on being ordained as a minister. He would serve there until 1882. Another young minister and teacher, C.R. Scott, sometimes shared duties with him.

By 1883, the American Missionary Association dropped the name Woodbridge and listed their minister and teacher at *Havelock* as Rev. Z. Simmons of Dudley and Mrs. G.A. Rumbley of Philadelphia.

Georgiana Rumbley was the last teacher to serve the AMA school at Havelock.

A note in the AMA's 1884 annual report, which showed no minister, said "a church was formed in 1871 at (Janesville) or Woodbridge, N.C. but has been a long time without a pastor, and is scattered. It is hoped that it will be reorganized in the coming year."

It wasn't meant to be.

After 1884, no Woodbridge or Havelock station for the missionaries was ever again listed in the annual AMA publication *The Field*.

The Woodbridge Legacy

Before the war, local slaveholder George Wolf Perry wrote, "Every man who is endowed with common sense can better tell what a negro requires than he can himself." [b]

Despite the outward altruism, some within the Northern missionary community – including Edward Bull – appear to have brought a similar mentality of racial superiority to their Southern outreach.

In the end, the former slaves desired no new masters. They neither sought nor welcomed – over the longer term – the novel paternalism offered by self-appointed saviors from the North. After centuries of being dominated by other white patriarchs, they made clear by their actions that

---

[b] *A Treatise on Turpentine Making*, 1859.

they longed for freedom on their own terms, not as prescribed by others. They preferred their own churches, their own ministers, their own teachers.

Shared sensibilities reside in many human hearts: the determination to stand on your own two feet, to have some property, to raise a family, to enjoy a taste of liberty, and to be otherwise left alone in peace.

Over the next eighty years, the once-enslaved Africans settled the lands of southern Craven County – sometimes in prosperity, sometimes barely eeking by – but determined, after all this time, to control their own destinies.

Still, it's hard not to wonder what might have been. What if a selfless, charismatic minister had been teamed from the beginning with the skills and ardor of a Carrie Waugh? What if they'd worked fairer deals on land prices with the settlers? There might still be a Town of Woodbridge or even a City of Woodbridge just west of Slocum Creek.

And what became of it all ... and all of them?

Less than three years after leaving North Carolina, Mrs. Alicia Sarah Blood Brown died of tuberculosis, the illness with which she had struggled at Woodbridge. Her passing came at 4 o'clock in the afternoon on Tuesday, February 25, 1878. She and her husband Robert were then living in Leavenworth, Kansas where the AMA was doing work among the American Indians. She was buried nearby. Her obituary said she was 35. According to her obelisk-shaped granite grave marker, she was 36. No one knows what happened to her school bell. [c]

Carrie E. Waugh, the Congregationalist warrior, lived to be 85. Born on October 25, 1835, her death came on August 20, 1921. She is buried among family in the Hillside Cemetery in Scriba, Oswego County, New York.

The political capital earned during the Civil War ran out for Bull and the rest of the North Carolina Republicans in the late 1800s. In 1892, Edward Bull was making a living promoting agricultural fairs and selling honey. He became well-known in beekeeping circles and was an award-winning honey producer.

He was alone now. His wife, Jane, appears to have left years before for New England. His boys were grown and gone. His Woodbridge land long since reverted to AMA ownership, he eventually migrated to northeast Florida. In 1903 and 1904, he was pastor of the Pilgrim Congregational Church in a railroad village, Pamona, today called Pamona Park. He lived beside a small lake. Later, he was a deacon at the church. He worked as a supply pastor preaching occasionally at other churches around Putnam County, sometimes marrying people, sometimes officiating a funeral.

He died in Pamona, Florida on September 15, 1913. He was 83.

---

[c] *The Leavenworth (Kansas) Weekly Time*, March 7, 1878; Find A Grave memorial 126792009.

Four days later, the local newspaper, the *Putnam News and Advertiser*, said his body was to be "shipped to his old home in Massachusetts for interment." But Bull was not from Massachusetts. He was from Connecticut. Congregational Church records say he was buried in Danbury. *The Middletown Press* of Sept. 22, 1913, says he was buried in Centerbrook, Connecticut's Nott Cemetery, today a part of that town's old and massive Central Burying Ground. The cemetery's records do not list his grave. Searches by the author on the ground in Connecticut, with the enlisted help of professional historians, amateur historians, and local historical societies, have led to the conclusion that the grave of Edward Bull is lost. No one ever marked his final resting place.

And Woodbridge?

Its post office went dormant on October 7, 1881, when the first Havelock post office was established.

Though several parcels of the missionary land were still occupied by black families – including the Cullys – into the late twentieth century, not a trace of Woodbridge remains. All of its buildings have long since fallen to ruin. The only tangible evidence that it ever existed are hundreds of documents in archives and libraries around the country.

The former Utley Plantation on which Woodbridge was founded contained 615 acres. After subtracting all the lots and pieces of land sold over nearly three decades, 511 acres remained. On April 12, 1899, the American Missionary Association conveyed its ownership of the land to the Blades Lumber Company for $605.[d]

Today, much of western Havelock is built upon it.

---

[d] Craven County deed book 129, pg. 114.

A Country Harmony

Southern Craven County after the War Between the States, like most of the South, was a place where infant mortality was high and life-expectancy short; where women married young – as girls really – and men married often, sometimes taking vows with younger sisters in chronological order as their older siblings died in childbirth. Fevers were annual reapers of souls and all kinds of peril – wild animals, fire, gunshots, trains, drowning – were as common as the change of the seasons. Most people struggled. Henry David Thoreau was on to something when he said that the mass of men leads lives of quiet desperation.

But they stayed busy. Marrying and visiting and going to town. The "Havelock district," as it was often called, wasn't a separate place from New Bern as is often thought today. It was an extension, a suburb, populated by the same people and intertwined branches of the same families, who moved back and forth from summer to winter. Some who had a farm in the country also kept a residence in the city. The train was their trolley car. We see examples time and again of people who lived at Havelock, but regularly went to church in New Bern.

In 1884, Havelock was described as "a village to surrounding farms." The farm village at the crossing of the main county road and the railroad was the hub where people came by horse and buggy, mule cart, or on foot to catch the train, to buy supplies, pick up mail, and socialize.

There was no electricity in the homes, churches, or country stores, and there would not be for many decades. There was no indoor plumbing. Outhouses were the standard. There was no running water. Water came from a hand pump or well, and had to be carried into the house in buckets. There was no hot water unless you heated it over a wood stove with wood you or someone in the family cut and split by hand. There was no refrigeration. If you wished to eat, you or someone in your family plowed, planted, fertilized, and hoed. You grew, shelled, shucked, dug, peeled, picked, and gathered. And killed, skinned, dressed, or caught, gutted, and scaled. And then and only then, you roasted, boiled, fried, stewed, grilled, or baked whatever was going on your plate. Lighting was by oil lamp. People went to bed early. Everyday life was more akin to camping than to our modern world.

Farming was the standard occupation. There were two types. Subsistence farmers – the majority – farmed to keep the family fed. There were a few in southern Craven County, though, who made money at it. If a person wasn't farming or selling their labor to a farmer, the "log woods" were another way to earn your daily bread. Cutting trees, hauling them out of the woods with horses or oxen, "rafting" the logs by water to the sawmill, and sawmill work itself made for a tough, back-breaking, and dangerous life. Timbering went on at a level in the late 1800s and early 1900s that is hard to either imagine or believe. A great percentage of the old-growth woodlands in the southern end of the county – the majority of it, actually – was clear-cut. So much so, that when the 160,000-acre Croatan National Forest was established in 1936, the government put men to work *planting* trees.

The end of the 1800s and the beginning of the 1900s were economically tough times. It was a time when the South was still recovering from the Civil War, both economically and politically. It was a time when the traditional big moneymaker for southern Craven County – naval stores – was on the wane. It was a time of financial panics, Prohibition, and the Great Depression. People had to do what they could to survive and, for many of them, that meant taking the familiar, tried-and-true distillation technology of the turpentine business and creating something with a higher-octane rating: bootleg liquor.

As hard-scrabble as things were, however, here on the south shore of the Neuse River there was another industry both curious and unlikely: leisure and recreation.

And for the "city people" of New Bern, Havelock was their entertainment destination. They'd boat down to the beaches at Slocum Creek, to swim, camp, and picnic, as evidenced by this 1874 excerpt from *The Daily Newbernian*.

> DISPATCH. The steamer Raleigh, of the Pioneer Transportation Company, W. G. Harding captain, arrived at her wharf Wednesday evening at 10 o'clock, with full freight to merchants. Immediate preparations were made to discharge the cargo and put sufficient naval stores under deck to trim her for sailing; this was accomplished Thursday at 6 AM, and at 9 AM she left her dock on an excursion to Slocum's Creek, where the teachers and children of the Episcopal Sunday School had decided to have a picnic. Returning from the excursion at half past seven, a large freight of naval stores and cotton was put on board, and at 5 AM, she again left her dock for Norfolk.

The hunting and fishing were legendary. Hardly a week went by in the early 1900s when there wasn't an outdoor sporting story in a newspaper somewhere in the state headlining Havelock, Slocum Creek, or Lake Ellis. Southern Craven County became famous for rod-and-gun recreation. Groups of people and individuals from Durham, Kinston, Goldsboro, and especially New Bern "motored" or arrived by train. Many owned lodges or cabins on waterways and in the woods. Others might be members and guests of hunt clubs on nearby creeks and among the lakes in the dense forest southwest of town. The deer, bear, tarpon, and free-flowing moonshine whisky drew people – some of them certified celebrities – from as far away as Philadelphia and New York City to a rustic, pristine, and playful haven bordering on wilderness.

Eat, drink and be merry ... if you could afford it.

The Old Homeplace

The formerly booming plantation economy was hard-pressed after the collapse of slavery. Still, many people hung on to their old way of life the best they could. The transition to the new world of social relations went more smoothly along the southern Neuse than it did many other places. Relations between the races, though not perfect, weren't marred, as in other areas of the South, by violence or activities of an organization like the Ku Klux Klan. African American participants in an extensive oral history program conducted over many years by the University of North Carolina said for the most part that race relations were good. Bertha Mae George, for example, was quoted as saying, they "never had trouble with white people in Harlowe." Pauline Frazier used nearly identical words in a separate interview adding "white people were nice and they would visit." Both races shopped at country stores together, they said, like the ones owned by Henderson Godette, selling fuel and groceries in North Harlowe, and white-owned Russell's and Trader's with the same fare at Havelock.[a]

Over many years of interviews and discussions with white elders at Havelock, in particular, the author has consistently gotten the same opinion. Former Craven County attorney Jim Sugg grew up in the Havelock area. He agreed that "everyone got along just fine." Other researchers have shared the same conclusion.

In 1865, and the immediate aftermath of the Civil War, a one-room schoolhouse for black children at Clubfoot Creek was burned and its white female teacher warned by an individual in rude terms to stop educating the students there. Nevertheless, the schoolhouse was rebuilt and teaching continued without further incident.

Perhaps the heritage of North Harlowe residents who were free people for generations before the Emancipation Proclamation had an influence. Perhaps it was the shared poverty and struggle to merely keep food on the

---

[a] SOHP, K-121 and K-124.

George R. Fuller's fishing camp on Hancock Creek near Little Witness.
EBE/ECU. Cherry Point Property Photos, Image 753.1.e.14

table. The races lived close by one another, worked, and did business together.

An exemplar of the subject was George R. Fuller, a white landowner
with a fishing camp on the banks of Hancock Creek. Fuller's property, ten
acres known as Cherry Point tract 287, was immediately adjacent to the African American settlement of Little Witness, also called Toon Neck. Resident Leander Moore and Lillian Green remembered Fuller. Green said he
sharecropped with the families there. He was known for his generosity.
Based on his perception of his partner's needs, he sometimes didn't ask for
his share of the year's production. "The whole community loved him," she
said.

The affection for Fuller is a reminder of the affinity the same community – in almost the same spot – felt for the blacksmith, A. J. Sparks, to
whom we were introduced in the first chapter. If people want to get along,
along they will get.

As we have learned, the land where MCAS Cherry Point is today was
a well-settled and productive plantation district before the Civil War. After
the war, the white settler population waned during the years of financial re-
cession and depression that followed. Many of the old homeplaces remained, however. Some were taken over by the freedmen. Others were
rented out or used as weekend or vacation homes.

One example is Oak Lane Villa, the gracious home of the William Buys
family. Buys, an immigrant from Holland, purchased the home, stock barns,
and stables on 550 acres of Slocum Creek waterfront in 1880. The plantation
was on the east side of the creek at its intersection with Mill Branch and
immediately adjacent to the farm of James H. Hunter.

William & Mary Buy's Oak Lane Villa on Slocum Creek, 1919.
Photograph courtesy of the New Bern-Craven County Public Library.

Buys was born in 1847 and came to the U.S. as a young man in 1873 moving first to Illinois. Less than a year after taking up farming at Slocum Creek, his wife Nellie passed away leaving the widower with three young children. His second wife, Mary, came to the U.S. from Denmark in 1883 and they married the same year.

On August 11, 1912, the *Daily Journal* of New Bern described the Buys farm as "noteworthy for the way in which the owner has improved the property." The article called the home "a model dwelling" and commented on the "neat barns and outbuildings" all surrounded by large water oaks. "Leading out to the country road, a distance of about a mile, is a straight avenue of those trees on each side, making a beautiful driveway." The newspaper noted that Buys was "developing a fruit farm and vineyard. Last season, one-eighth of an acre of land produced four hundred gallons of Scuppernong wine."

At age 69, after farming the land for 36 years, William tried to sell his home and acreage in 1916. He never found a buyer. He died in 1918 and was buried at the family's cemetery under live oak trees beside the creek.

By 1919, Mary Buys had moved to New Bern, leaving Oak Lane Villa behind. In September of that year, she invited some friends to "camp" with her and her daughter at the empty farmhouse. One of the women, Louisa Shriner, took photos at the house and pasted them into an album with the

notation: "Camping at Oak Lane Villa. In September 1919 Mrs. Mary Buys went to her home at Slocum Creek to super-intend the picking of grapes. She asked several girls to go with her and camp in the vacant house. The members of the camping party were Mrs. Buys, Sara Buys, Laura Brinson, Gladys Sexton, Julia, Anna, Louise, and Sara Shriner."

Slocum Creek view from Oak Lane Villa, 1919.
New Bern-Craven County Public Library.

Mary Buys succeeded in selling the farm soon after. In March 1920, it was purchased by Ira Williams Shields, a wealthy and well-known tobacco planter from Durham. Shields

Mrs. Ruth Ross with workers in a farm field near Slocum Creek, 1919.
Photograph courtesy of the New Bern-Craven County Public Library.

Front and rear of gambrel-roofed Ross farm home at Beech Haven Farms, Havelock, 1919. The two-story structure no longer exists but was on what is today Slocum Road.   New Bern-Craven County Public Library

died there thirteen months later. On March 2, 1922, newspapers reported that "the home of Mrs. I.W. Shields, four miles from Havelock and one of the oldest and prettiest estates in that section, together with the stock barns and stables, was destroyed by fire." [b]

Across the creek neighbors of the Buys family were Robert H. and Ruth Ross. Robert Ross was a farm manager at the property on Beech Haven Farms Road, today's Slocum Road, which is one of the entrances to MCAS Cherry Point. The photo of Ruth Ross with some unidentified field hands, and the two views of the Ross home, are from the Shriner family photo album. They were taken in September 1919.

John B. Green III published the Shriner photos in his 1985 book *A New Bern Album*. In it, he commented about the style of the Ross home saying, "Although gambrel-roofed homes were common enough in New Bern, this is the only example of that type of home to be built in the county."

A gorgeous Craftsman-style depot was built at Havelock in 1901-1902 under the administration of James A. Bryan, president of the Atlantic & North Carolina Railroad. Its site was on the Lake Road side of the rail line at the intersection of the Beaufort to New Bern Road with the tracks. The depot was described as "forty by one hundred feet, with excellent waiting

James A. Bryan, president of the A&NC Railroad, took some heat for building such a large and stylish depot in 1901 near his plantation property at Havelock.

---

[b] *The Alamance Gleaner*, Graham N.C.

James Edgar White and Elizabeth Pate White, Havelock, circa 1895. EBE/ECU

room and office." The cost of the 4,000-square-foot train station $1,322.51. Bryan was criticized by outsiders for the lavishness of the Havelock depot. The critics said the Havelock depot would have been "appropriate and proper for Morehead City" and that a $500 structure would have done the job of replacing the "shed" that had served the stop previously. [c]

A new $621.70 water tower with a large, barrel-type tank was built down the tracks at Slocum Creek about 1902. The water tower serviced

---

[c] *The North Carolinian*, Raleigh, N.C., May 26, 1904, pg. 3.

steam locomotives. In the diesel engine era, its fallen and decaying remains were still visible beside the railroad tracks in the 1960s.

On the opposite side of the old Beaufort Road from the railroad depot and close to the Jesse Trader family, was the home of Ed and Elizabeth White. They were photographed (see previous page) about 1895 at the picket fence in front of their two-story house on what is today Miller Blvd. Ed holds a straw hat in his left hand and stands with a faithful spotted hunting dog at his side. Ed and Elizabeth were near newlyweds having just tied the knot on April 30, 1894.

James Edgar "Ed" White was born on November 18, 1869. His grandfather James Speight White was born in Craven County in 1806. His parents were George Washington and Lenora C. Hanks White. Ed's wife, Elizabeth Pate White, was born on September 24, 1876. She was a Wynne descendant through her mother, Sarah Jane Wynne Pate, born at Slocum Creek in 1851. Sarah was the daughter of W. H. and Elizabeth A. Wynne.

Like all the men just mentioned, Ed was a farmer. He also operated a country store at Havelock. The White Store was the polling place for a special school district election held May 9, 1910, and he was appointed as the registrar with Henry A. Marshall and T.L. Hill assisting. He was an avid hunter once photographed with a black bear he killed near Havelock. Despite ending his school career after the first grade, he was successful in supporting a large family including children Carl, Mary, and Glen.

The White's two-story Havelock country house had a tall brick chimney on the left side and a covered front porch. The home was gone and the lot vacant before the 1960s.

By 1920, the White family had moved to a farm near Granthan in Township 7 east of New Bern. Ed and Elizabeth died in 1950 and 1943 respectively and are buried at Cedar Grove Cemetery in New Bern.

Mrs. Schollenberger at Havelock

Maybe the Union soldiers were nostalgic. Maybe they circulated the word about the natural wonders of the area.

Maybe positive word-of-mouth spread among economic and social circles the locals couldn't fathom. For whatever reason, in the late 1800s and early 1900s, southern Craven County became a hit, a location, a place to be for the rich and famous of the northeastern corridor of the country.

Industrial magnates, sports stars, newspapermen, business tycoons, and sportsmen of every stripe could hardly wait to hop the train – or their private rail car – for the twenty-four-hour trip from New York City or Philadelphia to a backwoods paradise of hunting, fishing, and high-quality, free-flowing local booze on which no tax was payable.

Cartoonist Bud Fisher, above, created the first "comic strip" and his characters, Mutt & Jeff.

This pristine playground of the big river, creeks, and lakes was a place to pack your cares away, to relax, and have some fun.

Harry Conway "Bud" Fisher is credited with inventing the horizontal comic strip in 1907 starring his beloved characters Mutt & Jeff. Syndicated via the *San Francisco Examiner* of William Randolph Hearst, Fisher was soon a wealthy man involved with showgirls and racehorses. When he needed to unwind, it was off to Havelock, N.C. by train for some quiet time around Slocum Creek and the lakes district.

Fisher was one of a handful of truly famous personalities who frequented the area. There were other less-well-known but even more fabulously wealthy individuals, especially from the North, who hopped the train for a Carolina getaway. For the northern industrialists, in addition to relaxation, there was another attraction: unexpectedly cheap land. And plenty of it.

Just before the turn of the last century, Carrie Curran Schollenberger of Philadelphia bought 3,800 acres of land beginning near the Havelock railroad depot and stretching many miles into the forest south and west of the town. She paid the modern equivalent of more than one million dollars for it. She signed the papers on October 20, 1897. Then her husband, business magnate William S. Schollenbereger, Jr., did a curious thing. He immediately signed away to her his ownership rights to the property. [d]

Just off Lake Road and about two hundred yards south of the train station, the Schollenbergers soon built what would be the best designed home in Havelock, one of the finest in the county, a home that would have held its own against most others into the late 20th century.

---

[d] Craven County Deed Book 123, pp. 396, 429-32, 434 and 440.

Mrs. Carrie Curran Schollenberger of Philadelphia communes with a dog in front of her seven-bedroom manor home on Lake Road at Havelock, circa 1900.
EBE/ECU. Photo courtesy of Dr. John Kirkland of Charlotte.

William Schollenberger, Jr. was an outdoor sportsman and the home was built ostensibly for his family's country enjoyment and to entertain guests. It had seven bedrooms; two on the ground floor and five upstairs. There was a main entrance into a lobby with bay windows on each side. There were entrances in the front and back, which flowed into a salon with a fireplace suitable for social gatherings. French doors separated the salon from the formal dining room.[e]

The grand lodge had a backyard of nearly 4,000 acres replete with farmland, forest, and lakes. And, of course, there were servants.

In early 1898, Mrs. Schollenberger advertised for a cook and "a boy about twelve years of age as waiter. Must be well recommended."[f]

But with Mr. Schollenbereger spending much of the next few years either in Philadelphia or England and with Mrs. Schollenberger settling into Craven County society where she'd spend the remainder of her life, the purchase had the feel of a separation and a division of property.

The Schollenbergers had been introduced to the land tract by a Philadelphia real estate agent name David M. Hess. He'd been advertising the oversized parcel for several years and backed off his asking price of

---

[e] Author's interview with Natalie Sugg, March 7, 1984.
[f] *The Daily Journal*, New Bern, March 10, 1898, pg. 4.

$45,600, or $12 per acre. The Schollenbergers paid $35,000 or a little over nine dollars an acre.

William was the son of a Prussian immigrant who was a tanner of hides. William Schollenberger, Sr., born in 1826, grew his humble trade into a huge and lucrative Morocco leather company. The firm's four-story brick Philadelphia factory took up a city block. Then the father became an early proponents of oleomargarine but had to fight the entire dairy industry to get his product to market. Dairy lobbyists had succeeded in making margarine illegal. It was labeled "fake butter."

Amid their business battles, the massive factory of Schollenberger and Son was destroyed in a spectacular fire. The father and, particularly, the son were suspected of arson. It was hot news. In the end, they were vindicated and the insurance companies were forced to make a substantial settlement.

William, Sr. died in 1895 leaving a fortune to his son and namesake.

Though they lived in the deep forest country that abounded with lakes, navigable creeks, and wildlife, the Schollenbergers were a social hit in New Bern, just 15 miles directly up the rail line.

"Mr. William Schollenberger of Havelock was a visitor to the city yesterday," *The Daily Journal* noted on March 10, 1898. But a few months later, when the newspaper reported about a Thanksgiving party, Mr. Schollenberger was nowhere in sight. From an article dated November 24, 1898: "A number of New Bern young people went down on last night's train to Havelock … The occasion was a house party given by Miss C. Louise Schollenberger at her mother's country home at that place. The party will celebrate Thanksgiving Day and will continue the remainder of the week. The gentlemen took their guns and expect to find some sport in the fields. Those who went last night include Mr. and Mrs. Street of Philadelphia, now visiting here, Misses Kathleen, Margaret, and Isabelle Bryan, and Messers

Carrie Schollenberger poses for a photographer in her Havelock home, c. 1900.
EBE/ECU. Photo courtesy of Dr. John Kirkland of Charlotte.

Tom Waters, C.D. Bradham, F.S. Duffy, and D.R. Davis. Some others are expected tomorrow."

And the father wasn't around for his daughter's 1900 wedding to attorney D. L. Ward of New Bern.

From *The Morning Post* of Raleigh, February 9, 1900:

"New Bern, N.C., Feb. 8, Special. A brilliant wedding took place in the Christ Episcopal church yesterday afternoon at 4 o'clock, the contracting parties being Mr. David L. Ward, a prominent attorney of this city, and Miss C. Louise Schollenberger ...

D. L. Ward and Carrie Louise Schollenberger Ward on their wedding day in the salon of the Schollenberger home at Havelock, 1900.

Rev. T.M.N. George officiated. The church was filled with friends and acquaintances. Mr. Kearney, of Philadelphia, gave the bride away and Mr. W.L. Ward was best man. Miss Irene Peck was the pretty little flower girl. The ushers were C.D. Bradham, R.A. Nunn, D.R. Davis, and H.R. Bryan, Jr. There was a reception at the home after the ceremony, and the couple later took the steamer for an extended trip North."

Following the marriage of Carrie Louise to David Ward, the mother and daughter appeared from time to time in the society news columns of both Raleigh and New Bern newspapers. While maintaining the Havelock home, over time more of their activities were focused on New Bern.[g]

By the time the dissolution of the marriage between William, Jr. and Carrie Schollenberger was announced in 1909, Mrs. Schollenberger was living in New Bern.[h]

By 1915, the ownership of the home and acreage at Havelock had passed to David and Carrie Louise Ward. In that year, the property was sold to farmer Sidney E. Tilton and his wife, Katherine, who moved into the former Schollenberger home on Lake Road. Tilton had big plans for ditching, draining, and farming the thousands of acres around the lakes. The operation succeeded instead in lowering the water table and drying out the underlying peat, which soon caught fire and burned for years sometimes making the roads too smoky for travel. In 1920, a group of Greenville businessmen, including B. Bruce Sugg and Dr. Leon Meadows, bought the property in a series of transactions from Tilton.[i]

Prominent citizen Benjamin Bruce Sugg (1884-1975) founded the Star Tobacco Warehouse in 1914. He was a banker and served as Greenville's mayor. He was "a distant cousin" of Craven County farmer Wendell Davis Sugg. According to Sugg's wife, Natalie, the cousin soon asked W.D. Sugg to oversee the Havelock farm, which she described as "from the intersection of Miller and Church Road down both sides of Lake Road to Camp Bryan." The Suggs moved into "the run-down [Schollenberger] house" in 1937. The Suggs built barns and stables on the left-hand side of the road, hired a man named George Buck as a "hand," and built a house for him on the property. Even in need of maintenance, Mrs. Sugg said, "It was a most gorgeous house to be sure." She also spoke with admiration of Bruce Sugg who she described as "like a daddy to us."[j]

---

[g] *The Morning Post*, Raleigh, December 1, 1901, pg. 3.

[h] *The Philadelphia Inquirer*, July 7, 1909, pg. 8.

[i] Craven County Deed Book 206, pg. 463, July 9, 1915; W.J. Wynne, Jr., SOHP interview K-56, 1995; Craven County Deed Book 238, pg.234; Book 298, page 507.

[j] Interview with author March 7, 1984.

The arrow points to the Schollenberger dwelling on an unpaved Lake Road in the later 1920s. At right is one of the residential wings added to Havelock's one-room school house when it was sold to become a home about 1926. It sat at today's Church Road, Lake Road, Miller Blvd. intersection. The old post office shed, at left, was next to the railroad tracks, which were directly behind it. EBE/ECU

One of the other partners, Dr. Leon Meadows, would be another matter altogether. Meadows (1884-1953) was the second president of East Carolina Teachers College in Greenville. ECTC is today's East Carolina University. In 1944, Meadows was formally charged on sixteen counts of embezzlement from the college. In the value of 2021 money, the amount was more than a quarter of a million dollars. He was convicted on two counts in a 1945 trial and sentenced to three years in state prison.

After a few years on Lake Road, the Sugg family moved to a farm on Beech Haven Road, today's Slocum Road. By then the family consisted of the parents; three sons, William, James (the future Craven County attorney), and Thomas; and daughters, Bettie and Sarah. Mr. Sugg died young in 1962. Natalie Joyner Sugg (1910-1993) was a noted historian, genealogist, civic and social leader.

William Schollenberger, Jr. died in England. The date of his death and the place of his burial are unknown. Mrs. Carrie Curran Schollenberger (1853-1942) was buried at the Laurel Hill Cemetery in Philadelphia. Carrie Louise Schollenberger Ward (1875-1957) and David Livingston Ward (1860-1932) are buried together at Cedar Grove Cemetery in New Bern.

The former Schollenberger 3,800-acre tract at Havelock would be divided among the partners and sold off in pieces over many years. The old country dwelling home on Lake Road was left unoccupied for years. It continued to fall into disrepair until the 1960s when windowless, vandalized, and forlorn, it was referred to by local children as "the haunted house." Today, not a trace remains.

Society News

Columns of society news appeared in the New Bern newspapers each week from the various communities of southern Craven County. Once in a while, there was an actual news item but these were primarily congenial lists of people's comings and goings. Sometimes, for instance, James Hunter of Havelock would make the column just for riding the train to New Bern. Hundreds of these items were published over many years. Nevertheless, the few here are a good source of names and provide a glimpse of the quiet nature of the times gone by.

"*Bachelor* Items" in the news by an unnamed writer from June 2, 1897: "Miss Nannie Becton returned home Saturday from Cherry Point where she was visiting for a few days. Mr. Clyde Taylor and Miss Mamie Becton made a flying business trip to Beaufort. [*The term "flying" meaning "quick" in this instance.*] Rev. F.S. Becton preached Sunday night at Oak Grove and had a good attendance. Messrs. John Bowen and M.D. Taylor went out to Cherry Point last Sunday. A nice rain here, it is very much needed. Mr. C.F. Marshal of Winthrope passed through Bachelor Sunday on his way to Cherry Point. Mr. W.L. Harris is working on Adams Creek for a few days. Messers. Samuel Becton and Sons tug boat is very busy towing logs to and from Clubfoots Creek."[k]

A *Riverdale* list of December 13, 1905, said "Miss Margaret Fisher of this place has gone to Cherry Point to see her aunt who is sick. [*A number of the Fishers of Riverdale, and their affiliated families, had moved to Hancock Creek by this date.*] Mr. H.C.Wood has built a new piece on to his kitchen. Mr. Levi N. Latham of this place has been sick, but we are glad to say he is better now. Our public school is progressing finely under the skillful management of Miss Mittie Phelps. Miss Laura Latham was a visitor at Mrs. Jennie Cannon's Sunday. Mr. and Mrs. Levi Latham spent Sunday at Croatan. Mr. J.P. Fisher passed through our berg Monday en route to New Bern."[l]

Another *Riverdale* report appeared in the newspaper on December 13, 1906, from the pseudonymous "School Girl" who said the weather had been fair since Monday night's showers. "Mrs. J.T. Ives spent the day in New Bern last Friday. Mrs. B.B. Mallison is home from Spring Hope. Mrs. B.W. Ives was in New Bern Wednesday. Mrs. Lula Trader of Cherry Point was here yesterday. Mrs. A.D. Fisher and her daughter were in New Bern Wednesday. Mrs. B.B. Mallison returned from Pine Grove to her home at this place last Friday. [*The Mallison had the huge Egypt Plantation at Pine*

---

[k] *The Daily Journal*, New Bern, June 2, 1897.
[l] Ibid, December 15, 1905.

Grove]. Mr. J.B. Fisher and son spent part of the day in New Bern yesterday. Mr. and Mrs. C. Simpson spent the day in New Bern Monday. Miss Maggie Tucker who is teaching at this place is expecting to return to her home at New Bern tomorrow A.M. where she will spend Saturday and Sunday." [m]

Havelock, December 28, 1906, correspondent "B." writes "Mr. M.F. Russell of Cherry Point is spending the week with friends at this place. Mrs. J.E. White spent Tuesday night in New Bern. Mrs. E.A. Armstrong and daughter Zippette of Kinston are spending a few days here with friends and relatives. Miss May Lockey of Newport is the guest of Miss Georgia Godwin. Miss Nell Buys, a trained nurse in New York, has returned to spend Christmas with her parents Mr. and Mrs. William Buys. Messers. Clyde Jackson and Fred Bryan went to Harlowe Saturday to spend Christmas with friends and relatives. Mr. John Buys and his wife came home from Pennsylvania last Friday to spend Christmas with his parents. Mr. Ford Bryan was the guest of Clyde Godwin Monday night. Mr. and Mrs. John Hancock of Cherry Point are the guests of their mother at this place. Mrs. A.D. Rooks and son Cecil Dunn were guests of Mrs. James H. Hunter Sunday evening. We are glad to know Mr. R. Amans has improved his stock of chickens by buying some that lay eggs like gourds, twice a day." [n]

From *Havelock* on April 24, 1907, "Idle Hours" informed readers that "Mr. J.J. Trader moved in(to) our vicinity yesterday and his many friends are glad to have him as a neighbor. Miss Eliza Oglesby is spending this week with Mrs. R[*ufus*] Amans. Mr. W.Y. Wynne was in our village Thursday. Mrs. Mary Jackson who has been spending a few days with her mother in New Bern returned home Tuesday morning. Miss Sally Russell who has been spending a week at Newport returned home this morning. Miss Beulah Rooks was the guest of the Misses Georgia and Rena Godwin Sunday. Mrs. Lora Lawrence and children are visiting Mrs. S.G. Parker. Mr. Eliza Godwin was the guest of his brother, Mr. J.F. Godwin, Sunday. Master Earl Rooks who has been in the hospital for two weeks returned home Thursday and is getting along exceedingly well. Mrs. Addie Hill was the guest of Mrs. A.D. Rooks Monday evening. Miss Bessie Morton and little brother, Ashby, passed her Tuesday en route to New Bern. Mr. Orin Hill is spending a few days home on account of his hand burned. Mrs. H.G. Rowe and daughter Julia passed by Tuesday going to spend a few days with Mrs. Rowe's father. Mr. J.J. Ballard has been sick but we are glad to hear he is improving." [o]

The *New Berne Weekly Journal* of Oct. 11, 1907, announced that "Mrs. E.A. Armstrong [*Mattie Lena Armstrong of Havelock*] is spending a few

---

[m] *New Berne Weekly Journal*, December 18, 1906.

[n] Ibid, December 28, 1906.

[o] *The Daily Journal*, New Bern, April 27, 1907.

The Trader House was a Havelock landmark on the main county road after its completion c. 1910. Today, the former home of John Jesse Trader and wife Lula Ives Trader faces Miller Blvd. The grand and gracious country home is the largest to survive into the modern era. This was the boyhood home of Hugh Trader whose iconic country store across the road is one of the county's historic gems.

The farm home of Abner Parker Whitehead (1846-1925) and wife Margaret Dozier Whitehead (1855-1934) at Bachelor. Abner Whitehead descended from a family that settled in the Cherry Point area in the 1700s. Bachelor is east of Clubfoot Creek on Adams Creek. Road. The photograph, from the Margaret Wall Collection, is courtesy of John B. Green III and the New Bern-Craven County Public Library.

days at Cherry Point with friends and relatives." [*It was about two hours from Havelock to Cherry Point by buggy.*] The same paper on November 24, 1911, reported "The shadow party at the Cherry Point Schoolhouse Saturday night was quite a success. Our little village is 'booming' now."

The "special correspondent" for *Harlowe and North Harlowe* sent a 1908 report. "Miss Bessie Morton, accompanied by her little brother, Ashby, went to New Bern Saturday morning, where she went to the teachers' institute. They returned home Sunday. Mr. R.W. Ward has made a very remarkable improvement in his place by the erection of a nice wire fence in front of his place. Miss Laura Connor, of Thurman, is with her sister, Mrs. Jno. Morton, for a short visit. Mr. N.D. Bangert went to New Bern on the shoofly this week and returned Tuesday night. [*The "shoofly express" was a nickname for the A&NC railroad trains, which carried enough fish out of Morehead City for the line to be called "The Old Mullet Road."*] Mr. Albert Bangert, and a friend of New Bern, were here last week and spent the day with Mr. E.D. Bangert. They were on their way to Cherry Point. The school of Miss Frannie Knight at Blades closed last week and she is now spending a while with her aunt, Mrs. C.D.F. Bell. Mr. John S. Morton went to New Bern on business. Dr. Bilfinger came down this week to look at the plant in course of erection here. He returned home at New Bern by the shoofly yesterday. Mr. Lewis Baxter, who has been spending a while here with Mrs. Baxter and her parents left yesterday on the shoofly returning to his home in Petersburg. Dr. C.N. Mason was called to Winthrop Mills to several patients Tuesday of this week. He is kept quite busy now. Mr. W.F. Butler of Norfolk, Va., representing the Stief Piano Company was here last Saturday to tune the piano at the home of Mr. James R. Bell. Mr. W. B. Swindell of Morehead City was over today looking after getting some logs from some of our timber men. Mr. James R. Bell left for Havelock to take the shoofly to New Bern where he goes to spend a day on business." [p]

Note the various spellings of Slocum Creek in *Cherry Point* news for late August 1912: "Mr. F.F. Abbott was a business visitor at Slocums' Creek Sunday. Misses Bettie Mitchell and Gladys Wood were welcome visitors at Mrs. G.A. Russell's last Tuesday. Mr. W.Y. Wynne and family made a fishing trip to Slocum's Creek Wednesday. Mrs. Mollie Barnes is visiting friends and relatives at Newport, N.C. Quite a large crowd of New Bern people spent the day at Sloccum's Creek Thursday. Mr. and Mrs. John Williams, Mr. Robert Rowe, and Mrs. Sarah Gaskins of Croatan spent Tuesday fishing at Slocumb Creek. Messers. Fred and Ford Bryan of Havelock made a fishing trip to Slocomb Creek Wednesday. Mrs. L.C. Jones of Soccom's Creek has gone to spend a month at Blount's Creek. We

---

[p] *New Bern Weekly Journal*, February 7, 1908.

are glad to know that school will soon start and we will have our same teacher, Miss Sallie Russell, of Havelock. Mrs. W.T. Belangia and children have been very sick but are better now." [q]

The Hub of the Community

Of course, a church is and was considered holy ground. Souls are saved there. People baptized. Marriages consecrated. Funerals preached. And, as important, vital, and necessary those things are, in the villages of southern Craven County, in the 1800s and early 1900s, they were more. The churches were where people gathered for all sorts of reasons.

In an undated photograph from the early 1900s, Havelock Methodist Church in the midst of one of its expansions and renovations. EBE/ECU.

The community or social hall served as an impromptu town meeting room. In addition to prayer circles and study of scripture, men met to socialize, and to brainstorm about politics, and to puzzle over the important issues of the day. Women met to discuss their concerns and interests, for group projects, and social reasons. People gathered for birthday parties, baby showers, music recitals, lectures, choir practice, and club meetings. In times of trouble, it's where people gathered. If a child were missing, the search party was organized there. If there was a bell, it rang to summon help or to get people together to deliver urgent news. But the key functions were always Sunday school, bible study, and worship services.

If the community was a wheel, the church was the hub around which it spun. Through the church, you were received by the faithful when born and borne by the faithful at death.

The local churches served the people, but the people also served the churches. They became deacons and church mothers, some assisting in these and other roles for decades.

---

[q] *The Daily Journal*, New Bern, August 27, 1912.

If there weren't enough pastors, pulpits went empty. In horse-and-buggy days, a minister who served the Methodist Church lived in Newport and had responsibilities at other churches. In 1916, for example, a pastor named C.H. Caviness hop-scotched between churches in Craven and Carteret. A minister who filled in at a church was called a "supply" and Caviness was supplying several churches of what was called the Croatan District.[r]

"You'd be lucky to get a preacher once or twice a month," life-long church member W. J. Wynne, Jr. said. "But there was Sunday school held every Sunday."

Havelock Methodist was on the county's main thoroughfare, the New Bern to Beaufort road. Just a little further up the Beaufort Road toward New Bern was the Havelock Christian Church. Down the Beaufort Road a few miles in the other direction was Little Witness Baptist Church.

At Havelock Methodist, there would be Christmas parties for the kids each year, complete with a hand-decorated Christmas tree and Santa Claus.

The church was heated by a wood-burning stove.

"When I was a boy growing up, we didn't have electricity yet," Wynne noted. "They had electricity that came into Newport from Morehead City. They had electricity that came down to Tom Haywood's Store [at Croatan] from New Bern. There were not enough customers for the power company to think they could afford to build a line for maybe two dozen families."

Havelock wouldn't get electric service until the 1940s at the advent of MCAS Cherry Point.

Power or no, churches functioned. Sometimes truly large gatherings were held. Like in February 1911: "News from Pine Grove Station by J.S. Bell, Pastor In Charge." Our quarterly [A.M.E. Zion] conference was a harmonious one, encouraging and inspiring. Sunday was a high day, it being Passover day, quite a number of people favor us with their presence from New Bern, Beaufort, Morehead City, Pilgrims Rest, Hymans, Little Witness, and Havelock. The presiding elder was at his best in all his services. Sunday night we close with a love feast and general class meeting. The Holy Spirit was indeed felt in some of our hearts. The presiding elder, Rev. Mayboy, deacon Collins, and deacon Cully serving. The total amount collected for all purposes, $54.46. Thus ended a glorious quarterly meeting. The Lord's name be praised."

The local churches had many roles. There was another important mission for the churches as well: burying the dead. Not only preaching funeral and comforting families but providing a final resting place for the deceased. A graveyard.

---

[r] *The Morning New Bernian*, December 7, 1916, pg. 2.

The largest burying ground in Havelock is at the United Methodist Church on today's Miller Blvd. Many members of the community's earliest families are there. But it's not the only church cemetery by far.

Where Pioneers Rest

Taylor. Adams. Hancock. Hardesty. Mason. Pelletier. Garner. Bell. Dudley. Foreman. Gooding. Guthrie. Connor. Rigdon. Sabiston. Small.

These names, and many more found on the headstones of the Harlowe United Methodist Church cemetery, occur repeatedly on deeds, land grants, marriage bonds, contracts, and other documents dating back to when every-

Harlowe United Methodist Church

one in the colonies was ruled by a king. A good percentage of the more than four hundred individuals buried there were born before and survived the War Between the States in the mid-1800s.

The classic brick chapel with its signature lightning-rod sphere hovering above its steeple sits beside the old Beaufort Road 11.8 miles down Highway 101 from Cherry Point's main gate and just a few hundred yards into Carteret County. Despite being across the county line, the church has long been a mainstay of the Harlowe district and until 1919 was part of the same Methodist "circuit" as its Havelock counterpart.

The word *circuit* harks back to a time when ministers on horseback rode long, lonely miles from one un-pastored church to the next. In a 1974 history of the church and the Harlowe community, Rev. Edgar F. Seymour put it this way:

> "There was one solitary preacher, a stranger to every citizen of the State, belonging to a people who were unknown to all that dwelt in this vast extent of territory … and that herald of the Cross, with his horse, saddlebags, Bible, and hymn-books, trusting with a firm and unwavering faith in the God that had redeemed and pardoned him through the blood of his Son, came pioneering this

unexplored realm, and carrying the 'glad tidings' of the personal salvation that he had experienced in his own consciousness, to those that sat in the region of darkness and shadow of death'."

Founded in 1834, the church serves an area named shortly after Capt. Christopher Dawson sold a piece of land at a creek-head of the Newport River to a newcomer named John Harlow in 1712. The district's earliest maps reflect the name.[5]

Among those interred there are David W. and Sarah A. Morton, born in 1823 and 1828 respectively. Sarah Morton died in September of 1897, almost eight years after her husband. Aristotle Connor was born on August 28, 1825. He was 58 years old when he died on February 20, 1884. Also buried together in the Harlowe cemetery are a long-lived couple, Daniel Bryan Dickinson and wife, Senia F. Dickinson. Born in 1826, she was in her eighty-sixth year when she died in 1912. Her husband, born in March 1825, had just celebrated his ninetieth birthday when he died in April 1915. The Dickinsons' headstone carries the epitaph: "They are not lost, but gone before."

While we have thrust First United Methodist and Harlowe UMC into the limelight here, there are many other churches, black and white, that have given spiritual sustenance to generations in southern Craven County, and today give a resting place to their dearly departed.

The graves of the pioneer Whitehead family – and many more – are at Oak Grove United Methodist, for instance. And we've previously mentioned the Core Creek Church, which was built for the place of his birth by philanthropist Fairley Dickinson.

Among the storied places of worship are the Croatan Presbyterian Church, Croatan Free Will Baptist, the Craven Corner Church, Hyman's Chapel, Pilgrim's Rest United Church of Christ, Zion Temple, and St. Antioch Missionary Baptist Church at Great Neck. Each has a history, some stretching back more than a hundred years. Pine Grove African Methodist Episcopalian Zion Church, for example, was organized by 1865. It's thought Little Witness had done so about the same time. Green Chapel Missionary Church at Hickman Hill was founded in 1861, and, as we mentioned, the First United Methodist Church of Havelock, founded in 1878.

This is not only sacred ground on which we tread, but dangerous ground as well if we have failed to mention one of the old churches with ancient burying grounds. Our apologies if we have. The point is simply that the headstones and grave markers at these places of worship, not only

---

[5] Book 2, page 695, Craven County Records.

memorialize the deceased but also preserve some of our most valuable archaeological and historical data.

School Days, School Days, Dear Old Golden Rule Days

"Miss Lala Ewell who has been teaching the public school at Cherry Point for four months past came up to her home, the school having closed last week. A rosette party at the home of Mr. B.T. Borden was the concluding feature. Miss Ora Borden came up with Miss Lala to visit her," recorded the *Daily Journal* of March 13, 1895.

Miss Ewell was one of many school teachers who taught the educational basics to the children of southern Craven County. We remember a few others here.

Julia Arms had a school in the village of Hancock Creek. "Mrs. Marie Buys of Havelock has arrived to assume her duties as teacher in the graded school of New Bern," said the *New Bern Weekly Journal* of September 29, 1905. Nellie Buys was listed at age 20 as a school teacher. Henrietta Dixon was "Havelock's popular teacher." According to the *Daily Journal* of March 19, 1908.

"Maggie" Fisher was teaching school at Hancock Creek with her aunt, Julia Armes, in 1907. *The Daily Journal* of June 27, 1907, has them attending church together in New Bern. Etta Nunn "came home from Havelock yesterday where she has been teaching school," the same paper said on April 16, 1898. Missouri Russell taught at the Cherry Point school. Sallie Russell was a public school teacher at Cherry Point, according to John G. Johnson's *N.C. Yearbook and Business Directory. The Morning New Bernian* of November 3, 1917, said she "spent the weekend here [*in New Bern*] with relatives."

Margaret Thorpe lived near Cherry Point at the village of Hancock Creek and was also a teacher taught at the school run by Julia Armes, in 1907 and possibly 1908.

Minnie Vynes was "quite a successful teacher at her "school near Havelock." Her school put on entertainment to raise money for the local Methodist church, we are told. Maggie Tucker taught school at Riverdale, according to the *New Berne Weekly Journal* of December 18, 1906.

Jennie Willis of New Bern taught at Havelock in 1891. *The Daily Journal* of February 15, 1891, said she "returned home yesterday morning from teaching at Havelock." Mrs. W.J. Wynne was a public school teacher at Havelock in 1914, according to the *N.C. Yearbook and Business Directory.*

These are just a handful of the area's teachers through the years. As we mentioned in a previous chapter, the county's "common schools" began operation for white children in the 1840s. Many teachers have come and gone.

Havelock's one-room school was located across the road from the end of Gray Road at its intersection with the old Beaufort Road. In 1923, nineteen children and two teachers were present the day this photo was made. In the front row from left are Mary Williamson, Louise Garner, Lila Wynne, Bertie Lee Smith, Elaine Wynne, Thomas Jackson, Opal Ketner, Kenneth Ketner, Annie Mae Garner, and teacher Annie Franks Reel. Second row from left, Charles Jackson, Scott Williamson, Bill Jackson, Louellen Armstrong, Leslie Muse, "Doc" Hill, Bernard Ketner, and Ethel Ketner. Back row, teacher Rosalie Wynne, unknown, and Fred Bryan. EBE/ECU

Havelock's one-room schoolhouse was located on the Beaufort Road, today's Greenfield Heights Blvd. directly across the road from and at its intersection with Gray Road. Farther down Greenfield Height's Blvd. toward New Bern, an original schoolhouse for black children, and nearly identical to the white school, was still standing in 2021. [t]

A Visit to the School at Havelock, 1902

Miss Leah D. Jones of Craven County, one of the supervising teachers in the practice school of the North Carolina State Normal College, in promoting better educational conditions in several North Carolina counties, was a guest of the William Buys family of Slocum Creek during the summer of 1902. Her first-person account of her observations at Havelock follows.

"July 3d, I went to Havelock, twelve miles from New Bern, on the A. & N. C. railroad. I reached there at half-past ten in the morning. Marie Buys, a

---

[t] Photographs of both schools appear in the book *Historic Images of Havelock and Cherry Point, N.C.*

normal graduate, met me, and together we went from house to house, visiting every home in the district except one, which was three miles away.

"The school-house was … unfurnished, save with rude benches. It was situated in a pretty bit of woods, back some distance from the road, and if the underbrush had been cut away and walks made, would have furnished very attractive grounds. We planned the walks while I was there. On my first visit, we interested a young girl who went with us to that school-house and to the homes in the district. There were only about eighteen children in the district.

> "One of the committeemen of the school said there was no use talking education or beautifying school-houses to those [Havelock] people; that they were blockheads and that the committeemen should fix things to suit themselves."

One of the committeemen of the school said there was no use talking education or beautifying school-houses to those people; that they were blockheads and that the committeemen should fix things to suit themselves.

"Miss Buys' father invited the Havelock Sunday-school to have its picnic in his yard. He had also invited people from other villages and neighborhoods so that I had a chance to talk to forty or fifty people from Croatan, Havelock, Harlowe, North Harlowe, Adams' Creek, and Hancock's Creek. After dinner was over the yard was strewn with paper, box-tops, etc. I gave an object lesson by suggesting that we should not leave our friend's yard in such a condition, and the litter was soon collected and burned.

"One gentleman from Croatan went home from this meeting and stirred up the neighborhood by cleaning up the school-yard, the church-yard, and the grave-yard. Miss Mamie Hill of Havelock, the young woman who went around with us there, got the people together and cleaned up the Havelock school-grounds, scoured the floors and washed the windows of the school-house, and planned for a basket party to raise money to whitewash the house. The whitewashing was postponed on account of the breaking out of smallpox in the village. A second attempt was made, but another case of smallpox prevented it, and I have heard nothing from there since.

"Saturday morning, July 5th, I left Havelock." [u]

The Havelock school, mentioned by Miss Jones and visible behind the school children in the nearby photograph, was closed in 1925-26. According to W.J. Wynne, Jr., who missed starting school there by a single year, the

---

[u] *The Woman's Association for the Betterment of Public School Houses in North Carolina, Connor, R. D. W., 1906.* Source: Southern Historical Collection, UNC-Chapel Hill.

"powers-that-be wanted the Havelock kids to stop off at Croatan, but Croatan was just a two-teacher school and the people at Havelock wanted a better school for their kids."

To get the school kids to Brinson Memorial on the Neuse River east of New Bern in the 1920s, they hatched a plot. The local one-room schoolhouse, owned by the people of Havelock, was sold for cash to an individual. The building was moved down the street to the corner of Lake Road. "Wings" were added to each side by the new owner for additional space. The structure became a personal residence and was used into the 1970s.

The proceeds from the schoolhouse sale went to buy a truck chassis in Detroit, Michigan. This was driven to the Hackney Body Shop in Wilson, N.C. where a bus body was added to it. The bus was painted orange, the first such vehicle in North Carolina to be used to transport children to school. Wynne said the state later adopted the style, added some yellow to the color, and North Carolina buses have been the color ever since.[v]

With the school bus, the Havelock students were transported to and from the Brinson school each day it was in session.

In a time when many children didn't finish school – the period from the end of the Civil War to the end of the Great Depression – occupational options were limited even for high school graduates. Several sources have said repeatedly that there were three choices: Farming, the log woods, and making, transporting, or selling illegal liquor.

This isn't one hundred percent true, however. As we've just seen individuals could be schoolteachers. People were barrel makers, fishermen, blacksmiths, doctors, cooks, and hunting guides. Some people went into business, opening country stores, or dealing in horses and mules.

Nevertheless, opportunities were primarily in the trio of occupations mentioned so often. We'll explore the logwoods and farming later. For now, let's take a look at what was behind Door Number Three.

---

[v] W.J. Wynne, Jr., SOHP interview K-56, 1995.

Goin' to Atlanta

Author's note: Years ago, when we wrote about moonshine and bootlegging in the first Havelock history book, *In This Small Place*, the names of those who participated in the illegal trade were not printed. It was written in 2005 that we would use "first names, nicknames or aliases" but that "every word is true as rendered" to the writer. Attributing facts is important in this line of work so, in retrospect, that appears to be some pretty thin gruel. Nevertheless, we're sticking with it, more or less, in telling this part of the story about an illegal vocation that flourished in southern Craven County for half a century.

Those curious readers desiring to know who got caught in the moonshining trade between 1900 and 1950 will find that old news stories are searchable online. And those familiar with the area may not be surprised by the family names to be found in those stories.

There are three exceptions to what has just been said. Fred Solomon Nelson went on the record in a 1995 interview recorded by a researcher from the University of North Carolina. Nelson spoke candidly about his experiences, and those of his father, Walter Nelson, on their Nelson Town farm. The family of Sidney "Sap" Hardy gave permission for use of his remarkable portrait made with one of his moonshine stills at Havelock. And Adam Cully, who knew much about the bootlegging trade without ever saying how.

Others appearing herein are sources of information and were not necessarily involved in making, selling, or transporting "shine."

The first thing to know is that it's a hard way to make a living.

There were no lazy men in this line of work. Most years, moonshine liquor – distilled in equipment that looked like it came from the lab of a mad scientist – was the only cash crop.

"It's how we bought shoes," one person said.

Asked why someone would make and sell illicit whiskey and they'd suggest that "starvation" was the only alternative. That was overstating things, of course. Barring some calamity, nearly everyone could grow, shoot, or catch all the food they needed. But if you wanted to do more than subsist, there had to be a source of income.

Setting up a still was laborious and complicated. Whether a person built the still or bought one, it took cash money, or something substantial in trade.

A site was needed that had the contradictory attributes of being easy to get to and hard for law enforcement to find. There had to be a source of water, which might mean sinking a well. Once the still was built and all its supporting apparatus was ready, the process took constant supervision. There was acquiring the ingredients, mixing the mash, timing the fermentation, running the distillation process, putting the product in barrels or jars, transporting it, and selling it, while not getting robbed, or caught by the law.

Adam Burt Cully was the last person in Havelock to get around in a mule cart. Adam, the grandson of Eliza Ann Cully, lived in the family's ancestral home on former American Missionary Association land. The Cully farm was across the railroad tracks at the terminus of a dirt path at the end of Manila Street in the city's western half.

Adam (1900-1969) was a friendly, polite, even humble man. He was tall and thin. He dressed like a farmer in plain, sturdy, sensible clothes. Work boots. Brimmed hat. If you needed a bushel of sweet potatoes, a mess of greens, a load of firewood, or the tilling of a garden, Adam was your man. He and his aged mule were a big hit with the kids, black and white.

He took the time one day, many years ago, to explain to the author the making of a little moonshine liquor. He also threw in tips on the fine points of avoiding arrest around the still site.

Craven County Corn liquor, the then-ubiquitous CCC, earned during the Depression a standing for quality that some say stretched to New Jersey, New York, Massachusetts, and beyond. Many in the Havelock-to-North Harlowe section took great pride in both its quality and well-earned fame.

Mayor D. M. Clark of Greenville inadvertently helped popularize the brand name during a 1921 meeting of the North Carolina Anti-Saloon League in Greensboro. Speaking of the area including southern Craven County, Mayor Clark declared that "whiskey stills are as thick as fleas on a dog's back." He said "raising corn, cotton and tobacco had been abandoned" in favor of the manufacture of illegal "monkey rum" that he designated Craven County Corn. His comments using the name and the initials made frontpage regional headlines.[a]

North Harlowe earned the bulk of the credit. A statewide newspaper said in 1923 that it was "that little corner of Craven county which has given Craven a National reputation for its famous 3 "C's," which when being correctly interpreted, means: *Craven County Corn*." [b]

Historian, author, and university professor David Cecelski, while in graduate school in Boston, recalled meeting an old man who had run a

---

[a] *The Charlotte (N.C.) News*, February 3, 1921, pg. 1.

[b] *The News and Observer*, Raleigh, September 25, 1923, pg. 16.

"speakeasy," an illegal bar in Baltimore during Prohibition. When the man learned that Cecelski was not only from North Carolina but also from Craven County, he said with enthusiasm, "Oh, my goodness! We had three brands at my bar in the 1920s, and you could always count on CCC!" [c]

It was impossible in the 1960s to navigate the woods anywhere around Havelock and not come across former still sites. Excavations, old boilers and their various parts, copper coils, and stacks of Mason jars with corroded lids were like archaeological artifacts along the southwest prong of Slocum Creek and in the woods around Don-Lee Heights, Greenfield Heights, Indian Hills, and Gray Road.

These clandestine discoveries led to questions and Adam was willing to provide answers. Some of the talk about thumpers, worms, doublers, running, and slopping back was over the youthful observer's head but the broader concepts were easy enough to understand.

Making moonshine was "like baking a cake." He said you had to follow a recipe. The best recipe. Measure things. Get time and temperature right. If you didn't, you could "burn the liquor." If you never put in anything but the best, the pure stuff, you'd come out with a product that was "strong, but easy to take."

He said the constable or revenue agents had to catch a person in the act of producing moonshine to make an arrest. The most dangerous time was when the mash was fermenting because it took a while for the mixture to set up just right in big wooden boxes built for the purpose.

To be on the safe side, Adam said a person could take a spool of black Clark-brand thread and tie it to a sapling near a still. Then the fellow could walk a big circle around it in the woods, all the time unspooling the thread. Once a circle was completed, the hypothetical moonshiner would tie it off and leave. When you returned to the still, he said, you'd check to see if the thread was broken. If it was, you'd know someone else had been there and might be lying in wait. In that case, you could either go home or go some safe distance away and watch to see who was there.

"'Cause you don't want to go to Atlanta," he explained.

The Atlanta Federal Penitentiary was the home-away-from-home for those caught and convicted of bootlegging in eastern North Carolina.

Adam said conversations went like this:

"I haven't seen Willie in a while."

"Yeah, he's down to Atlanta."

Despite their best efforts and tricks-of-the-trade, more than a few men in southern Craven County involuntarily visited 601 McDonough Blvd. SE in the Georgia capital over the decades. It opened in 1902 as the largest

---

[c] SOHP, K-56, UNC-CH, 1995.

FEDERAL PRISON, ATLANTA, GA.—4

A 1920s postcard shows the federal penitentiary in Atlanta, Georgia.

prison in the country. It held 3,000 inmates. When the liquor business was best, the 1910s-1940s, the arrest and conviction rate was high. A typical sentence was one year with some served at hard labor.

Federal prohibition of the manufacture, sale and transportation of alcohol began with the passage of the 18th Amendment to the Constitution in 1919 and ended with the passage of the 21st in 1933. North Carolina however, was the first state in the South to enact a statewide prohibition. It began in January 1909 and North Carolina's laws against alcohol remained in effect for years after federal prohibition ended.

The newspapers of the period regularly ran stories of those arrested at still sites or for transporting liquor. Many of those arrests were in southern Craven County. These accounts document that both races were involved in all aspects of the trade and about equally likely to wind up behind bars.

African Americans farmed, worked in the logwood, or made CCC, said W.J. Wynne, a Havelock native, and former Craven County commissioner. "That was the only jobs available for blacks," he said. "Lots of moonshine was made at that end of the county," referring to Cherry Point before the base, North Harlowe and Adams Creek. "It was against the law ... but people had to live somehow. They'd get caught, serve prison sentences, and return to moonshining."

Wynne noted that Havelock people also made moonshine, "not just the Harlowe crowd."

"There were white people and black people, both," he said. "The white people had more money and could make more sophisticated stills. And they knew how to get it to market and not get caught. A lot of the black people worked for the white people in that business."

Much of the liquor was sold on the local market but "a lot of it was bootlegged out of the county, to other parts of the state, and other parts of the country," he said.

Fast cars were used, and an untold amount left on steamers, barges, and fishing boats. "At one time, some even got shipped on the freight train out of here," he said.

"This was anything but a prosperous place," he said. "Havelock had the big river, the Neuse out there. Hancock's and Slocum's Creek was the waterway. Then, down Lake Road, we had what we called the lake section. Hunting clubs that drew people from all over the country … like at Camp Bryan. But nobody here had a lot of money."

Revenuers Make Headline News, 1921

"ARRESTED IN STILL RAID: Is Now In Jail, Awaiting $500 Bond – Raid Was Made Near Havelock. Revenue Officer W.D. Allen brought another alleged moonshiner to town late yesterday. [He] was caught at a still about five miles east of Havelock early yesterday morning by the revenue officer. It was said that [he] was actively engaged in the manufacture of liquor and that the still was running at the time the raid was made. The still was of 35-gallon capacity. [He] was brought here and placed in jail. His bond had been fixed at $500 but it has not been forthcoming." *The New Bern Sun Journal* September 17, 1921.

"ARRESTED MEN ON SUSPICION: Were Seen At Still During Raid Last Week. [X], white, and [X] colored, who are alleged to have been seen at a still at which [a different X] was arrested last week are now being held under warrant. They waived examination and the bond was fixed at $500 each. They are still being held in the county jail. The still was about two miles from Havelock. When the officers made their recent raid the two men ran away but they were recognized and arrested subsequently." *The New Bern Sun Journal* September 19, 1921.

"MAN ARRESTED RUNNING STILL: Federal Prohibition Agent Allen made a raid at the head of Hancock's Creek, in the Havelock section, yesterday and succeeded in surprising [X] in the manufacture of corn liquor. He offered no resistance and was taken to Beaufort where he will be given a hearing before the U.S. Commissioner and probably bound over to await trial in the next term of federal court." *The New Bern Sun Journal* September 22, 1921.

Sidney M. Hardy (1897-1936) of Havelock with a moonshine still of his own design and construction. Hardy, known by the nickname "Sap," was a skilled auto me-chanic by trade. He was also sought after for his innovative distillation know-how. In his Harold Lloyd spectacles, a straw hat pushed back on his head, and with a cigarette dangling from the corner of his mouth, he sat for a portrait in the woods near his Gray Road home in the 1920s, about as self-assured as a man can be.

Photograph courtesy of the Hardy family. EBE/ECU.

"ANOTHER STILL RAIDED: The war on illicit stills in Craven county continues with unabated vigor. Revenue Officer W.D. Allen telephoned Sheriff Williams last night that he had succeeded in making another raid between Havelock and Harlowe and had captured a large copper still, together with considerable equipment. No one was at the still at the time the raid was made, although it showed signs of recent activity." *The New Bern Sun Journal* September 27, 1921.

Gunfire in '22

"REVENUERS" RUSH PLACE, FIND TWO STILLS: A hundred rounds from rifles and shotguns fired over the heads in warning was not enough to halt the march of revenuers in the "Cahooky" section, five and a half miles east of Havelock, off the New Bern-Beaufort road at noon today and the raiders headed by W.D. Allen, prohibition enforcement agent, captured two copper stills of a total capacity of 16 gallons along with several thousand gallons of mash. The operators escaped.

"Mr. Allen with W.C. Rector, another prohibition agent, and Deputy Sheriff W.C. Gaskins, were winding up their march through two miles of swamp, when as they stepped out on a ridge, shots rang out several hundred yards away, coming they believe as a warning to them, and at the same time as a signal to the operators from sentinels that surrounded the place.

"The officers rushed the plants but found them deserted." *The News and Observer*, Raleigh, February 1, 1922.

Machine Guns at the Courthouse

Tension ran high in 1924 when the speeding Cadillac of a North Harlowe rum-runner struck and killed a 12-year-old girl on the two-lane Central Highway in front of the Croatan school. The car was reported to have been traveling "at a dazzling speed" when the child was hit. The impact catapulted her forty-eight feet through the air.

Newspaper reports said "whiskey runners use that highway as their speedway" and that people along the stretch were familiar with both the car and its driver from his frequent high-speed passes.

The child was the niece of Tom Haywood. The accident occurred in front of his famous Croatan store on what is today US 70 a few miles west of Havelock. Haywood refused the offers of the distraught bootlegger to transport the child to the hospital in New Bern. Haywood loaded the victim in his car and sped away from the scene. All efforts were useless. The head, neck, and leg injuries were beyond the benefit of medical care.

Word of the tragedy and its cause spread quickly as did news of the bootlegger's arrest and the seizure of his load of liquor contraband. As a crowd assembled near the county jail in New Bern, local authorities were on the phone to N.C. Governor Cameron Morrison. Hearing their concerns, Morrison promptly ordered National Guard Battery D to the scene.

A heavy, black, all-caps headline ran across the entire front page of *The Morning New Bernian* newspaper: CHILD KILLED ON HIGHWAY BY RUM RUNNER'S CAR.

The news account said, "Soldiers took their stand at the jail, mounting two machine guns on the lawn at 6:30 last night, but, while hundreds gathered for the next hour, there was no disorder nor indication that the fears of the authorities might materialize. The batterymen remained on duty throughout the night."

The excitement wasn't over though. The troops fired on the automobile of one of their men who didn't properly identify himself as he was reporting for duty. The single round missed the driver by inches, passed through the car, and no one was injured.

A Cadillac of the early 1920s

The rum-runner, who had been out of jail on appeal of a previous conviction, was quickly swept out of town to a Raleigh jail and whatever mayhem the local authorities had feared never came to pass.

The driver of the speeding car went to prison, of course. The child, Edna Williams, was buried in the Croatan community cemetery across the highway from her uncle's country store. [d]

Flying Packard Goes Through Town With Cargo of Craven County Corn was another *New Bernian* headline, this one from September 26, 1923.

"Running at a rate of 80 miles per hour or better, a white man driving a Packard automobile outdistanced a member of the local police in a race out Trent Road and made his escape toward Pollocksville," the news account began.

Police had been tipped off that a car "loaded with whiskey" was on the way. They posted themselves at the Trent River bridge, the local chokepoint for stopping moonshiners. The driver pulled over for the officers, got out,

---

[d] *The Morning New Bernian*, November 26, 1924, pg. 1.

and approached their car, but when one of them said he believed there was "something in the car" the driver climbed back into the Packard and "left there like a bird." The New Bern car gave chase reaching its maximum speed of 65 miles per hour. The Packard was soon out of sight.

Blind Tigers, Watchdogs, and a Bar at Slocum Creek

- "A recent train derailment at Havelock caused blind tigers [*a nickname for people who sell moonshine*] to flock from the woods in large numbers, according to reports had here. The train was delayed several hours. Hardly 10 minutes had elapsed before men and women, mostly negroes, were surrounding the train with suspicious packages. Trade was fairly heavy." [e]
- "When I started up, I was fourteen years old," said a man who grew up to be a successful and well-known name in Havelock. "A regular job paid twenty cents a day but there were no regular jobs. They put me in a little skiff boat with a cane pole at the edge of the creek where anyone coming in had to pass. I was a watchdog. If a stranger came along, I was supposed to holler 'I got a fish. I got a fish,' and go to jerking on the line like I had something on it." [f]
- Reuel Henry Pietz, in a college thesis about the growth of the south shore of the Neuse River, came to the conclusion that "the attempts by authorities to stop the practice of illegal liquor manufacture helped develop a close-knit community, distrustful of strangers and making them loyal to their own people, even though they did not all agree that whisky-making was proper. Local people were assumed to be good and outsiders were believed to be bad." [g]
- Working on a tip, revenue officers raided an alleged distiller's barn at Slocum Creek in 1913. They didn't find a still. They found "the most complete barroom they ever saw." There was whiskey and beer in bottles and jugs of every kind, and glassware for the use of the patrons. Since government officers in those early days couldn't make an arrest or even confiscate booze unless there was evidence of a sale, and since no one on the premises was willing to swear that they had purchased whiskey or beer, they left the barn "not well pleased with the outcome of their long trip to Slocumbs Creek." [h]

---

[e] *The Daily Free Press*, Kinston, March 28, 1923, pg. 1.

[f] Interview by author, 1998.

[g] Reuel Henry Pietz, *The Impact of the Cherry Point Marine Corps Air Station Upon Local Settlement*, 1964.

[h] *The Daily Journal*, New Bern, December 13, 1913, pg. 1.

How One Guy Got Caught

They call it "moonshine" because so much of the activity is at night, under the light of the moon. But it was a moonless night when revenue officers raided a still in North Harlowe three-quarters of a mile off Highway 101 in the late 1930s.

One of the men helping to run the still that night was young and strong. He'd grown up in these woods. Played in these woods. He knew every nook and cranny, every walking trail, deer trail, and rabbit trail for miles around.

Now, with the surprise arrival of revenue officers, he was running like his life depended on it, he told family members who later told the writer.

He'd always known that in a foot race in these woods, especially in the dark, nobody could catch him.

So why couldn't he shake this white guy?

He'd been running like mad for ten minutes and this one was right behind him the whole time. He'd dodged and weaved, cut one way and other, and the man was still on his tail. He'd hit a trail and run down it. The guy was right there. Finally, in desperation, he crashed into thick brush, ran for about a hundred yards, and dove to the left into some bushes. He laid there holding his breath. As still as rock. As quiet as moss.

The lawman walked right up to him and said, "On your feet. Let's go."

What are you going to do? The young moonshiner stood up, was handcuffed, and the two of them started making their way out, back to the others, back to the cars, and no doubt on to jail.

After walking for a few minutes, though, the moonshiner couldn't stand it any longer. He said, "Man, I just gotta know."

"Got to know what?" The lawman said.

"How did you keep up with me like that?"

"It was kind of easy," the lawman said. "The flashlight's on in your back pocket."

Moonshining at Nelson Town

Fred Solomon Nelson says he was seven years old when his daddy started making moonshine.

Walter Nelson entered the trade the same year the federal government enacted Prohibition, 1919. He was 24 years old. Operating from the family's 131-acre farm at Nelson Town, at the center of what is today the Marines' airbase, he'd stay in business for the next twenty-two years. As a result of his hard work, ingenuity, and luck, Nelson grew to be as close to wealthy as a man could be in economically depressed southern Craven County.

Before he became a moonshiner, Walter Nelson worked at a sawmill on Hancock Creek near the village of Cherry Point. The son said his father was the "head block-setter." Starting in the log woods at an early age, Walter Nelson worked himself into the second most important position at the sawmill.

The boss of that team was the sawyer. He stands behind the saws, some of them five feet tall, and runs the control levers and winch that moves the log along the carriage. The block-setter *rides* the carriage toward those spinning sawblades. After the sawyer makes the first cuts, the block-setter calls the shots on the rest of the milling cuts for the log.

Some consider it the most complicated job in the sawmill. It's the hardest to learn because the block-setter has to keep all the calculations in his head for the various thicknesses of boards to be made. He must think two or three moves ahead "like a chess player," some say, to maximize the amount of useful lumber yielded by the log.

You have to be smart and you have to think fast to be a block-setter.

For reasons of his own, Walter set up a still on his farm in 1919, made whiskey, and sold it. He never looked back. He'd continue to farm, growing his own corn and other crops. But the main crop was the shine.

Through the years, Walter Nelson earned a reputation for making good whiskey. He was one of the suppliers who prided himself on finessing the best product; one of the reasons CCC was in such demand.

Fred said there was plenty of competition. Even white people came in and set up stills. They hired others to work for them. Nonetheless, there were plenty of thirsty customers – a nation full of them – and they sold all they could make.

His father owned his own still. He used sugar, meal, and wheat bran to make the mash. They tried molasses sometimes "but it made bad whiskey." They called it rum.

Walter made moonshine, plenty of it, but he rarely hauled it. That was another layer of danger. And he found over time that people would come in and buy it right there on the farm. Individuals would come and drink. They'd buy what they wanted for themselves and others. Some entrepreneurial sorts would buy in large quantities so they could re-sell the product, making it a wholesale-retail operation. Fred said, "a lot of them came from Newport."

"They would sell it to their friends," he said. "If they didn't have money, they would bring a hog's head to trade. Especially in 'Hoover's time.' [*The Great Depression beginning, more or less, in 1929.*] They would trade hog's heads or sides of meat. Sometimes corn. During Hoover's time, there wasn't much money."

Fred said that bootlegging was "the quickest way to make money." At a regular job, a working man made five cents an hour to a dollar a day.

The Walter Nelson House at Nelson Town, 1941. At top, prosperous farmer and moonshiner Walter Nelson lived in one of the area's finest homes on a 131-acre farm. The graceful and spacious two-story house featured multiple porches and chimneys. The Nelson family lived for four generations in the middle of what is today MCAS Cherry Point. The settlement was begun at the end of the Civil War by Nelson's grandfather, former slave Smith Nelson. At bottom, a few of the farm's numerous outbuildings are shown. including a barn, pack house, and stable. Two vehicles are visible, a pickup truck, at left, and a sedan, at right.

Edward Ellis Collection. ECU. House image 753.1.e.27, barns image 753.1.e.27a

If you worked on the farm, you made fifty cents a day for ten hours of work. If you grew tobacco, you'd get ten cents a pound, which "wasn't enough to pay the fertilizer bill."

His first job was washing dishes at the Hotel Villa in Morehead City, a vacation place for white people who came on an excursion train from the western parts of the state. When the Depression idled that business, Fred was laid off. Bootlegging seemed like a reliable way to earn money. When jobs were scarce, people depended on it.

The money was good, but whiskey-making wasn't without risk.

"Sometimes customers would rob you," he said without elaboration. And, of course, you could get arrested for bootlegging.

If the federal agents, the revenuers, caught a moonshiner, they'd wind up in the federal penitentiary in Atlanta. But if convicted on county or state charges, a man might end up "out on the road" wearing stripes on a chain gang.

Fred said some of the county officers would accept a bribe. "A few of the federal officers would, too," he said.

As the fame of CCC grew, customers began to show up from Kinston, Goldsboro, and Raleigh. Sometimes business was slow and customers wouldn't come to buy. Then you had to make of choice of waiting or risking the extra exposure of hauling liquor yourself.

From CCC to CCC, and back

Fred quit the business because of Katie. He married Katie Toon in 1935. They knew each other from childhood. They'd stay married for the rest of their lives and have many children together.

She supported her husband and his work. She remembered Fred's time moonshining. In talking about it once, she recalled one particular customer, a Mr. Cotton. Cotton was a tall man and liked to drink liquor. It must not have hurt him any. Katie said he lived to be a hundred and five. She said they all drank back then but "didn't get drunk like they do now." There were good times.

"You could go out at night and nobody would bother you," she said.

Still, she worried. She didn't want Fred to get caught, or get hurt. She asked him – she told him – that he needed to quit. So, he pulled away from the business in 1935 at age 24 and took a job with the federal Civilian Conservation Corps. There's a certain odd irony, or coincidence, or symmetry in leaving the sale of CCC to go to work for the CCC. But that's what he did.

The CCC camp was on the opposite side of the New Bern highway from Hickman Hill. There were 200 black men from all over the country working under white foremen. Fred was one of twelve locals hired. Most of them were made "assistant leaders" since they would be there as the other men came and went.

The CCC was created by the government to get men out of the big cities and away from the need for welfare assistance. In Craven County, the CCC men were busy in the Croatan Forest. They were building roads and planting trees. They also fought forest fires. They worked a regular schedule but were on call twenty-four hours every day. The pay was $30 a month.

"That was a lot of money," Fred said. "One dollar a day."

White men had originally worked at the camp where they were. When the black camp was activated west of

Fred Solomon Nelson

Havelock, the white camp moved to Pine Cliffs, to the east down Highway 101.

The men at the camp wanted to drink. Fred knew how to make it. For a couple of years, he rotated between the two different sets of Cs before going back to moonshining full-time in 1937.

Close Calls

Walter Nelson's twenty-two-year run of good luck almost came to an end one day. His son said the father was moving an entire wagonload of whiskey when a revenue officer passed right by. The inattentive officer glanced at the man and moved on.

When Fred was discharged from the Civilian Conservation Corps camp and went back to making liquor, Katie was as worried as ever. She talked to him about it often.

"She said, *the man's going to catch you*," he recalled.

There were a lot of Alcohol Beverage Control officers. All of them white. One, in particular, was named Cox. He made himself familiar. Cox and the others would come down to the area and stay overnight. Sometimes things would be quiet with the revenue officers for a long time. Then, sometimes, all of a sudden, they'd start pulling one raid after another. Some of it was routine police work, but some of it was pure politics. A new prosecutor trying to make a name for himself. An ambitious officer looking for a promotion. During the Depression, law enforcement jobs were precious and valuable. The men with badges wanted to hang on to them.

One morning, it was past time for Fred to have left the house to work at his still, but Katie kept after him, all but begging him not to leave.

"That morning I kept saying, please don't go," she said. "And you know something. You know I'm telling the truth. As he was getting ready to go, the man was walking down the side there, going on down there, just before [Fred] got there."

They had found Fred's still. They knew the time he went there. That morning they had moved in to take him, but, because of Katie, he hadn't yet left his house when the law arrived.

"They had to catch you in the act," he said. [i]

But She Didn't Know Who

Pauline Frazier was born into the close-knit community of Frazier Town east of Clubfoot Creek in 1911. Everybody knew everybody and had for generations.

Some of her ancestors had been slaves but others had not. There was Indian blood in her lines, so much so that one of the ladies in the family claimed to be from Hawaii.

As a child, Pauline walked to her school next to the Craven Corner Missionary Baptist Church on Adams Creek Road. And into her thirties, she lived in the heart of the liquor trade.

"Mr. Henderson (Godette) had a store and so did Old Man Sweet," she said, explaining that Sweet was also a Godette. She said he sold "knit-knacks" and cakes and drinks, but Henderson Godette sold groceries. She said people didn't sell liquor in stores. It was made in the woods and sold in their houses. She said people came to Frazier Town to buy liquor. But sometimes the customer was an "undercover man." Then someone would get arrested.

She said that in general the law "didn't give people a hard time in Harlowe." The trouble was in New Bern if you had to go to court. Bootleggers almost always went to jail when they were caught.

In 1996, at age 85, Pauline recalled that white people along Adams Creek Road also made whiskey. Those who didn't could buy it "from the colored people, if they were friends."

---

[i] Fred S. Nelson, SOHP K-40, 1995.

THE MISSING PORCH POST – The Arts & Crafts style of architecture from the 1880s onward included "pillar and post" construction on front porches. An empty pillar with missing porch post, like the one left of the front door above, was an invitation along Highway 101 from Havelock to Beaufort, to come and buy a drink or a jar of moonshine. Although the trade is long gone, a few homes along that stretch of road are still missing a post to the present day. Artwork by the author.

"They never was trouble between the races," she said.

She knew that Havelock, Cherry Point, and North Harlowe were the centers for a lucrative whiskey-making business for decades in the first half of the twentieth century. She knew the product was generally high-quality. She knew many people were in the trade.

"A lot of people did that back then," she said, but she didn't know who. [j]

Postscript: Did Havelock Have a Chicago Mob Connection?

We found a curious 1928 story with the awkwardly-phrased title *Havelock Shipment Liquor, To Chicago, Reaches Norfolk*. It reported that "assorted liquors valued at more than $100,000" had been seized in Norfolk. That would be over $1.5 million in 2021. It was the largest haul in their local history. The booze was in a boxcar and the paperwork for "200 barrels of sweet potatoes" showed that the shipment came from Havelock, N.C.

---

[j] Pauline Frazier, SOHP K-124, 1996.

The sender was A.C. Raynolds, Norfolk. The shipment was to Bathistini Brothers, Chicago. The address was in a big Chicago produce market.

Police found fourteen barrels of sweet potatoes in the middle of the car at its big, sliding door but the rest of the barrels held liquor. And here's the most curious part. It wasn't moonshine. It wasn't CCC. The Norfolk police found 100 cases of cognac, 25 cases of imported single-malt Scotch, and more than 300 quarts of rye whiskey.

"It is believed that the liquor was loaded aboard the car at Havelock after being brought into the Neuse River by way of Pamlico Sound and the Atlantic and the car seized here is only part of the cargo of some rum ship," the news story concludes.

The local word-of-mouth has always been that booze went out of Havelock on the train. This news story tells us how it was done. But the local lore was *always* about moving homemade corn whiskey, not about the international smuggling of name-brand liquor.

And Chicago? In 1928, notorious gangster and crime boss Al Capone was at the apex of his power in control of the Chicago mob. Is it likely that so much booze could be shipped to Chicago without mob involvement?

The questions multiply. According to the story, a train carload, or more, of liquor was offloaded from a ship in North Carolina coastal waters, was loaded on a smaller boat or boats. It was then off-loaded somewhere in a local creek, from which it was somehow transported to the Havelock railroad depot, and was packed into a boxcar!

Who could have arranged such a thing?

How many people were involved?

What happened to the rest of that shipload?

Was this a one-time event or an ongoing operation?

The Havelock-to-Chicago story was very thinly reported. It is only printed in a few North Carolina newspapers. We found ours in the *Roxboro (NC) Courier*, of all places, dated March 28, 1928. Searches for A.C. Raynolds and the Bathistini Brothers had been a dry hole.

Until...

A Breakthrough in the Chicago Mob Connection

Not Bathistini Brothers, but *Battistini* Brothers.

According to its masthead, *The Chicago Packer* was "Dedicated to the Interests of Commercial Growers, Packers, Shippers and Receivers of Fruits, Vegetables, Melons, Etc." The industry's newsletter reported on

Havelock Shipment Liquor, To Chicago, Reaches Norfolk

Norfolk, Va., March 25.—Assorted liquors valued at more than $100,000 according to prevailing bootleg prices and the biggest single seizure of such contraband ever made by the Norfolk police, was discovered this morning in a box car on the Norfolk Southern railroad tracks. The freight bill shows the shipment originated at Havelock, N. C., and was billed as 200 barrels of sweet potatoes. The consignor was given as A. C. Raynolds, of Norfolk, and the consignee as Bathistini Brothers, 102 South Water market, Chicago.

The car contained 100 cases of cognac, 25 cases of imported malt and more than 3,000 quarts of rye whisky. Fourteen barrels of sweet potatoes were placed in the middle of the car at the doors. The police received a tip last night that the car was coming into Norfolk on its way to Chicago and several officers armed with a search warrant were in the Norfolk Southern yards when the freight pulled in.

It is believed the liquor was loaded aboard the car at Havelock after being brought into the Neuse river, by way of Pamlico sound and the Atlantic and the car seized here is only part of the cargo of some rum ship.

The Roxboro (NC) Courier, March 28, 1928, pg. 7.

December 16, 1922, that Sam Battistini had been re-elected as a director of the Chicago Fruit and Vegetable Shippers' Association.

The association represented thirty firms in the South Water Market produce district "that are engaged in the carlot and less-than-carlot shipping business to the jobbing trade in the territory." A "carlot" is a boxcar load. Battistini and his unanimously-elected fellow directors and officers were installed at a well-attended dinner meeting in "the clubrooms of the Chicago Produce Club."

Samuel Morino Battistini's older brother and business partner was Jacob Frank Battistini. The older brother went by the name Jack. Jack and Sam Battistini had been born in 1888 and 1889 respectively to Frank and Harriet *Battistine*. Their father was a French immigrant. With an apparent eye toward fitting in and better business, the boys Italianized their names to Battistini in Mafia-ruled Chicago.

The Chicago mob made its living off Prohibition crime. It was the country's major trafficker in illegal liquor. The iron-fist ruler during its heyday was Alphonse Gabriel "Scarface" Capone, a chubby Italian with a winning smile and a heart as hard and cold as glacial stone. Arguments rage to this day over how many men he killed in one evening with a baseball bat at a fancy black-tie banquet. The scores range from one to three with two smashed heads being the consensus. After the savage killings, the dinner continued.

U.S. census data for 1910 shows Jacob Battistini, 22, and Samuel Battistini, 20, living with and apparently supporting their widowed mother through their work at a Chicago "commission house." A commission house is a brokerage that deals in stocks and bonds. In this case, it also dealt with commodities, specifically fruits and vegetables. Soon after, Jack and Sam formed their own firm, Battistini Brothers, at 102 South Water Market in the heart of the city's busy produce district.

The transit records for the *SS Cuba*, an excursion vessel that ran from Key West to Havana, show that Samuel Battistini, 34, and Harriet Battistini, 66, were passengers on January 26, 1921. Books have been written about Cuba's central role in supplying liquor to the United States during the Prohibition era. In the early days, Cuban rum was the major product for clandestine deliveries to U.S. ports.

That's why we have the terms *rum-runner,* and *rum boat,* and why the three-mile offshore limit was nicknamed the *rum line.* As the Coast Guard got more sophisticated in its tactics, the business shifted to less-trafficked southern U.S. waterways. The product mix changed as well. A variety of branded alcohol began to be legally shipped from England to Cuba for not-so-legitimate transshipment to American consumers.[k]

There is, of course, no record of the Battistinis' involvement in smuggling, but they *were* in the shipping business, and the mysterious March 1928 news story specifically cites the firm as the receiver for the load of "sweet potatoes" from Havelock, N.C.

Sammy Battistini, however, would not have been there to help unpack the "produce."

Headline: *Excitement Kills Man During Storm.*

"Sam Battistini, 35, a leading wholesale fruit dealer of Chicago, died of apoplexy following his submersion in waters of Lake Gogebic, 36 miles from here Saturday afternoon. Excitement, caused by a squall, which suddenly came up, is believed to have caused his death. Excited, Battistini stepped from the boat into eight to ten feet of water before the boat reached the dock. His body was pulled out immediately, but life was extinct."[1]

Apoplexy is a stroke. On Lake Gogebic Death Certificate #13, the coroner ruled that Sam's August 23, 1924 death was caused by "accidental drowning." The "informant of death" was a man named George J. Mahoney.

Seven months after his trip to Cuba, Battistini was buried in Chicago under a headstone engraved "Our Sammy."

A little less than four years later, the load of illegal liquor left from Havelock disguised as sweet potatoes. The shipment was valued at an astonishing 100,000 1928 dollars, and it was destined for 102 South Water Market, Chicago, when it was waylaid at Norfolk.

The next we hear of Jack Battistini is his bold block advertisement in *The Chicago Packer* that he was leaving the business "effective as of December 1, 1931." A news

story in the same publication, dated December 11, said Battistini had "severed all relationship with the business enterprises known as Battistini Brothers, the Hi-Ball Celery and Vegetable Company, and the Service Fruit

---

[k] *A Thousand Thirsty Beaches: Smuggling Alcohol from Cuba to the South during Prohibition*, Lisa Linquist Door, 2018.

[1] *Kenosha (Wisconsin) News*, August 25, 1924.

and Vegetable Company and is no longer connected with any of the above styled firms."

One of the men taking ownership of Jack Battistini's three entities – including the ironically named "Hi-Ball Celery" – was none other than George J. Mahoney who had been with Sammy Battistini when he died of excitement.

In 1937, after the end of the federal prohibition of the manufacture, sale, and transportation of alcohol, Jack Battistini announced he had opened a new produce business doing "car lot brokerage and distributing." [m]

He lived until 1974 reaching the ripe old age of 86.

Summation

Even with the additional facts, questions linger. A novelist could bend the story in many directions. In one version, Mother Battistini is a criminal mastermind pushing her boys into the smuggling trade. In another, young Sammy decides to get in on the action and sets up his illegal importing operation, only to be discovered and deep-sixed by mobsters, who then force the big brother to act as a front for Capone's gang. Or maybe, Jack was just a good soldier all along, and Sammy really slipped off the boat.

Who was A.C. Raynold, whose name was spelled *Reynold* in some other reports? How many Battistini shipments went undetected? But, for us, the most mysterious part is how folks who appear by all available evidence to have been backwoods moonshiners in southern Craven County fit into this international tale of intrigue. Was there a Mr. Big at Havelock?

One surmise is that some individual or individuals – like the ones in the next chapter's *A Sportsman's Paradise* section – learned that the Havelock crowd had devised a railroad smuggling system and took advantage of it. We have no reason to suspect any of the people mentioned there, but hundreds of other well-connected individuals came to the area in the 1920s, the names of whom we may never know.

The story is ripe for further investigation. We encourage readers to do so. Maybe you'll get a book or movie deal out of the project.

Unfortunately, all the old-time players are long gone. None are left to question. But all of them said – every time they mentioned local liquor leaving on the train – that potatoes were involved.

---

[m] *The Chicago Packer*, February 6, 1937.

Making Ends Meet: 1890-1940

"It's very hard to get hold of any money."

-- Schoolteacher Alicia Blood
Woodbridge (Havelock), N.C.

The first immigrants from Europe dug in to survive wherever they landed. A generation or two later, other opportunities arose and people loaded their Conestoga wagons and headed west. Southern Craven County experienced a major out-migration when *Go West Fever* struck at the beginning of the 1800s.

Tennessee, with lots of newly-opened lands, became a hot destination, as did Alabama and the Northwest Territories. People began to move off the North Carolina coast in droves, some of them abandoning land claims to relocate.

The Quakers, early civilizers of the area, pulled out en masse.

The devastation of the Civil War and the collapse of the lucrative naval stores business brought the second round of people moving out of Craven County in the late 1800s.

One was C.H. Hunter.

Collins Hughes Hunter was born on the banks of Slocum Creek near Havelock N.C. in 1863, the height of the War Be-

HAVELOCK MERCHANT – A young Collins Hunter as he would have appeared during his Havelock years when he was a store keeper, postmaster and railroad agent.

tween the States. As we've learned, his father James H. Hunter was a Confederate scout and courier engaged in dangerous clandestine activities in eastern North Carolina territory occupied by Union forces from 1862-1865. Collins was the third generation of the family living on the south shore of the Neuse River.

Before the war, the Hunters presided over a sprawling 500-acre plantation on what is now the Marine Corps airbase at Cherry Point.

As a young adult Collins Hunter – known for much of his life by his initials, C.H. – was an early postmaster and country shopkeeper near the railroad tracks at Havelock. The place was a stop on the Atlantic and North Carolina train line and young Hunter was also a station agent for the A&NC, selling passenger tickets and handling freight.

General store operators near train depots often augmented their income by contracting to send and receive mail which moved with the passage of the daily train. Collins appears in the archival records of the U.S. Post Office as postmaster at Havelock in 1887.

All commercial activity within the tiny hamlet of Havelock was concentrated around the intersection of the Old Beaufort Road with the A&NC railroad tracks. The course of Old Beaufort Road today is followed by Greenfield Heights Blvd. and Miller Blvd. So, Hunter's store was one of a series of mercantile businesses in the vicinity of, but pre-dating, today's preserved local landmark, Trader's Store.

The late 1800s were hard times for southern Craven County and many people moved out for greener pastures. The plantation economy had been impoverished by the turmoil of the 1860s. It had never recovered. Now, with

ROXBORO GROCER – C.H. Hunter holds his daughter, Mary, while sitting next to his wife, Betty Dudley Hunter, in the early 1900s in front of what may be their Roxboro residence. At right, Collins's father, James H. Hunter, sports his finest duds and a handsome cane during a visit. In later years, the elder Hunter, a long-long resident, farmer and civic leader in Havelock, made Roxboro his final home.

the advent of metal-hulled steamships, forest-based industries that serviced the wooden ship trade were on the wane.

Looking for more opportunities than Havelock afforded, Hunter visited Roxboro, in Person County north of Raleigh-Durham near the Virginia border. He liked the looks of the place and bought two lots there. As of May 1890, the name C.H. Hunter began to appear in the "Roxboro Courier" newspaper as a "Staple and Fancy Grocer" selling meat, meal, flour, lard, syrups, sugar, coffee, and canned goods. His motto, the ads proclaimed: "Low Prices and Square Dealing."

C.H. Hunter's Store was a hit and so was C.H.

His elderly father, Jim Hunter, a linchpin of southern Craven County his entire life, would soon follow his son to a new home.

The Havelock area had lost another hard-charging businessman and his family. The drip, drip, drip of outmigration would continue until the population of Havelock, once an active and prosperous locale, was down to about one hundred by the end of the Great Depression.

Jim Bryan and Southern Craven County

But don't turn out the lights, or *lantern,* quite yet. The vacuum caused by Hunter's departure seems to have been quickly filled. In 1896, there were four (!) general stores operating in the vicinity of Havelock. The proprietors were John DePorte, M.N. Fisher, Jr. (at Hancock's Creek), J. L. Gorrell, and Edward M. Piver.

The magistrates for Township Six were J. H. Barnes, Dock Cooper, Andrew Jackson Chesnutt, James H. Hunter, E.H. Hess, John D. Pittman, and Benjamin E. Williams with Edward D. Russell at Havelock.

This information comes from the 1896 edition of *Branson's North Carolina Business Directory*, which was something like today's chamber of commerce membership guide. Branson's also listed the prominent farmers at Havelock.

Several names we would expect to see: Jim Hunter, Henry Marshall,

Maj. James A. Bryan

Edward D. Russell, and Benjamin Williams. Others included W.H. Mallison, W.H. and J.D. Pittman, Mrs. Emeline "Emily" Rowe, Andrew J. Rowe, Mrs. Mary L. Taylor, T.W. Brame, J.L. Stevenson, and G.T. Tippett.

But also listed as a farmer at Havelock was James A. Bryan.

Why should that come as a surprise? Maj. James Augustus Bryan was a New Bern businessman. He served as mayor of the city. He was president of the Atlantic & North Carolina Railroad. But he was also an heir of Richard Dobbs Spaight, former North Carolina governor killed in an infamous duel, who once owned most everything from the Trent River to the Carteret County line. That included much of the land surrounding Havelock and the lake section west of town.

Bryan owned the dam and mill site that Spaight had built circa 1786. His land holdings around Havelock totaled 57,484 acres, according to an 1899 report prepared for Bryan by Edward Jack. In case you haven't made the connection yet, he's *the* Bryan of *Camp Bryan*.

Bryan liked the southern end of the county enough that he had a house off Lake Road and put in his own rail stop nearby to make his travels to and from the county seat more convenient and impressive. Despite his ties to New Bern, he was a regular presence in southern Craven County.

Among his assets was the 15,000-acre Lake Ellis Plantation. There, he had both farm fields and turpentine pine trees. The amount of acreage varied because he would sometimes drain one of the lakes to plant special crops like rice. Yes, *rice*.

James A. Bryan's Lake Ellis Plantation was off Lake Road near Havelock.
Image courtesy of John B. Green III.

Of the rice, a newspaper reported that "at Havelock and adjoining the McLean's Hollander settlement, in this county, is a luxuriant rice field of 70 acres cultivated by Mr. J.H. Hunter." A rider on horseback going through the field found the rice plants "were seven feet and one inch tall in height, reaching his shoulder when sitting in the saddle." [n]

There were thousands of acres under cultivation for a variety of crops. Some of the farmland was rented to area farmers, but on February 18, 1881, the *Charlotte Democrat* newspaper reported that Bryan himself had a yield of 606 pounds of lint cotton per acre at Havelock. One week earlier, the *Wilmington Weekly Star* wrote: "James A. Bryan, Havelock, Craven county, takes the gold premium of $15, having produced on one acre near Lake Ellis, 102 ½ bushels of rice. This acre was not manuered but was in a position to be supplied with the proper amount of water at all time from the lake."

Bryan also had livestock: Holstein and Jersey cattle, Jersey Red, Poland, China and Essex hogs, sheep, and mares.[o]

Hunter and Bryan knew one another through their time in the Confederate army where Bryan had earned his rank. Hunter aided Bryan in management of the plantation and, in addition to his farm at Slocum Creek, cultivated some land there himself.

In the 1880 agricultural census, Hunter is shown renting from Bryan 640 acres of tilled land and 15,341 acres of woodlands. He valued his own Slocum Creek farm at $30,000. At an inflation rate since then of 25-to-one, that's about three-quarters of a million dollars in 2021. He reported $300 in farm implements, $200 worth of livestock, and a production value for the year of $7,000 ($175,000 in 2021). He had one horse, 18 hogs, six chickens, and had produced fifty dozen (600) eggs. He had three milk cows and had made 150 pounds of butter. He'd killed four cows for meat plus two cows died that year.

On his rented acres at Lake Ellis Plantation, he produced 11,875 bushels of corn on 475 acres, ten bales of cotton on 25 acres, 1,500 bushels of potatoes on 60 acres, and 18,480 pounds on 80 acres, substantially increasing his farm income.

In a regular farm report in 1887, D.W. Morton near the Carteret County line said his cotton and corn were "pretty fair" but the weather had been too wet for the past ten days. J.L. Taylor of Adams Creek said the "crops were promising" and he didn't have "too much cotton planted." Benjamin F. Borden on "Hancock Creek, near Havelock: too wet, cotton good stand, bugs bad on corn, prospects pretty fair for a good crop." And W.B. Flanner at

---

[n] *The Daily New Bernian*, September 6, 1880.
[o] *New Bern Daily Journal*, June 2, 1887.

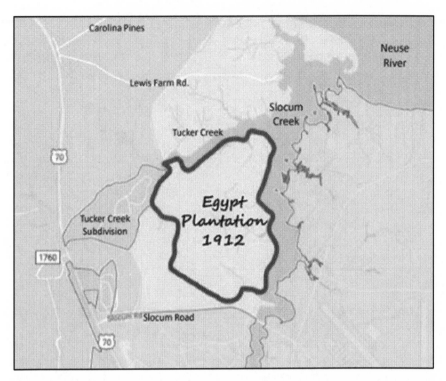

The 1912 location of the 1,700-acre Egypt Plantation is shown on a modern map of Slocum Creek, the Tucker Creek Subdivision and Carolina Pines above. To-day's US 70 approximates the route of the old county main road, the New Bern-to-Beaufort road of colonial times. Egypt Plantation was owned by the Mallison family and was part of a thriving farm section that stretched from Slocum Creek to Riverdale. The site is now part of MCAS Cherry Point, as is the land to the right of Slocum Creek.

Croatan indicated things were about average. His cotton wasn't coming in as well as last year, bugs were eating his corn "badly," and "it had been too wet the last few days."[p]

Lake Ellis wasn't the area's only big farm. The agricultural district from Slocum Creek west to Riverdale, known as The Croatan, included the 1,700 acres operated by brothers W.H. and Benjamin Bynum Mallison. It had been known in earlier times as the Pate farm. In 1892, the Mallisons were planning to build a new residence and move there by summer. Primary crops there were potatoes, peas, and tobacco.[q]

---

[p] *New Bern Daily Journal*, June 9, 1887.
[q] *The Daily Journal,* New Bern, Jan. 5, 1892 and January 12, 1899.

In 1912, the Egypt Plantation Company bought the property from the Mallison estate and made headlines when they announced a new-fangled 45-horsepower gasoline tractor would be used to plow and clear the land. The new owners said they thought the work could be done with the tractor "Cheaper Than by Horse Power."

The farm had three miles of Slocum waterfront and the "main dwelling," apparently the one built by the Mallisons, was described as colonial architecture "very appropriate to the site, being on a high hill overlooking Slocum Creek, and surrounded by large elms of several hundred summers."

Major crops were to be cotton, corn, hay, wheat, and all types of vegetables. The farm had "a pasture for hogs, sheep, cattle, and goats."[r]

The majority of the farms were smaller than Lake Ellis and Egypt, of course, but farming was the number one occupation. Those listed as farmers in the era's censuses, both black and white, approached ninety percent.

The Racial Makeup of Southern Craven County

Using 1930 as the benchmark, black and mixed-race families outnumbered white families two to one in the lower half of Craven County. In Townships five, six, and seven, a total of 720 households are listed. Of those, 213 are shown as white and 507 black. African American families were 70.4 percent of the population.

In Township Seven, 390 households are shown in 1930. Of those, 107 are white (27.4%) while 283 are African American (72.6%). In Township Six, of 152 total households, 63 are white (41.4%) and 89 are black (58.6%). Of Township Five's 178 households in 1930, 43 were white (24%) while 135 were black. The percentage of African American households in Township Five was 76 percent.

Extrapolating from the existing 1930 census data, the total population of southern Craven County, from the Trent River to Adams Creek, was about 4,383. African Americans numbered 3,068 while 1,297 were white; about a 70%-30% racial divide.[s]

Considering the available data, the population numbers seem to reflect both the legacy of the plantation chattel slavery culture and the ability of whites to out-migrate in higher numbers. In earlier eras – colonial times to just before the Civil War, for example – the split had been closer to 50-50.[t]

---

[r] *The Daily Journal*, New Bern, August 11, 1912.

[s] Federal census date for 1930 accessed on familysearch.com.

[t] *The History of a Southern State*, H.T. Lefler and A.R. Newsome, University of North Carolina Press, 1954 pp. 118-119.

African Americans, like the Michael and Martha Toon family pictured above, were the bulk of the population in southern Craven County in the early 1900s. Toon was a farmer and his extended family gave the name *Toon Neck* to a settlement off Highway 101 near its junction with Hancock Creek. The village was also known as Melvin, because of its post office, and Little Witness because of its church. The Toons' 31-acre farm was on Melvin Road, which ran from the highway into what is now MCAS Cherry Point. During the 1930s, 70 percent of the Craven County's inhabitants south of the Trent River were black. Photograph courtesy of Wade Fuller. EBE/ECU.

While many African Americans and mixed-race individuals farmed or worked as laborers, others found employment in the timber industry, and as fishermen or boatsmen. Some were skilled craftsmen.

In the 1920s, W.H.F. Johnson, George Fenner, and Henderson Godette were house builders. Thomas Bell built boats. William Whittington and Jacob D. Becton worked as logging contractors. Martin Davis was a painter. Bettie Godette, Daisie Harris, and Melvina Robinson were public school teachers. Rev. A.R. Andrews was a Methodist minister and George Alonza was a merchant.[u]

Others were entrepreneurs.

In 1912, ten black men of Havelock formed a mutual insurance company. George Cully, Abraham Dennis, Allen E. Whittington, Isaac H. Carter, George W. Benjamin, W.T. George, A.E. Pelham, D.C. Cooper, George W. Chance, and A.L. Cully were chartered by the secretary of state's office to operate the Grand Lodge of Home Protection of North Carolina.[v]

---

[u] U.S. Census, 1920, Townships Five and Six, Craven County.

[v] *The News-Record*, Marshall, N.C., December 6, 1912. pg. 8. "A.L Cully," may be Alvania Cully, wife of George Cully. The article misspells George's name as "McCully."

A mutual insurance company is owned entirely by the policyholders and may pay dividends to the policyholders from any profits earned.

A Sportsmen's Paradise

As we've mentioned, another moneymaker was what we now call "tourism." Vacationers, campers, hunters, and fishermen flocked to Slocum Creek and the lakes of southern Craven County in the late 1800s and early 1900s. They came as individuals, in groups, and as families. The region had incredible word-of-mouth and steady publicity through the printed word.

The Sportsman's Gazetteer and General Guide of 1883 was 977 pages of advice for hunters and fishermen. It had this to say about Craven County:

"New Berne is easily reached from New York by rail or by water direct, or by water via Baltimore and Norfolk steamers. To go to the lake region, take the cars at New Berne on the Atlantic and North Carolina Railroad, for Havelock Station, sixteen miles distant.

In the vicinity of Havelock Station is a heavily wooded country, vast pine uplands, and swamps where gum, maple, and other trees grow in dense profusion. Five miles from the station is Lake Ellis, a round lake about three miles in diameter, and nearly connected with it are four or five other sheets of water. Some of these lakes are open water; others are grown up, like Lake Ellis, with grass, through which a punt [*a flat-bottom boat with a square bow*] can be easily pushed.

These lakes are the resort of thousands of wild geese, black ducks, and mallards, very few of any other kind being found there. The dry swamp known as Long Lake, to the south and west of the above chain of ponds, is an excellent place to hunt bears, panthers, and wild cats. The pine ridges in the vicinity offer excellent deer hunting.

As but a few persons about New Berne hunt in these forests, there are but a few guides to be had. Sailing down the Neuse River from New Berne, the yachtsman will pass several good shooting points, one of which – Slocum's Creek, about eighteen miles from the city – is a resort for various species of ducks. In these woods colored guides can be had for 75 cents to $1 per day, finding themselves in provisions.

Black ducks and Canada geese are found in large numbers.

The fishing … is of great variety and excellent, including trout, drum, bluefish, and other varieties."

Such advice was commonplace and drew a veritable parade of sports figures, politicians, and the well-to-do from the big cities.

Most have heard that the world-famous baseball great, Babe Ruth, spent much of his off-time in the woods around Havelock. Many of the local families have passed down cherished stories of "The Babe" (1895-1948) taking a drink in someone's kitchen, visiting the sick, signing a kid's

BABE RUTH BAGS DEER AND DUCKS ON INITIAL HUNT

King of Swat Is Enjoying Annual Hunting Trip in Havelock Section of State.

Babe Ruth, king of swat in baseball and one of North Carolina's foster sons, is back in Tar Heelia for his annual hunting trip in the Havelock section. Every year Ruth comes to North Carolina to hunt and get his leg muscles in shape for early baseball practice.

On the hunting trip with the Babe is Bud Fisher, renowned originator of the comic-cartoon, "Mutt and Jeff," and Frank Stevens, intimate friend of the Bambino. Mrs. George H. Ruth is expected to join the party at Camp Bryan, Sunday.

The sultan of swat reported bagging a large deer and several ducks in his initial hunting round Tuesday. Both Ruth and Stevens, dressed in hunting outfits, displayed hunting licenses very prominently.

The last sentence of the story from the *Daily Tar Heel*, December 8, 1932, was a little dig as The Bambino had been fined for hunting without a license on an earlier trip.

baseball, or simply being seen walking down the road. Other notables include Christy Mathewson (1880-1925), who pitched seventeen seasons for the New York Giants; the aforementioned cartoonist, Bud Fisher (1885-1954); and Frank Stevens, son of a renowned New York ballpark concessionaire, Harry M. Stevens, credited by some with inventing the hot dog. Frank eventually inherited the business and the title "The Hot Dog King."

During a visit by Mathewson and Stevens in 1912, their companions were noted to be New York City police Lieutenant George Schoenick; Professor John Henry Larkin of Columbia University; Walter A. Bass, governor of the New York Stock Exchange; New York politician, and judge Charles Dodd; "and other well-known New Yorkers." [w]

N.C. Governor Thomas Bickett; former secretary of the Navy and publisher of the Raleigh *News & Observer*, Josephus Daniels; former Olympic athlete and prolific novelist Rex Beach; and several Fort Bragg generals are listed as 1928 visitors. [x]

And never forget, one of the big draws was the high-quality, free-flowing moonshine available to each and every one of them. Here in the heyday of Prohibition, they could drink away from the public eye and the scrutiny of law enforcement.

The rich and famous were just the tip of the iceberg. The bulk of the trade was in everyday folks who followed the lead of the notables.

[w] *New Berne Weekly Journal*, December 13, 1912.

[x] *Asheville (NC) Citizen-Times*, by Gertrude Carraway, December 30, 1928, pg. 3.

For instance, the *New Berne Weekly Journal* of Oct. 11, 1907, announced that Mr. R.H. Satterthwaite, of Colleton, S.C., and Mr. G.L. Turnage, of Hugo, N.C., are spending a few days at Camp Liberty, Cherry Point, N.C., fishing and hunting."

A few from 1916 alone: *The Kinston Daily Free Press,* June 8, 1916: "Smithfield Boy Scouts are camping at Havelock."

The Raleigh News and Observer, August 2, 1916: "Messrs. E.E. Warrick and F.B. Crowson returned yesterday from Havelock where they have constructed house tents in which the families are to spend the summer. They say fishing is unusually good this season, and that life at Havelock is exceedingly pleasant."

The Albemarle Enterprise, August 17, 1916: "Mrs. S.H. Milton and son, Clifton, returned a few days ago from a camping trip near Havelock. In the party which they joined were Mr. and Mrs. F.B. Crowson of Goldsboro."

The Raleigh News and Observer, December 13, 1916: "Off to Havelock. Col. W.T. Dortch [*of Goldsboro*] and a party of friends, leave tonight for the Colonel's lodge near Havelock, where they will spend several days fishing and hunting."

The fish stories sound like fish stories: "A boat arrived last night about ten o'clock with four or five thousand grey trout, which were caught in a Dutch net at Cherry Point."[y]

For outdoorsmen, Camp Bryan, in the heart of the lakes district, was a heavenly natural retreat. Rustic cabins and primitive conditions were part of the charm for wealthy men from big cities. As mentioned in the hunting gazetteer above, bears, deer, alligators, and an occasional cougar were hunted.

As an example, one visitor, Mr. F. Harding of Patterson, N.J., made headlines for his hunting prowess in the local woodlands. Harding "succeeded in killing a large 400-pound bear" at Havelock in 1893, according to a news report. Such stories were common. They were reprinted across the country and added further to the area's fame.[z]

The larger game was taken along with rabbits, squirrels, turkeys, doves, quail, and ducks of all kinds. The lakes named Long, Little, Great, and Ellis gave plenty of opportunities for the freshwater anglers as well.

Around the turn of the last century, local notable James H. Hunter oversaw the operations of Maj. James A. Bryan's Lake Ellis Plantation. This including running the hunt club. Speaking of a 1903 hunting party from Raleigh and Goldsboro, a front-page newspaper account says, "When they reached Havelock, they stopped at Mr. J.H. Hunter's well-known

---

[y] *The Daily Journal*, New Bern July 24, 1896.

[z] *The Daily Journal*, New Bern, January 10, 1894.

Dave Sampson, at left, and Ben Joyner at Camp Bryan near Havelock in 1920.
Photo courtesy of John B. Green III and the New Bern-Craven County Public Library.

clubhouse." The trip was fatal for one creature of the forest. "While trying to regain the lost trail," the story reported, "they ran into a large Panther cat coming toward them, and without waiting for orders the entire party blasted away and the sixty-pound beast fell dead."[aa]

Over many years, two of the main characters at the camp were Dave Sampson and Ben Joyner. Everything from cooking to guiding to taking care of the camp and its guests was in their job descriptions.

And they were interesting characters.

Dave Sampson was born September 5, 1853, to a woman enslaved on the Fisher plantation at Riverdale. Dave's mother, Hannah, was sold when he was a little boy. He was raised by the Fishers. Michael N. Fisher, the owner of the plantation, had told his female slaves that they would be sold if any of them delivered a mulatto child. Hannah told him that the father of her child was indeed a white man, an itinerant teacher who had boarded at the Fisher home for a time. True to his word, Fisher sold the woman away from the plantation but the family's biographer assures his readers that it was "to a planter well-known to the Fishers and who provided well for his slaves."[bb]

Dave received special attention from the Fishers and was a playmate of their children. As a man, he stayed close to the family and worked for them for years after the Civil War and as occasions later arose. He was bright,

[aa] *The Gastonia Gazette*, January 2, 1903, pg. 1.
[bb] P.W. Fisher, *One Dozen Eastern North Carolina Families*, page 75-77.

genial, and well-known throughout the area. A cook and caretaker for many years at Camp Bryan, he was a particular favorite of many of the visitors.

When Babe Ruth visited, he insisted Dave prepare all his meals and considered the prize cook's collards and cornbread to be sheer delicacies. According to New Bern historian and journalist Gertrude Carraway, Sampson "probably knew more national celebrities and sportsmen than any other person in the entire region."

The 1920 census lists David Sampson, 68, a mulatto male, born about 1852 with his wife, Mary (Marry) Jane Mitchell Sampson, 55; son Alford, 33; and daughters, Annie, 31; Effie, 27; and Rose, 19. All were shown as single and mulatto. All could read and write in a time when not everyone did.

The first home Dave built for Mary was a ten-foot by twelve-foot log cabin with a chimney made of sticks and mud. Later, that had evolved into a fine home and a small productive farm.

Dave's intrepid professional sidekick of many years at Camp Bryan was Ben Joyner.

Well-known in his own right, Joyner had been born about 1855. In 1910, his wife, Matilda, was a seamstress. They'd been married 10 years and had 9 children. He was 55 and she was 40. Nathaniel, 11; Ernest, 10, Johnny, 9; Marieta, 7; Frank, 4; Isaac and Jacob, 2; and Melvina, 1, count among his children. But these were but a few of his kids.

In 1914, the 58-year-old Joyner made statewide news as a man with 33 offspring who married an 18-year-old girl. Joyner was born in 1856 making him just five when the Civil War began. He grew up to be a renowned hunting and fishing guide. His home was a log cabin on the shores of Ellis Lake. [cc]

In the 1920 photograph on the previous page taken in front of a rustic building at Camp Bryan, Sampson holds a couple of birds while Joyner has a raccoon firmly in his grip. There is little in the forests of eastern North Carolina that can't be made fit to eat and country people didn't hesitate to partake of raccoon.

Here's how: "Skin and dress him. Remove the 'kernels' (scent glands) under each front leg and on either side of the spine in the small of the back. Wash in cold water. Parboil in one or two waters depending on the animal's age. Stuff with dressing like a turkey. If you have a tart apple, quarter it and add to the dressing. Bake to a delicate brown. Serve with fried sweet potatoes." [dd]

[cc] *Western Carolina Democrat*, Hendersonville, October 8, 1914.

[dd] Kephart, Horace; *Camping and Woodcraft*, 1917, pg. 321.

Wildcats of Havelock

Great Lakes Well No. 2 began drilling outside of Havelock on November 24, 1924. Despite its number, this was the first exploratory oil well drilled in North Carolina. Breathless news stories worked investors and speculators into a frenzy and there were complaints of not enough stock to go around. The Great Lakes well was the first of many as drillers from Louisiana and Pennsylvania poured in.

Newspapers across the state were mad for the details. Headlines blared:

An oil rig in the forest west of Havelock.
New Bern-Craven County Public Library

- "Will Start Well Near Havelock Soon."
- "Oil Prospectors Go to Havelock."
- "Very Rich Oil Sands Reached at Havelock"
- "Interested Business Men Look on as Drilling for Oil Continues at Havelock."

The Carolina Syndicate, the Pennsylvania Drilling Company, Carolina Petroleum, and the Great Lakes Drilling Company each raised money, shipped equipment by train, and mobilized roughnecks to drill holes from 2,300 feet to a mile deep into the promising geology a couple of miles west of town. Lawyers salivated over the paperwork.

In one offering, Great Lakes Drilling sold $75,000 worth of stock. One syndicate meeting in Sanford raised $4,000 in two hours. Megabucks lumberman W.B. Blades and land baron Col. Charles S. Bryan (Maj. Bryan's son), both of New Bern, got in on the action with Col. Bryan leasing 52,000 acres all around Havelock to the "wildcat" exploration firms.

Since you haven't seen any refineries in the area, it probably won't be spoiling the story to just go ahead and say they never found a drop of black gold near the lakes, in the forest, or anywhere else. Nevertheless, they were magnificently persistent.

"Drilling For Oil to be Resumed: *Drilling for oil on the property of the Great Lakes Drilling Company at Camp Bryan, near Havelock, will be resumed, according to one of the few official statements which have been issued by B.G. Banks, engineer in charge. And the officers and directors of the company, representatives of the Chamber of Commerce of the eastern part of the state, and the public generally are invited to be present and see the beginning of the new well.*"

By the end of it all, 128 exploratory wells were drilled before it occurred to the prospectors to consider that Dr. Collier Cobb was right. The renowned geologist, author, former Harvard professor, and chairman of the Department of Geology at the University of North Carolina exclaimed all through the hubbub, "There is no oil in North Carolina."

In the end, the newspapers that hyped the affair grew a little snarky. *The Williamston Enterprise* offered this on May 22, 1931: "Some sections of Eastern Carolina are becoming anxious to get oil wells going. They are talking of boring wells in Perquimans and Lenoir Counties. The stock of these new projects is not listed on the regular exchanges yet. It might be easier to buy stock in a Havelock well over in Craven County. There is large amount of stock in the bottom of that deep hole over there which can no doubt be bought cheap now." [ee]

One wit said, "They didn't find enough oil to fill an ant's motorcycle."

Looking on the bright side, the influx of oil field workers was probably a boon to the corn liquor trade.

Working in the Logwoods

A sawmill is a roaring, hissing conglomeration of dangerous machinery broadcasting the clatter-bang clap-trap of a hell-bent locomotive; syncopated by a high scream as the saw bites wood. It's a place of sweat and sawdust. It's a place where jaggedy-sharp blades as tall as a man subdue the largest logs in the forest or, in a single moment of inattention, remove a hand, an arm, or a leg with surgical precision.

Sawmills, large and small, were numerous. Some ran on water power, like Spaight's Mill and James Davis's, both on Slocum Creek. Others were

---

[ee] For example, *The Daily Free Press*, Kinston, May 13, 1916; *The Franklin Times*, November 7, 1924; *The Daily Advance*, Elizabeth City, May 16, 1924.

powered by steam. The Taylor and Temple Sawmill operated by steam at Clubfoot Creek in 1885. Several turned trees into boards on the west side of Hancock Creek, including A.N. Weaver's and Webber & Reems.

The logs themselves were bone-crushers. There are myriad ways to be maimed or killed working in the logwoods. Colossal pines and hardwoods, true giants, bigger than any now in the forest, fell to the earth all day. They groaned. They cracked. They bumped hard enough to make the ground bounce. Falling limbs, splitting trunks, rolling logs, all could put a man in an early grave. Still, the work was there for anyone bold enough, or needy enough, or both, to take it.

What went on in southern Craven County in the first decades of the twentieth century was the kind of wild abandon that modern causes like the Sierra Club rail against today. Tens of thousands of acres of ancient, old-growth forest full of trees hundreds of years old were whacked down whole-sale like grass before a weed-eater.

One tree was so big that a photographer was engaged to transport his or her heavy, bulky camera gear into the forest between New Bern and Havelock to make a portrait of a six-man logging crew posed on its stump. The rugged-looking men weren't jammed together either. They were spaced apart, some with their gleaming, double-handled saws standing on end beside them.

W.J. Wynne, Jr., born in 1919, said almost all of Cherry Point was clear-cut when he was a boy. Riverdale was a thriving rail hub where

Roper Lumber Co.'s substantial Clubfoot Creek sawmill was located on Matthews Point at the end of Temples Point Road. A marina was at the location in 2021. Source of image: American Lumberman, April 27, 1907. Courtesy of Jerry Jackson.

workers loaded log trains. For a time, it had a small commercial district including lodging and a café.

It was outfits like Blades, Rowland, and the Roper Lumber Company that did the job. Roper was established in 1865 and headquartered in Virginia. In the late 1800s and early 1900s, it owned or controlled 800,000 acres of forest land, much of it in eastern North Carolina. They owned what would become the Croatan National Forest and intended for every tree in it to be turned into lumber. When Roper was at its peak, it was said to own trees equal to four billion board feet of timber.

Roper was so big that they created whole towns, Roper, N.C. and Winthrop, N.C. being examples. They owned three hundred homes for their employees. At a time when northern Carteret County and southern Craven County were sharing a doctor, Manly Mason, M.D. of Newport, Roper had its own staff of physicians.

Above, old growth pine trees just before harvesting by the Roper Lumber Company in a southern Craven County forest near Clubfoot Creek, 1907. Below, housing for Roper black workers at Winthrop on the eastern bank of Adam's Creek near the Neuse. Winthrop and Winthrop Mills boomed for many years, but no longer exists. Images: American Lumberman, April 27, 1907. Courtesy of Jerry Jackson.

In 1907, Roper had 150 miles of logging railroad, 23 locomotives, 250 train cars, 12 sawmills, three planing mills, two shingle mills, eight stores, 12 tugboats, 16 barges, three schooners, and 3,000 workers.

Roper had a massive operation on Clubfoot Creek. One of their industrial-sized sawmills squatted at the mouth of the creek on Matthews Point. The length of the Clubfoot Creek was taken up with storage buildings and wharves that serviced a small fleet of boats. Excess logs were floated in huge "log rafts" to New Bern where Roper had an even bigger sawmill. These activities required the skill and muscle of many men.

Census data shows a strong percentage of the male population was in the logwoods. Some worked part of the year at farming or fishing and worked in the timber for another part.

And like moonshine, southern Craven County lumber traveled far and wide: "Shipping News. The Schooner *J. Dallas Marvel* cleared for Cherry Point. There she will take a load of lumber for Washington, D.C." *The Daily Journal*, New Bern, June 2, 1896.

It was the former Roper lumber mill that caused the Great Fire of New Bern in 1922. Smaller plants were just a spark away from disaster as well.

Headlines in the *Daily Journal* on July 22, 1900, read: "Milling Plant Burned. Saw Mill, Dry Kilns and Lumber of Reams & Co., at Hancock Creek."

And the story: "Fire was discovered in the dry kiln of Reams & Co. at Hancock creek at 9 a.m. Saturday morning, which spread to the sawmill, both being destroyed, with about one hundred thousand feet of lumber in the kiln. The loss is estimated at $12,000 to $15,000 with insurance of about half the loss. The sawmill had a capacity of 30,000 feet a day."

Helming the Post Office, 1923

Though not distinguishable in the nearby photo, the crude, carved signboard above the window read P.O. HAVELOCK. It was to this 180 square foot two-room, wood-framed structure that farm families and others of the rural countryside came to receive their letters, postcards, and packages before and during World War II.

The postmaster was life-long resident Walter James Wynne, Sr.

Another resident, Carlilie Fenner Hill, said Wynne had "a little shed with little pigeon holes in it" where he sorted the mail. The mail moved on the train that ran from Morehead City to Goldsboro and back each day moving letters and small parcels in both directions.

Wynne headed one of those farm families that traced its local ancestral lineage back into the 1700s. He oversaw the mail at Havelock from 1923 to

Farmer and postmaster W. J. Wynne. Sr. at the Havelock Post Office c. 1940 near the intersection of Lake Road and the A&NC railroad tracks. The vintage auto is pointing down Lake Road. The Schollenberger mansion was on the right a few hundred feet ahead. The house was visible beyond the tree in the original of this picture. Photograph courtesy of the late Mrs. Lila Wynne Simmons, daughter of the postmaster.

1945 and gathered in the deliveries and correspondence for other post offices further away from the rail line.

His humble and unadorned post office was located on a narrow strip of land between unpaved Lake Road – which can be seen going toward the south in front of the 1939 Plymouth sedan above – and the Atlantic & East Carolina railroad track immediately behind the building. Central Highway 10, today's Church Road, and Miller Boulevard ran nearby. Rough stones stacked at the entrance functioned as steps. Inside, two rooms were divided by a counter. There were combination mailboxes but most customers just had their mail handed to them across the counter by postmaster Wynne, or often by his wife, Maude, who some folks claim actually ran the place.

With mail arriving daily by train, a series of small post offices operated near the same location – the intersection of the railroad and the old Beaufort Road – beginning in 1881 when Dutch immigrant William Leauhout opened the first one with the name Havelock. His name was also spelled as *Leanhout* in official records due to difficult-to-read cursive handwriting.

John Dinker, another Dutchman, replaced Leauhout for a few months of the same year before handing duties to resident Edward D. Russell. Russell and members of his family, including John I. Russell and Sallie E. Russell, shared postal services from then until Wynne took over, except for a few months in 1887 when local store-owner Collins H. Hunter handled the trade.[ff]

There had been another small post office at the same site in 1861, next to the railroad, just before the start of the Civil War. It was established by local farmer A. J. Chesnutt who called it *Spaightsville*. The Spaightsville post office was closed by war's end, but, based upon the appearance of the building, it could have been the same one Chesnutt used decades before.

The daily trains not only delivered mail for Havelock residents, but also for other small post offices to the east. Thus, Russell regularly handed off mail sacks to postmasters from Harlowe, North Harlowe, Melvin, Becton, Bachelor, and Cherry Point.

Old Havelock and Cherry Point

The local community, remembered by those arriving at the time of Cherry Point base construction, was one winnowed down by the Great Depression. The oil wells had failed. The logwoods had been clear cut. The Great Depression bore down hard.

Area resident Moses Moore, known to generations of students as Havelock High School's custodian, said with ironic good humor that people here didn't lose their jobs during the depression ... because they didn't have any.[gg]

While the property where Cherry Point would be built had many homes and farms, Havelock's immediate population had dropped to about 100. There were a few homes strung out along the highway that arced through town on what is now Greenfield Heights Blvd. and Miller Blvd., crossing the railroad tracks and passing in front of Trader's Store. Most of the homes and families of old Havelock were clustered on Gray Road.

As they had been for decades, Saturdays were busy as African Americans arrived in the vicinity at Trader's and the railroad to catch weekly bus and truck rides for shopping in New Bern.

Trader's is reputed to have been the supply source for the moonshine trade. An inordinate amount of sugar was sold there. In fifty and one hundred pound bags. Industrial quantities of yeast. Pallets of Mason jars. And more. All available on credit at Trader's. Hugh Trader's store usually

---

[ff] **For more on the Dutch colony at Havelock, see *Whatnot* section, Part III.**

[gg] SOHP, interview K-39, by William Jones.

featured a large soft drink advertisement painted on its side by one supplier or another. Coca-Cola and 7 Up being examples. The store also offered a wide variety of groceries and goods including fuel, horse collars, overalls, kerosene lamps, tools, and patent medicines. Like many country stores, it was the Dollar General of its day. And the social nexus of village life.

At the top of the small hill near the east prong of Slocum Creek, Frank Russell's filling station and store operated very much the same way. Travelers on the highway stopped there for fuel and something to eat. Russell's store was convenient for the residents of the African American settlements between Hancock's Creek and Slocum's Creek.

In 1940, there was still no electricity for Havelock or the black settlements.

But there were thousands of people on the river's south shore, nonetheless, as there had been for two hundred and forty years.

Granted, their numbers had dwindled substantially under the weight of the Great Depression.

Some gave up the struggle and went elsewhere.

So, there were not as many as there had been in times past.

And not so prosperous.

But alive, growing up, growing old.

Working, courting, marrying, giving birth, being born.

Living, loving, breathing, laughing.

Crying, suffering, dying, and burying their dead.

In old Havelock, old Cherry Point, and the black settlements in between, there were laborers on the railroad, on the highways, with the WPA, in the logwoods, and at the sawmills. And farmhands and helpers numbering in the hundreds. There were farmers and loggers and mill workers. Gas station attendants, fertilizer salesmen, maids, and machine operators. There were postmen, inspectors, seamstresses, and sales ladies.

They're all in the census records.

There was a white public school teacher, Leona Tolson; a black public school teacher, Louise Redding; and a midwife, Josephine Blake. There was a caretaker for a hunting lodge and one for a fishing lodge, and a fire tower lookout. There were auto mechanics and pensioners, fishermen, and grocers. And foremen of farms, forestry, sawmills, highways, and the railroad. There were four men doing time in the Atlanta Federal Penitentiary for moonshine, and a couple in the state sanitorium, most likely because of it.[hh]

In 1940 as noted previously, there were no less than four named communities between the creek banks of Hancock and Slocum. Cherry Point Road – the route from Highway 101 to the river – was ornamented

---

[hh] United States Census, Township 6, Craven County, 1940.

with scores of family farmsteads and hundreds of acres of rich, cultivated fields bordered by maturing pinelands.

There were tobacco barns, smokehouses, pack houses, outhouses, birdhouses, sheds, shops, fences, chicken yards, hog lots, stables, corrals, pastures, beehives, orchards, shade trees, and gardens for both vegetables and flowers. There were boat docks with skiffs and cruisers, fishing piers, net stakes, channel markers, and swimming beaches. And nestled along the spectacular river and creeks were comfortable recreational retreats for individuals, firemen, policemen, and companies from New Bern, Kinston, Goldsboro, and Durham, to name only a few. [ii]

Nelson Town and Tar Neck were well-settled and active farming enclaves of close-knit households, with a sideline in corn liquor. Both had been founded by former slaves shortly after the warfare of the 1860s. Their neighbors in the predominantly white village of Cherry Point had a post office, a cemetery, and a boat harbor. Cherry Point people also had their active tourist trade, including leisure rentals for fishermen, hunters, and carousers. These visitors kept the residents not only occupied year-round but also supplied with ready cash. And Melvin, N.C. – also known as Little Witness – was a village with its own United States Post Office, postmaster, named streets, farms, a Baptist church, graveyards, and a public schoolhouse.

Despite all that, a few decades later an authoritative and well-circulated Craven County history book would boldly state: "During the summer of 1941, the site [of Cherry Point] was just a vast stretch of swamplands." [jj]

[ii] Cherry Point property photographs, 1941, Edward B. Ellis, Jr. Papers, ECU.

[jj] *The Heritage of Craven County, Vol. 1*, 1984, "Marine Corps Air Station Cherry Point," article L59, pg. 38.

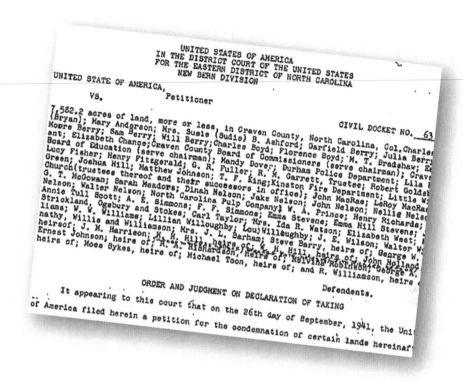

A portion of one of the condemnation lawsuits for Cherry Point land.

The Right of Eminent Domain

The North Carolina Pulp Company was by far the largest conveyor of property – 4,911.3 acres – to the federal government for the construction of Cherry Point Marine Corps Air Station in 1941. No other entity or individual exceeded three hundred acres.

The retrieval and review of the firm's corporate records from the N.C. Secretary of State's office – SOSID #1765197 – indicates that North Carolina Pulp was a Delaware corporation owned by members of a Wisconsin family named Kieckhefer. John W. Kieckhefer was the president. Under its parent company, the Kieckhefer Container Co., the firm engaged in the timber, pulpwood, and paper business. North Carolina Pulp was formed December 4, 1937, and was dissolved December 30, 1960. It had no apparent ties to the State of North Carolina, the Navy, or the U.S. Marine Corps.

Kieckhefer Container Company was a financial powerhouse; an early innovator in corrugated cardboard shipping boxes and paper milk cartons. Through a stock transaction that made national business headlines, John Kieckhefer's holdings merged with those of Weyerhaeuser Timber Company in 1957. *The New York Times* spotlighted the story. Afterward, Kieckhefer (1887-1970) was among the wealthiest men in American with a reported net worth that would push the billionaire range today.

Nothing in the company's N.C. Secretary of State corporate filings refers to the 1941 land seizure by the federal government, but based on the scope of Kieckhefer's overall holdings and operations, the condemnation of the land titled to North Carolina Pulp appears to have been a minor matter.

For others around Cherry Point, however, there was nothing minor about it.

Fred Solomon Nelson's house was brand new. He, his wife, Katie Toon Nelson, and their four children would be moving into the home in a matter of days. Built on land given to him by his father, Walter Nelson – the prosperous leading man of the Nelson Town community – the home had clapboard siding and a standing seam metal roof. It was built with a crawl space on brick piers for good ventilation. Fred had outfitted his home with a comfortable covered front porch and was looking forward to using the new smokehouse he'd had built out back. He'd paid cash for all of it.

As a moonshiner, Nelson must have had reservations when, on a warm afternoon in 1941, a white man drove up in a dark, late model automobile. He identified himself, asked Fred's name, and then served him with some folded sheets of paper. It wasn't a warrant. The papers included the *Order and Judgment on the Declaration of Taking* from the federal court petition by the United States of America for the condemnation of his small farm tract. He had thirty days to be off the property.

Fred was the fourth generation of his family on the land and had lived there all his life. In and out of slavery, Fred's great grandfather, Smith Nelson, had lived nearby. Smith Nelson bought seventy-five acres at the site from Rufus W. and Abigail F. Bell in 1880. Sam B. Nelson, Fred's grandfather, was born into

Fred and Katie Nelson's new farm house and smokehouse on MCAS Cherry Point Parcel 288 as it was photographed on September 15, 1941. *EBE Collection, ECU. Image 753.1.e.27b*

slavery in 1860. After the Civil War, Sam farmed and logged around Havelock and Cherry Point. About 1920, he acquired a 500-acre plantation on the east side of Slocum Creek that had been owned by a white neighbor and former Confederate cavalryman, James H. Hunter. It was where Fred's father was born. Fred had been born at Slocum Creek, too.[a]

It was almost a standard practice in the timber business to have a team of lawyers constantly challenging people's land deeds; especially people who would find it hard to defend themselves. Many old deeds were flawed because trees and other perishable landmarks had been used within them to designate boundaries and landmarks. Over the years, several timber firms had worked the area and the original five-hundred-acre Nelson Town tract had been whittled down by more than half.

Emma West Bell, a granddaughter of Sam B. Nelson, said he had a "more or less deed."

"That means sometimes it's good," she said, "and sometimes it's bad when you have those kinds of deeds."

Still, the remainder was enough for all the Nelsons, their related family members, and neighbors to not only subsist but make a go of it. Walter Nelson, even after gifting away land to family, lived in a fine two-story home in the middle of 131 acres.

But now Uncle Sam had come for the remainder of their acreage.

The government paid Fred Nelson the tax assessment value of $10 per acre – not the then-current market value –for his land; a few hundred dollars total for the farmland and the new home. It was eighteen long months before he saw any of it.

By then, their new home at Nelson Town had been unceremoniously bulldozed, and he and Katie had moved a world away from all they had ever known. Nelson had no money to build another home. New Bern was the only place they could find something to rent.

Fred said his wife cried for six months.[b]

The power of governments to take land for public use is old and nearly universal. In other countries, it's called land acquisition, or compulsory purchase, or expropriation. Under U.S. federal law, it's known as the right of eminent domain and flows from the wording of the Fifth Amendment to the

---

[a] Bell to Smith Nelson deed, Craven County Book 83, pp. 403-404, March 5, 1880.

[b] The bulk of interview material for this chapter is drawn from the remarkable recordings and transcripts of the Southern Oral History Program (SOHP) Collection #4007 in the Southern Historical Collection, Wilson Library, University of North Carolina-Chapel Hill; plus supplemental interviews by the author.

Constitution: "… nor shall private property be taken for public use, without just compensation."

The founding fathers were following the recent lead of the French here. France had recognized a property owner's right to compensation for taken property in 1789. *The French Declaration of the Rights of Man and of the Citizens* states, "Property being an inviolable and sacred right no one can be deprived of it, unless the public necessity demands it …"

The concept of "just compensation" is required to lighten the financial burden put upon the property owner for the benefit of the public.

In making the case for eminent domain, some sources demonstrate its ancient standing by citing the Old Testament story of King Ahab offering Naboth compensation for a vineyard near Ahab's palace in the city of Jezreel. A close reading of biblical 1 Kings 21:1-19, however, reveals that through the intrigues of King Ahab's wife, the infamous Jezebel, instead of the man being compensated for his land, he was actually murdered near the city's gates, and "dogs licked the blood of Naboth." After which, they killed Naboth's son to prevent his claim of inheritance.

So, in weighing the propriety of eminent domain, that's probably not a good example.[c]

Emma Hill Davis was seven "when the base came." Fifty years later the memories and emotions were still fresh. She remembered her neighbors, these rural individuals, and families who were uprooted from their generational homes. They were forced to go, she would say, nearly empty-handed. She remembered they received no assistance in moving. They would never again have land to farm. For many, there would be nowhere to live except in a rental house on a postage stamp lot in a city.[d]

"They were very upset," she recalled. "They were devastated for life."

She also remembered her peanuts.

Emma loved the fresh, plump peanuts the family grew each year on her great-grandparents' farm at Nelson Town. For her, they were a treat still moist from the sandy ground. So much better than the store-bought kind. Sometimes country kids would sit in the shade of the peanut stack, shell the fat goobers, and eat them until their bellies hurt.

On the last day before they had to be off their land for good, her elders were scrambling to move the remainder of their possessions from the only home the child had ever known. It would be their last chance to retrieve what things they could salvage from the farm. But the seven-year-old girl,

---

[c] Eminent domain, legal definition of, freedictionary.com; Singer, Isidore, Ph.D., Entry for 'Right of Eminent Domain'. 1901 The Jewish Encyclopedia.

[d] SOHP, taped interview K-36 by Karen Kruse Thomas, 1995.

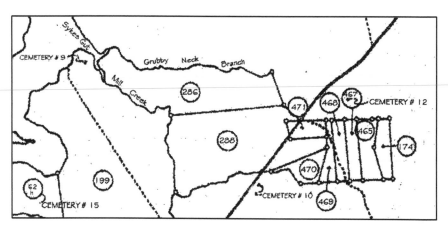

The Nelson Town settlement in 1941 with Slocum Creek at left. The diagonal line passing left to right was the Cherry Point Road from Highway 101 to the village of Cherry Point on the Neuse River. Walter Nelson lived on Tract 288. The home of Nelson Town's founder Sam Nelson and his wife, Dinah, was on Tract 468. Nellie Nelson, Tract 174; Elizabeth West, 465; Lila Fenner, 467; John Nelson, 469; Norman Nelson, 470; Jake Nelson, 471; Mrs. Ida R. Watson, 286. By the time the map was created a law firm owned Tract 199, and Craven County owned 62h. Four cemeteries appear on this small section. The proper name for Grubby Neck Branch is Hunter's Branch. Excerpt of *Cherry Point Ownership Map of 1941*, EBE/ECU.

as seven-year-olds do, was thinking about peanuts and that she might not have any more for a long time.

While they always grew peanuts, the family's main selling crops were cotton, tobacco, and corn. On the farm, they had all they needed to be self-sufficient. They grew most of their food. They only had to buy a few things like salt, sugar, flour, and cloth. Trees had been planted to yield fruits at different times of the year. They had grapevines. And strawberries. At the dinner table, Emma said, they ate pork, some beef, and plenty of garden vegetables like butter beans, string beans, okra, collards, cabbage, and rutabaga. She didn't care for rutabagas.

The farm was also stocked with turkeys, ducks, chickens, hogs, and guinea hens. They ground their own corn. One of the few things they had to buy was rice, which could be purchased in Havelock. When they didn't have cash, they traded eggs for rice. At least once a week they ate fresh fish to take a break from pork.

Fish usually came from Slocum Creek. Big enough to be called a river elsewhere, Slocum was near at hand; its water beautiful and clear. A woman named Aunt Teema was a whiz at fishing. Catching fish was a livelihood for some in the community and she was "a good fisherwoman," according to her niece. "When the water got low, she would go in there and catch fish. She had a dip net to dig them out." [e]

Emma grew up in the home built by her great-grandfather, Sam B. Nelson. His old homeplace was an L-shaped two-story house on ten acres. Downstairs was a kitchen, dining room, and a big screen porch that they called the "cooler." There were two bedrooms upstairs. Emma remembered how she loved to walk down the pretty wooded lane from the house to the barns where the plows and other farm equipment were stored.

While all the grown-ups were busy that last day in 1941, Emma went after peanuts. She hurried out to the vine-laced stacks and filled a small burlap sack to the brim. She carried the bag back to the near-empty house and placed it on a shelf. It wasn't until the family was driving away that she realized she'd forgotten the peanuts.

"I was so sad. I always hoped someone would go back and get those peanuts for me," she said. "But they never did."

Emma Hill Davis's roots were deep on her home ground, especially with community pillars Sam Nelson (1860-1929) and Dinah Nelson (c.1874-1939) as great grandparents.

Dinah Nelson's mother, Eliza Jane Phillips, had been a slave in Duplin County, between Jacksonville and Fayetteville. After New Bern was captured and became Union territory, the family legend is that Eliza "escaped by water" and made it to freedom there. The puzzle of the story is that Duplin County is landlocked and the major river within the county is the narrow beginnings of the Cape Fear, which leads to Wilmington but not New Bern. Just east of Duplin, however, are the headwaters of the Trent River. The most direct modern driving route from Duplin County to New Bern is more than 70 miles long. The twisting, convoluted path of the Trent is easily twice that. What a trip that would have been during the Civil War. No matter how Eliza Jane Phillips came to freedom, family members have never forgotten the story of her remarkable feat.

Emma counted off her relatives. Walter Nelson was her uncle; Fred Nelson, one of the cousins. Norman and Jacob Nelson were great uncles. Elizabeth West was her aunt and Lila Fenner her maternal grandmother.

There were more Nelsons, plus brothers, sisters, and cousins, but Emma said the people were spread out at Nelson Town. They had elbow room and were "not all clustered together."

Her paternal grandmother and namesake was Emma Hill who married Alexander Hill. After Alex died, the grandmother remarried to a man named

---

[e] SOHP, interview K-236 with Sudie Green by Angela M. Hornsby, 1999.

John Stevens; making her Emma Hill Stevens, the one person who remembered the grave of a man named Sparks in the first chapter of the book.

Emma Davis named the other places near where she had lived. There was Tar Neck, just south of Nelson Town, with a lot of families like the Johnsons, Berrys, Hollands, and Fishers. There were Doves and even more Nelsons at Tar Neck.

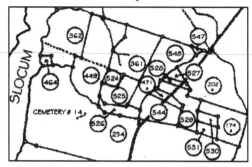

Tar Neck

Then there was Toon Neck, another name for Little Witness. At the intersection of Highway 101 and Hancock Creek, it was the biggest settlement with the most families. Her grandmother Hill lived there. The Richards lived there. Alex Hill's brother Josh also lived at Toon Neck. Emma said Alex Hill had a son named Henry who married a woman named Louisa. They had a large tract of land where they also raised corn, cotton, and tobacco. Emma recalled the large black grapes – muscadines – that she loved to eat at the Hills' place.

The H. H. Hill estate was 54.3 acres, Tract 235a, with a good bit of waterfront on Hancock Creek. As described by Emma Davis, the Henry and Louisa Hill house was similar to the Sam B. Nelson home – two stories but with a big bay window on the front.

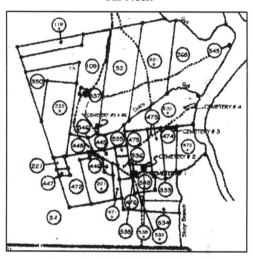

Toon Neck, "Little Witness," or Melvin

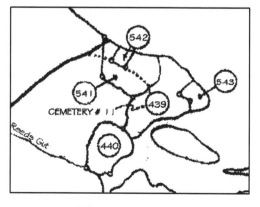

"Cherry Point," 1941

Emma went to the Melvin School at Little Witness. One of her teachers was Ruth Adams and another was Mrs. Walker. The number of children in school at Little Witness varied, but sometimes there were 35 to 40. Most people considered having their kids in school to be a good idea, but some couldn't go at all due to farm necessities. School was normally in session about six months out of the year. The schoolhouse was one room heated by a wood stove. The children were tasked with keeping it going. During the 1920s, Melvina Robinson was the teacher. Mrs. Robinson was married to James Robinson, the mail carrier from Melvin (Little Witness) to Harlowe. He founded the local Melvin post office in 1906, naming it for her. The school took the name as well.[f]

Emma went to Sunday School and church at Little Witness Baptist. After moving at age seven, she went to the one-room Cahoogue school where her teacher was Mr. Willis. Into adulthood, Emma attended the Hyman Chapel AME Zion Church on Highway 101.

She considered it a wonderful life ... until it ended.

More than a half-century after the fact, the gentle, soft-spoken woman could barely conceal her anger and profound sadness when talking about the families that were forced to move off their land at Cherry Point.

She used the word *upset* and *devastated*. Despite the condemnation settlement, she holds that they were "not compensated."

"They told us to move the best way you could, with nothing," she said. "When you're shoved out of your house with nothing, that's a great setback. It's a setback for life. [It was a] very devastating time."

She said most of the Cherry Point refugees, uprooted from their self-contained and tight-knit world, had no choice but to move from the area altogether, to other cities, counties, and states. Her family was among the few who found housing to the east down Highway 101.

She said it took them "three or four years to get paid." Some of the people died before their money came.

Little Witness Baptist Church was "a little place but all the people could get in there," said Mary Carter Stone. After reflecting on it for a minute, she said it wasn't much bigger than a living room. The church had "homemade benches."[g]

The church at Little Witness was perched on eight-tenths of an acre at the very heart of the settlement. It was the focal point of the community's social life, the weekly gathering spot, where people gave their lives to the Lord, where they sang, where they were married, and where their funeral

[f] SOHP, taped interview K-40, by Will Jones.

[g] SOHP, taped interview K-239 & K-233, by Angela M. Hornsby, 1999.

services were held. Stone said people needed and wanted "to get to their church and pray to *their* God."

In a 1999 interview, she recalled being there when the church was burned to make room for the military base.[h]

"I saw my father cry," she said. "And my grandfather two. And then I cried three. It was a sad time. That's all the blacks had of their own. And here they had to move from their homes. A lot of them moved to New Bern. A lot of the old ones grieved themselves to death. They never got over it."

She said her first cousin told her about "bulldozers and bones coming up out of the ground from the graveyard."

Many would speak repeatedly of their belief that graves and cemeteries were damaged, destroyed, and otherwise lost during the base construction process. Several said one near Little Witness was covered by a runway.

"The people had lost their homes and now they had taken the church, too," she said.

Stone's grandfather taught them all how to survive in the world. His motto was *Do for Yourself*. There was no welfare in those days. Besides, she said, "welfare is a form of slavery."

"You knew how to prepare for summer in winter. I lived in a period of time when God had put everything at my fingertips," she said, but "when the Cherry Point Marine base came in, people lost sight of God."

She said the community also lost its firm grip on self-sufficiency.

Another Emma, Emma West Bell said Little Witness Baptist was "a pretty church, painted snow white and well-maintained." It was a small wooden church on brick pillars with a steep A-roof and the "nicest steeple." She estimated that it held "150 people, maybe more." There were two services per Sunday: Sunday School at 10 a.m. and preaching at 11 a.m. Church members would gather again at 3 p.m. and in between "folks would visit other community members."[i]

[Another interviewee, Beulah Whitehead Ward, added that the steeple had a bell that was rung before services and during funerals. For her, the church symbolized the importance of religious faith to the community.][j]

[Sam Nelson's grandson, Fred Nelson, noted that there were times in its history when services at Little Witness came just once a month, based on the availability of minsters. He said Rev. Tom Gaskins served as a preacher there. Baptisms took place in nearby Hancock Creek.][k]

---

[h] Memories vary on whether it was burned or demolished with heavy equipment.

[i] SOHP, taped interview K-233, by Angela M. Hornsby, 1999.

[j] SOHP, taped interview, Coastal N.C. series K240, by Angela Hornsby, 1999.

[k] SOHP, taped interview K-40, by Will Jones, 1995.

Emma Bell's attendance began when she was "a toddler" and continued through the years "until the base tore it down."

Her grandfather, Sam Nelson, was a deacon of the Little Witness Baptist Church, and her grandmother, Dinah Nelson, was a "church mother." Getting the sacrament ready for the members was one of the duties of the church mothers; preparing the bread, wine, and linen. They visited the sick, carrying the communion to people too ill to come to church service. She said she was "raised up in the church" as was her family.

The church was the community gathering place. Each August on a Saturday, Little Witness pulled out the stops for a wondrous homecoming picnic. Tables in the churchyard groaned under the weight of fried chicken, ham, and every vegetable known to man. Ice was imported from New Bern to cool barrels of lemonade. There were pies and cakes galore.

In the church, Sam Nelson "took up collections and saw to the preacher's needs," according to Emma Bell. He made sure visiting preachers were fed. Some "long-time" preachers were James Anthony Stiles and Reverend Walter Green. After Rev. Stiles's wife died, he married a woman from the Cherry Point community.

Her father had worked on the railroad and for timber companies. She said he cut crossties earning from fifty cents to a dollar a day. She was the oldest of three children. By the date of her interview, her brother and sister were deceased.

The family home was a good size, what she called "a story and a jump." A large first floor and a smaller second. It was wood-framed with a shingle roof. Her chores included feeding chickens, bringing in buckets of water and firewood for cooking and heat, sweeping the yard, and taking care of the flowers. Oil lamps were used for interior lighting with lanterns for the outdoors. The lamps and lanterns regularly needed to be filled and cleaned of soot. Water was hand-pumped. With oil lamps as the only light, everyone went to bed early.

Baseball was a favorite childhood pastime played with neighbor kids. Sometimes they'd "rent a boat for 15 cents from Mr. Russell at Cherry Point and go fishing with the whites."

Emma had pleasant memories of the little village at Cherry Point. White folks lived there. She knew and liked George and Annie Russell. Good people. Then she thought about the cemeteries.

"They're all buried there," she said, referring to the Russell Cemetery near Hancock Creek and the river. "They're still there, you know. They didn't take their graves up, but they demolished ours."

According to the interview transcript, Bell said graves, marked and unmarked, were built over "to make room for the military base."

The Whittington cemetery, she recalled, was near the Cherry Point schoolhouse. It had a wire fence around it with a gate. As a child, Bell would marvel at the markings on the gravestones.

"They sure built over that one 'cause is no cemetery out ... all out of the woods," she said. "And they certainly didn't move it." It was certain that an aunt's grave was "built over," she said. "Cemeteries are supposed to be, you're not supposed to interfere with a cemetery," she said, struggling for words. "But ... they did. So, it's not a good feeling at all."

Traditional since colonial times had been the burial of the deceased on family land. An untold number of people were buried with no marker, or with one made of wood that was subject to the forces of the seasons, weather, fire, and insects. These were easily lost to time. Nevertheless, family members would recall where their people were buried even when their gravesites were no longer obvious to outsiders. Other gravesites, like the Whittington's, were more elaborate, with fences and engraved stones.

There are Whittington graves accounted for in the list of relocated burials at Cherry Point. Some Whittingtons are mentioned in Part II of this book. The list of Cherry Point graves, including Whittington burials, is in

Rare photograph. Taken Thursday, August 28, 1941, exactly two weeks ahead of the deadline for the former owners to be permanently off Cherry Point, two men, at right, and a boy, in the door, try to salvage what they can from a two-story pack house on Sarah Meadow's 168-acre homestead, also known by government officials as Tract 540. The photo shows one of the many farm buildings abandoned by those whose land was condemned for the creation of the Cherry Point air station. *EBE, Jr. Papers, Joyner Library, ECU. Image 753.1.d.16*

Part IV. It's possible, even likely, that the Whittington graves were relocated and Emma Bell didn't know about it. Her sentiments, though, reflect the overall hurt and resentment felt by many of the evictees.

"We didn't have no say so, no nothing, honey," she said. "They'd put your butt in jail," if not off the land by September 11. "They were supposed to pay something for the church, but I doubt they ever paid anything 'cause some of the people at the base died before they got their money. We was out three or three and a half years before we got one dime. They didn't pay 'em nothing what the land was worth. You went to the courthouse, what that land was valued at 50 years ago that, that's what they got."

The family moved from their farm to a Havelock rental house leaving behind their garden, chickens, fruit trees, crops, and much more.

"Lord, it was the worst feeling I ever had in my life 'cause we had … used to having everything." she said. "When we left out, we had collards as big as washtubs. And all we could do is bring four or five heads down here and we couldn't go back to get no more. We were out with nothing to eat."

Like many of those displaced by the condemnation, Emma Bell was later employed at Cherry Point. She worked in the cafeteria and did janitorial work, but she said she would have preferred to stay on the farm. "I would have been so much better off," she said. "A lot of people profited from the base, you know, but, honey, I'd have rather had my land."

Not everyone who lived on Cherry Point was prosperous.

Property photographs taken during the eviction process show a few houses that were nothing more than "tar paper shacks," the kind that was characteristic of the rural poor from the end of the Civil War into the Great Depression and after.

Many of the families lived on only a few acres. But even on a single acre, country people grew most of their food and got by, especially when supplies were supplemented by fishing,

Worse for the wear after its abandonment, the Will Berry home at Tar Neck, Cherry Point, on eight-acre tract 526. September 15, 1941. *ECU. Image 753.1.e.16*

hunting, chickens, and a milk cow. And, of course, as we have noted, there was moonshining.

Moonshine was a double-edged sword. Like cotton and tobacco, it was a cash crop. Many people in Havelock, Harlowe, and Cherry Point gained spending money from the liquor business. A few made quite a lot. But others succumbed to overconsuming the famous liquid corn.

Said Bertha Mae George: "People drank too much."

And some did time in prison.

Emma West Bell said a few families had a hard time making ends meet with adults and children sometimes going barefoot, even in church. She spoke of men she would see sometimes wearing "the raggediest clothes."

Still, many were able to stand up and take care of themselves. Even at times when they didn't have available cash, Bell said they always "had plenty of food."

They were poor but independent is how Bertha Mae George phrased it. With the bonus, she said wryly, of not having to rent from whites either.

Cherry Point was a double-edged sword, too.

Its cutting side meant the end of a way of life among the people on its land. The positive aspects included the monetary. Millions upon millions of federal dollars flowed into southern Craven County, creating jobs and op- portunities. With it came the fresh blood of people with new ideas who ar- rived from all over the country. They rapidly jump-started southern Craven County – which in some ways had been stuck in the 1800s – to a more mod- ern way of living than had previously imaginable.

The advent of Cherry Point shattered an old culture but brought an un- expected economic boom. Hundreds of people were hired each month in 1941 and 1942. Thousands were soon engaged in building the air station. Even some of those displaced later came around to view things differently.

James George, Sr. said that when the base opened it "brought about a change." He said many people found work and, suddenly, "there was more money" than ever before. "The base was a blessing," he said.

Speaking of Cherry Point, Sudie Green said, "That's what made eve- rybody get up on their feet, you know, 'cause it give everybody jobs." Her husband was able to work as a janitor at the base for 30 years and he helped others get jobs there, too. She said he "made good money." He was able to put savings in the bank and at the same time buy the family a new home, bigger than the one they had before. She said they had electricity and bought clothes and furniture from Montgomery Wards.

Lineda Carter put it simply: "The base made things better."

She did domestic work on the air station, caring for children and clean- ing houses for officers. People on the base were nice to her and friendly.

Early base employee Willie Jenkins signed his ID badge with an X at top right.

They came from everywhere, Florida and Pennsylvania. She said they treated her well and she would make five dollars a day, which was more than she ever made before.

"Once people worked on the base, they wouldn't go back to the farm," she said.

Women initially found jobs in the mess halls and cleaning houses, but later took on roles at the big aircraft maintenance facility called Overhaul and Repair (O&R).

Lillian Green said many of her relatives went to work at Cherry Point. The base gave people a way to make a living. "Everybody ate," she said. "Everybody was happy."

She noted, though, that some families were "scattered" and others left altogether to find opportunities up north.

Black people weren't the only ones who lost land. The Russell family surrendered Cherry Point and its quiet, peaceful way of life. New Bern businessman George Fuller had to give up his new hunting and fishing camp on the banks of Hancock Creek. And M.T Bradshaw was forced to move away from a riverfront farm so lovely that they'd one day build a social and dining club for officers on his former land.

Havelock farmer W.J. Wynne, Sr. would lose his farm as well. Despite that, a son, Walter J. Wynne, Jr., would later say the base "made the economy so much better."

Wynne would become a long-serving county commissioner giving him a unique perspective on Craven's dynamics. He acknowledged that the African Americans who were dispossessed of their land suffered the most but thought that, in the end, things happened for the best.

"My daddy used to tell me he had it rough," Wynne told an interviewer. "He says that the depression we saw when I was a boy was nothing like the depression ... well, they never knew what prosperity was. Really, they didn't. Until after the 1930s depression [ended]. They really didn't. Because, living down there, you made your living with your hands, doing whatever you could. Sawing wood in the lumber business, catching fish, shooting game to eat, having a little garden, and a farm. This sort of thing. They didn't go hungry but they didn't have any conveniences like ... no running water; no electricity."

In a few short years, the colossal military project radically changed that hard-scrabble reality for the better.

"Blacks benefited from Cherry Point as much as whites," he said.

The settlements of Tar Neck, Nelson Town, and Little Witness were founded by ex-slaves after the Civil War. Asking nothing from others, they simply sought the right of self-determination, the same sacred human impulse that had been held in ultimately high esteem by the enlightened founders of the republic.

These newly-freed people found refuge between the creeks of Slocum and Hancock; upon the very ground where many of them and their forebears had been enslaved. They cherished their freedom: to live as they wished to live, as best they could ... and to be left alone. They existed, and generations of these families thrived for 80 years in the pine woodlands of coastal Carolina, not burdening others and never soliciting anything from anyone. In their own way, they flourished. They made a place for themselves. They lived in peace.

But change, they say, is inevitable. And despite the initial surprise and heartache, even former bootlegger Fred Solomon Nelson started over.

He went to work at Cherry Point clearing land and then shifted into a successful 20-year civil service career. In the beginning, he was a truck driver hauling and delivering fuel around the base, often passing through the former sites of Tar Neck and Nelson Town. Later, he was a power plant worker not too far from his family's old homeplace.

Katie and Fred Nelson raised ten children and saw them through New Bern city schools.

And Fred didn't have to moonshine ever again.

Marines and sailors at MCAS Cherry Point in 1943.

From the Halls of Montezuma to the Shores of Slocum Creek

It was dark. As dark a night as Walter J. Wynne, Jr. had ever seen; so dark that the two demolition men had gotten out of the jeep to walk ahead of him. Corporal Wynne had been ordered to get these ordnance specialists close to some particularly tenacious German-occupied pillboxes on the front lines. Headlights – lights of any kind – were out of the question. On foot, the pair of overtired tough guys guided the young enlisted man to prevent him from driving to his death off the narrow, twisting mountain road.

Wynne was *enlisted* in the sense that he wasn't an officer. He'd been drafted. He hadn't volunteered because he was needed on his father's farm in Havelock, North Carolina. But when his draft board letter came early in the war, he went. Now, in 1944, he was deep inside Germany with the 100th Army Division.

A half-hour before, he'd been trying to bed down in a sleeping bag when the colonel came in looking for his driver. Wynne was one of about a dozen guys sardined on the floor of a cramped room, hoping to get some shuteye in a commandeered house that was passing for the battalion's command post.

They'd punched into Germany through the old Maginot line, sometimes taking a defended position, being driven back, and having to take the objective all over again. What they'd been through recently would become known to World War II history as the Battle of the Bulge. Together with the others in the 100th, they'd muscled their way into some provincial town along the Neckar River on the way to Stuttgart.

The colonel had a little Italian kid for a driver. At the moment, he couldn't find his wheelman and was giving Cpl. Wynne some serious eyeball. Somebody had to take the two men from an explosives outfit up to the action and the CO knew that Wynne knew the way. With the colonel, he'd watched the fighting there all through the afternoon. From a strategic vantage, they monitored the surreal U.S. assault. Above their heads, daredevil acrobats wheeled aircraft through doppler whines. One after another, fountains of angry yellow sparks erupted, then puffs of white, and three beats later, a thud you felt in your chest. The crackle of small arms echoed from busy infantry who risked all against the stubborn enemy bunkers. There were concussions, flames, smoke, and whiffs of cordite. It was like watching a Hollywood movie. Almost.

That night the demolition men had arrived to see what they could do about it. And, as Wynne had apprehended, he got the dangerous nod from the colonel to take the officer's jeep and deliver the men to the battle line.

The two bedraggled soldiers looked like they hadn't slept in days. "They were so tired, I felt sorry for them," Wynne recalled five decades later. "And I felt sorry for the task they had ahead of them when they got there."

The rutted path was up the side of a mountain. He knew Nazi infantry was at the top but they might be waiting anywhere in the night's blackness.

"When we left it was so cotton-picking dark that they walked in front of me with white handkerchiefs," he said.

Progress was painfully slow. About halfway to the top, they came upon a battalion ammunition truck hanging off a ledge. "It didn't go over but it had missed that much of the road that it was about to go," he said. "We wiggled our way around it."

With the demolition men's hankies leading the jeep and Wynne picking the route among the mountain paths, he got them close to the objective. He pointed the men the rest of the way, whispered a farewell, and watched them melt into the gloom. Then he turned the jeep around and headed back down the dark mountain alone.

"I just creeped," he said. "You can see in the dark after your eyes get adjusted, just a wee little bit. Like I said, I was creeping so if I did hit a soft place, I could stop before I went over. It was hairy. I'll never forget it."

Before joining the Army, Wynne hadn't been away from his southern Craven County home for more than one night at the time except for a single trip to visit relatives in Charleston, S.C. After long training at Fort Bragg, N.C., and Fort Jackson, S.C., he and the rest of the 100th had boarded Liberty ships at a New York City pier for the perilous ocean voyage to the European war zone.

While crossing the Atlantic, they'd encountered what he called "the worst storm I've ever seen." Many men got sick and others were hurt as the ship was thrown about by the angry seas. Wynne was injured when he fell in a shipboard shower. The wound to his foot became badly infected. After the ship entered the Mediterranean and the troops disembarked at Marseilles, France, he was ordered to an Army hospital for treatment.

W. J. Wynne, Jr., U.S. Army, WWII

At what was the primary hospital for care of the battlefield wounded, the gravity of his circumstances dawned clearly upon the young soldier for the first time.

"I had the living daylights scared out of me," he said. "There were people coming off the frontlines. Legs shot off. Arms shot off. They told us about the [weapons] the Germans were using, 'screaming-mimis.' They scared the fire out of me."[a]

There are things you're better off not knowing.

Before leaving Marseilles for the front, Wynne witnessed a group of German POWs as they were killed by a falling brick wall. The prisoners were demolishing a building he described as "20 to 30 feet tall" when it collapsed. The men were crushed, killing or injuring all of them.

None of the observers reacted to the accident. "Nobody batted an eye," he said. "This was the first I saw of what war was."

After leaving Marseilles on a troop train, he passed other trains – some fifty freight and passenger cars long – that had been destroyed by aerial

---

[a] A type of World War II German rocket artillery with a distinctive sound after firing.

bombing and strafing. Just blown to pieces. There were herds of cattle dead in French pastures. They'd swollen to three times their normal size and been left to rot. Though some of the things he saw worried him, maybe frightened him, he carried a sense of homespun optimism even after he was thrown full-tilt into the fray.

"When you're 21 or 22, single, in perfect health, and you didn't know what getting tried was, I'm not sure you thought that much about death," he said. "Or that the next one might get you. Besides, they kept us too busy. You didn't have enough time to think about it."

But some things left strong impressions long after the war was over. There's no accounting for what the mind singles out.

Wynne remembered snow had covered a lot of the dead soldiers who had been killed but were unrecovered during the brutal winter battles of 1944. "When the snow started melting … they had laid there all winter; a long time under all that snow."

He'd carry that image forever.

"I saw my share of combat," he said. "You better believe I did."

Quoting many before and since, he added, softly, "War is hell."[b]

While He Was Gone to War, They Built the Base

When W.J. Wynne was called to military service, Havelock, N.C. was a sleepy railroad stop with two country stores and a population of around one hundred. A Cherry Point Marine Corps airfield was "mostly talk." When he returned at war's end, however, the placid realm of his youth was all but unrecognizable.

"It was an entirely different place," he said.

Electricity had arrived at long last. There were as many as 20,000 people in town and on the base. Wynne said, "honky-tonks were everywhere." New houses had sprung up including former farm fields converted to trailer parks. There were new gas stations. New stores. New churches. There was even a barbershop. Taxis were running around town. Trucks were rolling, planes were flying, and two new railroad spurs now channeled long lines of train cars into MCAS Cherry Point. There were so many automobiles that there was rush hour traffic, and military policemen standing on barrels on Highway 101 directing it on and off the base.

"On base," they'd demolished or burned old homes, farm buildings, and vacation camps. The forest had been harvested for miles, stumps removed,

---

[b] Parts of this chapter are based upon historian David Cecelski's 1995 recorded interview # K-56 with W.J. Wynne, Jr., as archived in the Southern Oral History Program, Southern Historical Collection, Wilson Library, University of North Carolina at Chapel Hill.

The Cherry Point School was the first modern school built in southern Craven County. Local students attended, but it was funded by the federal government in the early 1940s to meet the needs of the dependent children of Cherry Point's military personnel. It faced Havelock's Cunningham Blvd. at the intersection of Jaycee Street and was built on former W.J. Wynne, Sr. farmland. EBE/ECU.

and the land bull-dozed flat and level. Drainage projects were completed, pipe and electrical lines laid, and endless miles of new roads cut, graded, and paved. At the center of things, they built an impressive, colossal X of runways with a control tower for the largest Marine Corps airbase in the world. Runways were lined with aircraft and with a string of hangars, each much bigger than anything east of Raleigh.

An entire Marine air wing had moved in. Aircraft filled the skies.

There was nothing left of Tar Neck, Little Witness, Nelson Town, or village of Cherry Point. But everywhere you looked in those old places stood a new building, a construction project underway, or ground being prepared for one.

Wynne, who had grown up at Havelock, said he had a hard time recognizing the place and pinpointing exactly where some things had been before he left for service. He readily acknowledged, though, that the economy was much, much better.

Where the Wynne family's extensive farm fields had been south of Highway 101 was now a thick patchwork of government housing. The mile-long farm paralleling Highway 70, in what is now Havelock, belonged to Walter J. Wynne, Sr. He was a descendant of pioneers and was born and raised on Hancock Creek. Some of his colonial forebears lay buried in the family's old cemetery near Slocum Creek.

In 1941, Wynne, Sr. owned acreage from unpaved Highway 101 to today's Wynne Road in Havelock. The Wynne farmland, condemned by the federal government, was soon completely developed. It was used for the construction of the Cherry Point School, a combination community center-chapel, and housing.

The chapel accommodated both nondenominational Protestant and Catholic worship services, weddings, and funerals. Substantial housing complexes called Flat Tops, Splinterville, and Fort Macon were also built on the former Wynne farm. The Flat Tops were single-story homes with a roof canted toward the back to drain rainwater. These were built closest to Highway 101. Splinterville housing units, in the center of the property, were connected like one- and two-story apartment buildings. The Fort Macon neighborhood was quadruplex and duplex multi-family homes on the east end of the former farmland. These developments eventually aged out and were demolished, but many of the streets are still visible on satellite maps.

By 2021, Havelock city park, the municipal police, fire, and rescue building, and Walter B. Jones Park would each occupy a portion of the Wynne farm site, as would Craven Community College, the Havelock Public Library, and a new Havelock Elementary School.

The former base chapel served for many years as Havelock's first town hall and city hall, until a new city hall was built at the site.

A Harrier jet monument keeps watch over it all.

W.J., Jr. was surprised when he learned his father had lost the farm. He said the land went "awful cheap" and the family got little money for it. He was also surprised at what – and how much of it – had been built there while he was away.

"I plowed a two-horse or two-mule team out there when I was boy," he said. "We had tobacco. We raised cotton one year, but cotton was on the way out. The boll weevil killed it. The reason you raised tobacco is you made more money in it."

Wynne, along with brother Clay and sister Lila, spent his youth doing field and farm work. The family had hogs and cows. They planted soybeans, but not to eat or sell. "We'd put young cows in those fields to fatten up and be sold," he said.

Havelock city park between Cunningham Blvd. and US 70 was his father's hog pen. "It was a cypress pond," he said. "It's filled in a whole lot, but the water stood out there year-round. The reason it was his hog pasture was that we didn't have to pump any water to it."

He said that where the elementary school and city hall stand was where they had sod barns and tobacco barns.

"My grandfather [William Yarrow 'W.Y.' Wynne] lived on the other side of the road [US 70]," Wynne said. "There's a two-story house there that's probably the oldest house in Havelock."

Of his father, Wynne said "Daddy was born on Cherry Point. My grandfather owned land down there. Daddy used to ride those log rafts to New Bern when he was a boy. He worked in the logwoods ... My mother was a school teacher at one time. She taught school at Cherry Point. I think that's where Daddy met Mama and married her."

He said during his earlier lifetime people "either farmed, worked in the logwoods, or made moonshine liquor."

When he returned from the war, however, thousands of local people had found another alternative: Marine Corps Air Station Cherry Point, N.C.

MCAS Cherry Point Before Pearl Harbor, 1941

In a rare September 7, 1941, aerial photo below, the "X" marks the location of the future main gate and Pass and ID Office of today's MCAS Cherry Point. Major points of interest are noted with numbers and text boxes in the image of early base construction.

For example, the number 1 at the bottom left is where US 70 and Highway 101 separated seventy years ago. The split was just east of the small bridge over the southeast prong of Slocum Creek. Highway 70 then

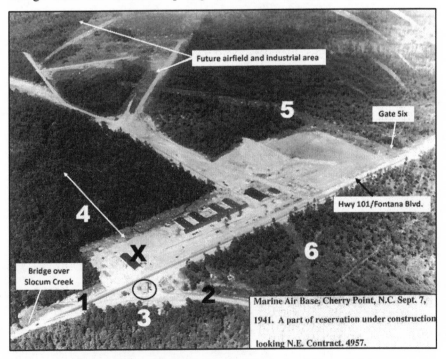

Photograph from *Historic Images of Havelock and Cherry Point.*

continued to the east toward Morehead City on the route marked by the number 2, which today is a part of Roosevelt Blvd. The familiar four-lane highway through town wouldn't exist for two more decades. Highway 101, today called Fontana Blvd within Havelock city limits, is marked by a text box and arrow. The route to Beaufort is toward the right.

The circle above the number 3 encloses Russell's Service Station and store, one of only two places in Havelock with a payphone in 1941. Local legend is that the phone there had a line of expectant callers 24 hours a day in the early months of the air station.

While most of old Havelock shopped at Trader's Store, Russell's was the one used most often by the hundreds of local people who lived on Cherry Point before their eviction around 1940. A remnant of the Russell store is thought to still be incorporated within a building on the triangle of land at today's intersection of Fontana and Roosevelt boulevards.

The arrow above number 4 illustrates the approximate route of today's Roosevelt Blvd. on the air station. At number 5, the beginnings of Cunningham Blvd. are visible as is the clearing for a railroad line onto the base at number 6.

None of the buildings visible along Highway 101 exist at the location today. They were considered temporary structures used during the construction period and were later moved, cannibalized, or demolished. The one just below the X was moved further into the air station and became one of the wings of the Training Building.

Other marked places are the current location of Gate Six at the intersection of Cunningham and Fontana, the first main gate; and the clearing that would become the approach to runway 5R and the base's industrial area. "A" Street would be just off the top edge of the photograph.

The old aerial photo was made under government contract Number 4957 exactly three months before the Japanese attack on the U.S. Pacific fleet in Hawaii. The identification label at the bottom right was a part of the print. The image proves beyond question that base chronologies stating that construction began "17 days before Pearl Harbor" are incorrect.

The End of the Deadly Savannah Swamp

The introductory chapter of the book began with an explanation of the use of dynamite in 1941 to drain wet areas for base construction. In the fourth chapter, the "low and wet savannah" was located, mapped, and described, along with an explanation of its suspected deleterious effects on the health of those living nearby. As we learned, that swampy place at the center

270 of the territory between Slocum Creek and Hancock had inconvenienced

of the territory between Slocum Creek and Hancock had inconvenienced and plagued settlers and their children for 200 years.

In modern times, scientists and medical researchers determined that the anopheles mosquitoes of Cherry Point's central savannah swamp had long been responsible for the highest rate of death from malaria and other mosquito-borne diseases anywhere in the State of North Carolina.

Before water management and land clearing could begin in earnest, the mosquitoes had to be killed. Or at least suppressed.

To attack the deadly threat, the military brought in a heavy-hitter, Lieutenant Kenneth Ellsworth Anderson, USNR. A former Cornell University scientist, Anderson was called to the war effort and made commanding officer of U.S. Malaria Control Unit #8. Before the war was over, Unit #8 would also wipe out mosquito-breeding areas in Morocco, Corsica, Italy, the Philippines, and Puerto Rico.

At Cherry Point, Lt. Anderson employed a spray boat, a biplane, a "skeeter jeep," mobile power sprayers, and a small army of workers to attack mosquitoes with fuel oil and a new "wonder chemical," DDT.

The plus-or-minus 11,000 acres of Cherry Point were crisscrossed with sixty streams emptying into the nearby creeks and river. Forty-four marshes of various sizes were identified for draining including the colossal savannah at its center that measured a mile long, four hundred feet wide, and three feet deep.

Used on the larger streams, the spray boat carried 300 gallons of oil. Men sprayed on foot along the smaller waterway. The spray plane was specially designed Stearman N2S-3 "equipped with a centrifugal force atomizing head, [to expel] liquid DDT in the form of a heavy fog which descends on a strip 150 feet wide with each run." The plane sprayed over the entire base while concentrating on the wooded areas. It was normally flown in the still air of the early morning.

Dichlorodiphenyltrichloroethane was later banned for its harmful effects on the environment but under its initials, DDT, it was considered a miracle tool in the 1940s. It worked quickly on mosquitoes directly exposed to it and was deadly to insects that came in contact with surfaces coated by the sprayers. DDT didn't kill the mosquitoes directly but short-circuited their nervous systems causing them to "run themselves to death."

The final weapon in the Unit #8 arsenal was devised by Lt. Anderson and created by the base's new public works department. The "skeeter jeep" was a regular jeep that was fitted with a DDT spray tank and used the vehicle's exhaust to lay down a thick cloud of insecticide as it plied "the built-up areas of the base" at night.

Inspection teams constantly roamed the landscape. They were individually armed with portable oil sprayers as much for self-protection as to thwart the mosquitoes and their larvae.

Former Cherry Point resident Julia Hooks said her husband worked long days on the mosquito abatement project, making the best pay he'd ever earned. Though the base officially opened in the first half of 1942, Moses Moore, one of the early workers there, said land clearing went on for years,

Timbering had long been one of the key industries of southern Craven County. As previously noted, a major activity of "working in the logwoods" from the colonial era onward was cutting ditches to drain the land. The Navy's construction team found a plentiful supply of people with extensive experience in ditching and drainage already on the ground here. They added the labor-saver of modern explosives technology to get the job done at record speed.

During just the first six months of the initial phase of base construction, 16,000 feet of ditches were dynamited, 12,000 feet were opened with draglines cranes, and Cherry Point laborers dug a whopping 24,000 feet the old-fashioned way – by hand.

Even with that, it took three months for the central savannah swamp to drain. [c]

MCAS Cherry Point, World War II and beyond

A Grumman J2F Duck, a single-engine amphibious biplane, was the first aircraft to land on Cherry Point's new runways. The commanding officer, Lt. Col Thomas J. Cushman, ensured his place in history by personally initiating "Cunningham Field" flight operations with the touchdown at 1:45 p.m. on March 18, 1942. The field, named for the first Marine aviator, became MCAS Cherry Point two months later.

The Duck was used as an air-sea rescue aircraft from the mid-1930s through World War II. Powered by a 750-horsepower piston engine, the biplane carried a crew of two and cruised at 155 mph. The aircraft circling over southern Craven County and touching down at Cherry Point have evolved quite a bit since then.

If placed end to end, Cherry Point's runways are more than six miles long; long enough that in 2007 the command was tasked with "providing emergency landing contingency services for the Space Shuttle Orbiter Vehicle and astronauts." [d]

---

[c] "Marine Corps Air Depot Wins Mosquito War," *Wilmington Morning Star*, July 22, 1945.

[d] MCAS Cherry Point, Air Station Order 3121.1A, March 29, 2007.

Initially, however, Cherry Point was home for North American B-25 Mitchell bombers called PBJs by the Marines. The B-25s were flown by the 22nd Squadron of the Army Air Corps who'd been sent to fight off Nazi submarines that were wreaking havoc with coastal shipping along the Outer Banks. A Navy aircrew operating from Cherry Point in 1943 would get credit for sinking a German U-boat in the Atlantic off North Carolina.

'A' STREET, ROOSEVELT, BEFORE & AFTER – The same streets on MCAS Cherry Point are shown above in late 1941 and below some years later, illustrating the magnitude of base construction. Above, smoke from land clearing fires is seen in the distance. 'A' Street, at center, and Roosevelt Blvd. in the foreground are unpaved. The swampy "savannah" discussed in the book had been in the area at the top of the photo before it was drained and filled. Below, in 1962, with roads completed, the 75 acres of massive hangars housing the aircraft maintenance facility, Overhaul & Repair (O&R), are at right center above the warehouses of Navy Supply. The main Navy Supply building is left center. A runway is at upper right in the photo below. Since 1941, Cherry Point construction has paused occasionally, but never stopped. EBE/ECU.

One of the units trained at Cherry Point for World War II in the Pacific was VMF(N)531, the first night-fighter squadron of the Marine Corps. The pilots of 531became the first in the Marines or Navy to engage Japanese aircraft using the then-new radar technology.

Watching neighbors come and go, the local civilian population lent support to Cherry Point personnel as its war-fighters and their planes and helicopters engaged in America's fights in Korea and Vietnam. All of

The Neuse River is at the top, with Slocum Creek at left and Hancock Creek at right in this aerial photo of Cherry Point runways taking shape in early 1942. Highway 101 is in the foreground. When the photo was made, Little Witness Road and its farm fields, was still visible below the runways at right. EBE/ECU

A Vought F4U Corsair on a Cherry Point runway during World War II.

Havelock knew when the Marines went on full alert during the Cuban Missile Crisis in the fall of 1962. They saw them off when they were called to service again for Operation Desert Storm. They've watched and waited for them in Iraq, Afghanistan, and other actions around the globe.

It's probably impossible to count the number of Marines and sailors who have passed through the gates of the base since 1941, but they've come from every state in the union and several foreign countries. The new blood of Cherry Point and the new civilian jobs brought by the base in general and its big aviation maintenance facility, in particular, transformed the local economy and culture.

Flight Path to the Future

One of the early transformations was that people quit using coal and wood for heat and cooking. W.J. and Clay Wynne converted the store their father started into a gas station, garage, and heating oil distribution business. At one time, "Wynne Brothers" had four tanker trucks servicing home heating accounts across the southern end of the county. The business became a landmark on the highway in east Havelock. They operated their enterprise until they retired in 1968.

Clay Wynne was a driving force in the incorporation of the Town of Havelock in 1959. He served on the first town board and as Havelock's second mayor, succeeding George Griffin. He was the first town manager. W.J. became a leader in county government and the push for rural electrification.

It was quite a transition for two boys who grew up with mule-power and candlelight. "It was a different way of life," W.J. said. "It had been a country place. So much happened in a relatively short period of time."

Despite all the changes, Wynne accentuated the positive when he sat down at his Wynne Road home in 1995 for an interview that was frequently interrupted as Cherry Point jets flew low and slow overhead.[e]

He commented on how quickly "things sprang up around here" and Havelock, for a time, became a boomtown. "People had money in their pockets" because the base was employing so many of them with good-paying jobs. He said the federal education dollars sent to support the base made the local schools better than they could have been otherwise. He said the federal aid had been "critical for the schools."

Wynne said the military people fit in well with the community and the relationships between the base and the civilian side were generally good over the years. He, his wife, Lillian, and his sons, Jay and David, made many friends in the Fort Macon housing development bordering their yard. His

---

[e] SOHP #K-056 by David Cecelski, 1995.

children went to school with, played with, and befriended military kids. They attended church together and interacted in social, sports, and community events.

In the end, Marine aviation found a home on the shores of Slocum Creek, Hancock Creek, and the mighty Neuse. And in the few short years of the 1940s, Havelock was changed more than any other town in North Carolina. It was dragged unceremoniously and without warning from its wood-fired, lantern-lit world into a new and tumultuous 100-watt future.

To make sure everyone had electricity, Wynne joined the board of directors of the Carteret-Craven Electric Membership Cooperative in 1952. The EMC's president for 16 years, he was still serving as a director in 1995.

Well-liked and trusted, he was repeatedly elected as a Craven County commissioner. During the 22 years of his tenure in office, he represented the people from the Trent River to Adams Creek; the entirety of southern Craven County.

It was fitting. There had been Wynnes here since at least 1750 when James Wynn bought a 150-acre plantation on Slocum Creek. His deed, preserved in Craven County Deed Book No. 1, was witnessed by both a Hancock and a Slocum.[f]

Since before the American Revolution, through generation after generation, beside the river and between the creeks, the family had always been on this land. They had always been farmers.

In his home on the last remnant of the last Wynne Farm, Walter James Wynne, Jr. lived under the flight path of Cherry Point's main runway for the rest of his life.

He told everyone who asked that he didn't mind the noise.

---

[f] Craven County Deeds, Book 1, pp 486-487.

PART II

THE WHISPERERS

"These facts are calculated to awaken serious reflection in every thinking mind. – Neither temporal dignities nor popular favor, not even the 'arms of an Angel,' can shield any mortal from the common lot of all."

From a column entitled: "Death."
Poulson's American Daily Advertiser
The early 1800s

Traversing Hallowed Ground

Now we make a radical departure from the narrative form that has propelled us thus far. Part II is more a list than a story, though the story is alive in every detail. Herein are the cemeteries and individual graves, some known and many lost, that give testimony for those who have gone before us. We set out to listen to whispers from the past. Those whispers are stronger here.

Engraved stones in the cemeteries scattered from Riverdale to Croatan and Havelock, Cherry Point to Harlowe and Adams Creek have left for us remarkable clues to the area's rich history. While this section provides information and photographs gleaned from local gravestones, several caveats are in order.

The contents herein are by no means complete. Some cemeteries and single burial sites unknown to the author have surely been overlooked. An unimaginable number of graves were unmarked, especially among those individuals and families of less prosperous circumstances. Many times, graves were memorialized only by crudely constructed wooden crosses or carved wooden grave markers that have succumbed to the onslaught of time. We know of one graveyard at an African American church on the old Beaufort Road – Highway 101 – where nearly the entire collection of wooden markers was destroyed in a forest fire.

A 1985 archeological report for Cherry Point states: "*Most of the graves recorded in 1941 lacked markers*" [emphasis added]. It also notes that the majority of graves in the nearby Little Witness community were memorialized only with small metal frames containing paper inserts that quickly became illegible.

Add to those factors that settlers here tended to consider the peaceful vistas of the riverfront bluffs an ideal resting place for loved ones, and that many of these bluff-top cemeteries have been washed away over time by the ceaseless erosion of the Neuse River's south shore. While we can document European settlement here from 1702, the oldest surviving graves in southern Craven County date from more than a hundred years later.

The conclusion is that only scant remnants survived for interpretation. Perhaps ten graves are unknown for each one now evident. And possibly many more. In any event, each remaining nugget is precious for the understanding of our heritage in general and, in particular, to interested descendants of those whose information has survived.

Today, each marked grave, or nameless depression in the soil, should remind us also of the tender care of family and friends for their lost loved ones.

Edward Salter was born here in 1861 during the War Between the States. An infant when the Union army invaded Craven County, he was 64 years old at the time of this death and burial at Cherry Point in 1916. His wife had this carved on his headstone:

> Dearest husband thou hast left us.
> And thy loss we deeply feel.
> But 'tis God that hath bereft us.
> He can all our sorrows heal.
> Yet again we hope to [meet thee].
> When the day of life has fled.
> Then in heaven with joy to greet thee
> Where no farewell tears are shed.

Though valuable in the extreme, it's fortunate that gravestones aren't our only source of information. The county's register of deeds is full of data about the southern half of Craven. So's the census. And then we have the old newspapers. In a single newspaper, *The Daily Journal* published in New Bern from 1882 to 1914, for example, the word "Havelock" appears 3,717 times; not bad for a place often said not to have existed until MCAS Cherry Point was built in 1941. And then there are references to and stories about Slocum Creek, Hancock Creek, Cherry Point, Croatan, Pine Grove, Harlowe, Clubfoot Creek, Adams Creek, Lake Ellis and to individuals and places-names long forgotten.

And there are dozens of other newspapers to consider, some published at the same time and some earlier.

In all, the critical mass of information – enough for an encyclopedia – coalesces into a solid picture of this distant, horse-drawn world. Ninety percent of the families were tied to the farming of produce, cash crops, livestock, and turpentine. There were multi-generational farms and plantations of unimaginable size spread every one to five miles with 500 acres seeming to be just average.

From the beginning, it had been about the land. Half-starved survivors of a European nightmare, where savage wars had raged for generations, risked all to cross the ocean for North America. On the old continent, Catholics were working as hard as possible to kill the Protestants, while Protestants were equally diligent in their work. Letters written home from eastern North Carolina in the early 1700s are almost heartbreaking in their pleadings to friends and relatives to escape their homelands and come and feast on the freedoms and bounty of the New World.

A final note and an important one. This work is not, nor is it intended to be, a comprehensive list of cemeteries and burials in the greater Havelock area. Such an all-inclusive accounting of graves and graveyards is beyond the scope of this work and, more candidly, beyond the capabilities of the author. To illustrate this point, midway through this project, Debra Newton-Carter, a friend who is a highly skilled historian and genealogist, touched base with direction to yet another cemetery.

In that sense, the effort is incomplete. Other discoveries are yet to be made. But these sites and individuals, with their details and stories, appear primarily because they came to our attention, one way or another, in an earnest attempt to discover, study and document early settlers and later residents, some of whom were previously unknown or otherwise forgotten.

We hope that the burial grounds and persons included – whatever their limitations may be – will remind the reader of the vast number of people who have lived their lives, passed on, and been buried in southern Craven County during a period of more than three hundred years.

Our further hope is that the information disclosed will be both an inspiration and a useful catalyst for local historical and genealogical research by others in the future.

Graves on US 70 near Carolina Pines. Croatan FWB Church at right.

Some Old Cemeteries of Southern Craven County

Batts Cemetery, between a convenience store located on Ketner Heights Boulevard at the US 70 Access Rd. and a former furniture store building. The small cemetery with African American burials and marble headstones in a low brick enclosure was intact in the 1960s but destroyed and paved over during construction of the original store on the site, circa 1970s. Photo of location, *Havelock Progress* newspaper article, November 1976.

Benjamin Family Cemetery, a small African American graveyard off Greenfield Heights Blvd. across from Westgate subdivision and the location of an old black one-room schoolhouse. Currently eight burials, mostly from the modern era. Most prominent burial "Book" Benjamin.

Blades cemeteries, three are known to us in the area east of Blades Road near Clubfoot Creek: the **George** Family Cemetery with at least 175 burials, the **Carter** Family Cemetery, and the **Jesse Godette** Family Cemetery.

Cherry Point cemeteries, traditionally numbered CP 1- CP 16, usually with tract numbers corresponding to Cherry Point ownership map circa 1941. Each contains from one burial to a hundred or more, many unidentified. Abbreviated CP 1, CP 2, CP 3, etc. CP 2, for example, is the **Winn, (Wynn or Wynne) Cemetery**, on tract 538-A on the 1941 Cherry Point ownership map. Also, see Little Witness Church below. For a map, see *Cemeteries and Farms at Cherry Point, 1941* at the front of the book.

Chesnutt Cemetery, in a farm field at a sharp turn in Tebo Road. Burials include Eborn, Conner, Hardison, Haskett, Ives, Scurlock, Smith, and Williams.

Craven Corner Missionary Baptist Church Cemetery, Adams Creek Road, a large African American cemetery with more than 200 marked burials, a few dating from the early 20th century. Comprehensive list online at findagrave.com, but some of the oldest burials are unmarked.

Croatan Community Cemetery, across US 70 from the location of the old Croatan store ("Tom Haywood's Store," later the Country Store at Croatan, operated until 2017 by Charles and Martha Davis family of Havelock.) The Croatan cemetery contains the grave of former Craven County Commissioner and local celebrity Tom Haywood, founder of the Self-Kicking Club of America.

Dennis-Wynne Cemetery, about one mile south of Carolina Pines, on the east side of US 70 access road, just south of Hazeldale Lane. In woods behind old plantation homesite.

First United Methodist Church Cemetery, (FUMC) behind the church on Miller Blvd., Havelock, N.C. The original church building dates from circa 1880.

Fisher-Latham Cemetery (New), is located halfway down East Fisher Ave. at Riverdale. Well-kept.

Fisher Cemetery (Old), further down East Fisher Ave. near Neuse River. Many and possibly all graves washed away by storms.

George Family Cemetery is located in North Harlowe and is likely to exceed 200 burials. Prominent family names there include Becton, Carter, Fenner, George, Godette, Miller, Moore, Richard, Sparrow, and others.

Harlowe United Methodist Church, twelve minutes from Havelock on Highway 101 (the Old Beaufort Road), the church had its beginnings in 1834. The cemetery memorializes many of the earliest names of the pioneer period.

Hickman Hill cemeteries, three cemeteries on Hickman Hill Loop Road, Havelock, are maintained by Green Chapel Church.

Hyman Chapel A.M.E. Zion Church, 2180 Highway 101, Havelock. More than 200 burials.

"Little Witness" also known as Melvin, N.C. was one of several African American communities on what is today MCAS Cherry Point. It was located northwest of the intersection of Highway 101 with Hancock Creek and included Little Witness Baptist Church, a post office, a school, and named dirt streets. None of these exist today. All residents were relocated through condemnation proceedings enabling the construction of a Marine base. A cluster of burial grounds within the old community's boundaries is counted among the MCAS Cherry Point cemeteries. Some of the graves have been moved and consolidated. Cemeteries have been named or numbered more than once in the past 75 years resulting in some conflicting records. CP 1 through CP 6, and CP 16 – also known as "Site C" – are all within proximity of one another. Many burials are unidentified.

Marshall Cemetery – What began as a family and slave cemetery in the early 1800s was used by African Americans into the modern era. It's behind Indian Hills and in Greenfield Heights along the railroad track. It was a part of the 1816 565-acre Marshall plantation, one of several in the immediate area dating to colonial and post-colonial times. The boundaries of Greenfield Heights are approximately contiguous with those of the original Marshall plantation, which was occupied by the William Henry Marshall family at the time of the War Between the States. Burials are likely to have begun in the 1700s. Most occupants are unknown. In the late 1800s and after, it was referred to as the "old cemetery." Some graves were disturbed by construction activity in the 1970s. It's conceivable that there are hundreds of burials. It's mentioned in the 1928 Craven County deed in Book 284 Page 190 and others.

Magnolia Plantation Cemetery (Lovick / Shute), among the oldest burial grounds in the Neuse River basin. Within Carolina Pines, by bluff near the river, now on private property. Dates from the 1700s. Many graves were washed away by storms and damaged by vandalism. Because of other burials, it's also known as the Lovick and/or Shute cemetery.

Mount Olive Cemetery, at the west end of Fisher Avenue, Riverdale.

Oak Grove United Methodist Church, Adams Creek Road, beyond North Harlowe and Craven Corner in the Bachelor area, about eight miles north of Highway 101. Large graveyard with burials dating to the early 1800s and possibly before. Paul, Taylor, Adams, Becton, Salter, Jackson, Belangia, and Whiteheads are among the prominent family names prominent.

Physioc Cemetery, primitive, nestled deep in the Croatan National Forest between Cahoogue Landing and Little John Creek. On hilltop surrounded by Forest Service cable fence. First visited February 26, 1984, by the author after seeing information on rare 1930s-era Civilian Conservation Corps map. Two marble headstones and evidence of additional burials (2 - 4 depressions within a fenced-off area). Headstones were broken but upright. Cemetery leaf-covered at the time but otherwise in good shape.

Rowe (or Pittman) Cemetery, within the median of US 70 and access road near Carolina Pines, at the intersection of Lewis Farm Road.

Saint Joseph Methodist Church, exact location protected off Waterscape Way south of West Thurman Road. About three dozen burials.

"Siddie" (City) Fields: From a book in the New Bern library: "Twp. 5. Located in City "Siddie" Fields area of Croatan National Forest near Harlowe [at real Cherry Point]. Erosion problems caused by the Neuse River destroyed this cemetery. With permission of a [Whitehead] family relative, forestry personnel relocated tombstones to Oak Grove Methodist Church Cemetery on Adams Creek Road. The stone of Rhoda Whitehead, a daughter of John Whitehead, was found among rock and ship's ballast stones; this stone was left on the site."

Simpson Cemetery – East side of Wilcox Road near the intersection with County Line Road in Riverdale community.

Taylor-Bell Family Cemetery, Bachelor, more than 60 burials including Jane P. Hancock Taylor and Joshua E. Taylor buried in 1860, and four-year-old Elijah E. Taylor, 1862. Names include Salter, Elliot, Harris, and Bell.

Tolson Cemetery, small Civil War-related cemetery in Croatan National Forest west of Havelock. The precise location is a secret to protect the cultural heritage significance of the site and the burials.

Whitehead Cemetery, see Siddie Fields.

Williams Cemetery, in an isolated farming area south of Tebo Road, is listed in a cemetery book at KR. Family names include Boyett, Caton, Eborn, Williams, and Wood. Some wooden markers.

Williams-White Cemetery, On the north side of Catfish Lake Road about one mile west of US 70, just beyond Carolina Pines from Havelock. Several members of prominent pioneering families of Havelock are here.

Willis Cemetery, Township Five off Adams Creek Road (SR 1700). Turn left onto dirt road SR 1701, then right on SR 1702 after about one mile. The cemetery in a field on left has four known burials.

As the headline says, these are some *old cemeteries. This is not a comprehensive list. Some, maybe many, are unknown to us, and others are yet to be discovered.*

ABBREVIATIONS:

AAF = African American female
AAM = African American male
a.k.a. = also known as
AMA/ARC = American Missionary Association records at the Amistad
      Research Center, Tulane University
ARC = Archaeological Resource Consultants report 1985
c. or circa = about, approximately
COD = cause of death
CP = Cherry Point
CP with number = Old Cherry Point cemetery. See map at front of book.
EBE/ECU = Edward B. Ellis, Jr. Papers, Joyner Library, ECU
ENCGS = Eastern North Carolina Genealogical Society
Esq. = Esquire, often means the person is an attorney
FUMC = First United Methodist Church Cemetery, Havelock
HIHCP = *Historic Images of Havelock & Cherry Point* - Ellis
ITSP = *In This Small Place* - Ellis
i.e. = in other words
inst. or instant = when referring to date means *this month*
KR = Kellenberger Room, New Bern Craven County Public Library
MCAS = Marine Corps Air Station
MUM = mulatto male
MUF = mulatto female
OR = Official Records of the War of the Rebellion
ORN = Official Records, Navy, War of the Rebellion
q.v. = which see
SHC = Southern Historical Collection, UNC-Chapel Hill
SOHP = Southern Oral History Program, Collection 4007, SHC, UNC-CH
ult. or ultimo = when referring to date means *the previous month*
USFS = United States Forest Service
WF = white female
WM = white male

Some Old Burials in Southern Craven County

Many, many graves are gone and forgotten. The earliest burials known to us in the greater Slocum Creek area include a man born before the American Revolution and a husband and wife who were themselves descendants of early settlers of the Neuse River basin.

The bedboard headstone of George Lovick (c. 1765 – 1798) is nestled on the riverfront at Carolina Pines west of Slocum Creek, the ancient site of the massive Magnolia Plantation established by his ancestors in 1719.

The gravestone of Sallie Jones of Cherry Point says she died in 1813. Her husband, Evan, was buried beside her four years later. The Joneses were a prosperous family whose plantation was situated at the junction of the Neuse River and the east bank of Slocum Creek. And it was there they were buried more than 200 years ago.

The following is a list created from known burials and lost graves primarily around Havelock and Cherry Point. The information comes from headstones, grave markers, vital records, news stories, archaeological lists, obituaries, maps, family members, and other researchers. The sources of each fact are too numerous to list. The information is deemed to be accurate but, with this quantity of details, errors of fact and transcription are inevitable. The overall purpose of the list is to demonstrate the sheer number of people who have lived, died, and been buried in the communities of the Neuse River's south shore, and to provide a springboard for future research by others.

Adams, Catherine, see Piner, Catherine   WF
Aman, infant   WM
A baby buried at FUMC was born March 18, 1904, and died April 2, 1904, 15 days old. The infant was the son of Rufus (born c. 1860) and Corinne W. Aman. The father, Rufus, registered to vote in Twp. 6, Oct. 29, 1904. The child appears to be the first burial at FUMC.
Armes (Arms), John W. and Maria F.   WM & F
They are mentioned on son's (Philip J. Armes) gravestone at a Cherry Point Cemetery, CP 7.
Armes, Julia Thorpe   WF
She was born c. 1854 at Hancock Creek, the daughter of Benjamin William Thorpe and Eliza Hope Whitehead Thorpe. She was the head of the school at the village of Hancock Creek. A personal news column noted that she was ill in Beaufort in late 1909. She died March 6, 1910, according to *The Daily Journal* of New Bern, March 8, 1910. The news story noted: "Remains taken to her home at Hancock's Creek, where they were interred in the family

burying ground." Based on the newspaper and other information that pin-points the family cemetery, she was buried in what was later designated CP 7, though the burial is unrecorded by base officials.

Armes (Arms), Philip J.   WM

He was born on January 2, 1848. The son of John W. and Maria F. Armes, he was a native of Virginia. He married Julia Thorpe of Hancock Creek. He was a farmer in Craven County and a resident of the village of Hancock Creek. He died March 5, 1896, and was buried in Hancock Creek commu-nity cemetery; later Cherry Point cemetery, CP 7, tract # 540.

Armstrong, Eloise (Sarah), see Hardy   WF

Armstrong, Mattie Lena Russell   WF

She was born on January 24, 1882, though her death certificate says 1883. She died on August 9, 1953, at 11 a.m. She was 70 years of age. Her death certificate was signed by her colleague, Manly Mason, MD, of Newport. COD: coronary thrombosis. The informant of death was one of her daugh-ters, Mrs. Thelma Armstrong Norris. Funeral services were by Willis Fu-neral Home of New Bern. She was buried at FUMC on August 12, 1953. She was the daughter of Edward D. Russell and his first wife, Sarah Eliza-beth Meadows. She was a housewife, midwife, community medical care-giver. At 18, she married Earnest Alonzo Armstrong on October 2, 1900, at the Havelock Methodist parsonage with Rev. R. B. John officiating. Ed Bangert was the best man. She appears in the 1940 Craven County census as a widow. Children, see Earnest Armstrong below. According to Mrs. Bobby (Sandra) Hardy, in the early 1900s, Mattie was the local unofficial "doctor" and served as midwife for many babies, black and white. She treated other illnesses and injuries with popular folk medicines like sugar, castor oil, kerosene, and turpentine. Worked in concert with Dr. Manly Ma-son of Newport. [*From EBE interview September 7, 1984*]

Armstrong, Earnest Alonzo   WM

He was born about 1858 or 1866. Census data conflicts. In 1900, he was living in the household of Sylvester Reems as a boarder and cook. He oper-ated a two-story country store near the current site of Trader's Store. The store was known locally as "Armstrong's Grocery." He was a native of Mar-yland, according to the 1910 census. He was the husband of Mattie Lena Russell. Married on October 2, 1900, Havelock Methodist parsonage, Rev. R. B. John officiated. Ed Bangert, best man. He was 37. She was 18. He was appointed by the county commissioners as a local registrar of births and deaths. He served as justice of the peace at Havelock in 1914. He was the Voluntary Township 6 Forest Fire Correspondent in 1917. He was the father of Zippiette Armstrong, George Allen Armstrong, Monzelle Armstrong, Thelma Armstrong, Sarah Eloise Armstrong, Louellen Armstrong, and Ear-nest Woodrow Armstrong. He appears in the 1930 Craven census at 63 years old but mysteriously disappeared without a trace from Havelock sometime before 1940. His wife was listed as a "widow" in the census of 1940. Death date and burial place are unknown. [*Sandra Hardy interview, 1984*]

Armstrong, George Allen   WM
He was born August 24, 1903, at Cherry Point, North Carolina. He was a single white male, farmworker, self-employed who died December 8, 1920. COD: croupous pneumonia, Buried at FUMC, December 10, 1920. The attending physician was Raymond Pollock, MD. Undertaker D. B. Lilly, Newport. His parents were Earnest Alonzo Armstrong and Mattie Russell Armstrong

Armstrong, Monzell Russell   WM
He was buried at FUMC with his brother, George Allen Armstrong. He was born November 26, 1905, and died at age 19 on September 15, 1925. There was no death certificate at Craven County, but he was thought to have succumbed to pellagra, a disease of the skin resulting from severe vitamin deficiency.

Armstrong, Thelma (see Norris)   WF
Armstrong, Zippiette Elizabeth   WF
"Zip" was born on December 27, 1901. She lived in Old Havelock on Gray Road and was the daughter of E.A. Armstrong, a Havelock grocer and shopkeeper, and Mattie Armstrong, who served the area as a midwife. She was the granddaughter of Edward D. Russell, a Havelock farmer, and postmaster. She was the sister of Thelma Armstrong Norris and Eloise Armstrong Hardy. She appears in an article, *Havelock Progress* newspaper of September 18, 1976, talking about local burials and other matters. She died September 7, 1984, and was buried at FUMC. Armstrong family information and photographs appear in *HIHCP*.

Atkinson, Laura J.   AAF
She was born c. 1918 and was the daughter of George and Viola Atkinson. She died June 30, 1930, at age 11 or 12. COD: unknown. No obituary or census data has been found. She was buried at Little Witness Church cemetery CP 1. Her burial was officially identified after 1985.

The Barnes Family of Cemetery CP15

Barnes, Caroline, see Garner, Caroline Barnes   WF
Barnes, Francis M., "Frank"   WM
He was born in December 1831. He was a farmer who lived west of Havelock near the Lewis Farm Road area. (Living "next door" to John R. Barnes, born 1860, in both 1880 and 1900 census). His wife was named Susanna(h) (1883-1900), and their children were: Mary E., born 1859; Caroline, born

1861; Delila, born 1863; James H., born c. 1866; Joel Henry, born 1874; William L., born 1881. He was widowed and age 68 in the 1900 census. He died June 16, 1909, at age 76. He was buried at CP 15.

Barnes, Joel Henry WM

Born May 20, 1874, he was the son of Francis M. "Frank" Barnes (1831-1909) and Susanna Barnes (1838-1889). He died August 18, 1907, at age 33, and was buried at CP 15.

Barnes, John R. WM

He was born c. 1850. In the 1880 census, he was an unmarried farmer living in Township 6, Craven County. His first wife, Murphy E. Barnes, lived from 1850-1900. They had a daughter Maggie who was born in 1882 and died at 15 in 1898. His second wife, Dinksie (Dinkie) Barnes, was born c. 1868. Their son, Willie J., was born in 1909 but died in 1911 at the age of 15 months. In both 1880 and 1900, he was living "next door" to Francis M. "Frank" Barnes, relationship unknown. In 1800 and 1890, he was living on Lewis Farm Rd. in the area west of Havelock. In 1910, he was living in New Bern and working as a planer at a lumber mill. He died at age 73 on December 10, 1929, and was buried "in the Barnes family burying ground." His obituary said he "was a member of one of the oldest families in the county" and "died on the old Barnes homestead" near Croatan.

Barnes, Maggie WF

She was born October 27, 1882, the daughter of John R. Barnes (born c. 1860) and first wife, Murphy E. Barnes (1850-1900). She died October 14, 1898, at age 15. She was buried in CP 15.

Barnes, Murphy E. WF

She was born March 26, 1850, and was the first wife of John R. Barnes (born c. 1850). She was the mother of Maggie Barnes (1882-1898). She died on her birthday, March 26, 1900, at age 50, She was buried with other family members at CP 15.

Barnes, Susanna, (Susannah) WF

She was born on November 21, 1938. She married Francis M. "Frank" Barnes (1831-1909). For her children, see Francis Barnes above. She died June 1, 1889, age 50.

Barnes, Willie J. WM

He was born November 8, 1909, the son of John R. & Dinksie Barnes. He died young on March 2, 1911, at age 15 months, and was buried in the family graveyard at location CP 15.

Barnes, William "Willie" L. WM

Born May 9, 1881, he was the son of Francis M. "Frank" Barnes and Susannah Barnes. He was a general farmer in Township 6, Craven County. In the 1910 census, he's listed as the "head of household" at age 25 (indicating his birth in 1885). At the time, his wife, Mollie Garner Barnes was 21; his baby daughter, Bessie, was age nine months; his sister-in-law, Izora Garner was 15; and James Thorpe, a nephew, 17, was in the home as a laborer on the "home farm." William Barnes died on March 16, 1917. According to his headstone, he was 35 years old. He was buried at CP 15.

Comments on the Barnes Families: (1) While they were buried in CP 15 on the east side of Slocum Creek (see Cemetery map, p. xv), based on the order in which the census lists were made, they appear to have lived on the west side of Slocum Creek among the Rowes, Pittmans, and Belangias (Bellangers). The area would be west of Havelock near or along the county road in the area between present-day Tucker Creek to Lewis Farm Road, near present-day Carolinas Pines. Present-day Slocum Road was then Beech Haven Farm Road and was a shortcut from Cherry Point to the county road and New Bern. The shortcut was accomplished by rowing, rafting, or ferrying people, produce, lumber, and so forth across Slocum Creek at the peninsula now known as Ordnance Point. (Visible on the cemetery map immediately above the number 15.) Therefore, it is conceivable that this family and others might have crossed Slocum Creek to bury their dead in the established cemetery there, while not living on the east side of the creek.

(2) Caroline Barnes Garner is the only Garner with a headstone at CP 15, but her brother William L. Barnes was married to a Garner (Mollie) and also had her sister (Izora Garner) in his household in 1910.

(3) As mentioned above, the John R. Barnes family and the Francis M. Barnes family were long-term "next door" or "next farm" neighbors. They're listed side-by-side in both the 1880 and 1900 censuses. The census taker would have traveled house-to-house. The federal census records for 1890, including Craven County, were destroyed in a fire at the Commerce Department in Washington, D.C. on January 10, 1921. The family's proximity to other named families supports the theory explained above that they lived between Havelock and Croatan.

(4) Other members of this large, intermarried, and extended family may have been buried at CP 15 in unmarked graves or in graves where the headstone did not survive to the mid-twentieth century.

The Batts Family on the Beaufort-New Bern Road

Batts, Amos (misspelled as "Baattes" in the census)   AAM
He was born c. 1865 and died after 1920. He attended the AMA's Woodbridge School under teacher Carrie E. Waugh in 1878. He was said to have been a "logger, farmer, and father of a large brood." He was a railroad laborer during the 1920s. He married Mary Frances Manning Batts in 1887. Among their children were Ernest, Amos, Hester, Minnie, and the uniquely

named Mary F., Jr. He owned 10 acres of land on the "Central Hwy." in Havelock, according to an 1891 tax list. This parcel was one of the lots of the Woodbridge community founded by the American Missionary Association about 1870. He was the son of Isaac Batts, a farmer, born c. 1828, and Hester Batts, born c. 1830. The siblings of Amos were Sarah, born c. 1869, and William Henry, born. c. 1871. His children were Amos, Jr, Earnest, Hester A., Minnie, and Mary Frances, Jr. He and his wife Mary sold one acre of land on April 6, 1910, on what was then the New Bern to Beaufort Road and is now Greenfield Heights Road, to the Craven County Board of Education for the construction of a one-room school house for black children. The transaction was attested by Justice of the Peace James H. Hunter and is recorded in county deed book 187 on page 381. Amos Batts was buried in Batts family cemetery near the intersection of US 70 and Ketner Heights Blvd. More details about the cemetery are in the *Havelock Progress,* November 1976.

Batts, Amos, Jr.   AAM
He was born in Havelock on September 10, 1891. He was listed as a laborer in the census. His wife was named Laura. He was the son of Amos and Mary Batts. He died at age 38 of kidney disease and was buried March 14, 1929, in Batts Cemetery.

Batts, Earnest   AAM
He was born April 1892 and died February 5, 1926, at age 34 when he was accidentally run over by Norfolk Southern Railroad train behind what is now Don-Lee Heights in west Havelock. He had been a laborer for the Blades Lumber Company. He was the son of Amos and Mary Batts. He was buried in Batts Cemetery. See "Batt's Inquest" in the chapter *Peril and Drama in the News,* Part III.

Batts, Isaac   AAM
He was a former slave and a settler at Woodbridge. He also appears on an 1877 list of Lake Ellis tenant farmers of James A Bryan.

Batts, Laura   AAF
She was the wife of Amos Batts, Jr.

Batts, Mary Frances Manning   AAF
She was born 1876 in Beaufort County, the daughter of Larkin(s) Manning. She died July 22, 1925, at age 49 after four or five years of heart trouble. She was the wife of Amos Batts and mother of Amos, Jr., Earnest, Hester A., Minnie, and Mary Frances, Jr. She was buried in Batts Cemetery. Mentioned in the *Havelock Progress,* November 1976.

Batts, Minnie   AAF
She was born on February 18, 1900. She died at age 14 of pellagra, a vitamin deficiency disease causing skin rashes and lesions. She was the daughter of Amos and Mary F. Batts. She was buried in the Batts Cemetery.

NOTE ON BATTS CEMETERY: Saul Lofton and **Hester Wallace** may also be buried in Batts family cemetery.

COMMENTS ON BATTS CEMETERY: The author, at the time a reporter for the *Havelock Progress* newspaper, wrote about the Batts Cemetery in November 1976 in a series of articles about graves that had been disturbed around the city. The Batts family cemetery was located west of Ketner Heights Blvd. near its intersection with US 70. The lowered access lane there was the original two-lane course of the "Central Highway" and later two-lane US 70 itself. The small cemetery with grave markers was immediately adjacent to the road and was partially covered by asphalt when a convenience store was built at the intersection in the late 1960s or early 1970s. Several black families had lived along the road who were descendants of Woodbridge settlers from the 1870s. The newspapers are preserved at the Havelock Public Library.

Area burials continue:

Belangia, Cornelia, see Shelton   WF

Bell, Emma West   AAF
She was born Nov. 7, 1921, at Havelock. She died October 30, 2003, in Fayetteville, N.C. She is featured in the chapter of this book entitled *The Right of Eminent Domain.*

Bell, Stellecta A.   WF
She was born on June 22, 1823. She was the wife of A. G. Bell. She died December 27, 1910, at age 87. She is buried at the Oak Grove United Methodist Church.

Benjamin, Booker T., "Book"   AAM
He was born April 7, 1912, at Havelock. He was said to have been raised on "Old Road" (Old Beaufort Road, which is modern Greenfield Heights Blvd.). He had four brothers and six sisters. As an adult, he lived on old family land at 401 Greenfield Heights Blvd. across from Westgate. He worked as the custodian at West Havelock Elementary School, later renamed Arthur Edwards Elementary. His wife was Violar; his son, William; and his daughter, Thelma. He died January 9, 1972, after a brief illness at age 59. He was buried in his yard off Greenfield Heights Blvd. across from the old black one-room schoolhouse. The burial site is now called the *Benjamin Family Cemetery*. His funeral services were by Oscar's Mortuary, New Bern. Before his death, he had objected to the disturbance of the Marshall Cemetery in Greenfield Heights by home construction. He was the son of George W. Benjamin and Lydia Cooper Benjamin. See *Havelock Progress* article and photographs by Eddie Ellis: *"Can Booker T. Rest in Peace?"* November 1976.

Benjamin, Lydia (also spelled Lida and Aida)   AAF

The wife of George W. Benjamin, she was the mother of Booker T. and William Benjamin, and others. She was buried in the "old cemetery" (Marshall). She is referred to in a *Havelock Progress* article, November 1976.

Benjamin, George W.   AAM

He was born April 1, 1864, and died April 9, 1928. He was a student at the AMA's Woodbridge School under teacher Carrie E. Waugh in 1878. He was a farmer on land he owned and also a skilled carpenter for most of his life. He married a woman named Lydia and was the father of Booker T. Benjamin. Jenny Benjamin appears on an 1897 deed with George. His death was due to blood poisoning after a foot infection. Manly Mason, MD, was his attending physician. He was buried in the "old cemetery" (Marshall) off Greenfield Heights Road. He had another son named William. He's mentioned in the *Havelock Progress,* November 1976.

Benjamin, William   AAM

He was born on November 23, 1920. He died at age 18. He worked as a farmhand on the family's land. He was the brother of Booker T. Benjamin and the son of George W. and Lydia Benjamin. He was fatally stabbed in a fight at North Harlowe receiving a wound to his heart. He was buried in the Marshall Cemetery. See *Havelock Progress*, November 1976.

Benjamin, Viola (Violar) Bennett   AAF

She was born February 1, 1910, in Craven County. She was the wife of Booker T. Benjamin and was widowed in 1972. She died December 8, 1997, aged 87. COD: acute myocardial infarction (heart attack). She was buried in Benjamin Family Cemetery.

BENJAMIN FAMILY CEMETERY   other AA burials

William Thomas (Ben) Benjamin 1930-2005 Korean War Veteran
Bessie Benjamin Davis 1910-2012 (age 102)
Jennie B. Davis 1914-1989
Luke Lane Davis 1913-1997
Thomas Leo Benjamin Moore 1953-2006 USAF
William Ray Benjamin Moore 1949-2005 U.S. Army Sgt. Vietnam

NOTE ON BENJAMIN LAND: Ancestor George W. Benjamin and wife Jenny bought a total of 36.25 acres of contiguous land in two transactions in the area of what is now 401 Greenfield Heights Road in 1885 and 1887 with a partner, U.S. Colored Troops veteran Abraham Dennis. The land was purchased from the Marshall family: William H., Henry A., and Frank P. Marshall. George Benjamin acted "as agent" in the 1887 sale. In 1897, George and Jenny Benjamin sold Dennis one of the two parcels measuring 21.25 acres keeping 15 acres for themselves, all according to Craven County records. More information on the Marshalls and Dennis appears in this list.

Area burials continue:

Berry, Anna "Annie" M. Nelson   AAF

She was born in Craven County on October 20, 1876. She was a home-maker, a farmer, and a midwife. Her father, Aaron Nelson, was born c. 1828, was a farmer on what is now Cherry Point. Her mother, Lucy Nelson, was born c. 1850. Annie married Stephen Berry (1879-1930). Their children were Clarence, Samson, James A., and Annie E., according to the 1920 census. She died August 20, 1926, aged 49, and was buried at the Little Witness Church cemetery, CP 1. Her burial was identified after 1985.

Berry, Ernest Lee   AAM child

Died as a baby, October 12, 1936, age 16 months old. He was buried at CP 1, Little Witness.

Berry, Elizabeth   AAF

She died on February 27, 1935, at age 25. She was buried at CP 1, Little Witness.

Berry, Ollie   AAM

He died in 1939 and was buried at CP 1, Little Witness. Ollie Moore Berry is listed as the owner of Tract 534, a 12.7-acre parcel bordering on Shop Branch, a tributary of Hancock Creek. Berry's land was in the Little Witness (Toon Neck) community and near the Old Beaufort to New Bern Road, today called Fontana Blvd. or Highway 101.

Berry, Pearsey   AAM

He was born in 1912 and died on April 14, 1933. The son of Josephine Berry, he was buried at Little Witness, according to Kathryn Moore via Findagrave.

Berry, Steven (Steve)   AAM

He was born c. 1879 in Craven County. He was the son of George and Maggie Berry. He married Annie M. Nelson. He was a farmer, fisherman, and laborer in the "log woods." He is shown as the owner of the 4.6-acre Tract 530, Cherry Point Ownership Map of 1941, on the Slocum Creek side of the base near today's Roosevelt Blvd. For his children, see Berry, Anna above. He died on August 6, 1930. He was 51 years old. COD: Heart disease, according to Manly Mason, MD, of Newport. Tom Haywood of Croatan was the registrar of the death. He was buried at CP 1, Little Witness on August 12, 1930.

The Bordens on Slocum and Hancock Creeks

William Borden was one of the first men of Carteret County. He was a Quaker from Rhode Island who moved to North Carolina in 1732. The first meeting of the Quakers in Carteret County was held at his home on Harlowe Creek in 1733. He acquired a *lot* of land. Bogue Island, where Atlantic

Beach is, was originally called Borden's Bank. He was Carteret County's largest landowner of the 1700s.

William Borden (1689-1749)   WM

Abstract of last will: Son: "William ('my manner plantation' and also 800 acres of land on Harlor's [Harlowe] Creek and Core Creek). Daughters: Alice Stanton, Katherine Borden, Hannah Borden, Sarah Pratt. Nephew: William Borden. Brothers: Thomas Borden, Benjamin Borden. Sister: Amy Chase. Executors: Benjamin Borden, Henry Stanton (son-in-law), Susannah Borden (wife). Witnesses: Samuely Newby, Joseph Newby, Joseph Robinson. Will proven before Gab. Johnston, Governor, at Edenhouse." [Immediately across the Chowan River from Edenton.]

Borden, Benjamin Sr.   WM

Will: Signed with [X] – 11 December 1833 / August Term 1841 – "To grandchild, Nancy Borden, daughter of my son John Borden deceased a tract of land in Carteret County on the Newport River…to Harlows Creek …provided that if she dies without heirs, the land goes to my son Franklin George Cockburn Borden. "Provided further that whereas I have sold a certain Lot of ground on Portsmouth to which said Nancy Borden was entitled and which descended to her from her Grandmother Nancy Borden deceased— Now if the said Nancy Borden …should refuse to release my estate from all claims on account of said land" then the above devise is void. All the remaining estate to son Franklin George Cockburn Borden. If George should die without heir, the property to go to my friends John Coart and Samuel Hyman. Executors: John Coart and Samuel Hyman. Wit: David B. Gibson, Asa Conner, Matthew Williams."

Borden, Benjamin F., Jr.   WM

Will: 26 August 1875 / 25 March 1886 – "Hancocks Creek, Craven County, N.C. In the name of God Amen. I Benjamin F. Borden, Jr. being week of body but of sound and disposing mind and knowing the uncertainty of life do make and declare this my last will and testament. First I lend unto my beloved father during his life all of my property real and personal and after his death I give unto my beloved brother Barclay D. Borden all of my property of any discription to him and his heirs forever. In witness whereof, I hereunto set my hand and seal this 26th day of August 1875. B.F. Borden. Wit: J.B. Duffy, Charley Jones." [Recorded in Book E, pages 404-405]

Borden, Eliza Hope

Will: 9 May 1863 / March 9, 1872 – "I lend to my beloved husband Benjamin F. Borden all of my property both real and personal during his lifetime then I give it to the child or children that I may have by him surviving him at his death. But if there is no child or children, then the property to go to my three last children by my first Husband Benjamin W. Thorp namely William Julia and John. Three heifers given to the three oldest children Sarah,

Carolina, and Margret. Trustee Suthy Pittman to be Executor. Wit: W.H.
Rand, Francis Mace." [A note along with the probate indicates that there
was a marriage agreement between Borden and wife providing that Mrs.
Borden should have sole use of the property during coverture, with a power
to dispose of the same by any written document in presence of two witnesses. The will, evidently, was contested by some of the children of the
first marriage.]

Borden, Barclay D.   WM
He was born in Craven County, January 1849. (Birth/age records vary significantly). He was the son of Benjamin F. "Frank" Borden and Tryphena
Wynne Borden. His siblings were Benjamin F., Jr., born c. 1844, and Joseph, b. circa 1846. His step-mother Eliza Hope Thorpe Borden from August 20, 1857. Farmer at the village of Cherry Point. He died on January 18,
1923. COD: accidental drowning in Neuse River. Grave marker says age 76
years; death certificate says 74 years old. He was buried in the old Cherry
Point Cemetery, January 20, 1923, "Hancock Creek Landing." He was a
widower at the time of death. His death was reported by George A. Russell.
Undertaker D. G. Small, New Bern. J. S. Hartsfield, coroner. Photo of Borden in *HIHCP*

Borden, Benjamin Franklin, Sr. "Frank"   WM
He was the father of Barclay D. Borden. He was a farmer at Cherry Point
and owned 1,000 acres of land on the east side of Hancock Creek. He was
born c. 1819. He married Tryphena Wynne, April 11, 1843 (died before
1857). Their children were: Benjamin Franklin, Jr., c 1844, (listed as
"farmer" at age 16); Joseph, c. 1846; and Barclay D., c. 1849. He married
Eliza Hope Thorpe, August 20, 1857. Their children were, sons, W. B.; John
B.; A. J.; and one daughter, Hope Borden. Frank and Eliza took in the children of Benjamin William Thorpe after his death. They also had Mary E.
Whitehead, 20, seamstress, in their household in 1860. On October 16,
1895, "Miss Hope Borden and Mr. S. W Reams [*or Reems*] were united in
the holy bonds of matrimony ... at the residence of the bride's father, Mr.
B. F. Borden," according to the newspaper. The wedding took place in the
evening with numerous friends of the bride and groom assembled to witness
the ceremony." Justice of the Peace J. D. Pittman officiated, "after which,
all partook of a splendid supper." The Reams were next-door neighbors to
the Borden, Arms, and Fisher families at Hancock Creek. Sylvester W.
Reems owned a sawmill there. *The Daily Journal* of New Bern, Thursday,
June 24, 1897, reported: "A large and greatly respected gentleman, Mr. B.
F. Borden, died Wednesday afternoon at his home on Handcock's Creek."
He had been in his 78th year of life. He died, June 23, 1897. His burial
location is not known. No marked grave or other record has been located.

Borden, Eliza Hope Thorpe   WF

She was the second wife of Benjamin F. Borden, Sr. They married on August 20, 1857. She died February 17, 1910, at home in Beaufort, N.C., age 71. Her funeral was held at Baptist Church, Beaufort. Her place of burial is unknown. The children of Frank and Eliza Borden were born at Cherry Point, and surviving at the time of her 1910 death: Dr. W. B. Borden, U.S. Army surgeon, Fort Bayard, N.M.; Dr. John B. Borden, U.S. inspector of steam vessels, Charleston, S.C.; Dr. A. J. Borden, druggist, Norfolk, Va.; and Mrs. [ ] Burkhead, Norfolk, Va.

Borden, Tryphena Wynne   WF

She was the first wife of Benjamin F. Borden, Sr. and mother of Benjamin F., Jr.; Joseph; and Barclay D. Borden. She died before 1857. Her burial is likely to be in Wynne, Hancock Creek, or "Old Cherry Point" cemeteries.

NOTE ON BORDEN LAND: Bangert, Sebastian -- February 1886 / 28 June 1886 -- of New Bern ... "to his Son Albert H. Bangert, the entire tract of land known as the Borden Land in Craven County on Hancocks Creek which I bought at a foreclosure sale from B.F. Borden and others."

Area burials continue:

Bragg, Golda P.   WF

Nicknamed "Goldie," she was born February 5, 1900, and died at her Havelock home early morning, September 9, 1906, at age six. She was the daughter of J. M. And Cora A. Bragg. She was buried the evening of her death at FUMC.

Brandt, Antje Visser Buys   WF

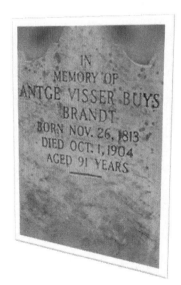

She was born in Holland on November 26, 1813. A Dutch immigrant of 1873, she was the mother of William Buys. In America, she called herself "Anna Brand." Lived on Slocum Creek. She died October 1, 1904, and was buried at CP 9, tract 199. "Death of Mrs. Anna Brand: Mrs. Anna Brand died Saturday, October 1 at the home of her son Mr. William Buys at Slocum Creek, aged 91 years. Mrs. Brand was a native of Holland but had been a resident of this country for many years. She lived in Chicago for several years." *New Bern Weekly Journal* October 7, 1904.

Briggs, Joseph E.   WM

He was born June 11, 1849, and died March 21, 1905. He was buried at the Oak Grove Methodist Church cemetery.

Brinkley, J. B.   Lost Grave   WM
The Wilmington Dispatch (Wilmington, N. C.) December 24, 1916: "The
body of Mr. J. B. Brinkley, of Havelock, who died suddenly at Jacksonville, on the
previous day, passed through New Bern last night in route to the former place,
where it will be interred. Mr. Brinkley went to Jacksonville early in the week, intending to make his home there, but was taken ill and death followed a few hours
later. The funeral service was conducted from Croatan church this morning at 11
o'clock by Rev. W. B. Everett, of this city, and the interment made in the family
burying ground near that place."
No grave or Brinkley "family burying ground" has yet been identified in the
region around Havelock and Croatan.

Bryan, Betty M.   WF
Her former Havelock residence was at 152 Bryan Blvd. She was born July
20, 1900. She was the wife of Frederick P. Bryan. She died March 18, 1986,
and was buried at FUMC.

Bryan, Edgar Ford   WM
He was born on June 3, 1891. He was listed as a farmer in the 1920 census.
He died December 25, 1954, at 63 years of age. Services by Pollock funeral
home. He was buried at FUMC on December 28, 1954. He was the son of
Edgar W. Bryan and Minnie Merritt. He married Serena "Rena" Conner.
Rena was listed as a railroad agent at Havelock in the 1920 census. The 1930
census showed their children as Minnie Marjorie, Robert Fort, Merrell
Gibbs, and Edgar F. Jr. He was a World War I veteran and worked as a
heavy equipment operator. Later in life, he lived at Route 4 Box 652, New
Bern in a mobile home

Bryan, Edgar William   WM
He was born in 1851, the son of Wright William Bryan of Onslow County.
The mother's name is undiscovered. He was the husband of Minnie Merritt
Bryan. He was a farmer. His children were Edgar F.; Frederick P.; and Lula
B. Bryan. He's on the voter registry of Township 6 on October 14, 1906, at
age 48. He died October 16, 1925, at age 73-74. His death certificate lists
his birthdate as Dec. 1855, and date of death as Nov. 12, 1925, age 70. He
was buried at FUMC on November 15, 1925. The informant of his death
was E. F. Bryan. COD: heart failure due to high blood pressure, according
to S. M. Blalock, MD, of Havelock, attending physician. Services by Newport Coffin Company, Newport North Carolina.

Bryan, Frederick P.   WM
He was born October 11, 1889, in New Bern and died at Havelock on April
3, 1955, at 9:05 PM at age 65. COD: "heart, immediate," according to C. O.
Connor, MD, Havelock, attending physician. He was buried at FUMC Cem-
etery, April 5, 1955. He was retired. He was the husband of Betty M. Bryan.
His former residence was at 152 Bryan Blvd., Havelock. He was the son of

Edgar Bryan and Minnie Merritt, a World War I veteran and the father of Ernest Bryan, Sr. He was the grandfather of Russell, Bonita, Rusty, Joelle Bryan.

Bryan, Lula, see Jackson   WF

Bryan, Merrell G.   WM
He was born February 27, 1926, and died May 6, 1948. He's buried at the FUMC cemetery. No death certificate has been found at the Craven County offices. The COD was thought to be a cerebral hemorrhage. He had worked at Cherry Point.

Bryan, Meriel (Merrill) (Merrell)   WM
He was born April 13, 1870, in Onslow County, North Carolina. He died in Raleigh, December 18, 1915, at the State Hospital while being treated for a long-term illness. He was 45 years of age. He was buried at FUMC. He was never married. He was the son of Wright William Bryan (1825-1915) and Susan Hunter (Onslow County?). He had two brothers, Edgar William Bryan, and Capt. A.L. Bryan.

Merrill Bryan

Bryan, Minnie R. Merritt   WF
She was born on August 9, 1861. She died June 3, 1925, and was buried at FUMC on June 4, 1925. She was 65. She was a housewife and married to Edgar W. Bryan. His children included Edgar Ford Bryan, Frederick P. Bryan, Lula B. Bryan. She was the daughter of Frank Merritt and Mrs. Murphy of Jones County. COD: flu and pneumonia, nephritis, and heart trouble. She was said to have been sick for about a month before death.

Bryan, Serena "Rena" Connor   WF
She was married to Edgar Ford Bryan in 1895. She was a railroad agent at Havelock, according to the 1920 census.

Bryan, Serena Hill, see Hill   WF

Bryant, Mindora McCray (McCrae)   AAF
She was born April 21, 1898, in Craven County, the daughter of Turner McCray (1841-1928). She married Alonzo Bryant who was born c. 1893 and worked as a laborer on the highway. They owned their home, free and clear, and lived near the New Bern Road, which is another name for Beaufort Road - Highway 101. Their children were Estella, born 1918; and Luke, born about 1918. She died on June 20, 1925, at age 27. (ARC in error). Her cause of death was tuberculosis. She was buried at CP 1, Little Witness.

Bryant, Reta   AAF
She died on December 29, 1925. She was four years old. She was buried at CP 1, Little Witness.

Buck, Julia F., see Piner   WF
Buys, Anna   WF
She was born January 17, 1876, and lived on Slocum Creek. She died November 24, 1917, and was buried at CP 9, tract 199. She was the daughter of William and Nellie Buys.

Buys, Antje Visser, see Brandt   WF
Buys, Marie   WF
She was born c. 1880. Maiden name unknown, she married one of the Buys men. According to an article in the New Bern Weekly Journal of September 29, 1905, "Mrs. Marie Buys of Havelock has arrived to assume her duties as a teacher in the Graded School" (in New Bern). She was a graduate of the North Carolina State Normal College and is mentioned in the story *The School at Havelock 1902* in Part I: *A Country Harmony.*

Buys, Nellie   WF
She was born April 17, 1847, lived on Slocum Creek, and died September 23, 1881. She was the first wife of William Buys, and mother of Anna, John, and Nellie Buys. She was buried at CP 9, tract 199.

Buys, William   WM
He was a Dutch colonist at Havelock. He was born July 28, 1847, in Holland and lived on Slocum Creek. He was the husband of Nellie Buys. The 1880 census lists William, 32, a farmer who came to the US in 1873; Nellie, his wife, 33, "keeps house," also born in Holland; Margaret, 7, born in Holland; Anna "Annie," 5, born Illinois; John 3, b. Illinois; and Nellie, 11 months, born in Illinois. In the 1900 census, William, 52; Mary, second wife, age 39, was born in Denmark, who came to US 1883 and married William the same year. In the home are a son, John, 23, listed as a farmer; daughters, Nellie, 20, a school teacher; Nancy, 16, a student born in Illinois; and son, William H., 14, born Illinois. Also, in the household was his mother, Anna Brandt (Brand), 86, from Holland, who arrived in the US in 1900. He was a farmer with property on the east side of Slocum Creek about one mile below its mouth. He was on the voter registry for Township 6 on October 29, 1904. He advertised his land for sale in newspapers across the state in 1916. The asking price was $50 per acre. This appeared in the Winston-Salem Journal and other newspapers: "FOR SALE – I WANT TO SELL within 60 days my beautiful situated home with 500 acres of land on Slocumb's creek. Address William Buys, Havelock, N.C." He didn't find a buyer for his property called "Oak Villa." He died September 27, 1918, and was buried at CP 9. His headstone's epitaph reads "Kind, upright, honest and true."

The Buys family is mentioned in Part I, *A Country Harmony.*
Area burials continue:
Canaday, Cannedy, Canada. See Kennedy
Cannon, Addie G., see Hill

Cannon, Mary Elizabeth Godwin WF
She was born May 16, 1859, and died July 4, 1923, at 65 years of age. She was buried at FUMC in Havelock. She was the widow of C. C. Cannon. Her COD is unknown. There was no undertaker. She was born in Jones County, the daughter of William Mundine and Jane Godwin. The informant of death was E. J. Godwin.

The Chesnutt Family at the Fork of Slocum Creek

Chesnutt is a name found with various spellings for the same individuals in Craven County marriage, deed, census, and other records. The most common form for this Havelock group is Chesnutt or Chesnut, but Chestnut is also found occasionally. For consistency here, we'll stick with the first spelling.

Virginia Zuckerman (1924-2020) was a descendant of Harvey Chesnutt. She was also the wife of Winchester, Virginia Mayor Charles M. Zuckerman. In the late 1980s, Mrs. Zuckerman provided genealogical information gleaned from the family's Bible and other sources for Havelock settlers Owen and Keziah Chesnutt, parents of Andrew Jackson Chesnutt. Other data has been added to hers through local research and fieldwork.

Owen Chesnutt's plantation was established before 1830 at the fork of the east and southwest prongs of Slocum Creek. [*For the location, see Letter "F" on the Cemeteries and Farms Map at the beginning of the book.*] We have neither a birth date for Owen nor a purchase date for the land of Slocum Creek. It appears, however, that Owen Chesnutt may have had forebears there. The names John and Jonathan Chestnut appear on an 1815 county tax roll that shows John Chesnutt owning 120 acres in the appropriate area. [*See the Captain John S. Smith district list herein*]. An 1854 land advertisement by William G. Bryan in *The Atlantic*, a New Bern newspaper, indicates that the land of Chesnutt was formerly Spaight property. It seems likely that a previous generation of Chesnutts purchased the land from Richard Dobbs Spaight who died in 1802 when Owen was a child.

In any event, the Chesnutt plantation was at today's location of Graham A. Barden Elementary School and the Slocum housing area. It was about 500 acres in size; fairly standard for plantations of the period. Most people grew food for subsistence, kept chickens, milk cows, and so forth, but one old Civil War-era map, the Branch map, shows that Chesnutt was also a turpentine farmer. That would be quite typical, too, as tapping the sap of the loblolly and longleaf pine and processing it into turpentine, tar, and other products in a class called "naval stores" was a way to make ready money, as has been previously stated several times.

[As noted many times before, in the mid-1800s, an unbelievable quantity of naval stores and timber were shipped out of the Slocum Creek area. The shipping news for a single week in May 1867, as reported by the *New Bern Journal of Commerce* listed these three arrivals of cargo: Schooner *Emma Elizabeth* under Capt. Black from Slocum's Creek; schooner *Marietta*, under the command of Capt, Godett, from Handcock's Creek; and the schooner *Dolphin*, with a man named Hill as the master.]

Here are the details on the Chesnutt family at the fork of Slocum Creek. **Owen Chesnutt** (WM) and **Keziah Stanly** (WF) were married on February 17, 1827 (Family Bible). Owen died September 8, 1860, and was "buried near Havelock, N.C." Keziah Stanly Chesnutt died Oct. 26, 1863, "buried near Havelock, N.C."

The family Bible notes a Havelock burial, but their exact grave locations are unknown. Standard practice would have been burial on their land.

The children of Owen and Keziah Chesnutt: **Jeasteen (Chestene)** born February 17, 1828 (Her grave marker says Feb. 26, 1828). She married Elijah M. Dudley of Slocum Creek, January 25, 1848, and died May 4, 1860, age 32. She was buried at the Old Sabiston Cemetery in Morehead City; a son, Jonathan was born September 10, 1829. Death and burial information is unknown; a son, **Readmon S.** was born October 1, 1832. He died September 21, 1871, and was buried at Croatan, N.C.; a son, **Andrew Jackson** was born April 1, 1835 (see additional information below); a son, **Danneal (Daniel) H**. was born August 9, 1837. He died November 5, 1843, at age six; Twins: **Ann Jain**, born October 3, 1839. Death and burial unknown; **Marianne (Mary Ann)** was born October 3, 1839. She died, May 1, 1860, age 20; **Kezia**, born October 14, 1842, Death and burial information unknown. Sisters Marianne and Jeasteen died only three days apart suggesting a common illness.

Chesnutt, Andrew Jackson (aka "A.J." and Jackson)   WM
He was born April 1, 1835, at Slocum Creek on the South Side of Neuse River. He was the son of Owen Chesnutt (born c. 1804) and Kezziah (Kezia) Stanly Chesnutt (born c. 1806), who were married January 26, 1827, according to Craven County records. At 15, in the census of 1850, A.J. is listed as a "farmer" along with his father. At 25, in the 1860 census, he's listed as a "merchant" living in his father's house at Havelock. He operated a small store near the intersection of the A&NC railroad with old Beaufort Road. In 1861, he also became the postmaster of the short-lived "Spaightsville" post office in his store at Havelock near the railroad. His postal venture was interrupted and ended by the Union army's invasion in 1862. In 1870 at age 35, he's listed as a farmer living alone with a 16-year-old white "housekeeper," Sarah. He was a member of the county Democratic Party Executive Committee. In 1880, at age 45, he's at his Havelock farm with his wife,

Laura, age 23. They had two children, Annie, age seven, and Harvey, age one.

Andrew Jackson Chesnutt and Laura Virginia Williams were married on June 16, 1870. The wedding ceremony was at "Mallison's," a plantation at Pine Grove. Pine Grove is a name that still appears on many official maps identifying an area just west of Havelock that at one time had both a rail stop and an election polling station. It is in the general area of today's Hickman Hill and Tucker Creek subdivision. The 1,400-acre Mallison Plantation stretched along three miles of Slocum Creek frontage with a mile-long tree-lined entry road (today's Slocum Road) off the then-existing County Road, also known as the New Bern to Beaufort Road (Old Beaufort Road), today the course of US 70. The bride, Laura Virginia Williams, who was born circa 1855, was 15 or 16 (or younger, according to the census) at the time of her marriage to 35-year-old A. J. Chesnutt. Laura was the daughter of Benjamin E. Williams, Jr. and Mary Elizabeth "Bettie" Hunter Williams. Read more of the Williams family under the listing for their names herein.

Rev. A. J. Chestnutt is listed as Township 6 Justice of the Peace in county marriage records of 1895.

The children of Andrew Jackson Chesnutt and Laura Virginia Williams Chesnutt are from the family Bible. The birthplace of all of these children was Havelock, Craven County, North Carolina. They include **Redman S.**, born April 20, 1871, and died September 21, 1871, at age six months; **Annie Laura**, born February 26, 1873. She later married James Marion Gorrell at the Methodist Church in Havelock on December 3, 1891. The Gorrells were a prosperous Havelock farm family. (Pronounced gor-ELL); **James**, who died 1937; and Annie Laura who died in 1939; both buried in Lynchburg, Va.; **Harvey Jackson**, born August 22, 1879, who died June 28, 1882, age two years and ten months, and was buried at Croatan, N.C.; **Harvey Jackson (2)** born August 8, 1884, and died 1964. He was buried in Rock Creek Cemetery, Washington, D.C.; **James Millard**, born March 20, 1892. Died 1951; buried in Lynchburg, Va.

Andrew Jackson Chesnutt died Feb. 20, 1896, at age 60, He was buried with his wife's family in the William-White Cemetery, Catfish Lake Road, Croatan. Laura Virginia Williams Chesnutt, wife of A. J. Chesnutt, died December 15, 1911. She was about 56 years old. She is buried in Catlett, Va. A number of the children had migrated to Virginia by then.

Area burials continue:

Croom, Jesse James   WM
He was the husband of Rebecca J. Croom. He was born December 25, 1829, and was still living in 1900. A Croom ancestry site says he died May 11, 1910, but his place of death and burial information unknown.

Croom, Rebecca Jane   WF

She was born April 2, 1832 (a census document says April 1830). She died December 17, 1910, and was buried in FUMC. Her headstone says "Mother." She was the wife of J. J. Croom (census has him as Jesie J. and Jessee J. Croom)

Interesting matter. The Croom name is known in local records since colonial times, but these Crooms were a farm family from Bladen County around Elizabethtown. In 1870, in addition to Mr. and Mrs. Croom and their seven children, they had living in their household eight others; men, women, boys, and girls from age 8 to age 68; that the census identified as "paupers." All of the Croom children had titles, such as "laborer" or "assistant."

Mrs. Croom's name was spelled "Rebecky" in that document.

In 1900, they were still in French Creek Township of Bladen County, but now just the two of them with a grandson, James, age 17. J.J. Croom, 71, was listed as a farmer with the grandson as a farm laborer. Rebecca was 70. She'd had 11 babies and nine were still living.

How Rebecca got to Havelock, why she's buried alone at FUMC, and what became of the rest of them we didn't know until we found that a man named H. P. Croom, age 33, listing J.J. Croom as an immediate ancestor, registered to vote in Twp. 6 on October 29, 1904. In the 1910 census, he wasn't in Craven County anymore. But that year's census for French Creek in Bladen County, N.C., lists a 39-year-old farmer named Henry P. Croom living with his wife, Kittie, three young sons … and an 81-year-old father names Jessie J. Croom.

Also, Caroline E. Croom, age 66, a "pensioner" and a native of Ohio is listed in the 1900 census as living on Cherry Point.

No Crooms were listed in the Havelock phone book 1976. Possibly unrelated, a Miss Croom was a teacher at a Clubfoot Creek school for black children when it burned down in 1865.

Cully, (Culley) Adam Burt   AAM
He was born at Havelock in 1900. He died in 1969 and was buried at a Hickman Hill cemetery. He was the son of William "Octavius" and Annie Smith Cully. His father was a farmer and his mother was a seamstress. He had four sisters: Leona (Blealock), Eliza, Izora (George), and Beulah (Harrison). One death record has his name as *Adam Birt Culley*. His headstone reads *Adam Burt Culley*. He lived in a dwelling on 17 acres near the A&EC railroad tracks at the end of Manila Street in Havelock on what had been "Missionary Land" of the American Missionary Association's failed Woodbridge community. His grandfather was also named Adam. His grandmother, Eliza Ann Cully, bought the family's land for $68 from the American Missionary Association on March 18, 1887. Adam traveled around Havelock on a mule cart. For additional information about him, see the chapter *"Goin' to Atlanta"*

Cully, (Culley) George W.   AAM
He was born December 27, 1869, and was a farmer in Havelock. His wife, Alvani was born in 1872. They had a son named William A. who was born in 1895. George Cully died December 6, 1919, and was buried at CP 1, Little Witness. He was the son of Wm. H. and Nancy E. Cully, who lived next door and kept a servant in residence.

Davis, Emma Louise Hill   AAF
She was born October 28, 1932 at the African American settlement of Nelson Town, founded by former slaves after the Civil War on what is now MCAS Cherry Point. The daughter of James Emanuel Hill and Carlilie Fenner Hill, she married Herbert Joseph Davis in 1957. They had three children. Herein, she is featured in the chapter *The Right of Eminent Domain*. Due to an obituary of an individual of the same name, she was erroneously listed as deceased in the early printings of this book.

Dennis, Abraham (a.k.a Ezekiel Nottingham)   U.S.C.T.   AAM
A free man before the Civil War, he enlisted in the United States Colored Troops under the assumed name of Ezekiel Nottingham. He was born in Norfolk, Va. c. 1844. He was a farmer in Virginia before the war. He joined for a three-year term in the Union army, at the original organization of Company G of the 36th Regiment of U.S. Colored Infantry, at Yorktown Va. on Oct 18, 1863. He was nineteen years old and five feet eleven inches tall. He has 24 pages of records in Fold3 and was present at every muster but one. A record of the company's service shows: "Duty at Norfolk and Portsmouth, Va., until April 1864. At Point Lookout, Md., District of St. Mary's, guarding prisoners until July 1864. Expedition from Point Lookout to Westmoreland County April 12–14. Expedition from Point Lookout to the Rappahannock River May 11–14, and to Pope's Creek June 11–21. Moved from Point Lookout to Bermuda Hundred, Va., July 1–3. Siege operations against Petersburg and Richmond, Va., July 3, 1864, to April 2, 1865. Battle of Chaffin's Farm, New Market Heights, September 29–30. Battle of Fair Oaks October 27–28. Dutch Gap November 17. Indiantown, Sandy Creek, N.C., December 18 (detachment). Duty north of the James River before Richmond until March 27, 1865. Appomattox Campaign March 27-April 9. Occupation of Richmond April 3. Duty in the Department of Virginia until May. During the war, the regiment lost a total of 224 men during service; 8 officers and 79 enlisted men were killed or mortally wounded, 5 officers and 132 enlisted men died of disease. Moved to Texas from May 24-June 6. Duty along the Rio Grande, Texas, and at various points in Texas until October 1866." At the end of the Civil War, the "colored troops" were sent out west to fight the Indians. Nottingham mustered out as a corporal at Brazos, Santiago County, Texas at the end of his term on October 18, 1866. He bought farmland and made his home on what was the New Bern to Beaufort Road

(and is now Greenfield Heights Road) in 1885 with neighbor George Benjamin. He had married Rebecca Canada, 21, a seamstress of Havelock on March 6, 1885. Baptist minister Rev. W.H. Cully performed the marriage service, which was witnessed by George Benjamin. Dennis, Benjamin, and four other African American men incorporated a mutual insurance company in 1912. Dennis applied for a Civil War Pension at New Bern with his military service name changed to Abraham Dennis with service in Company G. 2nd Regiment, U.S. Colored Infantry on April 6, 1889, and again on April 27, 1908. He died at Havelock on October 16, 1919. His widow, Rebecca Dennis, filed for a widow's pension at New Bern on November 5, 1919. He was the son of Abraham Dennis and Lener Hammond. His Craven County death certificate has his name as "Abram Dennis." His burial location is unknown. Rebecca Dennis *may* have been the daughter of Squires Cannady and Matilda Aldridge.

Dennis, Leon WM
He was born December 10, 1897 (or 1898). His parents, William Nash and Laura Hancock Dennis. For siblings, see William Nash Dennis's entry below. He died June 16, 1918, at New Bern General Hospital. COD: appendectomy on June 11, followed by the fatal onset of pylephlebitis, a type of blood poisoning often fatal in the pre-antibiotic period. He died at 1 P.M. Dr. Richard Duffy of New Bern was the attending physician. He was buried June 17, 1918, next to his father in second burial at Dennis-Wynne Cemetery.

> **1918:**
> **W.N. and Leon Dennis, father and son, deaths exactly six months apart.**

Dennis, William Nash WM
He was born March 9, 1868, the son of Isaac (Jasia) Dennis and Caroline Whitehurst Dennis. He was nicknamed "Dennie" as a child. The family lived in an area just west of Havelock called Pine Grove. He was a merchant, Township 6 by 1900. He worked as a locomotive engineer on the Atlantic and North Carolina Railroad by 1910 and until his death. His wife was Laura Hancock of Havelock. She was born c. 1876. Their children were: a son Luther, born 1895; a son Leon, born 1897 (died June 16, 1918, six months to the day before father); daughter Carrie, born 1899 (thought to have died as an infant); daughter Jessie Louise, born May 5, 1901, later married Caleb J. Wynne; son Jack, born c. 1906. He died 5 A.M., January 16, 1918, age 49. COD: "tuberculosis of the lungs" complicated by diabetes after three months of illness. The informant of death was Thomas E. Haywood of Croatan. Registrar of death was Earnest A. Armstrong of Havelock. He was buried June 17, 1918, the first interment at Dennis-Wynne Cemetery.

Deport (De Porte, Deporte), John WM

Moved to Havelock from Michigan as one of the Dutch settlers. He was a farmer and is on the 1891 tax list, which showed that he owned 300 acres of land at Lake Ellis. He married Rachel Taylor on January 13, 1885. A.J. Chesnutt, justice of the peace, performed the ceremony, and C.H. Hunter, G.W. Rigdon, and Edward D. Russell were the witnesses. He was the grandfather of Golda Bragg. Burial details are unknown.

Deport, Rachel Taylor WF

She was born July 25, 1852, and died November 7, 1927, at age 75. Engraved on the headstone is "Gone but not forgotten, J. W. R." She was the wife of John Deport (or DePort) and grandmother of Golda Bragg. She was buried at FUMC.

Dewey, Annie AAF

She died August 20, 1926, at age 40 making her presumed birth year c. 1886. She was buried at CP 1, Little Witness.

Dickinson, David Owen WM

See the chapter, *Rebel Spies of Southern Craven County.*

Dove, Virginia AAF

She was born c. 1869. Her husband was William E. Dove, a farmer. They lived near Beaufort Road (now Highway 101). Her children were John, who at 25 was working "in the timber woods"; and Charlotte, who was 14 years younger than John. Virginia died June 7, 1932, at age 64. She was buried at CP 1, Little Witness.

Dove, William E. AAM

He was born c. 1865. He farmed and lived near Beaufort Road, (Highway 101). He was married to Virginia Dove. For the names of his children, see Virginia Dove above. He died at age 63. Burial at Little Witness, CP 1.

Dudley, Christopher WM

He was born on July 28, 1821. He was a farmer and owned a 700-acre plantation on the river between Slocum and Hancock Creek. He was one of the signers of the School House Petition of 1849. He married Susan J. Slade on April 24, 1845. The couple lost two children at Cherry Point: Susan C., at age 5 in 1853; and Christopher, age 3 in 1857, before Christopher Dudley died at age 37 on November 18, 1858. Susan then left the Neuse River plantation and moved into her father's and mother's home in New Bern. She was living with her parents, Zach and Narcissa Slade, when the Civil War reached New Bern in 1862. Before the war was over, she lost four more children, probably to yellow fever. Susan N. died in 1863 at age five; Hugh, 14, in 1864; Sarah, 13, in 1865; and Mary Ann, 19, also in 1865. All members of the family are buried at Cedar Grove Cemetery in New Bern.

Dudley, Susan J. Slade WF

She was born March 8, 1826, in Craven County. Lived at Slocum Creek. She married Christopher Dudley in 1845. They had six children. She died

March 5, 1893, at age 66. She's buried at Cedar Grove in New Bern. See more under Christopher Dudley above.

Fenner, Joe Early   AAM

He was born September 16, 1890, the son of Charlie H. Fenner, who was born 1873, and Rock H. Fenner, who was born May 1870. His sister, Carlilie, was born in December 1888. He was a farmer at Cherry Point and Blades, N.C. He married Lola (Lela) (Lalee) Ora Nelson. Their children were Rosa Lee Fenner, and Carlilie Fenner, who was born August 17, 1918. He was a patient at State Hospital in Goldsboro in 1930. He died November 28, 1930, at age 39. His cause of death was listed as pellagra, a severe disease of the skin. He was buried at CP 1, the Little Witness Cemetery. His name and date were noted in 1941 from small metal-and-paper undertaker's markers. No such marker was present in 1985.

Searching for the Lost Graves of the Fisher Family

FISHER-LATHAM CEMETERY: Before the War Between the States, the sprawling plantation, stately home, and daily existence of Michael Nelms Fisher and his wife, Elizabeth Ann Pelletier Fisher, were like something from the movies. Think "Tara" from *Gone with the Wind* and you won't be too far off the mark. A multitude of slaves worked the fields and cared for livestock while house servants did the laundry, cleaning, and cooking. Maids, valets, and coachmen were always at hand. An illustrative family tale is of one of the Fisher children requiring a slave boy to lay boards in front of him as he moved about one day so that his new shoes wouldn't have to touch the ground.

Michael Fisher was the scion of a multi-generational family of eastern North Carolina wealth, achievement, and prominence. The Fishers owned thousands of acres along the south shore of the Neuse River. The family bought, sold, traded, and inherited tracts – 1,600 acres, 575 acres, 225 acres -- among the creeks of Clubfoot, Hancock, Slocum, and Otter, and lands around Lake Ellis southwest of Havelock. And they had relatives, neighbors, and business connections in all those places.

As further examples of their dealings, in April 1801, Fisher's father paid Philip Turner for a deed "to 450 acres on the south side of the Neuse River between Hancock's Creek and Slocum Creek," within the boundary of today's local military base. The size of the plantation land tracts was often staggering. Michael Nelms Fisher later sold 850 acres to Elijah Dudley and a whopping 3,425 acres to Benjamin William Thorpe. B. W. Thorpe was one of the largest landowners at Cherry Point and a key player in this part of the story.

Fisher's manor-home commanded his main farm of some 1,200 acres spreading along and away from the river shore, across the county road and railroad line, deep into the forest just northwest of Havelock.

But then, suddenly, their idyllic world was thunderstruck.

On March 13-14, 1862, after most of the Fisher clan had taken a precarious refuge in New Bern, Union naval forces ascending the Neuse River put enough cannonballs through the family's white bluff-top mansion to render it uninhabitable. The Fishers would forever hold that the Yankee vandals were engaging in unprovoked and malicious target practice. The Union fleet would later claim they were receiving fire from Southern mobile artillery at Fisher's Landing, which may indeed have been the case in the chaotic movements preceding the battle for New Bern.

The end of the war would find the Fishers, Craven County, and the South as a whole economically devastated. Elizabeth Fisher was dead from yellow fever. Michael was broken. "Tara" would never return. But just a trace of the Antebellum splendor is preserved in the old cemeteries still being cared for on East Fisher Road

Some names from newer Fisher (Latham) Cemetery   WMs & WFs

Hughes, J. J. & M. L.

Latham, L. N. & E. B.

Horton
Fisher
Dudley
Simmons
Boyd
Wood
Watson
Smith
Pelletier

Also marked and inscribed at the Fisher cemetery
- Infant son of E.E & Grace Fisher August 25, 1933.
- In memory of **Alvina F. Latham**, daughter of Brian H. and Margaret Smith Latham, first wife of John S. Fisher and mother of Joseph P. Fisher. Born July 10, 1847. Died 1878. Buried at the old Fisher cemetery.
- **Joseph Pelletier Fisher** February 4, 1874, to December 6, 1942.
- **John Slade Fisher**, son of Michael N. Fisher from January 26, 1844, to November 16, 1917, Sgt., Company G, Second Regiment North Carolina Junior Reserves CSA.

- **Emma Jane Watson**, daughter of John H. and Frances Morton Watson, January 26, 1858, to August 9, 1940. Second wife of John S. Fisher.
- In memory of his third wife, **Elizabeth Fisher,** and, born April 23, 1821, died September 12, 1863. [*Elizabeth died during a disastrous yellow fever epidemic in Union-occupied New Bern.*] Buried in New Bern. Daughter of Peter and Tamar Weeks Pelletier.
- Big monument with three columns. On the reverse, in memory of **Michael Nelms Fisher**, born November 8, 1809, died December 21, 1868, buried at an old cemetery near the river washed away by storm erosion. Son of Michael and Frances Dudley Fisher.
- And others known and unknown.
- *Fisher information recorded by the author, February 25, 1984.*

We've spoken previously of missing graves.

Michael Nelms Fisher died on December 21, 1868, just three years after the war's end. He was 59. With no coffin within their means, Fisher's sons, Michael, Jr., and John – who had faced extreme adventures and adversities of their own during the North-South conflict — fashioned a casket from some spare pine lumber. They buried their father in the family graveyard with a large but uninscribed stone as his monument.

Clues to the Missing Fishers & Thorpes (Hancock Village)

Hancock Creek today forms the eastern boundary of the Marine's Cherry Point air station. About halfway down the creek, during the second half of the 1800s, was the village of Hancock's Creek. In 1874, Michael Nelms Fisher, Jr. married Margaret Thorpe, daughter of the long-time Cherry Point family of Benjamin William Thorpe (c. 1816-1856). Margaret had inherited a 200-acre farm adjacent to her family home. After the marriage, according to the family's history, *One Dozen Eastern North Carolina Families*, by P.W. Fisher, Michael Fisher, Jr. traded Margaret's brother, John Thorpe, land that Fisher owned elsewhere for an additional 200 acres next to that of his new wife. Thus, the Fishers came to own a 400-acre farm on Hancock Creek. In addition to farming the land, Michael operated a small general store and served as postmaster for the village.

Incredibly, five of the children died of a recurrent disease, known locally as "the dreaded fever," and were buried in the family cemetery at Hancock Creek. Their farm and home were on land that is now part of MCAS Cherry Point next to the aforementioned deadly savannah swamp.

Fisher children (WM/F) buried in lost graves at Hancock Creek, Cherry Point; probably (CP 7):

Lula Fisher

She was born on February 24, 1875. The daughter of Michael N. Fisher, Jr. and Margaret Thorpe Fisher. She died on October 16, 1879, at age 4. She was buried in the Fisher family cemetery at the village of Hancock Creek.

Roland Nelms Fisher

He was born on July 7, 1877. He was the son of Michael N. Fisher, Jr. and Margaret Thorpe Fisher. He died April 4, 1880, at age 2. He was buried in the Fisher family cemetery.

Alban Fisher

He was born in 1879, the son of Michael N. Fisher, Jr. and Margaret Thorpe Fisher. The grave marker says "Died a child." He was buried in the Fisher family cemetery.

Julia Olive Fisher

She was born on March 14, 1883. Also, the daughter of M. N. Fisher, Jr. and Margaret Thorpe Fisher, who died c. 1895, at age c. 12. She was buried in the Fisher family cemetery.

Margaret "Maggie" Thorpe Fisher (the daughter)

She was born March 14, 1887, the daughter of M. N. Fisher, Jr. and Margaret Thorpe Fisher. She became a teacher at the district school, Hancock Creek, in 1907. She died of "the dreaded fever" in 1908, age c. 21, and was buried in the Fisher family cemetery.

In 1898, Margaret Thorpe Fisher, the mother, died at age 48. Michael Fisher, Jr. would live on at his Hancock Creek Village farm until 1902, so where else would he have buried his wife but in the family cemetery?

A clue to the location of these graves is that Cherry Point Cemetery # 7 (CP 7) is situated where the village of Hancock Creek was. And people named Thorpe and Armes had the only surviving gravestones. The young teacher, Maggie Thorpe Fisher (1887-1908), taught at the Hancock Creek school of her aunt, Julia Thorpe Armes (q.v.), her mother's sister, who was born and raised at Hancock Creek. She was the widow of Philip J. Armes (1848-1896) (q.v.). Mrs. Julia Armes was socially prominent in Craven County and Carteret County. She owned a country home at Hancock Creek called "Live Oak Hill." An 1891 tax roll shows an Armes property of 225 acres on Hancock Creek. Social events and visitors made the news from time to time. Live Oak Hill was lovely enough that one New Bern couple, George and Elizabeth Henderson, honeymooned there in 1908, according to the announcement of their wedding in the newspaper. Philip Armes headstone survived in Cherry Point cemetery # 7.

Mrs. Julia Frances Thorpe Armes became ill in 1909. She tried recuperating in Beaufort before being admitted to "Dr. Taylo(e)'s hospital at Washington, N.C.," according to her front-page obituary in the New Bern *Daily Journal*, March 8, 1910. She died "on March 6th after a long illness

... in the 57th year of her age. Her remains were brought to New Bern yesterday morning and then to her home at Hancock Creek, where *they were interred in the family burying ground.* Members of the family and friends accompanied the remains from here." [Emphasis added].

The other surviving headstone of CP 7 was Caroline R. Thorpe (1846-1867), Margaret Thorpe the elder's sister. This would seem to provide sufficient evidence, both circumstantial and logical, to conclude that these Fisher children and Mrs. Margaret Fisher were buried at CP 7.

One final installment of the story. Michael Nelms Fisher, Jr., who had by now moved the few miles back to Croatan, died on January 8, 1905. According to the family's published history: *"His body was taken to Hancock Creek and interred in the family burying ground there."*

So, in addition to the Fisher children and Mrs. Armes, we can add to the lost graves at Hancock Creek Village, and to CP 7 itself:

Fisher, Margaret H. Thorpe   WF
She was born in 1850 at Cherry Point. She was the daughter of Benjamin William and Elizabeth Hope Whitehead Thorpe. She married Michael Nelms Fisher, Jr., on January 8, 1874. She was 24. She lived at Hancock Creek village farm (Cherry Point). She was the mother of Lula Fisher (1875-1878); son, Roland Nelms Fisher (1877-1880); son, Alban Fisher (b. 1879, died in childhood); daughter, Marcell (Marselle) Nelms Fisher (1881-1955); daughter, Julia Olive Fisher (1883-c. 1895); and daughter, Margaret Thorpe Fisher (1887-1908). Margaret H.T. Fisher died 1898, c. 48. She was buried in the family burying ground at Hancock Creek, Cherry Point; CP 7.

Fisher, Michael Nelms, Jr.   WM
He was born September 25, 1842, at the Fisher Plantation, Croatan, N.C. He was the son of M.N. Fisher, Sr. and Elizabeth Ann Pelletier Fisher. He had seven brothers and sisters, one step-brother, one step-sister. He married Margaret Thorpe of Cherry Point on January 8, 1874. He was 31. For children, see Margaret Fisher above. He was a farmer, a merchant, and the postmaster of the village of Hancock Creek, Cherry Point. His two-story home was all but destroyed by fire in 1887. He died on January 8, 1905, at age 62, and was buried at Hancock Creek Village.

And one more: Remember that Michael Fisher traded land with his new bride's brother, John Thorpe? The *New Berne Weekly Journal* of November 8, 1907, carried the story of the *"Death of John M Thorpe. Mr. John M Thorpe, age 60 years, died of pneumonia at the Stewart Sanatorium* [New Bern] *Saturday evening.* [November 2, 1907] *He has been a resident of Craven County all his life living in the vicinity of Havelock and Newport. The burial took place Sunday at the family burying ground ... on Hancock Creek."*

Which we understand to mean that John Thorpe is also buried at CP 7, too. See. Thorpe, John M.

Adults and children in unmarked graves at Cemetery CP 7, Village of Hancock Creek

Mrs. Julia Francis Thorpe Armes

Alban Fisher

Julia Olive Fisher

Lula Fisher

Mrs. Margaret H. Thorpe Fisher

Miss Margaret "Maggie" Thorpe Fisher

Michael Nelms Fisher, Jr.

Roland Nelms Fisher

John M. Thorpe

Michael Nelms Fisher, Jr.

Area burials continue:

Fulshire, Mary D   WF

She was born on July 5, 1805. She was the wife of William Fulshire. She died December 21, 1857, at aged 52, She was buried at the end of Adams Creek Road on the property that was the L. S. Paul farm in 1980. The information is from an ENCGS listing.

Fulshire, William   WM

He was born on January 15, 1812. He was the husband of Mary G. Fulshire. He died on January 5, 1857, at aged 42. He was buried at the end of Adams Creek Road on the property that was the L. S. Paul farm in 1980. The information is from an ENCGS listing.

Garner, Caroline Barnes   WF

She was born on March 12, 1861. She was the daughter of Francis M. "Frank" & Susanna(h) Barnes of Havelock. She married Denard B. Garner, after 1900 (Caroline was "single" in that census), She died September 21, 1906, at age 45, and was buried at CP 15. Also, see *"The Barnes Families of Cherry Point Cemetery 15"* above.

George, Addie   AAF
She died September 24, 1926, at age 18. She was buried at CP 1. No Craven County death record or U.S. census entry is found.

German (Germann), William B. ("Bill")   WM
He was born December 19, 1909, though December 15 is recorded on his 1940 draft card. He was a native of Peoria, Illinois, the son of Jacob Germann, a house carpenter from Germany, and Lydia Germann who was from Iowa and of German descent. He had one brother and two sisters. His last name is pronounced with hard G like *girl*. In the 1920 census, his parents listed their country of origin as Switzerland. By 1930, Jacob and three children had moved to Township 6. Jacob was a cabinet maker in a cabinet factory. William registered for the draft in 1940: Age 31, 5'8" 140 pounds, brown hair and eyes. He listed his occupation as "self-employed." He lived in a two-story, wood-frame home in an isolated pine savannah at 1801 Lake Rd. The house was on the left before the second curve on Lake Road. He had a phone number listed in the 1984 Havelock directory. He never married and was said to have lived as a hermit. As a child, he attended the old Havelock school c. the 1920s. He died on January 30, 1985, at age 75. The graveside service was by Rev. Charlie Rice. He was buried at Cedar Grove Cemetery in New Bern. Services by Cotton Funeral Home. He was survived by one sister, Lydia T. White of Morrisville, N.C.

Gibbs, Estelle (Estella)   AAF
She was born on February 23, 1918. She was the daughter of Alonzo and Mindora Bryant and married Glendell Gibbs, a butcher, who was born c. 1918. They had a son, Glendell, Jr., born c. 1935. They resided in New Bern. Estella died June 21, 1940, at aged 22. COD: unknown. She was buried at CP 1, Little Witness.

Godette (Godett), Blango   AAM
He was born in 1881 and died on April 15, 1927, at aged 46. He was buried at Little Witness Church cemetery, CP 1. His gravesite was identified after 1985. No obituary or census data has been found. [Godette's name has been misspelled as *Bango* is some obituary databases. *Blango* is a family name appearing in Craven County. It is common for another family's name to be given to a child his first name. He appears in the article *Logging Camp Robbed* in the chapter of the book called "Peril and Drama in the News".]

Godwin
Marker at FUMC, no name, no date.

Godwin, Caro Clinton   WM infant

He was born August 6, 1904, and died October 26, 1904. Age two months. He was the son of Jaby F. and Elizabeth C. "Lizzie" Godwin and was buried at FUMC.

Godwin, Carolina (or Caroline) Taylor   WF

She was born around 1828, a native of Havelock. She was the wife of Joseph Godwin. She was the mother of children, Louvenia (Lavinia), Mary, Jabez (Jaby), Harriet, Cora, and Elijah Godwin. No death or burial information is found.

Elijah Godwin   WM

No death or burial information; though he was living in 1880.

Godwin, Jabez F. (Jaby or Jabie)   WM

He was born on February 10, 1862, at Havelock during the Civil War and died there January 18, 1920, at age 57. He was buried in FUMC on January 20, 1920. He was a farmer. COD: double pneumonia. He was the father of Georgana, Clydia, Rena, Lillie, Edward, and Caro Clinton Godwin. He married Elizabeth C. "Lizzie" Godwin. His parents were Joseph Godwin and Carolina Taylor of Havelock. For his sibling, see Carolina Taylor Godwin above. The undertaker, Joe K. Willis and Company of New Bern.

Godwin, Joseph   WM

He married Carolina Taylor and was the father of Jaby (Jabez) F. Godwin. No death or burial information is known.

Godwin, Joseph Clyde   WM

He was born on February 22, 1892. His gravestone says "MM2 USNRF World War I." He married Essie Davis. He died May 28, 1952, at age 62, and is buried at FUMC.

Godwin, Lizzie (Elizabeth)   WF

She was the mother of Caro Clinton Godwin and wife of J. F. Godwin. No death or burial information is known.

Godwin, Louvenia   WF

She was born in 1861. She died April 7, 1933, at age 72 years. She was buried at FUMC.

Goodwin, E. J.   WM

He was the father of James Carlisle Goodwin and husband of Lula Goodwin. No death or burial information is known to us. He is listed on the gravestone of James Carlisle Goodwin, an infant's burial at FUMC.

Goodwin, James Carlisle   WM infant

He was born in August 1905 and died in October of the same year. He was the son of the E. J. and Lula Goodwin and was buried at FUMC.

Goodwin, Lula   WF

She was the mother of James Carlisle Goodwin and wife of E. J. Goodwin.

No death or burial information is known to us. She's listed on the gravestone of her infant's burial at FUMC.

Hardesty, Infant   AAM

He was born and died May 31, 1928. The grave marker says, "Son of Daisy Hardesty." Daisy A. Hardesty was the daughter of Willie and Georgia Hardesty. She was born c. 1914. The child's burial was at Little Witness Church CP 1, though one list said CP 16.

Hardy, Sarah Eloise (Armstrong)   WF

She was born on April 22, 1911. She died on March 15, 1936, at 24 years of age. She was buried at FUMC. She was married to Sidney M. "Sap" Hardy and was the daughter of E. A. Armstrong and Mattie L. Russell Armstrong. The informant of her death was Mrs. J. C. Norris. COD pneumonia, according to Manly Mason, M.D., of Newport. The undertakers were Bell and Jones (W. H. Bell) of Morehead City.

Hardy, Sidney M, "Sap"   WM

He was born January 3, 1897, in Beaufort County and died at Havelock on May 29, 1936. He was 39 years old. He was buried at FUMC on May 30, 1936. COD pneumonia, according to Manly Mason, M.D., of Newport. He was the husband of Sarah Eloise Armstrong, who died two months earlier also of pneumonia. He was the father of Bobby Hardy; and father-in-law of Sandra Hardy. He was the son of J. A. Hardy of Greene County and Maggie White of Beaufort County. He lived in the Gray Road area of old Havelock. He was a professional auto mechanic but was skilled at building moonshine stills. He is pictured with a moonshine still in *HIHCP, the* Havelock Historical Exhibit at the Havelock Tourist Center, and in the chapter *"Goin' to Atlanta"* in this book.

Haywood, Annie Bell   WF

See entry under *Lovick/Magnolia Plantation Cemetery.*

Haywood, Thomas E.   WM

This remarkable man was born on August 4, 1893, in Croatan, N.C. He was the well-known and popular proprietor of "Tom Haywood's Store," on the main highway west of Havelock near Catfish Lake Road. For decades, the well-appointed country store was a landmark and regular stopping place for travelers largely due to the national fame of the quirky "Self-Kicking Machine" set up in July 1937. The Kicking Machine garnered lots of national publicity in newsreels, magazines, and newspapers across the U.S. Haywood, the founder, and president of the Self-Kicking Club of America even appeared in Ripley's "Believe It or Not!" President Harry Truman made a rolling stop to see the contraption in 1948 on a pass through the area. The kicking machine featured a series of leather shoes on a rotating wheel that delivered quite a punch when the crank handle was turned. The gimmick

TOM HAYWOOD AND THE KICKING MACHINE

SOURCE OF IDEA? This old newspaper advertisement looks suspiciously like the famous Haywood Kicking Machine, above. One of Tom's Croatan neighbors, Wilbur Herring, actually built the contraption for Tom's country store. Perhaps this promotion from Schnapps Tobacco was their inspiration. *The Albemarle Enterprise* Dec. 21, 1906.

This man bought a supply of tobacco without acquainting himself with the distinctive taste of SCHNAPPS Tobacco, which has the cheering qualities that gratify his desire to chew, and at less expense than cheap tobacco.

and Haywood's sparkling personality pulled in a lot of business for the strategically located filling station and store on the state's central highway, now known as US 70. For years, it was a must-see tourist attraction on the way to and from Atlantic Beach. Haywood was a farmer with a hundred acres at Croatan. He was a Craven County commissioner, Township 6 justice of the peace (1914), Voluntary Township 6 Forest Fire Correspondent (1917), and census official, along with other accomplishments. He died in 1955 at the age of 61. He was buried at the Croatan Community Cemetery, almost directly across the highway from the location of the country store, along with his wife, Julia Haywood

(1895-1962). The original Kicking Machine? It's in the state's history museum in Raleigh.

Area burials continue:

HILL Plot at FUMC   WM/F
Father, Jesse Hill, was born June 14, 1848, and died July 4, 1920, a cooper by trade. COD "Old age," per death certificate; Mother, Elizabeth F. Hill was born on April 29, 1856. She died September 11, 1929; Son, Jesse E. Born April 22, 1890, died September 16, 1920; Daughter, Serena Hill Bryan, was born April 19, 1895, and died December 1, 1939; Thomas Lewis Hill, was born June 27, 1877, and died October 15, 1929; Addie G. Cannon Hill, the wife of Thomas, was born May 11, 1886, and died April 22, 1912.

Hill, Carlilie Fenner   AAF
Carlilie Fenner was born in North Harlowe on August 17, 1918, the daughter of Joe Early Fenner and Lela Ora Nelson. She was the wife of James Emanuel Hill, and mother of Emma Louise Hill (Davis). Her obituary was in the *Sun Journal* on December 5, 2005, and December 6, 2005.

Hill, Emma (see Stevens)   AAF
Hill, William Henry   AAM
He was born during the Civil War on July 27, 1864. He was self-employed as a farmer. His wife was Crisanna ("Chrissie") who was born c. 1886. He had a son named Urashford who was born c. 1911. He lived on Melvin Road, which turns off Highway 101 onto what is now Cherry Point. He died on August 16, 1928, age 64, and was buried at Little Witness CP 1.

The Hollands of 'Cravensville'

Among the white settlers on the south shore of the Neuse River at Slocum Creek during the late 1700s and early 1800s was the large, prominent, and prosperous Holland family. Some early obituaries include:

Huldah Holland, 1821: "DIED. At Slocumb's Creek, on the third instant [*i.e., the third of this month: December 3, 1821*], Mrs. Huldah Holland, wife of William Holland, Esq. *Centinel* (New Bern) December 15, 1821.

William Holland, 1836: "DIED. At his late residence in this county [on Slocumb Creek], William Holland, Esq. His memory will be long cherished by a large circle of acquaintance, to whom he was endeared by his many benevolent and disinterested actions." *New Bern Sentinel* December 21, 1836. He was a justice of the peace at Slocum Creek in c. 1811 and founded the first post office [Cravenville or Cravensville] in southern Craven County in the year of his death. It was taken over by his son and operated until a virulent fever killed several family members in 1841.

Hylliard Holland,1838: "Died. At his residence on Tucker's Creek, in this county, on Sunday the fourth instant [*i.e., the fourth of this month; November 4, 1838*], in the 37th year of his age, Mr. Hylliard Holland. The deceased was a kind and affectionate husband, an obliging neighbor, and most estimable man." *New Bern Spectator* November 16, 1838.

Some other family members were at Slocum Creek were:

Philemon Holland (1), July 31, 1768-September 28, 1841, had a plantation at Slocum Creek. He was married to Sally Rowe Holland. He was described as a "prosperous farmer." His sons included Philemon, Barney, and Richard Dobbs Spaight Holland. He died at age 73 in an epidemic with other family members. Burial place unknown.

Sally Rowe Holland, wife of Philemon Holland. He lived at Slocum Creek. Birth and death dates, and burial information unknown to us.

Barney Holland, July 10, 1816-September 12, 1841, age 25, lived at Slocum Creek and was the son of Philemon and Sally Holland. He died in a fever epidemic. His place of burial is unknown. A news story on his death said he was "a very fine young man, much beliked by virtuous people."

Richard Dobbs Spaight Holland, June 24, 1828-September 6, 1841, age 13, lived at Slocum Creek. He was the son of Philemon and Sally Holland. He died in a fever epidemic with other family members and his place of burial is not known.

Philemon Holland (2), 1822-1892, married Margaret A. Pigott Holland in January 1846. They had eleven children. He had a plantation at Slocum Creek. He is buried at Cedar Grove Cemetery in New Bern.

Margaret A. Pigott Holland, 1829-1902, was the wife of Philemon Holland, married in 1846, and mother of eleven children, including Henrietta, Sarah, Philemon, Pearl, Lidia, Margaret Ann, Hughes, and Leah. She was the daughter of Col. Levi and Eliza Dennis Pigott and was born in Carteret County. She was the sister of famous Civil War spy Emeline Pigott. Margaret lived at Slocum Creek. She is buried at Cedar Grove Cemetery in New Bern.

Philemon Holland (3), 1859-1886, was the son of Philemon and Margaret A. Holland. He married Keziah Marchant. He farmed at Slocum Creek. He is buried at Cedar Grove Cemetery in New Bern.

Stephen D. Holland, 1829-1878, lived at Slocum Creek and is buried at Cedar Grove Cemetery in New Bern.

Keziah Ives Holland Bell, 1826 (or 1827)-1858, married David Wilkinson Bell in Craven County on July 23, 1845. She was the daughter of Philemon Holland and Keziah Marchant. She died in September 1858 and is buried at Cedar Grove Cemetery in New Bern.

Three generations of the Holland men had the biblical name, Philemon. More information on the family is in the chapter *The School House Letter of 1849* in the "Death in a Low and Wet Savannah" section. A map in that chapter shows where one of the Holland plantations was located. Many African American Hollands are thought to descend from their slaves.

Area burials continue:

Holland, Annie Mattie   AAF Infant
She was born November 1927 and died July 12, 1928. She was buried at Little Witness CP 1 (CP 16).

Holland, Charles E.   AAM
He was born on March 3, 1880, the son of John R. and Emily J. Holland. He was a farm laborer at Little Witness. He died on February 21, 1908, at age 27, and was buried in Little Witness, CP 14.

Holland, Dortha McCray (or Carter)   AAF
She was born on April 20, 1909, at Havelock, N.C. She was the daughter of Turner and Josephine Carter Holland. She was married to Joseph Holland. She died June 26, 1936, at age 27. She was buried at Little Witness Church CP 1 (CP 16),

Holland, Emily J.   AAF
She was born in December 1848. She was the wife of John R. Holland. They married c. 1877. Their children were: Matilda A., born December 1870; Melvina, born November 1871; David W., born June 1874; Millie J., born December 1875; Charles E., born March 1880; Mary L., born August 1882; Jacob, born December 1886; James H., born December 1888; Georgia P., born February 1890; and George H. C., born September 1895. Emily died in 1930, at age c. 82. She was buried in CP Little Witness.

Holland, Infant   AAM
This boy was born and died May 11, 1928. No other information was found.

Holland, Jacob   AAM
He was born on December 24, 1886. He was the son of John R. and Emily J. Holland and lived at Little Witness. He died April 26, 1907, at age 20, and was buried CP Little Witness.

Holland, John R.   AAM
He was born on November 10, 1838. He was the husband of Emily J. Holland. They married c. 1877. He was a farmer at Little Witness. He was a deacon of the Craven Corner Missionary Baptist Church for 30 years. At his death, his fellow members of the Grand United Order of Odd Fellows and the Household of Ruth of Melvin, N.C. placed a "Resolution of Respect" in the *Daily Journal* of New Bern. It said that "the church has lost one of its strongest pillars ... the community one of its best citizens, and the race one of its brightest examples of integrity and honesty, his family a devout husband and loving father." For his children, see Emily J. Holland above. He died September 17, 1911, and was buried at Little Witness. He's mentioned in the first chapter, *A Man Called Sparks*.

Holland, Millie J.   AAF

She was born in December 1875, the daughter of John R. and Emily J. Holland. She lived at Little Witness. Her death date is unknown to us. She was buried CP Little Witness.

Holland, Minerva "Minnie" Pasture Holland   AAF

She was born in 1898 and died on December 30, 1918. She was buried at CP Little Witness.

Holland, unknown

Two burials at CP Little Witness.

MISSING AFRICAN AMERICAN HOLLANDS. Despite the pair of newly-identified Holland burials immediately above, many Hollands remain unaccounted for. As elsewhere, numerous Cherry Point graves are either unmarked or unidentified. In most cases, the graves weren't permanently marked following the burial. Officials at Cherry Point have attempted over the years to discover and identify unknowns buried aboard the air station. Other Holland family members are buried at Greenwood and Cedar Grove cemeteries in New Bern.

Holton, Barbara Parsons   WF

She was born on March 25, 1783. She was a member of a family from the Hancock Creek area and lived at Cherry Point with her husband, Lot Holton, who became a wealthy turpentine farmer. They married on August 18, 1803. She was 20. He was 22. She died on July 8, 1823, at age 40. She was buried at CP 8. See Lot Holton below.

Holton, Lot   Lost Grave, maybe   WM

He was born on October 6, 1780. He was a wealthy plantation owner at Hancock Creek with 370 acres and three slaves (per Capt. John S. Smith District list of 1815). He had twelve slaves listed in the 1830 census. He was a producer of naval stores for export. He married Barbara Parson on August 18, 1803. The Parson's 988-acre plantation was on Hancock Creek and close to Holton's.

From 1985 Cherry Point archeological report (ARC) of Cemetery 8: *"The 1941 cemetery survey originally recorded that only unmarked graves were present. At an unknown later date, this entry was corrected to include the one marker present."*

Barbara Holton's double marker referred to above – and viewable in the appendices of this

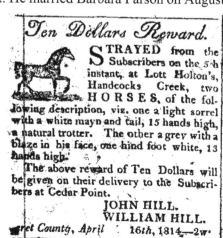

Ten Dollars Reward.

STRAYED from the Subscribers on the 5 'th instant, at Lott Holton's, Handcocks Creek, two HORSES, of the following description, viz. one a light sorrel with a white mayn and tail, 15 hands high, a natural trotter. The other a grey with a blaze in his face, one hind foot white, 13 hands high.

The above reward of Ten Dollars will be given on their delivery to the Subscribers at Cedar Point.

JOHN HILL,
WILLIAM HILL.

——et County, April   16th, 1814—2w.

book – included her husband's name. It recorded Lot Holton's birth date as October 6, 1780, with a space to be filled in upon his death. It never was. This tends to indicates Lot Holton was not buried there. That was the supposition when Barbara Holton's marker was found, and of the contract archeologists in 1985. They did not include Lot Holton's name on the list of Cherry Point burials. It seems likely he remarried. Following Barbara Parsons's 1823 death, there are two Lot Holton marriages in county records. These are to Charity Smith in 1832, and Ferebee Daw in 1839 when he would still have been a marriageable 59 years of age.

Not surprising in light of the era's fluidity of spelling, Holton's first name sometimes appeared with a double "t", as evidenced by a notice above of lost horses in the *Carolina Federal Republic* of New Bern in 1814.

In the United States Census for both 1820 and 1830, Lot Holton is living on the south shore of the Neuse River among other neighbors known to reside there, including Jeremiah Parsons, Michael Fisher, Stephen Winn, and Dexter Gibson. He was prominent enough that a later trustee sale notice refers to the main road from the mouth of Hancock Creek to the Beaufort Road – across what is now Cherry Point – as "the old Holton plantation road." [a]

In 1840, Lot Holton pulled off a neat trick. He appears in the county census for south of the Neuse and also for north of the Neuse as "Lott" Holton. In 1840, that area was still a part of Craven County and would remain so until Pamlico County was carved out of Craven and Beaufort counties in 1872.

One explanation for appearing in two places is that the censuses were conducted at different times during the year and Holton relocated in between them. The original of the north side census for that year displays a sworn and signed statement that it was completed on October 20, 1840. The south side census, however, is undated.

As noted, in 1839 a Lot Holton married Ferebee Daw and on the north side in 1840 he's enumerated among several Daw neighbors, suggesting he moved so his new wife could be close to her family. The overland trip at the time from Hancock Creek to, say, Arapahoe or Bayboro would have been several days each way.

The 1985 ARC study also surmised that a reason his gravestone was unmarked with a death date was that sometime following his first wife's death, Holton remarried and moved across the Neuse River to what was then northern Craven County. The census data lends support to that conclusion. Circumstantial as it may be, Holton families still reside in Pamlico today.

But there's another explanation.

---

[a] Reams and Webber, *The Daily Journal* (New Bern) December 25, 1900

A check of the 1830 census also finds a Lott Holton living north of the Neuse River and this time he's surrounded by other Holton families. Five Holton heads-of-households are living in a row. This Lott Holton's name is consistently spelled with a double "t". He, too, has a plantation. He, too, is a slaveholder.

So, there were two Lot Holtons; one on each side of the river. Northside Lott did the same thing his southern doppelganger did; he married one of the local neighbor girls, in his case Miss Daw.

This much speculation requires a theory summary.

There's no evidence that the Hancock Creek Lot Holton ever had any children. Early censuses did not name children but made tick marks for them and Southside Lot had none. If he never remarried perhaps, he *was* buried next to Barbara but there was simply no one invested enough in his life to have his death date chiseled in the couple's headstone.

Former Hancock Creek plantation owner Lot Holton's date of death is unknown to us. There's no will. No obituary. Determining if Lot Holton is buried next to Barbara would require *real* archaeological work with shovel and trowel or ground-penetrating radar. We don't expect that to happen any time soon. Lacking further evidence, all that can be said is that the location of his grave has yet to be documented.

Area burials continue:

Hunter, Collins Hughes, 1863-1951. Born at Havelock, he's buried in Roxboro, N.C. He's featured in the "A Country Harmony" chapter.

Hunter, Mary Elizabeth "Bettie," see Williams.

Hunter, Capt. John Stricter (Streeter) WM

A sea captain, he was the father of James H. Hunter and may have been the founder of the Hunter plantation on Slocum Creek. John S. Hunter was born September 3, 1792, and died July 11, 1865. He married Nancy Jackson on October 7, 1813, in Havelock. She was the daughter of Joab Jackson and Mary Carmott. They would have ten children. Grave unknown.

Hunter, John Noe WM

He was born February 15, 1859, on a substantial family plantation at Slocum Creek, Cherry Point. He died on April 23, 1905, and was buried at what is now called CP 10, tract 3F. It was a single grave near the intersection of runways after the base was completed. He was the son of James Howard Hunter and Mary Jane Noe Hunter and the brother of Bettie Hunter Williams (1864-1918). John was a member of a large and prosperous local family featured in the book *HIHCP*. His father is in the "Rebel Spies" chapter of this book. "Death of John N. Hunter. The death of John N. Hunter, son of Capt. James H. Hunter, occurred at his home in Havelock, on Monday, [April 23] the funeral taking place Tuesday. He was a timber man for the Blades Lumber

Company and was held in esteem. Complication of diseases caused his death." *New Bern Weekly Journal* April 28, 1905.

Missing Hunter Family Graves at Cherry Point

As highlighted in an earlier chapter, **James Howard Hunter (1824-1920. Buried in Roxboro, N.C.)** defended North Carolina against invasion by Federal troops as a cavalryman under Capt. Peter G. Evans during the Battle of New Bern. Later in the war, Hunter was a "scout," basically a Confederate spy on horseback who engaged in intelligence operations for the remainder of the war. He'd been wealthy in tar, turpentine, timber, and farming on his 500-acre spread at Slocum Creek before the war and he became even more prosperous afterward. See "Rebel Spies" chapter.

Hunter had eight children and family members who surely passed away at the large plantation home. His first wife, Mary Jane Noe Hunter died there. A second wife would as well. His father, an old sea captain, died there, and at least one of his children. See John Noe Hunter above. Like almost all large landowners in that era, Hunter had a cemetery on his farm. Today, its adjacent to the intersection of large air station runways.

James H. Hunter married Mary Jane Noe, the daughter of John Noe and Susannah Templeton, on March 6, 1858. Their children born at Havelock were John Noe Hunter, born February 15, 1859; Charles F. Hunter, born July 19, 1861; Collins Hughes Hunter, born April 20, 1863; and Mary Elizabeth Hunter, born July 25, 1864.

He married Margaret Ann Ives on October 8, 1867. Their children born at Havelock were: Lizette Bell Hunter, born December 17, 1868; Julus Louis Hunter, born September 2, 1871; Margaret Jackson Hunter, born January 18, 1872; and Charles Duffy Hunter, born September 19, 1874.

He married Caroline Hardison of Croatan on November 24, 1881. They had no children.

The 1985 Cherry Point archeological survey said of Cemetery number 10, the one located on Hunter's former domain: "Local informants in 1941 estimated 100 graves were present. Only one marker is present." That marker belongs to J. H. & Mary J. Hunter's son, John N. Hunter, who died in 1905. One hundred burials. One marker. No one will ever know who else rests there beneath the "Sound of Freedom" today.

Also, see Betty Hunter Williams.

Area burials continue:

Hyman, Baby Boy   AAM

He was born and died on January 25, 1930, and was buried at the Little Witness Baptist Church in Havelock.

Jackson, James Clennie   WM
He was born on July 28, 1880. He was the son of William Henry and Mary
W. Jackson and the husband of Lula Bryan Jackson. Their children were
Herbert J., William Edgar*, Charles F., and Thomas B. Jackson. Following
the death of his first wife, he married Lila Mae Taylor of North Harlowe on
May 25, 1918. In the 1920 Census for Township 8, Oaks Road, New Bern
lists J. C., 39, electrician, John C. Roper Lumber Co.; Lila, 20, wife; Herbert, 18; William, 13; Charles, 10; Thomas, 5. He died December 13, 1964,
aged 84, and was buried at FUMC. [*William Edgar "Bill" Jackson (1907-
1993), a former state highway employee, was head of a well-known Havelock business family after the establishment of MCAS Cherry Point. He married the former Louise Margaret Trader (1906-1985), a businesswoman in
her own right, a daughter of Jesse Trader, and sister of Hugh Trader. The
Jacksons are buried at Cedar Grove Cemetery in New Bern.]

Jackson, Lula Bryan   WF
She was born on April 11, 1886. She married James C. Jackson. She was a
housewife and high school graduate. For children, see James C. Jackson
above. She was the daughter of Edgar Bryan of Onslow County and Minnie
Merritt of Jones County. She died June 3, 1915, at age 29. COD: tuberculosis. She was said to have been "sick for almost two years." She was buried
at FUMC on June 4, 1915.

Jackson, Mary Matilda Casey   WF
Born May 13, 1852, she was from Township 5 near Adams Creek. "Wife of
W. Henry Jackson" is engraved on her gravestone. She was the mother of
James Clennie Jackson, 1880-1964; Horace T., 1883-1966; and Charles C.
1887-1965. She died on January 8, 1920, at aged 67, and is buried in the
Oak Grove Church Cemetery on Adams Creek Road.

Jackson, William Henry   WM
He was born on April 4, 1847. He was a farmer in Township 5, Adams
Creek. He went by "Henry." He was the husband of Mary Matilda Casey
Jackson and the father of James Clennie Jackson, 1880-1964; Horace T.,
1883-1966; and Charles C. 1887-1965. He died August 20, 1905, aged 58,
and was buried at the Oak Grove Church Cemetery on Adams Creek Road.

Jones, Bryan and Sarah J. Winn   Lost Graves   WM/WF
They were the parents of Martha E., Gilley A. Cooper, and Elizabeth H.
Jones. They lost three baby girls in seven years; 1843, 1848, and1850.
County marriage bonds list "Bryan Jones" marrying "Sarah I. Winn" Feb-
ruary 23, 1841. Other sources have the mother as "Sarah J." No death or
burial information for either. Likely burials at family cemetery CP 9.

Jones, Elizabeth H.   WF
She was born on January 24, 1842. She died on June 17, 1843. She was 17

months old. The daughter of Bryan and Sarah Winn Jones, her burial was at
CP 9, tract 199.

Jones, Evan   Lost Grave   WM

He was an early settler at Cherry Point and a Welsh Quaker pilgrim. He
arrived on Neuse with his brother, Roger, c. 1710. His plantation was on the
Neuse at the mouth of Slocum Creek, the site of Cherry Point's "consolidated club." Slocumb Creek was early identified as "Evan Jones pasture
creek" in Book 1 Craven County deeds. He was a turpentine farmer. His
name was on the county list of colonial freeholders and jurymen, 1723. He
was elected twice as borough representative for New Bern 1731-1733 and
1736-1737, per Alan Watson. Death date and burial unknown.

Jones, Roger   Lost Grave   WM

He was an early settler at what we now call Cherry Point. A Welsh Quaker,
he arrived with brother, Evan, c. 1710. He lived on Neuse River near the
mouth of Slocum Creek. He was a turpentine farmer. He was killed in 1711
or 1712 when Indians attacked his brother Evan's plantation. Chased
through the woods when working at a tar kiln. Some sources say he was
beheaded. Precise death date and burial place unknown.

Jones, Evan   WM

Likely the grandson of the original settler named Evan Jones. He lived on
the family's Neuse River plantation, which had been established c. 1710. He
was born in 1757. He died on March 21, 1817. He was 60 years of age,
according to Cherry Point cemetery records. However, *The Raleigh Register*, in its newspaper edition published March 14, 1817, stated that his death
occurred on Feb. 20. He was the husband of Sally Jones. He was buried at
CP 13, tract 461. [*More members of the Evan Jones family appear in the
DIED section of the book.*]

Jones, Gilley A. Cooper   white infant

She was born on November 22, 1848. She died on June 27, 1850, at the age
of 17 months. She was the daughter of Bryan and Sarah Jones. Buried CP
9, tract 199.

Jones, Martha E.   white infant

She was born on February 13, 1847. She died on February 27, 1848, at the
age of 12 months. She was the daughter of Bryan and Sarah Jones. She was
buried at CP 9, tract 199.

Jones, Sally   WF

Early settlers of what we today call Cherry Point. She was born in 1761. She
died on February 24, 1813, at 62 years of age. She was the wife of Evan
Jones. She is buried at CP 13, tract 461.

*MORE ON THE JONESES under *Whatnot* in Part III*

Kennedy, Squire(s)   AAM

Also found as *Kanady, Canaday, Cannedy, Canada*

He was born c. 1864 in Havelock. He was the son of Allen Kennedy of Lenoir County (1834-1880) and Sylvia "Silvie" Orum of Havelock (1840-1880). In 1920, he was living in Township 5 and working as a farmer. He married Sarah Ward of Beaufort (1873-1955) on March 18, 1895. They were married by Rev. A. J. Chestnutt, a Township 6 Justice of the Peace. Their witnesses were George W. Cully, and Charles and Walter Kennedy. He was the father of John, Jessey, Ada, and Squire, Jr. In 1930, he was living in New Bern; working as a laborer in a lumber mill. His occupation was listed as "contractor" on the death certificate. He died before January 14, 1931. COD: apoplexy. His burial was at the Greenwood Cemetery in New Bern.

Ketner, Calvin Pless ("C.P."), aka Calhoon K. & Cathern K.   WM
He was born c. 1886. He was a farmer. The residential subdivision, Ketner Heights, was built on the family's land and named for the family. He lived in a two-story farmhouse near US 70 at what is now Stonebridge in Havelock. His first wife was named Maggie. They married c. 1906. He died on June 1, 1957, at aged 72. Services were observed at St. Andrew's Lutheran Church in New Bern. He was buried at the New Bern Memorial Cemetery. At the time of death, he was survived by his wife Zella Kelly Ketner. His children included: Kenneth, Opal, Vernon A., and Sterling; several step-children.

Ketner, Donald Wayne   WM infant
He was born June 29, 1947, and died the next day, June 30, 1947. He was the son of S. W. and Beatrice Ketner. The child was buried at FUMC.

Mother & Son

King, Elizabeth "Bettie"   AAF
She was born c. 1838 and died October 9, 1928, aged 89-90. She was buried at the Little Witness Church Cemetery on what is today Cherry Point. There's quite a bit of disparity within the records about Mrs. Elizabeth "Bettie" King's age. But despite an apparent gap of almost fifty years between them, there's no doubt the man buried beside her in the Little Witness Church graveyard was her son, Johnny.

King, John F.   AAM
The son of Elizabeth "Bettie" King, he was born c. 1898. His grave marker at CP1, the Little Witness Cemetery, indicated he died January 24, 1939, at age 41.

John King's father – and Bettie's husband – was Stanley King. They married in 1880. Stanley King was a preacher, born in Craven County in March 1850, but living with Bettie in Goose Creek, South Carolina in 1900. He was 50.

330

When we find Bettie next, it's in the 1910 Craven County census. Rev. King is no longer in the home. "Elizabeth" is listed as the head of household and gives her occupation as farmer, a rare but not unknown designation for a woman. Son "Johnny" is 19 and working as a teamster, using horses, mules, or oxen to drag sawlogs to the mill of a timbering operation near their residence on Cahoogue Creek Road in Havelock. During that period a big lumber conglomerate, the Roper Lumber Company, was clear-cutting the old-growth trees from Carteret County to New Bern. There was plenty of work.

Bettie's age is listed as 57 in the year's census. That would make her birth year about 1853 instead of 1838, aligning her age more typically with that of her husband's. And Johnny's age of 19 in 1910 adjusts his birth toward 1891, dropping the age gap between mother and son from 49 years to a more likely 38.

In the 1900 census, when Bettie was living in South Carolina with her husband of 20 years, her birthdate was listed as March 1851. That's the most specific date we have for her. If correct, she was 77 when she died in 1928.

In 1920, Bettie King was living with her son, "Johnnie," aged 27 on the New Bern Road, which we take to mean the Beaufort-to-New Bern road, today's Highway 101. Bettie is no longer farming. John is. And it must have been good for him because, according to the records, he only increased eight years in age during the ten years since the last census.

The census-taker often moves house-to-house gathering his information. Based on Johnnie King's neighbors we surmise he and his mother were living somewhere between Little Witness (Melvin, N.C.) and Cahoogue (*Cahooca* in the census) Creek Road. Also in the home at the time was Johnnie's recently acquired wife, Clara, aged 30, and Johnnie's stepdaughter, Malissa Godette, age eight. Clara's listed as "wife" and Bettie is listed as "mother."

John King married Clara Whittington four years earlier, on New Year's Day 1916. A Baptist minister, Rev. T. M. Gaskill, tied the knot, and David W. Holland, W. A. Cully and John McCray, all of Havelock, signed as witnesses to the ceremony. The bride was the daughter of Allen and Sarah Whittington of Havelock, both of whom are shown by Craven County Marriage License No. 2035 to be living. Father-of-the-groom Stanley King, however, is listed as deceased, explaining his absence from Bettie's home. John King's age is shown as 24, once again confirming a birthdate in the 1891-92 range.

At the time of her 1928 death, someone reported – and someone recorded – that Bettie King was born in 1838 – making her 89 or 90 years old. We can only say that the death records are significantly out of line with all the other records of her life. With good numbers or bad, she was buried at

Little Witness, a village still bubbling with life as the Great Depression grew nearer.

And life went on.

Johnnie and Clara never had kids of their own, but Le Roy Godette joined his sister Malissa in the home. They were listed in the census as stepson and stepdaughter. The four of them continued to live beside unpaved "Highway No. 101," nears its intersection with Cahoogue Creek Road, and only a few doors down from her father.

As years rolled by, John King became ill and stopped farming. It got worse toward the end of 1938. On January 24, 1939, he died of kidney disease and its complications. His wife, Clara, was the informant on the death certificate. She told Dr. Manly Mason of Newport and a county registrar that John was born in 1898 and that he was 41 years old, figures that appear from other records to be off by six or seven years. But that's what they wrote down on their official documents and that's what followed him to his grave at Little Witness. It wasn't long after his funeral service was spoken that the ground began to rumble with airfield construction and World War II-era bombers and fighters commenced take-offs and landings within a few hundred feet of his resting place.

There's another curiosity on Johnny's death certificate. Upon the printed lines to name Clara's husband's dead father, a man she'd never met, the information is recorded correctly as Stanley King, born in Craven County, North Carolina. But for the name and place of birth of the mother, a woman she had known and lived with for years, registrar Clyde J. Morton, wrote at a slant across the space that the information was "not obtainable."

In fairness, there's no way to know the reason. Maybe the registrar forgot to ask or misplaced his notes. Maybe Clara was so upset she couldn't think straight. It's not something we'll figure out all these years later.

Clara E. Whittington King never remarried. She moved to New Bern and died of breast cancer in 1961. Born in 1899, she was 62. Her burial was in New Bern's Evergreen Cemetery. She couldn't be buried beside Johnnie. Cherry Point, by then the flying leathernecks' largest airbase, had been closed to new burials for twenty years.

Area burials continue:

Latham, see entry below *Williams, Mary Elizabeth "Betty" Hunter*

Lockey, Henry E.   WM

He was born on July 28, 1884. He was the son of John (d. before 1900); Susan Goodwin Lockey (1861-1940). In 1900, at age 16, he was working as a day laborer and living in Newport. He was the third of seven children: four boys, and three girls. He died on May 8, 1909, at age 24. He was buried at FUMC.

Lofton, Saul   AAM
He may have been buried in the Batts family cemetery. He was mentioned in *Havelock Progress* newspaper article, November 1976. Other details about him are unknown.

Recovering the Distant Past One Marker at a Time

LOVICK (SHUTE) / Magnolia Plantation Cemetery

Lovick, George WM
George Lovick is one of the earliest preserved burials known to us. He died on May 13, 1798. He was "Aged thirty-three years." He is buried at the Magnolia Plantation Cemetery, on private property at Carolina Pines.

In the early 1700s, the Magnolia Plantation consumed much of the land east of present-day Stately Pines, off U.S. 70 west of Havelock, running to Slocum

Magnolia Plantation gravestones
Edward Ellis photo

Creek, within the boundary of the modern MCAS Cherry Point. The entirety of today's Carolina Pines was once part of Magnolia Plantation, which is thought to have covered 1,250 acres.

For more than a hundred years, the Lovick family held sway there, beginning with a 1719 land grant to John Lovick, a planter and colonial surveyor. He and his brother, Thomas, were among the Welsh Quakers who settled on the south shore of the Neuse River along Slocum, Hancock, and Clubfoot creeks in 1710, the same year New Bern was founded by Swiss and Germans. Roger and Evan Jones arrived with the same group as Lovick. Lovick and his plantation would thrive. Eventually, there would be a

LOVICK CEMETERY HEADSTONES recovered by Gail and Doug Lindeman from the site of the 18th century Magnolia Plantation cemetery. Two of them are more than two hundred years old. Top left is Mehitabel Jones Lovick with husband James Lovick at top right. Sally Lovick's marker is the best preserved of the lot. The oldest for George Lovick is bottom right.
Douglas Lindeman photos.

gracious plantation home on the farm known as Magnolia Plantation.

A portion of the property was later owned and operated as Magnolia Farm by Mr. and Mrs. Josiah J. Hughes before being sold in the 1960s for real estate development.

Two Carolina Pines residents, Doug and Gail Lindeman, took voluntary stewardship of the old Lovick cemetery, which is today on private property. The burying ground has suffered the ravages of time. It's thought that storms have washed away graves and there's been damage; possibly from farming, and apparently from vandalism. But even the small number of remaining headstones recovered and interpreted by the Lindemans prove that Magnolia Plantation's cemetery is one of the oldest in the counties of Craven and Carteret. Known burials there include:

George Lovick 1765-1798, aged 33, WM
Sarah "Sally" Lovick, wife of George, 1765-1817, aged 48, WF
James Lovick, their son, 1794-1831, aged 37, WM, and
Mehitabel Jones Lovick, 1797-1827, age 50, wife of James, WF.

There's no reason to believe these are the first burials in this location. At least some, and maybe many, would have gone before.

Two more headstones recovered by the Lindemans are of later dates. Not heard so often today, the Shute name has a long and venerable history in

DIED

On the 20th inst. near Slocumbs Creek, Craven County, Mrs. SARAH LOVICK, relick of Mr. George Lovick.

The Carolina Federal Republic published at New Bern, November 29, 1817, noted the death of Mrs. Sarah Lovick, suggesting Sally was her nickname. The date of death is given as the 20th, one day off from the headstone. *Relick* or relict is an archaic word for widow.

Craven County with the records of the family beginning to appear in the late 1700s. But this pair of Shute graves convey a somber tale of others interred at the Magnolia Plantation Cemetery.

See these under their alphabetical headings:

Shute, Almira Cordelia "Ellie" Holland   WF
Shute, Fred Pauline   WF

And yet another unmarked Lovick Cemetery grave was discovered by accident in the preparation of this book:

Haywood, Annie Bell   WF

In research of other matters. we came across evidence of another burial in the Lovick graveyard. From the *New Bern Weekly Journal* of December 13, 1907.

"Died, At Croatan, December 9, Annie Bell [Haywood], the daughter of Mr. and Mrs. Thomas E. Haywood, at the age of eight years. The burial services were conducted by Mr. B[enjamin] E. Williams, and the interment made in the Lovick family graveyard on Slocumbs Creek. The funeral will be prepared at the Croatan Presbyterian Church, by Rev. S. H. Isler of Goldsboro, Friday night, of this week."

No headstone for Annie Haywood is evident today, nor was one found in a cemetery survey by the Eastern North Carolina Genealogical Society during the winter of 1980. There's other historical and anecdotal evidence that graves have been forever lost at Magnolia Plantation. The author has been told stories that exposed caskets were once seen after a hurricane. The number of lost and unmarked graves may never be known but, thankfully, interested neighbors like the Lindemans keep watch.

Area burials continue:
Lutz, Irvin A. WM
According to his headstone at FUMC, he was born in 1892 and died in 1953.

Recalling a Woman Named Love

Midwife, community "doctor," washerwoman, mother, and grand-mother. Lova "Lovie" McCabe (1836 – 1916) was all these things and more. An African American female, she was born in southeast Craven County near Slocum Creek when Andrew Jackson was President of the United States – and the day after Arkansas became the twenty-fifth star on the American flag. She came up in the wood-fired, horse-and-buggy world of the early nineteenth century. But she'd survive the War Between the States and lived into the age of the Wright Brothers' flyer and Henry Ford's Model T automobile.

Today, the primary reminder of the 79 years of Lovie McCabe's life is an arched marble gravestone. Her marker shelters under shade trees at Pilgrims Rest Christian Church near the junction of Temples Point Road and the old stretch from Beaufort to New Bern, now known as N.C. Highway 101.

Grave of Lova McCabe
Bernd Doss Photo

But we know more. The first time we see her existence in writing, in the 1870 census, it says her name is Love.

By 1910, six years before she died, Lovie was a widow living with her daughter Alice, son-in-law, John H. Perry, and a house full of kids – ten in all – on farmland just east of Havelock. She was having more than a little trouble hearing, speaking, and seeing, possibly the result of a stroke or some other curse of aging, but the census taker for that part of the county – by the name of Godette – carefully marked down that Mrs. McCabe had served as a mid-wife, and what's more, he wrote out that she was a "woman doctor." It's a great tribute for an elderly black lady who could neither read nor write.

Before the war, there were a surprising number of free people of color in southern Craven County. Possibly chief among the reasons was that a majority of the original white European settlers on this part of the Neuse were Quakers; many of them from Wales. The Quakers, in general, were opposed to enslaving anyone. The Quaker antipathy for chattel slavery may have been a catalyst for migration to the area of many black people freed at the time of the American Revolution. Perhaps the two things worked together as a social siphon to draw more and more. By 1860, nearly half of the *free population* of what is today Township Six, Craven County, N.C. was of African descent.

A peaceable kingdom existed here for a while; an uncharacteristic anomaly compared to the stereotype of the slave South. Locally, for a few scant decades, the historical record supports the view that blacks and whites lived side-by-side as neighbors, did business together, traded, exchanged services, bought and sold land, communed socially, even romantically, and reasoned with one another. Black people learned to read and write. They had their trades and occupations and worked on their own account.

There were, no doubt, lines that could not and would not be crossed. It wasn't a perfect world. Neither is the one we live in today. But, according to our best reckoning of the facts, compared to other parts of the South in 1860 – where 90 percent of the entire African American population was in chains – society seems to have been both functional and civil in this corner of Craven County.

Having said all that, Lova McCabe does not appear on the 1860 list of Free Inhabitants of "Gooding's District." That doesn't prove she was a slave. There might be other reasons for her missing the list. But the absence of her name points the probabilities in that direction. Whatever the case, she'd live 53 of her years after the Emancipation Proclamation.

In addition to her grave maker, we find her first in 1870 and present these other facts below.

McCabe, Lova "Love" "Lovie"   AAF

She was born (according to her grave marker) on June 16, 1836. Her maiden name is unknown. She was married and "keeping house" in the 1870 census. Her age was first listed as 50 (but she'll get *younger* as time goes by). Her husband was Sciffeo (Cifeo) "Zip" McCabe, age 57, a farm laborer. By 1870, she has children: daughter, Betsy, age 14, born c. 1855; son, Sciffeo, age 11, born c. 1860; son, John, age eight, born c. 1861; and son, Charles, age four, born c. 1865. Ten years later, in 1880, she's only aged four years, according to the census, to 54. Her husband, Zip, is 65 and still farming. They have Bettie, age 20; John M., 17; Charles, 15; Alice V., 12; William H., eight; and Mary E., age four.

The national 1890 census was lost in a fire so our next update is 1900. She's a widow now. She works as a "washerwoman." She was born in North Carolina and so were both of her parents, it says. She can't read or write.

She's living in the household of her son-in-law, John Perry, 36, who earns his daily bread hauling logs to the sawmill. Although twenty years have passed since the previous census, her birthday count had increased by just 14 years to the age of 68. That would mean she was born in 1832, not 1836 as shown on her grave marker.

This brings us to the final entry.

In April 1910, the census "enumerator" for Township Five, Jesse P. Godette, found her still living with her daughter, Alice V. Perry, 37, and husband John, 44. Godette recorded that Lovie was 84, altering her birth-year a full decade earlier than the one chiseled on her stone. The census says John and Alice had been married 23 years, which made them 21 and 14 respectively at the time their marriage commenced. In the intervening years, Alice had borne 12 babies. Godette recorded that eight of the Perry children were still alive, but named 10 residing in the home.

There's Sylvester, 22, working at "odd jobs;" Ailsy, 20; Elihu, 17, helping on the farm; Pauline, 15; Laura G., 12; James A., 10; Alice V. C., nine; Agnes, four; Narrine C., three; and Sarah A., one.

Perhaps two were grandchildren. Except for the youngest, almost all could read and write.

Lovie's marked boxes on the census form tell that she was "deaf, dumb and blind." But the old midwife and woman doctor would live almost exactly six more years before being laid to rest with the other deceased pilgrims of her church.

We'll never know how many babies she helped bring into the world, how many fevers she soothed, or how many hands of friends, neighbors, and family members she held as they heaved their last breaths. We'll likely never know what her life was like as the War Between the States extracted its feast of blood in eastern North Carolina. There's much we do not know, but that solitary markers testify that Lovie McCabe was here. And an administrator's records prove she lived. And common sense tells us that as a wife, mother, grandmother, and great-grandmother, she loved and was loved.

Area burials continue:

McCray, Ambrose   AAM
He was born in 1905. He died on April 8, 1935, and was buried at CP 1, Little Witness Cemetery.

McCray, Catherine   AAF
She was born in 1911, the daughter of Josephine McCray. She died June 9, 1933, at age 21 or 22. The informant of death was Walter Nelson. She was buried at the Little Witness Baptist Church Cemetery.

McCray, John   AAM
He died on August 21, 1940, and was buried at CP 1, Little Witness.

McCray, Josephine Carter   AAF

The wife of Turner McCray, she died on July 25, 1936, at age 60, making her birth year 1876. She was the daughter of Henry Carter and mother of Catherine McCray. She was buried at Little Witness.

McCray, T. AAM

He died in 1923 and was buried at CP 1, the Little Witness Cemetery.

McCray (McCrae), Turner AAM

He was born on January 2, 1841, in Carteret County. He was a slave on a plantation between Slocum and Hancock Creek. According to local lore, he was "sold down to Georgia." He escaped because "the Lord told him to go home," and returned to Havelock. In freedom, he farmed on what is now MCAS Cherry Point. He was married to Josephine McCray. He was the great-grandfather of Katie (Mrs. Fred) Toon Nelson. He died March 2, 1928, at age 87, and was buried at CP 1, Little Witness.

Mallison –

"DIED, At Pine Grove, Craven County, Tuesday, November 1ˢᵗ, **Charles C. (Mallison)**, son of Thomas H. and Mrs. Fannie Mallison, aged two years and six months." "FUNERAL of Mr. Mallison's Child – The remains of the infant child of Mr. Thomas H. Mallison, whose death is noticed elsewhere [i.e., noted elsewhere in the same edition of the newspaper], were brought up on the afternoon train yesterday and buried in Cedar Grove Cemetery, Rev. Mr. Eason, of the Baptist Church, ministering." *Daily Commercial News*, New Bern, Thursday, November 3, 1881. Thomas Mallison was one of the county's wealthiest men; a successful farmer and business leader. His 1,400-acre farm and estate bordered Slocum Creek at "Pine Grove," which today is in the Tucker Creek / Hickman Hill vicinity of west Havelock. Mallison was often in the news simply for making a business trip to the city by train. For example, in October 1881, this appeared in a print: "T. H. Mallison, one of the principal farmers of Craven county, was in New Berne yesterday." While many farms had their own burying grounds where generations of one or several families were interred, New Bern's Cedar Grove Cemetery was the destination of choice for the county's well-to-do and socially prominent.

Area burials continue:

Manning, Larkins AAM

Believed to have been a slave before the Civil War, he was one of the settlers at Woodbridge. He purchased lots 18 and 19, totaling 14.5 acres from the American Missionary Association on January 5, 1881, for $58, or $4 per acre. His birth, death, and burial information is unknown to us. His daughter, Mary Frances Manning (1876-1925), married Amos Batts (q.v.) of Havelock.

Manning, Mary Francis, see Batts AAF
Marshall, Henry A. WM

He was the 12-year-old spy at Havelock Station featured in the *Rebel Spies of Southern Craven County* chapter of the book. He was the author of the important article *"A Boy's Recollection of the Battle of New Bern"* in 1913. The son of William H. Marshall and Sarah J. Perkins Marshall, he was born in November 1849. He had two brothers, George H. Marshall, born c. 1853, and Frank P. Marshall, born c. 1853. He was a plantation owner at Havelock, farming what is now the Greenfield Heights neighborhood. In the 1870 census, at age 20, he was listed as a law student. In 1880, he was listed as a store clerk. He married Elizabeth A. (Tatum) Harget (1862-1884) who appears to have died at the 1884 birth of their child, **Eleanor Eborn Marshall**. Eleanor became a famed New Bern school teacher and principal. She had a school, Eleanor Marshall Elementary, named in her honor. It stood at the corner of Rhem Avenue and First Street until it was demolished in the 1980s. Henry farmed and dealt in land but he worked much of his life as a professional surveyor. In 1891, he owned 784 acres at Havelock. He was a justice of the peace at Havelock for Township 6 in 1914 and a voting registrar in 1920. He died near his birthday in 1935 at age 86. He was buried at Cedar Grove Cemetery in New Bern with his wife and daughter.

Marshall, James   Lost Grave   WM

He was the father of William Marshall and the grandfather of Henry Marshall. A planter at what is today Havelock, he married Eva Brittain on August 4, 1800. It was from Joseph Brittain, thought to be his father-in-law, that James bought two parcels of land in the 1816-17 assemblage of his 600-acre plantation on the New Bern to Beaufort Road at the heads of Slocum Creek and Wolfpit Branch, where Greenfield Heights is in Havelock today. A map of his plantation appears in the chapter *Rebel Spies of Southern Craven County*. He married a second time to Mehatabel Holland, a daughter of the prosperous Holland planter family of Slocum Creek, on June 20, 1815. They had at least two sons, William, born about 1817, and James, born about 1830. We don't have birth or death dates for James. Based on his first marriage, he was probably born before 1780. In 1820, he's in the census living among neighbors named Winn, Holland, Brittain, Rowe, and others. There are five in the household plus four slaves. He appears in the 1830 and 1840 census with 11 and nine slaves respectively. In 1850, James Marshall is absent from the census and his oldest son, William, is listed as head of the household, suggesting that he had passed away in the interim. As was typical in that era, the farm had a graveyard. It would have been normal for his burial to taken place there.

Marshall, William H.   Lost Grave   WM

He was born about 1817. The son of James and Mehatabel Holland Marshall, he grew up on a large plantation at what would become Havelock. A map showing its location appears elsewhere in the book. He was one of the most prominent men of southern Craven County, a political leader, and one of the stars of our story. He inherited a 600-acre plantation from his father at the head of the SW prong of Slocum Creek. In addition to farming, he worked as a surveyor. He was skilled as a mapmaker. He invested heavily in large tracts of land. He became a member of St. John's Lodge #3, a Masonic Lodge in New Bern in 1852. Under the direction of Walter Gwynn, he was instrumental in surveying the route of the Atlantic & North Carolina Railroad from New Bern to Morehead City in 1853. He developed and became the head of a spy ring during the Civil War. His exploits are recounted in the "Rebel Spies" chapter of this book. He was the 1850 census taker for the southern end of the county. As such, he would have visited the homes of everyone in the county, and been known by all. He listed himself that year as a 33-year-old farmer with a wife, Sarah J., 26, and one infant son, Henry, age ten months. He married Sarah J. Perkins of Slocum Creek on June 1, 1847. In addition to Henry, who was born in November 1849, they had two other sons, George H., born c. 1852, and Frank P., born c. 1853. Also, in the household in 1850, was James, a 20-year-old student we believe to be his younger brother. J. H. Marshall was a lieutenant in the Confederate army during the war. He later moved to Beaufort and became a farmer. He's found there in the 1880 census at age 50, married to Ann Thomas, 45. The William H. Marshall farm value in 1850 was $900 or $2,365,200 in 2018 dollars. William Marshall owned property in New Bern and sometimes lived there. Through son Henry, he was the grandfather of the famed New Bern educator, Eleanor Marshall. Though we know a great deal about him, we don't know when he died or where he's buried. He didn't appear in the 1910 census, so it's likely he was deceased by then. We know in his advanced age he was living at the Havelock plantation with his son Henry as the head of the household. There was a large, old cemetery at the plantation. With no evidence to the contrary, it seems logical that he was buried on the farm.

Martin, Willie O.   AAM

He was born on July 30, 1907, the son of Jacob C. and Izora Whittington Martin. He was a farmer on what is now MCAS Cherry Point. He died on January 31, 1930, at age 22. He was buried at CP1, Little Witness.

Matthews, Joseph Luther   WM

He was born in 1849 and was the son of John and Mariah P. Matthews. He died in 1906. He was buried at the Oak Grove Methodist Church Cemetery on Adams Creek Road.

Moore, A. F.   AAM

Father of Nannie and Maudie Moore. Spouse of M. C. Moore. This person was mentioned on daughters' gravestones at CP 5 – 6, tract 52, the "old cemetery."

Moore, Delia   AAF

Her birth and death dates are not known. She was buried at Little Witness.

Moore, M.C.   AAF

She was the mother of Nannie and Maudie Moore and wife of A. F. Moore. She's mentioned on daughters' gravestone, at CP 5 – 6, tract 52, the "old cemetery."

Moore, Maudie E.   AAF

She was born on February 12, 1892, and died on August 30, 1898, at age six. She was the daughter of A. F. And M. C. Moore. She was buried at CP 5 – 6, tract 52, the old cemetery.

> The inscription of the double marker of the Moore children reads:
> "Our Darlings Together in Heaven"

Moore, Nannie K.   AAF

She was born on June 7, 1890. She died on July 9, 1895, at age five. She was the daughter of A. F. and M. C. Moore. She was buried at CP 5 – 6, tract 52, called the "old cemetery."

Moore, Odious   AAM

He was born on September 14, 1915, and died on March 4, 1916, at age five months. He was buried at the Little Witness Church Cemetery.

Merritt, Minnie, see Bryan

Muse, Chellie (Chelly) Lucas   WF

She was born on August 1897 in Wilson County, N.C. In 1920, she was living in Wilson County, Black Creek Township with her husband Finney Muse, a general farmer. She listed herself as a laborer on the home farm. She died in Craven County on June 18, 1921, at age 23, and was buried in the Pittman - Rowe Cemetery.

Muse, John William, Sr.   WM

He was born on April 15, 1889. He married Emma Beacham Brite in 1916 and worked as a general farm laborer. One source said he later worked in law enforcement (deputy sheriff). He had a son, Herbert A. Muse, who was in born 1919. Other children included Lesley (Leslie), Irene, Ralph, Herbert, and John. He died on November 23, 1930, at age 41, and was buried at the Rowe-Pittman cemetery.

Muse, Leslie James   WM

Born on October 5, 1911, he was the son of John William Muse, Sr. and Emma Muse. In the 1920s, he attended Havelock's one-room school. He died on November 11, 1974, and was buried at the FUMC cemetery. He was the husband of Victoria Lee and father of James, Shirley, and Thomas Muse.

Muse, Victoria May Lee   WF

She was born May 12, 1912, and died July 26, 1953. She was buried at FUMC cemetery. She was the wife of Leslie James Muse and mother of James, Shirley, and Thomas Muse.

Nelson, Athalia C. Fenner   AAF

The wife of Walter Nelson, she was born October 14, 1885. She died January 10, 1969, and was buried at Hyman Chapel, Havelock.

Nelson, Blanchia McCray   AAF

The 19-year-old married daughter of Turner and Josephine McCray died of burns on January 4, 1916, in a household accident. According to registrar E. A. Armstrong: "Death caused by fire burns. Caught fire from the fireplace where she was cooking. She turned from the fireplace to pick up her baby when her skirt caught afire. There was no one in the house but small children. She ran [*unreadable*] and when help came, she was too badly burned to live." She was born October 24, 1896. Burial was "near Melvin" on January 6, 1916. Little Witness Church Cemetery.

Nelson, Charlie   AAM

He was born in 1915 and died in 1941. He was one of the last people buried at CP 1, the Little Witness Baptist Church Cemetery.

Nelson, Dinah   AAF

According to family tradition, she was the daughter of a former slave, Eliza Jane Phillips, who escaped to freedom during the Civil War. Mrs. Nelson was born c. 1874. She lived at the Nelson Town community, which was founded by her husband, Sam B. Nelson. She died on June 18, 1939, at 65 years of age. She was a "church mother" of Little Witness Baptist. She was buried at CP 1, Little Witness. She's mentioned in the chapter *The Right of Eminent Domain*.

Nelson, Fred Lee   AAM

[*We include this obituary, more recent than the others herein, to illustrate how the Nelson family, in particular, and other families in general, have spread since the establishment of MCAS Cherry Point in 1941.*]

Fred Lee Nelson, 70, died in Queens Village, N.Y., on Friday, January 29, 2010, at the L.I. Jewish Hospital, New Hyde Park, N.Y. The son of Fred Solomon Nelson. Fred Lee was born in Havelock in 1940. He attended the New Bern City Schools. He was employed at New York City Hospital as Director of Hospital Maintenance.

His funeral service at Little Rock M.B. Church with the Rev. James Stephens, pastor, and Rev. De' Ves Toon, eulogist, officiating. Burial was at Hyman Chapel Church Cemetery, Havelock.

At the time of his 2010 death, he was survived by his wife, Mary Hill Nelson of the home; his mother, Katie Toon Nelson of Brunswick, Ga.; four sons, Fred Lee Nelson Jr. of Charlotte, Darryl Nelson of Fort Mill, S.C., Demetrius Nelson of Queens, N.Y., and Romel Nelson of Queens, N.Y.; three daughters, Lisa Watson and Rosalind Nelson of Queens, N.Y., and Lisa Harris of Virginia; six brothers, Robert Nelson of Havelock, Ramon Nelson of Willingboro, N.J., Larry Nelson of Randolph, Mass., Bishop Curtis Nelson of Stoughton, Mass., Etroy Nelson of Waldorf, Md., and Bishop

Gerald Nelson of Dorchester, Mass.; two sisters, Thelma Nelson and Mittie N. Waye, both of Brunswick, Ga.; and 10 grand-children.

Nelson, Fred Solomon   AAM

He was born on February 26, 1911, at Nelson Town near Havelock. He was the son of Walter and Penny Nelson. He married Katie Bell Toon on October 14, 1935. (Katie Toon was born March 11, 1918). After losing his home in the establishment of MCAS Cherry Point, he worked on the base for 30 years. He died October 1, 2005, and was buried at the Hyman Chapel AME Zion Church Cemetery. He is featured in two chapters in this book, *Goin' to Atlanta* and *The Right of Eminent Domain*.

Nelson, James   AAM

He died in 1929 and was buried at CP 1, Little Witness.

Nelson, Sam B.   AAM

The son of an enslaved man named Smith Nelson; Sam Nelson was born a slave in southern Craven County on March 4, 1860. He was the husband of Dinah Nelson and head of the prominent Nelson family. He grew the Nelson Town settlement on what is now Cherry Point in the early 1900s to 500 acres of land from the 75 acres purchased by his father in 1880. He was a farmer and early contract mail carrier. He served many years as deacon of Little Witness Baptist Church, Havelock. One of his children was Walter Nelson. He died September 20, 1929, and was buried at CP 1, Little Witness.

Nelson, Walter   AAM

He was born at Nelson Town, Cherry Point on December 22, 1896. He was the son of Sam B. and Dinah Nelson. He married Athalia C. Fenner. He was the father of Walter Allen Nelson (1919-1960) and Fred Solomon Nelson. He was a prosperous farmer with a substantial home on 131 acres, known as government tract 288 after its condemnation for the construction of the Marine air base. He was the leader of the Nelson Town settlement, founded by his grandfather Smith Nelson and father Sam B. Nelson. After MCAS Cherry Point opened, Nelson moved to New Bern. He owned and operated a "wood yard." He was already a widower when he died of a cerebral hemorrhage at 809 Miller Street in New Bern on December 11, 1959. He was 63. His death was reported by his son, Fred. He was buried at the Hyman Chapel AME Zion Church Cemetery in Havelock on December 16, 1959.

Norris, Corbett   WM

He was born c. 1894. He was a highway inspector on the Central Highway, which later became US 70. He retired as a foreman with N.C. Highway Department. He married Thelma Armstrong of Havelock. For his children, see Thelma Armstrong Norris below. He died at Havelock on January 21, 1973, and was buried at Gethsemane Memorial Park in Morehead City.

Norris, Thelma Lena Armstrong   WF

She was born March 8, 1909, at Havelock, the daughter of E.A. and Mattie Lena Armstrong, and granddaughter of Edward D. Russell. The family lived on Gray Road. She married Corbett Norris (1893-1973) of Beaufort. The couple was said to have had the first automobile in the Havelock area, a Model T Ford. She was featured with a photograph in *Havelock Progress* newspaper article, November 18, 1976, talking about early burials in Havelock, including that of her grandfather. She died on February 25, 1997. Her funeral service was at FUMC on Feb. 27, 1997, with burial at Gethsemane Memorial Park, Morehead City. She was survived by four sons, George Thomas Norris, John Corbett Norris, Jr., and (adopted son) Robert Hardy, all of Havelock, and Monzell Norris of New Bern; two daughters, Mattie Marie Wallace, and Betty Lou Nethercutt of Havelock, according to the *Sun Journal*. Thelma was generous in helping the author learn about Havelock's history.

Nunn, Etta, see Wynne   WF
Pate, George D.   WM
He died May 26, 1920, and was buried at CP 13, tract 461. His headstone inscribed: "In memory of George D. Pate whose stay on earth was 86 years – died May 26, 1920."

Pate, Laura C., see Wynne   WF
Paton (Paten, Payton), Redmond (Redman)   AAM
He was born c. 1866. He owned 10 acres of land on Slocum Creek (*The Daily Journal* – New Bern March 7, 1894). He died on July 26, 1926. He was 60 years of age. He was buried at CP 1, Little Witness Baptist Church.

Physioc, Eliza Hope Cox   WF
She was born circa 1789 (or 1809). She died April 1, 1839, 50 years of age (number unclear, possibly 30 years of age). She married Joseph Physioc on February 15, 1827. She is buried beside her husband in the small Physioc cemetery on U. S. Forest Service land east of Hancock Creek. White marble headstone and footstone were broken, but upright on February 26, 1984. Elegantly carved bed-board-style grave markers begin with the words "Sacred to the memory of..." There's more Physioc information in *ITSP*.

Physioc, Joseph   WM
He was born circa 1786 and married Elizabeth Hope Cox, February 15, 1827. A witness to the marriage was Elijah Clark. Physioc was a prominent plantation owner from an equally prominent family that was at the forefront of southern Craven County, business, social, and political affairs for generations. Other well-known male family members, often found in county land and estate records, included William, Peter, and Thomas Physioc. Joseph served on the county court and was a justice of the peace at Slocum Creek

Joseph Physioc's 1841 headstone, broken but upright in 1984.

c. 1811. He was presiding magistrate Craven County Court of Pleas & Quarter Sessions in 1825. His plantation was east of Hancock Creek in the Cahoogue Creek area. He died on October 27, 1841. He was 58 years, one month, and 24 days old. He's buried beside his wife, Eliza, in the Physioc cemetery. His and his wife's headstones were the only ones to survive into the modern era. A small number of sunken depressions were evident in the 1980s. Joseph's first marriage on August 30, 1805, was to Contentnea Evans, a widow. A chapter is dedicated to the Physiocs in *ITSP*.

Piner, Catherine (Catherine Piner Adams)   WF
She was born on May 31, 1910, at White Oak, Carteret County. She died on April 25, 1968, at age 58. She was buried at FUMC.

Piner, Edward L.   WM
He was born July 9, 1926, and died on January 17, 1965, at age 38. He served in the United States Naval Reserve during World War II. He was buried at FUMC.

Piner, John R.   WM
He was born on January 25, 1885, at White Oak, Carteret County. He was a farmer. He married Julia F. Buck. Their children were Ruby, born c. 1909; Catherine, born c. 1911; Walter Buck, born c. 1913; Edna, born c. 1915; and Edward L. Piner, July 9, 1926. John Piner died on January 29, 1969, and was buried at FUMC.

Piner, Julia F. Buck   WF

She was born on November 11, 1888, at White Oak, Carteret County. She died May 16, 1947. She was the wife of John R. Piner. For children, see John Piner above. She was buried at FUMC.

Pollock, Rachel   AAF
She was born at Rocky Point in Pender County, N.C. in 1897 and died at Havelock on January 7, 1935. She was buried at Little Witness.

Powell, Emma Jane Rowe Wynne   WF
She was born in November 1873. Her parents were David and Emily Susan Pittman Rowe. She married Caleb J. Wynne circa 1893. Following Caleb's early death, she married Kenyon Percy Powell in 1902. She was the mother of two Wynne children and three Powell children. She died at age 60 on March 2, 1934, and was buried in the Rowe-Pittman cemetery.

Powell, Kenyon (Kinyon) (Kinion) Percy   WM
He was born in Pamlico County on June 4, 1876. He worked in "the log woods" and became a timber foreman. He married Emma Rowe Wynne on September 7, 1902. He was the father of Rosann, Minnie F., and William A. Powell. He died on August 3, 1943, at age 67, and was buried in Rowe-Pittman Cemetery.

Prichard, Rosa Lee   AAF
She was born in 1914 and died in 1941. She was buried at the Little Witness Baptist Church Cemetery, CP 1.

Rhodes, W.H.   WM
A married man who operated a sawmill, gin, grist mill, and general store at Beech Haven in the early 1920s.

Rice, Lota Troy Hardesty, see Rice, Richard G.   WF

Rice, Richard Grantham, Sr.   WM
He was born October 18, 1901, in Beaufort and married Lota Troy Hardesty (1903-1981) of Harlowe on June 14, 1928. In the 1940s, the family lived on Miller Blvd.-Greenfield Heights Blvd. in the area of Old Havelock. He worked for the U.S. Postal Service. She was a homemaker. Richard and Lota had four children: James Dudley, Donald Darden, Richard Grantham, Jr., and Elizabeth Alice "Betty" Rice. Richard Rice, Sr. died on July 1, 1968, and is buried at Greenleaf Memorial Park at Trent Woods.

Richards, Jimmie Lee   AAM
He was buried at CP 1, Little Witness. His headstone reads "age one year eight months."

Robinson, James B.   AAM
He was born on February 8, 1877. He was the founder of the post office and postmaster at Melvin, N.C. He was married to Melvina Robinson. James and Melvina were pillars of the Little Witness community. He died on March 10, 1929, and was buried at CP 1, Little Witness Baptist Church.

Robinson, Melvina Cully   MUF

She was born near Havelock on November 15, 1875, the daughter of William Henry and Nancy E. Harkley Cully. She was married to James Robinson who founded and named the Melvin, N.C. post office, in what is now the southeast quadrant of MCAS Cherry Point, after her. They lived in the Little Witness-Melvin area. Melvina was a teacher at the African American community's "Melvin School." By the time she died at age 70 on December 19, 1945, the base had closed all the old cemeteries so she could not be buried next to her husband at Little Witness. She was interred at Evergreen Cemetery in New Bern.

Rooks, Asa David, "Acy" "A. D."   WM
He was born on September 5, 1859. He was a farmer and storekeeper, who was listed as a merchant in the *N.C. Yearbook and Business Directory* for 1914. His store and two-story house were on what is now Greenfield Heights Boulevard. He owned a farm near Lake Ellis southwest of Havelock and provided fuel wood to the Atlantic and North Carolina Railroad in concert with James A. Bryan. In 1914, he was a railway agent at Havelock. His wife was Katie Rooks. He served on the Havelock school committee. He was pronounced dead on March 30, 1927, at 68 years of age, at New Bern General Hospital, Dr. R. N. Duffy of New Bern attending. COD: hardening of the arteries. The informant of death was his son, Earle A. Rooks of New Bern. He also had sons named James, Leroy, and Cecil, and daughters, Beulah and Hazel. He was originally buried in the Havelock Christian Church yard located near the Atlantic Baptist Association parking lot at 602 Miller Blvd. He was interred beside his friend Peter Schaufhauser. A story and photo of overgrown graves appeared in *Havelock Progress of* November 18, 1976. Both graves were later moved to FUMC.

Rowe, Andrew Jackson   WM
He was born on August 21, 1871. His wife, Hattie, was born circa 1879. He was a general farmer with a large family and lived in the Lewis Farm Road area just off the Central Highway (today's US 70). His close neighbors were Ed and Ella Belangia. His children listed in the 1920 census were Minnie, 21; Etta, 16; Sallie, 12; Jim, 10; Claud, eight; and Lena, two years and two months. He died July 24, 1936, at 64 years of age. He was buried in the Rowe (Pittman) cemetery.

Rowe, David   Civil War Veteran   WM
He was born on July 30, 1843. He was a farmer who gave service in the War Between the States. He enlisted in the 10th North Carolina troops, 1st NC Artillery, in February 1862. He was the husband of Emily Susan Pittman, who was born in 1842. He was the father of Emma Jane Roe, born in 1873. He died at age 51 on February 20, 1895, and was buried in the Rowe (Pittman) cemetery west of Havelock.

Rowe, Emily Susan Pittman   WF

She was born on March 12, 1842. She married David Rowe (1843-1895) and had a daughter, Emma Jane Roe Powell (1873-1934). She died on January 9, 1913, at age 70. She was buried in the Rowe-Pittman Cemetery.

Rowe, William J.   WM

He was born on January 12, 1868. He lived at Pine Grove west of Havelock and died on March 18, 1939. He was buried at the Rowe-Pittman Cemetery.

Russell, Annie Breslin   WF

She was born in 1872 in Belfast, Ireland, the daughter of Anthony and Madge Breslin. She died June 12, 1935, at Cherry Point, N.C. She was 63. She had a strong Catholic faith and her family sometimes took a boat up Neuse River to New Bern to attend services. She was the wife of George A. Russell. Her children included Anthony, born at Havelock 1898; and Edward, Madge, Mary Lillian, and Helen, all born at Cherry Point. She served as postmistress at Cherry Point, operating the mail service from her small home. She was buried among her family at the old Cherry Point community cemetery, now known as CP 11. Flowers were on her grave when it was visited by the author on February 21, 1984.

Russell, Anthony Joseph   WM

Born in 1898, he was the son of George A. and Annie B. Russell. He was a farmer, a fisherman, a worker in the family's fishing shop at the village of Cherry Point, a fishing guide, and a caretaker at a nearby hunting lodge. He was the husband of Missouri Russell and father of Dorothy Lillian (died at birth), Verna Frances, and Vida Russell. He was a member of Woodmen of the World. He was buried at CP 11, the family cemetery near Hancock Creek. Though early European settlers and Africans, both slaves and freedmen, were interred there even before the United States was founded, Anthony J. "A.J." Russell is the last person ever buried at the village of Cherry Point, and one of the last to be buried on what is now the Marine base. Born in Havelock on December 31, 1898, he died young. Russell was just 42. But he passed from this life on May 7, 1940, surrounded by his large extended family including a wife, daughters, friends, and neighbors in the small Neuse River village next to Hancock Creek. His funeral was preached a few days later in the old community cemetery. But with the construction of the new Marine Corps base beginning, all the residents soon moved away leaving behind their homes, their farms, and their burying grounds.

Russell, Dorothy Lillian   white infant

She was born and died on October 26, 1926. She was the daughter of Anthony J. and Missouri Hill Russell. She was buried at old Cherry Point Cemetery, CP 11.

Russell, Edward Borden   WM

He was the son of G. A. Russell and Annie Breslin Russell, born at Cherry Point on December 23, 1901. He died December 27, 1911, at age 10 from a gunshot wound to his side after a gun fell from a horse-drawn farm wagon and accidentally discharged, according to Margaret Trader, 2007. He was buried at the old Cherry Point community cemetery, CP 11. Flowers were on his grave when it was visited on February 21, 1984.

More information and many photographs of the Russell family in HIHCP

Smallpox Drama Hits Russell Family at Havelock, 1902

Russell, Edward Davis   WM

He was born on November 29, 1840, in Jones County. He died on August 9, 1902, at his Havelock home. Cause of death: Smallpox. He was the third Havelock Postmaster (1881-1887). He married Sarah Meadows of Jones County. Sarah was said to have come "directly from England." They had a

MAP: Due to fear of smallpox, Edward Russell was quickly buried just out the backdoor behind his home at the southeast corner of what is today the Indian Hills subdivision, and near the Atlantic Baptist Association headquarters on Miller Boulevard. A depression in the ground and a broken headstone were still visible in March 1984. A photograph of the grave was printed in the *Havelock Progress*, 11/18/1976. More information in *HIHCP*, page 29. (*EBE map 1984*)

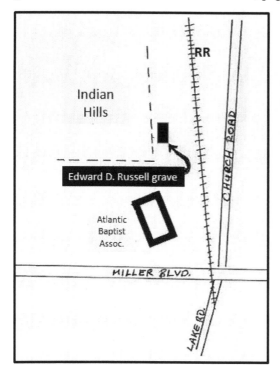

Farmer, postmaster, and smallpox victim, Edward D. Russell. His gravesite map at left.

daughter, Mattie Lena in 1882. After Sarah's early death, his second marriage was to Rebecca Jane Garner. They had a son, Richard, and a daughter, Sallie. He was the grandfather of Thelma Armstrong Norris, Zippiette Elizabeth Armstrong Eloise Armstrong, and others.

The death from smallpox of Russell, a well-known citizen of the county and former postmaster, created quite a bit of public concern and the newspapers both criticized the handling of the matter and simultaneously tried to reassure the public that everything was well-in-hand. During the crisis, the *New Berne Weekly Journal* expressed concern. From the August 8, 1902 issue:

"There is another cause for complaint in this matter. Last Monday a doctor was in town who was attending the case of smallpox in Havelock. He was under the influence of liquor and though he may have taken precautions against the infection he should not have been allowed to travel out of his town and after he arrived here his own talk was sufficient to put him under quarantine.

"The person at Havelock was reported yesterday to be in a dying condition; that being the case, the doctor's presence in this city on Monday was extremely hazardous. The doctor was warned in the town of Newport not to mingle with people and on his continuing to disregard their wishes he was placed in the guardhouse there Wednesday."

As published in *The Farmer and Mechanic*, Raleigh, N.C., the Associated Press carried the story *Havelock Mail Ordered Fumigated* on August 9, 1902, with the dateline of Washington, D. C.:

"It developed today that the case in a post office building and North Carolina exists at Havelock, and not at New Bern, as stated yesterday. The postmaster at Havelock, John I. Russell, has a serious case of smallpox. Railway mail officials have ordered that all mails from there be fumigated, and the supplies of the office have been ordered destroyed after an accounting has been made."

Thus, the Associated Press corrected the location but gave the wrong name for the Havelock postmaster. An announcement of the death in *The Daily Journal*, published at New Bern the next day, Aug. 10, 1902, carried sad news but was calculated to reassure a scared public:

"Edward Russell, the small pox patient at Havelock, died yesterday morning. He was the father of the postmaster there and is said to have lived in part of the building [i.e., the post office was within the Russell home]. Mr. Russell died in the pest house [i.e., the house where the smallpox was] and everything that was contaminated with the disease during his sickness will be properly disposed of."

A newspaper called *The Goldsboro Headlight* carried this report on April 14, 1902. "The post office at Havelock, Craven County, has been ordered by the government to be burned on account of a fatal case of smallpox which afflicted the postmaster."

The local records of the Havelock postal services don't always match with the official records of the National Archives. Other facts sometimes don't match up either. For example, when Edward Russell became ill with smallpox in 1902, it was reported far and wide that he'd contracted the disease through his mail handling duties. The post office was fumigated, according to news reports, and then ordered to be burned. It's doubtful that the burning occurred since the mail was being dispensed from a room of the Russell home adjacent to the train tracks. Nevertheless, news accounts were published stating that John I. Russell, who's in the official records as the postmaster at Havelock during that time, had died of smallpox. In further confusion, the modern brick post office, which is now City Hall in New Bern, was ordered to be burned because it was thought the smallpox outbreak was there. Fortunately, the order was quickly countermanded.

Russell, Marcus Frank   WM
He was born in 1884. He married Beulah L. Rooks in 1908. He died on Monday, September 7, 1942, at age 58. His funeral was held at FUMC on September 8, 1942. He was buried in the "family graveyard" at the church but never got a permanent marker. His obituary was published in *The Times* (New Bern) on September 11, 1942. The son of Edward D. and Sarah Russell, he had been a hunters' guide for many visiting celebrities and built the first "filling station" at what was then the fork of Highway 70 and the old Beaufort Road (Highway 101). This location is across the street from the current main gate of Cherry Point, where a real estate office was located in 2020. According to SHC interviews with residents of that era, the Russell station also sold groceries and was the store of convenience for people at Tar Neck, Nelson Town, and Little Witness. The only local competition was Trader's store. According to Mrs. Bobby Hardy (Sandra), Thelma Armstrong's uncle, Frank Russell,

operated a small café or "coffee shop" at the store in the 1930s and early 1940s. Dogs would lay on the floor. Frank had a monkey. Thelma's sister, Zippiette, "used to tell how the customers didn't like the way the monkey would swing down from the curtains" and put his hand in the sugar bowls. "He always had quarters in his pocket when no one else did." Mrs. Hardy said. "Uncle Frank liked to hang around with famous people. Babe Ruth took a drink of liquor in our old house kitchen with Uncle Frank. Bud Fisher who wrote a cartoon strip for the funny papers used to walk up and down Gray Road with Babe Ruth when they stayed at Camp Bryan." Russell was also known to have been associated with the moonshine trade. According to his obituary article, Russell "was born and reared in the Havelock section of the county" and was "one of the best-known residents." After operating the service station for many years, he moved to Tennessee but had come home ill several months before his death. According to The Times: "Surviving the deceased are his widow, Leona Russell, and two children, Frank, Jr., and Rudene, a daughter. There is also a brother, James E. Russell of Cambridge, Md., and two sisters, Mrs. Mattie Armstrong of Havelock and Mrs. Sally Wynne of Four Holes, S.C." He is featured with a photograph of the "filling station" in *HIHCP*.

Russell & Rooks: A dramatic (and romantic) elopement

"The [New Berne Weekly] Journal has received news of a clandestine marriage of Havelock. Sunday, Mr. Frank Russell of Cherry Point, and Miss Beulah [L. Rooks], the attractive daughter of Mr. A. D. Rooks, of Havelock, being the happy conspirators.

The parents of the young people were violently opposed to the union and thought they had broken up the courtship. Mr. Russell had dutifully left home and secured employment at Oriental, many miles away and across a wide river from the home of his heart's delight. She had apparently forgotten the very existence of her true knight and lover.

Miss Rook is, or was, the organist at the chapel at Havelock. Sunday school met at 2 o'clock and the pretty musician was at her instrument. During the reading exercises she was seen to quietly retire from the room, and when the time came for more music the organ was dumb, and Miss Beulah was o'er the river, and far away with Frank...

It transpired that a number of Mr. Russell's friends at Oriental, appreciating the situation and sympathizing with his forlorn condition, gallantly manned a couple of launches, took him aboard, and steered the course to the land over which his star of hope was shining.

A landing was made on the banks of the creek near the chapel and a secret emissary dispatched to confer with the lady who soon made an appearance, and amid a profuse shower of congratulations, the reunited lovers embarked and sailed away to the shiny shores of Pamlico County, were standing upon the bow of their rocking vessel, they were joined together in the bonds of holy wedlock...

It is said that the parents were [inclined] to take to the warpath and overtake their disobedient children, but the broad waters of the Neuse intervening, they returned to their homes and early became reconciled. An invitation to return has been extended and forgiveness promised." [as published June 9, 1908]

Russell, George Allen WM
He was the leading man of the old village of Cherry Point where Hancock Creek met the Neuse River. He was born on June 9, 1876. He worked in 1900 as an "edger" at Webber-Reems Sawmill at Cherry Point. He was a farmer, and widowed, at the time of his death. COD: acute myocarditis, according to G. M. Henderson, the coroner. He was the husband of Annie Breslin Russell and the son of Edward D. Russell and Sarah Meadows Russell. He died on June 14, 1936, at 60 years of age. His funeral service was at Cherry Point, June 15, 1936, with Catholic priests officiating; Father Gorman of Morehead City and Father Julian of New Bern. A membership in Woodmen of the World is noted on his gravestone. Flowers were on his grave when it was visited on February 21, 1984. From obituary in *The Beaufort News* of June 18, 1936: "His late wife proceeded him to the grave by one year. Surviving is one son, A. J. Russell of Havelock, and three daughters, Mrs. Darrow Wetherington, Mrs. John J. Trader, Havelock, and Mrs. Eugene Blalock, Raleigh. Interment of the body was made in the family burial grounds at Cherry Point." He was buried at the old Cherry Point community cemetery (CP 11, tract 439) near Hancock Creek.

Russell, John I. WM
He was the Havelock Postmaster from June 1898 to July 1914, according to USPS records, National Archives, page 170. He was born in Jones County on January 28, 1872. He was the son of Edward D. and Sarah Meadows Russell, both of Jones County. He was married to Ida Russell. He was a farmer. He died on January 19, 1921, at 48 years of age. COD: heart failure. He had been ill for a month. He was a member of Woodmen of the World. He was buried at FUMC.

Russell, Mattie Lena, see Armstrong.

Russell, Missouri Hill WF
She was born in 1904 and the wife of Anthony J. Russell. She taught at the old school at Cherry Point. She had a daughter, Dorothy Lillian, who died at birth in 1926. She was the mother of Verna Francis, born in December 1929, and Vida, born in 1934. Death and burial information unclear.

Russell, Rebecca Jane Garner, "Becky" WF

She was born March 11, 1854 (Census says March 11, 1855). She was the second wife of Edward D. Russell. They married c. 1890. She was widowed at her husband's death of smallpox in 1902. She was the mother of Sallie E. Russell (Wynne) and Richard C. Russell. She was postmistress at Havelock following her husband's death (1910, 1920 U.S. Census) and, assisted by son Richard, as a "mail carrier" c. 1910. She lived in a house on Gray Road, old Havelock. She was a member of the household of C.M. and Sallie Wynne in 1930 at age 76. She died March 4, 1936, and was buried at FUMC. She's in a family portrait in *HIHCP*.

Russell, Richard C.   WM
He was born on February 27, 1893. He was the son of Edward D. and Rebecca J. G. Russell. He's listed in the 1910 census as a Havelock mail carrier. He was a member of Woodmen of the World. He died on July 5, 1913, and was buried at FUMC. His portrait as a child is in *HIHCP*.

Russell, Sarah "Sallie" E., see Wynne   WF
Russell, Wilbur L.   White infant
He was born on July 8, 1912, and died on September 13, 1912. He was the son of M. Frank and Beulah L. Russell. Died of "Fever, probably malarial in origin." He was buried at FUMC.

Russell, Veda Kathleen   WF
She was the daughter of Anthony and Missouri Russell, born at Cherry Point, September 14, 1932. She later lived in "old Havelock school" after it was moved to the corner of Miller Boulevard and Lake Road. Married name Veda Garner. Died June 20, 2004. Buried at Morehead (Greenwood).

Sampson, David   AAM
He was born a slave in Riverdale on September 5, 1853. "Dave" lived to the age of 78. He was a famous and popular cook at Camp Bryan in the lakes section near Havelock. He married Mary Jane Mitchell and they had four children: a son, Alfred, and three daughters, Annie, Effie, and Rose. He was buried in the Mount Olive Cemetery at Riverdale in January 1932, near the Fisher Plantation where he was born. He's featured in the chapter of this book called *Making Ends Meet, 1890-1940*.

Schaufhauser (Schoffhauser), Peter   WM
He was born in Yugoslavia in the 1870s. He immigrated to the United States about 1905. He listed his occupation in the census as a carriage maker. Around Havelock, he worked as a handyman and "bee raiser." He was a friend and/or employee of A. D. Rook. He died on November 5, 1934. COD: acute alcoholism and high blood pressure. He was buried in the Havelock Christian churchyard on old Beaufort Road (today's Greenfield Heights Blvd.) by Rook's grave. Both of the graves were later moved to FUMC. A story about the graves' discovery with photographs is in the *Havelock Progress*, November 18, 1976.

Shelton, Cornelia Belangia   WF

She was born July 15, 1850, in Craven County. She was the wife of Joseph Shelton but was widowed by the time of her death. She passed away on April 12, 1916. She was 66. She was buried at FUMC. She was the daughter of William Belanger of Edgecombe County. On the death certificate, the mother's name is listed as "unknown" even though the informant of death was William Belanger of Cherry Point. The cause of her death was listed as pneumonia.

Shelton, Joseph   WM

He was born on September 8, 1846. He was a farmer at Havelock and married to Cornelia Shelton. He died of pneumonia on October 10, 1915, at Fairview Hospital in New Bern. He was 69. He was buried at FUMC.

Shute, Almira "Ellie" Cordelia Holland   WF

She was born into the locally prominent Holland family on December 10, 1854. Nicknamed "Ellie," she was the wife of Macon Metts "Make" Shute, a farmer, and timberman, born 1858. She was the mother of daughters, Mettie, who was born 1888; Freddie P., born 1890, (next page); and Effie C., born 1892. Family members said she was "a good cook and a good neighbor." She liked to fish and make clothes for herself and her daughters. Mrs. Shute died of a stroke on May 9, 1916. Thus, according to their carved stone markers, in a period of just over two months, 57-year-old Mack Shute buried first his wife, and then one of his three daughters on

Descendant of a local pioneer family, Ellie Holland Shute, at left, was the mother of Freddie Shute, following page. Mother and daughter died just weeks apart in 1916.

a silent bluff above the Neuse River in the old Lovick-Magnolia Plantation Cemetery.

Shute, Fred Pauline   WF
She was born March 4, 1890, the daughter of Macon Metts and Cordelia A. Shute, above. She got her odd name in honor of an uncle who died young. She called herself "Freddie" and told people her middle name was *Palmetta*. Like her mom, she was a talented seamstress. She worked as a salesperson at the Kress retail store in downtown New Bern and also worked at the Wooten photo studio. She died July 20, 1916, of a kidney infection just two months after her mother's funeral. She was buried in the old Lovick graveyard overlooking the beautiful Neuse.

Singleton, Marietta   AAF
Died on February 28, 1935. Buried at CP 1, Little Witness. No other data found.

Simmons, Lila Wynne   WF
She was born on July 1, 1914, at Havelock. She was the daughter of W.J. Wynne, Sr. and Maude Wood Wynne. She grew up on Gray Road and her father's farm in the middle of what is today modern Havelock with her sister, Elaine, and brothers, W.J., Jr., and Clay Wynne. She married Roland Cornell Simmons (1911-1964). She died on March 2, 1995, at the age of 80. Mrs. Simmons was kind in teaching the author about old Havelock. Among many other things, she told of how, as a child, she helped her father pump water from Slocum Creek into a big wooden water tower beside the railroad tracks for the resupply of steam locomotives that stopped twice daily. She is buried beside her husband at the Amariah Garner Memorial Cemetery in Newport.

Simmons, no first name   WM infant
The child of R. C. and Delila Simmons was born and died on April 30, 1941. Burial was at FUMC.

Smith, Cedric   AAM
He was born circa 1901. He lived in a cinder block house on Highway 70 between Westbrook and Ketner Heights. See *Havelock Progress* newspaper article, November 23, 1976.

Smith, James Ambrose   WM

He was born on December 31, 1900. He was a native of Oklahoma. He was a first sergeant in the United States Marine Corps Reserve during World War II. He died on February 26, 1956, and was buried at FUMC.

Sparks, Unknown   Male   **Now identified in Chapter 1**
A former Cherry Point landowner and resident, Emma Hill Stevens, reported that a man named Sparks was buried in the small cemetery of unmarked graves called CP 4, Tract 235-A. No other details about the man were remembered. Now identified in Chapter 1.

Stevens, Emma Hill   AAF
She was born on May 29, 1891. She was a Little Witness resident and landowner and identified in the ARC Study of 1985. She appears on Cherry Point Property Map of 1941 as the owner of 21.3-acre Tract 475. She died on January 26, 1976, and was buried at the Hyman Chapel AME Zion Church cemetery in Havelock.

Stowe, Herbert DeLambert   WM
He was a Charlotte businessman who owned a 3,000-acre farm at Havelock 1880s. He was born on September 22, 1831, at Stoweville in Gaston County NC. He was a school teacher before he joined the 37th N.C. Regiment. He was made captain of the commissary on March 13, 1861, at New Bern on the staff of Col. C.C. Lee. He participated in the Battle of New Bern but resigned on July 25, 1862, due to a medical condition. He was a Gaston County farmer, a wealthy Charlotte businessman, a magistrate, judge, and state legislator. He became chairman of Farmers Mutual Fire Insurance. His visits to New Bern, his real estate purchases, and his farm advice were noted in *New Bern Daily Journal*. He was involved in a lawsuit with the Bryce family. His death on February 8, 1907, at age 75, was front-page and second-page news in *The Charlotte News*. He is buried at the Steele Creek Presbyterian Church Cemetery in Charlotte.

Sutton, unknown
The birth and death dates, sex, and race unidentified. The burial was at Little Witness.

Sykes, Daisie Bell   AAF Infant
She was born May 6, 1927, though Craven County death certificate No. 478 lists May 7, 1927. She was the daughter of Jessie and Nicie (Nicy) Johnson Sykes, the granddaughter of Moses and Kissie Sykes. She died May 12, 1927, when she was just six days old. COD: whooping cough. She was buried at CP1, the Little Witness Baptist Church Cemetery.

Sykes (Sikes), Ennis   Lost Grave   AAM
He was born in June 1845. In the census of 1870, at age 25, he is married to Ruthie Sikes, 24, and they have a baby daughter, Julia, age 3. He's shown as a farm laborer. Ennis was later the husband of Nancy Paton (Peyton) Sykes, who he married c. 1885. He lived on Tar Neck Road at Little

Witness. He was a farmer, who could not read or write, but owned his farm free and clear. By 1910, he had nine children of which five were living. Known children were Nancy, born April 1887; John, born July 1889; Freeman, born March 1891; and Ann M., born June 1897. He died before 1924 but other death and burial information is unknown.

Sykes, Kizia (Kissie) (Kizzie) Styles   AAF

She's become, for better or worse, Havelock-Cherry Point's best-known ghost story; a tale of her nightly prowls in search of her lost children. Some of these "reports" can be found on the internet; even on MCAS Cherry Point's official website. Despite all that, little is known about her. What facts there are sometimes conflict. Her name is found as *Kissie* on her gravestone, and as Kizzie and Kisia in census records. We know that she was the daughter of Elizabeth Styles, yet one authoritative source gives her name as Kitsann *Turner*. She was born in May 1877, according to the 1910 census; 1878 from the 1910 census; or 1876-77 from the 1920 census. Her headstone disagrees with all the census records. At CP 1, Little Witness, it read "Age 40 Yrs." Adding 40 from the census ages would mean her death came sometime between 1916 and 1918, but the 1920 census shows her alive at age 44. Her death certificate of May 2, 1929, gives her name as "Kizzy" and states that she was 46. That would make her birth year 1883. The cause of death was listed as "acute food poisoning." She married Moses Sykes. Their children were Benjamin, born in December 1898; Jessie, 1903-1970; Henry, born c. 1906; and Moses, Jr., born c. 1909. All of them appear to have reached adulthood. In the 1900 census, Kissie is listed as a "laundress." Benjamin and Jessie are listed in the 1920 census as lumber company laborers. The 58-year-old mother-in-law "Lizzie" Styles, a widow, is shown in the Sykes household in 1920. They lived in the Tar Neck settlement. *Mose* Sykes is listed on the Cherry Point property map as the owner of 19-acre Tract 529, which would have put the Sykes's home near the intersection of today's Sixth Avenue and A Street in the heart of Cherry Point's industrial area. The name Sykes is likely to have come down from a white, slave-owning family with a plantation on Slocum Creek. Slaves often took on the family name of their owner. Jacob Sykes was an early white settler on land that includes a small bay on the east side of the creek, known to this day as Sykes Gut. This site lies in proximity to the land owned by Moses Sykes and with Kissie Sykes's original burial place ... where witnesses swear they've seen her ghost.

Sykes, Moses   Lost Grave   AAM

He was born in October 1873, according to census records. He was born in 1880, per his death certificate. He was the son of Ben and Mary Sykes of Havelock. He was a farmer and "timber piler" for a lumber company. He married Kissie Ann Styles. Their children are listed in *Kissie Sykes* above.

He died on October 15, 1935, at age 55, per his death certificate. COD: apoplexy, which is unconsciousness or incapacity resulting from a cerebral hemorrhage or stroke. While his death certificate No. 13 states that his burial was at Little Witness Cemetery, Havelock, his gravesite was unmarked and the exact location is unknown. He is not listed in records of Cherry Point burials for 1941 or 1985.

Sykes, Moses C. (Moses Sykes, Jr.)   AAM
The son of Kitsann and Moses Sykes, he was born December 12, 1910, at Havelock. He worked as a laborer, died at age 26, and was buried at the Little Witness Baptist Church Cemetery.

Sykes, (Sikes) Nancy Paton   AAF
She was born on May 1855 or 1856. Her mother was Bettie Paton. She was the wife of farmer Ennis Sykes. They married c. 1885 at her mother's house. They lived on Tar Neck Road near Little Witness. By 1910, they had nine children of which five were living. Children known include Nancy, born April 1887; John, born July 1889; Freeman, born March 1891; and Ann M., born June 1897. Nancy Sikes died on February 25, 1924, at age 68. By the time of her death, she was a widow, so Ennis was no longer alive. She was buried at CP 1 Little Witness.

Sykes (Sikes), The Missing   Lost Graves   AAM&F
The Sykes family was large and many of them are unaccounted for. From the 1870 census, living next door to Ennis Sikes was Riley Sikes, 24, his wife Eliza, 25, and daughter, Francis, aged one. Also, nearby, was Simon Sikes, 35; Silva, 25, female; and Freeman Sikes, 19; Anthony Sikes, 65; Chaney (Chancy), 25, female; John, aged one. The men were listed as farm laborers; the women, "keeping house." In 1880, there was Lucy, 40, and Julia, 13. In 1910, Annie, 11. None of their burials are known.

Tate, Hannah McCray   AAF
She was born in 1902, the daughter of J. C. McCray of Halifax, N.C. and Josephine Carter of Craven County. She was a widow by the time she died at 32. She was buried at the Little Witness Church Cemetery.

Taylor, Alvina Canady (Cully)   AAF
She was born on March 31, 1874 (Death certificate said March 1, 1873). She was the daughter of Alvin Canady of Pitt County and Sylvia Orum of Carteret County. She married Charles Taylor. The informant of death was William A. Cully of New Bern. She died at age 51 on February 27, 1925, and was buried at CP, Little Witness Baptist Church Cemetery.

Taylor, Carolina, see Godwin   WF
Taylor, Rachel, see Deport   WF
Thompson, Julia Berry   AAF
She was born in 1905 in Havelock and died on February 19, 1939. She was the daughter of William Berry and Betty J. Nelson Berry, both of Havelock.

She married Billie Thompson. She worked as a domestic and cook. She died of pneumonia. She was buried at CP, Little Witness Church.

Thorpe, Benjamin W.   WM
"Died. At his residence in this county, on the 21ˢᵗ ultimo [*last month*], Mr. Benj. W. Thorpe, about 40 years." – New Bern *Union*, December 1, 1856. Benjamin W. Thorpe, a long-time resident of the village of Hancock Creek, was one of the county's wealthiest men and largest land holders. He was born c. 1816 – 1819. His wife was Eliza H. Whitehead. "In Carteret County, on the 28ᵗʰ August [1840], by J. W. Hunt, Esq., Mr. Benj. Wm. Thorpe to Miss Eliza Hope Whitehead." *Newbern Spectator*, September 5, 1840. The marriage bond was issued in Craven County, on February 26, 1841. Their children were Sarah V., born c. 1844 (seamstress, 1860 census); Caroline R., born c. 1846; Margaret H., born 1848 (or 1850); William B., born c. 1850; Julia F., born c. 1854; John D., born. c. 1856; Benjamin Thorpe died "at his residence in this county" on November 21, 1856; at age "about" 40, per *The Weekly Union* (New Bern). His burial is likely to have been in what we now call Cherry Point cemetery no. 7 (CP 7). His children were taken in by farm neighbors, Benjamin F. and Elizabeth Borden of Cherry Point. All were living in the same household 1860 census.

Thorpe, Caroline R.   WF
She was born on July 8, 1846, and died on January 30, 1867, age 20 years, six months, and 22 days. She was the daughter of Benjamin William and Elizabeth H. W. Thorpe. She was buried At CP 7, tract 540.

Thorpe, Edwin D.   WM
He owned a large plantation on Hancock Creek and more land at Clubfoot Creek and the real Cherry Point. He married Sidney Ann Read on February 28, 1846. He was one of the schoolhouse petitioners in 1849. We don't have his birth and death dates but his estate was filed in 1851.

Thorpe (Thorp), John M.   WM
He was born c. 1847. He was the son of Benjamin William and Elizabeth Hope Whitehead Thorpe. He was the brother of Caroline R. Thorpe and Margaret Thorpe Fisher. He died at the Stewart Sanatorium, New Bern, on November 2, 1907. He was 60. COD: Pneumonia. He was interred at the family burying ground, Hancock Creek, on November 3, 1907 (CP 7).

Tolson, Benjamin F.   WM
He was born on October 28, 1849. Benjamin Tolson and his family moved to Havelock in early 1891 to engage in farming and the mercantile business. Tolson, a widower, took over the operation of a store previously owned by Collins H. Hunter, a merchant and Havelock postmaster. After two years he moved back to New Bern. *The New Bern Weekly Journal* reported Thursday, January 18, 1894: *"Death of Mr. B. F. Tolson. Mr. Benjamin F. Tolson died at his residence in this city at 1 AM Tuesday the 16ᵗʰ of catarrhal*

pneumonia, aged 44 years. Mr. Tolson was the brother of Mr. J. J. Tolson, a prominent merchant of New Berne. He lived for a number of years in the city, but the last three years he spent in farming— two at Havelock and one at Bellair" [a large plantation farm west of the city of New Bern]. He died January 16, 1894, and was buried at the Wildwood Community Cemetery, Carteret County, N.C.

Tolson, James Henry, Capt., CSA WM

He was born on September 3, 1841, the son of Vine Allen Tolson, Sr. and Abigail Oglesby of Croatan. He was a veteran of the War Between the States serving in Company B, 67 NC Infantry. He was instrumental in the Confederate intelligence operations at New Bern. After his service, he taught at the Harlowe Creek Academy and Newport's Peabody School. He never married. He died on September 23, 1875, at age 34. He is buried in the Tolson Cemetery in Croatan National Forest west of Havelock. The exact location is a secret. Capt. Tolson is mentioned in the *Rebel Spies* chapter of the book.

Tolson, Vine Allen, Sr. WM

Upon his death on September 16, 1889, the *Daily Journal* of New Bern eulogized Vine Allen Tolson in a rare front-page obituary. "Through the seventy-seven years of his history he has served the people long and faithfully as a magistrate and school committee-man," the Journal said. "It can truly be written over his grave, here lies an honest man." Born on February 1, 1813, he became a mainstay farmer at both Croatan and Havelock. He was twice married, and the father of a large brood. He donated the land for the Croatan Presbyterian Church. He was descended from Craven County settlers who worked the land at Otter Creek in the early 1700s. He was named after a famous county politician and banker, Vine Allen. He was dedicated to the creation and perfection of the "common schools" serving on the local board for decades. Tolson was said to

Vine Allen Tolson

be bright, entertaining, and well-read. By the time of his death, he owned 750 acres of farmland in southern Craven County. He's buried among family in the Tolson Cemetery at Croatan.

Tolson Cemetery – Some other burials.

Elizabeth Hardison (1811-1886)

Holland M. Tolson (1824-1899), wife of Vine Allen Tolson, Sr.

Elijah R. Tolson (1858-1925)

Robert E. Lee Tolson (1865-1930), son of V.A. Tolson, Sr.

Toon, Marland   AAM infant

This baby was born January 10, 1925, and died on January 19, 1925, aged nine days. Burial was at CP, Little Witness.

Toon, Walter M.   AAM child

He was born circa 1919 and died at seven years old on December 7, 1926. He was buried at CP 1, Little Witness Baptist Church Cemetery.

Toon, Webster   AAM child

He was born on May 15, 1919, and died on December 8, 1926. It has been suggested to us that this was possibly *Mike W. Toon*, grandson of Mike and Martha Toon. The child was buried at CP1, Little Witness Cemetery.

Trader, Earnest Ives   WM infant

He was born and died on January 21, 1905, the son of J. J. Trader and Lula Trader. He was buried at FUMC.

Trader, Elsie Willis   WF

She was born on August 16, 1905. She was the wife of Hugh A. Trader. She was co-operator of Trader's Store in Havelock until her husband's death in 1961 and its sole operator afterward. She died on October 3, 1981. Her funeral service was held at FUMC on October 6, 1981. Her burial followed at Bay View Cemetery, Morehead City. She was survived at death by her daughter, Cherry Trader Roycraft of Havelock, and son, Hugh A Trader, Jr. of Waukegan, Ill.

Trader, Hugh Arlington   WM

He was born on April 30, 1899. He was the son of John Jesse Trader, a farmer from Virginia, and Lula Ives Trader of Riverdale. His siblings included John, Harris, Louise Margaret (later Mrs. William Jackson), Allen, and Ivey Elizabeth (later Mrs. Lewis Bryan). In 1920, Hugh was a farm laborer. His first wife, Dora Stevenson, was the daughter of J.J. Stevenson of Bellair. She died in a Norfolk hospital at 1 P.M August 24, 1925. Her body arrived in New Bern by train the same evening. The funeral and burial, "attended by a large crowd from the community" were the following day at Beech Grove Church in New Bern. He later married Elsie May Willis c. 1928. The couple had two children, Cherry and Hugh, Jr. In 1930, Trader listed himself as a merchant. By 1940, he was the owner of a "retail grocery store." He was the proprietor and operator of locally-famous Trader's Store on Central Highway 10. He died of cancer on November 30, 1961. He was 62. His funeral service was at FUMC on December 2, 1961. His burial was at Bay View Cemetery in Morehead City. Rev. R. L. Pugh and Rev. Woody Caviness officiated. Masonic honors were conducted at the graveside. Mrs. Trader continued operation of the country store after her husband's death.

Trader, John Jesse   WM

He was born October 24, 1865, in Accomack County, Virginia, the son of John T. and Elizabeth Harris Trader. He grew up on the family farm, the third of seven children. He moved to Havelock with a lumber company in the 1890s. He married Lula Ives of Riverdale on May 28, 1898. The marriage would last for 49 years. In 1900, the family was in Black River, Georgetown, S.C. where Trader was working as logging superintendent. His children included Hugh, age one, and a second son, John J., born in S.C. Other children, all born in N.C., were Horace, Louise, Allen, and Ivy. In the 1910 census, his profession was listed as "Lumberman." According to a news account, "he spent many years in the lumber business and owned numerous acres of farming land in the Havelock-Cherry Point area." He died at home on May 18, 1947, at age 82, "following an extended illness." His death certificate listed his occupation as "Farmer" in "rural Township 6." COD: Bronchial pneumonia. Dr. Manly Mason of Newport, attending. He was survived by two daughters, Mrs. Wm. E. (Louise Margaret Trader) Jackson and Mrs. Lewis M. (Ivey Elizabeth Trader) Bryan of Havelock. Four sons, Hugh A. and John J. Trader of Havelock, Allen T. Trader of Newport, and Horace B. Trader of Raleigh. His funeral services were on May 19, 1947, at the Shaw-Harris Funeral Chapel with Baptist minister Rev. Robert L. Pugh officiating. Interment followed at Cedar Grove Cemetery, New Bern.

Trader, Lula Ives   WF

She was born on October 7, 1876, in Township 6, Craven County. She was the daughter of W. Henry Ives of Craven County and Louisa Caraway Ives of Pamlico County. She was the youngest of four children. Her mother died when she was a small child. In the 1880 Craven County census, her name is given as *Louisa*. Her father was a farmer at Havelock. She would live at Riverdale, Black River-Georgetown, S.C., and Havelock. She married John Jesse Trader, 34, of Virginia, on May 28, 1898. She was 21. The ceremony was performed by Methodist minister Rev. F. S. Becton at the home of her brother Bryan. For children, see J.J. Trader above. They made their home in Havelock. She died on November 17, 1951, at Kafer Memorial Hospital, Broad Street, New Bern. Her funeral service was on November 18, 1951, at the Shaw-Pollock funeral chapel. Rev. R.L. Pugh of New Bern and Rev. Langill Watson, pastor of "Havelock Methodist Church" (FUMC) officiated. Her pallbearers were Amos Connor, William Tolson, Dewey Connor, Clyde Connor, Charles Jackson, and Joe Hughes. Her survivors were the same as John Jesse Trader above. Her burial was at Cedar Grove Cemetery in New Bern.

Utley, Jacob, and Aplis   WM/F

A Free Will Baptist minister from Wake Forest, Jacob Utley was born in Raleigh on November 6, 1803. He was the owner of the 615-acre plantation at Havelock that became the American Missionary Association's Woodbridge station. His wife, Aplis, was born in Jones County in 1810. They married in 1851. Rev. Utley was a member of St. John's Masonic Lodge of New Bern from 1846. During the Civil War, he conducted a small school in the Silas Webb House in Morehead. Late in life, the Utleys took up residence at the Baptist Children's Home in Thomasville, which was intended to become a "home for aged ministers." No other ministers ever came. Aplis died on March 12, 1888. Jacob died sixteen days later, March 28, 1888. Both are buried in "God's Little Acre" at the state children's home.

Wallace, Hester   AAF
Possibly buried in Batts cemetery. See *Havelock Progress* newspaper, November 1976.

Weaver, A.N.   Lost Grave   WM
He was the proprietor of a sawmill at Cherry Point, having moved from Pennsylvania in 1890. He was drowned when a schooner hauling wood was overturned and broken up in a gale in the Neuse River near Cherry Point on Wednesday, November 8, 1893. Two other men of Clubfoot Creek, Lewis, and Cull Willowby, also drowned. The next day, Weaver's body "was recovered and buried at Cherry Point, his home since moving to this locality about three years ago," according to the *Daily Journal* of New Bern of November 12, 1893. He was unmarried and about 35 years old. No record of his grave is known. More details in the *Perils* section of this book.

Wetherington, Darrow   Lost Grave   WM
He was the father of Annie Virginia Wetherington and husband of Madge Wetherington. We were told years ago that he was thought to have been buried at Cherry Point, but the date and location were unknown. No other information was then available. Now we know that Amos Darrow Wetherington was born April 14, 1895, at Havelock, N.C. His father and mother were Amos T. and Virginia "Ginny" Eubanks Wetherington. He married Madge Breslin Russell and they had three daughters, Marie, Grace Hughlene, and Annie Virginia. Annie died three months short of her second birthday. In 1940, the family lived on the "Cherry Point Road," which at the time meant the road from Highway 101 to the village of Cherry Point at the Neuse River and Hancock Creek. "Darrow" died of pneumonia at Duke Hospital in Durham on January 13, 1960. He was 64. His death certificate said that his wife, Madge, was already deceased and that he would be buried at the "Family Cemetery," Havelock. The cemetery where other family members are buried, including two-year-old Annie, was on MCAS Cherry Point, which had been closed to burials since 1941. His funeral services were by

Willis & Ballard Funeral Home in New Bern, today's Cotten Funeral Home. After extensive searching, his place of burial remains unknown.

Wetherington, Madge WF

We were told years ago that she was thought to have been buried at Cherry Point, but the date and location are unknown. No other information was available. We have found that she was born Madge Breslin Russell at the village of Cherry Point on October 28, 1903. She was the daughter of George Allen Russell and Annie Breslin Russell. She was the sister of Anthony J. Edward, Madge, Mary Lillian, and Helen Russell. She married Amos "Darrow" Wetherington and had three daughters, Marie, Grace Hughlene, and Annie Virginia. Annie died three months short of her second birthday. In 1940, the family lived on the "Cherry Point Road," which at the time meant the road from Highway 101 to the village of Cherry Point at the Neuse River and Hancock Creek. They lived next door to Madge's brother A.J. and his wife, Missouri G. Hill Russell. Madge died at her residence on November 9, 1954, after being sick with cancer for two years. She was 51. Her death certificate states that she was buried two days later at the "Wetherington Family Cemetery." The location is not known to us but it could not have been at Cherry Point. Burials ended there in 1941.

Wetherington, Annie Virginia WF child

She was born on July 20, 1922, the daughter of Darrow and Madge Wetherington. She died on April 13, 1924. Her cause of death is unknown. She was buried at old Cherry Point Community Cemetery, CP 11 Tract 439. Her gravestone was topped with a lamb and the inscription reads "Gone to Be an Angel."

Whitehead, Abner Parker WM

He was born on October 24, 1846. He was a turpentine farmer at true Cherry Point and later farmed at Bachelor. He was the husband of Margaret Dozier Whitehead. He was the father of James Berttie Whitehead and Ivan B. Whitehead. He died December 12, 1925, and was buried at the Oak Grove United Methodist Church Cemetery.

Whitehead, Emily Starton WF

She was born December 26, 1839, and died August 23, 1908. She was the wife of Abner Whitehead, Sr. She was buried at the Oak Grove United Methodist Church Cemetery.

Whitehead, Ivan B. WM

He was born April 16, 1893, the son of Abner P. and Margaret D. Whitehead and brother of James Berttie Whitehead. He died May 24, 1913, and is buried at Oak Grove United Methodist Church.

Whitehead, James Berttie WM

He was born July 15, 1881. He was the son of Abner P. and Margaret D. Whitehead. Lived on father's farm at Bachelor. He was the brother of Ivan

Whitehead. He died January 11, 1899, and was buried at Oak Grove United Methodist Church.

Whitehead, Jeremiah Cherry   Lost Grave   WM

He was born about 1802. He went by the name Cherry. He married Sally Rice on January 1, 1828. While living at the true Cherry Point, he was a merchant and owned a store at the corner of Middle and South Front Street in New Bern. He "commuted" by centerboard sailboat to and from the city. He died unexpectedly and without a will in 1832, close to the time his father died. His family owned a large plantation. The location of his grave is unknown but it was likely washed away from the Whitehead family cemetery in Siddie Fields. According to family lore and local legend, Cherry Whitehead is the namesake of Cherry Point, though the name pre-dates his life by more than 30 years. See chapter, *Naming Cherry Point*.

Whitehead, John E.   WM

He was born March 9, 1858, and died December 31, 1938. He's buried at Oak Grove United Methodist Church.

Whitehead, John S. (Sr.)   WM

He was a wealthy planter with a large farm on the Neuse River. He died in 1832, the same year as his 30-year-old son, Cherry. The location of his grave is unknown but it was likely washed away from the family cemetery in Siddie Fields at the true Cherry Point.

Whitehead, John S. (Jr.)   Lost Grave   WM

He was born May 21, 1804. He died on February 8, 1878. He was buried at the Whitehead family graveyard, Siddie Fields, true Cherry Point, but relocated to the Oak Grove United Methodist Church by the USFS.

Whitehead, Margaret Dozier   WF

She was born on February 5, 1855. She married a planter, Abner Parker Whitehead. Lived at Bachelor. Mother of James Berttie Whitehead and Ivan B. Whitehead. She died September 30, 1934, and was buried among the family at Oak Grove United Methodist Church.

Whitehead, Rhoda   Lost Grave   WF

She was born near Hancock Creek about 1858 but her date of death isn't known to us. She was the daughter of John S. and Sidney Whitehead. Her gravestone was found among rocks and ships' ballast in the water at Siddie Fields, at the true Cherry Point on the former Whitehead Plantation. It was left in place by USFS when others were moved for protection to Oak Grove Church. The Whitehead graveyard had been disturbed by the erosion of the Neuse River.

Whitehead, Sidney Oglesby   WF

She was born in 1825 and died on April 28, 1892. Her grave is at Oak Grove United Methodist Church. She was originally buried in "Siddie Fields" at the real Cherry Point, but was later moved by the USFS.

Whittington, Allen Earl   MUM

Born August 5, 1853, he was a farmer. He lived on the Beaufort Road (Highway 101) and owned a logging camp four miles from Havelock, according to the *New Berne Daily Journal*, July 21, 1914. See the story in *Perils* chapter. He was the husband of Sarah Cully Whittington. For children, see *Sarah Whittington*. He died September 13, 1932, and was buried at CP 1, Little Witness.

Whittington, Sarah Francis Cully   MUF

She was born on November 6, 1860. She lived on Beaufort Road (Highway 101). She was the wife of Allen E. Whittington. The census listed children at home in 1920: Nora, age 21; William W., age 38, a logging contractor; Cassie J., son, age 30, a laborer in the logwoods; Reba, a granddaughter, age 9. Sarah died on February 10, 1922. She was buried at CP 1, Little Witness Baptist Church.

Whittington, William Washington "Willie"   MUM

He was born in May 1882. He was the son of Allen E. and Sarah F. Whittington. He worked as a teamster in a logging camp and lived on the Beaufort Road (today's Highway 101). He died on January 25, 1934, and was buried at CP, Little Witness.

Willoughby (Willoby), William R.   MUM

He was born in 1870. He was a farm laborer at Little Witness, according to census records, and lived on Melvin Road. He was the husband of Larrah (Lurrah) C. Willoughby, born c. 1872. Children at home in 1910 included John H., 18, a teamster at logging camp; Lemuel, 15, a laborer on the home farm; Chrissie Johnson, 23, adopted, a laundress for a "private family." Children at home 1920, only Sarah, age 7. William Willoughby died March 3, 1928, and was buried at Cherry Point, Little Witness.

They Ran Away Together ... and Made a Life

Williams, Benjamin E. and Mary Elizabeth "Betty" Hunter

Despite the vigorous objections of her prosperous Civil War hero father, 19-year-old Betty Hunter climbed down a ladder one night in 1883 from the second story of the family's Slocum Creek plantation house to run off with a man 14 years her senior. Betty's father, James Howard Hunter, owned a 500-acre creekfront farm on what is now MCAS Cherry Point. The township around Havelock was devasted by the war that hit hardest from 1862-1865, but Hunter had quickly recovered and was becoming one of the county's wealthiest men.

He considered his potential new son-in-law, Benjamin E. Williams to be, in the words of family legend, "nothing but a poor dirt farmer." Betty's suitor was from the Croatan side of Slocum Creek and that's where they'd make their home, in the Catfish Lake Road area west of Havelock.

Betty and her man, Benjamin, would make a go of it, become prosperous themselves, raise a family, and live out the rest of their lives together at Croatan in a home in the woods along the road and railroad tracks behind the church. The home no longer exists.

Benjamin eventually won over his father-in-law and they served together in civic and official capacities.

Betty and Benjamin Williams suffered a great deal of heartache, however, losing four of five children within their lifetimes. Three of the children didn't make it through their teens. Another died as a young adult and her widowed husband soon married another Williams daughter. The Williamses lost children in 1903, 1909, 1913, and 1914. A descendant said that word passed down through the family was that "one or more of the children died accidentally in the railroad tracks near their home." [b]

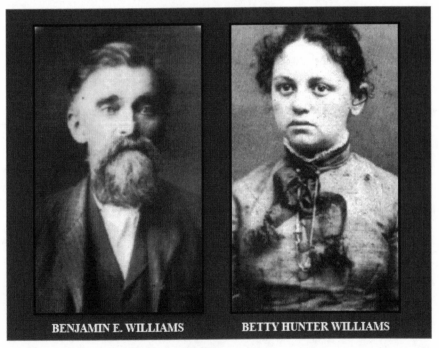

BENJAMIN E. WILLIAMS   BETTY HUNTER WILLIAMS

[b] Author's interview with Rev. Douglas G. Williams, Marshallberg, N.C., June 21, 2005.

And after all this time, Betty and Benjamin are still together today … in the small Williams-White Cemetery on the edge of the Croatan National Forest.

Williams, Benjamin Ethridge, Jr.   WM

He was born on June 9, 1850, at Croatan, the son of Benjamin E. and Nancy Williams. He married Mary Elizabeth Hunter, 1883. He was a farmer, but later entered the sugar cane grinding and molasses business. He was staunchly religious, trusted, and popular. He was one of the founders and an elder of the Croatan Presbyterian Church, in November 1883. He served on the school board, as a magistrate and census taker. His children were: Jane M., born 1887; Bettie, born 1891; Benjamin J., born 1892; James H., born 1894; and Charlie D., born 1897. Benjamin Williams died June 10, 1915. He was 65 years old. He's buried at the Williams-White Cemetery on Catfish Lake Road.

Williams, Mary Elizabeth "Betty" Hunter   WF

See the story above. She was born during the Civil War at Slocum Creek, on what is now MCAS Cherry Point, on July 25, 1864. She married Benjamin E. Williams of Croatan in 1883. She was a homemaker and mother. She died October 17, 1918, at age 54. She's buried at the William-White Cemetery.

These are the 11 children of Benjamin and Bettie Hunter Williams:

Bryan 1884-1919	35 years	
Mary Jane 1887-1913	26 years	
Triphene 1889-1959	70 years	
m. Levi Latham b. Dec. 8, 1885 d July 12, 1978		
children: Marie, Nina, Margaret, and Harvey*		
Bettie 1891-1961	70 years	
Benjamin J. 1892-1909	17 years	
James H. 1894-1903	10 years	
Charlie D. 1897-1914	17 years	
John H. 1899-1950	51 years	
Carl H. 1901-1946	46 years	
George F. 1904-1963	59 years (Doug Williams's father)	
Harvey B. 1907-1965	58 years	

* Marie Latham b. June 16, 1912, married Joe Hughes and lived at Carolina Pines. Margaret Latham Aversa of New Bern died in July 2009. Harvey Latham was born c. 1908 and died in 1974.

Williams, Jane " Janie" M.   WF

She was born in June 1887. She married C. B. Williams of Riverdale, becoming Jane Williams *Williams*. She died of an illness at age 25 in February 1913 and is buried in the Williams-White Cemetery.

Williams, Triphene "Phenie" "Fenie"   WF

Her nickname was pronounced *FEEN-ie*. She was born in March 1889. She married Levi N. Latham, a railroad section crewman, later the section master at Riverdale. They had four children. She died December 24, 1959, and is buried at New Bern Memorial Gardens.

Williams, Bettie W.   WF

She was born in April 1891. She married C.B. Williams of Riverdale, on June 2, 1914, becoming Bettie Williams *Williams*. She lived until 1961, dying at age 70. She was buried at Cedar Grove Cemetery in New Bern.

Williams, Benjamin J.   WM

He was born in 1892, died in 1909 at age 16, and was buried in the Williams-White Cemetery.

Williams, James. H.   WM

Born in August 1894, he was named for maternal grandfather, James Howard Hunter. He died in 1903 at age eight and was buried in the Williams-White Cemetery at Croatan.

Williams, Charlie D.   WM

He was born in August 1897 and died in 1914 at age 16. He was buried at the Williams-White Cemetery.

Williams, John   WM

He was born in August 1894. His death and burial information is unknown. *[For more information see,* Hunter, James Howard, *and associated listings. The Hunters and Williams are featured with photographs in* HIHCP.*]*

Willoughby, (Willowby) W.R.   MUM

He was born circa 1870. He died on June 15, 1928, at 58 years of age. In the 1920 census, he was age 49 and living in Township 5 on Melvin Road where MCAS Cherry Point is today. He worked for wages as a farm laborer. His wife's name was Larrah, age 47, and they had one child, a seven-year-old daughter, Sarah. He rented his home. He could read and write. Names of his nearby neighbors included Toon, Nelson, Dove, Berry, and Bryant. He was buried in CP 1, Little Witness Baptist Church Cemetery.

Willis, George Thomas, Jr., 1833-1867   WM

He was a farmer and Confederate soldier. He married Mary Ellis, 1837-1867. Father of James V., 1861-1865; and Sylvester, 1867-1867, son. They lived and are buried in the Adam Creek Road area. See *A Man Called Sparks*, Chapter 1.

Winn, see Wynne

Wood, Maude, see Wynne   WF

Woolvin(e), James E.   WM

He was born April 7, 1883, the son of Charles Woolvine. He registered to vote in Twp. 6 on October 19, 1906, age 24. He died April 22, 1909, age 26, and was buried at FUMC. No census data or obituary in Craven County has been found. The gravestone was legible when first surveyed by the author in the 1970s, but was illegible in 2018, and some websites marked it as "unknown" by that time.

Wynne, Caleb J.   WM

He was born c. 1857 in North Carolina. His date of death is unknown to us. He was the son of James H. Wynne and Lucy Thorpe who married in Craven County in 1844. He was the brother of Mary C., Martha J., and William "W.Y." Yarrow Wynne. His wife was Emma Jane Rowe Wynne. They married on New Year's Day 1893. He's buried in the Rowe-Pittman Cemetery.

Wynne, Caleb Joshua   WM

He was born on December 3, 1898. He was a farmer at Havelock, the son of Caleb J. Wynne (1857-?) and Emma Jane Rowe Wynne (Powell) (1873-1934). He married Jessie Louise Dennis (1901-1964) and their children were Albert Joshua Wynne (1925-1981), W. Ashford "Red" Wynne (1930-2001), and others, see Laura Dennis Wynne entry below. He was the brother of Mary C. Wynne (~1844-?), Martha J. Wynne (~1850-?), and William Yarrow Wynne (1861-1932). He died December 10, 1970, age 72, and is (thought to be) buried in the Dennis-Wynne Cemetery.

Wynne, Cye N.   WM

He was born February 15, 1895, and farmed at Havelock. He was employed later in life as an inspector for a lumber company. He married Sallie Russell Wynne, and their children were William E. Wynne, born c. 1922; and Richard A. Wynne, born c. 1929. He died October 5, 1949, and was buried at FUMC, next to Mattie Lee Wynne.

Wynne (Winn), Elizabeth Jones   WF

She was born circa 1788 and died December 27, 1842, at age 54. She was the daughter of Roger and Sarah Lovette Jones, and granddaughter of early settlers Evan and Elizabeth Jones. She was the wife of Stephen W. Winn. She was buried at CP 9, tract 199, with a lovely headstone shown in the final section of this book.

Wynne (Wynn), Elizabeth   WF

She's found in the 1870 Township 6 Census with her name spelled *Wynn*: Elizabeth, 42, head of household, keeping house. Her implied birth is c. 1828. Others listed in the household: William, 21, farmer; "At home," Sarah, 21; Susan, 17; Eliza, 15; John, 13; and Robert L., seven. Likely to be buried in Cherry Point cemetery 9, though the location is uncertain.

Wynne, Etta Nunn   WF

She was born March 19, 1898, and died September 6, 1910. She was the daughter of William Yarrow ("W.Y.") Wynne and Laura P. Wynne. She was buried at FUMC.

Wynne, Emma Jane Rowe, see Powell   WF
Wynne, Henry Clay   WM

He was born in Havelock, May 31, 1922, and named for his maternal grand-father. The son of W.J., Sr. and Maude Wynne, he was raised on the family farm and at old Havelock. He married Janice Lockey. He was a Havelock businessman, prominent civic leader, and a veteran of World War II. He was co-owner, with brother, W.J., Jr., of Wynne Brothers Texaco, an early gar-age, filling station, and fuel oil distributor, which they operated for more than 25 years. A photo of the station is in *HIHCP*. He was Havelock's sec-ond mayor and first town manager. He died September 2, 2014, aged 92 at Snug Harbor, Nelson Bay, Carteret County, and is buried in the Straits UMC cemetery. He is mentioned in the chapter *From the Halls of Monte-zuma*...and in Part III: Whatnot.

Wynne, Jessie Louise Dennis   WF
Born May 5, 1901, she became the wife of Caleb Joshua Wynne; mother of Albert J. Wynne (1925 – 1981); W. A. "Red" Wynne (1930 – 2001); Caleb E; daughter L. R.; and Jack Dare Wynne (1936-1995). She died December 31, 1964, age 63. Buried Dennis-Wynne Cemetery.

Wynne, Kenneth Lee   WM infant
Stillborn March 31, 1951. The son of Mr. and Mrs. W. J. Wynne, Jr. was buried FUMC.

Wynne, Lara C. Pate   WF
She was born June 13, 1860, and died November 6, 1943. The wife of Wil-liam Yarrow Wynne, she was buried at FUMC. She was the mother of W.J. Wynne, Sr.

Wynne, Mattie Lee   WF infant
Born and died June 11, 1925. Buried FUMC. Her marble marker has a lamb on top and reads "Sweetly Sleeping."

Wynne, Maude Wood   WF
She was born at Croatan on July 3, 1890, the daughter of successful Croatan farmer Henry Clay Wood (1857-1947) and Delialah Williams Wood (1859-1917). She was the wife of Walter J. Wynne, Sr., a farmer, and Havelock postmaster. Mrs. Wynne is said to have "run the post office." She was a teacher at Havelock's one-room school, September 1913 to June 1914, ac-cording to Rosalie Wynne. She was the mother of Lila, Elaine, W. J., Jr., and Henry Clay. She died at Havelock on April 23, 1983, age 92. She was buried at FUMC.

Wynne, Phillip Raymond   WM
He was born April 19, 1900, the son of W. Y. and Laura P. Wynne. He died at age 16 and was buried at FUMC. *The Morning Newbernian* reported Oc-tober 8, 1916: "Mr. Raymond Wynne died September 26, 1916. He had a host of friends and relatives who mourn their loss; to all, we tender our sympathies. He will be greatly missed by his associates at school where he always showed a deep inter-est. He is survived by his father and mother, Mr. and Mrs. W. Y. Wynne, one sister

Miss Rosa Lee, and three brothers Messrs. Walter, Herbert, and Cye Wynne. To the family, we would say look beyond the shadows and may the sweet consolation which God gives to his beloved ones sustain them in this sad hour. Our loss is Heaven's gain. With appropriate services conducted by the pastor, Rev. C. H. Caviness, and Rev. W. B. Everett of New Bern, the body was laid to rest in the family burying ground at Havelock." Thought to be CP 9.

Wynne, Rosalie (Rosa Lee) WF

She was born on August 14, 1902. The daughter of W.Y. and Laura Wynne, she was a public-school teacher. She died on April 21, 1985. She was 82. She's buried at FUMC.

Wynne, Sarah "Sallie" E. Russell WF

Born July 20, 1891, she was the daughter of Edward D. and Rebecca Jane Garner Russell, and sister of Richard C. Russell. She served as Havelock postmaster from July 6, 1914, to July 23, 1923, according to USPS records, National Archives, page 171. However, the 1910 U.S. Census shows mother Rebecca (R.J.) Russell as postmistress with Sallie unemployed. 1920 census lists Rebecca Russell again as Havelock postmistress and Sallie Russell as a teacher in public school. Sallie Russell married Cye N. Wynne c. 1920 and their children were William E., born c. 1922; and Richard A. born c. 1929. She died April 23, 1958, and was buried at FUMC.

Wynne (Winn), Stephen W. WM

He was born circa 1787. He married Elizabeth Jones on June 16, 1817, as listed in the marriage bonds book, Craven County. He was a prominent plantation owner with 1,300 acres on what is now MCAS Cherry Point. He was a civic and social leader. He's mentioned on his wife's grave marker. He died February 23, 1833, at age 45 years, 10 months, 24 days, and was buried at CP 9, tract 199.

Wynne, Walter James, Sr. WM

Born February 10, 1887, he was a Havelock railroad worker, farmer, and postmaster. The son of W.Y. Wynne, he was raised on a Hancock Creek farm. He worked in the logwoods and for a time followed the business to South Carolina. For the railroad, he operated the pump station at Slocum Creek. The Wynne farm stretched from Wynne Road, east of Walter B. Jones Park to Highway 101. It was taken from the family in the condemnation of land for the Cherry Point airbase in 1941. He was the husband of Maude Wood Wynne, and father of Lila, Elaine, W. J., Jr., and Henry Clay. He was the son of W. Y. and Laura Wynne. He died November 18, 1951, and was buried at FUMC. He appears in these chapters *From the Halls of Montezuma..., A Country Harmony,* and in Part III, Whatnot.

Wynne, Walter James, Jr. ("W.J.") WM

He was born December 7, 1919, the son of W.J., Sr. and Maude Wood Wynne, and raised at old Havelock and the family farm. He married Lillian

Garner Wynne (1920 – 2004). After distinguished Army service in Europe during World War II where he was awarded a Bronze Star Medal, he was a Havelock businessman and prominent civic leader. He co-owned Wynne Brothers Texaco, an early garage, filling station, and heating oil distributor, with his brother, Clay. Wynne Brothers operated for more than 25 years on Havelock's Main Street. A photograph of the business is in *HIHCP*. He had sisters, Elaine and Lila Wynne (Simmons). He was a multi-term Craven County commissioner, an advocate of rural electrification, and a long-time Carteret-Craven electrical co-op board member (Carteret Craven EMC). He died September 9, 1997, and was buried with three generations of his family at FUMC. He is featured in the chapter *From the Halls of Montezuma...* and appears in other chapters. See Index.

Wynne, William Yarrow ("W. Y.")   WM
He was born August 14, 1862, and died March 19, 1932, He was the husband of Laura C. Pate Wynne, and father of Walter J. (Sr.), Cye, Etta Nunn Wynne, Phillip Raymond Wynne, and Rosalie Wynne. He lived in old Havelock and was buried at FUMC.

Wynne (Winn) William   WM
He lived in the Slocum Creek area circa the mid-to-late 1700s, though his date of birth is unknown to us, he died in 1801. He was the father of Stephen Winn. County records show that he was overseer of the road from "Hancock Creek Bridge up to East Branch" by the Craven County Court, June Session, 1782. [East Branch *is an early name for the East Prong of Slocum Creek, which would have put Winn in charge of the stretch sandy road known today as Fontana Blvd.*] For more, see the chapter *Up the Creek*, and below.

The Missing Wynnes of Cherry Point

That's a pretty impressive list of Wynnes we've just run through. The Wynnes have, without question, one of the greatest longevities of residence of any of the families that settled around Slocum Creek and the area today known as Havelock. As you might expect from such early-arrivers, and according to Cherry Point's 1941 cemetery survey, some (maybe many) will be forever uncounted.

The oldest-known Winn (Wynn-Wynne) burials are today in a Cherry Point cemetery. According to our best documentation and records, the Wynne family is known to have lived exclusively on the east side of Slocum Creek in the 1700 and 1800s. That's where their old family cemetery was known to be in the late 20th century. Based on common custom it's reasonable that all of them would have been buried there from the earliest death after their settlement in colonial times. Some of their grave markers have not survived. Cherry Point Cemetery Number 9, where the Wynnes were buried, can be found in the final section of the book. Its location can be seen on a map of cemeteries at the beginning of the book.

Thomas W. Davis, Ph.D., was the principal investigator for an archeological survey at MCAS Cherry Point in 2002. Of the Wynne Cemetery, he wrote, "inferences based upon the known documentation suggest that there is a high potential for additional, unmarked burials in this vicinity. The sheer size of the historically reserved cemetery (one acre) argues for considerably more interments than currently are known. Among those buried in unmarked graves, the most likely candidates include James Wynne, the earliest family member, who requested specifically that he be buried "touching" his estate; William Winn and his wife Elizabeth; and Bryan and Sarah (Winn) Jones, whose three young children lie in marked graves. Children of James or William and Sarah Winn who died in infancy or early childhood also may be buried without the benefit of a permanent marker. Finally, one must remember that the bodies of esteemed slaves and servants frequently were interred within family cemeteries."

In addition to those just named, the report listed "Probable interments in Wynn Family Cemetery." These include Sally and Cressy Ann, daughters of William and Elizabeth Foscue Winn; James, Sarah, Tryphenia and William, children of Stephen and Elizabeth Jones Winn; Mary, Martha and Caleb, children of James and Lucy Winn; Stephen, Nancy, Sallie L. Susan, and Samuel, children of Bryan and Sarah Winn Jones; and William, Sarah, Elizabeth and Edwin, children of William (II) and Elizabeth Winn.[c]

The Cherry Point cemetery records of 1985 also note: *Cemetery 2 "Wynne Family": The cemetery survey notes from 1941 state only, "Overgrown with trees and brush – no markers, sinks visible – impossible to give an accurate count of the graves."*

This cemetery – spelled *Wynn* on the 1941 property owners map – is located in the middle of Little Witness, an African American settlement on the west side of Hancock Creek. How it came to be associated in the survey and on the map with the Wynne family name is something that the author has yet to understand. One possible – and speculative – explanation is that this is the location chosen to bury the enslaved people associated with the family's plantation of the 1700s and 1800s.

---

[c] *Phase I Archeological Survey of Nine Parcels at Marine Corps Air Station Cherry Point, Craven County, North Carolina*, R. Christopher Godwin & Associates, Inc., Frederick, MD, June 2002, page 26-31. R-9-Davis et al, 2002.

PART III

DEATH, PERIL & REAL ESTATE

DIED,

This is a chronological listing of some ancient obituaries for individuals of southern Craven County gathered over many years from old newspaper archives and other historical sources. Most of the men, women, and children listed here are buried in lost graves. The month has been spelled out. Otherwise, announcements are quoted substantially as they ran in the publications noted; except where brackets [ ] appear, indicating that clarifications and/or additional related information have been added by the author.

❖ BARRON - "On Wednesday last, died at his house in this town, after a tedious and afflicting indisposition, David Barron, Esq., a gentleman who, in the course of a few years, with great industry and assiduity, has acquired a handsome fortune, with a fair and unblemished character." *The North-Carolina Weekly Gazette* (New Bern) Friday, February 13, 1778. [*David Barron owned about 2,000 acres of land near present-day Havelock in southern Craven County including two large tracts touching Long Lake and Little Lake.*]

❖ JONES - Neuse River near Hancock Creek: "Allen Jones son of Comfort and Roger Jones, Jr. died October 14, 1792, at Hancock's Creek Age 7 mons." *Hardy Loftin Jones Bible* from DAR Library via Kellenberger Room, New Bern-Craven County Public Library.

❖ JONES - Neuse River near Hancock Creek: "Roger Jones, Sr. died November 1801 age 70 years." *Hardy Loftin Jones Bible* from DAR Library.

❖ JONES - "Roger Jones, Jr., son of Roger Jones, Sr. died at Hancocks Creek December 15, 1801. Age 41 years." *Hardy Loftin Jones Bible.*

❖ HYMAN - "At his seat in Craven County, Thomas Hyman, Esq." *Raleigh Minerva* November 26, 1807. NCGenWeb.

❖ WEST - "At his seat in this county, on Tuesday last, Mr. Richard West. In discharging the last sad duty of surviving friends, the tribute of respect to departed worth, we can, with great truth say, that through life, Mr. West, supported the character of a benevolent and honest man – his virtue will long endear his memory to his relatives and friends." *Newbern Herald*, Saturday, May 20, 1809.

❖ JONES - Neuse River near Hancock Creek: "Sarah Jones died January 9, 1810 age 75 years." *Hardy Loftin Jones Bible.* DAR Library. Also, from the *New Bern Herald* January 29, 1810: "At Clubfoots Creek in this county, on the 6th inst., Mrs. Sarah Jones, relict of Roger Jones, sen. [*Sr.*], aged 75. During her long journeys through life, she supported an unusual vivacity of mind, and strength of thought. She had been for many years a sincere professor of the Quaker religion, in which faith she continued till her death."

❖ HANCOCK - "In Craven County, on the 28th ult. [June 28, 1811], Mr. John Hancock." *Raleigh Minerva* July 19, 1811. [*Aged 23, NCGenWeb*]

❖ BELL - "On Sunday last, Mr. Reuben Bell." *The True Republican* New Bern, Wednesday, August 7, 1811.

❖ CARNEY – "At Adams Creek, in this County, on Friday the 17th inst., Mr. Robert Carney." *The Carolina Federal Republican* December 25, 1813.

❖ DICKSON - "Died in this Town on Thursday evening, James Dickson, Esq." *The Carolina Federal Republican* May 30, 1815.

❖ BORDEN - "In Craven County on the 8th [*March 8, 1816*], Mrs. Ann Borden." *Raleigh Minerva* March 29, 1816. NCGenWeb.

❖ JONES - "Died, At his plantation on Slocumb's Creek, on the 20th ult., Mr. Evan Jones." *The Carolina Federal Republic* March 1, 1817; *The Weekly Raleigh Register* and *Raleigh Minerva* March 14, 1817.

> **DIED,**
> At his plantation on Slocumbe Creek, on Thursday last, Mr. *Evan Jones.*

❖ LOVICK - "On the 20th inst. near Slocumbs Creek, Craven County, Mrs. Sarah Lovick, relick [*sic*] of Mr. George Lovick." *The Carolina Federal Republic* New Bern, November 29, 1817.

❖ FISHER - "In this town, on Tuesday last, Jonathan Fisher, eldest son of Michael Fisher." *Newbern Sentinel* April 4, 1818.

❖ ROWE - "At Slocumb's Creek, in this county, on the 25th ult. [*i.e., the previous month, August 25, 1820*] Benjamin, son of Amos Rowe, Esq. in the 8th year of his age." *Newbern Sentinel* September 2, 1820.

❖ PARSONS - "Of Peripneumony [*pneumonia*], on Thursday night, at his residence near Newbern [*actually Hancock Creek*]. Mr. Nathan Parsons, in the prime of his life, much regretted by his acquaintances." *Newbern Sentinel* December 30, 1820.

❖ BORDEN - "At Handcock's Creek, in this County, on the 3d instant, Mrs. Rebecca Borden, consort of Benjamin Borden, Esq. much lamented by all who knew her." *Newbern Sentinel* January 6, 1821.

❖ HOLLAND - Slocum Creek 1821: "Died. At Slocumb's Creek, on the third instant [*i.e., the third of this month: December 3, 1821*], Mrs. Huldah Holland, wife of William Holland, Esq." *Centinel* New Bern, December 15, 1821.

❖ DUDLEY - "Died in this county on Friday the 27th September 1822, Mrs. Mary Dudley, wife of Mr. William Dudley, aged 69 years, 10 months and 18 days." *Carolina Centinel* 5 Oct 1822.

❖ JONES - Neuse River near Hancock Creek: "Comfort Jones, the relict [*i.e., widow*] of Roger Jones and daughter of Henry Always [*misspelled Alwdy in transcription*], December the 16th August 1826." *Hardy Loftin Jones Bible* DAR Library.

❖ PHYSIOC - "At Handcock's Creek, on Saturday last [*October 28, 1826*], in the 64th year of her age, Mrs. Contentna Physioc, wife of Joseph Physioc, Esq. of this County." Newbern Sentinel November 4, 1826. [*Mrs. Physioc's grave is known, but its exact location is protected as a cultural resources site within the Croatan National Forest east of Havelock.*]

❖ LOVICK - From Slocum Creek: "Mehitable Content Lovick dau[*ghter*] of Comfort and Roger Jones, Jr. Died August 11, 1827, at Slocumb Creek age 31 years." *Hardy Loftin Jones Bible* from DAR Library.

❖ LOVICK - "At Slocumb's Creek, on Saturday 11th instant, Mrs. Mehetibel [*Mehitibel Judd*] Lovick, wife of Mr. James Lovick." *Newbern Sentinel* August 25, 1827.

❖ JONES - From Slocum Creek: "Hugh Jones. Son of Comfort and Roger Jones, Jr.. died May 9, 1831, in Gerard Co Ky. Age 32 yrs." *Hardy Loftin Jones Bible* from DAR Library.

❖ LOVICK - "In this place, on the 29th ult., [*i.e., May 29, 1831*] James Lovick, Esq. in the 39th year of his age." *New Bern Sentinel* June 3, 1831. [*Lovick was the owner of Magnolia Plantation on the Neuse River near Slocum Creek. His grave is known. See article within under his name.*]

❖ BENNERS - "On the 3rd Instant, Winnifred Benners, age 18 months 20 days, daughter of Lucas Benners, Esq." *Newbern Spectator* Nov. 18, 1831.

❖ WHITEHEAD - "On Wednesday last, aged 30, Mr. Cherry Whitehead." *New Bern Sentinel* April 18, 1831.

❖ WYNN - "At his plantation in this County [*on Slocum Creek*], on Saturday last [February 23, 1833] Mr. Stephen W. Wynn." *Newbern Sentinel* March 1, 1833. Also reported March 12, 1833, in the *Weekly Raleigh Register*. [*Wynn was buried in Cherry Point cemetery 9 (CP 9). More details in his alphabetical listing within the book above.*]

❖ MASON - "In this place, on the 4th inst. [*i.e., June 4, 1833*], in the 68th year of her age, Mrs. Nancy Mason, of Adams's Creek." *Newbern Sentinel* June 7, 1833.

❖ REW - "At Adams Creek, in this county, on Wednesday the 5th instant [*i.e., March 5, 1834*] Mrs. Francis Rew, aged 60 years, consort of Mr. Southy Rew." *Newbern Sentinel* March 14, 1834.

❖ DIXON - "At Slocomb's Creek, on the 12th inst., after a long and painful illness, Mrs. Fanny Dixon, relict of the late Capt. George Dixon, and daughter of William Holland, Esq., in the 30th year of her age. She was a member of the United Baptist Church, and died in full confidence of her Saviour." *Newbern Spectator* May 16, 1834.

❖ HANCOCK - "Died on the 24th ult., in the 19th year of his age, Richard G. Hancock, son of William Hancock." *The Spectator* Sept. 5, 1834.

❖ SARAH - "One old negro woman, Sarah, [*a slave*] … the old woman died in January 1853, and I buried her." Joseph Physioc, guardian, in the accounting of the property of his ward, Eliza Hope Whitehead, May 11, 1835. *Cherry Whitehead Estate*, Craven County, Image 86.

❖ HOLLAND – On Slocum Creek 1836: "Died. At his late residence in this county, William Holland, Esq. His memory will be long cherished by a large circle of acquaintance, to whom he was endeared by his many benevolent and disinterested actions." *New Bern Sentinel* December 21, 1836.

❖ TYRE - "Died at Slocumb's Creek, on the 9th instant [*February 9, 1837*], Mrs. Esther Tyre aged 74 years." *Newbern Sentinel* February 15, 1837.

❖ HOLLAND - Tucker Creek 1838: "Died. At his residence on Tucker's Creek, in this county, on Sunday the fourth instant [*i.e., the fourth of this month; November 4, 1838*], in the 37th year of his age, Mr. Hylliard Holland. The deceased was a kind and affectionate husband, an obliging neighbor, and most estimable man." *New Bern Spectator* November 16, 1838.

❖ JONES - Of Hancock Creek: "Henry Always Jones, son of Comfort and Roger Jones [*Jr.*] die[*d*] February 9, 1841, Age 51 yrs." *Hardy Loftin Jones Bible* from DAR Library.

❖ MASTERS - On Tuesday, 10th inst., Mrs. Lavinia Masters, in the 28th year of her age, consort of Dr. Samuel Masters." *The Newbernian and North Carolina Advocate* October 14, 1843.

❖ JONES - Of Hancock Creek: "Hardy Loftin Jones. Son of Comfort and Roger Jones Jr. died August 15, 1854, New Bern, NC age 61 yrs." *Hardy Loftin Jones Bible.*

❖ MASON - "Died, at his residence on Adams' Creek on the 14th ult. [*October 14, 1858*] Rev. Francis Mason, aged 63 years and 2 months ... The deceased had been a member of the Methodist Episcopal Church for 45 years – 35 [*years*] a class-leader, and the last 8 years of his life he had been engaged as a Local Preacher in proclaiming the Gospel of Christ." *The New Era and Commercial Advertiser* New Bern, November 2, 1858.

❖ REID - "On Hancock's Creek, the 2d of December 1860, Virginia F. Reid, wife of W.H. Reid and daughter of John S. and Nancy Hunter, in the 23rd year of her age. She was baptized on July 1856, and lived the life of a Christian up to her death, and was ready at the call of her Saviour to go. Her loss to us, though gain to her, cannot be replaced. John Ferguson." *The Biblical Recorder* January 9, 1861.

❖ WYNN[E] - "On Tuesday night, 24th instant, at the residence of her son-in-law, Mr. John Pate, Mrs. Elizabeth Wynn[e] in the 57th year of her age." *The Daily Journal* (New Bern) March 28, 1885.

❖ PEARTREE - "Died at his home at Havelock, Craven County, on Monday night, September 3, [*1888*] Mr. Stephen Peartree, aged 77 years." *The Daily Journal* New Bern, September 5, 1888. [*Stephen Peartree, born circa 1811, was a longtime resident of the Havelock area. He was a cooper – a barrel maker – by trade. Survived by wife Caroline*].

❖ RIDGON - "George Rigdon of Havelock, a farmer 68 years of age, died Sunday morning [*June 17, 1894*] of dropsy. He leaves a wife and several children. Our townsmen, Mr. J. C. Rigdon is one of his sons." *The Daily Journal* (New Bern) June 19, 1894.

❖ CHADWICK - "Mrs. Mary F. Chadwick, wife of Edward Chadwick, who was [*Havelock*] ticket agent and train dispatcher of the A. & N.C.R.R., died at her home in this city at 10 o'clock Monday night, aged 24 years." Newbern *Journal* reprinted in the *Wilmington (NC) Morning Star* February 8, 1895.

❖ MCCAFITY - "At Slocumbs' Creek on August 30, 1896, Thomas McCafity, aged 16 years. The deceased was a son of Mr. Alonzo McCafity, the interment took place at Lane's Chapel." *The Daily Journal* New Bern, September 2, 1896.

❖ MORTON - "Died November 26th, 1900, aged 14 years, 8 months, and ten days, Guy Morton, at the home of his father at Cherry Point, N.C. The body was taken to Harlowe Church for interment. A father and mother and several brothers and sisters are left to mourn this, their first great loss." *New Berne Weekly Journal* December 4, 1900.

❖ MORTON "Died of hemorrhagic fever at Cherry Point, Craven county, January 24th [*1901*] and was buried at Harlowe cemetery on the 26th. Blanch Borden Morton, daughter of Capt. M.F. and M.E. Morton, services conducted by Rev. Jiles. She was born November 22, 1882 ... a father, mother, three sisters, and two brothers survive her. She became a member of the International Order of the King's Daughters and Sons, November 8, 1896. In the year 1896, she united with Christ Church." *The Daily Journal* New Bern, January 30, 1901.

❖ CAVANAUGH - "Died at her home in the city yesterday afternoon Mrs. Mary L. Cavanaugh, age 43 years. She was a daughter of the late Henry J. Lovick. Her husband and son survive her. The funeral will be held this afternoon at 430 o'clock from the First Baptist Church of which she was a member. The remains will be carried on the evening train to Havelock for interment near that place." *The Daily Journal* New Bern, October 15, 1901.

❖ TAYLOR - "Mr. Isaac Taylor who is been very ill for several days, of pneumonia in this city [*New Bern*], died yesterday shortly after noon. The remains were taken by the A. & N.C. train to Havelock, and from there conveyed to Bachelor, the late home of the deceased, and will be interred today. Mr. Taylor was about 64 years of age, was wide and favorably known, and his death will be a sad loss to the community, in which he has so long made his home." *The Daily Journal* New Bern, April 8, 1902.

❖ BRAND - "Death or Mrs. Anna Brand. Mrs. Anna Brand died Saturday, October 1st at the home of her son, Mr. William Buys, at Slocum Creek, aged 91 years. Mrs. Brand was a native of Holland but had been a resident of this country many years. She lived in Chicago for several years." *New Berne Weekly Journal* October 7, 1904.

❖ THORP[E] - "Mr. John M. Thorp[e] age 60 years, died of pneumonia at the Stewart Sanatorium Saturday evening. He had been a resident of Craven County all his life living in the vicinity of Havelock and Newport. The burial took place Sunday at the family burying grounds ... on Hancock Creek." *New Bern Weekly Journal* November 8, 1907.

❖ THORPE - "We are sorry to note the death of Mrs. W.E. Thorpe [of Havelock], which occurred at the New Bern Sanitorium, Saturday morning," [*November 9, 1907*] *Daily Journal*, New Bern, of the same date.

❖ HAYWOOD - "At Croatan, December 9, Annie Bell [Haywood] the daughter of Mr. and Mrs. Thomas E. Haywood, at the age of eight years. The burial services were conducted by Mr. B[enjamin] E. Williams, and the interment made in the Lovick family graveyard on Slocumbs Creek. The funeral will be prepared at the Croatan Presbyterian Church, by Rev. S. H. Isler of Goldsboro, Friday night, of this week." *New Bern Weekly Journal* December 13, 1907.

❖ BRINSON - Death of Mrs. Brinson: "Mrs. Kitty E. Brinson died at her home on Broad Street [*New Bern*] Sunday evening [*June 21, 1908*], her death resulting from a stroke of apoplexy, which she had Friday. Mrs. Brinson was born near Havelock in October 1842 and has been a resident of New Bern for nearly 50 years ... She was married to William George Brinson." *The Daily Journal* (New Bern) January 23, 1908.

❖ BELL - Harlowe Funeral: "Mrs. Hannah Bell departed this life last Thursday the twelfth at the home of her daughter, Mrs. J. C. Long, at the advanced age of 70 years. She was laid to rest in the Harlowe Cemetery, Friday the thirteenth, the Rev. Futrell officiating at the burial." *The Daily Journal* (New Bern) May 19, 1908.

❖ ARMES - "At Dr. Taylo[e]'s hospital at Washington, N. C., on March 6 after a long illness, Mrs. Julia Francis Armes, in the 58th year of her age. Her remains were brought to New Bern yesterday morning and then taken to her home at Hancock's Creek, where they were interred in the family burying ground. Members of the family and friends accompanied the remains from here." *The Daily Journal* (New Bern) March 8, 1910.

❖ WYNNE - "In Loving Remembrance of Etta Nunn Wynne, who died of Hemorrhagic fever at Cherry Point, N.C., September 5, 1910, age 12 years 4 months and nine days." [*She was the oldest daughter of Mr. and Mrs. W.Y. Wynne, and was survived by four brothers and one sister.*] *New Berne Weekly Journal*, September 8, 1910.

❖ SHIELDS - "Mr. Ira W. Shields, one of the state's best-known tobacco planters, died suddenly at his plantation, known as Oak Lane Villa, on Slocum creek, Thursday night. The remains were shipped to Durham yesterday afternoon, passing through New Bern, for funeral and interment. The deceased was in his sixty-second year." *The Twin-City Daily Sentinel* Winston-Salem April 28, 1921.

❖ RUSSELL - "Funeral services were held last week for Mrs. Annie Breslin Russell, 62, wife of Captain George Russell of Cherry Point, the Rev. Father Francis Gorham, and the Rev. Father Gable of the Catholic Church officiating. Mrs. Russell died Wednesday afternoon after an extended illness. Interment was at the family cemetery at Cherry Point. Surviving are the husband; one son, Anthony John Russell, of Cherry Point; three daughters: Mrs. Madge Wetherington of Wilmington, Mrs. Lillian Trader of Havelock, and Mrs. Hellen McCullers of Raleigh, route 3. There is also one first cousin, John McHue of Southern Pines." *New Bern Tribune*, June 16, 1935.

Peril and Drama from the News

The news never stops. It certainly didn't stop – it didn't even slow down – in the 162 years between the first entry below from 1764 and the last blurb from 1926. These items have been gleaned from thousands of bulletins breathlessly published in county newspapers. This chronological offering refers to matters of the Havelock end of Craven. They're published as they ran in the publications noted, odd spelling included; except where brackets [ ] appear, indicating that additional information has been added by the author.

RAN AGROUND, ATE RATS: "A small sloop … employed as a lighter, as she was coming into the river, ran ashore on Brant Island, and filled; its people, by accident, lost their boat, and had no means to get ashore, and no vessel happening to go that way, they remained on board eight days without any provisions, except two rats which they catch'd in the mainsail: at length being likely to perish, they cut up the boom and made a raft of it, on which they happily reached the shore, after twenty-two hours in the water." *The Newbern Gazette*, December 7, 1764. [*Brant Island shoals, a long-time hazard to navigation, are near the mouth of the Neuse River.*]

CHILDREN STOLEN, RESCUED: "We learn that two men, one of whom passed by the name of Gibbs, a few days since kidnapped two free negro children in the vicinity of Handcock's creek, in the county. They were pursued and overtaken a few miles beyond Washington, and brought into this county, where the thieves effected their escape. The children, however, are in town, and will be restored to their parents." *Newbern Sentinel* April 17, 1819.

ARSON SUSPECTED: "I will give a reward of Fifty Dollars in cash, for information sufficient to convict the fellow that burnt the dwelling house at the mouth of Slocumb's Creek called Sandy Point. Eden T. Jones. September 10, 1825." *Newbern Sentinel*, February 26, 1825.

HAIL AND LIGHTNING: "After a Spring unusually cold, our Summer has commenced with unusual ardour. On the first instant, at 3 P.M. the thermometer rose in different situations to 88, 90 and 92 in the shade. In the evening of the same day a dark and portentous cloud arose in the eastern section of our horizon, and we learned that the neighborhood of Adams's Creek, it was accompanied with much hail, and that a negro woman belonging to Mr. Nathaniel Smith was killed by lightning." *New Bern Spectator* June 6, 1829.

KILLER PREACHER: "Elder George W. Carrowan is expecting to preach the 3rd of August at Slocumb's Creek." *Tarboro Press* June 11, 1842. [*The circuit-riding minister is later described in the annals of the Kehukee Primitive Baptist Association as "the notorious George W. Carrowan, whose conduct was disgraceful, and yet whose influence as pastor of the church was so great as to escape expulsion until he was tried and condemned for murder and committed suicide." In 1854, upon his conviction in a Beaufort County courtroom for the murder of a young male schoolteacher, Carrowan, 55, drew two single-shot pistols. He fired one directly at the heart of the prosecutor and then shot himself in the head. The prosecutor was only slightly wounded as a thick pocketbook in his coat slowed the bullet. In the chamber, the gunman's wife and three children witnessed the tragedy.*]

"PANTHER KILLED. A correspondent, writing from Slocumb's Creek, 15 miles below New Bern, says that Mr. William Rowe killed a panther [*i.e., cougar*] last Wednesday, measuring 5 feet from his nose to the root of his tail. He was caught in a bear trap and afterward shot. He has for some time past been committing serious ravages among the sheep, hogs &c. of the farmers in that region. Mr. Rowe is deserving of credit for ridding the neighborhood of such a dangerous visitor, thereby saving his own and his neighbors' bacon." *Wilmington (N.C.) Journal*, December 10, 1847.

NOTICE.

AT the November Term, A. D. 1830, of the Court of Pleas and Quarter Sessions of Craven County, the subscribers qualified as Executors to the last Will and Testament of *Joseph Brittain* deed. All persons indebted to the estate of said deceased, are requested to make immediate payment, and those having claims against the estate, will exhibit the same within the time prescribed by an Act of the General Assembly, or said Act will be plead in bar of their recovery.

STEPHEN W. WINN, }
WILL. PHYSIOC, Sr. } *Exrs.*

Slocumb's Creek, Nov. 15, 1830. 26kt.

WANTED.

Early Slocum Creek settler Joseph Brittain died in 1830 and two of the other prominent men of the community, Stephen Winn and William Physioc, gave notice as the estate's executors.

"DEATH BY DROWNING: A Free colored man, we learn, by the name of William Chance, who lived on Slocumb's Creek in this county, and who was in the practice of boating on the Neuse, was found drowned at the New County Wharf Dock in Newbern, on Friday morning last. A Jury of Inquest was held over the body, but owing to the absence of important testimony, they postponed the matter until Thursday next." *The Newbernian and North Carolina Advocate* June 4, 1850.

"MELANCHOLY DISASTER: We are pained to learn that during the severe blow which took place on Friday night week, as a boat, belonging we hear to Samuel W. Chadwick Esq. of New Bern was on her way down the river near the mouth of Slocum's Creek and having one white man by the name of Henry Silverthorne and five Negro men on board, she capsized and all on board perished." *Spirit of the Age,* Raleigh, North Carolina, January 18, 1854.

"FIRE: The [turpentine] Distillery of Mr. John D. Flanner was partially consumed by fire on yesterday morning. Loss estimated at $600." *The Atlantic,* New Bern, July 19, 1854. [*Think Flanner's Beach Road*].

"WILD BEASTS IN CRAVEN. Many of our readers may be ignorant of the fact that within 10 or 12 miles of New Bern ... bears, catamounts, and wild cats exist to such an extent, that it is with great difficulty hogs and sheep are reared. Such however is the fact, and we do not see the reason why our members of the Legislature do not take the thing in hand, have a law passed giving a bounty to the slayer, for every wild animal of the kind that may be killed. We were assured on our recent visit to that region, that something of the kind was absolutely necessary. There are other parts of this county and the state, that are infested in the same manner by wild beasts." *The Charlotte Democrat* January 27, 1857.

A WHOLE FAMILY DROWNED: "We are pained to learn that Mr. John Thomas and family – a wife, a lad and an infant were drowned last Saturday by the capsizing of his boat near Adams' Creek. The body of the little child was found floating in the water dead." *Newbern Weekly Progress* November 20, 1860.

"MORE PLUNDERING. We are informed of the theft of two mules and a cart from the premises of a negro man named N. Jackson, near Havelock Station. A reward of $50 will be given for their recovery." *Newbern Journal of Progress,* November 27, 1866.

BEAR VS. TRAIN: "Bear killed. —The freight train of the A. & N.C. Railroad killed a bear of the largest size, near Havelock, on Friday night instant. What bruin was doing on the track is not known, though it is conjectured that he intended to dispute the passage of the train." *The Wilmington (NC) Daily Journal* January 25, 1869, quoting *The New Bern Journal of Commerce.*

BILIOUS FEVER: "Sudden death of the wife of Col. S.S. Atwell, formerly of Bridgeport, Conn., and who since the war has been engaged in manufacturing and agriculture in North Carolina. Col. A. with his family lives on the "Ormsbee" Plantation at Slocom's Creek. About one week ago, he came to this city [*New Bern*] on business, was taken sick and confined to his room at the hotel until yesterday morning, during which time Mrs. Atwell was taken sick at the plantation, and died of billious fever Monday evening. Col. A was taken home

Col. S.S. Atwell

yesterday, although hardly able to be moved." *The New Berne Times*, July 21, 1869. [*Col. Seagar Schuyler Atwell (1836-1911) was a Union officer and commander of the Seventh Connecticut Volunteer Infantry. His wife, Georgia, was just 22 when she died at Slocum Creek near the notoriously deadly savannah swamp previously mentioned. Bilious fever is associated with excessive bile or bilirubin in the blood stream and tissues evidenced by jaundice, a yellowing of the eyes and skin. The most common cause is malaria spread by mosquitoes. Col. Atwell later returned to the North and remarried. He lived to the age of 75 and is buried in Rhode Island.*]

ARSON CHARGED: "A large crowd was in attendance [*at Mayor's Court*] yesterday attracted thither by the fact that two men had been arrested the night before on suspicion of being the incendiaries that had fired the stables in the rear of G. W. Dill's office. The men were colored, and named Ananias Fenner and Benjamin Carter. The evidence demonstrated that they are residents of Hancock Creek and had come up on the day of the attempt, with a boat load of wood ... and immediately after the alarm were found in their boat, they being the only persons found in the immediate vicinity. The evidence failed, however, to attach any guilt to these men and they were accordingly discharged." *The New Berne Times* May 17, 1871.

CONFLAGRATION: "James W. Gray, Esq., informed us that the fire now in progress in the Adams Creek vicinity, had already consumed about five miles of his fencing and that other landowners in that neighborhood were losing heavily from the same cause." *The New Berne Times* April 19, 1873.

NO AVERAGE GATOR: "On Thursday of last week, our townsman, Mr. Richard Williams, killed a large alligator at the junction of Slocum and East creeks, which measured 15 feet, 7 inches in length." *Wilmington Weekly Star* August 23, 1878, quoting the *New Bern Journal*. [*While it's conceivable that such a large animal was found in the North Carolina wilderness of 1878, it should be noted that the world's record alligator, 15'9" weighing 1,011 pounds, was killed in 2014 by an Alabama woman named Mandy Stokes.*]

DUCKS FEAR HIM: "Mr. B. F. Borden, who lives on Hancock's Creek, in this county, says that twice this year he has killed twenty-five wild ducks at a single shot." *Wilmington (NC) Morning Star*, December 11, 1878.

KEELED OVER: "John H. Cook, a native of New Bern, but for the past few years a resident, with his wife and children, of Slocum Creek, fell dead in the road near the creek, on Tuesday afternoon, of heart disease." *Newbern Nut Shell*, as reprinted in the *Goldsboro Messenger*, April 12, 1880.

SUDDEN DEATH: "Mr. C[ollins] H. Hunter, of Havelock, who was in the city yesterday, informs us of the sudden death of Mr. Henry Eborn, a young man of about 22 years who was just married in November last, which occurred at his residence in that neighborhood last Saturday night. He worked the road on Saturday, was at Mr. Hunter's store in the evening and purchased some goods, went home, ate supper as usual, and went to bed. About 9 o'clock his wife discovered that he was struggling for life, and by two o'clock he was dead." *The Daily Journal* (New Bern) March 8, 1884. [*C. H. Hunter, the son of James H. Hunter of Slocum Creek, was a store-keeper and postmaster at Havelock.*]

LODGE BROTHERS STEP UP: "Mr. Eugene Spencer, a gentleman from Cleveland, Ohio, who had visited this section with a view to engage in the lumbering business and who had made arrangements for the purchase of a sawmill at Havelock Station, was on Monday last taken suddenly ill at the Gaston House [*a New Bern hotel*] and died within a few hours, the cause of his death being heart disease. From papers in his possession, it was discovered that he was a Knight of Honor, and the Lodge of that Order in this city took charge of his remains, and on Wednesday forwarded the body, in a metallic case, to his relatives." *The Newbernian* May 29, 1880.

MILL DAMAGED: "Capt. A. E. Oglesby of Carteret County was in the city yesterday and told us of a terrible windstorm that passed near Andrews on Tuesday, about 12 o'clock. Two log houses were blown down and one negro boy was hurt. Fence rails were scattered in every direction, and at Havelock Mr. Terry's mill was damaged about $700." *Wilmington Weekly Star* April 25, 1884, quoting the *New Berne Journal*.

A GIFT OF RATTLESNAKE: "The large rattlesnake killed by Collins H. Hunter near Havelock last spring … has been nicely mounted and leaves on the *Shenandoah* [Steamship] today for Norfolk as a Christmas present from James H. Hunter, Esq. to our former townsman, Thomas J. Latham, Esq. He is over 7 feet long, has 13 rattles and a button, and is a terrible-looking monster for this section. He has been on exhibition at Dail's corner, where many went to see him." *The Daily Journal* (New Bern) January 2, 1885.

MILL ACCIDENT FATAL: "Last week, while the saw at Taylor & Temple's mill on Clubfoot Creek, in this county, was cutting a log, Samuel Martin, colored, who was assisting in the sawing, accidentally dropped the mallet which he was using to unlock the 'dogs' or irons which hold the log in its proper place on the carriage. He immediately stooped over the log to snatch up the mallet, when his arm was caught by the saw and cut off before the carriage could be reversed or the machinery stopped. Profuse bleeding followed for several hours, from which cause the unfortunate sufferer died next day." *Wilmington Daily Review* October 17, 1885, quoting the *New Bern Journal*.

AGROUND AT CHERRY POINT: "The steam tug *Taylor* of J.V. William's line, having in tow the two barges *Jennie Reed* and *Squires*, anchored at Gar Bacon shoals. The barges being anchored, the tug still retained its tow lines and endeavored to ride out the storm. Her cable parted, however, and the storm took her like a cork and threw her on Cherry point. Two hundred and fifty yards from floating water, where she lies now embedded in three feet of sand with a hole in its iron bottom, probably made by a stump, and several bushels of sand in her hold. One of the barges was seen yesterday, by a sailboat coming up ashore near where the storm struck them. The other barge has not been heard from up to this writing, though she is necessarily ashore somewhere not far distant." *New Bern Weekly Journal* August 25, 1887.

"AFLOAT AGAIN: The steamer *Annie* of the E.C.D. line, that was blown ashore at Cherry Point during the storm in August, has been gotten off and she arrived at her dock Friday in good shape. She has resumed her regular trips between this city [New Bern] and Elizabeth City." *New Berne Weekly Journal* September 29, 1887.

FISHER HOME BURNS: "Mr. M[ichael] N. Fisher's dwelling house [on Hancock Creek] near Havelock was destroyed by fire last Friday night. Loss about $1,500; insured for $1,000. All the furniture was lost except what was on the lower floor." *Wilmington Weekly Star* October 14, 1887, quoting the *New Bern Journal*.

HUNTING ACCIDENT: "We learned that on last Monday Mr. L. F. Tillery, formerly telegraph operator here, but now of Rocky Mount, who is visiting his father-in-law, Mr. Geret Vyne of Havelock, went out with a little son of Mr. Vyne for a hunt. In some way, young Vyne's gun went off unexpectedly and a great part of the load lodged in Mr. Tillery's back and shoulder. The shot, fortunately were small and Mr. Tillery was not seriously hurt, but we learned that his wounds were quite painful. He has many friends in the city who sympathize with him." *New Bern Weekly Journal* January 19, 1888.

HURRICANE OF 1887: "Mr. Geret Vyne of Havelock writes us that the storm on Saturday morning last damage the crops about one-third in that community. The fodder is all lost. A barn on Mr. Vyne's plantation was blown down and one mule killed. The house of Mr. and Mrs. Hoover in the neighborhood fell in so that they had to be assisted in getting out, but they escaped uninjured. We hear the damage to crops near the coast is considerable." *Wilmington Daily Review* August 25, 1887, quoting the *Newbern Journal*. [*Vyne was a prosperous, well-known Havelock farmer. His last name appears in news stories and other records as* Vyne *and* Vine, *and his first as* Garrett, Gerrett, Geret, Geratt, *and so forth.*]

MORE HURRICANE '87 MAYHEM: "The tug *Wm. F. Taylor* of Norfolk and the steamer *Annie* of the North Carolina Dispatch Company, are reported ashore near Cherry Point, Neuse River, eighteen miles below New Bern." *Wilmington Weekly Star* August 26, 1887.

BEAR IN THE CORN: "Mr. J. D. LaRoque, superintendent of Mr. J[ames] A. Bryan's Lake Ellis Farm, came up yesterday and gave us the following bear story. Late Tuesday evening, Mr. Elliott, living in the neighborhood, came through the farm and asked permission of Mr. LaRoque to go down to the cornfield and kill a bear. It was granted with the understanding that the bear *must be* killed. About fifteen minutes after Mr. Elliott left, a gun fired in the direction of the cornfield, and the halloing and two other shots which followed induced Mr. LaRoque and his force to go immediately to the relief of the man, who seemed to be in distress. Upon arriving they found Mr. Elliott in the wildest state of excitement, but he had [killed] the bear. He was in the field gathering roasting ears when Mr. Elliott came upon him, and although excited, Mr. Elliott's shots were well-directed enough to [kill the bear]. He was a very large one, but poor in flesh." *The Wilmington Daily Review* September 3, 1887, quoting the *Newbern Journal*.

"OX THIEF CAPTURED: Charles Bailey, col., of Newport arrived in the city yesterday morning with an ox belonging to Mr. E[dward] D. Russell of Havelock. Mr. Russell, finding the stall empty early in the morning, took the train for New Berne, arriving in advance of his ox, notified the butchers and Bailey drove in in good time to be taken before Justice Watson and transported to Craven Street hotel. [*Note: a euphemism for jail*]. He failed to give bond for his appearance at the next term of the Superior Court." *The Daily Journal* (New Bern) December 20, 1888.

HIT BY BOOM: "On Saturday night, the Schooner *Laurie*, a wood boat from Slocum's Creek, Isaac Rouse, colored master, and Ezekiel Chance, colored mate, left New Bern on its return trip under a fair wind and was making good time. When off Riverdale, Chance was struck by the fore boom and knocked overboard ... Chance yelled out and sank immediately. He lived at Slocum's Creek and had always been regarded as a negro of good character." *Wilmington Weekly Star* March 15, 1889, quoting the *Newbern Journal*. [*This schooner was a boat that carried wood, as opposed to just a wooden boat.*]

TICK ORDER CANCELLED: "An unparalleled order; some progressive thinker has advanced the idea that ticks on cattle at the season of the year when the luxuriant pasturage vegetation puts them in their most lethargic condition are promoted of their health by reducing their quantity of blood. For purpose of experiment and to supply those who hold such opinions but live in the regions where ticks do not abound, Dr. Kilborn, U. S. Veterinary surgeon, placed an order with Mr. James H. Hunter of Havelock for 10 bushels of the biting little creatures. It is needless to say that the order will remain unfilled -- the supply of ticks in this instant does not equal the demand." *The Daily Journal* (New Bern) August 17, 1890.

DOCTOR SAVES CHILD: "A little four-and-a-half-year-old colored boy, the son of John Peterson, who met with the accident of having a watermelon seed lodge in windpipe a week ago, and which it was found impossible to move, was brought up to the city yesterday from his home near Havelock and taken to Dr. Duffy's office where the windpipe was cut into and the seed removed, after which the little sufferer regained the use of his voice, of which he had been almost deprived, and now seems to be doing well." *The Daily Journal* (New Bern) July 23, 1891.

CAUGHT IN HIS OWN TRAP: "A colored man near Havelock named Sam Locker lost one of his legs by accidental shooting. Bears had been troubling his corn, and in company with another man he set two guns and a bear trap in the woods by the field in which the bears had been. In retracing their steps, they went back on a path in which one of the guns was set, thinking they were on one they had not previously traversed and the mistake was not discovered until Locker struck against the string attached to the gun, discharging it, the load of buckshot taking effect above the knee, mangling it so that the limb had to be taken off at the lower third of the thigh. [*The other man was apparently wounded as well*]. The operation was performed by Drs. C. and F. Duffy, assisted by Dr. Primrose. The operations were successfully performed and the patients are getting on as well as can be expected." *The Daily Journal* (New Bern) November 5, 1891.

KNOCKED OVERBOARD: "Henry Hardesty, colored, who lives at Hancock Creek was drowned near his home Tuesday [February 28, 1893] by being knocked overboard by the boom of William Collingswood's boat on the way to the city. The man could not swim and the wind was so severe and boat going so fast that assistance could not be given him in time. The body had not been recovered at last accounts says the New Bern Journal." *The Progressive Farmer* March 7, 1893.

"SUDDEN DEATH AT HAVELOCK. Mr. Ira Hancock, who for several years has been with Mr. J. H. Hunter of Havelock died from heart disease Monday and five minutes from the time he was attacked. He was plowing cotton at the time; his mother and daughter and Mr. Hunter were near him. He called the latter and as he turned to see what was the matter Mr. Hancock fell and died almost instantly. Mr. Hancock was originally from Carteret County. He leaves a wife and several small children." *New Bern Weekly Journal* May 25, 1893.

THREE MEN LOST. "The schooner Molly B., Capt. James Bell, colored, was turned over by the gale on Wednesday morning two miles from Cherry Point, Neuse River, while bringing a load of wood to Newbern and broken to pieces. Five men were aboard. The captain and another man escaped – one by clinging to the bottom of the little skiff; the other by clinging to a piece of the boat. Two colored men, Lewis Willowby and Cull Willowby were drowned. The body of the former was recovered; but that of the latter has not been found. They lived at Clubfoot Creek. Mr. A. N. Weaver, a northern gentleman and proprietor of a sawmill at Cherry Point was also aboard and was drowned. He moved here, we believe from Connecticut, about three years ago. He was about 35 years of age and not a man of family. His body at last accounts had not been found." *The Chatham (NC) Record* November 16, 1893, quoting the *Newbern Journal*.

BODY RECOVERED: "The body of Mr. A.N. Weaver, formerly of Pennsylvania, of whose drowning we told in our last issue, was recovered and buried at Cherry Point, his home since moving to this locality about three years ago." *The Daily Journal* New Bern, November 12, 1893.

TWO HUGE BEARS: "Mr. C. C. Cannon of Havelock had the good fortune to kill two huge bears on Mr. J. M. Gorrell's place. Each hind quarter weighed a hundred pounds and judging by this the very lowest estimate that could be put on the entire weight of each bear would be 800 pounds. This is immense. The bears were in fine condition, rolling in fat. They are living principally on gum berries found in the swamps and on late corn, which they steal. This species of game continues abundant in that locality and offers fine sport for those who like an exciting hunt." *Wilmington Weekly Star* December 15, 1893, quoting the *Newbern Journal*.

THIRTY-FIVE BEARS: "Mr. [T. H.] Mallison does not live far from the Havelock neighborhood where bears have been so plentiful this year. Bears visit his farm also, and he not only joins in hunting them but has captured numbers in traps. He has one trap in which he has caught thirty-five bears, and the trap is doing as good service today as the day it was first put into use. In addition to the thirty-five bears, a number of racoons, foxes, wild cats and dogs have all been snapped up and held in his firm embrace." *Wilmington Weekly Star* December 29, 1893.

BALLENGER RESIDENCE BURNED: "The dwelling of Mr. E. S. Ballenger of Havelock burned Tuesday. The fire caught from a defective flue. Not only was the house lost but all the contents -- the clothes of the inmates as well as the furniture. Mr. Ballenger has a wife and several children and the loss falls heavily upon him. He is a worthy man and has the sympathy of all who know him." *New Berne Weekly Journal* December 6, 1894.

TWO CHILDREN AND A PISTOL: "While two children were playing with the pistol Friday at the house of Mr. John Deport at Havelock, the dangerous plaything went off and seriously wounded the three-year-old daughter of Mr. J. M. Bragg of this city. The little girl had gone to visit Mr. [*John*]

Deport who is her grandfather. The other child is her half-brother and about 12 years old. He was holding the pistol at the time of the accident. The ball followed a downward course, going through the girl's neck and lodging in her shoulder. Mrs. Bragg is gone to Havelock to be with the unfortunate little girl. Mr. Bragg is now absent on the revenue cutter *Winona*. At last account the child was living but in critical condition." *New Berne Weekly Journal*, July 11, 1896. [*By some miracle, the child, Jessie E. Bragg, did not die and appears in the 1900 census at age seven. The half-brother, Newton R. Satterthwaite, was only 10 at the time of the accident.* ❖*Jessie's and Newton's mother, Cora Bragg, was the former Cora A. Small, daughter of the late Joshua Small of Harlowe. Newton was a product of her first marriage to S. H. Satterthwaite of Granville County. They were married near Havelock Station, May 9, 1883, by Rev. Edward Bull. The groom rode the morning train to meet his bride at Havelock "and the marriage was celebrated while the train was making its way to Morehead," according to a news account. "On its return the parties came to New Bern where they will reside."* ❖*The Satterthwaite's marriage didn't last and she later married J. M. Bragg, the father of the girl who was wounded by the pistol.* ❖*The Bragg's would have another daughter, Golda, in 1900. Sadly, they lost that child six years later and she's buried at FUMC. See Bragg, Golda. The Daily Journal of New Bern reported Sunday, September 10, 1905: "Goldie, the little daughter of Mrs. Cora Bragg, died at her home in Havelock early Saturday morning. Interment took place last evening."*]

"DROWNED IN THE CABIN. Like a rat in a hole, Allen Miller, a colored man, aged about 50 years, suffered a most horrible death Tuesday night. He was employed upon the piledriver owned by Maj. Dennison and slept in the cabin of the flat [*a barge*]. Yesterday morning persons about the cotton gin, at the market dock, noticed that during the night the flat had gone down. It been known that Miller slept aboard the boat, inquiry was made to learn of his whereabouts. He was nowhere to be found alive and a force of hands were once engaged to raise the flat. When the boat came to the surface a man with a hook dragged Miller from the cabin. He had been dead several hours and the verdict of the coroner's jury was that Allen Miller came to his death by drowning. He was from Havelock and leaves one child." *New Bern Weekly Journal* July 1, 1897.

ACCIDENTALLY SHOT: "A young man named Willie Tippitt of Havelock, son of Mr. George F. Tippitt, was accidentally shot Thursday afternoon. The young man was in the field after a load of fodder and had his shotgun with him. The gun hit against the cartwheel and went off, the load entering his shoulder which was badly lacerated. He was brought to New Bern on the morning train for medical treatment." *The Daily Journal* (New Bern) October 29, 1898.

"STRAYED OR STOLEN: One light bay mare, blaze in forehead, white around mouth, from my pasture at Pine Grove, near Havelock. Reward for her return. Lafayette Hardesty." *The Daily Journal* (New Bern) December 4, 1898.

BURNED IN THE FIELD: "Friday evening a field of dry grass and vegetation was being burned on a farm belonging to James A. Bryan near Havelock. Clifford Rogerson, son of Capt. William Rogerson of this city, stationed himself near a house to prevent the fire reaching it. After the fire had swept through, the other men came to where Rogerson had been stationed, and found that he had moved several hundred yards from his first position and that the flames had caught and burned him to death. The burial took place Saturday at Havelock. The deceased was 28 years old." *New Berne Weekly Journal* March 6, 1900.

VANISHED FROM VIEW: "Sarah Davis, an aged colored woman of this city, who was on the poor list and had a monthly allowance from the county, has mysteriously disappeared. She was last seen here December 8 and two days later she was seen on the county road between Havelock and Riverdale. It is thought that she may have wandered into the woods and become lost. The woman has a daughter here called Sarah Lovick. Any information may be sent to J. J. Baxter, County Commissioner." *The Daily Journal* New Bern, January 2, 1902.

CAIN, ABEL LOST IN NEUSE: "Sunday evening [*December 7, 1902*], people below Wilkinson's Point on the Neuse River, observed two young men in a sailboat, which apparently came out of Hancock Creek, on the opposite side of the river, trying to make the shore. One was doing the sailing, the other bailing out the boat, and both boat and men shortly afterwards disappeared from sight. The water was dragged later on, but nothing was found, neither was there anything visible of boat or contents. While nothing could be learned last night, it was thought that the occupants of the boat were Cain and Abel Powell who live near Croatan, and who were in the habit of crossing the Neuse River to visit on the east shore." *The Wilmington Messenger* December 9, 1902.

POST OFFICE HIT: "The post office of Havelock in [Craven] County was robbed one night last week of $29 in stamps and some money." *Asheboro Courier*, Asheboro, N.C., February 12, 1903.

"ACCIDENT AT HAVELOCK. George W. Cully, a colored man, who lives near Havelock, while attempting to alight from a moving train at that place Monday morning, fell and was very painfully hurt. Cully was brought to the city on the same train and received medical attention from Dr. Primrose. The hurt was not very serious, being only the result of a fall, the train not striking him." *New Bern Weekly Journal* May 5, 1903.

"AN EXPLANATION: Havelock, N.C., July 20, 1903. Laboring under the impression that Mr. H. A. Marshall had accused me of false swearing, I insulted him before the board of equalization, but finding I was mistaken I have apologized and we are now friendly. J. H. Hunter." *New Bern Weekly Journal* July 24, 1903. [*Henry Marshall and James Hunter, whose families had been in the Havelock-Slocum Creek area for generations, were prominent and successful community leaders and landowners. Each had achieved recognition for daring clandestine service during the War Between the States.*]

WRECKED AT CHERRY POINT: "The schooner *James Rumley* had a rough time of it Friday near Cherry point. She dragged her anchor from the north to the south side of the river, the crew being powerless to stop her. She capsized and is thought to be a total wreck. She is the property of Maurice Sultan of this city." [*New Bern*] *New Berne Daily Journal* October 13, 1903. [*Staunch Confederate sympathizer James Rumley of Beaufort kept an interesting Civil War diary from 1862-1865. It was published in 2009 via author Judkin Browning.*]

"MRS. [*CAROLINE*] BANGERT and her son, Mr. Albert Bangert, went to Havelock last night in response to a message announcing the serious illness of Mrs. Bangert of that place." *The Daily Journal* (New Bern) November 4, 1903.

CIRCUIT RIDER: "On the second Sunday I preach at three places: Riverdale, Havelock and Hancock's Creek. At Havelock, the crowds are better than formerly and I hope to be able to reach more of the people this year. Sometimes the crowds at the other points are small; and the work presents many difficulties." E. O. Johnson in the *Atlantic Messenger* (New Bern) October 1904. [*The Atlantic Messenger billed itself as "Devoted to the Relief of Baptist Destitution in Eastern North Carolina."*]

"A FIERCE WILD ANIMAL: Caught and Killed in the Environs of Havelock. Last Saturday Messrs. J. S. Brooks of [New Bern] and Edwin Bryant and son of Havelock were hunting for deer near Havelock. Their hounds were not successful in running down any of the game they were looking for but they did find a large catamount and chased him two or three miles before it was brought to bay. The animal fought fiercely but the dogs overpowered it and killed it bearing away from the struggle but few evidences of the affair in the shape of scratches. The dogs killed the critter without the aid of any man. It was a fine specimen of this rare animal and weighed about 75 pounds. It could have made considerable havoc in a barnyard if it had been given a chance." *New Bern Weekly Journal* Friday, December 16, 1904. [*Catamount is another name for a cougar, puma, panther, mountain lion; all the same animal. These big, long tail cats used to be a staple of local forests and, in those bygone days, were the major predator of deer.*]

GUN EXPLODED: "Herbert Wynne, about 15 years of age and the son of Mr. W. Y. Wynne, who lives a few miles from Havelock, while out hunting wild geese last Thursday night met with a very painful accident caused by the explosion of his gun. His hand was badly torn as far up as the wrist, and the thumb had to be amputated. Dr. C. N. Mason of Harlowe was called for his services and the patient is now improving." *New Bern Weekly Journal* January 24, 1905.

STRAYED: "A roan mare, brown mane, and tail, like hind legs, branded on jaw and thigh. Closely built. A reward of five dollars will be paid for information leading to recovery. Address Nathan George, Havelock, N.C." *The Daily Journal* (New Bern) May 9, 1905

"BOATMAN DROWNED. Frank Hyman, a colored man, was knocked overboard from the schooner H. B. Lane, Tuesday afternoon and drowned. The schooner plies between New Bern and Slocumb's Creek from here loaded with general merchandise. When just below Johnson's Point, a flurry came up which necessitated the taking in of the canvas, and while reefing the mainsail the man Hyman, a sailor on the vessel, was knocked overboard. He immediately sank and it is presumed that the blow stunned him before falling in the water. The unfortunate man lived in the neighborhood of Havelock. The body was dredged for Wednesday, but had not been found at a late hour in the afternoon." *New Bern Weekly Journal* August 11, 1905.

ARSON AT HAVELOCK SCHOOL: "Mr. W. A. Scott of Greensboro, Department Insurance Commissioner, and Mr. Samuel M. Brinson, County Superintendent of Schools, went down to Havelock this morning to make an investigation regarding the burning of the schoolhouse on last Friday. Superintendent Brinson says beyond a doubt it was of incendiary origin." *The New Bern Sun* February 10, 1909.

RATS AND MATCHES: "Early Sunday morning, the home of Mr. Moses Rowe, just below Havelock, in this county, was entirely destroyed by fire. There was nothing saved except the sewing machine, the loss being given at $550 with no insurance. It is thought that rats and matches furnished the combination that caused the fire." *New Bern Weekly Journal* May 11, 1909.

RICHARD RUSSELL SHOT: "The condition of Richard Russell, the young man of Havelock, who accidentally shot himself last Sunday, is reported to be favorable for recovery, although it looked very serious for him at first. He is still in the [Stewart] Sanitarium [sic]." *New Bern Weekly Journal* July 23, 1909.

EXCITING BEAR CAPTURE: "Henry Stephens and two boys, who fish net at Hancock Creek, were returning to the city with their catch when they espied a bear nosing around about the mouth of the estuary. Thinking to have a little fun, the boys went ashore and with shouts and missiles made the bear take water. The chase was continued with boat until way out in the Neuse. Bruin decided that the boys' fun had gone far enough and he would have a little himself, so he went for the boat. The crew resisted with oars and axe, his efforts to board until a lucky blow put the enraged creature out of business. In the fight one of the boys fell overboard almost into the bear's clutches and his feelings can better be imagined than described. The carcass, quite a large one but lean, was brought to town and sold to one of the meat markets." *New Bern Weekly Journal* July 27, 1909.

STRUCK BY SPOUT: "Mr. George Driggers, the young Norfolk Southern flagman who was painfully injured by being struck on the head with the protruding spout of a water tank near Havelock a few days ago, and who has been confined at the sanatorium, is sufficiently recovered to be able to be discharged from that institution." *The Daily Journal* (New Bern) September 16, 1910.

"ANOTHER HIGHWAY ROBBERY. While returning from a commercial trip to Newport, last Saturday afternoon Mr. C. T. Midgett, traveling salesman for F. S. Duffy medicine company, was held up by two Negroes and robbed. The robbery took place between Newport and Havelock on a lonely stretch of the pocosin road seven or eight miles an extent. [*Nine Mile Rd.*] Mr. Midgett says that he was driving along slowly not expecting to be molested, of course, when two Negroes appeared in the road a short distance ahead and came meeting him, one on either side. Reaching the horse's head and seizing the bridle, both of them presenting pistols, commanding him to throw up his hands which he did. They went through his sample case and secured five dollars in currency and 50 cents in coin. Mr. Midgett said that the Negroes were young men, dressed in blue overalls and he took them to be innocent timber cutters until they accosted him as related." *New Bern Weekly Journal* July 16, 1911.

"STRUCK BY LIGHTNING. Information received in this city yesterday stated that Oscar Grantham, a colored farmer who lives near Havelock, was knocked unconscious Wednesday afternoon by a bolt of lightning that struck a tree in his yard. Grantham had been working in his garden when the storm arose and had gone into the house and sat down in a chair near one of the doors. When the lightning struck the tree, which was near the house, Grantham fell from the chair and it took his family more than half an hour to revive him. The shock was felt by other members of the family." *New Bern Weekly Journal* Friday, July 21, 1911.

LOST IN THE POCOSIN: "Only those who have been there can know what it is to be lost in the pocosin after dark. Last week near Havelock, a Mr. Wynne and a colored man went into the pocosin near that place to look after a survey line. It became dark and they were unable to find their way out, though but a short distance inside the pocosin bounds. The Norfolk Southern train passing gave them the direction, but a turn lost them again. Finally, a party of friends started with bells and firearms, and it was only after some labor that the two men were found and got home. There was no special danger but who wants to remain in the Pocosin all night without preparation?" *The Daily Journal* (New Bern) October 24, 1911. [*Note: Pocosin is an unusual and dangerous form of elevated spongy swamp found around the lakes southwest of Havelock and in other parts of the Croatan National Forest. Barren, boggy and lacking in landmarks, a thousand acres of the ground the Indians called "rumbling earth" can be found there.*]

SHOT AT CHRISTMAS: "Miss Lily Godwin, who was accidentally shot in the left hand on Christmas day with a toy pistol and who has been in New Bern undergoing treatment from a physician, has returned home very much improved." *The Daily Journal* (New Bern) January 8, 1913.

WRECK DELAYS TRAIN: "*Six Freight Cars 'Jump' Track Near Pine Grove.* While in route from Beaufort to this city yesterday afternoon, six cars of local freight train No. 99, in charge of Conductor Coward and Engineer Hancock, were derailed at Pine Grove, a flag station between Havelock and Croatan, and it was necessary to send the wrecking train down from this city to clear the track in order to allow the westbound passenger train to proceed onto this city. Just how the wreck occurred is not known but it is supposed that the truck of one of the cars jumped the track and this caused other cars to follow. It was impossible to transfer passengers from one train to another in the westbound train was delayed there for more than two hours. Two of the railcars were empty, one was loaded with potatoes, another carrying a load of oyster shells and two were filled with merchandise. Fortunately, no one was injured during the accident." *The Daily Journal* (New Bern) April 2, 1914.

LOGGING CAMP ROBBED: "Blango Goddett charged with robbing camp. Brought to New Bern and placed in jail: Blango Goddett, colored, was brought to New Bern by M. F. Russell from Havelock yesterday and in default of a $250 justified bond was placed in the county jail to await the September term of Craven County Superior Court. Goddett was charged with breaking in the logging camp of Allen Whittenton [Whittington] about four miles from Havelock and stealing a considerable amount of the furniture from the sleeping quarters. Some of the goods were found on him when he was arrested. It is also alleged that he set fire to the camp, which was completely destroyed, but the evidence of that offense was not sufficient and he was given a hearing before Justice of the Peace H. A. Marshall yesterday morning on the matter of housebreaking and larceny. After hearing the evidence, probable cause was found and he was placed under a $250 bond." *New Bern Weekly Journal* July 21, 1914.

TUG HOLED: "The ocean-going tug *Columbia* is on the marine railways at New Bern with a hole in her bottom. The craft struck a submerged piling in Clubfoot creek." *Washington (NC) Daily News* December 14, 1915.

HEAVY FIRE DAMAGE: In Havelock section. "Mr. A. D. Rooks, one of Havelock's well-known residents who is spending today in New Bern, told in a graphic manner of the fierce forest fire which has raged in that section for the past ten days and which has done thousands of dollars' worth of damage to timber and other property. Mr. Rooks declared that it was due only to the efforts of the residence of the Havelock section that much more property was not destroyed by the fire which swept through that like a hurricane." *News & Observer* (Raleigh) April 25, 1916.

DESERTERS NABBED: "Returning this morning from Camp Glenn where they had been to carry four deserters who were captured in this city [New Bern] yesterday afternoon, Chief C. Lupton and policeman Edward Belangia nabbed three others. The men left camp yesterday afternoon and had walked through the country to Havelock. They boarded the train at that place this morning after purchasing tickets for Goldsboro and ran right into the arms of the officers. They are spending the day here in jail and will be carried back to Camp Glenn this afternoon." *Washington (N.C.) Daily News* August 10, 1916, quoting the *New Bern Sun-Journal*. [*Camp Glenn was a National Guard camp, 1906-1918, on Bogue Sound just west of old Morehead City. It also served as a naval refueling base during World War I. Ed Belangia resided and owned farm land just west of Havelock, where Belangia-Ballenger families lived for several generations.*]

BEAR KILLS HUNTER: "Durand Morton, an aged hunter of the Havelock section, was killed Wednesday of last week by a huge black bear, according to reports brought here by Col. W. T. Dortch, who has a hunting lodge near the scene of the tragedy. Mr. Morton was killed when he went to the aid of his dogs who were being worsted in a fight with the bear, two of them being killed. He went to their rescue with an axe. The bear knocked the axe from the man's hand and overcame him. He was mortally wounded, dying a few

minutes later." *The Wilmington Dispatch, The Kinston Free Press* and *The State Journal* (Raleigh). November 14-17, 1916. [*Morton was attacked and killed Wednesday, November 8, 1916. The informant, William Theophilus Dortch was born on a plantation in Nash County near Rocky Mount but later made his home in Goldsboro. He was a politician who served as a Confederate State Senator in North Carolina 1862-1865. He was an avid hunter and frequent, well-known visitor to Havelock. For many years Dortch entertained friend and influential guests at his hunting lodge, Camp Goldsboro, on Tucker Creek off Lewis Farm Road.*]

JEWELLER DISPLAYS SNAKES: "Two of the largest rattlesnakes ever seen in this part of the state were caught Monday near Havelock by one of the residents of that place and were yesterday on exhibit at Mr. J. O. Baxter's jewelry store, attracting much attention. The snakes, each more than five feet in length, were nabbed by the forked stick method or, in other words, the gentleman who caught them succeeded in getting close enough to the reptiles to place the forked stick just back of the head of each after which they were easily picked up and deposited in a wire-covered box. Each snake is equipped with a fine set of rattles and these have been kept in almost continued motion since their capture." *Wilmington Dispatch* October 3, 1917. [*For many decades, Baxter's elegant New Bern store was a fixture on Pollock Street before closing in the early years of the twenty-first century.*]

"OAKDALE VILLA, the home of Mrs. I. W. Shields, four miles from Havelock and one of the oldest and prettiest estates in that section, together with the stock barn and stables, was destroyed by fire." *The Alamance Gleaner*, Graham, N.C., March 2, 1922. [*The 550-acre Slocum Creek-front property was actually called Oak Lane Villa. It was the former home of the William Buys family before being purchased by a wealthy and well-known tobacco planter, Ira William Shields of Durham, in March 1920. Shields died there in April 1921.*]

BATTS INQUEST: Inquest will be held probably Tuesday [*February 9, 1926*] for Ernest Batts who was found mangled to death after he had been run over by a freight train on the Norfolk Southern Railroad tracks about a mile below Croatan [*see note below*] yesterday afternoon. Coroner J. L. Hartsfield viewed the body last night. The theory is well established that the Negro was attempting to jump on the moving train. The train conductor, who was riding on the engine, saw him jump before the accident. The body was badly crushed. The left arm and left leg were cut off and the trunk was horribly mutilated." New Bern *Sun Journal* February 6, 1926. [*Eyewitness description by area resident Adam Cully to the author located the place of the accident on the railroad tracks south of the Greenfield Heights Boulevard crossing in Havelock; behind the Don Lee Heights subdivision.*]

☞ NOTICE

Miscellaneous items in chronological order from the news, wills, and elsewhere provide a glimpse of life and death in times long passed. These excerpts in quotation marks are published – misspellings and all – as they ran in the publications or public records noted at the end of each; except that last names are capitalized and where brackets [ ] appear, indicating that additional information has been added by the author.

❖　❖　❖　❖

COLONIAL ROADS: An Act, for a Road from Core-Point, on Pamptico, [*Pamlico*] to New Bern, on Neuse River. Whereas a Road from Core-Point, to New Bern Town, would be of very great Use and Advantage to the Inhabitants of the upper parts of Neuse River in particular … all the Inhabitants settled on the South Side of Neuse River, from Slocum's Creek upwards, including Trent River; and all the Inhabitants in the Fork of Neuse; are hereby ordered to work on the Main Road that is to be laid out, by the persons hereafter appointed for that purpose. *Acts of the North Carolina General Assembly, 1722.*

… And Be It Further Enacted, by the Authority aforesaid, That Capt. Richard GRAVES, Capt. William Hancock, Mr. John Tripp, and Robert Turner Esqr., or any Three of them, are hereby ordered and Impowered to lay out the said Road from New Bern Town to Core-Point, within three months after the Ratification of this Act, under the Penalty of Twenty Pounds. *Acts of the North Carolina General Assembly, 1722.*

COLONIAL TAXES. "Notice is hereby given, That the Subscriber had appointed Mr. John Dillahunty, one of his deputies; and, in order to make easy and convenient to the People in General, Attendance will be given by said Dillahunty, and himself, at several Times and Places hereafter mentioned to receive Taxes … On Friday, 8th, at James Handcock, Slocomb Creek. On Saturday, 9th, at William Rutledge, Handcock's Creek. On Monday, 11th at John Bishop's, Clubfoot's Creek. On Tuesday, 12th, Thomas M'Lin's, Adam's Creek. On Wednesday, 13th, at Samuel Masters's, South River." *The Newbern Gazette,* January 17, 1764. [*This sheriff's notice of tax collection is the earliest appearance in print yet found of the name of* Slocum Creek.]

"RANAWAY from my Saw Mill on Slocomb's Creek, a Negro Fellow Named JOE, belonging to the Estate of James Wynn, deceased. He is a well sett Fellow, aged about 45, and has a very ill look. 'Tis supposed he is harboured at Core Sound, where he is well known. Any person that shall be found to harbor or entertain him, will be prosecuted with Rigour. James Davis." *The Newbern Gazette* July 6, 1764. [*Before the formation of the United States of America and when New Bern was the capital city of North Carolina, James Davis was the royal governor's official printer – including the printing of paper money – and the first newspaper publisher in the fledgling colony.*]

NEWBERN, December 14, 1764. "Since our last [issue], several Vessels arrived here from Northward, particularly a Sloop from Maryland with 57 Passengers, chiefly Families, who are to settle in the Province." *The Newbern Gazette.*

[FROM THE WILL OF] Akerman, Frederick [signed with an X] -- n.d. / September 1772 -- "sick and weak." To my well-beloved wife Althea Akerman, the plantation and land where I now live … To son Leonard Akerman land on Slocumbs Creek, one 3-year-old mare and two 3-year-old heifers. To son John Akerman two 3-year-old heifers, 1-year old mare. To daughter Sarah Akerman land on Hancock's Creek where William Heath now lives with all the female cattle thereon …" Source: KR [*Before the American Revolution, Frederick Akerman (also spelled Acreman) owned 640 acres on the east side of Slocum Creek and both sides of the old Beaufort Road just south of the Chesnutt plantation. The exact location or size of the Acreman-Heath tract on Hancock Creek is not known to the author.*]

[*FROM THE WILL OF*] "Bishop, John - 18 December 1780 / June 1781 – 'of Neuse River in Craven County' - To wife Rebekah all my cards, and my loomb and utensils … To son John a tract of land known as Pastor Neck that I bought of Jesse Holton on the west side of Slocumbs Creek, also one shot gun, shot molds, and bullet molds. To son Charles one Little plantation on the west side of the west prong of Slocumbs Creek near the road known by the name of Grave Neck. Daughter Alice land adjoining James Bishop, William Borden, Peter Phisioc [*Physioc*], and Thomas Austin. All debts due me to my children John, Alice, and Charles … Executors: Benjamin Stanton, Jr., Owin Stanton, Benjamin Stanton, Sr., and Joseph Dew, they also to serve as guardians. Wit: Peter Physioc, Joseph Brittain, Joseph Bishop." Source: KR [*John Bishop and Peter Physioc built a dam and mill on the southwest prong of Slocum Creek near the Beaufort Road in 1772. Bishop's ownership of cards and a loom indicates that he was a weaver, a typical trade for the period. We're left to wonder if the name "Graves Neck" Road indicates another lost cemetery.*]

HORSE STEALING: "The subscriber, living on Adam's Creek, in the lower end of the county, has in his possession, a chestnut HORSE about thirteen hands high – branded on the near shoulder TN. Said horse was taken from one Asa Simmons, who was arrested and has since been committed for horse stealing. It is supposed to belong to some person in Onslow County.

This owner may have it again by proving his property and paying charges. John West, Constable." *The North-Carolina Gazette,* New Bern, September 14, 1793.

"WANTS EMPLOYMENT in the Country. A Person qualified to keep School, to teach children the rudiments of their mother tongue, and initiate them in the first lines of science. Apply at the Printing Office." *The Newbern Gazette,* July 20, 1799.

[FROM THE WILL OF] Bratcher, Thomas [X]—19 December 1804 / March 1805—For the love, goodwill and affection I bear to my son Benjamin Bratcher the land and house where I now live. Son William Bratcher land joining the same where Susy Umphres did live on the west side of the east prong of "Slocum" Creek. Sons Roger and Asy Brathcher land to be equally divided on the east side

> *I intend to leave this state shortly.*
> **A[dam] TOOLEY**
> The Newbern Gazette, March 16. 1799

of the east prong of Slocum Creek. Rest of property to my wife [not named] for life or "widderhood." Exec: [not named]. Wits: Abram Griffen, Jesse [x] Hampton." Source: KR

FAIR WARNING: "I hereby caution all persons dealing with my Negroes – either my own, or those I hired – particularly from the purchase of Tar or Turpentine, without written permission, in due form, from me. As I have been much injured by this unlawful trade, I am determined to enforce the law, without discrimination, on all those who deal with said Negroes, and will give Twenty Shillings to any person who will make information that shall lead to conviction. William Holland. Slocumb's Creek." *Newbern Herald* September 30, 1809.

"FOR SALE, Valuable Tract of Land, Lying in Slocumb's Creek, Sixteen Miles below Newbern, containing Three Hundred and Fifty Acres. Any person wishing to purchase, may know the terms by applying to Mr. James Tooly off Newbern, or the Subscriber near Snow Hill, Green County, Adam Tooly." *The True Republican and Newbern Weekly Advertiser* March 26, 1811. *[Adam Tooly (Tooley) owned land on Hancock and Slocum Creek. He ran the cryptic notice boxed above in 1799, but apparently didn't leave the state as we find him in Greene County in 1811. His name appears on the H. A. Marshall map for James A. Bryan, 1899.]*

SOUTH SHORE, NEUSE RIVER 1812: "The Subscriber having been Swindled out of a valuable Estate of Lands and Negroes, by a certain "Thomas Jorden of the County of Hyde, hereby forewarns all persons from purchasing said property. Abraham Jorden. January 1, 1812. ||| We the Subscribers do hereby certify that we are personally acquainted with Abraham Jorden, and that from our knowledge of him, we are willing to testify that we believe him of sound mind and memory, and able to transact business. Philip Neale, Benj. Bordin [Borden], John Marchant, Willis Whitehead, John Johnson, John Whitehead, J[ames] T. Jones, James Jones, Abner Neale, Michael Fisher, Thomas Austin, Gideon Jones, George Cooper, B[enners] Vail, H. Dade." *The Carolina Federal Republican* (New Bern) February 8, 1812.

"TEN DOLLARS REWARD: Ran-away from the Subscriber on 28th July last, a negro man named MARCH. He is about 22 years of age, 5 feet nine or 10 inches high, of yellowish complexion; he was formerly the property of *Levi Fulshire*, Esq., deceased, and is at this time in Carteret County, and passes for a free man by the name of *John Codett*, and it is believed he has got a free pass. I will give the above reward to any person who will deliver him to me, or secure him and his papers in any Jail, so that I get him again. I forewarn all persons from harboring or employing him, as I am determined to enforce the law on all those who may be guilty. William Holland, Slocumbs Creek, March 15, 1814." *The Carolina Federal Republican* (New Bern) August 16, 1814. [*Particularly in the early half of the 19th century, runaway slave notices were common fare in newspapers. Publishers used woodcuts like the one shown here as illustrations. These were silhouettes of dark-skinned people in various states of dress, sometimes with a coat, a hat, or a bundle over the shoulder, and often in the act of running.*]

GOODINGS' PETITION 1814: "To the Honorable General Assembly, The Petition of Stephen Gooding of the County of Craven humbly sheweth. That he is the proprietor of a tract of land granted on the 23d day of November one thousand seven hundred and twenty-three [*1723*] to Simon Keller for one hundred and sixty acres situate on the head of Colemans Creek [*today's Tucker Creek*] at that time in Bath County but now in Craven County of which patent though certified to have been recorded is not to be found on the records of the Secretary's office. Your petitioner prays that the Secretary of State be authorized to record the said patent. November 1814, Stephen Goodings." Source: *Connie Ardrey* 2009 from North Carolina Archives, North Carolina General Assembly Nov-Dec 1814 Session Box 2 - Petitions (Concerning Land). [*Stephen Gooding(s)) would become prominent enough that in 1860 the U.S. Census labeled the entire greater Havelock area, roughly equivalent to today's Townships Five and Six, "Goodings District."*]

"MARRIED. At Beaufort on the 27th ult. Benjamin Borden, Esqr. of Craven-County, to Mrs. Rebecca Stanton, of this place." *The Carolina Federal Republican* (New Bern) March 8, 1817.

"LOST. On Wednesday evening last, an old red Morocco POCKET BOOK, containing several Notes of hand $ other papers of value; amongst them a Note of hand [*a promissory note*] against Mr. George Cooper for $200, the others not recollected. – Any person finding the Pocket Book and delivering it with the contents to the subscriber will receive a generous reward. John Bishop. All persons are forbid trading for the above notes. JB." *The Carolina Federal Republican* (New Bern) January 31, 1818. [*A January 16, 1765 tax collection notice listed "John Bishop's, Clubfoot Creek" as a meeting place.*]

"TO THE FREEMEN of Craven County. Fellow-Citizens. Our late representatives having declined a further tender of their services, I am induced, by the solicitations of many of my friends; to announce myself a candidate for your suffrages at the ensuing election, to represent you in the House of Commons. Abner Neale. Adams' Creek, July 23, 1818." *New Bern Sentinel*, August 1, 1818.

"TEN DOLLARS REWARD. Ran away from the subscriber on the 1st instant, a negro fellow named PRIMUS, about 30 years of age: he has a lameness in one of his hips, occasioned by a burn; one of his great toes is deformed by turning in; and his fore teeth are decayed. He formerly belonged to Evan Jones, deceased. I will give the above reward, and pay all reasonable expenses, to any person who will apprehend and deliver said fellow to me, or secure him in the jail at Newbern. Masters of vessels, and others, are forewarned from harboring, employing, or carrying him away, under the penalty of law. Stephen W. Winn. Craven county, September 15." *Newbern Sentinel* September 19, 1818.

"MARRIED, In this county, on Tuesday last, Capt. John S. Smith, to Miss Elizabeth Lovick, daughter of the late Mr. George Lovick." *Newbern Sentinel*, December 19, 1818.

"MARRIED, On Tuesday Evening last, at the House of Mr. Samuel Potter on Slocumb's Creek, Mr. Eden T. Jones to Miss Frances Potter." *Newbern Sentinel* April 3, 1819.

"MARRIED, on Wednesday last, at Mrs. Jones' on Handcock's Creek, Mr. James Lovick to Mrs. Mehitibel Judd." *Newbern Sentinel* April 15, 1820. [*Mehitibel (Mahetabel) Jones Judd was the widow of William H. Judd. They married in Craven County on July 25, 1816, per Ingmire. The Judds are the subject of first entry in the oldest existing parish record book of Christ Church in New Bern, which noted the baptism of two African American children. "May 6 (1818) – At the home of William Judd – Julia, a black female child aged about 6 years, the property of said Wm. Judd; sponsors William Judd, his wife, Mehitable Judd. Also, at the same time and place Laura, a black infant daughter of Pakey, a black man and property of*

Wm. Judd, and Sukey, a free black woman." Reported by Gertrude S. Carraway in her book Crown of Life *1940.*]

"TWENTY DOLLARS REWARD. Ran-away from the subscriber, about the third of March last, his Negro woman named SILVEY. Aged about 28 years, five feet two or three inches high; has one of her little fingers drawn up by a burn. – She is supposed to be lurking about Mr. Thomas Austin's, having her mother and brother at that place, or she may be about the plantation of Mr. James Lovick, where her husband lives. The above reward will be paid if she is delivered to me, or secured in Jail, so that I can get her again. I hereby caution all persons from harbouring, employing or carrying her away, as I am determined to enforce the law against all offenders without distinction. — Ten dollars will be given for information sufficient to convict any person offending in any of said points. Eden T. Jones. Slocumb's Creek, May 11, 1820." *Newbern Sentinel.*

"MARRIED at Slocumb's Creek on the 27th ult., William H. Ives to Sarah Rowe." *The New Bern Morning Herald & True Republican* May 12, 1820.

"NOTICE. The sale of the Perishable part of the estate of Robert W. Franklin, deceased, will commence at his late residence on Slocumb's Creek, on Friday, the 30th day of June, instant. John Franklin, Administrator." Newbern. *Newbern Sentinel* June 16, 1820.

"MARRIED in this town on Monday last, Mr. John R. Good of this town and Miss Margaret Ellis, daughter of Mr. Michael Ellis of this county." *Carolina Centinel* [New Bern] November 25, 1820.

"TO RENT, for the term of one year, Two Plantations. On the south side of Neuse River, fifteen miles below New Bern – one of which is at the mouth of Slocum's Creek – the other, known by the name Moor[e]'s, is a mile higher up the Creek. Both are under good fences, and in every respect ready for farming. For further particulars, apply to the subscriber, or to Mr. James Lovick. Hancy Jones." Slocumb's Creek, January 18, 1821. *Newbern Sentinel.*

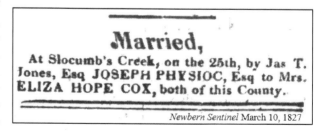

Married,

At Slocumb's Creek, on the 25th, by Jas T. Jones, Esq JOSEPH PHYSIOC, Esq to Mrs. ELIZA HOPE COX, both of this County.

Newbern Sentinel March 10, 1827

"MARRIED at Clubfoot's Creek in this county on Thursday evening last by Rev. Lemuel D. Hatch, Mr. Alfred Hatch to Elizabeth Vail, daughter of the late John Vail, Esq." *The Newbern Morning Herald & True Republican* May 11, 1822.

"MARRIED, At Mrs. Austin's on Handcock's Creek, on the 18th ultimo [December 18, 1823], Mr. James Bell of Carteret county to Miss Elizabeth Cooper of Georgia." *The North-Carolina Star* (Raleigh) January 16, 1824.

"Nothing has been heard from the CLUBFOOT AND HARLOW CREEK NAVIGATION COMPANY. It is presumed, therefore, that the proposed subscriptions by individuals to warrant further subscriptions on the part of the state to complete that work, have not yet been made." *Wilmington Free Press* April 16, 1824. [*The canal was an ambitious on-again-off-again project that eventually connected Clubfoot Creek with the Newport River as a shortcut for marine traffic from Beaufort to New Bern.*]

"NOTICE. On Monday, the first day of January next, at the court-house in New Bern will be hired for the year, 60 or 70 negroes: and at the same time and place, will be rented for the year, the PLANTATION owned by the heirs of Wm. P. Moore, deceased, on the Pembroke Road, adjoining the bridge: the plantation owned by the same person on Brice's Creek; and their plantation on Adams Creek. The lands and the mills thereon, and Clubfoot's Creek; owned by Michael N. Fisher, a minor; and the plantation at Pearson's point, owned by the heirs of Chris. D. Neil [Neale], deceased. Persons indebted to me, for the hire of negroes, or rent of land, are requested to make payment. Geo. Wilson." *Newbern Sentinel*, December 23, 1826.

LAND FOR SALE. "The undersigned wishing to remove to the westward offers for sale, that *Valuable Plantation* whereon he now lives, in the fork of Handcock and Cahooque creeks in Craven County. The situation is pleasant & as healthy as any in this section of the country, and for fertility of the soil, (with one or two exceptions) is certainly inferior to know place on the Neuse River between New Bern Ferry and Adams Creek. There are about 200 Acres of cleared Land under good fence, a considerable part of which will produce from 2 ½ to 3 barrels of Corn to the thousand or Cotton in the like proportion, and plenty to clear of the same quality, the Buildings are new and in good repair. – Also, two tracts of Piney Land in this neighborhood. Terms of sale will be made known by applying to the Subscriber on the premises. Joseph Physioc. October 20, 1827." *Newbern Sentinel.*

ADAMS' CREEK ROAD: "the subscriber gives notice that the Adams' Creek Road is now passable at his Mills on Long Creek, and that the Bridges are in good order. He also gives notice, that his Mills have undergone a thorough repair, and are now in complete order for grinding grain. Thomas J. Emery." *Newbern Spectator* July 12, 1828.

"JACK SANCHO. This beautiful and much-celebrated animal will stand the ensuing fall season at Mr. Nathaniel Smith's Otter Creek Plantation, and the subscriber's Farm, four miles from New Bern. SANCHO will commence the season at Otter Creek, on Monday the 1st of September, and will divide his time between his stands, by spending a week at each of them, alternatively. The terms of the season will be usual with him, and will be made known at his several stands. The season will expire on the 1st of November. August 27, 1828. Wm. S. Blackledge." *New Bern Spectator.*

"VEGETABLES. – We have received at our Offices, two radishes, raised at Adams' Creek, on the plantation of Nathl. Smith Esq. The largest weighs eight pounds, and measures fourteen inches in circumference, and twenty-one and a quarter inches in length. The curious horticulturalist is invited to call and see them." *Newbern Spectator* December 27, 1828.

"MARRIED, On Thursday the 1st of January, by the Rev. Mr. Mason, Mr. Thomas Ferguson, of this place, to Rebecca Wallace, of Adams's Creek." *New Bern Spectator*, January 10, 1829.

"MARRIED, at Slocumb's Creek, by William Holland, Esq., Mr. Dennis Watson to Miss Harriet Herrimon Rowe, daughter of Amos Rowe, Esq." *Newbern Spectator*, April 23, 1831.

"MARRIED, on Thursday the 26th ult., [May 26, 1831] at Clubfoots Creek, in this county, Mr. John Moore to Miss Martha A. Jones, daughter of Mr. Gideon Jones." *Newbern Sentinel* June 3, 1831.

"WE ARE REQUESTED to state that Joseph Physioc, Esq. is a candidate to represent this County in the House of Commons of the next General Assembly." *Newbern Sentinel* June 3, 1831.

"NOTICE. On Friday the 10th instant [June 10, 1831], at the Plantation of the late James Lovick, Esq. Will Be Sold, a quantity of Household and Kitchen Furniture at a number of Farming Utensils, Cattle, Sheep, Hogs, &c., on a credit of six months, for notes with approved security. Geo. Wilson, Executor. 2d June, 1831." *Newbern Sentinel.*

"MARRIED, in this town [New Bern], Thursday evening last by Rev. John Armstrong, Jr., Mr. John M. Jones of Edenton to Sarah Hancock, daughter of William Hancock, Esq." *The Sentinel* July 6, 1831.

"MARRIED, On Thursday evening the 5th instant, at the residence of Mrs. Ann Neal, on Adams's Creek, by Abner Neal, Esq., Mr. Elijah Taylor to Mrs. Elizabeth C. Dixon, daughter of the late Col. Philip Neal." *Newbern Sentinel* December 17, 1832.

"MARRIED, in Newbern, 7th inst., Dr. Samuel Masters of Washington, to Miss Lavenia J. Carraway." *The Weekly Standard* (Raleigh) May 29, 1835.

"MARRIED, On the 14th inst. by the Rev. James Jamieson, Mr. Francis Martin, of Adams' Creek, to Miss Esther Dixon, of this town." *Newbern Spectator*, December 16, 1836.

"CRAVENSVILLE, Craven County, July 1st, 1837, Doctor Duffy, Sir – I certify that my daughter was ill for near twelve months with Ague and Fever and that she was perfectly cured by taking part of a bottle of your Tonic Mixture, and that the remainder of the bottle cured a child of a neighbor and friend to who I gave it. Will Holland." *Newbern Sentinel* July 15, 1837. [*Here is an example of an early form of testimonial advertising; this one for a patent medicine of a local physician named Duffy.* Cravensville, sometimes Cravenville, *is the name of the earliest known post office serving the Slocum Creek area in what is today Havelock. It was established by the Holland family in the early 1800s. Ironically, William Holland would soon be the victim of a virulent fever that Duffy's elixir couldn't cure.*]

MARRIED: "In Craven county. Mr. Michael N. Fisher to Miss Francis C. Bailey." *The North-Carolina Standard* October 11, 1837.

"STEAM BOAT E.D. McNAIR will leave Newbern for Adams's creek every morning, during the continuance of the Camp Meeting at the latter place – Passage 50 cents. Apply on board to Wm. Farrior, or to J. & T.P. Burgwyn. July 27, 1838." *New Bern Spectator.*

BRIDGE THE TRENT: "Notice is hereby given, that application will be made in the next session of the General Assembly of this State, for passage of a law to construct a Bridge across Trent River at Swimming Point, near Newbern, and to open and lay off a Public Road, giving access to the same from the Beaufort and Pembroke Roads, through the lands of Richard D. Spaight and John R. Donnell, Esquires.

Charles C, Wilson	Thomas J. Emery
Henry G, Cutler	Thomas J. Pasteur
William R. Street	Thomas Singleton*
T.P. Burgwyn	Council B. Wood*
George W, Dixon*	Samuel Hyman*
John Williams	M. N. Fisher*
Henry Hall	Alexander H, Stanly
David B. Gibson*	Dennis Watson*
William Holland, jun.*	William H. Gooding*
Thomas J. Physioc*	Benjamin Tolson*
Joseph Physioc*	

Craven County, 4th Nov. 1838."

Newbern Spectator Dec. 14, 1838 [*Names with asterisks (*) known to have resided at or near Slocum Creek and Hancock Creek.*]

"ORPHANS APPRENTICED: No date [but c. 1840] —Grand Jury notice that the following boy be bound out: James Williams living on Otter Creek, south side of Neuse River … Alexander Price, orphan; Eliza Biggs, Mary Biggs orphans in the neighborhood of Mr. Hyman and [Lot] Holton on Hancocks Creek." [*KR Note: Alexander Price was apprenticed to Noah Price on 15 November 1842. When reported to them, local courts oversaw the apprenticeships of orphans to be cared for and learn a trade in a sort of foster home - guardianship arrangement.*]

"INCREASE IN LOG CABINS. On Saturday last, The Tippecanoe Club on Adams's Creek erected the Log Cabin in double-quick time. They commenced after breakfast, cut the logs, hauled them, prepared them, raised the building, covered and *completed it*, by four o'clock in the afternoon; and wound up their day's work by pledging the good cause in sparkling cider! The Harrison men are, "in earnest and not joking." *Newbern Spectator* August 8, 1840.

"FESTIVAL AT ADAMS'S CREEK. On the first Thursday (the 5th) of November, a Flag will be presented by the Whig Ladies of Newbern to the patriotick citizens of Adams's creek and South river, -- Those citizens have given a general invitation to the Whigs of the county to be present, and strong hopes are entertained that many Ladies will grace the ceremony and the feast with their presence." *Newbern Spectator* October 24, 1840.

TAX SALE: "On the Second Monday of November next, I will sell for cash at the Court House in Newbern, the following LOTS and Tracts of LAND, or so much thereof as will pay the Taxes due thereon for the year 1840, and cost of advertising ... Gooding's District,

[Acres............Name............		Tax due]
400	Seabrook, Moses W.	$1.35
50	Simpkins, Ezekiel	.17
50	Moore, Abel	.17
666	Whitehead, John S.	2.27
50	Whitford, Elinor	.17
75	Brown, Isaac	1.08
44	Carter, Thomas	.97
750	Holland, William	3.82
25	Chesnut, Owen per Chestnut, Isaac	.17

JOHN B. DAWSON, Sheriff, Newbern." *The Weekly Standard* (Raleigh) October 5, 1842.

EMANCIPATED SLAVES: "We learn that on Friday evening last. Messrs. Benjamin and Henry Mace, Executors of the late Joseph Physic [Physioc] of this county, left the port of Newbern for Philadelphia with twenty-one emancipated slaves under their charge. Mr. [Physioc] died a few years since, and left these persons free, making arrangements for sending them from the State, in accordance with the laws of North Carolina." *The Newbernian and North Carolina Advocate* August 6, 1844.

"RELIGIOUS NOTICE. There will be a Camp Meeting held on Adams' Creek, Craven Co., commencing on Friday the 7th of August next." *The Newbernian and North Carolina Advocate* New Bern, July 28, 1846.

"FOR SALE, the Sloop *Ida*, formerly owned by Wm. S. Wynne. She can be seen at Mr. Covert's Way. J. R. Franklin." *The Newbernian and North Carolina Advocate* December 19, 1848.

RAILROAD BUILDERS: "The Directors of this Company [*The Atlantic & North Carolina Railroad*] met in Newbern on the 16th inst., and were in session several days. We learn that the contract *[for building the railroad, its culverts, trestles, etc.*] from Newbern to Slocumb's Creek was awarded to C. B. Wood, Esq., and to Gov. [*John Motley*] Morehead from Slocumb's Creek to Shepard's Point." *The Newbern Journal* August 22, 1855. [*Council B. Wood owned a plantation between Havelock and Croatan and was an early Croatan postmaster. Governor Morehead was a politician, real estate promoter, and the namesake of the city that sprouted where the railroad ended after its completion in early 1858.*]

METHODIST MISSIONARY: "On December 20, 1859, the seventh day of its North Carolina conference in Beaufort, the Methodist Episcopalian Church – South appointed John Jones to the Slocomb Creek mission for the term of one year." *Wilmington Journal* December 24, 1859.

"A NEW POST OFFICE has been established at Havelock, in Craven County, immediately on the A.&N.C. Railroad, a few miles east of New Bern, by the name of Speightsville, Andrew J. Chesnutt, P.M. [*postmaster*]." *Newbern Daily Progress*, March 21, 1860.

"1100 ACRES of land for sale. The subscriber offers for sale a valuable tract of land, lying on Adams Creek, containing about 600 acres, and said by judges to be equal to any land in the State. Also, another tract lying on Hancock Creek, about 20 miles below New Bern and 3 miles from Havelock Depot, A & NC Railroad, containing 500 acres, and is well timbered with long straw pine, hickory and oak. For further particulars address the undersigned at New Bern, N.C. John N. Hyman." *Newbern Daily Progress* June 12, 1860.

DRAIN THE LAKES: "Notice! Application will be made to the next General Assembly, for permission to drain Lake Ellis, the Long Lake, Little Lake and Catfish Lake in the counties of Craven, Carteret and Jones." *The Southerner* (Tarboro, N.C.) November 10, 1860. [*Over many decades, massive efforts went into draining the lakes for agricultural purposes. Canals were dug, primarily with slave labor, all the way to the head and upper reached of Slocum Creek. In one extraordinary case, the Blackledge Canal was built all the way to the Neuse River, connecting at Dam Creek adjacent to present-day Carolina Pines. The Blackledge Canal was so large it appears on early maps. The original name for the road designated today as Lake Road was "the Canal Road." It was created on top of dirt thrown up from the excavation of a miles-long canal. Another road to the lakes was Gray Road.*]

LEVY ON LAND: "To John N. Hyman, Guardian of Samuel Hyman: You will take notice, that a Justices Judgment has been returned to this court by H. P. Whitehurst, one of the Constables of the County of Craven, in favor of George Allen versus said John N. Hyman, Guardian of Samuel Hyman, for the sum of $49.97 ½ cents, levied on the right and interest of John N. Hyman in, and to, 600 acres of Land on Adams' Creek, also 500 acres of Land on Hancock's Creek, three miles from Havelock's Depot, on the Atlantic & N. C. Railroad, adjoining the lands belonging to Gideon Jones's heirs and others on the head of Adams' Creek and adjoining Jerry Parsons, John Ferguson and others in the West side of Hancock's creek. And it appearing to the Court that said John N. Hyman is a non-resident of the state, it is ordered that publication be made in the New Bern Weekly Progress for six weeks, notifying him that the plaintiff will move for an order of sale of said land at the December Term 1860, of said court. W. G. BRYAN, clerk." *Newbern Weekly Progress*, November 13, 1860.

"A MESSAGE was received from the Senate transmitting the memorial of Kenelon [sic] Lewis and Wm. H. Lewis, asking that they may have control of the waters of Ellis and Little lakes, which lie within the bounds of their lands. Referred to committee on the judiciary." *The Weekly Standard* (Raleigh, N. C.) December 12, 1860. [*Kenelm H. Lewis and William H. Lewis, wealthy brothers from Tarboro, owned a large tract of land in the lakes area southwest of Havelock in the mid-19th century, which they operated as a slave plantation. The property was a part of the former Richard Dobbs Spaight and Donnell family land, and would later be owned by James A. Bryan.*]

Attention Neuse Cavalry!
Newbern Daily Progress, April 16, 1861

"NEW POST-OF-FICE. – A new Post Office has been established on the A. & N.C.R.R in the County by the name of Croatan and Council B. Woods,

Esq., is the Post Master." *Newbern Weekly Progress* December 3, 1861. [*Mr. Woods's post office suffered the same fate as the Speightsville post office opened at Havelock almost simultaneously by A. J. Chesnutt. When Union forces seized Craven County in March 1862, both would soon be out of business. Croatan post office later operated, 1874-1927.*]

"MORE HANDS WANTED, -- The subscriber desires several more hands for farm work, boys or girls, either will do. Address him at Newbern or Croatan, Craven County, N.C. E. Malett." *Newbern Daily Progress* February 12, 1862. [*One month later Union forces invaded Craven County.*]

"$100 REWARD. A Small Bay Mare, good traveler, belonging to Mr. Thompson at Croatan, was stolen from the subscriber from the Stable of Mr. Hill, at Havelock, on the night of the 21st. The above reward will be paid for the recovery of the Horse and detection of the thief. George W. Nason, Jr." *The New Berne Times* September 23, 1865.

ELECTION OFFICIALS: "Township No. 5 (Adam's Creek) – Registrar, Geo. H. Grover, J.P.; Inspectors of Election, John H. Nelson, S.B. Gaskell. Township No. 6 (Lee's Farm and Ives Precinct, near Havelock) – Registrar, Henry J. Lovick, J.P.; Inspectors of Election, Thomas H. Mallison, James H. Hunter. Township No. 7 (Wildwood – including James City and Evans mills) Registrar, Garrett G. Mouy, J.P.; Inspectors of Election, Geo. H. Potter, Gabriel Hardison. Election to be held at Hardison's." *The New Berne Times* August 5, 1869.

"AT THE COURTHOUSE DOOR in Newbern on Tuesday, the 9th November next, I will sell a tract of land lying in Craven County, East Fork of Slocum Creek and on Lake Ellis, being the divided interest of intestate in the lands purchased from the Donnell family by J. F. Speight, K. H. Lewis, and W. F. Lewis and containing 4000 acres more or less. Also, at the same time and place I will sell the undivided one-third interest of my intestate and about 12,000 acres, more or less lying in the counties of Craven, Carteret, and Jones, purchased by the same parties from the Donnell family. W. F. Lewis, administrator of Kenelm H. Lewis, deceased. Tarboro, N. C." *The Tarboro Southerner* October 21, 1869 [*The "East Fork" of Slocum Creek lies at the end of the creek's Southwest Prong.*]

> **"A correspondent at Havelock Station, signing himself, 'You Know Who,' is informed that we do not know him, and that we shall never publish anonymous communications."**
> *The New Berne Times*
> September 6, 1864

"MUCH NEEDED. A daily, tri-weekly, or even a weekly mail route between Adams Creek and this place [New Bern]. The people in that section are absolutely without any mail facilities whatever." *The New Berne Times* November 19, 1871.

OFFICIALS SWITCHED: "The following alterations were made by the County Commissioners in the list of Judges of Elections of Craven County: John R. Holland, vice Jessie P. Godet at Adams' Creek Precinct, Township No. 5. Jessie P. Godet, vice William Martin at Temple's Precinct, Township 5." *The New Berne Times* May 25, 1872.

ELECTION: "For County Surveyor. Henry J. Lovick received 2,697; Wm. H. Marshall received 1130." *The New Berne Times* August 13, 1872.

CAMP MEETING: "There

A Lost Dog! A Lost Dog! – I Have Loss My Dog! I Have Loss My Dog! I Got in contack with a Bare on the Thried Sunday in July and he followed the Bare off, and He is very Easey to tak up at any Body's House. He is a White and Black Dog with a Large Black Spot run down his Back. He is mostly a White Dog, with Black Spots on his Bock, and Yellow round mouth, from Handcock Creek Bridge, Belonging to Hardy L. Jones plantation.

[*An advertisement posted locally in public places caught the attention of* The Weekly Standard *(Raleigh) August 17, 1870.*]

will be a camp meeting at Adams' Creek, commencing 25th instant, and to continue one week. Able ministers will conduct services. The Bishop is expected to be present. Joseph Green, Elder." *The New Berne Times* September 17, 1872. [*Camp meetings were (and still are in some places) religious events held in the open air, a tent or other shelter, and lasting several days. They were popular, often nearly festive events, in that they involved visitation, socializing, and communal meals, in addition to prayer, gospel teaching, and spirited sermons, day and night.*]

STUMP SPEAKERS: "Rev. Edward Bull and Mr. George Green, Jr., went down to Havelock last night to make campaign speeches." *The Daily Journal*, October 2, 1890.

COMMISSIONER'S COURT: "The [Craven] county commissioners were in session yesterday… An order was passed making the cart way beginning at the foot of David Morton's Mill Road and running on the dam of said mill to B. F. Borden's landing at the mouth of Hancock's Creek a public road. The clerk was instructed to serve necessary notice on the supervisors of Township No. 5." *New Bern Weekly Journal* June 8, 1882.

ON THE STUMP: "Philemon Holland, Jr., A.W. Wood, and Robert Mallett addressed the voters at Croatan school house yesterday in the interest of the Democratic ticket. There was a good crowd out to hear them and enthusiasm evidenced." *The Daily Journal* August 16, 1884.

STEAM YACHT: "The government inspectors for this district were in the city yesterday and passed upon the boiler of Mr. Geret Vyne's steam yacht. It was pronounced O.K. and Mr. Vyne sailed it in for his farm at Havelock last night." The New Bern Daily Journal August 16, 1884.

WINDMILL GONE: "Cherry Point is minus the old windmill of Mr. Lot Holton, as I suppose it is also of the home of that old eccentric gentleman, which he kept ornamented with tin scraps revolving on high-burnished iron rods." *The Daily Journal* August 20, 1884.

❖   ❖   ❖   ❖

CLUBFOOT – HARLOWE CANAL: "…The latter, which is in process of construction, is on the same line as the old Clubfoot and Harlowe Canal, mention of which can be found on the statute books any time for a hundred years past. It was chartered about a century ago, and the statues are full of legislation concerning it. It is about to be actually completed in our own day and generation. Work is being vigorously pushed." *Wilmington Weekly Star* November 2, 1883.

"Work of the old Clubfoot and Harlow's Creek Canal (now New Bern and Beaufort) is progressing finally under the supervision of Capt. S. L. Fremont of Wilmington and Thomas P. Morgan of Washington, D. C., the contractors. The government is understood to favor the canal and the project is to establish a line of inland canals to Norfolk and the north. This section of Eastern North Carolina is improving and progressing." *Wilmington Daily Review* November 28, 1884.

"A party of steamboat men visited the canal on Friday, and thoroughly examined the route from Clubfoot creek through to the utmost difficult portion of Harlowe creek. These gentlemen examine the route with reference to immediately placing steamers on the canal to ply regularly between New Bern and Beaufort." *Wilmington Weekly Star* November 20, 1885. [*Also see April 16, 1824*]

❖   ❖   ❖   ❖

VISITOR: "Capt. H. D. Stowe of Mecklenburg [*County*], was in the city yesterday. He owns a [*3,000-acre*] farm near Havelock, in this county, and has recently purchased property in the city. Hope he will soon become one of us. The Captain was here on the day that this city was captured by General Burnside, and among the last to leave. He was on the staff of the lamented Col. C. C. Lee, of the 37th N.C. Regiment." *Newbern Journal* May 21, 1885.

SLOCUM MILL: "The machinery for Card and Gallop's mill at Slocumb's Creek arrived on Saturday might per Str. *Orinda." The Daily Journal* (New Bern) April 20, 1886.

DUCK! "Edward Stanly, the well-known Jones county sportsman, returned from Slocumb's Creek on Sunday last. Said his crowd had captured 192 ducks, most of which were shufflers and mallards, and 3 wild geese, having spent only three or four days in the sport." *New Bern Weekly Journal* January 27, 1887.

SLOCUM BRIDGE: "Allowances Made by the Board of Commissioners of Craven County at the Regular Monthly Meeting Held on the First Monday in May 1887 ... C. H. Hunter, for building bridge across east prong of Slocumb's Creek, $100.00." *County Commissioner Records.*

SLOCUM TRESTLE: "Slocumb's Creek [*A&NC RR trestle*] bridge has been thoroughly overhauled and repaired." *New Bern Weekly Journal* July 7, 1887.

HANCOCK MILL: "A new saw mill is being erected at Hancock's Creek in this county." *New Berne Daily Journal* December 29, 1887.

CRAVEN COUNTY FAIR 1888: "Taxidermist's Department. This exhibit is exceedingly fine and very interesting and cannot be excelled for elegance of workmanship and tasty display ... One alligator 12 feet long, mounted on a cypress log with an o'possum in his mouth. This monster reptile was killed on Hancock Creek three weeks ago by John Thomas, a lad of 16 years, while out on the bank eating this same o'possum." *The News and Observer* (Raleigh) March 17, 1888.

"THE BURNSIDE EXPEDITIONISTS. About 100 strong were expected to arrive Tuesday, but owing to the cold snap North, were unable to come. Only three put in their appearance on Wednesday night. These men were in the Burnside expedition that captured New Berne and were coming to celebrate the 26th anniversary of its downfall and visit the battlefield, etc. Their time of coming was rather unpropitiously chosen." *The News and Observer* (Raleigh) March 17, 1888.

BEFORE THE COURT: "8 November 1888--Abadeen McMillan 'of Slocumb Creek near J. H. Hunter' states that he and his wife have raised Susan Manny since she was about 8 years old. In February 1887, Susan gave birth to a bastard child named Lilla McMillon. In October 1888, Susan left, leaving the child with McMillon. The wife of Abadeen is Eliza. The child is to remain in the care of McMillon." Source: KR

NEWS NOTE: "Many Negroes are in camp at Havelock on the Atlantic and North Carolina Railroad, waiting for the labor agents to take them south. The cold, bad weather will accelerate the exodus without doubt." *The Richmond Dispatch* January 2, 1890.

"THREE NEW POST OFFICES have been established in Craven County. 'Bellair' on Neuse road about six miles from the city [*northwest of New Bern*], and 'Cherry Point' and 'Bachelor.' Both in the lower portion of the county near the Carteret line." *The Daily Journal* (New Bern) December 28, 1890.

HANCOCK CREEK ROAD: "Ordered, That the Board of Supervisors of Roads of township No. 6 examine the road passing from Hancock Creek through the lands of P[hilip] J. Arms, W[illiam] Y[arrow Wynne, C. J. Wynne, M[ichael] N. Fisher, William Cully and James H. Hunter, Agent, leading to the Beaufort to New Berne road and report condition of the same to the Board of Commissioners at their next meeting." *The Daily Journal* New Bern November 5, 1891. [*This is the main dirt road that ran from what is now Highway 101 through the middle of what is now Cherry Point. It passed through or beside the plantations of the citizens named and through the village of Hancock Creek, ending by the river at the village of Cherry Point at the old Cherry Point landing.*]

RETURNING BY STEAMER: "Mr. Henry J. Lovick, who has been off surveying at Havelock for the past week, returned home last night … Other passengers who came in [to New Bern] on the steamer Neuse were … Mrs. H. J. Lovick, returning from a visit to relatives at Pantego." *The Daily Journal* (New Bern) October 24, 1893.

BIG OTTER: "Mr. John Dennis of Slocum's creek was in the city yesterday with a very large otter skin which Mr. Isaac Mitchell killed at Slocum's Creek. The skin measured five feet and two inches from tip to tip and sold for $6.50." *The Daily Journal,* December 22, 1893.

"MARRIED—At the home of the bride's father, Mr. B. F. Borden, Miss Hope Borden and Mr. S[ylvester] W. Reams [or Reems] were united in holy bonds of matrimony, October 16, [18]'95, at 8 p.m., Mr. J. D. Pittman, Justice of the Peace, officiating. There were numerous friends of both bride and groom assembled to witness the ceremony, after which all partook of a splendid supper." *The Daily Journal* (New Bern) October 31, 1895.

TIMBER BUSINESS – "Mr. John Hill, a machinist [from New Bern], came down Tuesday [*October 22, 1895*] to do some machine work for the Cherry Point Lumber Co.; he returned Saturday. The company are making great progress in putting down the mill and will soon be ready for work." *The Daily Journal* (New Bern) October 31, 1895.

"BIGGEST OF WILD TURKEYS. George Russell claims to be the champion wild turkey killer of the season, and the wild turkey he shot last week at Hancock Creek, will be hard to equal, let alone beat. Dressed for the table, the turkey weighed eighteen-and-one-half pounds. The bird was a gobbler and his beard was twelve inches long." *The Daily Journal* January 30, 1900.

BIG FISH – "An unusually large sturgeon for these waters was brought in yesterday by two colored fishermen, Bill Anderson and G.R. Nelson. The huge fish was eight feet long and weighed 350 pounds. It was sold to Fernie Gaskill and Co. This huge fish was caught down the Neuse, near Slocum's Creek, in a sturgeon net…The roe [*caviar*]is the most valuable part…it was estimated that this one would furnish a keg of ore weighing 60 pounds." *The New Bern Journal*, via the *Wilmington Weekly Star* May 3, 1901.

"FIVE LAKES SOLD. The State Board of Education has sold to President James A. Bryan, of the Atlantic and North Carolina Railway, five freshwater lakes near New Bern. The lakes are called Great, Catfish, Ellis, Little and Long. The price paid was $4,800. The lakes cover about 6000 acres." *The Farmer and Mechanic* (Raleigh, N. C.) October 7, 1902. [*Early in its history, the North Carolina legislature placed undeeded swampland and other marginal lands under the ownership of the State Board of Education with the idea that the sale or development of the surplus property would eventually benefit the public schools. James Bryan was a wealthy Craven County businessman and politician with huge landholdings in the Havelock area. At the time of his purchase, Bryan stated that the land would be used as a game preserve. "Camp Bryan," a private hunting and fishing club, has existed ever since.*]

Telephony, 1901

"The final connections have been made so that the long-distance telephone is now in practical working order between this city [New Bern] and Morehead as well as the stations along the line of the Atlantic and North Carolina Railroad. The copper circuit wire was cut in yesterday and the service is very good and distinct.

There are three telephones at Morehead for use over the line … The service is direct from any local telephone here, it is only necessary to call up the central office and asked to be connected with Morehead, Newport, Croatan, Havelock, etc.

The service costs 30 cents to Morehead, 25 cents to Newport, and less for nearer stations.

The time allowed is five minutes which counts from the time communication is begun between the parties. The service will be a good one and a great convenience to the business public."

New Bern Weekly Journal
December 10, 1901

RAILROAD AGENT: "Mr. George Hill has been appointed agent and operator of the A. & N.C. [*Railroad*] station at Havelock." *New Berne Weekly Journal* June 30, 1905.

MELVIN, N.C.: "Melvin is the name of a new post-office located between Havelock and Newport." *New Berne Weekly Journal* March 30, 1906. [*Melvin's location description here is a little off. It was situated in the area of Little Witness near the intersection of the Beaufort Road (Highway 101) and Hancock Creek; on the eastern edge of present-day Havelock. In addition to being called Melvin and Little Witness, its residents also referred to the area as "Toon Neck." James Robinson was postmaster.*]

COLLECTOR: "Curator [H. H.] Brimley of the state museum returned yesterday from a special hop to Lake Ellis. He was after alligators and secured the heads and skins of eight, the largest 8 feet in length. The skins will be shorn and the heads mounted. The water in the lake is only 22 feet deep at most. Alligators were mainly speared, but some of them were shot, 25 caliber expanding bullets literally smashing their skulls. Many photographs were taken, and a number of reptiles and birds were secured." *The Semi-weekly Messenger* (Wilmington, N. C.) May 25, 1906. [*Herbert Hutchinson Brimley (1861 – 1946), a self-trained zoologist and native of Great Britain, was the director of the North Carolina Museum of Natural Sciences. Much of the museum's collection of birds, reptiles, and other fine animals was taken in and around the lakes, and in the adjacent swamps and forests, southwest of Havelock. Photographs of Brimley appear in* HIHCP.]

SCHOOL DISTRICT PROPOSED: "It is hereby ordered that an election be held in said [new proposed Special School] District, on Monday, May 9th, 1910, at J. E. White's store in Havelock, N.C., polls to open from 9 o'clock A.M. until 5 o'clock P.M., on said day, for the purpose of ascertaining the will of the people of said district ... Ordered further, that for the purpose of holding said election, Mr. J. E. White is hereby appointed registrar, and H[enry]. A. Marshall and T. L. Hill are hereby appointed poll-holders. Said officers are hereby authorized and empowered to conduct said election in the manner prescribed by law, for hold general elections as near as may be." *Clerk of Craven County Commissioners* from county records. Not dated.

[*THE COMMITTEE FOR A CENTRAL HIGH SCHOOL to serve Craven County was appointed by the county commissioners in 1911. Representatives from the southern parts of the county included:*] "J. S. Morton and J. E. White, Harlowe; A[sa] D. Rooks, H[enry] A. Marshall and T[homas] E. Haywood, Havelock; and G. L. Hardison and W. E. Moore, Thurman." *New Bern Weekly Journal* June 6, 1911.

"FISHERMAN'S LUCKY HAUL. While drag netting yesterday morning near the mouth of Slocumbs Creek, Ceasar [sic] Taylor, a colored fisherman, of this city, struck a school of rock fish and hauled in five hundred of a very large size. He sold his catch to a New Bern packer for 25 cents each, $150 for his load." *New Berne Weekly Journal* May 16, 1911.

MARRIED: "Last night, 7 o'clock, at the home of Mr. G.M. Oglesby, 108 Hancock Street, Mr. Walter J. Wynne and Mis Maude Wood were happily joined together in the holy bonds of matrimony, Dr. J.H. Summerell officiating. Mr. Wynne is a prosperous young man of Colleton, S.C, formerly of Cherry Point, this county, and his bride is the attractive daughter of Mr. Henry C. Wood, a well-known and substantial farmer who resides at Riverdale." *The Daily Journal* December 29, 1911.

VISITING HOME: "Mr. Hugh Trader of Havelock, who is attending the Dover High School, spent Saturday with his parents." *The Daily Journal* (New Bern) October 30, 1912.

33 KIDS, 18-YEAR-OLD BRIDE: "Ben Joyner, a negro ... and 58 years old, who bears the distinction of being the best guide in eastern North Carolina, came to New Bern yesterday from his little log cabin on the banks of Lake Ellis and went to the office of the register of deeds and secured a license to marry an 18-year-old girl. Usually there would be nothing of interest to warrant a write up of this length but in this case the facts are so strange that they seem like fiction. Joyner ... says he is the father of 33 children and out of this number 27 are now living in Carteret and Craven counties; and they are the pride next to his fishing and hunting trips. Despite the fact that there is a vast difference in the ages of Joyner and his new bride they seemed perfectly happy when they stepped up in front of a local magistrate to have tied the knot which will make them as one until death, or the divorce courts, place them asunder." *Western Carolina Democrat* (Hendersonville, N.C.) October 8, 1914. [*Ben Joyner, born in 1856, was a hunting and fishing guide and caretaker at Camp Bryan, southwest of Havelock. Among his clients were baseball legend Christie Mathewson and others in the category 'rich and famous.' Joyner appears with a photograph in the chapter* Making End s Meet: 1890-1940.]

CRABBING: "The arrival of Summer-time weather always means an ill omen for the variety of the crustacean family best known as the crab, and crabbing parties are almost daily hiking themselves down to Slocumb's Creek in quest of these crawlers." *The New Bern Sun Journal* May 25, 1920.

"NOTICE to voters in Sixth Township is hereby given that on account of inadequate facilities for voting at Lee's Farm, the Polling place at said Lee's Farm Precinct is changing to Pine Grove in the same precinct. This the 3rd day of May, 1920. W. E. LEE, Chairman County Board of Elections." *The New Bern Sun Journal* May 26, 1920. [*Lee's Farm was at today's Greenfield Heights. The precinct was similar to today's Township Six.*]

CREEK BAPTISM: "Quite a large crowd attended the picnic given at Slocumb's Creek Wednesday by the Free Will Baptist Sunday school. It was a very enjoyable day and those who participated were very enthusiastic in their praise for the manner in which it was conducted. What came as a surprise was the baptism of one of the ladies present, who asked this ordinance at the hands of the pastor, Rev. J.C. Griffin." *The New Bern Sun Journal* July 1, 1920.

SLOCUM CREEK FLOTILLA: "Tomorrow morning bright and early the ex-service men in Craven county, including their relatives and friends, will set sail from New Bern on board the steamers *S.J. Phillips* and *L.C. Ward* and a dozen or more smaller boats en route to Slocumbs Creek, where they are to spend the day enjoying the big celebration which the local post of the American Legion is to hold there. That there will be at least five hundred persons in the party is assured and the elaborate program, including a big dinner, will doubtless be greatly enjoyed by all who attend." *The New Bern Sun Journal* July 14, 1920.

"LOST, STRAYED OR STOLEN, one iron gray mule. Reward for return to C. N. Wynn, Havelock." *The New Bern Sun Journal* June 16, 1920.

PICNIC: "Members of the Sunday school of Christ Episcopal church and their friends are today enjoying a pleasant outing at Slocumb's Creek, leaving the city early on board the steamer *Phillips* and expecting to return late in the afternoon. Slocumb's Creek is one of the ideal picnic spots in this part of the state and many outings are held there each summer." *The New Bern Sun Journal* June 23, 1920.

TO RUN THE MILL: "Mr. and Mrs. W. H. Rhodes have moved to Beech Haven, a small station near Havelock where Mr. Rhodes will operate a saw mill, gin, grist mill and general store." *The New Bern Sun Journal* September 6, 1921.

[*Beech Haven, also called Beech Haven Farms, was located between the Central Highway (now US 70) and Slocum Creek, along what is now Slocum Road, an entrance road to Cherry Point.*]

"BUD FISHER is here today. Famous Cartoonist Passed Through Here This Morning – To Camp Bryan. 'Bud' Fisher, creator of 'Mutt and Jeff' arrived in New Bern this morning ... and left shortly afterward for Camp Bryan, where he will spend two weeks on a hunting trip. Geo. Nicholl of this city went with him. He is one of several prominent men who come to this section to enjoy hunting here. Among the others are Grantland Rice, the famous sports writer and Rex Beach, author." *The New Bern Sun Journal* November 10, 1921.

"LICENSES have been issued at the office of the register of deeds for the following couple: Alvin Dove, of Havelock, and Dereath Martin, of Blades." *The New Bern Sun Journal* December 15, 1922.

Estates & Real Estate

More interesting than it may sound, we submit here for the reader's edification a few examples of land and property transactions and offers to sell through the years in southern Craven County. Some of the properties are advertised by people wishing to migrate to western lands. Some are publicized as the results of deaths, some are ordered by the court, and some are simply a matter of property owners hoping to make a profit. Hundreds of similar examples exist in publication archives. Information in brackets [ ] added by author.

❖   ❖   ❖   ❖

"DEED – Craven Precinct, Bath Co., September 16, 1730, Christian Isler to Francis Brice, a certain parcel, Raccoon Neck, formerly sold to John Kinsey, south side of Neuse at head of Coleman's Creek, mine own property right as a good, perfect and absolute estate of inheritance: Test: Wm. Handcock, James C. Metcalf." County records of 1730 reprinted in *The Kinston Free Press*, October 7, 1914. [*Originally part of Bath County, Craven was broken out as a precinct in 1712 before becoming a county in 1739. Coleman's Creek is today called Tucker Creek.*]

"THE SUBSCRIBER also offers ... 300 acres patented by Patrick Conner, on the head of Clubfoot's Creek, the above land is well timbered for shipbuilding or making of Staves, which may be conveniently transported or conveyed to any part of core sound. Joseph Leech." *The Newbern Gazette* April 25, 1801.

"NOTICE is hereby given that the subscribers, agents of Mrs. Mary

FOR SALE,

The Land and Plantation whereon I now live in Craven County, on the Beaufort Road, about twenty one miles below Newbern, containing 606 Acres, with a good Dwelling House and all necessary Out Houses. The Land is suitable for the culture of Indian Corn, Peas, Potatoes, Cotton, &c. and has an excellent Range for Cattle and Hogs.

Also,

Three Hundred Acres on King's Creek, twenty two miles below Newbern, the growth of which is chiefly Pitch Pine, though it contains a large Swamp well Timbered with the best of Cypress.

This property will be disposed of at a fair price and on liberal credit.

For further particulars enquire of the Subscriber on the Premises.

Joseph Physioc,

March 18, 1811

Jones Spaight, are now ready to Lease the following property to wit, the plantation commonly called Claremont, with the Negroes, thereon ... and a Mill ... on Slocum creek, the above property will be leased for five years ... belonging to the estate of Richard D. Spaight, deceased. John West & Spyres Singleton, Agents." *The Newbern Morning Herald & True Republican* December 23, 1808.

"NOTICE. On Thursday the first day of August next, at the Dwelling House of the late Stephen Gooding, deceased, on Slocumb's Creek the Subscriber will expose to public Sale, all the perishable property of said deceased – consisting of cattle, horses, hogs, sheep, plantation tools, household and kitchen furniture, - Also the frame of a dwelling house with suitable weather boarding sufficient to enclose the same, with other articles too tedious to mention. For all sums not exceeding 20 shillings, cash will be expected. For all larger sums, notes of six months credit, with good security will be required. Thomas S. Gooding, administrator. Craven County, June 15, 1816." *The Carolina Federal Republican* New Bern July 27, 1816.

"NOTICE. It is hereby given, that Mary Dellamar, of Adam's Creek, is dead, intestate; and Letters of Administration on the estate have been granted by the Court of Pleas and Quarters Session of Craven County, to the subscriber. Creditors of said intestate are required to produce their claim to the subscriber, properly authenticated, within the time required by the Acts of the Assembly of the State, where they will be part of recovery by the operation of the said acts. James T. Jones, Administrator." *Newbern Sentinel* July 10, 1819.

"FOR SALE. 100 Acres of Land, situated on the South side of Neuse River, and West side of Adam's Creek, adjoining the lands of Mr. Nathan Smith and others, formerly the property of *John Young*, deceased. This land, I understand, is well set with timber, and not inferior, in point of fertility of soil. For terms apply to Mr. George Wilson, near New Bern, or to the subscriber. Joseph Bonner, Washington." *Newbern Sentinel* January 15, 1820.

"FOR SALE OR RENT. On accommodating terms, that valuable tract of land, lately owned by William C. Nelson on Adams' Creek – on which there is a large two-story commodious Dwelling House, with all convenient outhouses, an excellent Orchard, etc. – There are about 75 acres cleared – the fertility of the soil is well known in that neighborhood, and the situation is high and healthy, and very convenient to the waters for fishing, fouling etc. Frederick Jones." *Newbern Sentinel* January 27, 1821.

"FOR RENT for the term on one year– Two plantations on south side of Neuse River 15 miles below New Bern at Mouth of Slocum Creek - the other known by the name of MOOR'S, both under good fences, and in every respect ready for farming; Apply to Mr. James LOVICK or subscriber Hancy Jones - Slocumb's Creek." *Newbern Sentinel* February 17, 1821.

"VALUABLE LAND for Sale. The Subscriber offers for sale, on accommodating terms, the Tract of Land lately occupied by William C. Nelson, lying on the East side of Adams' Creek. Frederick Jones." *Newbern Sentinel* February 1, 1823.

"NOTICE. [*Leasing of property belonging to minors*] on Monday, the second of January next, at the courthouse in New Bern ... will be rented for the year: A Plantation on Brice's Creek, belonging to the orphans of William P. Moore, deceased; A Grist Mill, on Clubfoot's Creek, belonging to Michael N. Fisher, a minor; A plantation on Adams' Creek, belonging to the orphans of William P Moore, deceased. Persons indebted to me as the guardian of the above minors, are requested to make payment, as indulgence cannot be given to them. George Wilson." *Newbern Sentinel* December 31, 1825.

"NOTICE OF SALE by George Wilson – Plantation of James Lovick." *The Newbern Morning Herald & True Republican* June 3, 1831.

"NOTICE. Will be sold, at public sale, on Tuesday the seventh of January, 1834, at the subscriber's plantation, on Clubfoot's Creek, the following articles, viz. Cattle, Sheep, Cotton in the seed, Farming Utensils, Household and Kitchen Furniture, And a few young Hogs. Six months credit will be given, and notes with good security required. At the same time and place, will be offered for sale, the SAW and GRIST MILLS (on Long Creek, two miles below Clubfoot's Creek,) together with about 1,900 acres of land attached to the Mills. Conditions of the sale of Mills and Land made known on the day of the sale. Thomas J. Emery." *Newbern Sentinel* January 3, 1834.

"ADMINISTRATOR'S SALE. The public is informed that a sale of the effects of Hylliard Holland, deceased, will take place at his late residence on Tucker's Creek, on the eighth day of December next. The following are among the articles for sale: three cows, horses, cattle, hogs, household and kitchen furniture, a riding chair, the crop of corn, peas, potatoes, fodder, etc. A credit of six months will be allowed as usual, the purchasers giving notes with approved security. William Holland, Administrator. Craven County." *Newbern Spectator* November 16, 1838.

TO RENT,

FOR THE TERM OF ONE YEAR,

Two Plantations

ON the south side of Neuse river, fifteen miles below Newbern— one of which is at the mouth of Slocumb's Creek—the other, known by the name of Moor's, is a mile higher up the Creek. Both are under good fences, and in every respect ready for farming. For further particulars, apply to the subscriber, or to Mr. James Lovick.

Hancy Jones.

Slocumb's Creek,
Jan. 18, 1821. }—3w149

[A riding chair was a horse-drawn two-wheeled cart with a chair-like seat used to travel around the plantation or into town. Popular in the 1700s but falling out of favor in the 1800s.]

"ADMINISTRATOR'S NOTICE. The Subscriber, having been appointed administrator of the effects of the late Mrs. Ann Holland, gives notice to all who may be indebted to this intestate's estate to make immediate payment, and to all having demands against the same, to present them, duly authenticated, within the time limited by law. The public are also notified, that a sale of the property will take place on the 29th May, instant, at the house of the intestate on Coleman's Creek, consisting of a horse, cattle, hogs, household and kitchen furniture, corn, peas, etc. etc. Terms as usual William Holland, Administrator." *Newbern Spectator* May 24, 1839. *[Coleman's Creek and Tucker Creek are names for the same waterway west of present-day Havelock. William Holland founded the first post office in southern Craven County in 1836, calling it Cravensville.]*

> ## FOR SALE.
>
> A TRACT of Land situated on the west side of Slocumb's Creek, about four miles up the Creek, immediately on the road leading to New Berne, containing Seven Hundred acres of good Oak and Pine land. Any person wishing to purchase, had better call and see the Subscriber and examine the premises as it is a very desirable Tract and will be sold a bargain.
>
> WILLIAM BAILEY.
>
> Otter Creek, June 4th, 1849.   22 tj½

"SALE OF LAND, State of North Carolina, Craven County. In the case of John Milton Thorp, an infant, by his guardian, and etc., and Sidney A. Thorp. In equity. In obedience to a decree of the court of equity for Craven County, at the fall term of 1852, I shall expose to public sale at the courthouse in New Berne on Monday the 13th day of December next, the following described tracts of land, lying and being in County of Craven, and South side of Neuse River, viz: one tract lying on Hancock's Creek, being two-thirds of the Samuel Hyman land, purchased from said Hyman's two sons. Also, another tract of Land lying on the west side of Clubfoot's Creek, joining the land of John C. Washington (formerly Michael N. Fisher's and others) the same which formerly belonged to the late Stephen W. Wynn. The tract contains 550 acres, more or less. Also, another tract lying on the West side of Hancock's Creek, known as the Collin's place, containing 100 acres, more or less, adjoining the Frances Always' patent, and formerly the property of Thomas J. Physioc. Terms made known on the day of the sale. Wm. G. Bryan, C. & M. E. November 1, 1852." *The Newbernian and North Carolina Advocate* November 9, 1852.

"LAND SALE in Equity. By Virtue of a Decree of the Court of Equity for Craven County made on the October Term 1853, I shall expose to public sale at the Court House in New Bern on Monday the 13th day of March next, being the Monday of Craven County Court, a certain tract of land lying and being in the County of Craven on the South side of Neuse River in the fork of Slocum's Creek, adjoining the lands of Owen Chesnut (formerly Spaight's) containing 225 acres more or less, it being the property of Eliza D. Rowe. William G. Bryan, C. M. E." *The Atlantic* New Bern, February 21, 1854.

"1100 ACRES OF LAND for sale. The subscriber offers for sale a valuable tract of land, lying on Adams' Creek, containing about 600 acres, and said by judges to be equal to any land in the State. Also, another tract lying about twenty miles below New Bern and three miles from Havelock Depot, A&NC Railroad, containing 500 Acres, and is well timbered with long straw pine, hickory and oak. For further particulars address the undersigned at Newbern, N. C. John N. Hyman." *Newbern Daily Progress* December 10, 1859.

"VALUABLE TRACT OF LAND For Sale. The Subscriber, wishing to change his business, offers for sale a tract of land on which he now resides, lying immediately on the South side of Neuse River; 12 miles below New Bern, and 1 mile from Croatan Station, in a healthy and good neighborhood. Said tract contains about 400 ACRES. There is enough cleared and in cultivation for a two-horse farm. There is on the tract a good DWELLING HOUSE, together with all necessary outbuildings of a well-regulated farm. The farm is well adapted to the growth of corn, cotton, wheat, oats, etc. Marl is found in great abundance immediately at the plantation, of the best quality, and the only trouble or expense in using it on the farm, is the carting, as there is no digging after it. The advantage of FISHING, at all seasons of the year cannot be excelled at no place in the State for quality or quantity. The entire stock of the plantation, of cattle and hogs together with the crops on hand, farming tools, etc., will be sold with the land if desired. Persons wishing to purchase can, by calling on Mr. W. H. Marshall at New Bern, or Mr. Vine A. Tolson at Croatan Station, get any information that they may wish in regard to the land, and where to find the subscriber. Terms made easy. Craven County. William S. Bailey." *Newbern Weekly Progress* December 11, 1860.

"ENTRY CLAIM. State of North Carolina. Craven County. To George B. Waters, Entry Taker for Craven County: the undersigned Merrill and E. W. Bryan of Craven County, North Carolina, enters and lays claim to the following described piece or parcel of land in No. Six Township, Craven County, North Carolina, the same being vacant and unappropriated land and subject to entry, viz: Lying east of the head of Hancock's Creek, and bounded on the east of the Cully land, on the west by the old Bell land, and on the north by the Bell land and on the South by the land belonging to the

State, containing by estimation 1,000 acres more or less. Entered this 23rd day of March 1906, E. W. Bryan, Merrell Bryan." *The Daily Journal* New Bern. March 27, 1906.

Former Slave Smith Nelson Buys Land at Slocum Creek

On March 5, 1880, Smith Nelson bought seventy-five acres of land on what is now MCAS Cherry Point. The farm tract was the kernel from which sprang the Nelson Town community. The former slave bought the farmland from Rufus W. Bell and his wife, Abigail, of Carteret County for one hundred and fifty dollars. Two dollars per acre.

Smith Nelson's son, Sam B. Nelson, would increase the holding with the acquisition of land on Slocum Creek formerly owned by James H. Hunter. At its peak, Nelson Town encompassed about 500 acres owned by family and family-related members. Its residents were all former slaves or the descendants of enslaved people. Nelson Town's homes and farms were continuously occupied by the owners and their families from 1880 to 1941.

The deed described the land Smith Nelson purchased as being "*on the south side of the neuse river and the east side of Slocumbs Creek adjoining the land formerly known and owned by Lot Holton, Stephen W. Winn and Samuel Hyman and part of the grant to Obadiah Yarbroughs three hundred acres granted in 1761 butted and bounded as follows Beginning in the third line of the said Yarbrough patent and the corner of the late Stephen Cavanoe ...*"

It then lapses into descriptions of distances in surveyor's pole lengths, and landmarks like other people's property boundaries, stakes, and creek branches. The document is recorded in Craven County Deed Book 83 on pages 403-404.

Of Smith's seventy-five acres, the deed notes that it was "*the same heired to* [i.e., inherited by] *John Cavanoe from his father Lewis Cavanoe whose undivided interest was sold by J.C. Cole sheriff of Craven County on the 16th day of March 1824.*"

Hardy L. Jones, a Slocum Creek turpentine farmer and descendant of early settler Evan Jones, bought the land at the 1824 sheriff's sale. Jones split the land the next year with Stephen Cavanoe. One of those pieces appears to have been later acquired by a Bell family member.

Rufus W. Bell and Abigail F. Bell signed the deed. It was witnessed by J.R. Bell. Justice of the Peace R. M. Wicks certified the deed. James Rumley, clerk of the Carteret County superior court, and Probate Judge E. W. Carpenter also signed their portions of the document.

It seems reasonable to assume that Smith Nelson had been on a local slave plantation for most of his life. We don't know when he was born but since his son Sam was born in 1860, Smith might have been born anywhere between 1820 and 1840, meaning many years in bondage before his liberation in the 1860s.

As recounted previously in the book, Nelson Town was one of three communities on what is now the Marine base founded by ex-slaves shortly after the Civil War. More details appear elsewhere in the book but primarily in the chapter *The Right of Eminent Domain*.

The Mother of All Real Estate Ads

And then comes this whopper from William Holland of Slocum Creek. He caught the bug to go west along with many others who were leaving eastern North Carolina for potentially greener pastures elsewhere in the early 1800s. One of the problems facing those wishing to migrate to the lands in the West that were being opened up – such as Kentucky, Tennessee, Alabama, and the Northwest Territories – was trying to sell their land into a saturated market along with all the other people with the same idea. William Holland was a founder of one of the mainstay families of southern Craven County. He never did sell his land. He never did migrate to the west. His descendants would continue to live at Slocum Creek for several more generations. But his advertisement for the sale of his property from the November 9, 1822, issue of the Newbern Sentinel, *clearly indicates the kind of wealth that was possible for the area's early settlers.*

Notice.

THE SUBSCRIBER

intending to remove from this state, offers the following
Land & other Property
FOR SALE.

The Lands and Plantation whereon he now resides, containing 400 acres; about 150 of which are cleared and under cultivation, the remainder well timbered. On this plantation are, a good Dwelling House, new Barn, Kitchen, Stables, and all other necessary outhouses, the whole of which are in good repair. – Also, an excellent Orchard of the best-selected fruits – Apples, Pears, Peaches, Grapes, Figs and Plumbs. – It lies fifteen miles below New Bern on the south side of the Neuse River, immediately on the west side of the mouth Slocumb's Creek, and on the north side of Coleman's Creek – commanding a full view of the Neuse River for 30 miles down; and is one among the best and most convenient places for fishing and fowling, on the Neuse River.

ALSO, One other Plantation, known by the name of the Gibson Plantation, containing 270 acres; 80 of which are cleared and under cultivation; the improvements are, a Dwelling House, and good Orchard of Apples, Pears, Peaches and Figs. On this land may be got from 50 to 75,000 red oaks staves, and a great quantity of wood, very convenient to the water. It is bounded by Slocumb's and Glover's Creek; and is very well situated for fishing and fowling.

ALSO, Another piece of Land known by the name of Millford, adjoining the above, and bounded by Coleman's Creek. It contains 310 acres, with the exception of 75 acres (which have been sold out) – has no improvements but is well timbered and good land.

ALSO, Another tract of Land, known by the name of Pumpkin Neck, lying on the north side of Coleman's Creek, adjoining the above, and containing 236 acres. There are no improvements, but the land is good and well timbered.

ALSO, Another tract of Land, known by the name of Smithfield, lying on the south side of Coleman's Creek, and running up said Creek one miles and a half. It contains 300 acres, about 50 of which are cleared and under good fence, the remaining is well timbered, an excellent range for Cattle and Hogs. On this land is one of the best MILL SEATS on Neuse River; there is a dam 130 yards long, across the creek and of 35 years standing – and a never-failing stream. This situation, also, is remarkably good for fishing and fouling.

Also, Several Other Tracts of PECOSEN [*pocosin, a type of wetland with low-lying vegetation*] LAND, lying on the head of Coleman's Creek, 14 miles below New Bern, and near the main road. It will be described as I purchased it.

The first piece, known by the name of THE RED OAK RIDGE, contains 120 acres of the best-looking pocosin [*wetlands*] land, and the best growth that I ever saw.

The second piece, known by the name of THE FLAT RIDGE, contains 120 acres.

The third piece, known by the name of THE INDIAN RIDGE, contains 120 acres.

The fourth piece, known by the name of SWEEPALL'S, containing 120 acres.

ALSO, Another tract of Land on the road that leads from New Bern to Beaufort, and adjoining William Rowe's land. It contains fifty acres, nearly all cleared, and is good land.

A more particular description of the above lands is deemed unnecessary, as those in the neighborhood are acquainted with it; and those not acquainted, it is presumed, will come and examine for themselves before they purchase. – The whole will be sold together, or as it is described or, and lots to suit purchasers.

HE WILL ALSO SELL

his stock of

Horses, Cattle, Sheep and Hogs.

Among the horses are four likely colts, one of three years old, one of a year, one of six, and one of three months old, all thought to be of as good blood as any in the state and two good brood mares. There are about 50 head of Cattle, and several good pairs of Oxen, upwards of 100 head of Hogs, and a number of very likely Sheep.

ALSO, 100 barrels of Corn, A quantity of Peas and Fodder, Oats and Rice, A set of Blacksmith's Tools, Carpenter's and Cooper's Tools, One Scow [*a type of flat-bottomed cargo barge, often rigged for sailing*], and four Canoes – some of the best on Neuse River; Plantation Utensils, Household and Kitchen Furniture, and 12 or 14 likely Negroes.

To conclude, he offers all and every kind of property he possesses, on the most reasonable terms, and long credit, as he prefers selling at private sale.

Should he not sell off in four or five weeks, he will give further notice, and sell at auction.

W'm. Holland.

Slocum's Creek, October 25, 1822.

Whatnot

Here are things that didn't fit in elsewhere ... or that we forgot till now.

The Tale of the Bob-tail Horse

A story about the modern Wynne brothers was related by W.J. Wynne to the author: Clay and W. J., Jr. were farm boys in the 1930s. Their father owned a mile-long swath of land from what is now Fontana Blvd. to Wynne Road, on the east side of present-day Cunningham Blvd. and US 70. All the property occupied by Craven Community College, the Havelock Public Library, a Havelock school, Havelock City Hall, the Public Safety Building, and Walter B. Jones Park was once the Wynne farm. Havelock City Park, a cypress swamp at the time, served as Wynne's hog wallow.

In those Depression-era days, the afternoon train reached Havelock at 5:00 p.m., and the brothers were instructed to work in the farm fields until they heard the train whistle blowing. Riding their buggy home once at day's end, the horse pulling the buggy inadvertently slapped Clay across the face with its long tail. It stung him pretty good. Angered, the young man pulled on the reins, jumped from the buggy, whipped out his pocket knife, and proceeded to chop off the coarse hairs of the horse's tail.

After they arrived at home, W. J. Wynne, Sr. discovered the bob-tail horse, confronted the culprit, and began a stern lecture about the necessity of the tail to a horse for its protection from biting insects, for example. He ordered the much-chagrined youth to go and recover every hair of the horse's tail and then had him tie each one back onto the stub ends with sturdy knots one hair at the time. Afterward, the draft animal regained the semblance of a working tail, and, with many hours at the back end of a horse, Clay allowed that his lesson had been learned, W.J. reported.

The Railroad Comes to Southern Craven County

Few things have happened in the world of southern Craven County that changed day-to-day life as much as the opening of the railroad in 1858. All of a sudden, a person was able to climb down off a horse or mule, park the buggy, and hop aboard a railroad car for a trip to New Bern or beyond. The whole world opened up in a way it never had before.

For a hundred thousand years people had walked or ridden on the back of an animal making twelve or fifteen or, maybe, twenty miles a day, with

great exertion. And now you could ride 20 miles *in an hour*! It was a full-blown miracle.

You could get away from the dangerous river and the muddy roads – and ride, no matter what the weather.

And the engine's string of passenger and freight cars arriving at the station might be bringing anything or anyone.

Now, you could put a note on the train in the morning to a merchant in a town more than a day's walk away and your order would come back on the evening train.

And crazy as it sounds, you didn't even need a rail stop. No, you could wave a hat or hanky at the train, flag it down, and it would stop for you. Wherever you encountered it, the train would pull to a stop so you could hop aboard. Even if you just wanted a ride to the next farm.

Railway Chronology

1826: Following the lead of England, railroad construction begins in the U.S.

1828: Joseph Caldwell, president of UNC, publishes an article urging the state to finance a railroad to run horizontally across the entire state.

1840: Two railroads open in the state—the Wilmington and Weldon and the Raleigh and Gaston.

1848: NC legislature authorizes a railroad that will connect the eastern part of the state with the piedmont.

1854: The Atlantic and North Carolina Railroad was chartered, with the state providing two-thirds of the capital. John Motley Morehead, first president of the NCRR, gives a famous speech calling the railroad the state's "Tree of Life."

1856: The first train passes from Goldsboro to Charlotte.

1858: The Atlantic & North Carolina Railroad is completed, opening 95 miles of rail between Goldsboro to New Bern through Riverdale, Croatan, Havelock, and Newport to Morehead City, and later to Beaufort Harbor.

1862-1865: Union forces occupy sites on the railroad at Croatan and Havelock to protect the rails and trestle from Confederate forces. They are not successful.

The freight depot at Havelock was crucial to the logistics of Cherry Point base construction. The building was moved by rail from Riverdale in 1941 and placed on a foundation on the east side of the tracks at Miller Blvd. The bay window noticeable above was later added so that railroad employees inside could see approaching trains. Since this 2007 photo, the depot has been moved to a location nearby as part of a preservation effort.

1865-1870: Rebuilding and reconstruction after damage to tracks and neglect of rail corridor during the War Between the States.

1866: Efforts to consolidate the Atlantic and North Carolina with the NCRR are initiated, although it takes until 1989 to complete the merger.

1896: North Carolina leases the entire railroad to Southern Railway (later Norfolk Southern) for 99 years

1939: Begins operation as Atlantic & East Carolina Railway.

1941: Riverdale freight depot building moved by rail to Havelock on August 21. Material and equipment begin to flow on the A&EC "Mullet Line" for construction of the new Marine Corps base at Cherry Point; 32,000 carloads of sand and gravel in 1942 alone.

1950: Rail passenger service ends at Havelock and other Atlantic and East Carolina stops.

1989: Atlantic & East Carolina merges into NCRR, resulting in a consolidated corridor from Morehead City to Charlotte.

New Bern was founded as a city. It was settled by city people intending to create an urban environment. Beaufort was founded as a seaport. Immediate access to the Atlantic Ocean made it ideal for sea-going commerce and maritime culture.

Havelock, in contrast, was a railroad town. The very name of the place came with the completion of the Atlantic & North Carolina Railroad in 1858 and the whistle-stop was a water and wood station for trains for nearly 100 years.

A few examples of the importance of the railroad:

➢ When completed from Beaufort to Goldsboro, the 95-mile-long Atlantic and North Carolina Railroad—later called the Atlantic and East Carolina Railroad—connected southern Craven County with the outside world for the first time, opening a vital transportation link for farmers, lumbermen, business interests, and travelers. Previously, the trip to New Bern would have taken all day by horse, buggy, or on foot. By train, even with stops along the way, the trip was less than an hour.

➢ Mail and supplies came in, and timber, naval stores, and agricultural products went out of Havelock and southern Craven by steam train. Passengers moved both ways. This rail commerce helped foster a local economic boom in the mid-1800s.

➢ Within days of the beginning of the Civil War, a trainload of Confederate soldiers, the "Goldsboro Rifles," rolled through on their way to seize Fort Macon on Bogue Banks. The railroad tracks and trestles were protected and fought over during the Civil War. Federal troops built a log fort on the banks of Slocum Creek in early 1862, primarily to guard the rail line. Raiding Confederates burned the fort in 1864, burned the trestle, and tore up the tracks.

➢ Travelers, both rich and famous, came from as far away as Philadelphia and New York City to hunt, fish, and relax in the south shore countryside. Passenger trains passed through at least twice daily from 1858 until 1950. Baseball legend Babe Ruth is probably the most well-known of the people who routinely visited via the trains in the late 1800s and early 1900s. The trip from New York City was just 24 hours.

➢ A lot of high-quality, desirable moonshine was shipped from the area during Prohibition, smuggled aboard the train sometimes hidden in potato barrels or shipments of fish.

➢ The existence of the railroad was a critical element in the selection of Havelock as the home of the Cherry Point Marine Corps Air Station in the early 1940s. The current freight depot was moved to town at that time from Riverdale. Without the railroad, the base would have been built elsewhere. During Cherry Point's construction nearly everything, including the Marines and sailors themselves, was delivered by the trains of the Atlantic & East Carolina Railroad.

➢ The A&NC became the shortest railroad on the continent operating with diesel power in 1946, and it was fully "dieselized" in 1951. By 1958, the A&EC was absorbed by Southern Railway, which continues ownership of the line in partnership with the State of North Carolina.

As a note to researchers, Tryon Place Historic Sites and Gardens in New Bern holds a collection of A&EC Railway memorabilia including railroad maps, documents, photographs, artwork plus locomotive and train car models.

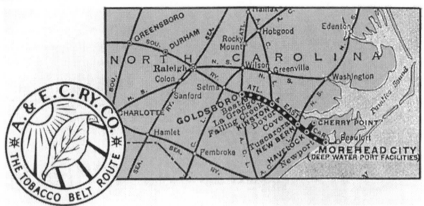

The Dutch Colony at Havelock

Woodbridge wasn't the only attempt to "colonize" southern Craven County. A man named C.W. McLean had ideas grandiose enough to rival Rev. Bull's. McLean billed himself as the local head of the American Colonization Society. About 1879, he made a tentative deal with James A. Bryan for a 25,000-acre tract of land running from just below the Havelock railroad depot along Lake Road toward Lake Ellis Plantation.

McLean expected Dutch immigrants from the Great Lakes region, Michigan in particular, to move south. He promoted cheap land with great farming potential. The land would be sold to the Hollanders at a nice markup, of course. By promising a quick sellout, McLean convinced Bryan to option the land at two dollars per acre.

The colonization plan attracted a lot of attention. The newspapers really liked the story. A Charlotte, N.C. paper wrote, "A colony of Dutch settlers is now locating at Havelock, halfway between Newbern and Morehead City, having purchased 25,000 acres of land, and we understand that the prospect is they will occupy the whole country." [a]

From a Wilmington, N.C. journal, "C.W. McLean, Esq., having completed the purchase of Donnell and Wade estates, which together contain twenty-five thousand acres of the best land in Eastern North Carolina, with splendid water power, left on Wednesday for Chicago and will spend the next two months in Illinois, Indiana, and Michigan, working among the English-speaking Hollanders." [b]

The paper said McLean's goal was "ten to fifteen families a month commencing in October" and a total of "fifty to seventy-five families during the winter."

The news report reveals a strategy to overcome what would be one of the big Dutch objections. Because the Dutch are acclimatized to cold weather, McLean planned to bring the farmers down beginning in October and settle them in the winter so they would already be tied to the land when it got *hot*.

The promoter was able to get the Dutch colony started. Visitors came to look. There were some initial buyers, too. Suddenly names like DePoorte, Shuringa, Vink, Dinker, Buys, Brandt, Leauhouts, Vyne, Schol, Van Vlissinger, Van Jacht, Vanarandenk, De Poothe and Kranjenbelt began to be heard in the area and mentioned in the local papers. Some would eventually be entered into the census.

But there was another flaw even worse than the heat. The pine wetlands of southern Craven County were of only marginal quality for mainstream farming. As we've seen over and over in the book, what grows best in the south shore area is pine trees. There was some good farmland around the lakes, but much of the land available to the Hollanders was swampy ground with acidic soil.

The Dutch are a hearty and industrious breed and some of them adapted. For one, William Buys moved to the area but, with partner Jacobus Schol, bought 550 acres of the productive plantation land along Slocum Creek. [c]

Garret Vyne tried to grow a variety of crops below Havelock with little success. He eventually found that he could harvest reasonable quantities of crabgrass and hay that he shipped out by train as cattle feed.

Most weren't so lucky. Those who expected to grow corn, cotton, and wheat were disappointed.

---

[a] *The Charlotte Democrat*, February 27, 1880, pg. 2.

[b] *Wilmington (NC) Daily Review*, June 9, 1879.

[c] Craven County Deed Book 82, pg. 442-443; see also Book 112, pg. 488.

The land sold slowly. Or not at all. Those who made deals for land found it hard to make enough money to pay for it. And the heat melted them.

Jim Bryan and C.W. McLean were soon in a relationship reminiscent of Rev. Bull and the AMA. Acrimonious letters were exchanged, with complaints about all manner of things, as McLean failed to make the magic happen.

Bryan wrote in his 1881 Lake Ellis account book, "Agreement with McLean obtained under false representation. viz., He would pay all moneys due me by Jan. 1 and would have enough of the land sold by that time to bona fide settlers to pay said sum. Wanted possession for the purpose of survey &c. McLean was to sell the Hollanders and establish a Holland colony; that was the object of my agreeing to sell to him. Agreement was based upon the establishment of a Holland colony ... and [McLean] represented would be made ten-fold more valuable than the entire tract in its pristine condition. In consideration of this representation price was $2 per acre." [d]

Some good came of it nonetheless. One of the Dutch settlers from Michigan, William Leauhouts, started the first Havelock Post office. He became the postmaster in 1881 and, even though he soon left for northern climes, the Havelock branch he started handled local deliveries for the next fifty years.

In the end, most of the colonists moved away. Bryan took the property back. McLean skulked off. And all the land is still growing pine trees to this day.

The *New Bern Weekly Journal* wrote the long-overdue obituary for the failed Dutch colony in 1907: "Mr. John DePorte of Havelock, was in the city, having just returned from a visit to relatives at Holland, Michigan. Mr. DePorte came here twenty-five years ago with a colony of Dutchmen, being of that nation himself, and settled at Havelock. The colony didn't thrive for some reason and the colonists returned to Holland, Michigan, from whence they came or became scattered elsewhere. Mr. DePorte was married at Havelock, settled down, and has become prosperous. He is the only one of the colonists to remain." [e]

The Joneses of Wales at Slocum Creek ... and beyond

The reader may have heard one too many times by now that Roger Jones was beheaded by Indians on the Neuse River near Slocum Creek in 1711 while his brother Evan escaped. Thus, we are skipping the first small part of the following Jones Family genealogical material "transcribed from

---

[d] James A. Bryan Papers, Southern History Collection, UNC-Chapel Hill.

[e] *New Berne Weekly Journal*, October 8, 1907, pg. 4.

a very old, undated paper, inherited by Catherine Boyd Browne from Mary C. Roberts with supplemental dates supplied by Miss Bessie Carmon, Oriental, North Carolina."

In addition to other information herein, we find several people who caught *Go West Fever*.

We pick up where Evan Jones "married Elizabeth, a daughter of Col. Thomas Lovick, the collector of customs at Beaufort, N.C. Mr. Lovick came also from Wales with his brother, John.

"Two children were born to Evan and Elizabeth Jones: Roger, b. 1731, d. November 1801, aged 70; Lovick. He married Abagail Parker.

"Roger married Sarah Lovette (b. 1735, d. January 9, 1810) a French lady, and to them were born ten children:

- Evan, married June 16, 1785, Betsy Turner; their three children: Elizabeth m. Stephen W. Wynne; Henry, never married; Eden, m. Fannie Potter.

- Roger, Jr. – d. 1801, m. Comfort Always d. 1826. Five children born: Henry A., b. 1790, never married, d. February 9, 1841, at New Bern at 51; Hugh married a Taylor and moved to Kentucky, had one daughter, Elizabeth Ann, m. Joseph Tomlinson, descendants there now, died May 9, 1831, Gerard Co., Kentucky, age 43; Mehitabel, m. James Lovick (1796-1827) Slocumb Creek; Hardy L., never married; Edward Roger, m. Louisa Cherry of Tennessee and their descendant live in that state.

- John (1764-1840) m. 1st – Susannah Saunders (1776-1815) at Green Springs. He was a successful and active businessman in New Bern and died respected and honored in the church and the community. Four children were born of them: Frances Ann Jones b. February 4, 1800, d. October 11, 1804; John Alex Jones, May 10, 1801-August 7, 1801; Mary Eliza Jones, b. December 12, 1802, d. November 20, 1873, m. John M. Roberts; Frederick John Jones, b. July 16, 1805, d. August 16, 1880, m. Hannah Shine, July 16, 1831, of Comfort near Cypress Creek, Jones County, N.C. Their children were Leah, Mary (married Rev. Lachlan C. Vass, May 9, 1867), John, Frederick, Nelly, and Edward. Hannah m. George Allen. Mary married Dr. Potter of Boston.

  John m. 2nd – a widow, Lucretia Hollister Bell (1780-1860). Through her influence, he became a Presbyterian and each now has a tablet on the Church wall in New Bern. Their children: William Hollister Jones, b. 1807, d. in Mississippi or Alabama, never married; Susan Margaret, 1808-1810; Sarah Susan, 1809-1811.

- William, m. Betsy Partridge, one daughter, Julia Ann, who m. Joseph Hall.
- Polly, m. Frederick Turner and moved to Tennessee.
- Lovick, (1771-1817), never married. Died in New Bern and is buried in Cedar Grove Cemetery.
- Sarah, m. George Lovick. Anne Elizabeth, Penelope, and James were their children. The latter was the grandfather of Hugh Jones Lovick.
- Frederick (1777-1828), m. Sidney Maria Daily (1792-1824). Four children were born to them: Lydia (October 10, 1810-November 24, 1835), m. Charles Shepard and had one son, Frederick, who moved to Alabama. Frederick m. Lydia and had two children, Mary and Louisa. After the death of Lydia, Shepard m. Mary Donnell, daughter of Judge Donnell, and mother of James Bryan and Mrs. Margaret Nelson; Ann Maria m. Thomas A. Borden, who moved to Alabama; George Lovick m. Madeline Clitherell and also moved to Alabama; and William Penn, d. in infancy (1819-October 21, 1826??).
- Gideon m. Julia Bigg and moved to Tennessee.
- Asa, the youngest of the ten married Sallie Bryan (1796-1838) and died childless. He and his wife are buried in Cedar Grove Cemetery. Said Mary C. Roberts was very fond of her Uncle Asa."

PART IV

APPELLATIONS

<u>Naming Havelock</u>

There was a big fight in New Bern about how to spell the town's name. The old-style was Newbern. That worked just fine for 150 years. But when the Union took the town in 1862, its minion quickly morphed to the more cosmopolitan *New Berne*. The locals were naturally rankled by this and as they slowly regained their political power in the waning years of the 1800s, a battle royal broke out *over spelling*. The brouhaha had to be settled in the legislature, the current style being the compromise winner.

Spelling wasn't the issue for the community that today bears the name Havelock. It was the name itself that was unsettled for as long as the county seat was arguing over one word or two, to "e" or not to "e."

Locally, folks tried on Neuse, Neuse River, Cravenville, and Spaightsville. We've seen a letter written from here in 1829 "return addressed" as "Craven, at Woodville." The Havelock name was first floated by the Atlantic and North Carolina Railroad for its wood and water stop at Slocum Creek when it opened the road in 1858. Even after that, a Northern minister tried in 1870 to change it to Woodbridge. He succeeded for a while, but in finest New Bern fashion, the locals fought back on that one, too, and Havelock stuck for good.

In explaining how the town got its name, please indulge us as we invoke the spirit of that pale-faced, straw-haired pop art icon – Andy Warhol. Warhol once said: "In the future, everyone will be world-famous for 15 minutes."

It was so for Andy, and so it was for Henry Havelock.

As naturally obscure throughout his life as a man can be, Havelock rose over six months in 1857 – through a series of truly brilliant and heroic battle victories in India – to be serialized in nearly every newspaper in the world, to be a name upon every English-speaking tongue and foreign tongues as well, and, in his dramatically-timely death, to be hailed a champion, mourned, eulogized, and nearly beatified on every continent save Antarctica.

Having been passed over twenty-two times earlier in his military career for advancement to the rank of captain, in the last half-year of his life he was rapidly ushered to the top of the ranks and knighted by Queen Victoria of England. Before he died, he was Major General Sir Henry Havelock.

Statues were raised in his honor. One in London's Trafalgar Square shares ground with Lord Nelson's Column. Cities around the world were named for him. There are two in Canada, two in New Zealand, and three in the United States. There's a Havelock Island in the Indian Ocean and – worldwide – an endless number of streets, schools, geographical features, and, at one time, even children named for him. East Carolina University holds a rare book collection of more than fifty volumes of biography about the man.

First and foremost, Henry Havelock was a devout Christian. Exceptionally fervent in his beliefs, exceedingly rigid in his manner, he was considered a "crank" by some who served with him in colonial India. Second, he was a consummate military man. In the end, he was an excellent leader and as good a general as ever took men into battle. Finally, he was a remarkable and devoted family man.

Besides his wife and children, his two lifelong passions were the odd combination of Bible study and the mastery of military tactics. He conducted himself without concern for the judgment of others focusing always on what he thought was proper and important. In the end, matters came out right.

Havelock was born on April 5, 1795, at Ford Hall, the family's estate at Bishop-Wearmoth, England. He was the second son of a prosperous shipbuilder, William Havelock (1757-1837).

Henry's mother, Jane, was responsible for the strong moral upbringing referred to in almost all accounts of his life. He was only 16 when he lost her guidance. She died in 1811.

Havelock's relationship with his father was tumultuous. The loss of his mother and his father's coming professional ruin only compounded matters. Due to unsuccessful speculation, William suffered financial troubles and lost much of his fortune in 1812. Henry and his father disagreed about the son's career. William wanted him to become a lawyer. That was the last thing on Henry's mind. In 1814, after a blow-up between the two, Henry left school. With the help of his older brother, also named William, he received a commission as a lieutenant in the British army. William had distinguished himself in several battles including Waterloo and got Henry a posting with the 95th Regiment on July 30, 1815.

A few years later the young lieutenant was ordered to India. The India of Henry Havelock's time, with its battles between the occupying British troops and the native population, was much like the American Wild West. British forces also engaged in nearly constant battle with Afghans and Sikhs. A young officer looking for experience could not have been in a better place.

During the long sea voyage to India, Havelock underwent the religious conversion that would color the remainder of his days. One biographer says Havelock embraced Christian principles following a violent storm at sea that nearly cost him his life. Another has it that during the long voyage around

Africa, a brother officer, Lt. James Gardner, was the instrument of his conversion. In any event, when Havelock arrived in Calcutta in May 1823, he was a changed man.

More changes were on the way. We are told that Havelock conducted himself well in battle. He took part in campaign after campaign in the hot, dusty land. In 1824, he took a fifty percent cut in pay to join the 13th Light Infantry in the First Anglo-Burmese War. The fighting lasted two years.

In 1829, Havelock married Hannah Shepard Marshman, the daughter of a famous minister, and became a Baptist.

Sir Henry Havelock

He gained rank slowly. In 1838, after more than 20 years of service, he was only a captain. That year he took part in the First Afghan War. Some writers have speculated that Havelock was often passed over for advancement because of his ardent Christian faith and his strong stand against alcohol. At one point, five other officers were promoted over him. Still, he was recognized for his skill on the battlefield. He was made a "Companion of the Bath," an honor close to knighthood. He also began drawing to him a group of like-thinking individuals whose temperance made them reliable soldiers.

One night there was an attack on a British barracks by marauding natives. The commander was told that the guard detail was drunk and unable to respond. The commander roared, "Call out Havelock's Saints. His men are never drunk and he is always ready." That night, Havelock and his troops did what needed to be done. The nickname "saints" for Havelock and his men had first been used in ridicule but came to be spoken with grudging respect. They were known for their faith, sobriety, and skill in battle.

The governor-general of India, Sir Henry Hardinge, would later say that Havelock "was every inch a Christian, every inch a soldier."

Havelock and his troops would rise before reveille to hold religious services. Sometimes they would go into the solemn darkness of a nearby

Buddhist temple and there, under the very gaze of the statue of Buddha, they would lift their voices in worship of their Christian savior.

The skill and faith of Havelock's Saints would be sorely tested in the whirlwind of history that was to unfold in 1857; a tumult that would rival any challenge ever faced by an army, and a series of events that would propel Henry Havelock to the very pinnacle of world fame.

By 1849, Havelock had been in India for 26 years. During that time, for lack of money to buy rank and because he was considered a grouchy eccentric by some, he had been passed over for promotion many times. Still, he had earned experience, medals, and respect for his conduct on the battlefield. He had fought in many campaigns, had horses shot from beneath him, and learned what it took to win in war. Slowly, recognition began to come. He was promoted to quartermaster-general of the Queen's troops in India, then to lieutenant colonel and brevet colonel. When the post of adjutant general opened in 1854, he was named to fill the position.

In November 1856, war was declared between England and Persia. Havelock, under Sir James Outram, was given a division to command and was ordered to the Persian Gulf. It was his last engagement before the Sepoy Mutiny, the bloody uprising that would make him famous.

Mutiny of the Sepoy

The Sepoy Mutiny of 1857 was avoidable but the British blundered.

Native troops known as the Sepoy were allied with the British occupying force in India. The British never numbered more than 100,000 inside a nation of millions. For the Sepoy, the relationship was as much financial as political. They were paid and supplied by the British to keep the native population in line. They were mercenaries, feared by the people, and could be heavy-handed and cruel in suppressing unrest.

The Sepoy were made up mostly of Hindus and Moslems. Hindus considered the cow to be sacred. The Moslems considered the pig to be unclean. In 1857, the British issued a new rifle to the Sepoy. In an exquisite manifestation of indifference, ignorance, or both, they also issued new cartridges that were greased with pig and cow fat. Pigs are taboo to Muslims. Cows are sacred to Hindus. The native Sepoy troops had to bite off the end of the cartridge before loading it into the rifle, thus having the objectional material enter their mouths.

They complained bitterly, but their word fell on deaf British ears. A Delhi unit refused to use the rifles. They threw down their weapons. At this, they were threatened at gunpoint by British soldiers. Naturally, fighting commenced. Within days, the word spread that native regiments at Delhi,

Ferozepore, and Meerut had mutinied. In a deadly, bloody struggle, Delhi was taken by the Sepoy.

When the native population saw that the Sepoy had rebelled, they took it as a signal that the time had come for a revolution. All over India, British embassies, compounds, and residences were besieged by angry mobs bent on killing the imperialists. All of the worst of human nature came forth, as it often does at times like these. Killing, rape, looting, and arson were rampant and the British men, women, and children were the objects of the wrath.

Havelock returned from his successful campaign in the Persian Gulf on May 19, 1857, and learned of the mutiny when he reached Bombay. He set out immediately to join a relief column marching on Delhi. The relief force was headed by Gen. George Anson, the commander-in-chief in India. The best up-country route was then in the hand of the mutineers so Havelock embarked on a ship called the *Erin*.

It was not a good trip. The *Erin* wrecked on the coast and he had to wait to be picked up by another vessel that was dispatched for him from Calcutta. Havelock reached Madras on June 13 and learned that Gen. Anson was dead. A local commander, Sir Patrick Grant, had replaced Anson. Havelock went with Grant and they arrived in Calcutta on June 17, five weeks after the start of the rebellion.

With India's military leadership in disarray, Havelock stepped to the fore. He was promptly given command of the entire force at Allahabad. His son, also named Henry, was with him now and served as his aide-de-camp. Havelock's orders were ambitious. He was to put down all resistance in the area, to move swiftly to support Sir Hugh Wheeler at Cawnpore and Sir Henry Lawrence at Lucknow, and, oh yes…to disperse and destroy all the Sepoy mutineers.

Within days Havelock's forces were charging toward Cawnpore, a central Indian city under siege by mutinous native troops. Havelock had heard on July 3 that many British soldiers and officials had been slaughtered there, but several hundred more European women, children, and a few men were still alive and surrounded in the fortress-like embassy.

With about one thousand soldiers, a few volunteer horsemen, and six cannons, Havelock moved across India during the hottest season of the year. By forced march he headed for his goal 126 miles away, stopping time and again to engage and defeat rebel forces. As Havelock's victories mounted, word began to be carried to Europe and England of his successes. Back home people were astonished by the brutality of the uprising and were waiting daily for dispatches from India. Nearly every newspaper in Europe carried stories of the Indian mutiny. The stories made it to America as well. Havelock's name began to appear in print around the world.

On July 15, Havelock again received word that the hostages were hold-ing out at Cawnpore; however, a hideous drama was unfolding, even as he marched to the rescue. The local rebel leader's name was Nana Sahib. He has been painted as a ruthless and corrupt criminal. Among his many crimes, he was alleged to have killed a man so he could steal the victim's wife.

The Nana, leader of the Cawnpore mutineers, told the British citizens trapped in the embassy that he wished them no harm. He said he merely wanted them to leave the place. He sent word that he would supply boats for their get-away on the river. For the hostages, the offer was most tempting. The mothers had very little water and food for their children. They were suffering from the heat and reeling from the shock of having seen husbands and friends killed. The thought of escape must have been irresistible. After much deliberation, they decided to go. Gathering what few possessions they could carry, the surviving men, women, and children left the compound where they had been held for weeks. Moving carefully, they made their way down to the river.

Soon most had boarded the boats. The rest were standing in long rows on the stone steps at the river's edge waiting for their turns. It was at that moment that Nana Sahib ordered the hidden guns uncovered and had his men open fire on the unarmed people.

They were slaughtered.

Amid screams and cries, only five men were able to make it to the op-posite river bank. All but one was hunted down and killed. That single sur-vivor lived to tell the tale of Nana Sahib's treachery.

After the butchery, the rebel leader moved out with 5,000 men to con-front Havelock and his force of less than 1,000. It would be one of the telling battles of the mutiny. The two armies met on July 16, 1857, a few miles outside of Cawnpore. Through what has been described as a "masterly flanking movement," Havelock used his forces to send Sahib's fighters into disarray. Members of Havelock's small force charged directly into cannons and right up the enemy's batteries and began capturing guns and turning them on the mutineers.

Fighting went on all day before the rebels were all killed or ran away. Nana Sahib fled the battlefield on an elephant. He is said to have escaped to Nepal and was never captured or punished for his deeds. *The Illustrated London News* later wrote, "the name of Nana Sahib will for the future stand conspicuous as that of the most ruthless and treacherous scoundrel who ever disgraced humanity."

Victorious against huge odds, Havelock and his men stopped for the night about two miles from the city. They had now marched the 126 miles under a blazing Indian sun, fighting and winning four major engagements against superior numbers along the way. The next morning, Havelock's forces entered Cawnpore.

LUCKNOW.—This city, in the Kingdom of Oude, for which Nena Sahib and Gen. Havelock are both on the march, contains 200,-000 inhabitants. In Lucknow there is a strong British garrison, which sabib, said to be four days ahead of Havelock, hastens to destroy, and Havelock to strengthen. Nena Sahib's forces outnumber seven times those of the gallant Highlander, but Havelock has repeatedly beaten him before against odds as great, and the garrison, it is believed, can hold out till the arrival of reinforcements. Fate may yet throw the miscreant Sahib, who, it seems, has not committed suicide, into British hands. Lucknow is an important point, and if taken by the Sepoys, will prove a formidable barrier between the British and Delhi.

The world watched. From a New Bern newspaper, the *Weekly Union,* October 21, 1857.

What they found is among the saddest scenes of human history. The bodies of the women and children were scattered along the river. Many of them had been dumped down a well possibly while still alive. The horror of the well would resonate in Great Britain becoming a long-remembered source of anguish and anger. One biographer cites Havelock's hold on his men as the reason few atrocities were committed against the captured mutineers: "The pitiful scene presented by the remains of their murdered fellow countrymen exasperated them to madness, but the firm hand of their commander held them in check."

The rigors of battle, the lack of a steady supply of food, and illness began to take their toll upon Havelock's small force. The decaying bodies did not help matters. Havelock moved his men outside the city for rest. He knew there was much to be done.

A force of 100 soldiers was ordered by the general to secure Cawnpore and deal with the dead. Soon Havelock and his remaining 800 fighters were marching again, this time to try and save another group of besieged English citizens at a town called Lucknow.

Back home in England, and in other parts of the world, readers waited anxiously for the next newspaper report of the fate of those in the Lucknow Residency. Trapped inside, surrounded and under attack, were mainly British civil servants and their families, many of whom would die as a result of the rebel onslaught. Having heard of the horrors of Cawnpore, the public had good reason to fear the worst at Lucknow. Havelock was their one hope.

At Bithoor, outnumbered five to one, Havelock defeated a rebel force of 4,000. Taking personal command in the field from horseback, he would win nearly a battle a day for the rest of the march.

General Havelock, at center with white hair, is greeted by other British officers after fighting their way into Lucknow in one of the final battles of the 1857 Sepoy Mutiny in India. Painting: *The Relief of Lucknow, 1857* by Thomas Jones Barker, National Portrait Gallery, London.

Throughout his career, Havelock had been denied promotions and command. Now at the height of his achievement, while literally, the whole world was watching his exploits in India, came word that Sir James Outram had been appointed to command the area where Havelock had skillfully assumed control. When Outram arrived with reinforcements on September 15, he found Havelock making preparations for a move on Lucknow. Outram then made a decision that one writer called "one of the most memorable acts of self-abnegation recorded in military history." Outram relinquished his rank and offered to accompany Havelock as a civilian volunteer.

When Havelock left Cawnpore on September 19, he was in command of 3,000 men. Under fire as they crossed the Ganges, Havelock's force would fight for the next 60 days almost without ceasing. He drove the enemy from Mungalwar, captured Bunnee, and attacked the Allumbugh, a fortified position within sight of Lucknow where the hostages were held.

The fight became urban warfare. Nearly all of the enemy forces had concentrated at Lucknow for what was expected to be the major event of the conflict. The two sides fought fence to fence, bridge to bridge, building to building, in a fierce contest for possession of the city. Havelock's force fought its way in among the enemy finally reaching the residency where the British citizens were housed. There was unimaginable relief for the captive countrymen in the compound.

The British residency in Lucknow had been a spacious, elegant building inside a large walled compound. It served as both embassy offices and quarters for the British staff and their families. After being shelled for two months, the building resembled a huge block of Swiss cheese. The random and incessant bombardment had been a living hell for the people within.

Having fought its way to the center of the city, Havelock's force now had enemy troops on all sides. From the residency stronghold, he and his men, along with the rescued British citizens, began to dislodge the enemy from surrounding buildings and take more ground. It was not until another force, under the command of Sir Colin Campbell, arrived on November 16 that the Indians were brought under control. With the fall of Lucknow, the Sepoy Mutiny collapsed.

Upon the arrival of Campbell, Havelock learned that his fame had spread around the world. The 62-year-old soldier was informed he had been promoted to major general. He had also been knighted by the Queen of England as he fought his way across the dusty landscape of India.

The humble and unpretentious man and now regaled around the globe as Maj. Gen. Sir Henry Havelock.

The Death of General Havelock

There was profound shock and dismay across Great Britain upon news of the death of Maj. Gen. Havelock on November 24, 1857.

Stories of his exploits had been the only source of hope during the dark days of the Indian Mutiny in which thousands lost their lives. After years of laboring in obscurity, he had become a national hero. His name was known around the world.

Havelock died soon after his last battle was fought. Four days following the relief of Lucknow, he fell ill with dysentery. Dysentery, commonplace at the time, is a painful inflammation of the large intestine resulting in fever and internal bleeding. The 62-year-old soldier had been fighting for months under the blazing tropical sun. His last portraits show a skinny, tired-looking man.

> **Death of Gen. Havelock.**
> The Europa brings intelligence of the death of Gen. Henry Havelock, whose recent exploits in India have gained for him a world-wide reputation.

Weekly Union, New Bern, January 30, 1858

At his death, he was surrounded by many of his friends. His son, who would one day also be a major general, was with him, too. He told them that he was happy and content. "See how a Christian dies," he said.

Four days after he was taken ill, barely a week after his final battle, Havelock was dead.

News of his passing did not reach England until January 7, 1858, and the nation plunged into mourning. Every newspaper in England carried word of his death as did most in Europe and many in America. The *New Bern Union* reported the death of Havelock in India.

THE HAVELOCK.

The Sunday following the news of his death, a memorial service was held in his honor in every village, town, and city in England. At Havelock's home church, Bloomsbury Baptist, an overflow crowd of 1,000 had to be turned away and the service repeated the following week.

Even Queen Victoria was said to have been distressed by Havelock's passing.

In America, flags were lowered to half-mast in New York and Philadelphia, the first time this honor had ever been shown for a British citizen. America, which had fought multi-year wars with England in 1776 and 1812, had not acknowledged the recent death of the Duke of Wellington by lowering flags. But flags were lowered for Havelock.

An honorary editorial appeared in the *New York Times*.

Public donations were gathered for the construction of a huge bronze statue of Havelock in London's Trafalgar Square where it is to this day. In Guild Hall, the equivalent in London of City Hall, a bust of the general was placed and paid for with tax money.

Havelock's wife, Hannah, received such a pension by order of Parliament that the family was left comfortable for several generations. Havelock's son, Henry, who served gallantly as his aide-de-camp, was knighted and made a baronet.

Havelock was buried in India.

An excerpt from a biography by Sir Leslie Stephens says: "When the opportunity came, he proved himself to be a great military leader, and won the gratitude of his country."

Tales of Sir Henry's exploits were the talk of the year and captivated the imagination of the world. His story was covered in local newspapers, as was his death. The publication of his biography in England by his brother-in-law, John Clarke Marshman, was noted in a newspaper in New Bern.

An item of headgear invented and popularized by the general and common among his troops also bears his name. A cap cover with a flap hanging over the back to protect the neck from the sun is called a "havelock." It was used by the troops in India and was later worn by the French Foreign Legion and American soldiers during the War Between the States.

Havelock became a favorite inspirational symbol for Civil War soldiers. His name and likeness appeared on some common items purchased and carried by those soldiers. One is called a Union case. It was a little hinged book-like affair used to protect tintype portraits of loved ones. The Union cases were made from a primitive plastic called gutta-percha, which provided some water resistance. One of the most popular Union cases carried by soldiers in the war had a standing image of Sir Henry holding a sword and the name "Havelock" molded on both the front and back.

No known evidence documents the selection process for the name of the rail stop at the junction of the train tracks and the Beaufort Road in southern Craven County. Perhaps a single railroad bureaucrat had the duty. Perhaps local people and railroad officials agreed on the name. When the local crossing was named Havelock Station, the next rail stop was named Lucknow Station after Sir Henry's most famous battle. That name did not stick. It was soon changed to Shepardsville. Today, we call it Newport.

There is much more that could be said, but the important things are covered. Henry Havelock was a good father, a loving and devoted husband, a leader of men, a man of principle and superior professional skill. When called upon, he was ready to do his duty and accomplished, in a profoundly heroic manner, the tasks fortune laid before him.

Naming Cherry Point

*The name "Cherry Point" came from a post office established in the
area for the Blades lumber interest many years ago ... and the word
"Cherry" came from the cherry trees that used to grow there.*
                                   – The Heritage of Craven County, Volume 1, 1984

After a lifetime of consideration, we've concluded that the name
Cherry Point has nothing to do with a post office among cherry trees.

The apocryphal story is that the moniker sprang to life when the first
"Cherry Point" post office opened in 1890, near the "X" on the map below.
The first postmaster, David W. Morton, Jr. – we've been told – chose the
name because the place was in a grove of cherry trees. [a]

We'll explain our skepticism and propose a new theory in a moment,
but first, it might be good to establish where the real Cherry Point is located.

And it's not on the Marine airbase.

Cherry Point is a geographic feature on the south bank of the Neuse
River east of the modern MCAS Cherry Point. In fairness, the Heritage
Book got that part right. It's near the place where the N.C. ferry loads and

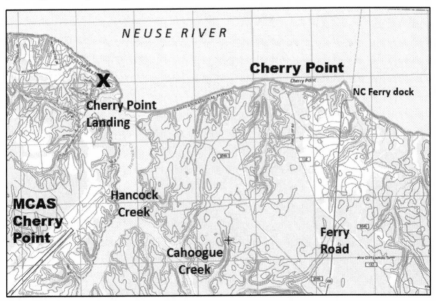

---

[a] For example, Carolina Telephone directories, without attribution, 1950-1980s.

unloads on its round trips to and from Minnesott Beach (Wilkinson Point) on the Neuse's north bank. To confuse things a little more, the area today is called *Cherry Branch* because a residential subdivision has grown up there that took its name from a small creek nearby.

Nevertheless, the words *Cherry Point* appears at that location on every official U.S. government map and chart, the name of the base notwithstanding. Cherry Point and MCAS Cherry Point aren't even in the same township; the base being in Craven County Township Six and Cherry Point being in Township Five.

So, what's going on here?

In much earlier times, boats were a major and, at times, *the* major mode of transportation. And you couldn't just dock them anywhere. The Neuse River can be exceedingly rough, and places with cliffs, marsh grass, and mud are certainly undesirable. A nice beach with a gentle slope up to the dry land would be a great place to put in, especially if there was some natural protection from wind and waves. Even in colonial times, the people who lived and farmed at Cherry Point recognized that a practical place to safely land a boat was just inside the mouth of Hancock Creek. Therefore, that natural cove became the "landing" for Cherry Point.

Kids making the most of Cherry Point Landing, Hancock Creek, 1920s. *EBE/ECU.*

The utility of Cherry Point Landing – as it came to be called – is confirmed to the present day by the fact that it's where the U.S. Navy built its boat docks and that the little harbor became the site of the marina that serves Marine Corps officers.

Long before the coming of the Marine Corps, a small village grew up around the landing. It was a wonderful place to keep a skiff or sailboat, a great place to fish and crab, and it made a dandy swimming hole for the kids. Over time the folks at the landing began to say, simply, that they lived at Cherry Point. The name sort of morphed westward.

As for cherries, in April 1711, Christen Jantz, a settler at New Bern, wrote a letter to his family at home in Switzerland. In it, he speaks of the quality of the land, plants like the wild grape, and things he had observed while exploring the countryside.

Jantz wrote: "Junker Michel told me they want to bring us wild or un-planted tree fruit; are not easy to find here. Cherries, I saw none." [b]

Of the black cherry or wild cherry, former N.C. state forester J.S. Holmes wrote that it's "a medium-sized tree, up to 70 feet high and one to three feet in diameter" and then added, "Black cherry as a tree is at its best *in the high mountains.*" [c]

Dozens of photographs exist of the old village of Cherry Point from about 1900 to 1940 including the home that served as a post office. In none of the photographs are any trees visible other than pine, oak, and live oak. The only fruit tree in any of the photos is a single peach tree about six feet tall in the garden of resident Barclay D. Borden.

In the settlement of the estate of Edward D. Thorpe of Hancock Creek in 1842, a large land tract he owned at Cherry Point was subdivided among the heirs. The proposed division lists trees on the property along Cherry Branch. Black gum, cypress, red oak, dogwood, and pine are mentioned, but no cherry trees. [d]

In two hundred years of old newspapers published in Craven County, we've found a single reference to the cherry tree. In 1811, a man named James Dixon offered for sale 6,000 acres, much of it swamp – "Pocosin of the richest kind, and may be conveniently drained," he said – extending from the heads of Brices and Slocumbs creeks back to Long Lake. On the land he notes, "The growth of its Poplar and Holly, both in great abundance of the largest size; White Oak, Red Oak, Beech, Laurel, Cypress, in great quanti-ties and of the first quality; Gums, Wild Cherry, &c., &c." [e]

Perhaps Dixon had cherry trees. Perhaps not. While only legend sup-ports the cherry-trees-at-Cherry-Point thesis, and many facts argue against their presence, it's impossible to prove they weren't there. Our surmise, however, is that the odds are exceedingly low that cherry trees grew in enough abundance to lend their name to a prominence on the banks of the Neuse River. What we can conclusively prove is that the name wasn't in-vented at the founding of the post office in 1890.

---

[b] *Swiss American Historical Review*, Vol. 45, No. 3, November, 2009.

[c] *Common Forest Trees of North Carolina and How to Know Them*, J. S. Holmes, De-partment of Conservation and Development, Raleigh NC, 1964.

[d] Craven County Wills and Estate Records, 1663-1978, image 14625.

[e] *The True Republican and Newbern Weekly Advertiser*, June 19, 1811, pg. 4.

In 1858, William G. Bryan, clerk of "the Court of Equity for the County of Craven" advertised in a New Bern newspaper the sale of 480 acres from the estate of W.H. Brinkley and his wife. The tract was described as being "situated on the South side of the Neuse River (at a point known as Cherry Point)." [f]

SALE OF LAND IN EQUITY.

W. H. Brinkley and wife, now deceased, and others. } In Equity

BY Virtue of a Decree of the Court of Equity for the County of Craven, I will expose to public sale on Monday the 19th day of April, 1858, being the Monday of Superior Court, a certain tract or parcel of Land, situated on the South side of Neuse River (at a point known as Cherry Point) containing about 480 acres, being the lands which were divised by the late Thomas Austen to his wife, Frances Austen.

Terms of sale made known on the day of sale.

WM. G. BRYAN, Cl'k & M. E.

March 8th, 1858.   [pr. adr. $5]   6w

A New Bern newspaper notice shows the name "Cherry Point" was
in use in 1858.

This is the earliest newspaper reference to Cherry Point and beats the post office story by more than three decades. It also proves that the post office was named for an existing geographic feature – that is, a point on the river named "Cherry" – and not for a grove of cherry trees surrounding the site of the post office established in 1890.

The Brinkleys received their land from relatives named Austin who were associated with an affluent family named Whitehead. During the mid-1800s, the Whitehead family owned a large plantation on the true Cherry Point east of Hancock Creek. The family lived there for generations and established a graveyard on a bluff overlooking the Neuse River.

[f] *The Weekly Union*, New Bern, March 30, 1858, pg. 3, col. 1.

It was only natural for families to choose the lovely bluffs along the river as the resting places for their deceased. The views from the river heights are so pretty it's easy to imagine people saying, "This is where I want to be buried someday." And many were, over the hundreds of years since first settlement.

The result of that sentiment is that a number of the graveyards have been badly encroached upon, or altogether destroyed, by the relentless erosion of the river's south shore. Single hurricanes have been known to cut fifty feet or more into the high banks of the Neuse. Some rather horrendous scenes of bones and exposed caskets have been reported over the years at these cemeteries.

The old Fisher family burial ground at Riverdale was lost in a hurricane and a similar fate befell the Whiteheads. In recent times, the U.S. Forest Service recovered some headstones from the river at the old Whitehead plantation site near the end of Ferry Road at Cherry Point. The USFS then moved all the Whitehead burials they found to the Oak Grove United Methodist Church on Adams Creek Road. That choice was made because a line of the family had migrated to the Bachelor area in the late 1800s and those relatives were buried in the Oak Grove churchyard.

Enter Cherry Whitehead

In the late 1980s, the author was visited at his newspaper office by a Whitehead descendant who was adamant that the point we're discussing had been named for her ancestor, Cherry Whitehead. She was the first person to inform us about what has turned out to be this prominent local family from a bygone time and to suggest an alternative to the post-office-in-a-cherry-grove scenario.

Asked what evidence there was in the matter, she responded that the family had always known it to be the case. It was named for Cherry Whitehead and that was that. She was convinced and convincing, but without a deed or even a birth or death date, there was nothing on which to hang one's hat.

In those pre-internet days, there was also no quick way to gather details on someone who'd been dead for, well, a long time. While a few Whitehead deeds were soon found, no mention of a family member named Cherry was forthcoming.

But a curious thing began to happen. Over the years, we heard from others, several of them older African Americans from the Highway 101 vicinity, that Cherry Point was named for a person. Always without evidence, but also always with an "everybody-knows-that" air.

We've referenced the Southern Oral History Program many times within this book. In a taped interview for that program, Emma West Bell said of Cherry Point, "the story goes that there was an old man named Cherry who had a lot there, hence the name." Pressed further on the matter, she immediately reverted to the cherry tree story, concluding finally, "That's where the name comes from, Cherry Point, because it was a lot of cherry trees down there." [g]

Despite the flip-flop, there was confirmation of some sort of persistent shared memory, especially among black folks, that Cherry Point was named for some*one*, not some*thing*.

In recent years, from a research standpoint at least, things have improved for the better. The internet and its digital indexing are a wonder.

Jeremiah Cherry Whitehead was born about 1800 to a prosperous family living on the Neuse River east of what is today MCAS Cherry Point. His family owned a plantation, but Cherry – he was always called Cherry – was a merchant and owned a storehouse at the corner of Middle Street and South Front Street in New Bern. He "commuted" by centerboard sailboat to and from the city. Such travel by boat was commonplace. Some families did so each week to attend church; the river often being a more reliable thoroughfare than the roads through the wet and muddy countryside.

He married Sarah "Sally" Rice on New Year's Day, 1828.

Of his involvement in civic affairs, we know that he served on a coroner's jury on June 1, 1831. The citizens on the jury were given the facts in the death of one David E. Anderson, alias H. Sullivan. The jurors, including Whitehead, determined the deceased to be "a lunatic person of insane mind" who committed suicide by cutting his own throat with a straight razor.

Cherry, too, died unexpectedly and without a will on Wednesday, April 11, 1832, at age 30, close to the time his father died. There was no obituary in the newspaper for Cherry's wealthy father, John S. Whitehead, Sr. Though it is speculation, this may have been because Cherry was better known in New Bern than his father living on the plantation down the river. Regardless, the lack of a known date of death for John Whitehead denies us the opportunity to understand whether or not father and son died close enough together for it to have been in a common accident or from a common illness. [h]

The same day Cherry Whitehead's obituary was published, there were three other death notices: a 76-year-old male, a 19-year-old male, and a nine-year-old female. That's a lot of deaths for one edition of the paper in a town the size of New Bern at the time. While some deadly fever may have

---

[g] SOHP, taped interview K-233, by Angela M. Hornsby, 1999.
[h] *Newbern Sentinel*, April 18, 1832, pg. 3.

been circulating, the number of obituaries that day may also be a mere co-incidence.

In the settlement of the father's estate, it's revealed that John S. White-head had tried to give the land of the real Cherry Point to his son. For an unknown reason, the son demurred. In his will, the father mentioned

NOTICE.

WILL BE SOLD, on Saturday the 28th instant, at the Store of the late Cherry Whitehead, in Newbern, all the GROCERIES, HOUSEHOLD AND KITCHEN FURNITURE, a CENTRE-BOARD Schooner, and various other articles belonging to the estate of said deceased. A credit of six months will be given, and the terms made known at the sale, which will commence at 11 o'clock A. M.

JOSEPH PHYSIOC, *Special Adm'r.*

April 17, 1832.

Joseph Physioc administered Cherry Whitehead's estate. He owned a plantation across Cahoogue Creek just south of the Whitehead's homestead, making him the equivalent of a modern next-door neighbor. *New Bern Sentinel*, April 16, 1832.

Cherry's disinterest in the "river land," so he substituted a hefty amount of cash instead. Sadly, Jeremiah Cherry Whitehead wasn't around to receive his inheritance. [i]

Almost every geographical feature around was named for people. Slocum Creek for settler John Slocum. Hancock Creek for settler William Hancock. Adams Creek for settlers Adam Ferguson, Senior and Junior. Wilkinson Point for the Wilkinsons. Johnson Point for the Johnsons. Clubfoot Creek for ... okay. Bad example. But you get the idea.

It was perfectly logical that the Whitehead family would have dedicated their big river bluff to the memory of their golden child, Cherry, who had lived well and died tragically young.

After much research and years of pondering the matter, we grew comfortable with the idea – and finally convinced – that Cherry Point was named for Cherry Whitehead.

---

[i] Craven County Estate Index, Vol. C, 1810-1839, image 379.

Until …

We recently found a North Carolina land grant to Thomas Austin dating from 1770 for land at Cherry Point. It's the smallest land grant we've seen at only 15 acres. It adds the minor parcel "Beginning at a Sweet gum [tree]" to the land Austin already owns at Cherry Point.[j]

Jeremiah Cherry Whitehead died in 1832. His obituaries stated that he was 30 years old; making his presumed birthdate 1802. Therefore, since we have a reference to Cherry Point from 1770 that pre-dates him by 32 years, it could not have been named in his honor, either at his birth or death.

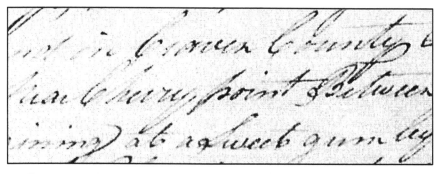

From a 1770 Craven County land grant to Thomas Austin at Cherry Point.

We've found no other record of anyone in the family having been called by the name. We've probed the genealogical line. There's no "Cherry, Sr." lurking about. So, we have no explanation for the lingering memory that this place on the Neuse River was named after a man who had once lived there.

Rampant Speculation

As John Lennon said in *Glass Onion*, "Well, here's another clue for you all."

And let's admit upfront that this one falls into the category of rampant speculation. The line of inquiry springs from the question: *If Cherry Point wasn't named for cherry trees or Jeremiah Cherry Whitehead, who or what could it have possibly been named for?*

If we consider how people were named in the seventeenth, eighteenth, and nineteenth centuries, it must be noticed that newborns often received the entire first and last name of some admired individual. We've mentioned before a man from the Croatan-Riverdale area, Vine Allen Tolson, who was named for a famous colonial-era man named Vine Allen. Everyone around

---

[j] N.C. Land Grant, entered July 3, 1770, entry no. 70, file #3851; Issued October 27, 1784, Book 55, page 292, Grant #108. MARS 12.14.50.3865.

southern Craven County whose name began with "George W." was named for George Washington. Benjamin F. Borden was named for Ben Franklin. A. J. Chesnutt was named after Andrew Jackson. A. H. Chesnutt was named for Alexander Hamilton. We even have Richard Dobbs Spaight *Holland.*

So, we wondered if Jeremiah Cherry Whitehead was named for someone named *Jeremiah Cherry.* If there was a Jeremiah Cherry, we'd have a family name that might be the source of the name for Cherry Point, just like John Slocum for Slocum's Creek or William Hancock for Hancock's Creek.

And by the miracle of the Craven County Register of Deeds office "Old Index Books," we not only found a man named Jeremiah Cherry but also that he owned land on the south shore of the Neuse River!

On October 6, 1821, Jeremiah Cherry and his wife, Mary Cherry, (yes, *Mary Cherry*) sold a tract "situated on the South side of the Neuse River between Adams's and Coats's Creek" to a man named John S. Nelson. [k]

Jeremiah Cherry died in Washington, N.C. on August 19, 1845, at the age of 79, making his presumed birth year 1766. Sources on the internet site *Find a Grave* contradict each other regarding Jeremiah Cherry, but one of them says he was born in New Bern on April 1, 1766. [l]

That would make him old enough for Cherry Whitehead to be named in his honor. What didn't seem to fit, however, was that he was only four years old when Thomas Austin received his 1770 Cherry Point land grant.

But, guess what? Jeremiah Cherry's father was named ... Jeremiah Cherry.

You may remember from earlier in the book that we found the Holland family with three generations of fathers and sons named Philemon. Cherry family histories on the internet indicate that *Jeremiah* was just as popular with them. There are men named Jeremiah Cherry alive in eastern North Carolina back to the era of Craven County's lost land records. [m]

Here, our speculations grind to a halt.

Try as we might, we have been unable to find other Cherry land ownership deeds or grants on the south shore of the Neuse River. And besides proximity, we have not made a connection between the Whitehead family and the Cherry family.

The matter remains for the present in the *History Mystery* file.

Further research, and some luck, will be required to determine the origin of the name *Cherry Point.* We may never know.

---

[k] Craven County Deed Book 43, pg. 122.

[l] *Wilmington (NC) Chronicle,* September 2, 1845, pg. 2.

[m] For example, *The Cherry Families of Early Norfolk County, Virginia and Northeast North Carolina,* John E. Young.

What we can say with utter certainty, however, is that the 2021 Wikipedia entry below for "MCAS Cherry Point," and many other similar claims elsewhere, are not supported by available evidence.

"On May 20, 1942, the facility was commissioned Cunningham Field, named in honor of the Marine Corps' first aviator, Lieutenant Colonel Alfred A. Cunningham. *The completed facility was later renamed Marine Corps Air Station Cherry Point, after a local post office situated among cherry trees.*"

The name Cherry Point was in use for a minimum of 120 years before the post office handled its first piece of mail.

❖ ❖ ❖ ❖

Lists of Names in Southern Craven County

1) Historic signatures

2) Old southern Craven County Post Offices

3) Other place names for the 'Havelock' area

4) Creeks, branches, "guts," features, and places

5) Owners from the Cherry Point Property Map of 1941.

6) Havelock landowners from Henry A. Marshall's *J.A. Bryan Land Map of 1899.*

7) Capt. John S. Smith District, Tax List 1815.

❖ ❖ ❖ ❖

A Collection of Signatures

Signatures of a few of the book's characters taken from correspondence, deeds, and other historic documents. On the previous page, signatures of William Handcock, John Slocumb, Richard Dobbs Spaight, William Holland, William H. Marshall as Justice of the Peace, James H. Hunter, and David O. Dickinson. Above, Joseph Physioc as Justice of the Peace, A.J. Chesnut, Edward Bull, Carrie E. Waugh, Alicia S. Blood, and Joseph Williams.

Old Southern Craven County Post Offices

POST OFFICE	1st POSTMASTER	DATES
Cravenville *	William Holland	1836-1842
Spaightsville *	Andrew J. Chesnutt	1860-1866
Adams Creek	Henry T. Foscue	1860-1866
Woodbridge *	Edward Bull	1873-1881
Croatan	James H. Tillian	1874-1927
Riverdale	Charles E. Mallett	1877-1920
Coohooca	Enoch F. Huskins	1880
Cohoogue	Enoch F. Huskins	1880-1885
Havelock *	William Leauhouts	1881-1945
Thurman	William H. Thomas	1885-1909
Harlowe	Joseph P. Godett, Jr.	1890
Cherry Point	David W. Morton, Jr.	1890-1932
Bachelor	Isaac Taylor	1890-1945
Cohoogue #2	Enoch F. Huskins	1891-1914
North Harlowe	James R. Bell	1893-1954
Blades	Gabriel A. Connor	1903-1929
Melvin	James B. Robinson	1906-1920
Becton	Emily Becton	1922-1931

* at Slocum Creek

Other Place Names for the 'Havelock' Area

Neuse River – Petition by settlers in 1706 for a "Court at Neus River." Earliest spelling *Neus*, *Nues, Nuse,* and *Nuce.*
Slocumb's Creek – Early 1700 to 20th century. Also, Slocumbe, Slocomb, Slocom, Slocum, and so forth. Locals pronounced the final 's' into modern times.
Hancock's Creek – Early 1700 to 20th century. Also, Handcock's, Hancocks. Locals pronounced the final 's' into modern times.
Capt. Smith's District – c. 1815

Cravensville or Cravenville – Post office by the influential Holland family 1836-1843; place name appears on early maps and even some from the Civil War.

Ives District – as a voting area.

Goodings District – c. 1860, a voting and census area.

Reev's District – some folks around Slocum Creek sometimes end up in this census district, which is theoretically adjacent to Goodings District.

Spaightsville – Post office by A. J. Chestnut 1861; operation ended by War Between the States but officially de-listed in 1866.

Havelock Depot – Earliest printed newspaper reference using *Havelock*.

Havelock Station – Probably so-called since 1858; seen in the newspapers during War Between the States.

Havelock District – General reference to the area used in newspapers for decades after 1860.

Haverlock – The most common misspelling of the name. In searches, use this, too.

Woods District – as a voting area.

Janesville – Used briefly as the first American Missionary Association name for its freedmen settlement on Slocum Creek. Named for Rev. Edward Bull's wife. Rescinded because another AMA outpost was already named Janesville.

Woodbridge – Another short-lived post office during the 1870s, and name of the AMA settlement on Slocum Creek; the subsequent name for Janesville.

Lee's Farm – as voting area. Lee's Farm, owned by Dalton Lee, was the former Marshall Plantation and, generally, today's Greenfield Heights.

Havelock – Name, selected by Atlantic and North Carolina Railroad officials, honors world-renowned late-1850s British war hero, Henry Havelock.

Creeks, branches, 'guts', features, and places

Note: Cherry Point tract and cemetery numbers are from the *Cherry Point Ownership Map of 1941* available for viewing online at the Edward B. Ellis, Jr. Papers, Special Collections, Joyner Library, East Carolina University.

Adams Creek – The most easterly of the four major creeks on the Neuse River's south shore after Slocum, Hancock, and Clubfoot. Named for early settlers Adam Ferguson and Adam Ferguson, Jr. Its northern portion forms part of the boundary between the counties of Craven and Carteret. See also *Creeks*.

Adams Creek Canal – Part of the Intracoastal Waterway (ICW).

Alligator Gut – Short watercourse flowing from the west into Slocum Creek just north of a peninsula now called Ordnance Point and the Slocum Road bridge.

Anderson Creek is a major branch of Slocum Creek flowing into it from the west near its mouth. The headwaters of Anderson Creek form the southern boundary of the Carolina Pines residential subdivision.

Bachelor – A rural community in Township 5, SE Craven County, off Adams Creek Road and east of Clubfoot Creek. At the time the community was debating a name for itself, a prominent local farmer had three unmarried adult sons. Someone suggested that what the place had the most of was bachelors. So it was.

Back Creek – A large arm of Adams Creek that flows into it from the east; south of Adams Creek's mouth of the Neuse River. It forms part of the boundary between Craven and Carteret counties.

Barney Branch – A tributary of Cahoogue Creek flowing in from the east; south of Still Gut (2).

Beech (Beach) Haven – A populated place west of old Havelock along mile-long, tree-lined Beech Haven Farms Road, a soil-surface lane on the approximate path of what is now Slocum Road, ending at Long Point (Ordnance Point). Scattered farms, a sawmill, cotton gin, grist mill, and general store were located there in the 1920s.

Beaufort Road – The road from New Bern to Beaufort dates from colonial times, and likely overlaid an older Indian route to skirt the deep water of creeks. Called the Old Beaufort Road, the Old Road, or the New Bern Road, it's now US 70 from New Bern to Havelock and Highway 101 from Havelock to Beaufort. It followed the current route of Greenfield Heights Blvd. and Miller Blvd. in Havelock until US 70 was routed through town c. 1960.

Big Branch is the easterly fork at the end of Mitchell Creek. The other one is Snake Branch.

Black Swamp – Part of the headwaters of the southwest prong of Slocum Creek; in Croatan National Forest and private game land near a group of lakes southwest of the city. See *Lakes*.

Blades – A rural, populated place in Township Five, Craven County, north of Highway 101 and North Harlowe, east of Temple Point Road, and west of Clubfoot Creek. Bears the name of the Blades Lumber Company, which once operated in the area.

Blue Billies Creek – Also *Blue Bellies*. It's the first creek crossed when heading north on Adams Creek Road after leaving Highway 101. A branch of Clubfoot Creek, which it enters from the east.

Brices Creek – One extremity of this deep, long and winding tributary of the Trent River at New Bern – Great Branch – reaches the village of Croatan, just northwest of Havelock.

Bounder Neck Gut – A tributary flowing into Hancock Creek from the west. Location of James Hyman Plantation c. 1803.

Buck Creek – An obsolete name for Cahoogue Creek. *William Stewart survey of 1762 (Craven County Land Grants).*

<u>Cahoogue (Cahooque, Kahookee, Cowhukey) Creek</u> is one of the major branches of Hancock Creek east of Havelock and Cherry Point. Pronounced ca-HOOK-ey. The name *might* come from the colonial "Kehukee" Primitive Baptist Association, which tried to establish a church in the area, or could be a residual Native American name; called *Cowhoqua* in 1759 James Black patent and 1762 William Stewart survey.

<u>Camp Bryan</u> – Historic private hunting and fishing preserve among the Lakes (q.v.) SW of Havelock; established within 6,000 acres James A. Bryan purchased in 1902 from the State of North Carolina for $4,800; accessed off from Lake Road.

<u>Caps Branch</u> – A major drainage feature in east Havelock flowing westerly into the East Prong of Slocum Creek; west of E. Main St. (US 70) near Annunciation Catholic Church.

<u>Catfish Lake</u>—The outlier from the other four Croatan National Forest lakes. This one is accessible via, you guessed it, Catfish Lake Rd, off US 70 at Croatan, west of Havelock. Also, see *Lakes*.

<u>Cedar Creek</u> is a ridge-and-ravine system of several branches draining from the west into Slocum Creek between Staff Capehart housing and Ketner Heights.

<u>Central Highway 10</u> – NC's first paved (concrete) mountains-to-coast highway, completed in the 1920s as two lanes on nearly the same route as US 70 today. Through Havelock, followed current Church Rd. and Miller Blvd., thus, Trader's Store was on the main highway.

<u>Cherry Branch</u> – The next creek to the east of the true Cherry Point; flows due north into the Neuse River. Near Ferry Road. Today, a residential subdivision claims the name.

<u>Cherry Point</u> – Not where the base is. The true Cherry Point is downriver east of the air station where the N.C. ferry docks on the south side of the Neuse. The name was first used in the 1700s. The area west of Hancock Creek's mouth had the name *Cherry Point Landing* – The shortened form was first used by the nineteenth-century village there, and then a post office at that location, and later for the Marine base. Sometimes spelled on maps as one word – *Cherrypoint* – as late as 1929.

<u>Cherry Point Landing</u> – Since colonial times, the westerly bank of Hancock Creek, just inside its mouth, was a sheltered harbor for docking boats and to load and unload cargo. The village took on the shortened form of the name: Cherry Point.

<u>Cherry Point Road</u> – While a portion of old US 70 east of New Bern bears the name today, before 1940, it was the name of a dirt road from Highway 101 to the old village of Cherry Point on the west side of Hancock Creek at the Neuse River. It was about seven miles long, passing through the settlements of Tar Neck and Nelson Town on its way.

<u>Clubfoot Creek</u> – Huge, north-flowing, it connects to the Neuse a few miles east of Havelock down Hwy. 101. Early written deed references say *Clubfoots Creek*. Some early maps – 1738, 1779, 1794, 1837 – show it as "Cutfoot Creek," but this may be a repeated "typo." Major tributaries are Mitchell and Guldens. Harlowe Canal upstream was dug long ago to connect to Newport River. ICW made it obsolete.

Indians called the creek *Hutosquock*, according to a 1706 land grant to John Lawson. Once called Clumsford Creek.

Clumfords (or Clumsford) Creek – Another name for Clubfoot Creek in use particularly around the time of the War Between the States. Also seen as "*Clubford's*."

Coaches Creeks and Coats Creek (also Coates, Coaties) -- There are two theories; one is that both are obsolete names for Courts Creeks. See below. The second is that a creek called by both names on the Neuse River west of Clubfoot Creek on the Neuse River has been filled in by storms. Temple family members of the area say this is true. Old land grant descriptions also tend to support Theory 2. [George Burgess patents of 1746 | Abner Neal patent 1787.]

Coleman's Creek – An older name for Tucker Creek, a tributary of Slocum Creek; named for early settler Robert Coleman before 1720. A land grant to Coleman in that year refers to the creek already bearing his name. [Book 2 | page 6 | November 6, 1720.]

Cowhoqua Creek – Name for today's Cahoogue Creek in 1762 land survey, which also refers to it as "Buck Creek." *William Stewart, Craven County land grants.*

Cowhuck(e) Swamp – A reference to Cahoogue Creek area, mentioned in 1845 200-acre land grant to Evan Jones mentions: Cowhuk(e) Swamp that runs into Handcocks Creek." Craven County land grant book 10, page 101.

Core Creek – In extreme eastern Craven County (and western Carteret County), a portion of Adams Creek and the area around it. Another *Core Creek* west of New Bern confuses matters sometimes.

Courts Creek is a split ridge-and-ravine system between Great Neck Creek and Great Neck Point in the Adams Creek Road area, flowing northwesterly into the Neuse River. Possibly aka Coaches Creek and Coats Creek, q.v. But maybe not.

Craven Corner – An African American settlement in SE Craven County's Township 5, along Adams Creek Road, probably dating from the colonial era.

Croatan – A populated place north of Havelock. Once a substantial farming center.

Croatan National Forest – 160,000 acres of federally-managed pine forests, lakes, saltwater estuaries, wetlands, and raised swamps called *pocosin* surround Havelock. Headquartered at Riverdale on US 70 northwest of the city.

Creeks – Four big creeks near Havelock parallel each other, all flowing north, all emptying into the south shore of the Neuse River. Slocum, Hancock, Clubfoot, and Adams creeks would be called rivers anywhere else in the country, but they're creeks here because the Neuse is so wide. Adams Creek is part of the ICW.

Crooked Run flows southeast and connects with Otter Creek near its mouth before flowing into the Neuse River.

Crosby's Landing – A place on the west side of Cahoogue Creek mentioned as a landmark in an 1801 land grant to Abner Whitehead, and others.

"Crossroads" intersection – Where Miller Blvd., Fontana Blvd. (Highway 101), and Main Street (US 70) meet in Havelock.

Crystal Lake – Small, man-made harbor on the west side of Slocum Creek accessible within Ketner Heights.

Cullie Creek joins Jonaquin Creek and then flows westward into Adams Creek, south of Dumpling Creek.

Cutfoot Creek – This is what Clubfoot Creek is called on the earliest maps from the 1700s, but, due to the absence of "Cutfoot" in county land deeds, it may be an error that got picked up by one cartographer after another.

Dam Creek is a pristine ridge-and-ravine system lying between the residential developments of Carolina Pines and Stately Pines. Its watercourses flow north and, depending upon rainfall, sometimes intersects with the Neuse River across a sandy beach. Mill operation there during colonial times.

Daniels Branch – A terminus of Tucker Creek on the west side of US 70 just north of the Hickman Hill – Pine Grove area.

Deep Branch – A tributary of Hancock Creek entering from the west; south of Highway 101 and below Matthews Branch.

Delamar Creek – A small stream flowing northerly into Adams Creek (the ICW) on the north face of Great Neck.

Dogwood Branch – A small tributary of SW Prong of Slocum Creek flowing from the north, parallel to and southwest of the Old Beaufort Road (Greenfield Heights Blvd.).

Duck Creek flows into Slocum Creek from the east, and near the mouth of Tucker Creek on Slocum's opposite bank. It's in the middle of Cherry Point Tract 42.

Doll's Gut – A tributary flowing from the west into Hancock Creek in the old Little Witness community near Highway 101 and north of Shop Branch.

Dumpling Creek flows westward into Adams Creek, south of Sandy Huss Creek.

Dupuis Landing – A boat landing on the west bank of Hancock Creek immediately south of Jack's Gut. Named for an early settler family there.

East Branch / West Branch – The terminus of the Southwest Prong of Slocum Creek, a short, swampy Y-shaped ravine in game lands near Lake Road south of the city. They're the point where man-made canals used to connect to drain one or more of four nearby lakes for agricultural purposes. (See *Lakes*).

East Branch / East Creek – From colonial and early post-colonial times to the mid-1900s, these are names for the East Prong of Slocum Creek. We also found it on a 1946 state highway commission map.

East Prong of Slocum Creek forks from the main creek at Graham A. Barden Elementary School, passes near the Crossroads intersection of Fontana Blvd. (Hwy. 101) with Main Street (US 70) and continues its course southward, deep into the Croatan National Forest.

Ellis Lake – Discovered by and named for early settler Michael Ellis who received a land grant there in the 1700s. Renamed by politicians for prominent Kinston resident and Camp Bryan member-manager Ellis Simon in the late twentieth century. See *Lakes*.

Flybus Branch was a small tributary of Trent Branch draining from a swampy savannah in the center of what is now MCAS Cherry Point. Both Flybus Branch and the big savannah succumbed to Cherry Point engineering. Named for a family of colonial settlers.

Frazier Town – An African American residential and farming area off Adams Creek Road.

Fredericks Gut – Obsolete name for a small creek on the west side of Hancock Creek near Shop Branch at Little Witness.

Glover's Creek – Named for colonial settlers in the Flanner's Beach area, and in use as late as c. 1822, but today called Otter Creek.

Goat Island – A peninsula at the mouth of Hancock Creek has been, at times, as many as three islands; Craven County deed book 370, page 390. The largest of these, making up the major portion of the peninsula in 2021, was once a place where goats were raised.

Godfrey Creek – East of Great Neck Point, it flows northerly into the mouth of Adams Creek. Early settler Matthew Godfrey owned land there before 1735.

Goodwin (or Godwin) Creek flows from the west into Tucker Creek at its intersection with Sandy Run. The head of Godwin Creek is near Lewis Farm Road.

Great Branch – The tributary of Brices Creek nearest Havelock. See *Brices Creek*.

Great Island – A small islet immediately east of Clubfoot Creek's mouth, completely covered in marsh grass.

Great Lake – See *Lakes*.

Great Neck – The large promontory of land at the intersection of the Neuse River with Adams Creek (the ICW). Transected by Adams Creek Road.

Great Neck Creek – A stream in Great Neck, east of Long Creek, flowing north into the Neuse River.

Great Neck Point – The peak of Great Neck on the Neuse River.

Green Springs – Riverfront area just south of James City.

Grubby Neck Branch – It flows into Sykes Gut and then into Slocum Creek forming the northern boundary of Cherry Point Tract 286. Properly called Hunter's Branch.

Guldens Creek flows west into Clubfoot Creek near its mouth.

Gum Branch – A multi-pronged, watercourse flowing northerly into the Neuse River just west of the Pine Cliffs Recreation Area at the true Cherry Point. About 1.2 miles long.

Gum Swamp – Large area of pocosin NE of Long Lake in the Croatan National Forest.

Gut – When referring to bowels or entrails, *gut* derives from a German word meaning *channel*. Ocean-going mariners call an inlet a gut, but the word also denotes a small stream or creek.

Hancock Creek – One of the major tributaries flowing from the south into the Neuse River and forming the eastern boundary of MCAS Cherry Point. Cahoogue Creek is one of its major branches. Named for early settler William Han(d)cock who had a plantation there as early as 1707. Handcock and John Slocumb were cousins.

Harlowe – A populated place on Highway 101 nine miles east of Havelock, near Adams Creek Road and the Carteret County line. Named for settler John Harlow, 1712 (Craven County Book 2, page 695). Also, see *North Harlowe.*

Harlowe Canal at the head of Clubfoot Creek was built with slave labor, in the late 1700s to mid-1800s. Connected the Newport and Neuse rivers as a shortcut from New Bern to Beaufort.

Havelock Station – Established at Slocum Creek as a wood and water supply point and freight/passenger stop in 1858 upon completion of Atlantic and North Carolina Railroad from Goldsboro to Morehead City. Named for British military hero, Major General Sir Henry Havelock, famous for his exploits in India during the Sepoy uprising of 1857.

Havelock, N.C. – Area was settled in the early 1700s. Named in 1858 for British General Sir Henry Havelock. Incorporated as a municipality on August 24, 1959. Home of MCAS Cherry Point.

Hunters Branch -- Flows into Sykes Gut and then into Slocum Creek forming the northern boundary of Cherry Point Tract 286. Likely named for early settler James H. Hunter who owned a plantation abutting it. Named Grubby Neck Branch on some maps. Identified as Hunters Branch on U. S. quadrangle series. Some old maps show it as a tributary of Mill Creek, just north of Moccasin Branch and parallel to Grubby Neck.

Hunters Creek – A tributary of the White Oak River system. Its headwaters reach up into the lakes area southwest of Havelock.

Hyman's Landing – a boat landing on the west bank of Hancock Creek about 1,000 yards north of Dupuis Landing. Named for the 19th-century plantation family there.

ICW – Adams Creek, east of Havelock toward Beaufort on Hwy. 101, is part of the grand Intracoastal Waterway. "The Ditch" is 3,000 miles long and runs from Boston to Brownsville, Texas. The Adams Creek section of the ICW connects the Neuse River with the Newport River.

Indian Landing – A narrow strip of land paralleling the north side of Highway 101 (Fontana Blvd) and intersecting the east prong of Slocum Creek on its east side is identified as "the Indian Landing" in old land documents and as the "Indian Landing Tract" on the H. A. Marshall map of 1899.

Isaac Creek enters Adams Creek from the east immediately south of Back Creek.

Jack's Branch or Gut – A tributary flowing from the northwest into Hancock Creek in the defunct village of Hancock Creek north of Squirrel Gut. Below Cherry Point Tract 540 and near Cherry Point cemetery 7.

Joe's Branch – A major drainage feature in east Havelock flowing north into the East Prong of Slocum Creek west of East Main Street (US 70). It's beaver country.

Jonaquin Creek joins Cullie Creek and then flows westward into Adams Creek, south of Dumpling Creek.

Jerry Bay is on the east bank of Adams Creek just south of Isaac Creek.

Jumping Run – Obsolete name from colonial times for a branch in the headwaters of Clubfoot Creek.

Kahookee Creek – See Cahoogue.

Kearney Creek – A ridge-and-ravine system south of Kellum Creek draining into Adams Creek, the ICW.

Kellum Creek – A small Great Neck stream flowing southeasterly into Adams Creek (the ICW).

King Creek – Flows due north into the Neuse River just east of Cherry Branch.

Lakes – Four substantial, yet seldom seen lakes lie deep in the forest southwest of Havelock off the aptly named Lake Road. Ellis Lake, Little Lake, Long Lake, and Great Lake are virtually surrounded by the national forest and private game lands. Home of famous hunting mecca Camp Bryan, among others. (Also see *Catfish Lake*). And try Google Maps.

Lake Ellis Simon – A re-naming for Lake Ellis, dating from the late twentieth century. Ellis Simon of Kinston was the general manager of Camp Bryan from 1933-1988.

Little John (or Littlejohn) Creek flows northeast into Hancock Creek south of Cahoogue Creek and opposite Jack's Branch on the other shore.

Little Lake – See *Lakes*.

Little Witness – African American community north of Highway 101 at its intersection with Hancock Creek. It had a church, school, post office, cemeteries, named streets. Also known as Toon Neck and as Melvin, N.C. (q.v.). Ceased to exist in 1941.

Little Witness "street" names – Of those known, Melvin Road, Little Witness Road, Tar Neck Road, and Hancock Road.

Long Creek – A Y-shaped ridge-and-ravine system near Bachelor and east of Clubfoot Creek flowing north into the Neuse River. A bridge on Adams Creek Road crosses it.

Long Lake – See *Lakes*.

Long Point – Traditional name of a peninsula in Slocum Creek near today's Slocum Road bridge that's been known as *Ordnance Point* since the advent of MCAS Cherry Point in the 1940s.

Lost Lake – An area of marshy savannah north of Great Lake and west of Long Lake. See *Lakes*.

Lucknow – Original name of the rail stop at Newport, derived from the place-name of Sir Henry Havelock's greatest military victory in 1857. Newport was also known as *Shepardsville* in various spellings.

Luke Rowe's (Rose) Gut – A small branch on the east side of Slocum Creek south of Ordnance Point, between Cherry Point Tracts 62 and 362.

Master's Mill – See *Mill Pond* below.

Matthews Branch flows into Hancock Creek from the west; south of Highway 101 and north of Deep Branch.

Matthews Point – A promontory of land at the junction of Clubfoot Creek and Mitchell Creek. Named for early settlers with a descendant still there.

MCAS Cherry Point – Marine Corps air station built primarily between Slocum Creek and Hancock Creek beginning in 1941. Dubbed Cunningham Field during construction, after first Marine Corp aviator Alfred A. Cunningham. It's included within the corporate limits of the City of Havelock.

Melvin—Name of the post office opened at Little Witness (Toon Neck) in 1906.

Mill Creek (Mill Branch) flows into Sykes Gut and then into Slocum Creek between Cherry Point tracts 199 and 286.

Mill Pond – The dam's still on the SW Prong of Slocum Creek. Was the site of Spaight grain and sawmill beginning in the late 1700s. Owned by Richard Dobbs Spaight, a signer of the U.S. Constitution, then by Dr. Samuel Masters, and later by James A. Bryan. Near US 70. Walk to it from the Havelock Tourist and Event Center.

Mill Pond Run – Crosses Highway 101 just east of Mill Pond Swamp.

Mill Pond Swamp – Wet area south of Highway 101, crosses highway east of Temple Point Road intersection.

Moccasin Branch is at the end of Mill Creek on the east side of Slocum Creek.

Mococks Creek – A source tributary at the head of Hancock Creek flowing east to west into it near the Carteret County line. Early spellings include *Mockcock* and "Indian"-sounding *Mocococ* and *Mococahawk*.

Mortons Mill Pond – Long and convoluted southwest branch of Clubfoot Creek, flows from west to east. Crosses Highway 101 just east of Adams Creek Road; crosses Blades Road and through North Harlowe.

Money Island – Small wooded islet in Slocum Creek near the location of original Cherry Point staff club, reputed to be the burial place of pirate treasure. It once changed hands in a poker game. Nearly washed away by 2018.

Mitchell Creek enters Clubfoot Creek from the west near its mouth. A good sailing marina is there. Mitchell has a tributary charmingly named Snake Branch. Wanna go?

Miry Branch flows into Sandy Run and then into Tucker Creek from the south.

Nelson Town – A settlement of the farms between Slocum and Hancock creeks begun by Smith Nelson in 1880 and expanded by his son Sam B. Nelson in the early 1900s. Divided among descendants and related families, it remained a populated place until 1941.

Neuse River – Runs some 275 miles from the Piedmont of North Carolina to the Pamlico Sound. About three miles wide as it passes Havelock and Cherry Point. All major local waterways flow into it.

Nuesiok Creek – A ridge and ravine system emptying into the Neuse River east of Hancock Creek and west of the true Cherry Point. Also, the name for the stretch of river shore there.

Newport – A town in western Carteret County seven miles from Havelock on US 70. Historian and author David Cecelski has determined that it was named by early settlers for their former hometown of Newport, Rhode Island. Also called Shepardsville during the 1800s. Location of the "Lucknow" rail stop circa 1858.

North Harlowe – A populated place east of Havelock on Highway 101 and north-west of Harlowe. At the Blades Road intersection.

Ordnance Point – The name since c. 1941 of the long, narrow peninsula in Slocum Creek, immediately north of the Slocum Road bridge, that had previously been known since the 1700s as *Long Point*.

Otter Creek – Ridge-and-ravine system flowing north into Neuse River at Croatan and west of Flanner Beach Road. Known earlier as Glover's Creek.

Paupers Island – Small area of high ground at the intersection of Goodwin's (God-win's) Creek with Tucker Creek.

Pine Grove – A farming and rural residential area immediately northwest of Have-lock in today's Tucker Creek – Hickman Hill area. Had a rail stop, loop road, and polling place in the 1800s to early 1900s.

Poplar Spring Branch – Nineteenth-century name for one of the two branches at the head of Little John Creek; probably the southerly one.

Reeds Gut – A tributary flowing from the west into Hancock Creek near its mouth just south of Cherry Point Tract 440.

Riverdale – A populated place by the railroad and county road north of Croatan, south of Thurman. A busy settlement as lumber transshipment center during clear-cutting of the forest; a post office operated 1877-1920.

Sandy Branch flows into Trent Branch from the east and then into the East Prong of Slocum Creek north of Fontana Blvd (Highway 101) and School House Branch. Roosevelt Blvd crosses it inside the Main Gate of MCAS Cherry Point. Some mod-ern maps have dropped the name Trent and label the system Sandy Branch.

Sandy Huss Creek flows westward into Adams Creek near its mouth. Just south of Winthrop Point and the Neuse River.

Sandy Point – The peninsula that nearly caps the mouth of Slocum Creek; so-called c. 1825. An area directly across the Neuse from New Bern is called the same.

Sandy Run is a tributary of Tucker Creek forming the eastern boundary of the Tucker Creek residential subdivision. Miry Branch is one of its arteries.

Sandy Run Branch – An obsolete nineteenth-century name for the Sandy Branch-Trent Branch system flowing into the East Prong of Slocum Creek.

Sassafras Branch – A three-pronged, ridge-and-ravine system flowing north into the Neuse River between Kings Creek and Temples Point.

School House Branch flows into the East Prong of Slocum Creek from the east near Fontana Blvd. (Highway 101) and is crossed by Roosevelt Blvd. immediately inside the Main Gate of MCAS Cherry Point. Site of 1800s county school. *Susan's Branch* was another name for it.

Shingle Landing – A place on Slocum Creek near Wolfpit Branch, mentioned in 1928 deed in Craven County Book 284, Page 190, 1928.

Shipyard Gut flows into Slocum Creek from the east just south of the creek's mouth. Shipyard Gut forms the southern boundary of Cherry Point Tract 461.

Shepardsville – Spelled in several variations, especially with double Ps, this was a name for Newport around the time of the Civil War.

Shop Branch – A tributary of Hancock Creek near where Highway 101 crosses the creek; on the creek's west side in the defunct community of Little Witness. Known in earlier times as *Shop Neck Branch.*

Shop Neck Branch was the name of Shop Branch before the twentieth century.

Siddie Fields – An area east of the true Cherry Point and near the mouth of King Creek. The former burial ground for the Whitehead plantation was there. Now controlled by USFS. Also found spelled "City Fields."

Slocum Creek – One of the major tributaries flowing from the south into the Neuse River and on the western boundary of MCAS Cherry Point. Slocum Creek splits into two prongs at Graham A. Barden Elementary School; the East Prong flowing under Fontana Blvd. (Highway 101), and the Southwest Prong flowing under US 70. Named for early-1700s settler John Slocum, its spelling has been tortured over the years. Major tributaries of Slocum Creek are Anderson Creek near its mouth and Tucker Creek farther upstream.

Squirrel Gut – A tributary flowing from the west into Hancock Creek in the old Little Witness area near Highway 101 and north of Doll's Gut.

Squirrel Point – A small promontory into Hancock Creek at the mouth of Squirrel Gut.

Snake Branch is the westerly fork at the end of Mitchell Creek. The other one is Big Branch.

South River is the next north-flowing tributary of the Neuse River east of Adams Creeks. It's in Carteret County.

Southwest Prong of Slocum Creek forks from the main creek at Graham A. Barden School. Crosses US 70 at bridges near Church Road, flows past Havelock Tourist and Events Center, under RR trestles, beneath a small bridge on Greenfield Heights Blvd. and continues into Croatan National Forest. SW Prong near RR was the area's commercial hub in the 1800s and early 1900s.

Spaight's Mill / Speight's Mill – see *Mill Pond* above.

Spe Branch – A northern fork near the end of Cahoogue Creek.

Still Gut – A tributary flowing from the south into Hancock Creek near its mouth between Cherry Point Cemetery 8 and Cherry Point Tract 291.

Still Gut (2) – Hey, there were *a lot* of stills! This one is a tributary of Cahoogue Creek flowing in from the east, north of Barney Branch on the Harlowe side of Hancock Creek.

Still Point – A promontory of land bounded on the east by Hancock Creek and on the west by Still Gut, just south of Cherry Point Landing. Turpentine distillery site before Civil War.

Susan's Branch is an obsolete name for Schoolhouse Branch.

Sykes Gut is a small bay on the east side of Slocum Creek, a little more than halfway to its mouth from Highway 101 and US 70 in Havelock. Sykes Gut splits into two branches which flow into it from the east: Hunters Creek and Mill Creek with Mill Creek being the more southerly. Likely named for settler Jacob Sykes (Sikes), here before 1775.

Tannyhills Creek is an obsolete name from colonial times for a tributary of Clubfoot Creek. See 1757 land grant to Abner Neale.

Tar Neck – A settlement of African American farmers in the southwest quadrant of what is now MCAS Cherry Point. Occupied by about two dozen families when condemned by the federal government for base construction in 1941.

Temples Point – The promontory of land on the west side of Clubfoot Creek at its junction with the Neuse River. Named for a family of early settlers who are still in residence.

Thurman – A populated place by the railroad and county road north of Riverdale, south of the Trent River near James City.

Tigersville – A steamer ferry stop on Adams Creek c. 1886.

Toon Neck – Another name for Little Witness, or a part thereof.

Trent Branch flows into the East Prong of Slocum Creek, from the east near Fontana Blvd. (Highway 101), north of School House Branch. It's crossed by Roosevelt Blvd. inside the main gate. One of its arteries is Sandy Branch, but with the twenti-eth-century re-engineering of the Trent-Sandy-Flybus branches by the military, some modern maps label the entire system as Sandy Branch.

Tucker Creek – A major tributary of Slocum Creek, which it enters from the west. The head of Tucker Creek crosses US 70 to the west of Slocum Road in Havelock. Sandy Run is one of its branches. First called Coleman's Creek, it was Tucker's Creek as early as 1838. Possibly named for Benjamin F. Tucker.

Turkey Gut – A small branch on the east side of Slocum Creek south of Luke Rowe's Gut.

Turkey Neck – A promontory on Cahoogue Creek near Hancock Creek. Name from colonial land grant of William Stewart 1762.

Turkey Point – A place on the east side of Slocum Creek mentioned as being part of Craven County land grant No. 218 to Charles Thompson dated January 22, 1773; described as being adjacent to the property of Edward Murphy and James Wynn (Win).

Turnagain Bay lies east of South River on the south shore of the Neuse River near its mouth. It's in Carteret County.

West Branch – See East Branch.

Wildwood – A name for the James City-Evans Mill section just south of the Trent River. (Also the name of a former A&NC rail stop east of Newport.)

Winthrop Point – Prominence at the confluence of the Neuse River with the east side of Adams Creek. Site of large Roper Lumber operation, Winthrop Mills, early 20th century.

Wolfpit Branch – Beginning in the swamp west of Greenfield Heights Blvd., it par-allels and crosses under railroad tracks behind the Wolf Creek residential subdivi-sion, flowing south into the southwest prong of Slocum Creek near the Tourist and Events Center.

Cherry Point Property Owners Map of 1941

Note: These owners gave up their land to make way for MCAS Cherry Point. *The Cherry Point Ownership Map of 1941* is available for viewing online at the Edward B. Ellis, Jr Papers, Special Collections, East Carolina University, or through the Havelock History page on the website edwardellis.com. Parcel numbers and acreage for each owner are listed on the map. The number in parentheses indicates multiple parcels per owner. The total acreage of this list: 8,046.8

Abernathy, Willis, and Williamson
Anderson, Mary
Ashford, Sudie B., Mrs.
Barham, J. L., Mrs.
Berry, Garffield
Berry, Ollie Moore
Berry, Sam
Berry, Steve
Berry, Will
Boyd, Charles & Florence (Claimants)
Bradshaw, M. T.
Bryan, Charles S., Col.
Bryant, Easter
Chance, Elizabeth
Craven County (2)
Craven County Board of Education
Cully, George W. (3)
Dove, Mandy, et al
Durham Police Dept.
Fenner, Lila
Fisher, Lucy
Fitzgerald, Henry
Fuller, G. R.
Garrett, R. M. (Trustee)
Goldsboro, Robert
Green, E. M. & Williamson, R. (Estate)
Harrison, J. M.
Hill [Stevenson], Emma
Hill, H. H. (Estate)
Hill, Joshua
Hill, W. H. (Estate)
Holland, John (Estate)

Johnson, Ernest (Estate)
Johnson, Matthew
Ketner, C.P.
King, T.F.
Kinston Police Dept.
Little Witness Church
Little Witness Church
    (Wynn Cemetery)
MacRae, John
MacRae, Turner
McGowan, George T.
Meadow, Sarah
Nelson, Dinah
Nelson, Ida R., Mrs.
Nelson, Jake (3)
Nelson, John
Nelson, Julia
Nelson, Nellie (2)
Nelson, Norman
Nelson, Walter
North Carolina Pulp Co.
Pate, George (Estate)
Prince, W. A.
Rawls, J.V. Estates,
    J.W. Burton,
    or Mrs. J.V. Rawls
Richards, Henry
Richards, Jim (Estate)
Richardson, R.A. (Estate)
Robinson, Melvina
Russell, George A.
    (Estate) (2)

Scott, Annie Tull, Mrs.
Simmons, F.F. & A.E.(2)
(Stevenson, see Emma Hill)
Strickland, Ogsbury & Stokes
Sykes, Mose(s)
Taylor, Carl (Timber lease from Sarah
 Meadows)
Toon, Michael (Estate)
United States (4)
West, Elizabeth

Williams, R.S. & W. W.
Williamson, R. & Green,
 E.M. (Estate)
Willoughby, Lillian
Willoughby, Lou
Wilson, J. E.
Wynn Cemetery (Little
 Witness Church)
Wynne, Walter J., Sr.

NOTE: During this period, the American Tobacco Company of Durham, N.C. conveyed its recreational property, "Lucky Lodge," on Slocum Creek to the federal government. However, the American Tobacco Company was not a party to the condemnation lawsuit, nor was it, or the Lucky Lodge tract, identified by name on the Cherry Point Property Owners Map of 1941.

Landowners from a portion of Henry A. Marshall's "James A. Bryan Map of 1899"

Note: In 1899 James Augustus Bryan, a Craven County man of wealth, accomplishments, and prestige bordering on nobility, decided to offer for sale nearly 58,000 acres of land he'd inherited and purchased throughout his lifetime. Much of it was farmland in and around today's Havelock, N.C. Bryan chose Havelock native and second-generation surveyor Henry A. Marshall to make the map and the following list of landowners is drawn from the Marshall rendering. The map can be examined in the Kellenberger Room of the New Bern-Craven County Public Library, or at the N.C. State Archives in Raleigh. Not all of the parcels' measurements were shown, but some representative acreages are given here to illustrate typical land holdings in that era.
"?" equals "difficult to read." Initials expanded to names within parentheses where known.

NAME / ACRES

Acreman, [Frederick] 600

Allison, David

Always

Always, H(enry)

Bailey, A.

Barron, D(avid) +/-2,000

Biggleston, Jos.

Bell

Bishop (& Physioc) w/ mill site 400

Blackledge (& Blount) 1,000

Blount & Blackledge 1,000

Blount & Leech

Borden, W(illiam)

Bratcher, Roger

Bratcher, T(homas)

Brice 200

Bruce 250

Burton 500

Canady

Chesnutt +/-500

Davis, J.

Davis, T.

Dawes (w/ Spaight & Singleton) 1,280

Dole (or *Bole?*)

Dry, William 1,280

Durton 500

Ellis, M(ichael) 640

Ellis, Richard (March 11, 1775)

Franklin

Foster, W. 150

Green, F. 200

Green, T. 200

Guard, Lydia 300

Haywood (& Spaight) 12,000+

Howard

Howe, Spaight & Davis 640

James, D.

Jones, A. L.

Jones, H.

Jones, H. A.

Jones, R.

Leech, Joseph (July 17, 1795)

Leech, Joseph (March 14, 1775)

Leech (w/ Blount)

Lewis, W. F.

Lovick, T.

Mallin's patent

Martin, Josiah

Marshall, H(enry) A.

McClure, Dr.

Perkins

Physioc (& Bishop) w/ mill site

Pollock, George +/-10,000

Rowe

Rutledge 200

Shaw, Robert 640

Sikes (Sykes), Henry (w/ church site)

Singleton (w/ Spaight & Dawes) 1,280

Singleton, S.

Smith, Basil (or Bazell)

Smith, B(asil) 445

Spaight & Haywood 12,000+

Spaight, R(ichard) D(obbs), numerous

Spaight, Singleton & Dawes

Speight, J. F.

Speight, Mrs. J. W.

Taylor

Tooley

Ward, D. L. ("D. L. Ward's entry")

Wicliff (Wycliff) 250

Other names on the map

Atlantic & NC Railroad
Brown, H. A., Esq.
Bryan, J(ames) A(ugustus)
Ellis (Lake)
Guion, H. T., Col.
Hancock (Creek)
Havelock

Hunter('s Creek)
Marshall, William H(enry)
Marshall, Henry A.
Neuse (River)
Slocumb (Creek)
Tucker (Creek)
Stanly

Other features on the map

"Indian Landing Tract" (Slocum
  Creek along Beaufort Rd.)
An abandoned Civil War cannon
  (just north of B&P mill tract)
A church (on Sikes parcel)

A cemetery (near Marshall tract)
Mill site (Bishop & Physioc)
Mill site (Spaight)

Capt. John S. Smith District, 1815

The names on the following list equate to a virtual "census" of the property owners in the early 1800s of southern Craven County and the modern Havelock vicinity. It's some of the earliest information of its type.

Captain Smith's District is roughly equivalent to today's Craven County Townships Five and Six, approximating the area from Croatan and Riverdale to Harlowe. We made the same comment about "Gooding's District" from the 1860 U. S. Census for Craven County, and the thirtieth name on the list is Stephen Gooding.

These are not the earliest settlers of the southern half of Craven, but some of them are the second or third generation of original families from the early 1700s; Evan Jones, and James and Thomas Lovick, for example.

The locations of property owned by many of the people on the list are known.

The Allways (or Always) families lived in the area around and between what is now Cahoogue Creek Road and Ferry Road along the Old Beaufort Road (Highway 101).

Benjamin Borden was east of Hancock Creek but also appears to have owned land on what is today MCAS Cherry Point.

The Chesnutts were in central "Havelock," though it wouldn't be called that until 1858.

Michael Ellis (no relation to the author) was southwest of Havelock on the lake that bears his family's name.

Fenno evolved into Fenner. Gaudett is now spelled Godette.

There is a *Hickman* Hill and a street in Havelock names *Ives*.

The Hollands were on Slocum Creek and its tributary, Tucker Creek.

Lot Holton was on Cherry Point.

The air base's golf course is located where the Evan Jones family once lived and farmed.

The Lovicks owned Magnolia Plantation, of which the land of today's Carolina Pines was a small part.

Isaac Perkins owned land on today's Cherry Point.

The Physiocs owned tracts on the east and west banks of Hancock Creek.

The Rowes' land would one day be Woodbridge.

The others were close by as well.

The list below is courtesy of the Kellenberger Room of the New Bern-Craven County Library.

1815 Craven County
Tax lists in Capt. John S. Smith District

Names	Free	Slaves	Acres	Value $
Allways, John	1	1	537	537
Allway, Meshack	1	2	781	1278
Allway, Boneta			125	350
Austin, Thomas		6	665	1765
Bailey, Jonathan	1	4	755	2000
Brittain, Joseph	1	4	250	150
Borden, Benjamin	1	7	1670	6000
Bratcher, Roger	1		233	233
Baker, William	1	1	50	50
Black, Henry	1	1		
Collins, Jesse	1	2	350	650
Carino, Sarah			200	200
Carter, George	1			
Chesnutt, Jonathan	1			
Chesnutt, John	1		120	70
Clash, Joseph	1			
Daniels, James	1			
Davis, James	1		420	2500

Ellis, Michael			640	640
Flybus, Archibald	1	1	175	250
Freeze, John	1	1	300	500
Foscue, John	1			
Foscue, Arthur	1			
Fenno, John			300	300
Fenno, Gambo	1			
Franklin, Robert	1	5	1015	3000
Foy, Frederick	1	22	5572	13000
Gaudet, Peter	1		100	100
Gaudet, Peter Snr.			120	120
Gooding, Stephen	1	3	500	500
Gaudett, George	1		300	150
Gaudett, James	1		200	200
Gaudett, John	1			
Gaudett, George	1			
Gibson, Ferebee	1	3	320	700
Gibson, Archey	1	1	100	100
Holland, Philemon	1	4	300	150
Holland, William		8	1000	4000
Do. for Ruth Smith		6	1200	1500
Hickman, Sally			160	160
Hickman, Shadrack				
Hatch, Durant, Esq.		28	1800	10000
Holton, Lot	1	3	370	1200
Hickman, Richard	1		300	500
Ives, Thomas P.		6		
Jones, Hardy	1	6	1260	1260
Ives, John M.	1	1	160	60
Jones, Evan		7	150	700
Jones, Gideon	1	9	1200	2400
Ives, John P.		3	466	466
Johnson, John			230	460
Kinsey, William	1	1		
Lovick, James	1	6	1000	2000
Lovick, Thomas		2		
Lewis, Joshua	1			
Moor, Jacob	1			
Marchment, John	1	1	366	400

Potter, Samuel	1	5	780	780
Perkins, Isaac			250	175
Parsons, Nathan	1	3	988	3952
Physioc, William	1		118	152
Rowe, Thomas	1	3	150	150
Rowe, Amos	1	1	200	275
Rowe, Benjamin		5	466	466
Stevens, Moses	1		170	75
Ditto for Elizabeth Stevens			220	55
Smith, Peggy			100	100
Smith, Seth	1		50	100
Smith, Archibald	1			
Smith, John	1	7	970	3000
Tolson, George	1		300	300
Tolson, John		2	310	310
Do. Heirs of Bynum Lewis			130	130
Do. Heirs of William Hamilton			50	50
Tolson, Winny			50	50
Thomson, Thomas	1	2	330	460
Winn, Stephen	1	3	1300	1300
Williams, William			175	300
Whitehead, John for Geo. Whitehead			150	150
Williams, John	1		50	50
Wood, Peter			40	150
Wilson, Ephraim			175	175
Williams, John	1		50	50
Whitehead, Abner	1		328	400
Whitford, Richard			175	225
Totals	56	158		

Historic Burials at MCAS Cherry Point

MCAS Cherry Point ARC Study, 1985

From 14 to 19 cemeteries have been identified at various times aboard MCAS Cherry Point containing marked graves dating as early as 1813. The cemetery count has changed over time because some graves have been moved and others consolidated.

Perhaps some of the challenges of understanding the old burial grounds at Cherry Point can be illustrated by a list generated when the Eastern North Carolina Genealogical Society (ECGS) attempted its survey there in the winter of 1980:

CEMETERIES

Craven County, Township 6. The following cemeteries are located within the boundaries of Marine Corps Air Station, Cherry Point, Havelock, N.C.

1. Off Hwy 101 through locked Forestry Gate
2. Off Hwy 101 through locked Forestry Gate
3. *Beyond runway near Hancock Creek
4. *Beyond runway near Hancock Creek
5. Relocated to #16
6. Relocated to #16
7. Near the end of Runway 5
8. Near Radar Installation
9. Near Picnic Area, turn left off Roosevelt Blvd.
10. Behind Bldg. 1225, 150'
11. Near Boat Dock, Hancock Creek
12. *Near Skeet Range
13. Relocated to #17
14. Relocated to #16
15. Relocated to #16
16. Left off Hwy 101, through locked Forestry Gate
17. Left off Hwy 101, through first locked Forestry Gate
18. *Near Officer's Housing
19. Located in woods behind Carolina Pines through locked Forestry Gate

*Not Found

In its comprehensive Cultural Resources Survey, accomplished under contract with the federal government, Archaeological Research Consultants (ARC) of Chapel Hill listed, in one of its report's sections, 15 graveyards found "on base" in 1985, similar to the ECGS findings five years before. Federal employees have continued the work in the years since. For example, old Cemetery 16, heavily overgrown – and with some graves missed in 1985 – has been re-designated "Site C." Additional burials have been identified and recorded there, both by work on the ground and by searching old local government records. In the course of research for this book, other burials – as mentioned in the text – have been identified or corrected as well. Nevertheless, the ARC cemetery survey information, containing valuable insights into the area's history, is reproduced here in its full form. The new data appears elsewhere in the book. It's transcribed from the original in its entirety for the benefit of researchers, students, genealogists, and the interested reader.

Be aware that in the research for this book we noted instances where the ARC conflicts with information engraved in stone, so to speak, and from the ECGS survey of 1980. We've found newspaper reports that differed from headstones, and census data that agreed with none of the above. Such errors are almost commonplace and normally minor. An example is Elizabeth Winn whose headstone says she died on March 23 at age 54, while the ARC said March 27 at age 54 [until we corrected it], but *The Daily Journal*, a New Bern newspaper, reported at the time: March 24 at age 57. And the family name is spelled with an "i" on the headstone and with a "y" in the obituary. In one of the most extreme cases, we found a newspaper announcement of a man's demise published several weeks before his headstone says he passed away.

Duplication standards of 1985 resulted in grave and gravestone photographs of only moderate quality. Photos in this appendix have been enhanced from the originals in brightness, contrast and, in some cases, sharpness for better viewing but are otherwise unmodified.

The following material is from the 1985 study entitled *A Cultural Resource Survey at U.S. Marine Corps Air Station Cherry Point, N.C* by Thomas H. Hargrove, Dennis Lewarch, Scott Madry, Ian Von Essen, and Charlotte Brown, Archaeological Research Consultants, Inc., P.O. Box 3296, Chapel Hill, N.C. 27514.

The cover sheet noted: "A report submitted to Archaeological Services Branch, National Park Service, Southeast Regional Office, Atlanta, by Archaeological Research Consultants, Inc., under Contract Number CX 500-04-0268. Funded by the United States Marine Corps."

It was stamped received on August 6, 1985.

■ Edward Ellis, February 2021

ARC STUDY 1985: CEMETERIES: MCAS CHERRY POINT, N.C.

"Cemeteries and their engraved stones proved to be the most informative historic sites at MCAS Cherry Point. This section presents information transcribed from each of the gravestones and photographs of representative examples. In 1941, when these cemeteries were first recorded and some were moved, surveyors recorded locations, inscriptions (in abbreviated form), and information supplied by residents about unmarked cemeteries (Dept. of the Navy 1941).

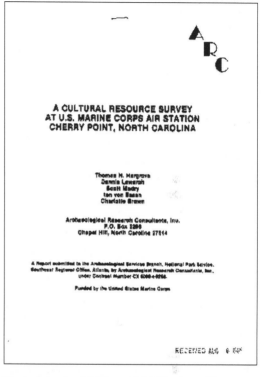

"The gravestones tend to provide a biased sample of information, however. Most of the graves recorded in 1941 lacked markers, and it is likely that slaves and less wealthy white residents had only wooden markers, if anything. Many of the residents of the black community around the Little Witness Church in the 1920s and 1930s (see Cemetery One) were buried with small metal and paper markers that have not survived the last 40 years.

"Although this group of gravestones is relatively small in number, we can see some changes through time, and comparisons can be made with the Burying Ground of Beaufort, about twenty miles away. The earliest markers at MCAS Cherry Point are those of Evan and Sally Jones, (1813 and 1817), a relatively prosperous family that lived near the Neuse River and the mouth of Slocum Creek. Their markers (Photo 14) have the "bedboard-shaped" profiles described by Benes for New England markers from 1670-1790. He attributes the use of this shape to the expression of a sleep metaphor, underlined by the normal presence of small footstones also shaped in the "bedboard" profile (Benes 1977:42). Such footstones also present in the Jones plot. The use of the "bedboard" profile at Cherry Point continued as late as 1840s, when it appeared in the Winn cemetery (see Photo 17 and 18).

"In contrast, the Burying Ground in the seaport of Beaufort also features the "bedboard" profile beginning around the 1790s, but it nearly disappears from there in the 1820s, to be replace by more elaborate and sentimental Victorian motifs such as the willow-and-urn, hands extended in farewell, or angels in flight. Crosses and cross motifs also became more common in Beaufort after the first quarter of the nineteenth century.

"At Cherry Point, the only example of the new Victorian type is the Holton stone, the largest in the inventory (Photo 5). Dating from 1823, the stone marks the burial plot of Barbara Holton, the wife of Lot Holton, a wealthy plantation owner and naval stores producer. Although Lot's name and birth date are inscribed on the stone next to his wife, he later remarried and apparently is buried elsewhere. Over Barbara's name is a hand extended in farewell, paralleling the expression of the inscription below. Over Lot's name is a heart, also a

> "In every case, the marked graves at Cherry Point are oriented with headstones toward the west and footstones toward the east. Tradition holds that this orientation ensured that the graves' occupants will face eastward, the direction from which resurrection will come."
>
> -- Cherry Point archaeological report / 1985

graphic representation of his own inscription. The relatively large size and elaboration of the Holton marker seems to correspond with the wealth of the family, but we should remember that the Evan Jones family markers, erected only a few years earlier, were much plainer although the Jones family was also quite prosperous (see Section 3.4).

"The elaborate and sentimental Victorian style apparently did not take root in the Cherry Point area. Later nineteenth century markers were either in the "bedboard" style or even plainer, featuring straight or arched but shoulderless tops (Photos.4 and10). In the meantime, Beaufort's markers from the 1840s onward began to display even more elaborate Victorian symbolism, including large, freestanding draped urns, broken columns, and obelisks. These do not appear in the Cherry Point area. Such elaboration was probably beyond the means of most of its residents, or perhaps they did not consider such displays appropriate.

"In the early twentieth century, some elaboration appears, and introduces diversity. Many stones were still in a simple style that featured a name outlined by rouletted lines and a short verse (see Photos 16 and 18). Others were more elaborate, with lamb motifs (Photo 13), a hand descending from a cloud (or rising into it) and holding a flower (Photo 2), crosses through crowns (Photo 9), and Masonic or other fraternal symbols (Photo11). Some featured only ephemeral metal markers; most of these have not survived (Photo 15).

"In every case, the marked graves at Cherry Point are oriented with headstones toward the west and footstones toward the east. Tradition holds that this orientation ensured that the graves' occupants will face eastward, the direction from which resurrection will come (Benes 1977:42). In every case but one, the inscribed faces of the stones face westward, away from the graves. The exception, the Hunter marker in Cemetery 10, has been broken off at the base and set upright, facing ease. It may also have originally faced west.

"Although we know of no published studies from N.C. that examine and compare gravestones in the region in ways long-since common in New England (e.g. Benes 1977; Deetz and Dethlefson 1978), we see no reason why it could not be done. Although the state lacks a recognized tradition of gravestone art in contrast to New England, it seems likely that anthropological and folkloristic studies of regularities and deviation in this area, given wide enough scope, could make useful contributions to regional and local history.

"Appendix 1 lists inscriptions for each of the marked graves and presents representative photographs of marker types discussed in this chapter." [237]

APPENDIX 1

CEMETERY 1
1. Son of W. H. & Nancy E. Cully
    G.W. Cully Born Dec. 27, 1869 Died Nov. 6, 1919
    Husband of A. L. Cully
    Peaceful be thy [illegible] slumber.
2. Sarah F. wife of Allen Whittington Nov. 6 1860 Feb. 10, 1922 Best mother, rest in sweet sleep, While friend in sorrow o'er thee weep.
3. Kissie Sykes Aged 40 years
4. James B. Robinson Born Feb. 18, 1877 Died March 10, 1926 Pride of Havelock Chamber 6091 – Havelock, N.C. [First Postmaster of Melvin, N.C.]
5. The following names were noted in 1941 from small metal-and-paper undertakers' markers. None of the markers seems to have survived.
    John King; Jan 24, 1939, age 42 years
    Charlie Nelson; 1915 – 1941
    James Nelson; died 1929

---

[237] Copy in quotes above, and following cemetery list, verbatim from Archeological Research Consultants 1985 survey for MCAS Cherry Point. Layout has been changed for clarity. Words in brackets [ ] added by author.

Dinah Nelson; June 18, 1939, 65 years
Joe Early Fenner; Nov. 28, 1930; 40 years old
Ollie Berrie; died 1939
Rosa Lee Prichard; 1914 – 1941
John McCray; April 21, 1940
Marietta Singleton; Feb 28, 1935
Jimmie Lee Richards; 1 year 8 months
Pollock
Estelle Gibbs; 1918 – 1940
W. R. Willoughby; June 15, 1928, Age 58
T. McCray; died 1923
Reta Bryant; Dec. 29, 1925, age 4 years
Mindora Bryant; died June 20, 1935
Addie George; Sept 24, 1926, 18 years
Virginia Dove; June 7, 1932, age 64 years
William Dove; 63 years old
Walter M. Toon; Dec. 8, 1926, age 7
Redmon Patton; July 28, 1926, 60 years old
Annie Dewie; Aug 20, 1926, 40 years old
Steven Berry; April 12, 1930, 51 years old
Elizabeth Berry; Feb. 17, 1935, 25 years
Earnest Lee Berry; Oct 12, 1936, 16 months old

CEMETERY 2 (Wynne Family) The cemetery survey notes from 1941 state only, "Overgrown with trees and brush – no markers, sinks visible – impossible to give an accurate count of the graves."

CEMETERY 3 Another unmarked cemetery, with an estimated 15-25 graves, according to Emma Hill Stevens, a nearby resident at the time of the cemetery survey in 1941.

CEMETERY 4 This cemetery also lacks markers, but the surveyors in 1941 estimated that three or four graves were present. According to their informant Emma Hill Stevens, one of the graves is the burial place of a man named Sparks.

CEMETERY 5 and CEMETERY 6 This cemetery preceded the Little Witness Church cemetery, according to the local informants in 1941. The informants also stated that about 40 to 50 graves were present, but only one was marked:
Our Darlings Together in Heaven
Nannie K. dau. of A. F. & M. C. Moore Born June 7, 1890, Died July 9, 1895

Maudie E. dau. of A. F. & M. C. Moore Born Feb. 12, 1892, Died Aug. 30, 1898

CEMETERY 7 In addition to at least one unmarked grave, this cemetery contains two stones:

1. Sacred to the memory of Caroline R. daughter of Wm. B. and Elizabeth Thorpe Born July 8, 1846, Died Jan 30, 1867, 20 years 6 mos. 22 days

2. Philip J. Son of John W. & Maria F. Armes Born Jan 2, 1848, Died March 5, 1896
"In the r[ ]ted Fork I'm resting,
Safely sheltered I abide."

CEMETERY 8 The 1941 cemetery survey originally recorded that only un-marked graves were present. At an unknown later date, this entry was corrected to include the one marker present: Barbara Holton was born Mar. 25, 1783, and died July 8, 1823
"Farewell dear husband, prepare to meet me in Eternity"
Lot Holton was born Oct. 6, 1780
"Here is my heart [illegible] to meet you in that happy life."

CEMETERY 9

1. William Buys Born July 28, 1847, Died Sept. 27, 1918 "Kind, upright, honest and true."

2. Anna Daughter of William and Nellie Buys Born Jan. 17, 1875, Died Nov. 24, 1917. "Faithful in the Lord's service until death."

3. Mrs. Nellie Buys Born April 17, 1847, Died Sept. 23, 1881 "In loving remembrance."

4. In Memory of Antge Visser Buys Brandt Born Nov. 26, 1813 Died Oct. 1, 1904 Aged 91 years

5. In Memory of Elizabeth H. Jones Daughter of Bryan & Sarah Jones Born Jan. 24, 1842, Died June 17, 1843. "Not youth, nor age, nor beauty Can evade the sentence Passed on man; Then parents Dear from grief refrain, for I Through Christ shall live again."
"Forgot by man but remembered By God"

6. [in original, Elizabeth Jones epitaph was erroneously numbered sepa-rately as paragraph "6".]

7. In memory of Elizabeth Winn Wife of Stephen W. Winn Who died Dec. 23, 1842, Aged 54 years. "Her ways were ways of Pleasantness, and all her Paths were paths of peace."

8. In Memory of Stephen Winn, Esq. Who departed this life Feb 23, 1833, Aged 45 years 10 months and 24 days

9. In Memory of Martha E. Jones Daughter of Bryan and Sarah J. Jones Who was born Feb. 13, 1842, And died Feb. 27, 1848

10. In Memory of Gilley A. Cooper Daughter of Bryan and Sarah Jones Who was born Nov. 22, 1848, And departed this life June 27, 1850 "Farewell, lovely babe, farewell, with me thou canst no Longer dwell. I hope ere long With thee to tell, that Jesus Has done all things well."

CEMETERY 10
Local informants in 1941 estimated 100 graves. Only one marker is present.
John N[oe], son of J[ames] H. & Mary J. [Noe] Hunter,
Born Feb. 15, 1859, Died April 23, 1905

CEMETERY 11
1. George. A. Russell June 9, 1876, June 14, 1936
   "Father is gone, but not forgotten."
2. Annie B. Wife of G. A. Russell Died June 12, 1935 Age 63 years
   "Mother's in heaven."
3. Anthony J. Russell Dec. 31, 1898, March 7, 1940
"Gone, but not forgotten."
4. Edward Borden Russell Born Dec. 23, 1901, Died Dec. 27, 1911
   "Rest in Peace."
5. Annie Virginia daughter of Darrow & Madge Wetherington July 20, 1922, April 13, 1924
   "Gone to Be an Angel"
6. Our Beloved One Dorothy Lillian daughter of Anthony & Missouri Russell
Born & Died October 28, 1926
7. B. D. Borden Died Jan. 18, 1923 Age 76 years
"Gone, but not forgotten."

CEMETERY 12 The 1941 cemetery surveyors' notes stated "No markers but sinks can be seen. Approximate area about 35 feet by 30 feet." No additional information is available.

CEMETERY 13
1. In Memory of Sally the wife of Evan Jones who departed this Life Feby 21st, 1813 Aged 52 years
2. In Memory of Evan Jones Who departed his life March the 2nd 1817 Aged 60 years
3. In Memory of Geo. D. Pate whose stay on earth was 86 years Died May 26, 1920
4. Edward Salter Born June 29, 1861, Died May 3, 1916
   "Dearest husband thou hast left us.
   And thy loss we deeply feel.
   But 'tis God that hath bereft us

He can all our sorrows heal.
Yet again we hope to [illeg.]
When the day of life has fled.
Then in heaven with joy to greet thee
Where no farewell tears are shed."

CEMETERY 14

1. In Memory of Charles E. Holland Born Mar. 3, 1880, Died Feb 21, 1908
"Thy will be done"

2. Jacob Holland Son of John R. & Emily Jane Holland Born Dec. 24, 1886, Died April 26, 1907
"Asleep in Jesus"

3. John B. Holland Born Nov. 10, 1838, Died Sept. 12, 1911. A member of the M. B. Church for 45 yrs. And the H. P. T.

4. Odius son of O. D. and Cordelia Moore Sept. 14, 1915, March 4, 1916

CEMETERY 15

1. Willie L. Barnes Born May 9, 1881, Died Mar. 16, 1917

2. Willie J. son of J. R. & Dinksie Barnes Born Nov. 8, 1909 Died Mar. 2, 1911
"Gone but not forgotten"

3. Maggie Daughter of John R. & M. E. Barnes Born Oct.27, 1882, Died Oct. 14, 1898

4. Murphy E. Wife of John R. Barnes Born Mar. 26, 1850, Died Mar 26, 1900

5. Susannah Wife of Francis M. Barnes Born Nov. 21, 1838, Died June 1, 1889
"We shall sleep, but not forever.
There will be a glorious dawn.
We shall meet to part no, never
On the resurrection morn."

6. Francis M. Barnes Born Dec. 26, 1832, Died June 16, 1909

7. Joel H. Barnes Born May 20, 1874, Died Aug. 18, 1907
"In the bright eternal city
Death can never, never come.
In his own good time, he'll call us,
From our rest to home, sweet home."

8. Caroline Wife of Denard B. Garner Born Mar 12, 1861, Died Sept. 21, 1906 "Gone Home"

Cherry Point Cemetery Photographs #1-18, ARC survey, 1985

1) Cemetery 1, Little Witness
Cemetery (eastward).

2) Cemetery 1, marker 2; Sarah F.
Whittington

3) Cemetery 1, marker 4;
James B. Robinson, [first
postmaster of Melvin, N.C.]

4) Cemetery 7, marker 1 in foreground

5) Cemetery 8, Holton marker
(eastward)

8) Cemetery 9, marker 5

6) Cemetery 9, overall view (eastward)

7) Cemetery 9, markers 7 and 6, left to right in foreground, markers 8 and 9, left to right in background.

9) Cemetery 9, marker 2

15) [Many temporary markers at
Cherry Point were illegible by
1985.]

10) Cemetery 10, John Hunter foot and headstones (westward)

13) Cemetery 11, marker 5

[*No photos marked 11 or 12 appeared in the original study.*]

14} Cemetery 13, overall view (westward). Left to right: Unknown; marker 2; marker 1; marker 3. Marker 4 is lying flat in the foreground.

16) Cemetery 14, marker 3

18) Cemetery 15, marker 7

17) Cemetery 15, overall view eastward)

Some Thoughts on Research

SOURCE OF DETAILS: Most of the information contained *in Part II: The Whisperers* is directly from headstones at the graves of the deceased. Some of the extraneous information and comments noted in the entries above, however, came from the word-of-mouth of family members of the deceased, neighbors, and old-time residents interviewed over many years. When possible, all information has been confirmed by the written source material, but, as researchers may understand, this is not always possible.

NO TRESPASSING: Some of the gravesites discussed in this publication are not on public lands. Those wishing to pursue the exploration of primitive cemeteries and graveyards are urged always to respect private property. Remember the law, the individual rights of others, and, as quaint as they may seem, the obligations of common courtesy, decency, and dignity.

RACIAL DESIGNATION: Before the mid-20th century, cemeteries were usually – but not always – segregated by race. It must be remembered that some graves and graveyards were moved and/or consolidated during the construction of Marine Corps Air Station Cherry Point in the 1940s. While the race noted with each burial is believed by the author to be accurate -- although a few have been left blank or marked unknown -- the serious researcher or genealogist may wish to consider the possibility that individual errors might have occurred.

SPELLING OF NAMES and names themselves were *very* fluid in earlier times. We've seen the same man's name spelled three different ways *in the same document*! The identical family's name would be spelled one way in one census and then a different way in the next. Same father, same mother, same kids, but an altered spelling of the last name. Thus, Belangia, Belanga, Belanger, Ballenger, and Ballinger are the same name. As are Winn-Wynn-Wynne, Dickinson-Dickerson, Cully-Culley, Rowe-Roe-Row, MacRae-McCray, Kennedy-Kannady or Cannady-Canada, so on and so forth. And don't even get us started on Weatherington! Then, there are *nicknames*. A person might be given a birth name and then be called something else forever after. Take the case of a Havelock girl, who, according to census records was named Sarah. But Sarah was known to everyone else for the remainder of her life as "Sallie." In no instance do we find further reference to the name Sarah in the long local history of Sallie Russell Wynne.

CONFLICTING DATA: Headstone dates and census data for a specific individual sometimes conflict, being off by a year or two. For example, Francis M. "Frank" Barnes, head of a large farm family in the Lewis Farm Road area west of Havelock, was born in December 1831. But his headstone in Cherry Point cemetery 15 (CP 15) indicates he was born in December 1832. That could be what we now call a "typo," but more than likely the case is explained by the fact that census data is submitted by the living person, and headstones are ordered based on the memories of survivors. The other side of this nickel is that people in the nineteenth century simply weren't as obsessed with birthdays as we are. Thus, an individual might be listed as 34 in a particular census, but two censuses (20 years) later, they'd be 50. In addition to typos, there are a couple of other explanations. Some folks back then weren't paying that much attention to their ages. They weren't being constantly asked their birthday on forms, weren't issued driver's licenses, didn't carry ID. So, they might just forget. Or approximate. And some people, as they get older, have been known to, well, fudge about their age a little, right? Each family's Holy Bibles were the state-of-the-art database for births, marriages, and deaths of that era, but even those have been known to have a typo or two of their own.

COD PNEUMONIA: As seen within, a noticeable number of deaths in Havelock were caused by pneumonia. The illness is normally a bacterial infection or flu virus. It causes inflammation of the air sacs in the lungs, which may then fill with fluid. The patient has a fever, some pain or discomfort in the side of the chest, short rapid breathing, and a raspy cough. It was often spread person-to-person by air droplets from coughing. Smoking, alcoholism, exposure to birds, like chickens, and farm animals increased the risk of acquiring and dying from the disease. Compared to other diseases of the time, a famous physician before the invention of antibiotics dubbed pneumonia "the Captain of the Men of Death." It's still the premier infectious killer in the world; fatal to four million people a year.

GRAVE DEPRESSIONS or "SINKS": Local custom, particularly in the 1800s, was that graves were only filled to within a foot of the top with dirt until a minister conducted services there. From time to time throughout its history, no minister – or no minister of the proper denomination – was available in the community. Clergymen often rode circuits and might only visit a particular town or village once a month and sometimes much less often. Thus, some of the graves were never consecrated and, therefore, never filled in. The other reason for "sinks" at the grave is the decaying of a wooden casket causing a collapse over time.

ACCESS TO CHERRY POINT GRAVEYARDS: The old family graveyards sequestered behind the gates of Marine Corps Air Station Cherry Point had traditionally been open in the past for visitation by individuals with a legitimate reason to do so — relatives of the deceased or historical researchers, for example. The starting point to discover the requirements for permission to visit any of the historic cemeteries aboard the air station has been Cherry Point's Communication Strategy and Operations Office (COMMSTRAT). An internet search will yield current contact information.

FURTHER STUDY: Among the best volumes of non-academic local history ever written is *One Dozen Eastern North Carolina Families* by Robert Primrose Watson "P. W." Fisher. Focused on the Fisher family of Riverdale and Hancock Creek, and their interrelated genealogical lines, the book renders a memorable portrayal of the past 200 years in Craven County. The inter-connectedness of families and the interdependence of people in an era when populations were tiny compared to today, plus the fragility of life and memories, are inescapable themes that run through this fine work.

INTERNET SEARCHES: When doing internet searches for Havelock data, also try the most common misspelling as well – HAVERLOCK.

POST OFFICES: For those who might research this in the future, local records of postal leadership don't precisely match those in the National Archives. For example, see Edward D. Russell's entry in *Part II: The Whisperers*.

OTHER INFORMATION RESOURCES:

1) Bound volumes of *The Havelock Progress* newspapers are held by the Havelock Public Library and are available to the interested public.

2) Microfilmed copies of the *Havelock News* and the *Sun Journal* are available for viewing at the Kellenberger Room of the New Bern – Craven County Public Library.

3) An extensive obituary index focused on Craven County is available at the Kellenberger Room's website.

4) A copy of the Cherry Point ownership map of 1941 listing graveyards and land tract numbers, can be seen online at Edward B. Ellis, Jr. Papers, East Carolina University. An original is at ECU.

5) A reminder: The family trees at Find-a-grave.com and the internet ancestry sites are often wonderful resources, but the genealogical information there is only as good as the skill of the donor.

6) Quadrangle maps. An incredible amount of information and detail is contained in the topographic map produced by the U. S. Geological Survey (USGS) covering the United States. The maps are usually named after local features. Begin on a computer by searching for *Cherry Point quadrangle map*, for instance. Other quadrangles will be connected to it. Older versions of the current maps are available online.

ADDITIONS, CORRECTIONS, COMMENTS: Errors, omissions, and misinterpretations by the author are likely for a work of this type. Additions, corrections, and comments are both anticipated and welcomed. They may be sent to his attention via email to flexspace2@aol.com, though, as confirmed by the characters of the book, this will be a limited-time offer.

INDEX

D

H

M

ACKNOWLEDGEMENTS

The course of research resulting in this book has run so long that hundreds of people have helped, taught, and encouraged the author. This is a partial list of those, living and deceased, who have his appreciation and gratitude.

Sandra Hardy
Charlie Markey
Charlie Potter
Lila Wynne Simmons
Adam Culley
Thelma Armstrong Norris
Donald R. Lennon
Dan Walker
Alice Bayer
William E. Jackson
Natalie Sugg
Jim Sugg
Gertrude Carraway
Margaret Latham Aversa
Cherry Trader
Johnny D. Oliver
Emma Hill Davis
June Rodd
Fred S. Nelson
Jean Bryan
Jack Murphy
Pat Bailey
W.J. Wynne
Clay Wynne
Eva Sermons
Arthur W. Edwards
Dick Tuttle
Irv Beck
Horace Mewborn
Marea Kafer
David L. Ward
Dr. John Kirkland
Pam Pafford
Diane Aversa Hodges

Veronica Ellis
Carmen Ellis Calmes
Beth Ellis DeMarco
Charles Raymond Adams
Bobby Stricklin
David Cecelski
Rev. Douglas G. Williams
James Muse
Debra Newton-Carter
Yvette Porter Moore
Dan Walsh
Linda & Harold Rawls
Jimmy Sanders
George Norris
Richard Rice
Kim Rice Smith
Betty Rice Slaughter
Dick Wynn
Pamela Miller
Michael Barton
Paula M. White
Sarah Koonts
Earl Ijames
Martha G. Elmore
Dale Sauter
Maury York
John R. M. Lawrence
Jonathan Dembo
Ralph Scott
R. Allen Humphrey
Steve Shaffer
Victor T. Jones
John Green
Margie Garrison

Nathaniel Glasgow
Earl Temple
Cathy Bayer
Joey Bayer
Jimmy Simmons
James Simmons
Margaret Trader
John Jackson
Jerry Jackson
Steve Massengill
Chris Meekins
Shugana Campbell
Lee Hampton
Chris Harter
Dr. Clifton Johnson
Claudia Houston
Mickey Miller
Susan Briley
Tom "Jet" Matthews
Jacqueline Nelson-Lee
David A. French

Wade Fuller
Douglas and Gail Lindeman
Bernd Doss
J. Troy Smith
Katie Fleck
J. D. Larimore
Tashamma Smith
Bob Kaylor
Suzanne Shell
Dianne Hassan
R. Allen Humphrey
David Wynne
Charlie Meyer
John Thomas
Bud Salter
Jimmy Smith
Virginia Zuckerman
Lindy Cummings
William Sidoran
Shirley Agen

Special thanks and recognition to Bill Benners – publisher, collaborator, and friend. His encouragement, skill, and untold hours of patient guidance were vital to the project.

The substantial contributions of others notwithstanding, responsibility for any errors of fact or conclusion herein rest solely with the author.

ABOUT THE AUTHOR

Edward Ellis was born in New Bern in 1950 and raised in New Bern and Havelock. In his early twenties, he began a career in the newspaper business that included roles as a reporter, editor, and managing editor of the *Havelock (NC) Progress*, managing editor of the *Garner (NC) News*, editor of the *North Carolina Farmer,* and the *South Carolina Farmer*, editor and publisher of the *Tar Heel Reporter* of the N. C. State Government Employees Association, Raleigh, N.C.

In 1985, under the banner of Ellis Publishing Company, he became the publisher of *The Windsock*, the official newspaper of Marine Corps Air Station Cherry Point, and in 1986 founded the *Havelock News*.

Since the purchase of Ellis Publishing Company by a national media firm in 1993, Ellis has concentrated his business activities on real estate ventures in North Carolina and Florida.

He began his research on the history of Havelock and southern Craven County in his early teens and was named Official Historian of the City of Havelock in 1984. He has written and spoken about the area's heritage for decades.

Through the years, he's collected documents, letters, interviews, prints, maps, surveys, artifacts, photographs, albums, collectible books, newspapers and other writings, which have been accepted as donations by archives including Tryon Palace Historic Sites & Gardens, the Southern Baptist Historical Collection, the State Library of North Carolina, the Kellenberger Room of the New Bern-Craven County Library, the Havelock Public Library, the New Bern Historical Society, the Town of Garner, N.C., the Heritage Center of Lenoir Community College, the Carteret County History Museum, UNC-Asheville, and MCAS Cherry Point.

Archives & History researcher ID, c. 1977

His major work – the Havelock, N.C. Historical Collection – is preserved as the *Edward B. Ellis, Jr. Papers* and the *Henry Havelock/British India Collection* at the Joyner Library, Special Collections, East Carolina University.

Ellis was instrumental in the creation of the Havelock History Exhibit for the Eastern Carolina Aviation Heritage Foundation. It's open to the public at the Havelock Tourist and Events Center.

Eddie and his wife, "Ronnie" Ellis, live in Melbourne, Florida.

This is his fourth book of local history.

Made in the USA
Columbia, SC
24 June 2022

62201218R00336